INTRODUCTION TO EXPERIMENTAL PSYCHOLOGY

DOUGLAS W. MATHESON
University of the Pacific
RICHARD L. BRUCE
University of Alaska
KENNETH L. BEAUCHAMP
University of the Pacific

HOLT, RINEHART AND WINSTON, INC.
New York   Chicago   San Francisco   Atlanta   Dallas
Montreal   Toronto   London   Sydney

INTRODUCTION TO EXPERIMENTAL PSYCHOLOGY

SECOND EDITION

Library of Congress Cataloging in Publication Data

Matheson, Douglas W. 1939–
   Introduction to experimental psychology.

   Includes bibliographies.
   1. Psychology, Experimental. I. Bruce, Richard Loren, 1938–
joint author. II. Beauchamp, Kenneth L., joint author. III. Title.
[DNLM: 1. Psychology, Experimental. 2. Psychometrics. BF181 M427i
1974]
BF181.M33   1974   150'.7'.24   73-15801
ISBN: 0-03-091541-4

PREFACE

In the four years since *Introduction to Experimental Psychology* was first published, a number of trends in behavioral research have been emerging. There is an increasing pressure to take the research out of the "sterile" environs of the laboratory, and to observe behavior in the more natural surroundings of the real world. The growing awareness that the experimental process and the experimenter himself can alter the subjects' behavior casts doubts on the generality of many research results. The increasing pressure by the public (via the federal government and other agencies) to protect the rights and integrity of experimental subjects curtails the research horizons enjoyed by researchers in the past.

Some psychologists have pointed to these factors as the early signs in the deemphasis of the role of the laboratory and the experimental psychologist in the study of behavioral problems. The argument is made that the important facts of behavior are not found in the precision of a psychophysical study or the construction of some new elegant method of channeling the animal's behavior in the laboratory; but rather in the naturally occurring behavior of the animal, particularly people. The new behavioral methodology includes methods for analyzing ongoing, natural behavior; means of contriving situations in the real world to stimulate and examine the behavior of interest; and ways to disguise the laboratory so thoroughly that the observed behavior is "relevant." While we have not yet reached the research elaboration of John Fowles' *The Magus,* the next sealed, addressed, and stamped envelope you find lying on the sidewalk could be a data point for a doctoral dissertation.

Since the laboratory is no longer the only playground for the behavioral researcher, the assumption is that the experimental psychologist (together with his nonsense syllables and lab rats) has become a sort of scientific dinosaur. Yet while the specific methodology of behavioral research is indeed changing, the rules for good research are essentially with us still. Relevant research (sometimes defined as research outside the psychology laboratory) is of no value unless the basic rules for observation and accumulation of knowledge are followed. This statement is equally true in the laboratory. Thus, the revision of an introductory text is very pertinent. The philosophical points discussed about scientific methodology, the methods of presenting, summarizing, and analyzing data, and the problems encountered in working with man or animals will always be a part of behavioral research. The phrase "scientific method" describes an attitude, a commitment to obtaining knowledge; and the tools and procedures reflect the advances in knowledge acquisition.

Since the issues discussed in the first edition of this text were stated in their general form, leaving the specific application to the individual researcher, there is little substantive change in the coverage for this edition. Many of the chapters are now supplied with more examples from recent sources.

A survey of statistical tests used in the research published in psychological journals during 1971 revealed that nearly 50 percent of the published research utilized some form of the analysis of variance as the statistical test. Consequently, the chapter on inferential statistics now includes a substantial addition to outline the logic and rationale of analysis of variance research; and four versions of the analysis of variance technique form an additional unit in the statistical tests section.

Introduction to Experimental Psychology was obviously intended to serve as a textbook in the first course in experimental psychology. It was also intended to serve as an undergraduate handbook to be used as a reference manual for dealing with specific research problems encountered after completing a first course. The organization of the chapters as well as the references at the end of each chapter were selected to provide direct access to answers to problems encountered at various times in the research process. The organization of this second edition has been modified to make this handbook feature more convenient. Section One contains a discussion of the theoretical and philosophical issues in behavioral research. Section Two now contains the material related to some of the practical, real-life problems involved during the actual data collection process. Sections Three and Four present various researchable ideas and examples as a means of encouraging the student to establish his or her own research interests. The new Section Four presents examples of undergraduate student research, indicating the range of topics that students may capably examine.

In addition to major and minor headings, summaries, and chapter review sections, there are three within-chapter tools used to organize the material. These three are marginal notations, italicized type, and bold face type. The italicized type is used to emphasize critical procedural details and precise wording or phrasing. Bold face type is used when a major, new term is defined. Marginal notations call attention to major concepts, label subsections, or emphasize terms and critical points.

We would like to express our sincere appreciation to all who have in various ways contributed to the process of producing this edition. The comments of students who have taken a course using the first edition as a text have been very helpful. Similarly, the comments and criticisms of colleagues have been useful and encouraging. We are particularly indebted to the reviewers of the manuscript for the second edition: Gabriel Gurski, University of California, Davis; Ralph Norman Haber, University of Rochester; Ron Offenstein, San Bernardino Valley College; and Charles L. Sheridan, University of Missouri, Kansas City. Although it is difficult to provide any sort of quantitative estimate, it seems that the greatest help has not been concerned with the content, but with the process of writing. To those who have directly assisted in creating, counting, correcting, and collating the final draft pages (particularly Judy Beauchamp and Gwenda Dalman-Nylen) we are grateful. Even less obvious, but equally important are the patience and forebearance shown to us by our colleagues, friends, and especially family members who indirectly had to bear the cost of our project.

Stockton, California   D.W.M.
Anchorage, Alaska   R.L.B.
Stockton, California   K.L.B.
February 1974

CONTENTS

INTRODUCTION TO EXPERIMENTAL PSYCHOLOGY

SECTION ONE
THE RESEARCH PROCESS

CHAPTER 1
The Scientific Approach to Knowledge

Man has an almost insatiable need to know. When not concerned with survival activity, he is preoccupied with the acquisition of knowledge. The patient research activity of a scientist, the gaggle of onlookers "rubber-necking" at the scene of an accident, the years you have spent in classrooms, and the politically motivated "bugging" of foreign legations and embassies dramatize the desire to know. Similarly, there is a tendency for man to share what he knows. Professional conventions and research journals, rumors and the office grapevine, the activity of professors and textbook writers, and newspapers and television news conferences demonstrate the desire to share knowledge.

The process of defining information as knowledge involves an interaction between man (the knower) and the environment of potential information (the to-be-known). Man does not assimilate all the information potentially available. Part of the process of acquiring knowledge involves evaluating the information that is received. Each individual may experience conflict between two criteria for evaluating the information he encounters. The first criterion is the highly subjective one of the potential information's relevance to the individual. There is a strong tendency for a person to emphasize information that is compatible with his previously acquired knowledge and to ignore information that is incompatible. The second criterion is the more abstract principle of "truth" or "reality." Here man is concerned with deciding if the information is compatible with the knowledge shared by all men. A three-year-old child may spend many hours playing with and talking to an imaginary playmate. That playmate is "real" and relevant to the child but is not "real" to the child's parents. Thus, the playmate is described as "imaginary," meaning the belief in its existence is not shared by others.

There are several ways to acquire knowledge. This book is concerned with one of these ways, the scientific approach, because research psychologists use the scientific approach. The scientist's approach consists of a particular set of rules for the acquisition and transmission of knowledge. By standardizing the criteria for "realness" and by specifying the rules for transmission of information, scientists minimize the chances for making errors. As previously stated, the rules of the scientific approach are not the only means of acquiring knowledge. In some cases other means may be more appropriate. The following sections briefly outline two alternative approaches that preceded the scientist's approach and which continue as useful approaches today.

THE ARTIST'S APPROACH

In the artistic approach, the artist attempts to organize information into a new knowledge structure. The artist utilizes his skills to present his unique perception to others in the form of an artistic product — painting, sculpture, a symphony, and so forth.

The sculptures of Michelangelo are well-known examples of the artistic approach. The huge, very lifelike figure of "David" represents the result of an extensive study of the human figure in all positions. Michelangelo dissected many cadavers and made hundreds of sketches in order to perfect his realistic portrayal of the human form. The artist's "Moses" is a better example of the artistic approach because the artist went beyond the goal of realism. Michelangelo transformed the written, biblical description of Moses into a fascinating marble statement. The intense expression of the face, particularly the eyes, and the wild flow of the hair and beard dramatically convey Michelangelo's interpretation of the strong character of the man. The artist's product (statue) represents a new organization of and source of knowledge unavailable to others in any other form.

A work of art, in addition to being a highly individualistic, subjective attempt to organize and present knowledge, may be an expression of a particular philosophical point of view. Michelangelo's sculptures illustrate the Renaissance conception of man. During the Middle Ages man was regarded as a "frail creature, in need of

God's grace and salvation." The Renaissance brought with it a sense of man's indi-viduality, creativity, and tremendous power. "In the mighty figures of Michelangelo the attributes of humanity invad[ed] Heaven itself" (Palmer, 1958, p. 52).[1]

THE RATIONALIST'S APPROACH

Another way of creating knowledge from potential information is the rationalist's approach. The rationalist arrives at knowledgeable statements about mankind or some other topic primarily through exercising logical (rational) analysis of basic information. The strict rationalist tries to avoid activities designed to increase the quantity of information available.[2] For example, a strict rationalist might attempt to answer the question "How does man learn?" by constructing a series of postulates based on existing information and opinion, but he would avoid direct observation of man in a learning situation. The avoidance of observation can be carried to ridic-ulous extremes as the following well-known anecdote illustrates.

> In the year of our Lord 1432, there arose a grievous quarrel among the brethren over the number of teeth in the mouth of a horse. For thirteen days the disputation raged without ceasing. All the ancient books and chronicles were fetched out, and wonderful and ponderous erudition, such as was never before heard of in this region, was made manifest. At the beginning of the fourteenth day, a youthful friar of goodly bearing asked his learned superiors for permission to add a word, and straightway, to the wonderment of the disputants, whose deep wisdom he sore vexed, he beseeched them to unbend in a manner coarse and unheard-of, and to look in the open mouth of a horse and find answer to their questionings. At this, their dignity being grievously hurt, they waxed exceedingly wroth; and joining in a mighty uproar, they flew upon him and smote his hip and thigh, and cast him out forthwith. For, said they, surely Satan hath tempted his bold neophyte to declare unholy and unheard-of ways of finding truth contrary to all the teachings of the fathers. After many days of grievous strife the dove of peace sat on the assembly, and they as one man, declaring the prob-lem to be an ever-lasting mystery because of a grievous dearth of historical and theo-logical evidence thereof, so ordered the same writ down.
>
> (Francis Bacon, quoted in Mees, 1934, p. 17.)

The artist's approach, the rationalist's approach, and the scientist's approach are all used to some extent at different stages of knowledge acquisition. The artist looks for knowledge conveyed in the "outstanding example," while the rationalist seeks the "general rule." The first two approaches are presented here in highly oversimplified form in order to provide some contrast to the following material on the scientist's approach.

[1] All references cited in the text, but not in the suggested reading list at the end of each chapter, will be included in a special section at the back of the book.

[2] The term "rationalist" as used here refers to a particular way of gaining knowledge. The word "rational" and its antonym, "irrational," are commonly used to summarize our evaluation of a person's behavior. In such a case "rational" refers to the degree of comprehensibleness of a behavior and the degree to which the behavior agrees with common sense. Even though there is a similarity in meaning, the term, as used here, should not be confused with the common usage.

THE SCIENTIST'S APPROACH

The scientific approach to knowledge draws from the artist's approach in that it involves the description of the world. The scientist draws from the rationalist's approach in that information is logically organized in a total body of knowledge.

One may still find remnants of preferences for one or the other approach within a science. In studying creativity, some researchers have produced knowledge about creativity by interviewing or otherwise studying persons generally accepted to be creative (for example, Wertheimer's [1945] study of Einstein). The approach has a distinctly artistic flavor. Others have studied creativity by carefully analyzing the logical properties behind creative problem-solving behaviors (for example, Duncker, 1945). This approach has a distinctly rational flavor.

The sciences differ in terms of their basic subject matter; and the techniques, procedures, and methods used by individual scientists depend on their research problems. However, all scientists (1) make a few basic assumptions, (2) study only restricted kinds of questions, and (3) have the same general goals. The shared assumptions, restrictions, and goals describe the scientific approach to knowledge.

ASSUMPTIONS OF THE SCIENTIFIC APPROACH

All approaches to knowledge are based on a few assumptions, premises, or basic beliefs. The assumptions of the scientific approach are: (1) order, (2) determinism, and (3) discoverability. Scientists assume that order pervades the universe. **Order** is a primitive, undefined term; however, to say that scientists believe in order is to say that scientists believe events happen in regular patterns. Scientists do not believe that events occur in a chaotic, chance manner.

Scientists assume that the occurrence of an event is determined by prior or antecedent events. The assumption of **determinism** is shared by all scientists; thus, psychologists assume that all behavior is determined. For example, a particular behavior such as choosing to buy one kind of car rather than another is assumed to be a consequence of the previous (antecedent) experiences of an individual.

The assumption of **discoverability** means that scientists expect to find answers to present scientific questions. Psychologists believe that eventually today's research questions about behavior will be answered. Of course, new questions are constantly being formulated, and new research is continually indicating that previously accepted answers are incorrect or incomplete. Therefore, scientific research is a continuous process.

RESTRICTIONS ON SCIENTIFIC OBSERVATION

Scientific observation must satisfy three requirements. First, the observations must be **empirical.** The scientist records relatively objective observations of events. Basic scientific information cannot be composed of speculations about unobserved events.

For example, electrons have never been observed, but the effects of electron movement have been observed in a Wilson cloud chamber. In psychology, learning has never been directly observed, but has been inferred from changes in the behavior of an organism. A second requirement is that the basic events and the observation of these events must be **public.** The observed events must occur in a manner, place, and time that allows the possibility of observation by others. The subjective observation of what is happening in one's own "mind" cannot be called scientific observation. Indeed, it is probable that a "mind" cannot directly observe itself (Hebb, 1969). A third requirement is that the observations must be **repeatable.** An observation by a single individual is not scientific unless it can be repeated. The details of the situation and the elements of the observation procedure must be specified in a scientific report.

Two types of observation are used in the scientific approach: naturalistic observation and experimental observation. Both types satisfy the above three restrictions.

Naturalistic Observation

The observation of events in their natural setting is called **naturalistic observation.** (See Chapter 2.) Naturalistic observers examine empirical, public events. Theoretically, these observations are repeatable, given that the events "naturally" occur more than once. The occurrence of the events is independent of the observer's behavior. For example, astronomers are naturalistic observers. The movements of the stars are not under the control of the observer, but they are empirical, public events, and the movements usually recur within a time span that allows a second observation.

Experimental Observation

The observation of events in a restricted setting is called **experimental observation.** Experimental observers make empirical, public, repeatable observations. In addition, experimental observations are made under controlled conditions. By **control** we mean that an experimental scientist manipulates the environment so that the critical events occur at a specified time and place. Manipulation allows the scientist to be fully prepared for precise observation. The experimenter is also assured that events will occur a second time, allowing verification of his observations under the same conditions. Finally, the experimental scientist can systematically vary the physical conditions to discover what changes in the events occur.

The three restrictions (empirical, public, repeatable) indicate that only certain types of problems can be studied with the scientific approach. The necessity for control further limits the experimental scientist. Supposedly, watching violent television shows leads human beings to aggressive behavior such as violent crimes. The problem cannot be directly studied by experiment because a scientist cannot control the rate of watching violent television shows, and he cannot publicly, repeatedly observe individual crimes.

THE GOALS OF
THE SCIENTIFIC APPROACH

The three goals of any science are: (1) understanding, (2) prediction, and (3) formulation of a systematic body of knowledge. The general goal of any approach to knowledge is **understanding.** Understanding is another primitive term defying clear definition in the dictionary sense. However, we all have some intuitive notion of the meaning of the term. For example, when we observe a child avoid a hot stove, we can agree that the child understands the relationship between the act of touching the stove and the resultant pain. Scientific understanding is the tentative acceptance of an explanation for the occurrence of an event. The acceptance is tentative because scientists know that through further testing another explanation may be developed.

Another goal of the scientific approach is **prediction.** On the basis of a given relationship between two or more events, the scientist specifies their probable future relationship. To a scientist, a prediction is but one step in the entire approach, for all predicted relationships must be tested.

A third goal is the **systematic organization** of empirical evidence into a **body of knowledge.** If a prediction is supported by repeated scientific tests, then the predicted relationship between observable events becomes a scientific fact. A systematic organization of these facts *and* the methods used to obtain them constitute scientific knowledge.

RESEARCH EXAMPLE

Weil, Zinberg, and Nelson (1968) conducted a series of experiments on the effects of marihuana smoking on human behavior. The research represents the first *experimental study* of marihuana intoxication. Previously, naturalistic observation of marihuana smokers at "pot parties" and incompletely reported observations of soldiers and prisoners indicated that smoking had little effect on tests of manual dexterity, but some effect on physiological measures such as pulse rate, overeating (hyperphagia), and pupil dilation. These observations were formally tested by Weil and his colleagues. They did not set out to prove or disprove popular dogma about marihuana. Rather, they wanted to find out what happens when someone smokes marihuana.

It took one year to get the study approved by university and governmental agencies. After approval was formally granted, it took two months to find nine willing, marihuana-naïve, male subjects, while eight chronic users of marihuana were easily found. All volunteers had to pass a comprehensive psychiatric interview.

The researchers set out to conduct an empirical, public, replicable, and controlled experimental study. The naïve subjects were taught how to smoke the cigarettes. During several sessions, the subjects smoked two cigarettes in a neutral, laboratory setting. The verbal interaction between the subjects and experimenters was minimized, and the physiological and psychological tests were given according to a rigid schedule. The subjects were not asked to describe their feelings about their experiences until after the final experimental session.

The amount smoked was rigidly controlled, and the presumed active agent in marihuana cigarettes was also controlled. At different times, the subjects were given placebos (cigarettes containing hemp without the active agent), low-strength cigarettes, and high-strength cigarettes. A **double-blind** procedure was used; neither the observers nor the naïve subjects knew, until afterward, which kind of cigarette was used in a given test session. During the sessions, the subjects smoked the different kinds of cigarettes in random order. All of the naïve subjects smoked each kind of cigarette.

Several measures of behavior were used. The physiological measures were heart rate, respiratory rate, pupil size, blood glucose level (related to hunger), and dilation of the small blood vessels of the eyes ("red-eyes"). The psychological tests included: (1) a test of sustained attention (signaling when a particular letter in a group was flashed on a screen); (2) a digit-symbol substitution test (substituting symbols for digits according to a code); (3) a self-rating scale of mood or feeling state; (4) a pursuit-rotor test (Section Two, Unit C); (5) an elasped-time estimation task; and (6) the subjects were asked to guess which dose they had received.

The naïve smokers experienced no mood reaction during their first session. The one exception was one man who said he wanted to get high. On the other hand, one naïve subject, who said he would not get high, never did, no matter what dosage he was given. The novices guessed right half of the time. They almost all guessed correctly when they had a placebo, but almost all guessed incorrectly when they had the strong dose.

There was a mild increase in heart rate 15 minutes after the naïve subjects smoked the cigarettes. The chronic users experienced a much greater increase in heart rate following the strong dose. There were virtually no changes in respiratory rate. There was no effect on pupil size, contrary to police and newspaper reports. At the 15-minute test, all but one subject indicated a significant "red-eye" effect from the high dose. There was no effect on blood-sugar level.

For both groups, the drug had no effect on the sustained performance test. The novices' performance on the digit-symbol substitution test decreased under the influence of the drug. The chronic users did slightly better on the substitution test following inhalation of the smoke. Similarly, the novices' performance went down on the pursuit-rotor test, but the chronic users improved. While they did well on the time-estimation task prior to smoking, four of the novice subjects overestimated the elapsed time after smoking. At the end of the experiment, the naïve smokers reported that they had not experienced the euphoria, visual or auditory distortions, or confusion that chronic users say they experience. On the other hand, the chronic users reported that the maximum dose produced strong "highs."

We have omitted some of the results and many of the procedural details of the experiment. The example indicates the large number of factors that must be controlled in an adequate experimental study of behavior. The controls are necessary in order to come to any definite conclusion about what kind of antecedent event leads to a specific consequent event.

RESEARCH HYPOTHESES

When he observes behavior that interests him, a psychologist asks questions about the reasons for the behavior. The questions automatically lead to possible answers, and the form of a question determines the form of the possible answer. Suppose a psychologist observes a caged leopard alternately circle to the right and then to the left. The question "Why didn't the leopard continue to circle in one direction?" may lead the psychologist to speculate that the leopard was physically tired of pacing in one direction. The question "Why did the leopard change to a new direction?" may lead him to think that the leopard was seeking as much variety as possible.

Before rushing into the laboratory to test his speculations, the experimental psychologist should state his idea in the form of hypotheses. An **experimental hypothesis** is the first formal step of an experiment and consists of a specific, potential explanation for the occurrence of an event. An experimental hypothesis must: (1) potentially provide a relevant answer to the specific question, (2) be stated as clearly and simply as possible, and (3) be capable of being directly supported or unsupported by the results of an experiment.

Since the researchers were mainly trying to find out what happens when people smoke marihuana, the Weil, et al., study did not contain any explicitly formulated hypotheses. However, there were a few implicitly formulated hypotheses based on the published observations of marihuana users. The research team expected that the subjects would: (1) develop "red-eyes," (2) experience an increase in heart rate, (3) exhibit decreased blood-sugar levels, and (4) behave less well on tests of manual dexterity and concentration. For the naïve subjects, all but the third hypothesis were supported.

Because the naïve and sophisticated subjects in the marihuana study were not tested under the same conditions, the researchers only suggest that it is possible that the observed differences between the two types of people may have been due to their different previous experience with the drug. From this study, we may formulate the experimental hypothesis that chronic marihuana smokers (more than three times a week on the average) will perform better on the pursuit-rotor test and the digit-symbol substitution test than novices (no previous experience with marihuana) when the amount inhaled and the strength of the dosage are equated for the two groups. The hypothesis is relevant to the question of what are the differences in reaction between naïve and sophisticated marihuana users. The hypothesis is clearly stated and can be directly tested in an experiment.

OPERATIONAL DEFINITIONS

The requirement that an experimental hypothesis be stated so that it is clear and directly testable is not easily attained. Even the apparently simple concept called "hunger" may not result in agreement among behavioral scientists. Bridgman (1927) introduced the idea of using operational definitions to delineate the meaning of an experimental hypothesis clearly. **Operational definitions** specify the terms in an experimental hypothesis according to the actions (operations) taken by the scientist to make the observations. Thus, the scientist may operationally define a hungry rat as one that has been deprived of food for 23 hours. There are a number of other possible definitions for the term "hunger" but with this operational definition established, everyone knows what the term means within the context of this experiment. Operational definitions provide a precise and replicable definition of a given term.

Consider another example. Suppose that a psychologist is interested in anxious behavior. He may operationally define anxiety in terms of cigarette smoking: a highly anxious person is one who smokes six or more cigarettes per hour and a less anxious person is one who smokes less than one cigarette per hour. Another psychologist may want to study creativity. He operationally defines a creative answer as any answer that is given by no more than five percent of his subjects. In the experimental hypothesis about marihuana, the phrases within the parentheses are operational definitions of chronic and novice marihuana users.

The use of operational definitions also serves to prevent the study of scientifically meaningless questions. A concept or variable that cannot be defined operationally cannot be measured. Without measurement, experimentation is impossible. Students frequently ask, "How can we change the mind?" The question cannot be answered until we know how to define and measure "mind." Without measurement, we could never know when "mind" had changed.

The use of operational definitions promotes communication between scientists, regardless of their specialties. Given an operational definition of intelligence (for example, intelligence is what intelligence tests measure), a physicist, a biologist, and a psychologist could intelligently discuss the concept.

MODELS AND THEORIES

Since a major goal of the scientific approach is the formulation of systematic bodies of knowledge, models and theories are a major element of the approach. Scientists and textbooks do not define the two terms consistently. Consequently, the following definitions were arbitrarily selected.

Models

A **model** is a set of symbols with an associated set of logical rules for manipulating the symbols. The symbols may be numbers, words, physical objects, or uncommon abstract forms. The rules may be explicit or implicit.

One general model of abnormal behavior is called "the medical model." Many forms of the medical model exist; however, they all state that abnormal behavior is primarily determined by physiological-biological events. The rules of the medical model are not clearly stated. Nevertheless, from the basic statement, the following corollaries are derived: (1) the treatment of abnormal behavior should primarily involve medical therapeutic tools such as drugs; (2) the use of the proper medical tools will correct the biological cause of the abnormal behavior; and (3) when the biological cause is corrected, the abnormal behavior will be cured. One implication of the model is that medical doctors should have control of the treatment of abnormal behavior.

We do not wish to impugn the applicability of the medical model, but we do wish to point out that a model, by itself, has no validity or truth value. It is just a model. Similarly, a store mannequin is a physical model of the human form. The fact that it is a model does not imply anything about how good a model it is. The mannequin is designed to display clothing; however, it would not suffice as a teaching device for a premed human anatomy class.

The model or set of models a psychologist believes in determines, to a great extent, the kind of research he does and the types of explanations he develops. If a person believes that human behavior is random, chance, chaotic, undetermined, or unordered, then he will not engage in experimental research on human behavior. A psychologist may believe that from the point of conception, all of an animal's behavior is determined by its experiences. If a psychologist believes in that model, then he will not engage in any research on the effects of chromosomal structure or "genes" on behavior.

Models are used to build theories. The value of a model is in part determined by the value of the resultant theory.

Theories

The construction of a theory involves relating the terms of a model to events in the physical world. That is, the symbols of a model are identified with a specific, operationally defined empirical event. The model with its set of identifications constitutes a theory. A **theory** specifies the probable relationship between real world antecedent and consequent events. A theory may be used to predict the occurrence of new consequent events and a theory may be used to explain what has happened in the past. Figure 1.1 schematically illustrates the structural parts of a theory.

The entire diagram represents a theory; only one part of the diagram represents the model. The identifications of symbols normally consist of operational definitions of empirical events, coordinated with the symbols of the model. Thus, the identifications are called **coordinating definitions.** The coordinating definitions must be explicit. When conceptualizing a model, the model builder may have implicit identifications in mind. Until the implicit identifications are explicitly formed into coordinating definitions, the model is only a model and not a theory.

In the discussion of their results, Weil, et al. suggest two possible theories to account for the observed difference between the reactions of the chronic and novice subjects. One of the theories is labeled the "psychosocial interpretation." The interpretation is that repeated exposure to marihuana reduces psychological inhibitions. The following paragraphs present our elaboration on and extension of the psychosocial interpretation.

Our model can be most clearly presented in equation form. The model is $p(H) = L + (E \times S)$. The rules include: (1) the value of $p(H)$ cannot be less than

0.0 or greater than 1.0, (2) the value of L varies from 0.0 to 0.4, (3) the value of E varies from 0.0 to 1.0, and (4) the value of S varies from 0.2 to 0.6.

In order to construct a theory, the model is provided with the following co-ordinating definitions. The symbol p(H) stands for the probability of a euphoric reaction and is defined as a subject's score on a self-rating, seven-point "mood" scale. Several different affective feeling states (moods) are described, and for each mood, the subjects indicate how they feel. The total response to the scale is transformed into a decimal score.

The symbol L stands for learning and is defined as the number of marihuana-smoking experiences. Each experience is limited to long puffs (20-second inhalation) of two 1.5 gram marihuana cigarettes. Each experience must be separated by at least 24 hours. The number of experiences is transformed into a decimal score with its maximum value reached at 50 experiences.

The symbol E represents the subject's expectancy of a euphoric reaction. The expectancy is defined as the score on a seven-point belief scale. The scale consists of several statements about the effects of smoking marihuana, and the subject indicates his degree of belief in each statement. The total score on the belief scale is transformed into a decimal score with the highest degree of belief yielding a score of 1.0.

The symbol S stands for the physical and psychological setting during the smoking sessions. The settings are rated on an hedonic (pleasure) response scale. The raters are trained to make consistent ratings, and the total score on the scale

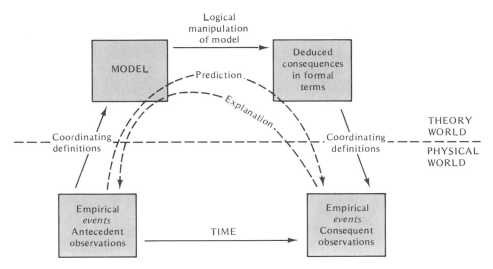

Fig. 1.1 Schematic presentation of the structure of a theory. The entire diagram represents a theory; one part of the diagram represents a model. The figure is modified from Coombs, et al. (1954), and Isaacson, et al. (1965).

is transformed to a decimal score. A negative setting gets a score of 0.2, and a very positive setting gets a score of 0.6. The model and coordinating definitions are summarized in Table 1.1.

TABLE 1.1. Marihuana Euphoria Theory.

Model	p(H)	=	L	+	(E	×	S)
Range of values	0.0–1.0		0.0–0.4		0.0–1.0		0.2–0.6
Verbal equivalent	probability of euphoria		learning		expectation		setting
Coordinating definition	score on mood scale		number of experiences		score on belief scale		rating on hedonic scale

The theory says that the probability of a euphoric ("high") reaction to marihuana cigarette smoking is equal to the measure of learning plus the multiplied measures of subjective expectancy ("set") and setting (physical and psychological environment). The antecedent observations are the measures of L, E, and S for each subject. The consequent observations are the measures of euphoric mood for each subject. The "deduced consequences in formal terms" (from Figure 1.1) are the results of adding and multiplying numbers as specified in the model. If a subject had at least 50 controlled experiences with marihuana, had a low expectancy score (0.1), and was placed in a moderately stimulating setting (0.5), then the theory predicts that he will have a mildly euphoric reaction [p(H) = 0.4 + (0.1 × 0.5) = 0.45]. If another subject has a highly euphoric reaction [p(H) = 0.9], we can use the theory to explain his behavior in terms of learning (0.4), his expectancy (1.0), and the moderately stimulating setting (0.5). As the example indicates, the major difference between explanation and prediction is that we predict what will happen and explain what did happen.

Evaluating Theories Theories can be evaluated in terms of two types of criteria. "Internal" criteria apply to the model portion of a theory. The internal criteria are: (1) clarity of terms in the model (for example, mathematical models tend to be very clear in comparison with models such as the medical model); (2) logical consistency of the model (models should not allow for logical contradictions between their parts); (3) deductive capacity (some models allow more possible deductions than others); and (4) parsimony (the relative simplicity of the model—all else being equal, the simpler model is preferable). "External" criteria apply to the relationship between the model and the empirical events identified with the model. The external criteria include: (1) clarity of coordinating definitions (if there is ambiguity regarding the relationship between the terms of the model and the operationally defined empirical event, then the researcher is not sure that he has an adequate test of the theory); (2) testability of the theory (some are more easily tested than others); (3) predictive generality (the theory that allows for more predictions and/or predictions that apply to a greater range of variables or more types of people is the better theory); and (4) degree of empirical support (the better theory is consistent with the greater amount of knowledge, both knowledge gathered as the result of testing the theory and knowledge gathered for other reasons).

The Value of Theories   A certain group of psychologists deplores the current emphasis on theory. Some of the reasons for their skeptical point of view include the following: (1) once formulated, a theory tends to take on an aura of "truth" and in some cases the followers of a particular theory have adhered to the theory in the face of conflicting data; (2) in the science of psychology, there have been several premature theories that have changed with every new observation; and (3) some theories have unnecessarily restricted research by suggesting that only certain areas should be pursued. As Hebb (1966, p. 316) suggested, "All theory needs to be held skeptically. . . . The time to be especially skeptical is when the theory says something cannot be so." It is obvious that theories, like any other tool, can be and have been misused.

Theories can be very useful. One major reason for constructing theories is that they are *general*. An attempt to list every potential relationship between antecedent and consequent behavioral events would require a computer with an infinite memory. Miller (1951, p. 86) illustrates the point with a physical example:

> For example, taking the type of substance as the condition and floating or sinking as the phenomenon, we need a whole series of laws such as wood floats, oil floats, paraffin floats, stones sink, metals sink, etc. Furthermore, there are likely to be exceptions, e.g., teakwood sinks and pumice stone floats. Thus the scientist is driven toward more abstract formulations, using such terms as *density* which do not directly refer to anything that is immediately observable. Stated in such terms, the law becomes: "A substance will float if its density is less than that of water." This law is more general; the specific cases, including the troublesome exceptions, may be deduced from it and a knowledge of the relevant conditions, namely the weight and volume.

Theories are also valuable because they can be used to make predictions about previously unexamined events. The density theory examined in the Miller quotation is a clear example. Theories guide research by suggesting potentially fruitful areas of investigation. Hull (1930 and 1943) constructed a theory of maze learning in rats. Some of his students (Dollard, Doob, Miller, Mowrer, Sears, Ford, Hovland, and Sollenberger, 1939) were able to use Hull's theory to develop research on human aggressive behavior.

The preceding pages outline the limits and complexity of the scientific approach to understanding behavior. Careful reading of these pages should leave you with more unanswered questions than you had on page one. To answer some of these questions, the following chapter examines the details of the scientific approach with emphasis on experimental observation.

REVIEW

Somehow any chapter discussing the scientific approach to knowledge (including this one) transmits the feeling that scientists live by a very restrictive set of rules. In actuality, the "rules" and "assumptions" are only a formalization of some agreed-on guidelines that have proved useful in the accumulation of knowledge. The most important feature of the scientific process is the data, not the rules. The use of operational definitions helps to tell in unambiguous terms what was really observed. The use of theories and/or models provides a framework for organizing the data. The rules and assumptions provide a common basis for making the observations.

Occasionally the pseudophilosophical issue is raised concerning the scientific value of a "one-of-a-kind" observation, since it does not meet the criterion of replicability. If the observation is made with scientific rigor, the data should not be declared illegitimate simply because of the inability to make another similar observation.

The artistic approach and the rationalistic approach emphasize other legitimate values in the accumulation of knowledge. Although the rules and assumptions of the scientific approach have proved valuable over many areas of investigation and over a long period of time, the student should not allow himself to be slavishly bound to a rigid set of criteria if it interferes with the data he wishes to observe.

SUMMARY

1. The assumptions of the scientific approach include: (1) the universality of order, (2) determinism, and (3) the discoverability of answers to research questions.
2. The requirements of scientific observation include: (1) observations must be empirical; (2) observations must be public; and (3) observations must be repeatable (replicable). Naturalistic observation does not involve the manipulation of the events by the scientist. Experimental observation does require controlled manipulation.
3. The goals of the scientific approach are understanding, prediction, and systematic organization of fact and method.
4. The Weil, et al. (1968), example indicates that many factors must be controlled in an experimental study of behavior.
5. An experimental hypothesis must be relevant, clear, and testable. An operational definition of a term is a description of how a scientist measures the term.
6. A model is a set of symbols with an associated set of logical rules. The rules may be implicit or clearly specified.
7. A theory is a model with coordinating definitions. Theories can be misused, but are developed because they are more general than a list of facts, they predict new relationships, and they guide research.

SUGGESTED READING

Bachrach, A. J. *Psychological research: An introduction.* (2d ed.) New York: Random House, 1965.

Bergmann, G., and Spence, K. W. Operationism and theory in psychology. *Psychological Review,* 1941, *48,* 1–14.

Bridgman, P. W. Remarks on the present state of operationalism. *Scientific Monthly,* 1954, *79,* 224–226.

Conant, J. B. *On understanding science: An historical approach.* New Haven: Yale University Press, 1947.

Coombs, C. H., Raiffa, H., and Thrall, R. M. Some views on mathematical models and measurement theory. *Psychological Review*, 1954, *61*, 132–144.

Kerlinger, F. N. *Foundations of behavioral research.* (2d ed.) New York: Holt, Rinehart and Winston, 1973.

Kuhn, T. S. *The structure of scientific revolutions.* (2d ed.) Chicago: University of Chicago Press, 1970.

Marx, M. H. (Ed.). *Theories in contemporary psychology.* New York: Macmillan, 1963.

Miller, N. E. Comments on theoretical models. Illustrated by the development of a theory of conflict behavior. *Journal of Personality*, 1951, *20*, 82–100.

Sanford, F. H., and Capaldi, E. J. (Eds.) *Advancing psychological science.* Vol. 1. *Philosophies, methods, and approaches.* Belmont, California: Wadsworth, 1964.

Siever, R. Science: Observational, experimental, historical. *American Scientist*, 1968, *56*, 70–77.

Townsend, J. C. *Introduction to experimental method.* New York: McGraw-Hill, 1953.

Turner, M. B. *Philosophy and the science of behavior.* New York: Appleton, 1967.

CHAPTER 2
The Basic Nature of Research

Why do students frequently fall asleep in lecture classes? The research process often begins with a question such as this. In seeking ways to answer the question, the scientist's first task is to define the behavior of interest. In this case the behavior is sleeping under certain environmental conditions: lecture classes. The subjects are students, and in order to have ready access to a pool of subjects, the scientist limits his question to college students at a particular college. For expediency the scientist further limits the population of students to those in a particular class in which lectures are regularly given. The researcher speculates about the possible causes of the sleeping behavior. The students may sleep because of internal bodily conditions such as fatigue due to lack of sleep, drug-induced somnolence, or perhaps they have just eaten a large meal. On a given day each bodily condition varies among the students—some may be very fatigued and others not at all. Thus, each bodily condition is a potential variable in the research on sleeping in class. The environmental conditions external to each student may also contribute to the sleeping behavior. For example, the room temperature may be too warm, the students' chairs may be softly padded, or the lecturer may speak in a dull monotone. Each of these conditions may cause sleeping. The researcher's task is complicated by the large number of potential causes of sleeping behavior. The usual method of attacking such a research question is to try to devise ways of eliminating potential causes so that only one or two are left, or at least to eliminate the minor causes, leaving only the most important ones. One way to determine the importance of a potential causative variable is to change the value of the variable and see if the frequency of the behavior changes. Thus, the researcher can change the room temperature to several different settings for several lectures and see if more or fewer students fall asleep. If there is no noticeable change in rate of sleeping, then temperature may be eliminated from the list of potential causes. Another way to determine the importance of a potential variable is to vary the time relationship between the occurrence of the potential cause and the behavior. Thus, the researcher may arrange to have his 1:00 P.M. lecture take place at a later hour or before the lunch period so that the effect of full or empty stomachs may be examined. If there is no change in sleeping rate, then the stomach-fullness variable may be eliminated. In a similar fashion the researcher may examine the effects of all the potential causes that he can think of and finally come to a statement about which variables seem to have the greatest effect on rate of sleeping in the particular class.

Research is the process of attempting to answer researchable questions. Frequently the research questions are generated by theories and the function of an experimenter is to examine the relationships between the antecedent and consequent events diagrammed in Figure 1.1.

VARIABLES

A **variable** is any condition in a scientific investigation that may change in quantity and/or quality (for example, room temperature, time and amount of food consumed, and so on). In contrast with a variable, a **constant** is something that does not change. If the investigator in the preceding example decides that the same professor will deliver all the lectures in the course, this factor is a constant.

Two main types of variables are studied in science: independent and dependent variables. **Independent variables** are controlled and manipulated by an experimenter. The experimenter chooses different levels of an independent variable to use in an experiment. An independent variable must have at least two levels (treatments). For example, a subject may smoke a marihuana cigarette or a placebo, or the thermostat in a lecture room may be set at 65° or at 75° (two levels of the independent variables). In psychology, independent variables fall into two general categories: (1) environmental variables and (2) organismic variables. An *environmental* variable is any characteristic of an organism's environment that may influence its behavior. For example, room temperature is an environmental variable. An *organismic* variable is any physiological or psychological characteristic of an organism. Sex, blood type, intelligence, degree of fatigue, and shoe size are all examples of organismic variables. The second type of variable studied in science is a dependent variable. In psychology, behavior is a **dependent variable.** In the preceding example, sleeping during lectures was a dependent variable. In an experiment, the experimenter manipulates independent variables and observes the effect on dependent variables.

Suppose an experimenter wants to determine the effects of drinking alcohol on handball playing. The independent variable may be operationally defined as the number of cans of beer consumed immediately before playing. The alcohol content of the beer is known, and the experimenter can manipulate the number of cans consumed. The dependent variable is operationally defined as the number of games won (the measure of behavior). The experimenter selects 12 male subjects who are all the same age and have equal handball-playing ability. The 12 subjects are assigned at random to six experimental groups of two subjects each. Both members of Group I receive no beer before each game. The subjects in Group II each drink two cans of beer before each game. The subjects in Groups III, IV, V, and VI each drink 4, 6, 8, and 10 cans, respectively, before each game. The levels of the independent variable, that is, the number of cans of beer for each group, are arbitrarily selected but operationally defined. These levels of the independent variable are also called treatments. Each subject plays every other subject, making a total of 66 games in the experiment.

The experimenter collects the data presented in Table 2.1. The data are represented quite easily by means of a graph. The components of a graph are shown in Figure 2.1.

TABLE 2.1.   Hypothetical Data from Beer-Drinking Experiment.

Group	Number of Cans of Beer Consumed (X)	Number of Games Won (Y)
I	0	21
II	2	17
III	4	13
IV	6	9
V	8	5
VI	10	1

The data from the experiment are plotted on the graph shown in Figure 2.2. The independent variable values (that is, 0, 2, 4, 6, 8, 10) constitute a set of numbers (X) that is placed on the X axis. The dependent variable values also represent a set of numbers (Y) that is plotted on the Y axis.

Relationships

A **relationship** is defined by the set of paired values of the independent and dependent variables. The set of six data points in the graph of Figure 2.2 defines the relationship between amount of alcohol consumed and number of handball games

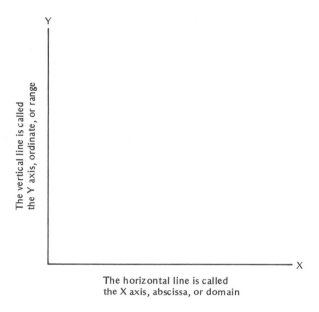

Fig. 2.1.   Components of a graph. The independent variable is usually plotted on the X axis. The dependent variable is usually plotted on the Y axis.

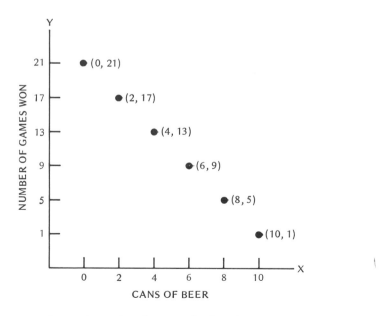

Fig. 2.2.   Data from example experiment plotted on a graph. The independent variable was the number of cans of beer drunk. The dependent variable was the number of handball games won.

won. The relationship may be summarized in simple English: "The number of games decreased as the amount of alcohol consumed increased."

Functions

One special type of relationship is called a function. Often psychologists state that the dependent variable, Y, is a function of the independent variable, X. Symbolically, $Y = f(X)$ where f means "is a function of." Mathematically, a **function** is defined as follows: if for every element in the domain (X axis) there exists *exactly* one and only one element in the range (Y axis), then the relationship between X and Y is a function. A relationship that is not a function can have more than one element in the range for each element in the domain. In the imaginary handball experiment, one could say that the number of handball games won is a function of the number of cans of beer consumed, since the plot of the data fits the definition of a function. For example, one may enter the graph in Figure 2.3 at any point along the X axis, draw a line perpendicular to the X axis to the function, then draw a horizontal line from the point of intersection to the Y axis. The value at the intersection of the horizontal line and the Y axis is the hypothetical Y value that would have been obtained if the X value had been used in the experiment. Briefly, if a value on the X axis is known, the value of the dependent variable can be determined from the function.

Figure 2.4 presents a nonlinear function in contrast to the linear function of Figure 2.3. Figure 2.5 presents a relationship that is not a function.

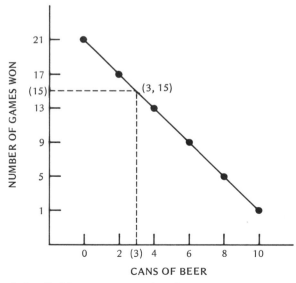

Fig. 2.3.   Data from the handball-beer experiment plotted on a graph (as in Figure 2.2). The plotted data points satisfy the definition of a function. The function is a straight line (linear) function. The dotted lines indicate how to infer probable values of the dependent variable (15) from hypothetical values (3) of the independent variable.

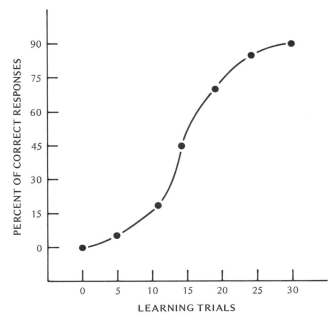

Fig. 2.4. Data from a learning experiment illustrating a nonlinear (curved) function. The percent of correct responses is a nonlinear function of the number of learning trials. The curvature of the function indicates that the rate of learning was slow during the beginning trials and ending trials. The rate of learning was fast during the middle trials (10–25).

Theoretical Constructs

Psychologists often use terms like "learning," "motivation," "perception," and "thinking" to describe relationships between variables. These terms are generally called **theoretical constructs,** and they symbolize or label the relationship between two operationally defined variables. When properly used, they have *no meaning other than the observed relationship.* A graphed learning curve (Figure 2.4) represents the construct "learning." The relationship illustrated in Figures 2.2 or 2.3 may be labeled with the theoretical construct "drunkenness" or "intoxication."

A recent study on interpersonal attraction illustrates the use of several independent and dependent variables in the same experiment (Kleinke, Staneski, and Pipp, 1972). Pairs of college students, each consisting of one male and one female student, were placed in a laboratory room and told to talk to each other for 15 minutes about any topic they wished. The discussion topics were unimportant to the study. The females were assistants (confederates) of the experimenter. The pairs were observed through a one-way viewing mirror. Three independent variables were manipulated and four dependent variables were measured in the study. We will not discuss all of the variables here. Two of the independent variables were: (1) amount of time the confederate spent looking at the male subject, 90 percent or 10 percent gazing time; and (2) level of attractiveness of the confederate, high

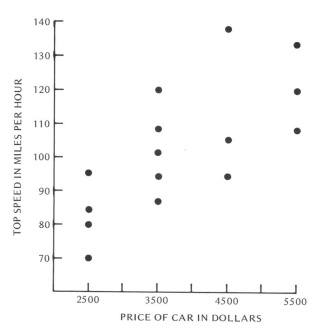

Fig. 2.5. Graph of the relationship between original price of cars and their top speeds. There is a relationship between the two variables (as price increases, speed usually increases). However, identically priced cars have different top speeds, thus, speed is not a function of price.

or low attractiveness as judged by raters who were otherwise uninvolved in the study. Two of the dependent variables were: (1) total conversational time during the 15-minute period, and (2) the males' ratings of the female confederates in terms of polar adjectives, that is, the females were rated on their degree of friendliness on a scale ranging from friendly to unfriendly, degree of warmth (warm to cold), sincerity (sincere to insincere), attentiveness (attentive to ignoring), politeness (polite to impolite), and interestingness (interesting to boring).

Main Effect   When the relationship between a single independent variable and a single dependent variable is easily and directly summarized, the summary statement is sometimes called the *main effect* of the variable. Among the important results of the interpersonal attractiveness study are several main effects. One of these was that the female confederates who gazed 90 percent of the time were rated as more attentive than those who gazed only 10 percent of the time. A second main effect was that highly attractive females were consistently rated more favorably than lowly attractive females.

Interactions   Sometimes two or more independent variables interact with each other in terms of their effect on a dependent variable. An *interaction effect*

Interaction   occurs when the observed effect of one independent variable changes as a function of a second independent variable. The independent variables of attractiveness and amount of gazing time interacted in the Kleinke, et al. study. The male subjects rated the attractive girls more favorably when the girls gazed 10 percent of the time than when they gazed 90 percent of the time. However, the males rated the unattractive girls much less favorably when they gazed 10 percent of the time than when they gazed 90 percent of the time. Thus, the effect of the gaze condition depended on the attractiveness of the girl.

Occasionally interactions can be spectacular. For example, moderate amounts of alcohol can be consumed by most people without harmful effect. And there are many wild mushrooms that are not only harmless but enthusiastically gathered for their flavor. One species of mushroom has the interesting quality of being completely harmless unless it is eaten within three days of the time any alcohol is consumed. It seems that the mushroom and the alcohol in the person's system interact to cause a significant loss of motor control, partial anesthesia of the extremities, and other symptoms of nervous system impairment.

Measurement Both the beer-drinking–handball study and the interpersonal attractiveness experiment employed measurement. *Measurement* is the assignment of symbols (usually numbers) to objects or events according to a set of rules. In a research study, the values of the independent and dependent variables are determined by measurement. In the handball-beer study, measurement involved counting the number of beers consumed and number of games won. In the interpersonal attractiveness experiment, among other things, time of talking, physical attractiveness, and friendliness were measured. The meaning of measurement is determined by the rules of measurement. The rule for measuring the time of talking in the attractiveness experiment was the rule that a clock be started as soon as the two people in the room started talking and the clock stopped when they were not talking. The clock cumulated times during the 15-minute period so that the measure for each male subject was a total talking time score in seconds. A measurement procedure initializes a set of pairs of numbers, the first members of each pair being the object or event to be measured and the second member of the pair being the number assigned to the object or event according to the measurement rule. Thus, in the attractiveness experiment the subjects were numbered (for convenience) and the set of pairs of numbers consisted of each subject number paired with a single time score.

Measurement

Researchers must carefully determine that they are measuring the variables they think they are measuring. Many colleges routinely ask students to evaluate teachers. It is often assumed that teaching effectiveness is measured by scores on the student evaluation forms. Rodin and Rodin (1972) examined the relationship between an "objective" measure of teaching effectiveness (what the students learned) and a "subjective" measure of teaching effectiveness (ratings on teacher evaluation forms). There were 293 students in an undergraduate calculus course. There were 11 teaching assistants (instructors) for the course, each with one recitation section (one instructor had two sections). The students were required to learn 40 specific procedures ("40 paradigm problems") and were tested with a specific problem for each paradigm procedure. The final grade in the course was completely determined by (measured by) the number of problems passed. The students were allowed up to six attempts to pass each problem. The students rated the instructors at the end of the quarter. They graded the instructors using the usual letter grade system in the usual way with A = 4, B+ = 3.5, B = 3, and so on. The average course grade of the students in each section was paired with the average student rating of the instructor. The relationship between the two sets of measures was negative and approximately linear. The three instructors with the lowest subjective scores had the highest objective scores (average student grades). The instructor with the highest subjective measure had the lowest objective measure. Student evaluations of instructors probably do measure the social skills and personal qualities of an instructor; however, this research indicates that student evaluations do not measure how much students learn from a course. "If how much students learn is considered to be a major component of good teaching, it must be concluded that good teaching is not validly measured by student evaluations in their current form" (Rodin & Rodin, 1972, p. 1166).

CONTROL OF VARIANCE

In the ideal experiment, all of the observed measures of the dependent variable are attributable to the manipulations of the independent variable. In the handball example, the relationship between beer consumption and handball performance is obvious. If the experiment were actually conducted, athletic ability, tolerance to alcohol, or lucky bounces of the ball might alter the observed relationship. There are innumerable factors—organic and environmental, contemporary and historical —they may affect the behavior of a subject at a given time. All of these factors working together, in addition to the independent variable, may elevate or depress the scores obtained by a subject in an experiment. It is the task of the experimenter to discriminate between changes in behavior due to the independent variable and other sources of variation.

The variation in observed scores on the *dependent variable* is called **variance.** Variance may arise from three general sources: (1) subject factors, (2) environmental factors, and (3) experimenter factors. In other words, the behavioral data obtained in an experiment is the product of: (1) the heredity, history, and present state of the subject; (2) the nature of the environment; and (3) the characteristics of the experimenter and/or the measuring device. Factors in any of the three categories may be manipulated as independent variables in behavioral experiments. Once the factor of interest has been selected, the researcher must control *all* other factors that contribute to the variance of the dependent variable. The ability of an experimenter to control the sources of variance in an experiment is a major feature of experimental observation. In order to understand methods of control, the basic characteristic of variance in the measures of the dependent variable are examined in the next section.

Primary Variance   An experimenter manipulates the independent variable in order to observe certain changes in the dependent variable. The observed, *consistent* variation in behavior related to the independent variable is called **primary**

variance (also called systematic variance, experimental variance, or between-groups variance). As implied by the term, primary variance is the major reason for conducting the experiment. Another way to think about it is that primary variance is sought by the experimenter (in other words, is wanted variance), while all other variance is unwanted.

Secondary Variance   The unwanted variation in the measures of the dependent variable may be divided into two categories. If the measure of the dependent variable is changed in a *consistent* fashion by some factor other than the independent variable, the change is called **secondary variance** (sometimes called extraneous variance). Secondary variance is the product of an unrecognized variable.

A magician depends on secondary variance, since he deliberately misdirects the audience about the causes of his tricks. To the experimenter, however, secondary variance presents a problem in determining relationships. In the beer-drinking experiment, for instance, it might be argued that the observed impairment in game playing resulted from the excess fluid weight some players had to carry around, rather than from intoxication.

Secondary variance can be the result of a variable that elevates or depresses all of the measures by a constant amount without altering or interfering with the desired relationship. For example, the length of a maze directly affects the time it takes the subject to run the maze. It is more common, however, to find that an extraneous variable *interacts* with the independent variable to enhance or reduce the effect of the independent variable. It seems likely that both fluid weight *and* intoxication *combined* to cause the observed effect on handball-playing ability. In such a case, it is difficult to determine how much of the observed data is due to the independent variable and how much is due to the extraneous or secondary variable.

The terms primary and secondary refer to the *intent* of the experimenter when designing the research. Both types of variance result from antecedent events. Either type of variable can be the major source of variance in any given experiment. The same variance in behavioral data may be labeled primary or secondary by two different experimenters depending on their own research orientation. During the course of an experiment, an alert researcher may find that altering the research plan to pursue a source of secondary variance is more interesting than further investigation of his original hypothesis. Thus, secondary variance can become primary variance to a researcher who switches to another experimental hypothesis.

Error Variance   The second category of unwanted variance, error variance (sometimes called within-groups variance or random variance), results when some factor affects the observed data in an *inconsistent* fashion. Error variance is the result of many factors that render a particular measure inaccurate. One source of error variance is the use of an inappropriate measuring instrument. For example, inconsistent data may result from using a 12-inch ruler to measure a city block, or using a bathroom scale to measure small quantities of chemicals. Another source of error variance is the use of inconsistent experimental procedures. Any changes in the treatment of individual subjects will increase inconsistencies in the observed data. Individual scores may vary considerably if some subjects are allowed eight to nine seconds to perform a task, and others get 11 to 12 seconds for the same "10-second" task. The effect of an error source is to increase the variability of the data, making it difficult to isolate the effect of the independent variable.

The primary problem facing an experimenter is to arrange his experimental conditions so that he can obtain data that specify the relationship between the independent variable and the dependent variable. The key to obtaining such data is the use of adequate and appropriate control procedures. Kerlinger (1964, p. 280) says of control:

> According to this principle [control], by constructing an efficient research design the investigator attempts (1) to maximize the [primary] variance of the variable or variables of his . . . research hypothesis, (2) to control the variance of extraneous or "unwanted" [secondary] variables that may have an effect on his experimental outcomes, but in which he is not interested, and (3) to minimize the error or random variance, including so-called errors of measurement.

Maximize Primary Variance

A well-designed experiment provides good control of irrelevant factors. An experimenter cannot completely eliminate secondary and error variance; however, good research is that which yields the desired information, not just superb control of secondary and error variables. If the noise level in a dormitory is so high that one cannot hear one's favorite radio or TV program, it may be more satisfactory to turn up the volume than to attempt other control procedures. Similarly, there are certain methods available to an experimenter that enhance the effects of the independent variable (primary variance) so that it is more easily discerned from the background variance.

Extreme Values of the Independent Variable   One way to increase the effect of an independent variable is to choose extreme values. Occasionally a variable automatically falls into two diverse classes such as male-female. In other cases, the experimental conditions represent a selection of the extreme values on a continuum. A classic example of this technique is found in a study by Tryon (1940) where a large number of animals were run in a maze task. In terms of maze-learning ability, the top 5 percent (maze-bright) and the bottom 5 percent (maze-dull) were selected and mated within each group. The top 5 percent of the offspring from the "maze bright" group were mated and the bottom 5 percent of the offspring from the "maze-dull" group were likewise selected and interbred. After several generations of selective breeding, Tryon produced two strains of animals in terms of maze-learning ability. Note that the selection of extreme values resulted in the loss to this experiment of 90 percent of the available subjects. In some cases, the extreme values method may be too extravagant to be seriously considered. An example of selecting extreme values of an environmental factor would be to condition animals to discriminate between black and white instead of shades of gray. Of course, if extreme values are used, the effects of intermediate values of the primary variable are not determined in the study.

Optimal Values of the Independent Variable   Occasionally the choice of extreme values of the primary variable will not maximize the observed effect.

Animals that have not been deprived of food probably will not run in a maze to find food. Animals that have been deprived of food for five days may not run in the maze either! It is not uncommon to find that as the measure of the independent variable is increased, the measure of the dependent variable will increase, level off, and then decrease. (See Figure 2.6.) If a variable yields an "inverted-U" relationship, intermediate values of the independent variable are advisable. If other research indicates that particular values of the independent variable will maximize primary variance, use these optimal values. The point of looking at optimal values to be used is to maximize the chance of detecting an effect if it exists.

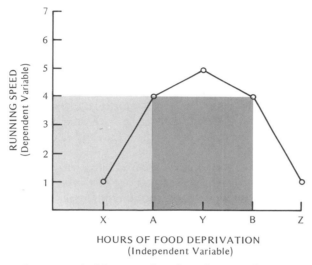

Fig. 2.6. An example of an "inverted U" function. The independent variable is hours of food deprivation and the dependent variable is maze-running speed. The A and B values of food deprivation yield identical dependent variable scores.

Several Values of the Independent Variable   Often the experimenter does not know the optimal values of the independent variable. The arbitrary choice of two values may lead to the conclusion that the variable has no effect on behavior. (See points A and B in Figure 2.6.) In general, the experimenter is best advised to run the experiment using several values of the independent variable (**parametric research**). An advantage of the parametric approach is that it increases the probability of choosing optimal values of the independent variable. Most importantly, it allows the experimenter to determine the nature of the relationship precisely.

Control of Secondary Variance

Historically, psychologists moved into the laboratory to obtain better control over secondary variables. Subject factors such as age or past experience can have an effect on the data and often are not controlled. Other factors may not be so obvious.

Laboratory Research

For instance, male rats will press a bar more often in a bright environment than females (Sackett, 1963). The sex factor may not be controlled in bar-pressing studies. The term "laboratory rat" conceals an important potential source of secondary variance. There are differences between the behavior of pigmented and albino rats in laboratory situations (Beauchamp, 1968). Since some experimental laboratories establish and maintain their own highly inbred animal colonies, it might be interesting to compare the behavior of each of these strains. Strain differences are usually not studied, but might explain some differences between similar experiments run in different laboratories.

By limiting extraneous factors, the experimenter clarifies the effect of the independent variable. However, not all extraneous factors can be controlled in the laboratory. Diverse factors such as time of day, amount of sleep, blood-sugar level, or an impending examination may markedly affect a subject's performance. Subjects are remarkably adept at picking up cues from the experimenter. Animals' utilization of experimenter feedback is illustrated by a study that found that rats learned a difficult maze discrimination in a suspiciously short time. Subsequent investigation revealed that the animals were learning to run to the (correct) side of the maze where the experimenter was standing. Another example occurs in counseling and interviewing where the responses of a subject may differ depending on the sex of the interviewer (Rosenthal, 1967).

Secondary variance also occurs when a measuring technique is biased. A **biased measure** is one that yields scores that are distorted in a consistent way. For example, biasing can occur when the experimenter must decide which object the subject looked at first. If an experimenter *expects to find* a certain phenomenon, he is more likely to find evidence for this phenomenon than an unbiased observer. Rosenthal (1966) discusses a number of examples of the experimenter effect. The data suggest that any researcher should be especially careful to guard against inadvertently introducing a bias because of his expectations. Several control procedures may be employed once an extraneous factor is identified as affecting the experimental data.

Elimination of the Secondary Variable A desirable control technique is to eliminate a secondary factor from the experimental situation. Occasionally this is accomplished effectively by hanging a sign on the door stating "Quiet Please, Experiment in Progress." The influence of the experimenter may occasionally be eliminated by placing a screen between the subject and experimenter.

It is possible to decrease the effect of experimenter bias by having a laboratory technician collect the data. If the technician is not informed which subjects are in the experimental conditions, he is less likely to bias the results with his expectations (**single-blind technique**).

Hold the Secondary Variable Constant Some secondary factors such as gravity, temperature, or time of day cannot be eliminated from the experimental situation. Since any variation in these factors could alter the experimental results, the alternative is to hold these factors constant. Treating all subjects in the same manner will sometimes allow the secondary factors to affect performance equally.

If temperature affects the performance of students on an anxiety test, then one can control the temperature variable by holding it constant.

Matching Subjects on a Secondary Variable Suppose an experimenter wishes to determine which of two study conditions facilitates learning. He must be concerned with the relative intelligence of the subjects in each learning condition. The hold-constant method of control would require a large number of subjects, since all would have to have the same score on an IQ test. As a result, a large number of subjects would be rejected. It is possible to utilize more of the available subjects by selecting several pairs of subjects, *matched* on IQ score. One of the subjects in each pair may be assigned to the first study group and the other subject to the second study group. The IQ factor will contribute equally to the scores of each group, and any consistent difference between the groups will be the result of the differential study conditions. Unless each subject in the original sample can be matched, some subjects will have to be rejected, or the matching procedure must be made less rigid. The last alternative weakens the effectiveness of matching. Matching is easier if a large number of subjects are available. Matching on one variable does not control for other possible sources of differences between matched subjects.

Subjects as Their Own Control A major subform of the matching method is the use of subjects as their own control. In general, the procedure consists of obtaining more than one measure of behavior from each subject. Using subjects as their own control may involve obtaining a measure before and after the introduction of the experimental treatment. The purpose of the procedure is to reduce the influence of subject factors on the total variability in the experiment. Fewer subjects are required than with the usual matching method.

Randomization Suppose the experimenter has no IQ measures. His best procedure for reducing the influence of secondary factors is to assign the subjects to groups by a random method, such as flipping a coin. With a random assignment procedure, both groups have an equal chance of getting a highly intelligent subject, or a very dull subject. Random assignment theoretically will equate the groups on average intelligence or any other factor. Random assignment is used in most experiments because it controls for the effects of unmeasurable and/or undiscovered secondary factors.

Random assignment is usually accomplished by means of a table of random numbers. (See Appendix D.) A **random-number table** consists of numbers from 0 to 9 arranged in a random sequence. There is no known pattern or rule that will account for the sequence of numbers shown. (Human beings do *not* make good random-number generators, primarily because they cannot bring themselves to call out the same number several times in succession, an event that can and does occur in a random sequence.) The table in Appendix D presents numbers in groups of five for reading convenience. To use the table in assigning the subjects to the treatment conditions, the experimenter enters the table at any point. He usually does this by closing his eyes and placing a pencil tip somewhere on the page, but more exotic and superstitious methods work equally well. He then reads a sequence of digits in any direction. After a sequence is obtained, he alphabetically lists the

Random Assignment

name of a subject beside each number. All subjects paired with even numbers are assigned to one condition, and all subjects with odd numbers are assigned to the other. Assigning numbers from 0 to 4 to one condition, and from 5 to 9 to the other works as well. The method of obtaining a random-number sequence is unimportant, provided the experimenter does not always enter at the same point and collect his numbers in the same direction. If he requires more than 10 digits in his assignment scheme, he can list the numbers in pairs or larger groups.

If the researcher requires an equal number of subjects in each of his groups, he continues to sample until one of his groups is full, then the other group (assuming there are two groups) is automatically filled with the remaining subjects. If there are three groups in his experiment, he might state that the numbers 1–3 constitute the first group, 5–7 the second group, and 8–0 the third group. (Note that the number 4 is ignored because 10 cannot be evenly divided by three.) Four groups can be obtained by first obtaining two groups, and then randomly dividing them in two. If the research requires that the groups be balanced by sex (equal numbers of each sex in each group), then the experimenter randomly assigns subjects to groups one sex at a time. The number of ways to select a random sample is limited only by the researcher's ingenuity. A coin or dice can be used to select a random sample, but a table of random numbers is the best (most unbiased) method.

A table of random numbers may be used to select subjects, assign subjects to conditions, determine the order of subject appearance in the experiment, choose stimuli, establish the sequence of stimuli in the experiment, and govern the pattern of reinforcement to the subject.

Note that it is still *possible* to assign randomly only bright subjects to one group and only dull subjects to the other. Such an event is more likely with small groups than large groups. If randomization is used to select a large sample, the probability of selecting an unrepresentative sample decreases (for example, a sample of only obese people from a college population). Therefore, as the number of subjects increases, randomization becomes more effective as a control procedure.

Systematizing the Secondary Variable   Another method of dealing with a secondary variable is to make it an independent variable. Suppose an experimenter wished to determine whether rats were more active in a light environment or a dark environment. As previously mentioned, male and female rats differ in activity when exposed to short test periods of light and dark. The experimenter must choose some method of controlling the effect of the organismic variable, sex. He could eliminate the variable by holding it constant, that is, he could choose to work with only one sex. In which case, the conclusions could not be generalized to both sexes. He could assign the sexes to each group, randomly, or he could balance the groups by assigning an equal number of males and females to each experimental condition, thus making sex an independent variable.

By using sex as an independent variable, the experimenter will find that he can recover more information than by randomization or holding constant. Suppose that the experimenter has a group of 10 males and 10 females, which he divides into groups of five males and five females. (The proper method of assigning *each*

individual male or female to a group is to use a table of random numbers.) The
design is summarized in Figure 2.7. The experimenter has four groups of subjects:
five females in the light condition (I); five females in the dark condition (II); five
males in the light condition (III); and five males in the dark condition (IV). In order
to evaluate the effect of the brightness variable, the experimenter combines the
data from Groups I and III and compares it with the combined data from Groups
II and IV. The operation is represented in the table by comparing column L, which
represents all of the subjects in the light condition, with the data from column D,
or all of the subjects in the dark condition. The experimenter now has the desired
comparison of the two environmental conditions with the secondary factor, sex,
systematized.

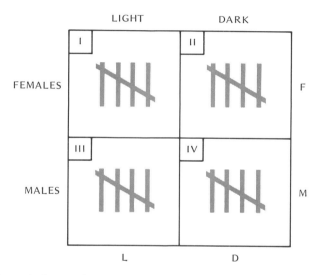

Fig. 2.7.   A 2 x 2 matrix showing four groups of five subjects each. Sex is an organismic, independent
variable. Brightness is an environmental, independent variable. Each tally mark represents a single subject.

Notice that the experimenter can also run a comparison to see if there is any
activity difference between males and females. By recombining the data from
Groups III and IV (all male subjects) with the data from Groups I and II (all female
subjects), the experimenter can compare the sexes under matched environmental
conditions. Sex and brightness both become independent variables, *all in the same
experiment!* Furthermore, the experimenter can determine if the combination of
the two variables produces an interaction effect.

Conservative Arrangement of a Secondary Variable   Occasionally the experimenter may not care if a secondary variable is uncontrolled in an experiment,
so long as the results are not greatly affected by the variable. In such cases, the
experimenter may choose to arrange the conditions so that the effect of the secon-

dary variable can only weaken the primary variance. Since *conservative arrangement* consists in the experimenter's deliberately stacking the cards against his hypotheses, he can be even more confident if his hypotheses are supported. Suppose an experimenter wants to test for learning in cockroaches. He can put the subjects in an apparatus where they can choose between a light and a dark compartment. Whenever the subjects enter the dark compartment, they are given a shock. After several shocks, the cockroaches should learn to stay in the light compartment and to run to the other compartment when the lights are switched. The learned response is opposite to the normal preference of cockroaches for dark places. Therefore, if the subjects do learn, the experimenter can conclude that the results are due to learning and not to the cockroaches' natural preference for darkness. Since any other procedure for controlling the secondary variable would produce even stronger results, the technique is known as a conservative arrangement of the secondary variable.

Minimize Error Variance

As stated previously, error variance is any *inconsistent* variation in the measure of the dependent variable. It is the product of a multitude of factors, each of which may change a particular score at the instant of observation. To guarantee that his observations are as accurate and meaningful as possible, the experimenter must try to minimize error variance.

A major component of error variance is identified by the term **individual differences.** Because of differences in the heredity and past history of experimental subjects, variability in responses must be expected. Individual differences also result from uncontrolled and uncontrollable factors in the environment that affect each subject differently.

Another major component of error variance results from the methods employed to gather, quantify, and analyze data. No matter how elegant the experimental procedures, the results of an experiment may be inconclusive if the measurement is not adequate. Thus, **measurement error** must be reduced.

The first problem in choosing a measurement procedure is the selection of an appropriate measurement technique. If the measuring device is too crude or too refined, the resulting data will not be very meaningful. The measurement technique should be able to discriminate between the performance of subjects. It would be ridiculous to use a creativity test that yields equivalent scores for all subjects. On the other hand, too fine a measure produces "noise" that can confound the interpretation of a relationship. Measuring running time in a maze to the nearest ten-thousandth of a second would also be ridiculous.

Psychologists are often faced with the problem of deciding how to score a particular observation. In classical conditioning research, one is sometimes faced with the question "Did the response occur or not?" Prior to an experiment, it would be best if the experimenter spent some time establishing unambiguous criteria for measuring responses.

A third component of measurement error involves the analysis of the data.

A number of statistical procedures may be used in analyzing the results of an experiment. If the experimenter uses an inappropriate statistical procedure and/or makes errors in his calculations, his conclusions may be inaccurate.

SAMPLING AND GENERALIZATION

When designing a research project, an experimenter would like to generalize his conclusions to the behavior of a large number of organisms that will never be in an experiment. The larger group of individuals is called the population. The **population** is defined as the set of all of the subjects of interest and is usually specified for each experiment. Examples of populations are: all living organisms, all mammals, all humans, all United States citizens, all United States college students, all students at a particular college, all students taking a particular class, students who sit in the front row of that class, and so on.

The group of individuals used by the experimenter constitutes a sample of the population. A **sample** is defined as a part (subset) of the population. The descriptions of the data obtained from a sample (such as the average score) are called **statistics,** while the corresponding descriptions of a population are called **parameters.** Statistics are used to estimate values of the population parameters. The accuracy of an estimate depends, among other things, on the nature of the sample.

The question of how well the sample statistics estimate the parameters of the population is of vital concern to both the experimenter and to the person reading the results of the experiment. Both the experimenter and the reader are interested in generalizing from the sample to the population. To use a sample statistic with confidence, the experimenter must ascertain that it is both valid and reliable.

Validity of the Sampling Technique

Validity is defined as the degree to which a measure actually reflects what it is supposed to measure. A sample statistic is valid if it closely approximates the population parameter. The validity of a statistic is reduced if the sample is *biased* in one of two ways. First, the sample may include individuals who are not members of the population. Inadvertently including a few married college students in a study intended to measure premarital sexual behavior might alter the conclusions a great deal. The conclusions may be perfectly accurate, but there is no way that the experimenter can make conclusions concerning the population of interest if the sample is not a subset of that population.

A second way biased samples arise is through selecting a sample that is not *representative* of a population. If you want to study the effects of height on self-concept, you do not study only short people. Another example is the now legendary *Literary Digest* presidential poll of 1936, which predicted the landslide election of Landon as President. The *Literary Digest* questionnaires were sent only to persons whose names appeared in telephone directories. Later it was discovered that an important segment of the population, those people who did not have telephones, voted overwhelmingly for Roosevelt. The conclusions of the poll were probably correct for people with telephones. Still another example is a movie review made with the audiences' common interest in mind. A subscriber to both *PTA Monthly* and *Playboy* might find some widely different reviews of the same movie.

An experimenter can be confident of his results if he is sure that very few of the elements in the population are excluded from the sample by the sampling technique. A biased or invalid sample yields data that is altered in some consistent fashion away from the parameter values. Obviously, large random samples are more likely to be valid than small samples. A valid sample is often referred to as a **representative sample.** Notice that the concept of validity, when applied to sample statistics, is similar to the concept of secondary variance.

Reliability of the Sampling Technique

Reliability is defined as **consistency.** A sampling technique is reliable if several samples from the same population yield similar data. In most cases, the reliability of a sampling technique is directly related to the size of the sample. If it were possible to eliminate the sources of secondary and error variance in behavioral data, a sample of size one might suffice. Most behavior, however, is highly variable. It would be unwise to draw conclusions concerning the characteristics of a child based on a single, 15-minute sample. The conclusions from such data might be correct, but the experimenter cannot be sure.

Selecting the sample size depends on two major factors. First, the amount of work and/or expense involved in collecting the data usually increases linearly with the size of the sample. The reliability of the obtained data increases proportionally to the square root of the number in the sample (Cantril, 1944). Thus, each additional subject in the sample contributes a decreasing impact on the reliability of the data. There are no arbitrary upper or lower limits to the acceptable size of a sample. The usual criteria for this decision involve establishing how much time and/or money you feel the study is worth, and collecting the maximum size sample within these limits. Secondly, the nature of the research design may dictate the minimum number of subjects required. For example, certain statistical analyses require that at least two subjects be measured under each experimental treatment. Within cost limitations, the larger the sample size the better.

Reliability can be defined in terms of amount of error—the more error the less the reliability. That is, if measurement error is high in an experiment, the data are not likely to provide good population parameter estimates. Suppose there is a "true" measure of some variable, the value of which is unknown to an experimenter. Through observation the scientist obtains a measured score that can be considered to be composed of a true score and an error score. That is, the observed score equals the true score plus error. The smaller the error, the closer the observed score approximates the unknown "true score."

SAMPLING TECHNIQUES

There are several sampling techniques available. The following techniques vary in their usefulness to the experimental psychologist.

Bellwether Samples

Occasionally the social psychologist has access to information that indicates that particular subsets of a population are unusually accurate in reflecting the behavior of the entire population. A case in point is national voting behavior. Broadcasting companies hire professional polling organizations to select certain "bellwether precincts" based on the similarity of their voting patterns to that of the nation as a whole. By analyzing the vote of the selected precincts, the networks can sometimes predict election winners before all the votes are collected.

Quota Samples

In most cases, the experimenter does not have the necessary information to select bellwether samples. He may, however, have knowledge concerning the characteristics of the population that help him select a representative sample. For example, in studying human behavior, a sample containing approximately the same number of males and females will be more valid than a sexually biased sample (such as a sample that is 90 percent females).

If the sample is selected in such a manner that it matches certain characteristics of the population, it is known as a quota sample or representative sample.

One method of quota sampling is to divide the population into subgroups (strata) each sharing different characteristics; then to sample from these subgroups so that the proportions of the sample match the population. Voter prediction pollsters are careful to obtain samples that match the population in terms of socioeconomic status, political affiliation, urban-rural environment (and since 1936, possession of telephones). A good stratified sample may be almost as valid and reliable as a census would be; however, the technique demands a very large expenditure of time and effort. Even if a sample is stratified along a single dimension, such as income level, the experimenter should select from each subgroup at random.

Random Samples

If the entire population is potentially available to the experimenter, he can use the table of random numbers to select the sample. That way, each subject in the population is equally likely to be chosen. Random selection makes it highly unlikely that the sample will be biased. As in controlling secondary variance, randomization allows the experimenter to control for unknown factors. Random sampling tends to distribute both secondary and error variance equally among experimental groups.

Available Samples

Most of the psychological research data on human behavior is generated by samples of college students who happen to be available to the experimenter. Animal psychologists rely most frequently on the laboratory rat as a source of data. It has been said that if we discover another life form in the exploration of outer space, the experimental psychologist will not be able to tell much about its behavior patterns unless the experimenter can study its equivalent of the laboratory rat and college student.

The experimental psychologist occasionally finds it difficult to select a representative sample of a population. By necessity, he must use the elements of the population available to him and his budget. He should carefully discuss his conclusions in relation to the actual population sampled, because the actual population sampled differs from the population he would like to have sampled.

The basic nature of experimental research is the control of variance. The general methods of the control of variance are outlined in this chapter. The following four chapters specify some of the research designs that can be used. The designs vary in terms of which types of variables are controlled and how well they are controlled.

REVIEW

If you have not learned the difference already, go back and review the difference between an independent variable (one manipulated by the experimenter) and a dependent variable (the resulting behavior). This is the crux of any experiment, and the terminology should become second nature to you.

The remainder of the chapter is devoted to various aspects of controlling variance. The term variance, in this case, applies to the variation in the dependent variable. Thus, "variance" is differences in measures of behavior. The classification of variance into primary, secondary, and error relates to the relationship of the changes in behavior to the aim of the experiment. The behavior that is directly attributable to the independent variable is the primary variance for that experiment. Secondary variance is behavior that can be traced to causes other than the independent variable. Error variance is behavior that cannot be traced to a single cause. Obviously, the ideal experiment would have only primary variance without the other two effects clouding the issue. The remainder of the chapter outlines some accepted ways to approach this ideal.

A subtle, but important, concept has been smuggled into the presentation of this chapter. The idea that the behavior observed in the experiment might be due to factors other than the independent variable has important ramifications to the researcher. Even more important is the fact that we can sometimes break down the observed behavior into its component parts and determine the relative effect of the various sources. This ability to analyze variance into its component parts is the basis of inferential statistics.

SUMMARY

1. In psychology, an experimenter manipulates the independent variables (environmental or organismic variables) and observes the effect on dependent variables (behavior).
2. A relationship is a set of pairs of scores formed by pairing the scores on one variable with the scores on another variable. A function is a special type of relationship.
3. A theoretical construct is a label for a relationship between certain independent and dependent variables.
4. Variance describes the variation observed in behavioral measures. Variance may be divided into three categories: primary variance, or systematic variation, which occurs as

a result of the treatment conditions; secondary variance, or systematic variation, resulting from extraneous factors; and error variance, or random variation, resulting from extraneous factors.

5. Sources of variance may be divided into three categories: subject factors, environmental factors, and experimenter factors.

6. Experimental control is the arrangement of the sources of variance so that primary variance is maximized, secondary variance is controlled, and error variance is minimized.

7. Maximizing primary variance is accomplished by manipulating the independent variable so that extreme values, optimal values, or several values are used.

8. Control of secondary variance is accomplished by manipulating extraneous factors so that their effect is eliminated, constant, matched, measured, randomized, systematized, or conservatively arranged with respect to the dependent variable.

9. Minimizing error variance is accomplished by minimizing individual differences, reducing measurement error (both data collection and analysis), and minimizing environmental changes.

10. A sample is a randomly drawn subset of a population; the statistics drawn from a sample are estimates of the parameters of the population.

11. Samples are described in terms of their validity, how accurately they reflect characteristics of the population; and their reliability, how consistent the measures would be if several samples were taken.

12. Sampling techniques include: bellwether samples, quota samples, random samples, and available samples.

SUGGESTED READING

Kerlinger, F. N. *Foundations of behavioral research.* (2d ed.) New York: Holt, Rinehart and Winston, 1973.

Lastrucci, C. L. *The scientific approach: Basic principles of the scientific method.* Cambridge, Mass.: Schenkman, 1963.

Plutchik, R. *Foundations of experimental research.* New York: Harper & Row, 1968.

Rosenthal, R. *Experimenter effects in behavioral research.* New York: Appleton, 1966.

Rosenthal, R. Unintended communication of interpersonal expectation. *American Behavioral Scientist,* 1967, *10,* 24–26.

Selltiz, C., Jahoda, M., Deutsch, M., and Cook, S. W. *Research methods in social relations.* (Rev. ed.) New York: Holt Rinehart and Winston, 1959.

Sommer, R. Hawthorne dogma. *Psychological Bulletin,* 1968, *70,* 592–595.

Wolman, B. B., and Nagel, E. (Eds.) *Scientific psychology: Principles and approaches.* New York: Basic Books, 1965.

CHAPTER 3
Introduction to Research Design

Chapters 3 through 6 present the basic types of research designs used in psychological investigations. A **research design** is a fundamental plan for research, including the assignment of subjects to the levels of the independent variables, the procedures for the specification of the independent variables (and manipulation of them in experimental research), and the operational definitions of the dependent variable measures. Thus, the research design specifies how most of the variance sources are controlled in a study. As indicated in Chapter 1, the term scientific research includes both experimental and nonexperimental ("naturalistic observation") research. Experimental research requires the controlled manipulation of an independent variable. The title of the text indicates that we are primarily concerned with experimental research; however, naturalistic research designs are included in this chapter.

NATURALISTIC OBSERVATION

Naturalistic research involves the observation of behavior without the manipulation of an independent variable by the experimenter. Occasionally, the scientist has no alternative but to use naturalistic observation. For example, the migratory patterns of wild fowl, or some of the courting and mating behaviors of many species, can only be observed in a natural setting without manipulated independent variables. In other cases, the researcher may prefer to use a nonexperimental research design after deciding that the manipulation of an independent variable may create an artifical situation that significantly affects the validity of the subjects' behavior. That is, it may be the case that a particular behavior of a particular species (including human beings) in a laboratory situation may be directly affected by the fact of observation under controlled conditions. For example, college students who are aware of being subjects in a study may, under certain conditions, modify their behavior either to please the experimenter (particularily if the researcher is their instructor) or to mislead the experimenter (which sometimes happens when the subjects and experimenters are all students). In addition, the researcher may decide to use a naturalistic design because of a concern for the generality of the results. The behavior of captive animals in a zoo or laboratory setting probably differs in significant ways from the behavior of the same species in a natural, "wild" setting. For example, the frequency of overt homosexual behavior in laboratory monkeys appears to be considerably higher than the related frequency in the natural setting. Note that independent variables (and dependent variables) are measured in naturalistic research. The difference between naturalistic and experimental research is the degree of control of the independent variables by the researcher. The levels of the independent variables occur naturally (without the researcher's help) in naturalistic research but are selected and made to occur by the experimenter in experimental research. There are several forms of naturalistic observation that vary in terms of the number of subjects involved and degree of control of the organisms' environment.

Case Studies

A case study is a longitudinal study of a specific individual's behavior. Usually, as many different measures of behavior as possible are recorded. Case studies are commonly used by clinical psychologists. However, case studies have been undertaken for the purpose of determining the normal trend of changes in behavior. For example, Lenneberg (1962) conducted a case study of a boy with a congenital disability for the acquisition of motor speech skills. The medical and family history of the boy was examined. Physical examinations and psychological tests were given and the boy's vocalizations were recorded for four years. The boy learned to comprehend English fully, yet could not speak it. The case study demonstrated that comprehension of a language does not require babbling in infancy or imitation of adult speech. Examples of case studies include almost any biographical report.

Case studies may also be used with nonhuman species. Jones and Kamil

(1973) describe a study of tool making and tool using in the Northern Blue Jay. A laboratory-reared jay was kept in a large suspended cage with newspapers beneath the wire floor. By chance, food pellets collected on the ledges formed by wooden supports at the sides of the cage. The jay was observed to tear pieces of paper from the pages of newsprint, and to use the pieces as tools to rake the otherwise unreachable food pellets on the ledges close enough to eat. The animal had been maintained under food deprivation conditions several times during its 16 months of life. Jones and Kamil speculate that the jay acquired its tool-making and -using behavior because of the combination of (a) food deprivation, (b) food pellets just out of reach, and (c) available newspapers. They recorded many instances of the tool-using behavior on film. Subsequently, they manipulated the presence or absence of food and the food deprivation state of the animal and verified that the tool-using behavior was dependent on hours of deprivation and the presence of food pellets on the ledges. (Five other jays in their colony have been observed making and using the paper rakes; apparently they learned by imitation of the first jay.)

Natural Environment Studies

In natural environment studies (also called field studies or field research) the behavior is observed in the "wild" or home environment. No deliberate changes are made in the environment, except that attempts may be made to hide the observer. Observations may be made continuously or a sequence of observations may be collected either at fixed or random time intervals. Jane Goodall (1963) spent several years living with a group of chimpanzees near Lake Tanganyika. She observed that chimps use straws to get termites out of rotten trees: the first recorded observation of tool usage by animals in their natural environment. She (van Lawick-Goodall, 1968) has also studied cranes in their natural environment. She observed that cranes also use tools; they pick up rocks and hurl them in order to break the shells of ostrich eggs.

Fawl (1963) observed 16 children for a complete day in their normal, natural surroundings. Among other things, he found that the children averaged about 16 frustrations (blocked from attaining a goal) per day. In previous laboratory reseach, when children were frustrated they displayed marked aggressive behavior. In Fawl's study the children's usual response to naturally occurring frustration was very mild (if they showed any response at all). The children did not usually exhibit aggression when frustrated in their normal environment.

Contrived Natural Environment

The subjects are brought into a constructed facsimile of their home environments. With the exception of insects, the facsimile must, of course, be smaller than the home environment. The ant colonies available in any pet shop, and modern zoos, represent contrived naturalistic environments. Because of the reduction in size of the environment, and the consequent limitations on the freedom of the organism, the observer must be very careful in generalizing his observations to organisms in their "home" environment. Contrived environments are developed to allow greater possibility of observation. For example, nocturnal animals that are insensitive to red light may be displayed in red illumination.

Klopfer (1963) placed sparrows in a room containing pine and oak foliage on their perches. There was an equal number of each type of perch. The chipping sparrows preferred the pine perches and the white-throated sparrows showed no preference. Because Klopfer controlled (manipulated) the type and number of perches, the study is really an experiment. It is included here as an example of a contrived natural environment.

Correlational Studies

Correlational studies (Chapter 6) are designed to determine the degree of relationship between two variables. At least one of the variables is not under the control of the experimenter. Such a variable could be an organismic variable (for example, personality introversion) or an environmental variable (for example, moon phases). Bradburn (1963) found that "father dominance" was negatively associated with need for achievement in Turkish junior executives. The measure of the organismic variable, father dominance, was the age at which the subject was separated from his father (by death of choice).

Correlational studies may involve the case-study technique and natural or contrived natural environments. In addition to manipulated variables, an experimental research study may include variables that are not under the control of or manipulated by the experimenter. That subpart of the experimental research project that is concerned with the relationship between an uncontrolled independent variable and the dependent variable or variables may be designated a "correlational study."

Correlational studies may be much less complicated than the above example. Sechrest (1965) found that there are more erotic inscriptions (graffiti) in men's than women's rest rooms. The difference was less in the Philippines than in the United States. Ross and Campbell (1965) found that a crackdown on speeding in Connecticut was not related to the number of traffic fatalities.

Rosenhan (1973) conducted a correlational study concerned with mental hospital admission procedures, psychiatric diagnosis, and the perception of life in a mental hospital. The study did not involve the manipulation of an independent variable, so it is an example of nonexperimental research. The study consists mostly of the anecdotal description of the experiences of eight people in 12 nonrandomly selected mental hospitals and is *not* an example of tight research design. However, it is an interesting example of a crude correlational study.

Eight "sane" (not seriously pathological in any way) people including Rosenhan sought voluntary admission to 12 mental hospitals. (It was not reported how many went to more than one hospital.) Each person told the admitting psychiatrist of hearing unfamiliar voices saying "empty," "hollow," and "thud" (auditory hallucinations). Other than using false names and occasionally fake occupation descriptions, the fake auditory hallucinations plus the request for voluntary commitment constituted the totality of their abnormal ("insane") behaviors. In all cases except Rosenhan's, the nature of the research was unknown to the entire hospital staffs. All of the people were admitted to the hospitals; in 11 cases the admitting diagnosis was schizophrenia and in the remaining case, manic-depressive psychosis. From this data one can conclude that those who seek voluntary admission to mental hospitals will probably be admitted. Further, the behavior of seeking admission is probably sufficent to yield the diagnosis of schizophrenia. (Auditory hallucinations of the type described are not a symptom of schizophrenia.)

Length of hospitalization ranged from seven to 52 days and average confinement was for 19 days. The pseudo-patients were told by Rosenhan that they would have to get out by their own devices, except that they could not tell the truth about being part of a research project. The psuedo-patients stopped hearing "voices" immediately after entering the hospital and behaved as "sanely" as they could from that point. The one "abnormal" behavior was that they constantly kept notes on their experiences. During their hospitalization, the eight were given nearly 2100 tranquilizers (which they threw in the toilet, the way some of the other residents also disposed of their pills). The experience of being in the hospital was very negative to the "Rosenhan" eight. It was boring and frightening because of the depersonalization involved in most hospital settings. While a large number of the other patients voiced suspicions about the psuedo-patients ("You're not crazy. You're a journalist or a professor."), none of the hospital staff verbally or in writing questioned their diagnosis. None of the patients was released from the hospital on the basis of mistaken diagnosis. All were released with a diagnosis of schizophrenia "in remission."

Rosenhan concluded that the diagnosis means the patient is still schizophrenic, but no longer exhibits symptoms. There is some confusion about this and other points, as indicated in a set of 15 letters criticizing the study (Fleishman and others, 1973). When a person volunteers for admission to a mental hospital and lies about his behavior in order to get in, then does not reveal that he has lied, he will probably stay there for a while.

Naturalistic Observation Measurement

Unobtrusive Measures   One of the major features of natural environment observation is that it allows the observation of naturally occurring behavior without the restraints and limitations of a laboratory setting. In order to maintain the natural feature, the researcher must often resort to unusual measurement techniques that do not alter the normal patterns of behavior. Wildlife photographers may use telephoto lenses and elaborate camouflage and spend several months to record the ongoing behavior of wildlife species. Radar has been used to study bird migration. Using this technique, it has been discovered that birds do not drift in crosswinds when flying over land in the daytime (Schmidt-Koenig, 1965). Webb, et al.(1966), present and discuss a number of measurement techniques that may be applied to human behavior without the subject's awareness of the observation process.

The note-taking behavior by the pseudo-patients in Rosenhan's study is an example of unobtrusive measurement. The notes were records of patient and staff behaviors. Patient writing behavior (compulsive or not) is not uncommon on a mental hospital ward. The hospital staff paid no attention to the note taking except to record occasionally that the patients were writing a lot.

As another example of unobtrusive measurement, students of human behavior occasionally dress to fit in with a skid-row environment. In their disguises they observe the "drunks and bums" loitering on the streets. One common observation is that the people carrying small brown paper bags are most frequently engaged in conversation by others. Also little action takes place in the middle of the blocks; rather, street corners are the site of skid-row social activity.

Inventories and Questionnaires   Inventories and questionnaires may be used if the researcher feels that the measurement process will not alter the ongoing behavior. Political values, moral and ethical standards, religious views, or personality traits may be measured by scoring the subject's answer to questions directly related to the variable of interest.

There are a large number of ready-made inventories that are available as measurement devices. Ready-made inventories have the advantage of being constructed by someone sophisticated in test and measurement theory. Ready-made inventories have been field tested, which provides some normative data for comparison with other groups. Many ready-made inventories have evolved from earlier instruments that were improved. Buro's *The Sixth Mental Measurements Yearbook* (1965) contains information on many current mental tests. Anastasi (1968) also presents information and criticism on many types and kinds of tests. In addition, new inventories are continually being presented in psychological journals.

The construction of an adequate questionnaire or inventory is a difficult, time-consuming process. We have seen many students attracted to the questionnaire approach because of its apparent simplicity, ease of data handling, and relevance to their research question. These apparent positive characteristics of questionnaires are often misleading.

If the only way to collect the data relevant to a research question is to construct an inventory or questionnaire, then first consult a reference such as Nunnally (1970) or Oppenheim (1966). The high probability of erroneous wording of questions by the beginner and the excessive amount of work involved in analyzing the data from a questionnaire lead to the strong recommendation that the beginning student avoid the questionnaire technique.

Generally speaking, a questionnaire yields better results if the respondent is allowed a variety of choices (**a summated scale**) rather than a yes-no answer scale. A widely used type of summative scale is Likert-type scale. Each test item offers the respondent several degrees of agreement and disagreement. For example, if an item on an anxiety scale states, "I always perspire during tests," the possible answers could be, (1) strongly agree, (2) agree, (3) undecided, (4) disagree, and (5) strongly disagree. This scale permits the use of items that are not manifestly related to the attitude or behavior being studied (Selltiz, et al., 1959). For example, a question such as "Do you like cut flowers?" is ostensibly concerned with gardening, but may be scored in terms of aggressive tendencies. The numerical value of responses to

Likert
Scale

items concerned with a trait are summarized to obtain a single measure of that trait. Summated scales are simple to construct and usually provide reliable results if the questions or statements are devised properly. The choice of certain words or phrases is crucial to the subject's response. For example, questions with "should" or "ought to" provide an indication of the idealized policies of an individual. Questions phrased "Would you do . . . ?" involve a personal prediction of the subject's behavior in a specific situation. Consequently, great care should be taken in making up test items in questionnaires. (See *Newsweek*, July 8, 1968, pp. 23–27 for errors often encountered.)

Advantages of Questionnaires

Questionnaires and inventories have certain advantages over other means of obtaining dependent variable measures. For example, interviews are often very expensive in terms of time and money. Inventories can be administered to large groups of subjects at the same time and can usually be machine scored. Also, tests and questionnaires can be sent through the mail, which provides subjects that otherwise might not be obtained. One problem, however, with mail-outs is that many people will not respond to a mail-out test. In order to insure a large enough sample, it is a good idea to send out about three times as many questionnaires or tests as you need. Otherwise your sample would probably be too small. A third advantage comes from the standardized and impersonal nature of tests. Subjects will respond more honestly on a test if they are sure that their identity is protected. Psychological testing is considered by many to be an invasion of privacy (Ruch, 1967). It is the tester's moral and legal responsibility to protect the person who takes the test by keeping his scores anonymous. Once in a while a tester may wish to obtain information about how certain groups will respond to an anonymous test. Suppose one had a mail-out test that measured racial attitudes, and the tester wanted to know how plumbers, doctors, lawyers, and engineers would respond to the test. The tester could print the test in four different colors and send a different color to each group. Using this procedure he could determine the score of each and still maintain each individual's anonymity.

Hollender, Luborsky, and Scaramella (1969) performed a simple, chauvinistic study on body contact and sexual enticement. They predicted that women like to be held or cuddled because it reduces anxiety and serves as a source of gratification. The experimenters sampled 39 women who had been admitted to a psychiatric hospital for relatively acute disorders such as neurotic depression. The subjects were given a questionnaire that contained ten items. The items included statements such as: "When you are upset, it is comforting for you to have someone hold you"; and "To get another person to hold you, you use persuasion." The subjects rated themselves as high, moderate, or low on these ten questions. Subsequently, the subjects were asked two additional questions: (1) "Do you use sex to get another person to hold you?"; and (2) "Do you make a direct request to be held?"

The responses to the questionnaire were self-rated by the subjects into low, moderate, and high categories. These measures constituted an intensity measure. The results were that every person who scored high on the first ten questions concerned with the need to be held, also said they used sex to achieve body contact;

whereas not a single subject who scored low said they used sex to be held. Those who scored moderate fell in between the high and low scores.

The experimenters "concluded" that sexual intercourse is often bartered for contact comfort, and that the intensity of the need to be held or cuddled related highly to the frequency with which sex is used to entice contact. The experimenters also "concluded" that sex is commonly used by women to entice men to hold them and also that the need to be held is sometimes a determinant of promiscuity.

Let us examine the study first with respect to the variables, and, second, with respect to the generalization of the results. There was no manipulation of an independent variable. The levels of the first variable were determined on the basis of a test, thus the subjects assigned themselves to groups. The body-contact scale served to measure an organismic variable. The major dependent variable was the response to the last two questions. By asking only two questions, the experimenters restricted the number and kind of measures obtained and, therefore, the amount of information obtained. It might have been better to obtain more measures of behavior to correlate with the other variable.

With respect to the generality of the results, the experimenters concluded that sex is "commonly used by women to entice their husbands to hold them and, also, that the need to be held is sometimes a determinant of promiscuity," (Hollender, et al., 1969, p. 191). Based on their sample of women from a psychiatric hospital, the above conclusion is *not* tenable. The authors state their results as though the results indicate that *all* women use sex to entice body contact. The experimenters did not *randomly* sample from a *large population* of women, and therefore their conclusions can only generalize to the women at that particular hospital who were diagnosed as having relatively acute disorders.

EXPERIMENTAL DESIGNS

To illustrate the advantage of an experimental design, we will examine a television commercial (a highly restricted form of naturalistic observation in a contrived naturalistic setting). A man is shown applying a certain preparation to his hair and, immediately after, is shown in the embrace of a pretty girl. The manufacturer of the preparation wishes the viewer to infer that there is a relationship between the independent variable (application of hair tonic) and the dependent variable (attention from girls). Is such an inference justified in this case? It is impossible to tell. A number of alternative hypotheses could account for the observed behavior of the girl. The young man may be kissed by many girls, no matter what the condition of his hair. Some other product (after-shave lotion, mouthwash, elevator shoes, and so on) might be the real cause for the observed behavior. It is also possible that the girl is very friendly. It could be that the entire sequence was performed at the request of an advertising agency. Thus, although hair tonic might be the important variable, we cannot eliminate any of the alternative hypotheses without additional information. If we can determine that the young man is only attractive to girls when he uses the hair preparation, or the girl is attracted only to men who use the preparation, we could be more confident in our conclusions. We need a reference point (control) in order to evaluate our results. An ideal reference condition would be to observe the same individuals under the same conditions, except that the young man would not apply the hair preparation. If the observed behavior were different, we could attribute the change in behavior to the change in the independent variable.

It is impossible to make the two observations under identical conditions. The fact that the observations cannot be made at the same time and in the same place, forces the experimenter to make his comparisons under less than optimal conditions. Any condition other than the independent variable that is different between the two observations, may serve as a source of secondary variance and invalidate inferences drawn from the data. As stated in Chapter 2, variations in behavior measures arise from three general sources: (1) subject factors, (2) environmental factors, and (3) experimenter factors. As sources of secondary variance, these three categories can be labeled: (1) individual differences, (2) outside influences, and (3) experimental contamination. Examples of **individual differences** include the species, maturation, and past experience of the subjects in the experiment. **Outside influences** are any environmental changes, other than the independent variables, between two observations. Examples of outside influences with human subjects include time and location of observations, intervening world or local events that affect the subject, or distracting events that occur during the data collection. Outside influences in animal research might include pinching the animal's tail in the door of the apparatus, inadvertently feeding animals that are supposed to be deprived, or providing discrimination cues other than those manipulated in the experiment. **Experimental contamination** is a term that applies to the changes in the subject's behavior as a direct result of the data-collection process. Experimental contamination includes anything that would change the subject's score on a second observation as a result of the first observation. For instance, learning, fatigue, or frustration may carry over to a second measure. Experimental contamination also occurs when the data collection process alerts or *sensitizes* the subject to the treatment condition. Subjects may respond quite differently to an independent variable if the subject is sensitized by a pretest measurement. An experimenter uses a research design to control for potential secondary variables. The choice of a design is based on data-collection limitations and the secondary variables that seem most likely to be relevant.

Control of Subject Factors

Two methods of controlling subject factors in an experimental design are (1) to make the treatment *groups* equivalent on some measure and/or (2) to provide that the *subjects in a group* are similar with respect to some variable prior to the administration of the treatment. Random assignment theoretically equates the groups with respect to all variables so that the average score of one group should equal the average score of another. Matching groups of subjects also increases the likelihood that the averages will be equal. Any difference between the averages is called **between-groups variance.** The second method is achieved by matching the subjects *within* each group on some variable. The effect of matching is to minimize the **within-group**

variance (for example, control of individual differences). Before the treatment is administered, between-groups variance and within-group variance should be minimized. The independent variable should produce a difference between previously equivalent groups. In most studies, after the treatment is administered, between-groups variance should be increased, and within-group variance should remain unchanged.

Notice that the important dimension of research is to make *comparisons* and not to describe the behavior in numerical form. There is a common misconception that the ability to express any observed behavior in some precise numerical form makes the observation much more "scientific" than less quantitative description. The important factor is not "What is the most precise measure that can be obtained from my observation?" but rather, "What level of measurement gives the most useful information?" The observation that an animal learned to choose the maze path that led to food may be much more informative than the observation that it traversed the maze in exactly 140 paces.

Research designs do not necessarily solve the problem of error variance (measurement error). The choice of a measurement device, whether it is a counter, recorder, or human observer is not a function of the research design. It should be obvious, however, that the observations taken in any experiment will be more useful if an appropriate measuring technique is used. Similarly, multiple observations are more likely to be representative than a few observations.

One-Shot Case Study (Poor Design)   The hair preparation example is labeled a **one-shot case study** and is symbolically summarized in Table 3.1. The symbol X represents the experimental condition; Y_a represents an after observation (measurement of the dependent variable);—means no pretreatment measure (before observation) was taken; and time moves from left to right. The treatment was the application of the hair preparation and the after observation was the embrace.

Measurement Decisions

TABLE 3.1. One-Shot Case Study.

Group	Before Observation	Treatment	After Observation
1	—	X	Y_a

A one-shot case study provides a very weak basis for inferring any relationship. Data comparison is a crucial aspect of the research process; consequently, the one-shot case study is not included as a legitimate research design, because it does not permit comparison.

For illustrative purposes, each of the following designs is presented in terms of a specific model, and the model is evaluated. The student can use these models as a basis for developing a design that is best suited for his research hypotheses. The addition of certain control procedures will increase the value of a given design. Similarly, two or more of the designs presented here as separate entities can be combined for a more controlled test of a hypothesis. Such modifications are encouraged, since each model is not intended to serve as an arbitrary standard for "good" or "bad" research designs.

Guide to Research Design Descriptions

One-Group Designs:
Subjects as Their Own Control

One-group designs involve the observation of a single group of subjects under two or more experimental conditions. Each subject serves as his own control by contributing experimental and control scores. One-group designs are intended to control for individual differences. If the experimenter is primarily interested in the change in the behavior of each individual due to the experimental treatment, a one-group design should be considered.

One-Group Before-After Design

A one-group before-after design consists in observing the subjects at some time prior to the onset of the experimental condition (Y_b) and comparing that performance with a similar observation made during or after the treatment (Y_a). This type of design is called a before-after design, referring to the temporal relationship of the observations to the experimental condition. The data are analyzed by comparing the before and after scores for all subjects.

TABLE 3.2. One-Group Before-After Design.

Group	Before Observation	Treatment	After Observation
1	Y_b	X	Y_a

Function   A before-after design provides a direct measure of the change in the behavior of each subject under two observation conditions. It may be used when the experimenter knows that the experimental condition will occur, and that he can observe his subjects prior to and after its occurrence. Before-after designs are occasionally employed experimentally to evaluate the effect of propaganda on the attitudes of individuals.

It is not necessary for a researcher to be the one creating the experimental condition. It is possible to use this design naturalistically to observe the effectiveness of national advertising campaigns on political attitudes throughout an election year campaign.

Advantages   The difference between the before and after scores, in the absence of a treatment effect, should be minimal. Because subjects serve as their own control in a one-group before-after design, additional subjects for a control group are not required. If the subjects are continuously available for observation (such as zoo animals) or periodically available (school children or weekly sensitivity group meetings), a before-after design is particularly convenient. If the experimenter has access to a before measure, and the experimental condition includes all available subjects, a one-group design will be useful.

Limitations   A one-group before-after design leaves a large number of secondary variables uncontrolled. Any outside influence that occurs between the two observations may account for an observed difference. For example, measurement of racial attitudes before and after a documentary film on race relations may be changed substantially if a race riot occurs between the observations. If one observation is made on a Friday and the other on the following Sunday, the difference in days of observation may also account for the observed differences in behavior.

If the time between two observations is more than a few days, the intervening learning and maturational processes may produce a change in behavior. Before-after designs are particularly vulnerable to experimental contamination.

The process of collecting the before data may also alert the subject so that he is particularly sensitive or resistant to the experimental condition. If the subject has just completed a questionnaire on racial attitudes, he might be quite cynical about any attempts to alter those attitudes with a propaganda film, or he might be particularly susceptible to the arguments presented in the film. A before-after design requires that two observations be made for each subject. If the subject is not available during one of the observation periods, the other observation must be discarded. If the subjects are not selected at random, then any observed difference between measures may be due to some unknown factor.

Statistical Analysis The phrase "subjects as their own control" means that the behavior of the one group of subjects is measured before administration of the treatment and the before measure is compared with the after measure obtained after treatment. That is, the subjects' behavior after the treatment is compared with the control measure of their behavior before encountering the treatment. The comparison of the two sets of measures may be accomplished with a significance of changes χ^2 test if the data consists of frequency counts of subjects falling into two categories before and after the treatment (Unit D2). Alternatively, the sign test may be used—if the dependent variable measure consists of ranking the subjects before and after treatment (Unit D1). Finally, the related groups t test (where the two related "groups" are the before scores and after scores of the subjects) or randomized-blocks analysis of variance (Units D4 and D5, respectively) may be used if the measures are at least interval level numbers (Chapter 8).

Comments A one-group before-after design is relatively weak because it does not control many secondary variables. Probably the most important problem is the effect of being observed. If the data can be collected without the awareness of the subject, this design may be quite useful. However, a one-group before-after design is seldom used unless supplemented with additional control procedures (for example, matching or counterbalancing with matching).

Time-Series Design

A time-series design consists in collecting multiple observations before treatment and comparing the observations with observations made during or after treatment. A time-series design is an extended form of the before-after design.

TABLE 3.3. Time-Series Design.

Group	Before Observation	Treatment	After Observation
1	Y_{b1}, Y_{b2}, Y_{b3}	X	Y_{a1}, Y_{a2}, Y_{a3}

Function   The experimenter measures the change in the behavior of the subjects under at least three observation conditions. In a time-series experiment, several observations are obtained at fixed time intervals. Once a trend (baseline) has been established, the experimental treatment is introduced and the experimental observations are continued. Any discontinuity in the observations that occurs after the onset of the experimental treatment is attributed to the treatment.

A discontinuity may occur in one of two ways. First, it may be that the observations change consistently over time, in which case the experimenter must examine the data for any deviation from the expected trend. We might record the performance curve of human subjects solving long addition problems. We announce that scores on this task are related to the intelligence of the subject. Performance may level off for a few problems. We would conclude that the announcement impaired arithmetic performance, since the observed performance did not increase at the same rate as before the treatment.

Another way to observe a discontinuity is to measure the performance of the subjects repeatedly until there are no significant changes in scores. Once such a baseline (operant level) has been established, any changes (increases or decreases in rate) after the introduction of the treatment may be attributed to the treatment. This type of design is very popular in behavior modification research where only one subject is used (sometimes called an **N = 1 experiment).**

Advantages   Time-series experiments utilize relatively few subjects since the subjects serve as their own control. The fact that multiple measures are obtained from each subject, both before and after the treatment, reduces the probability of a single erroneous observation. The fact that the subjects are observed several times prior to the treatment also reduces the probability that the subject is behaving atypically because of the observation process. The trend provides a measurement of the maturational and learning effects occurring during the period of the experiment. These effects can then be statistically controlled by measuring the departure from the established trend created by the independent variable.

Limitations   A time-series design does not control for the effect of outside influences (secondary variables) that occur in the same time interval as the experimental condition. Thus, the experimenter must be alert for any such coincident events. Because several before measures are made, there is an even greater possibility for experimental contamination than in a before-after design.

Since multiple observations are made, the experimenter must schedule more time for the collection of data. It also means that all of the subjects must be available for several observations, which usually results in the loss of a higher proportion of subjects. In addition, if the before condition is too rigorous or too monotonous, performance may be altered due to fatigue or boredom.

Statistical Analysis   The average before scores and average after scores or selected ("representative") before and after scores may be compared with the same techniques listed under the one-group before-after design. Sometimes the data from a time-series study may be statistically analyzed with the "goodness of fit" slope analysis technique outlined in Unit D6. A straight line is fit to the average before

Baseline

measure and average after measure and the slope of the straight line is tested to see if it is reliably different from zero.

An important problem in a time-series experiment is to determine which scores will be analyzed. In the case of a trend of changing scores, Campbell and Stanley (1963, p. 43) suggest comparing the before and after trend at the point where the treatment occurred. In some cases, a graphical presentation may illustrate the discontinuity and help in analytical procedures. If the data consists of a constant pretreatment baseline and a different posttreatment level of performance, the experimenter may find comparing an average score in each condition is adequate.

Care must be taken in analyzing time-series data, since the effect of the treatment must occur within the time period being analyzed. If you were to conduct a drug study with a time sample every ten minutes, it would be important to your data analysis to know when the drug becomes effective.

Comments   A well-conducted time-series experiment yields data that may be clearly interpreted. Time-series experiments are best applied to behavior that occurs periodically. Many industrial settings, school settings, and hospital or other institutional settings provide ideal situations for time-series studies.

Counterbalanced Experimental Conditions Design

Rather than collecting all observations in one block, it is sometimes possible to intersperse the treatment and observation conditions. The subject is first given treatment one and an observation (Y_{a1}) is made, then the procedure is repeated for treatment two, repeated again with two, and again with one. (See Table 3.4.) In this case, we obtain two measures under treatment two and two measures under treatment one. The sequence of administration of treatment is sometimes referred to as ABBA sequence. Our version of this term is that a counterbalanced design involves a 1221 sequence where the ones and twos are subscripts of the treatments X_1 and X_2. Counterbalanced means balanced sequences or orders of treatments or experimental conditions. In a 1221 design, the sequence of treatments 1,2 in that order occurs once and the sequence of treatments 2,1 in that order occurs once. Thus the sequences are balanced. The counterbalanced design is not a before-after design, rather it is an after-after-after-after design where there are two levels of the independent variable.

TABLE 3.4. Counterbalanced Experimental Conditions Design.

Treatment	X_1	X_2	X_2	X_1
After Observation	Y_{a1}	Y_{a2}	Y_{a3}	Y_{a4}

Function   A counterbalanced design provides a different kind of experimental control than other one-group designs, while retaining the feature of subjects serving as their own control. If the experimenter suspects that experimental contamination factors such as learning or fatigue may systematically alter successive observations, he may use the trend estimation technique of the time-series design; or he may counterbalance his experimental conditions so that they are more likely to be equally affected by the contaminating factor. By arranging his conditions in a 1221 pattern, and computing an average score for both observations in each condition, the sequential factor may be cancelled.

Advantages   Being a one-group design, counterbalanced presentation uses fewer subjects than two-group experiments, and the subjects provide their own control data. Time-related variables such as maturation, learning, outside events, frustrations, or fatigue are controlled by the data-collection sequence rather than by later statistical manipulation. A counterbalanced design is usually concerned with relatively short-term experimental variables, meaning that all four observations can be made on the subject in a short period of time. A single data-collection session results in less data loss due to subject defection.

Limitations   A counterbalanced design is based on the assumption *that all time-related secondary variables are essentially linear* in nature. That·is, the effect of the change from trial one to trial two will be the same as between all other adjacent trials. If the actual effect of these time-related variables is a nonlinear relationship to the behavior, they are not adequately controlled. Sufficient time must be allowed between each of the observations, otherwise the data will be contaminated by *carry-over* from the previous trial condition (Gaito, 1958). Suppose a study involves measuring eye-hand coordination under two stress conditions. Suppose that performance on the experimental task normally improves with practice. In order to control the practice effect, the experimenter uses a counterbalanced conditions design. The experimental task is also tiring. If the experimenter failed to allow the subjects to recover from the fatigue encountered in trial one (under treatment X_1), then performance on trial two (under treatment X_2) would be affected by the treatment and fatigue. Obviously, the comparison of the effects of the two treatments would be contaminated by such carry-over.

Carry-over

Statistical Analyses   The average performance under experimental condition X_1 is calculated and the average under X_2 is also calculated. The two averages are compared to determine the differential effect of the two conditions. The specific statistical technique depends on the level of measurement of the dependent variable. The techniques to be used are those listed for the one-group before-after design.

Comments   A counterbalanced design requires fewer observations than the time-series design. To counterbalance even more thoroughly, half of the subjects may serve under the 1221 sequence, while the other half experiences a 2112 sequence. Using both counterbalanced orders provides control for any peculiar effects which may result from a particular presentation order. The data from the two presentation orders may be combined (by treatment) for analysis.

REVIEW

To be successful in sorting out the primary variance from the error variance, a research design must provide at least two measures of behavior. In the classic case this is usually summarized as an experimental observation and a control observation. The experimental observation and control observation are identical in all ways but exposure to the treatment. The assumption is that both groups contain all of the effects of secondary and error variance sources. Consequently the *difference* between the control behavior and the experimental behavior can be attributed to primary variance. In the latter portion of this chapter, the one-group designs provide an example of subjects serving as their own control. In this case, the subjects are observed under standard observation conditions and a base rate or control measure is taken, and then a corresponding observation is made after the subjects have been exposed to the treatment or the independent variable.

The other designs that are presented in this chapter present a bit of a problem to the authors of a textbook in experimental psychology. The usual emphasis is placed on the elegance of the control procedures, and a basic requirement for most experimental psychologists is that there be some control group or control score to compare with the experimental group. Technically speaking, the various naturalistic observation procedures that are presented in this chapter often lack this vital feature of having a corresponding group for the purpose of comparing the effects of the primary variance source. Although elegance and cleverness in devising appropriate controls in experimental research is desired, do not be fooled by the relatively brief treatment of the naturalistic observation procedures. In some cases, these are the only ways that it is possible to collect data that are meaningful.

SUMMARY

1. Naturalistic observation does not involve manipulation of an independent variable. Four types of naturalistic observation are: case studies, natural environment studies, contrived natural environment studies, and correlational studies.
2. Unobtrusive measures are measures of behavior that do not alter the normal (natural) pattern of the behavior. Inventories and questionnaires are often cheap, efficient ways of collecting data; however, the beginning student is encouraged to use ready-made inventories and questionnaires rather than to attempt the construction of his own.
3. An experimental design is a plan or program for research, including the assignment of subjects and manipulation of the independent variable.
4. Three general sources of secondary variance are: (1) individual differences, (2) outside (environmental) influences, and (3) experimental contamination.
5. Any differences between the average scores of the treatment groups is called between-groups variance. Within-group variance refers to the amount of individual differences between the subjects within a group. Before administration of the experimental treatment, both between-groups and within-group variance should be minimized. After the treatment, between-groups variance is expected to be increased.
6. A design must allow the experimenter to make comparisons, otherwise it is not an experimental research design.
7. A poor design is the one-shot case study, which does not allow comparison.
8. One-group experimental research designs all involve the use of subjects as their own controls.
9. A one-group before-after design consists in the administration of a pretest (before measure), treatment, and posttest (after measure) to one group of subjects. The subjects may be randomly selected or naturalistically observed. The design does not control for several possible sources of outside influence and experimental contamination.

10. A time-series design consists in obtaining several measures of the subjects' behavior before introducing the treatment, after the treatment, and often at several points during the administration of the treatment. A time-series design provides control for many of the secondary variables not controlled in a one-group before-after design.
11. Given that the subjects are going to be observed under at least two treatment conditions, one can counterbalance the order of the conditions. A counterbalanced design is used when one suspects that experimental contamination will affect the scores of the subjects.

SUGGESTED READING

Campbell, D. T., and Stanley, J. C. *Experimental and quasi-experimental designs for re-search.* Skokie, Ill.: Rand McNally, 1963.

Gaito, J. Statistical dangers involved in counterbalancing. *Psychological Reports,* 1958, *4,* 463–468.

Johnson, H. H., and Solso, R. L. *An introduction to experimental design in psychology: A case approach.* New York: Harper & Row, 1971.

Nunnally, J. C., Jr. *Introduction to psychological measurement.* New York: McGraw-Hill, 1970.

Oppenheim, A. N. *Questionnaire design and attitude measurement.* New York: Basic Books, 1966.

Runkel, P., and McGrath, J. *Research on human behavior: A systematic guide to method.* New York: Holt, Rinehart and Winston, 1972.

Selltiz, C., Jahoda, M., Deutsch, M., and Cook, S. W. *Research methods in social relations.* (Rev. ed.) New York: Holt, Rinehart and Winston, 1959.

Webb, E. J., Campbell, D. T., Schwartz, R. D., and Sechrest, L. *Unobtrusive measures: Non-reactive research in the social sciences.* Skokie, Ill.: Rand McNally, 1966.

CHAPTER 4
Two-Group Designs

A two-group design consists in observation of two groups of subjects experiencing different levels of the independent variable. In most two-group designs, the two levels of the independent variable are the presence or absence of a treatment. The subject in the **experimental group** experience a treatment (nonzero level of the independent variable) and the subjects in the **control group** experience no treatment (zero level of the independent variable).

Two-group designs provide a very strong basis for measuring the independent variable. The two groups are designed to be essentially equivalent except for exposure to the treatment condition. When compared with the one-group designs, two-group designs have two significant advantages. The observations on the two groups can be made at essentially the same time so time-related secondary variance (such as age, weather, or current events) is eliminated. Two-group designs also avoid the experimental contamination found in one-group designs. Often a pre-treatment observation can contaminate the results of the posttreatment measure. With the two-group design, the potential contamination effect of the before observation is either eliminated or distributed equally in the two groups.

Two main categories of two-group designs are presented: (1) independent two-group designs and (2) related two-group designs. Independent two-group designs involve random assignment of subjects to groups, and related two-group designs involve matching the groups.

INDEPENDENT TWO-GROUP DESIGNS

In all independent two-group designs (except the static group comparison designs), the two groups are *independent* because every subject has an equal chance of being assigned to either the experimental group or the control group. That is, there is no known relationship between the subjects in the experimental group and the subjects in the control group.

Static Group Comparison Design (Poor Design)

The static group comparison design provides for the comparison of one group of subjects that has experienced a treatment condition with a control group that has not experienced treatment. Observation conditions for the two groups are kept as similar as possible to provide a comparative basis.

TABLE 4.1. A Static Group Comparison Design.

Group	Before Observation	Treatment	After Observation
1	—	X	Y_{a1}
2	—	—	Y_{a2}

Function   A static group comparison is an *ex post facto* design (the comparison is made after the unplanned occurrence of the "treatment"). In *ex post facto* research, the independent variable is not manipulated. Consequently, the static group comparison is not an experimental research design. The independent variable is the occurrence of some natural event experienced by a group of subjects (Group 1). The researcher *then* tries to locate a group of subjects (Group 2) who have not experienced the event ("treatment"), but are apparently equivalent in other respects.

Comparing behaviors of the same species of animal in captivity (in a zoo) and in the wild exemplifies a static group design. Static group comparison might allow the experimenter to comment on the effects of captivity on behavior. As another example, Webb, et al. (1966), cite an unobtrusive study of psychologists who attended a convention. Individuals with long hair tended to prefer clinically oriented symposia (lecture or discussion meetings), while those with short hair preferred experimental research symposia. Note that these observations were made before 1966 and hair length might not differentiate the two groups now.

Advantages   The static group comparison is sometimes the only way to study certain kinds of behavior. If the experimenter has collected data from a number of subjects who have experienced a treatment condition and does not have access to any before observations, the static group design will give him a crude basis for comparison. If the "treatment" involves exposure to a cataclysmic event (flood, earthquake, or A-bomb explosion) an experimental design is impossible.

Limitations   A static group comparison depends entirely on the subjects in the two groups being basically equivalent, except for the treatment effect. If the groups are different at the beginning of an experiment, any difference between their behavior after the treatment is given may be due either to the treatment or to the initial differences. Because the static group comparison is an *ex post facto* design, there is no way for the experimenter to assure himself that he has obtained groups that were equivalent. With respect to the zoo example, at least one obvious initial difference between the animals in a zoo and the animals in the wild is the ability to escape capture. Without equivalent groups, any conclusions drawn from a static group comparison are questionable.

Statistical Analysis   Descriptive statistical comparisons of the two groups may be made using graphical techniques (Chapter 7) or measures of central tendency or variability (Chapter 8). Inferential statistical analysis for the purpose of generalizing the results of the study to a larger population of subjects is *not* possible because the subjects observed are not randomly sampled from a population (Chapter 10). However, nonstatistical analysis and generalization may occur.

Comments   Except for pilot studies or some naturalistic observations, the static group comparison design should be avoided. Although any group difference may be related to the experimental condition, it is difficult to separate this relationship from naturally occurring differences between groups. Many beginning students inadvertently use a static group comparison design. By collecting subjects for the experimental and control conditions under different circumstances (time, place, or group membership), the students may be comparing static groups.

Before-After Static Group Comparison Design (Poor Design)

The before-after static group comparison design involves a combination of the one-group before-after design and the static group comparison. A before-after static group comparison design is used when the experimenter cannot randomly assign the subjects to the experimental and control groups, but wishes to use a more powerful procedure than the static group comparison. The initial observations (Y_{b1} for Group 1 and Y_{b2} for Group 2) made on each group may be compared to determine whether the two groups are initially equivalent.

If the two groups are the same on the before observation, then a comparison of the after observations (Y_{a1} and Y_{a2}) is appropriate. If, on the other hand, the before observations reveal an initial difference between the two groups, any post-treatment comparison must include a correction for the initial difference, for example, by consistently adding or subtracting the initial difference to the after scores.

TABLE 4.2. A Before-After Static Group Comparison Design.

Group	Before Observation	Treatment	After Observation
1	Y_{b1}	X	Y_{a1}
2	Y_{b2}	—	Y_{a2}

Function   A before-after static group comparison design is intended to provide some control for group differences when the experimenter cannot assign the subjects to form equivalent groups. That is, the design is used when randomization or matching is impractical. The design allows the experimenter to estimate the equivalence of his two groups and provides the opportunity to correct for initial differences. The before-after static group comparison design requires that the experimenter have access to both the control and experimental subjects before and after the experimental treatment, and therefore can be used only in cases where the experimenter can anticipate the treatment condition, or where he may rely on before measurements collected before the study was contemplated.

Advantages   Outside influences (secondary variables) should affect both groups equally, because the dependent variable measures are taken during the same time interval. Experimental contamination is measured by comparing the difference between Y_b and Y_a scores of the control group (Group 2) and may be used to correct the experimental group (Group 1) data.

Limitations   The subjects are not randomly assigned to the two groups. Even though the before measures are equivalent, unknown consistent differences (secondary variables) may account for differences in the after observations. The before observations may introduce experimental contamination by sensitizing the subjects to the independent variable. For example, in a learning experiment, the before measures may give the subjects a cue on how to solve the learning task.

Statistical Analysis   The statistical analysis described for the static group comparison design is appropriate here. The difference between the average before and after scores of each group may be calculated $(Y_a - Y_b)$. Then the difference between the two differences $[(Y_{a1} - Y_{b1}) - (Y_{a2} - Y_{b2})]$ would be examined. Again, no inferential statistical analysis is appropriate because of the lack of random sampling.

Comments   The before-after static group comparison design may be employed when the experimental and control groups are already formed and available to the experimenter. Many educational studies involve the introduction of a new class curriculum to a class or to an entire school. Suppose a school introduces a new language laboratory in the Spanish program. The school may evaluate the effectiveness of the laboratory by comparing the language skills gained by students using the laboratory with the skills shown by similar students in another school not using a language laboratory. Any factor, such as socioeconomic level, may dictate that a certain type of student is enrolled in one or the other school and may contribute a biasing effect. In addition, any differential treatment as a result of group membership, such as differences in curriculum or teachers, will also contaminate the results.

Randomized Two-Group Design

The essential feature of *all* randomized two-group designs is that the experimenter assigns the subjects randomly to the experimental and control groups. (Randomization is indicated by R in Table 4.3) Inferences about the effects of the independent variable are drawn by comparing the dependent variable scores of the two groups.

TABLE 4.3 A Randomized Two-Group Design.

Group	Assignment	Before Observation	Treatment	After Observation
1	R	—	X	Y_{a1}
2	R	—	—	Y_{a2}

Function   A randomized two-group design contains a major control feature not employed in the two previously mentioned designs. The experimenter randomly assigns his subjects to one or the other group prior to observation. As discussed in Chapter 2, randomization controls the effects of a large number of potential secondary variables.

Advantages   The random assignment of subjects to groups theoretically controls for differences between the two groups. By assuming initial equality between the two groups, the data analysis is comparatively simple. Additionally, a single observation of each subject eliminates secondary variables such as learning or fatigue (experimental contamination).

Limitations   The experimenter must be able to assign his subjects to the experimental and control groups prior to the onset of the treatment. If the two groups are observed at different points in time, there is a possibility that intervening events occurring outside of the experiment may affect the dependent variable measures. Time of observation should be controlled.

Statistical Analysis   For the purpose of describing and summarizing the data, the appropriate tabular and graphic techniques (Chapter 7) and the appropriate measures of central tendency and variability (Chapter 8) may be used. The inferential statistical analysis (Chapter 10) depends on the level of measurement and other characteristics of the dependent variable measure. At the nominal level of measurement with frequency counts of the number of subjects falling into at least two categories within Groups 1 and 2, the two independent groups or median χ^2 tests (Unit D2) are appropriate. At the ordinal level of measurement the Wilcoxon-Mann-Whitney test (Unit D3) may be used. At the interval or ratio level of measurement, either the technique of using a two independent group t test (Unit D4) or a two-group (simplest form of multilevel) analysis of variance (Unit D5) may be used.

Comments   The major difference between the randomized two-group design and the static group comparison design is random assignment of the subjects.

Although the randomized two-group design is commonly used in the laboratory to obtain maximum control of environmental conditions, it is also used for field studies.

Before-After Two-Group Design

The procedure for the before-after two-group design is: randomly assign the subjects to the experimental and control groups, obtain a before measure of each group's performance, expose one of the groups to a treatment, and then compare the scores of the two groups on some subsequent measure. A before-after two-group design offers the advantages of random assignment of the subjects along with a measure of the initial characteristics of each group. If the before scores indicate that the two groups are equated, a comparison of the after scores is sufficient. If, however, the before scores are different, that fact must be taken into account in the data analysis.

TABLE 4.4. Before-After Two-Group Design.

Group	Assignment	Before Observation	Treatment	After Observation
1	R	Y_{b1}	X	Y_{a1}
2	R	Y_{b2}	—	Y_{a2}

Function   As mentioned earlier, random assignment is a control method that theoretically equates two groups of subjects. However, it is possible to make a biased assignment to the two groups. A biased assignment will interfere with the interpretation of the data. The before observation in this design allows the experimenter to test whether or not his assignment procedures did equate the groups initially on the dependent variable measures.

Advantages   The before-after two-group design provides a control for group differences by the random assignment procedure. It also provides a partial check on the effectiveness of the control procedure. Outside influences are minimized between groups, since the before and after observations occur at the same time for each group. The effects of outside influences that occur between the before and after measures may be estimated by the differences between the Y_{b2} and Y_{a2} scores. The effect of any experimental contamination factors can also be estimated by the Group 2 before-after differences.

Limitations   The major limitation of the before-after two-group design is that it requires a fairly large sample of subjects in order for the randomization procedure to be effective. The before measure is used to examine the equivalence of the two groups on the dependent variable. Even if they are equivalent on that measure, they may not be equivalent on other (secondary) variables not measured by the dependent variable. Those secondary variables may interact with the treatment to affect the after dependent measures. A second limitation is that the before observation may sensitize the experimental group (Group 1) to the treatment.

Statistical Analysis   The statistical techniques indicated for the randomized two-group design are appropriate for the randomized before-after two-group design. The before measures for each group are compared first. If there are no differences between the two groups (Y_{b1} and Y_{b2} scores), then the after measure for the two groups may be compared without regard to the before scores. However, if there are significant differences between the two sets of before measures, then some statistical correction for the difference should be made. The computationally simplest correction is to subtract the before score from the after score for each subject, then analyze the resulting two groups of difference scores ($d = Y_a - Y_b$, where d = difference) using the technique appropriate to the dependent variable measure. That technique would be either the two independent groups χ^2 test, median χ^2 test, Wilcoxon-Mann-Whitney test, t test for two independent groups, or multilevel analysis of variance (Section Two, Unit D). There are other appropriate ways to handle the existence of before measure group differences; however, they are beyond the scope of this text.

Comments   A before-after two-group design controls all three major sources of secondary variance. The design provides a strong basis for discovering any relationship between the independent and dependent variables.

Randomized-Blocks Design

A logical extension of the randomized two-group design is the randomized-blocks design. The purpose of a randomized-blocks design is to make the groups more homogeneous prior to the treatment. At the outset of an experiment the design controls both the between-groups and within-group variance. Suppose, for example, that we wish to study the effect of tactile feedback on the perception of a visual illusion. It is reasonable to suppose that visual acuity will have some relationship to the perception of the illusion. So the variable of acuity is controlled by "blocking" the subjects. A randomly selected group of 24 subjects is given a visual acuity test. On the basis of the test, the subjects are assigned to three blocks: "good," "average," and "poor." There are four subjects in the good block, 12 in the average block, and eight in the poor block. Half of the subjects in each block are randomly assigned to the experimental group (symbolized by BR in Table 4.5, where B stands for block and R stands for random assignment within each block). The other half are assigned to the control group (Group 2). Consequently, each group contains two "good" subjects, six "average" subjects, and four "poor" subjects.

TABLE 4.5. Randomized-Blocks Design.

Group	Assignment	Before Observation	Treatment	After Observation
1	BR	—	X	Y_{a1}
2	BR	—	—	Y_{a2}

Function   The variability of the acuity premeasure is evenly distributed between treatment groups by the assignment procedure, thus ensuring similarity of the groups on that measure. The between-groups and within-group variance is thus controlled.

Limitations   The randomized-blocks design requires additional experimenter effort in assigning subjects. The blocking variable must be significantly related to the dependent measure. The between-groups variance minimization effect of random assignment to groups within each block depends on the number of subjects. Ideally each block would contain a large population to be sampled and a large number of subjects would be randomly assigned to each group. If there is an interaction between the treatment and blocks, the data analysis becomes complicated. (See Chapter 5.)

Statistical Analysis   The statistical analysis technique appropriate to the randomized two-group design is apppropriate here. This includes the two independent groups χ^2, median χ^2, Wilcoxon-Mann-Whitney, t test for independent groups, or multilevel analysis of variance (Section Two, Unit D). If the dependent variable is measured at the interval or ratio level (Chapter 8), then the most appropriate inferential analysis technique is the randomized-blocks analysis of variance (Unit D5).

Comments   A randomized-blocks design offers considerable control for individual differences. If the blocking variable is highly related to the dependent variable and a sufficient number of subjects is available, the design is extremely useful.

RELATED TWO-GROUP DESIGNS

Related two-group designs involve the observation of an experimental group and control group that have been matched (Chapter 2) on some criterion. Because of the matching procedure, each individual in the experimental group may be indentified with his counterpart in the control group. There are still different subjects in the two groups but they are matched on some common criterion. Thus, the scores may be thought of as occurring in pairs, with matched subjects contributing a score in each condition. The procedure minimizes the between-groups variability at the outset of the experiment. The decision concerning which of each pair of subjects is assigned to the experimental group should be made using the table of random numbers. The random assignment of the pairs to the conditions controls for inadvertent bias as a result of the matching procedure.

Match-by-Correlated-Criterion Design

A match-by-correlated-criterion-design involves two groups that are matched on a measure that is related to the dependent variable.

TABLE 4.6. Match-by-Correlated-Criterion Design.

Group	Assignment	Before Observation	Treatment	After Observation
1	M	—	X	Y_{a1}
2	M	—	—	Y_{a2}

Function Matching (M) by correlated criterion allows the experimenter to compare the scores of matched subjects in the experimental and control conditions. The design requires that the experimenter have access to records that allow him to match the subjects prior to the experiment. For example, an experimenter might wish to equate two groups in terms of physical ability before evaluating a new physical education program. If the school records include physical ability scores, the experimenter could use these records to assign the students to the old and new physical education programs.

Advantages Matching is efficient in controlling individual differences (that is, between-groups variance). Outside influences (such as changes in the weather) are controlled by taking the experimental and control observations at the same time. Experimental contamination is not an important factor except for the possible effect of the before measurement. The ability to compare each individual score with its matched counterpart allows the experimenter to evaluate the *change* in performance due to the independent variable. A matching design is more sensitive to small experimental effects (for example, small differences in levels of the independent variable) than designs using random assignment.

Limitations The matching criterion must be highly related to the measure of the dependent variable or the matching procedure will be of little use. The matching procedure must reduce the between-groups variance of the observed scores or it will not be effective. It should be noted that the subjects within each group may *also* be matched, which reduces the within-group variability. If the experimenter uses a matching design inappropriately (match on noncorrelated criterion), he does not strengthen the design and weakens the inferential statistical analysis.

Statistical Analysis The inferential analysis (Chapter 10) depends on the level of measurement and other characteristics of the dependent measure. At the ordinal level of measurement with both groups' scores ranked, the sign test (Unit D1) may be used. At the interval or ratio level use the *t* test for related groups (Unit D4) or the randomized blocks analysis of variance (Unit D5). In the case of the analysis of variance each pair of matched subjects forms a "block," so there are as many blocks as there are subjects in a group.

Comment If the matching criterion is highly related to the dependent variable, use this design.

Before-Match-After Design

In the before-match-after design, a before observation is made with the specific intent of using the before data to match the experimental and control subjects (similar to a match-by-correlated-criterion design).

TABLE 4.7. Before-Match-After Design.

Group	Assignment	Before Observation	Treatment	After Observation
1	M	Y_{b1}	X	Y_{a1}
2	M	Y_{b2}	—	Y_{a2}

Function Matching the groups allows the experimenter to compare the scores of matched subjects in the experimental and control conditions. The design requires that the experimenter pretest the groups before the administration of the treatment and collection of the after measures. The statistical analysis is then applied to the after observation.

Advantages A before-match-after design has the advantages listed under the match-by-correlated-criterion design. Individual differences are specifically controlled by the choice of design. Since the before scores are collected to accomplish the matching procedure, the matching criterion must be relevant to the experiment. Outside secondary factors are controlled by limiting the time difference between after observations of the two groups. Experimental contamination factors may be estimated by comparing the before and after scores obtained from the control subjects.

Limitations The before-matching procedure introduces one possible experimental contamination factor. The before observation might alter the experimental subjects' responses to the experimental treatment. The subjects are required to be available for both the before and the after measures.

Statistical Analysis Since the subjects (and groups) are matched on the basis of the before measure, there is no purpose in statistically examining the before measures. The after measures may be examined with exactly the same techniques listed for the match-by-correlated-criterion design: sign test, t test for related groups, or randomized-blocks analysis of variance (Units D1, D4, or D5, respectively).

Comments If used inappropriately, the control procedures themselves may interfere with the interpretation of the data.

Yoked Control-Group Design

A yoked control-group design consists of manipulating the environment (X') of a control subject so that the treatment conditions correspond to those of an experimental subject. Occasionally subjects in an experimental group each encounter different exposures to the treatment due to their own performance. For example, if a subject must learn to avoid electric shock, a subject who learns the task quickly experiences less total shock. In human verbal retention experiments, a major problem is to control for differences in the original level of learning. There is a need to match the subjects in terms of the amount of practice and particular sequence of learning experiences. This may be accomplished by "yoking" pairs (or triples if necessary) of subjects together. The yoking may occur through physical means (as in the case of oxen yokes) or through more indirect procedures such as the programmed sequence of experiences two subjects receive. For example, if the subject controls the reinforcement conditions he receives by pushing a bar or lever, then a record of the exact frequency and rate of bar pressing can be kept. The control subject can be exposed to the reinforcement conditions according to that record. The yoked control-group design matches the subjects in terms of time and procedure. A control-group subject is exposed to the same quantity of experimental conditions as the experimental subject. The treatment consists of a particular order of the experimental conditions. Statistical analysis is applied to the differences between the scores of the matched subjects.

TABLE 4.8. Yoked Control-Group Design.

Group	Assignment	Before Observation	Treatment	After Observation
1	R	—	X(X')	Y_{a1}
2	R	—	(X')	Y_{a2}

Function   A yoked control-group design specifically controls for secondary factors introduced as a result of the subject's participation in the experiment. Brady's (1958) experiment on "executive monkeys" provides a good example of a yoked control design. Brady found that monkeys who were warned of an impending shock by the onset of a light could learn to avoid the shock by pressing a bar before the shock was turned on. He also found that prolonged exposure to this situation caused the animal to develop massive stomach ulcers. Brady could not be sure whether the ulceration was the result of the responsibility for turning off the shock or a natural response to being shocked. Brady solved the problem with a yoked control design. The experimental animals were placed in a shock-avoidance situation with a warning light and a lever, which if pressed would terminate the shock. The control animals were placed in an identical apparatus; however, manipulation of the lever did not control the shock. Both apparatuses were interconnected so that both animals experienced the same sequence and number of lights and shocks (X'). (Brady named his experimental animals "executives" and the control animals "employees" based on the decision-making process.) The "executive" animals all developed ulcers, while the corresponding control animals did not. Brady concluded that ulceration was indeed an "executive" malady.

Advantages   When the experimental situation involves the introduction of a number of unusual situations simultaneously, a yoked control design may be necessary to isolate a significant factor. Individual differences are controlled by randomly assigning the subjects to each group (although preexperimental matching is also feasible). Outside influences, including those introduced by the experimental situation, are controlled by this design. Experimental contamination factors are also controlled by yoking the experimental and control subjects.

Limitations   The manipulations necessary to create a yoked control condition increase the cost involved in the research. Often these manipulations require the construction of complicated equipment.

Statistical Analysis   The statistical analysis to be used is exactly the same as for the match-by-correlated-criterion design. The possible techniques include: the sign test (Unit D1), the t test for related groups (Unit D4), and the randomized-blocks analysis of variance (Unit D5). In the case of the analysis of variance, each yoked pair of subjects forms a "block."

Comments   A yoked control design may be employed when the relevant variables are known.

REVIEW

Each of the two-group designs presented in this chapter warrants more than the usual careful study by the student. The classic two-group designs presented here epitomize solutions to research problems that are accomplished through careful research design. In many cases, when researchers are discussing their data, they reduce it down to a two-group comparison, although the design itself may be a more complicated type of experimental design. Thus, careful study of the differences between the two-group designs presented here will provide useful clues in understanding more complicated designs. The major problem addressed by a researcher using a two-group design is to assign the subjects (or to arrange the treatments) in such a way that the two groups are essentially equal. If the researcher can assume that his two groups are initially the same, then any difference observed in the behavior is easily attributed to the independent variable, which is the reason for conducting the experiment.

Pay particular attention to the difference between the randomized group procedures as opposed to the procedures under the matched groups designs. The randomized groups procedures involve assigning subjects to the groups in such a way that the average *group* scores are equivalent without paying attention to the individual subjects within the group. The matched procedures, on the other hand, match the subjects in each in the experimental and control group. Thus each subject observed under the experimental condition has a corresponding subject in the control group generating control data for his score. Although the difference may seem trivial at the present time, it becomes a very important factor when the researcher analyzes his data. In order to select the right statistical technique for data analysis, the researcher *must* understand the difference between matched designs and randomized designs.

SUMMARY

1. In most two-group designs, an experimental group receives a treatment and a control group receives no treatment (zero level of the independent variable). Two-group designs control for experimental contamination.
2. A static group comparison design is a poor design and a naturalistic research design because: (1) the subjects are not randomly assigned to the groups and (2) the independent variable is some natural occurrence that is not manipulated by the experimenter.
3. A before-after static group comparison design is an improvement over a static group comparison design because the pretests provide a measure of preexisting group differences. However, the lack of random assignment of subjects to groups makes the research conclusions suspect and the research design is a poor design.
4. A randomized two-group design is a better design than the static group comparison design. A randomized two-group design requires that the number of subjects be large enough so that the randomization procedure has a good chance of producing approximately equivalent groups.
5. A before-after two-group design requires that the subjects be randomly assigned to the

two groups. The addition of a before measure provides a check on the effect of randomization. As long as the before measure does not sensitize the experimental group to the treatment, a before-after two-group design is an improvement over a randomized two-group design.

6. A randomized-blocks design involves blocking the subject on a variable related to the dependent variable and randomly assigning the subjects within each block. If the blocking and dependent variables are significantly correlated, then a randomized-blocks design provides more control of between and within variance than a randomized two-group design.

7. A match-by-correlated-criterion design involves two groups of subjects that are matched in pairs. Each member of a pair is randomly assigned to the treatment groups. Instead of grouping subjects in blocks, the subjects are matched in pairs on the criterion measure. The criterion measure must be correlated with the dependent variable.

8. In a before-match-after design, the subjects are given a before measure, then matched in pairs on that measure. A before-match-after design is a direct extension of a match-by-correlated-criterion design.

9. A yoked control-group design consists of matching subjects in groups according to the experimental situation rather than on a correlated criterion measure. In a well-conducted, yoked control-group design, only one situation difference between the two groups is allowed to occur. Usually, subjects are randomly assigned to the two groups. A yoked control-group design is expensive and requires knowledge of which variables are relevant; however, it provides excellent control.

SUGGESTED READING

Campbell, D. T., and Stanley, J. C. *Experimental and quasi-experimental designs for research.* Skokie, Ill.: Rand McNally, 1963.

Kerlinger, F. N. *Foundations of behavioral research.* (2d ed.) New York: Holt, Rinehart and Winston, 1973.

Selltiz, C., Johoda, M., Deutsch, M., and Cook, S. W. *Research methods in social relations.* (Rev. ed.) New York: Holt, Rinehart and Winston, 1959.

CHAPTER 5
Multiple Treatment Designs

A multiple treatment design involves more than two levels of the independent variable or more than one independent variable in a single experiment. Multiple treatment designs usually require more subjects but yield more information than one- or two-group designs. The number of variables and the number of levels of each variable in a single experiment are determined by the research hypotheses, the experimenter's imagination, the available research tools, and the availability of subjects. The subjects in various groups may be randomized, matched, or both. The dependent variable(s) must be the same over all treatments. The research may involve multiple measures on a single dependent variable or measures on several dependent variables. For example, the subjects' reading comprehension may be tested several times; or the subjects may be tested on reading comprehension, reaction time, and typing skill in the same experiment. Clearly, multiple treatment designs can be complex.

MULTILEVEL DESIGN

A multilevel design consists of several levels of the independent variable. Usually several independent groups are exposed to different levels of treatment, including a zero level (no treatment control group). Occasionally, one group of subjects will be exposed to each level of the design (**repeated-measures** multilevel design). In the independent groups version, the subjects are randomly assigned to groups, and the groups are randomly assigned to the levels of the treatment. (See Table 5.1.)

TABLE 5.1. An Example of a Multilevel Design.

Group	Assignment	Before Observation	Treatment	After Observation
1	R	(Y_{b1})	—	Y_{a1}
2	R	(Y_{b2})	X_1	Y_{a2}
3	R	(Y_{b3})	X_2	Y_{a3}
4	R	(Y_{b4})	X_3	Y_{a4}

There may be pretests [indicated by (Y_{bi}) in Table 5.1] of each group. As is the case in the before-after two-group design, initial differences between the groups complicate data analysis. If you have time, the groups may be matched on the pretest measures; or you may subtract the before score from the after score for each subject, then analyze the remaining difference scores. Before measures are not necessary to a multilevel design; however, as indicated in the preceding chapters, pretests normally improve a design. In one sense, a multilevel design is several two-group designs being run simultaneously.

Speech anxiety may be measured in two ways: (1) behavioral measures in a speech-giving situation of performance, such as various mannerisms as well as number of words spoken per unit of time, duration of silences, and number of "ahh" and "duh" utterances; and (2) subjective measures of fear in a speech-giving situation, such as self-reports of confidence and ability in making a speech before an audience, and self-report inventories of social avoidance and fear of negative evaluations. There are two forms of therapy that have been successfully applied to cases of speech anxiety: group insight and group desensitization therapy. Group insight therapy involves attempting to make the client aware of his self-verbalizations and internalized sentences that contribute to his maladaptive behavior. The client is encouraged to examine possible incompatible self-instructions and other behaviors incompatible with his negative verbalizations. The therapy is based on the assumption that maladaptive self-verbalizations are instrumental in producing anxiety. The clients discuss the irrational and self-defeating aspects of such verbalizations and internalized sentences emitted while thinking about the speech situation. Group desensitization therapy involves group training in relaxation techniques, constructing a group hierarchy of the anxiety-provoking speech-giving and other social situations, group training in visualizing (imagining) each of these elements, and pairing the relaxation experiences with the imagined speech-making scenes, slowly moving from the least anxiety-provoking scenes to the most anxiety-provoking scenes in the hierarchy. The group should come to be less sensitive (desensitized) to the anxiety-producing situation as a function of associating relaxation (incompatible with anxiety) with the imagined speech-making scene. The theory behind desensitization is that a person cannot be both anxious and relaxed at the same time.

Meichenbaum, Gilmore, and Fedoravicius (1971) conducted a well-controlled study of the relative effectiveness of the two therapies on speech anxiety. A combined desensitization-insight treatment condition was employed with a desensitization treatment and an insight treatment condition in a multilevel design. **Placebo** In addition a "speech-discussion" placebo control group was employed; in the group the subjects met with the therapist and discussed neutral (nonanxiety-provoking) topics. The group was included to control for nonspecific group-treatment factors such as expectation of relief, suggestion, therapist-patient relationships, and group spirit resulting from frequent group meetings. Two therapists were involved in the study; each therapist used each of the four "techniques" with a group of five or six people (making eight treatment groups). A control group of nine subjects was placed on a "waiting list" and measured for any improvement over the period of the study while waiting for treatment. Thus, a total of nine groups were involved in the study and all nine received both objective and subjective measures of speech anxiety before and after receiving eight weeks (one hour per week) of group treatment. In addition, the subjective measures were taken three months after the end of treatment to measure the durability of the effects of the therapy treatment.

Several dependent measures of both types were used. In brief, the results indicated that the insight and desensitization therapies were about equally effective on all measures. The combined desensitization and insight therapy and the speech discussion "therapy" were about equally effective as measured by the mannerisms/behavioral measures and a self-report anxiety checklist, and both were less effective on these measures than insight or desensitization alone. Except with the "ahh" mannerism, the combined desensitization-insight therapy was as effective as either therapy alone in all other measures, and the speech-discussion treatment was less effective. Being on a waiting list did not lead to any improvement. The same general pattern of results showed up on the three-month later subjective measures except that the speech-discussion group got significantly worse than the other groups.

Detailed examination of the data from the insight and desensitization groups indicated that desensitization was more effective for those subjects who experienced anxiety only in formal speech situations. The insight therapy was more effective with those subjects who suffered anxiety in a variety of situations including speech making.

Function   A multilevel design allows the experimenter to evaluate several levels of the independent variable under comparable conditions. He can determine:

(1) that the treatment does or does not affect behavior, and (2) the effect of varying levels of the treatment. As indicated in Chapter 2, a multilevel design is used for *parametric* research. Multilevel design research indicates the presence of a linear (straight line) or nonlinear (curved) relationship between the independent and dependent variables. A graph of the average score for each group usually portrays the main feature of the data.

Haber (1958) studied affective judgments as a function of deviations of temperature from the adaptation level. Subjects adapted both hands to water of a given temperature (adaptation level). Then they placed each hand in different buckets containing water at different temperatures. The subject removed his hand from the least pleasant temperature. The subjects were tested several times with various degrees of difference in temperature (a repeated-measures, multilevel design). Slight increases or decreases in temperature from the adaptation level were preferred by the subjects. Greater differences (colder or hotter) were felt to be unpleasant. In summary, the graphed data points formed a "butterfly" or "M-shaped" curve. (See Figure 5.1.) Such information could not be obtained with a two-level design.

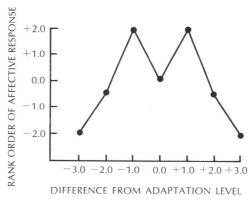

Fig. 5.1.   A hypothetical M-shaped curve. The ordinate contains the observed rank of affect, and the abscissa presents the measure of difference from adaptation level.

Advantages and Limitations   Multilevel designs are extensions of the two-group designs (See Chapter 4.) The advantages and limitations of the corresponding two-group designs generally apply to multilevel designs. As indicated, multilevel designs usually require more subjects than simpler designs.

Statistical Analysis   The analysis of variance (Section II, Unit D5) is most appropriate to the multilevel design given an interval or ratio level of measurement. In the analysis of variance of a multilevel design, the effects of all levels of a variable such as type of therapy can be assessed simultaneously. If the dependent variable is measured at the nominal level then the multiple group χ^2 test (Unit D2) is appropriate. If the dependent variable is measured at the ordinal level, use the

Kruskal-Wallis one-way analysis of variance by ranks (Kirk, 1968). (That test is not included in this text.)

Comments A multilevel design can be used in a pilot study where the experimenter is primarily interested in finding the most effective treatment level for subsequent experiments (finding "optimal values," Chapter 2). It is also useful for determining the parameters of an independent variable that two-group design research has shown to be effective.

FACTORIAL DESIGNS

A factorial design involves all possible combinations of the levels of two or more independent variables. Thus, the effects of two or more independent variables can be measured in a single experiment. A factorial design may be a related design (where each subject experiences all of the treatment conditions), or it may be independent (where different groups of subjects experience a single treatment). In Table 5.2, each independent variable (A and B) has two levels (1 and 2). There are four combinations of the two levels of each variable (the four quadrants: I, II, III,

TABLE 5.2. An Example Factorial Design.

		Variable B	
		B1	B2
Variable A	A1	I	II
	A2	III	IV

and IV). The example is called a 2×2 factorial design; a given factorial design may involve more levels of each variable (for example, 3×5, 2×4, and so on). A factorial design may involve more variables than two (for example, $2 \times 2 \times 2$, $2 \times 2 \times 2 \times 2$, and so on). Or, a factorial design may involve any combination of levels and variables (for example, $2 \times 3 \times 5$, $3 \times 2 \times 9$, and so on). A different group of subjects can be randomly assigned to each quadrant of the design. Variable A might be the number of hours of food deprivation (24 and 48) and Variable B might be the number of hours without sleep (36 and 72). (See Table 5.3.) The subjects in Group I would not be allowed to eat for 24 hours or sleep for 36 hours. The subjects in Group II would not be allowed to eat for 24 hours or sleep for 72 hours. The subjects in Group III would not be allowed to eat for 48 hours or sleep for 36 hours. The subjects in Group IV would not be allowed to eat for 48 hours or sleep for 72 hours (the really unpleasant condition).

The experimenter might see what effect the combination of the two variables has on final exam scores.

Function Factorial designs are efficient, since data concerning the effects of two or more variables are simultaneously collected from each subject. To evaluate the effect of variable A, compare all of the scores under treatment A1 with all of the scores under treatment A2. Combine the scores of quadrants I and II to determine the average performance under treatment A1, and combine the scores in

TABLE 5.3. Hypothetical Factorial Design.

<table>
<tr><td></td><td></td><td colspan="2" align="center">B
Hours of Sleep
Deprivation</td><td></td><td></td></tr>
<tr><td></td><td></td><td align="center">36</td><td align="center">72</td><td></td><td></td></tr>
<tr><td>A　Hours of Food</td><td>24</td><td align="center">I</td><td align="center">II</td><td>I + II ⎱</td><td rowspan="2">Difference is Main
Effect of A</td></tr>
<tr><td>Deprivation</td><td>48</td><td align="center">III</td><td align="center">IV</td><td>III + IV ⎰</td></tr>
<tr><td></td><td></td><td align="center">I + III</td><td align="center">II + IV</td><td></td><td></td></tr>
</table>

Difference is *Main*
Effect of B

Simple Effects:	effect of B under A_1: I vs. II
	effect of B under A_2: III vs. IV
	effect of A under B_1: I vs. III
	effect of A under B_2: II vs. IV

Interaction Effect:
The difference between I and II (I $-$ II) vs. the difference between III and IV (III $-$ IV), or the difference between I and III (I $-$ III) vs. the difference between II and IV (II $-$ IV).

quadrants III and IV to determine the average for A2. The effects of the two levels of B are equally represented in the two combinations of quadrants (I-II and III-IV). To determine the effect of variable B, compare all of the B1 scores with all of the B2 scores. Thus, add the exam scores of quadrants I and III to determine the average score for 36 hours without sleep, and add the scores for quadrants II and IV to find the average score under 72 hours of sleep deprivation. The average effects of the independent variables are called the **main effects** of the design.

　　The effects of the two levels of B under *each level of* A, and the effects of A under each level of B are called the **simple effects** of the design. The researcher can see what effect the different hours without sleep have when the subjects have gone without food for 24 hours, and also when they have been food deprived for 48 hours. In the same fashion, one can determine the differential effects of food deprivation under each level of sleep deprivation.

　　The effect of both levels of B under both levels of A is called the **interaction effect.** It could also be worded as the effect of both levels of A under both levels of B. As indicated in Chapter 2, an interaction effect occurs if the effect of one variable (for example, food deprivation) depends on the level of another variable (for example, sleep deprivation). The presence or absence of an interaction is determined by comparing the effect of the B variable at the first level of the A variable (I $-$ II = effect of B at A_1) with the effect of the B variable at the second level of the A variable (III $-$ IV = effect of B at A_2). Thus, the data are examined to find any *difference between differences,* or the two simple effects of B are compared to determine if they are approximately equal or not.

　　Kamin and Schaub (1963) studied conditioned emotional responses (CER) as a function of conditioned stimulus (CS) intensity. Hungry rats were pretrained to bar-press for food. Four times during the daily two-hour bar-pressing period, a three-minute noise (CS) was turned on. During the noise period, the bar turned on an electric shock. After five days of training, the noise CS was presented *without shock* during the CER *extinction period.* The magnitude of the CER was operationally defined as the number of bar presses during the three-minute noise CS presentation divided by the total of: (1) the number of bar presses during noise CS, plus (2) the number for three minutes prior to noise CS. Symbolically, CER = (number of CS presses) ÷ (number of CS presses and prior three-minute presses). The smaller the ratio, the greater the magnitude of CER. In other words, a high CER (number approaching zero) means that the animal reduces its bar-press rate during the noise. The independent variables were: (1) the intensity of the noise CS (strong and weak) during acquisition and (2) the intensity of the noise CS during extinction. Part of the study involved a 2×2 design where the dependent variable was the magnitude of CER. The results during extinction are presented in Table 5.4 (where S = strong and W = weak).

TABLE 5.4. Average Magnitude of CER during Three Extinction Days.

		Acquisition Noise CS	
		S (strong)	W (weak)
Extinction Noise CS	S (strong)	.06	.28
	W (weak)	.29	.19

Modified from Kamin and Schaub, 1963.

Analyzed separately, the two independent variables (level of acquisition and extinction noise CS had, on the average, a slight, inconsequential effect on CER magnitude. However, the interaction between the two variables was substantial. **Interaction** An interaction exists when the effect of one variable depends on the effects of another variable or variables. That is, the effect of extinction noise CS intensity depended on the level of noise CS intensity during acquisition. Another way of stating the same interaction is that during the extinction period, the effect of the acquisition conditions depended on the extinction conditions. Notice that the acquisition treatment effect was accentuated under the strong extinction noise CS, but not the weak extinction noise CS. Similarly, the extinction treatment effect was accentuated under the strong acquisition noise CS. Thus, the strong-strong (S-S) group exhibited a high CER magnitude as compared to the strong-weak (S-W) and the weak-strong (W-S) groups. In general, the rats tended to bar-press less during the noise when the acquisition and extinction levels were the same.

An interaction is most clearly comprehended when the data is presented in graphic form. The information presented in the preceding paragraph is summarized in Table 5.4 and Figure 5.2. One of the independent variables (acquisition noise CS) is mapped onto the abscissa (horizontal line) and the dependent variable (CER magnitude) on the ordinate (vertical line). (See Chapter 7 for a discussion of graphing.) The two levels of the other independent variable (extinction noise CS) are represented by the two lines on the graph. The interaction is denoted by the fact that

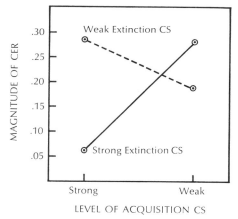

Fig. 5.2. Graph of CER magnitude as a function of level of acquisition and extinction noise CS intensity. Data from Kamin and Schaub (1963). The higher the number on the Y axis (ordinate), the weaker is the conditional emotional response (CER). The strong-strong condition yielded the greatest CER.

the two lines are *not parallel.* The lines do not have to cross on the graph. The crossed-lines form of an interaction is a special case. If an experimenter conducted a test of one variable using only one level of the other variable, he would make one kind of conclusion. If the same experimenter tested the same variable using the other level of the second variable, he would make the opposite conclusion. Clearly, the "crossed-lines" interaction indicates the importance of factorial designs.

In order to illustrate a lack of an interaction, the Kamin and Schaub (1963) data will be modified. Table 5.5 contains the artificial scores created for the example. The scores from Table 5.5 are graphed in Figure 5.3. The lines in the graph are parallel; they do not cross as in Figure 5.2. In Table 5.5, the first row is the same as in Table 5.4; to create the second row, the constant of 0.07 was added to the two numbers in the first row (that is, $0.06 + 0.07 = 0.13$, and $0.28 + 0.07 = 0.35$).

TABLE 5.5. Average Magnitude of CER during Three Extinction Days.

		Acquisition Noise CS	
		S (strong)	W (weak)
Extinction Noise CS	S (strong)	.06[a]	.28
	W (weak)	.13	.35

[a] Numbers created expressly to illustrate a lack of interaction.

Thus, the difference between the two scores in the first row equals the difference between the two scores in the second row that is, $0.28 - 0.06 = 0.22$ and $0.35 - 0.13 = 0.22$). That result was insured by adding the constant to the two values in the first row. What this means is that the effect of the extinction noise CS is to add a constant amount (0.07) to the effect of the acquisition noise CS. Thus, there is an *additive* relationship between the two variables. If the extinction noise CS added

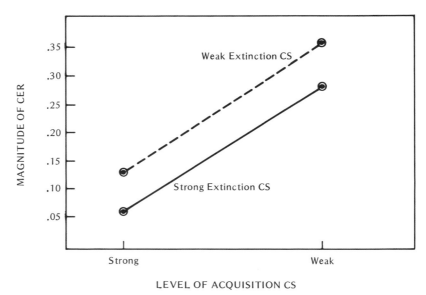

Fig. 5.3. Graph of CER magnitude as a function of level of acquisition and extinction noise CS intensity. The higher the number on the Y axis (ordinate) the weaker the conditioned emotional response (CER). Numbers were created to illustrate lack of interaction (additivity). The two lines are parallel.

or subtracted a nonconstant amount to the effect of the acquisition noise CS (as in Figure 5.2), then the relationship between the two variables would be *nonadditive*, or, in other words, there would be an interaction between the two variables.

Randomized-Blocks Factorial

A particular form of a factorial design is called the randomized-blocks design. (See Chapter 4.) Sometimes the experimenter wishes to control for individual differences between his subjects but does not have the necessary facilities for subject by subject matching. Using the randomized-blocks design, he can match the experimental and control groups in terms of groups (blocks) of subjects. Suppose that you want to study the effects of two methods of teaching on the learning performance of college sophomores. You expect that the intelligence of the subjects might affect your dependent variable. So, you divide your subjects into two blocks: a high-intelligence block and a low-intelligence block. Subjects in each block are randomly assigned to each treatment group. Thus, you have a 2×2 factorial with one "blocking" variable (intelligence) and one treatment variable (method of teaching). The advantages of the design are similar to those obtained with matching techniques, but since individual subjects are not matched, an independent-groups statistical test is used with the data.

Repeated-Measures Factorial

Another particular form of a factorial design is called a repeated-measures factorial design (sometimes called a split-plot design). In the repeated-measures design, the subjects each experience all of the levels of at least one variable. That variable usually consists of learning trials or some similar variable under which several measures of the subjects' behavior are taken. The simplest example of a repeated-measures factorial would be 2×2. For example, the subjects might be given two trials at learning a motor task. One group would attempt to learn under a high motivation condition (30 1974 dollars or their inflationary equivalent) while the other group would attempt to learn under a low motivation condition (30 1974 pennies or their inflationary equivalent, if it exists). The change in performance of the task across the two trials would be determined. The trials variable is the repeated (related-groups) variable; the motivation variable is a nonrepeated (independent-groups) variable. The design combines the advantages of subjects-as-their-own-control designs with the advantages of independent groups designs.

Advantages and Limitations   Factorial designs increase the amount of information provided by each response. In a factorial design, each measure of behavior provides information about at least two variables. *Only* factorial designs allow the experimenter to study all possible interactions between variables. Other designs (not covered in this text) provide some information about certain interactions, but other interactions are confused (confounded) with main effects.

In order to evaluate the interaction effect clearly in a factorial design, at least two measures of behavior should be observed under each combination of variables. Usually, this means that at least two subjects are included in each cell of the design table. As the number of variables increases, the number of possible interactions rapidly increases. With two variables, only one interaction is possible. With three variables (A, B, C) four interactions are possible: an AB interaction, an AC interaction, a BC interaction, and an ABC interaction.

Statistical Analysis   Given an internal or ratio level of measurement of the dependent variable, the most appropriate statistical technique is the analysis of variance for a factorial design (or randomized-blocks factorial or repeated-measures factorial) described in Section Two, Unit D5. At the nominal level of measurement, the multiple independent group χ^2 test (Unit D2) is appropriate for a factorial design but not a randomized-blocks factorial or repeated-measures factorial.

Comments   A factorial design is often used as an indicator of "sophisticated" research. If the data collection techniques are inadequate and the statistical analyses inappropriate, the fact that a factorial design was used, will not save the research.

SOLOMON FOUR-GROUP DESIGN

As compared with two-group designs, the Solomon (1949) four-group design uses additional groups to control for the effects of additional secondary variables. It is a particular form of the factorial design in which one independent variable is the administration of pretests. The four-group design is presented in Tables 5.6 and 5.7. The subjects are randomly assigned to the four groups.

Function   The design is an outstanding example of careful control of secondary variables through multiple "control" groups. Each individual group was discussed in Chapters 3 and 4. The Solomon four-group design consists of the before-after two-group design combined with the randomized two-group design. The limita-

TABLE 5.6. The Solomon Four-Group Design (Standard Presentation Form).

Groups	Before Observation	Treatment	After Observation
I	Y_b	X_1	Y_{a1}
II	—	X_1	Y_{a2}
III	Y_b	X_2	Y_{a3}
IV	—	X_2	Y_{a4}

TABLE 5.7. The Solomon Four-Group Design (Factorial Presentation Form).

		Pretest	
		Yes	No
Treatment	X_1	I	II
	X_2	III	IV

tions of each two-group design are handled by the combination of the two into a four-group design. You can determine the effects of the before measure (pretest), the effects of the experimental treatment, the effects of the treatment uncontaminated by the pretest, and the effects of the pretest by treatment interaction. The pretest performance of Groups I and III can be *combined* to estimate the scores of Groups II and IV had they been pretested. The effects of pretesting can be discovered by analyzing the differences between the after scores of Groups I and II and the differences between the after scores of Groups III and IV. Finally, the interaction between pretest and the treatment variables can be determined.

Solomon and Lessac (1968) maintain that the design is the "minimum design" required for a study of the effects of deprivation or enrichment on the development of behavior. The effects of environmental restriction or enrichment may be due to the deterioration or enhancement of already developed capacities, or the retardation or acceleration of the rate of development of behavioral capacities. Using a two-group design, it is not possible to discriminate between the alternative explanations, as can be done with the Solomon design. For example, an experimenter hypothesizes that early environmental stress affects later emotional stability. He tests the hypothesis by exposing half of his subjects to a series of electric shocks (X_1) and the other half of his subjects to no shock (X_2). Half of the shocked and nonshocked subjects are pretested on emotionality, and all four groups are given the after measure of emotional behavior. A high score indicates emotional instability or excitability. Suppose that the average *pretest* emotionality scores were: Group I = 15, and Group III = 15. The average *after treatment* emotionality scores are presented in Table 5.8.

The shock experience led to a decrease in emotionality (average of Groups I and II compared to average of Groups III and IV). If he had used only Groups I and III, the experimenter would have made the erroneous conclusion that the shocks had little effect on emotionality. If he had used only Groups II and IV, the experimenter would have overestimated the effect of the shock. The pretest performance

TABLE 5.8. Average Emotionality Scores In the Hypothetical Early Experience Study.

	Pretest		
	Yes	No	Average
Shock	I 10	II 20	15
No Shock	III 12	IV 30	21
Average	11	25	

of Groups I and III was less than the after performance of Group II, indicating that the shock experience contributed only part of the decrease. The pretest served to decrease the later measures of emotionality as indicated by the difference between: (1) the combined average of Groups I and III versus the combined average of Groups II and IV, (2) the difference between the posttreatment averages of Groups I and II, and (3) the difference between the posttreatment average of Groups III and IV. Finally, an interaction between pretesting and shock treatment occurred. That is, the pretest decreased the effect of the shock (the greater difference between Groups II and IV compared to Groups I and III), but both shock and the pretest combined to decrease the measure of emotionality. The fictitious data indicates that early shock retards the development of emotionality to the usual high level.

Advantages and Limitations   For a study of a two-level independent variable, a four-group design provides a great deal of control of secondary variables, particularly the before observation variable. The four-group design can be generalized to a factorial with more than two levels of the primary variable, or a factorial with more than one primary variable. A four-group design requires more subjects than a two-group design. If a pretest is meaningless or not possible, then a four-group design is inappropriate.

Statistical Analysis   The techniques listed for the factorial design are appropriate here since the Solomon four-group design is a factorial design. These include: the multiple independent group χ^2 test (Unit D2) and analysis of variance for factorial designs, randomized-blocks factorial, and repeated-measures factorial (Unit D5).

Comments   The experimenter should closely examine the advantages of a four-group design over one of the two-group designs. If the additional control warrants the increase in complexity, a four-group design should be employed. It is particularly appropriate in the case of developmental research where a pretest is meaningful.

REVIEW

Although two-group designs are elegant in their simplicity, they present the researcher with a difficult problem. The selection of one particular two-group design over another means that the experimenter must make an either/or choice as far as some of the factors controlled in his experiment are concerned. Multiple treatment designs get around this problem by simultaneously conducting two, three, four, or more, two-group designs in a single experiment. Sometimes the additional groups are used to investigate various levels of a single kind of treatment. Other times, several treatments can be simultaneously investigated in a single experiment. The multilevel design is this kind of addition of two or more of the two-group designs in the previous chapter.

When the experimenter begins to combine his treatments so that groups of subjects receive two or more treatments simultaneously, not only does he achieve the advantages of the multiple treatment design in terms of several levels of treatment measures, but he also can measure the interaction between two or more treatments. Interaction is an important concept and deserves careful study in this chapter and in the following chapters where it will periodically appear. Since approximately 50 percent of the published research articles in psychology journals involve research designs that include potential interactions, the importance of understanding the concept is self-evident.

SUMMARY

1. Multiple treatment designs contain more than two levels of an independent variable, more than one independent variable, or both.
2. A multiple level design includes several levels of a single independent variable and is necessary for parametric research.
3. A factorial design contains all possible combinations of the levels of two or more independent variables.
4. Factorial designs are efficient, since data concerning the effects of two or more variables is simultaneously collected from each subject.
5. The main effects of a factorial design are the averaged effects of each independent variable.
6. The simple effects of a factorial design are the effects of one independent variable, under one level of another independent variable.
7. Two variables "interact" when the effects of one variable depend upon the effects of the other variable. Graphically, an interaction is indicated by nonparallel lines.
8. Only factorial designs allow the analysis of all possible, unconfounded interactions.
9. A randomized-blocks design is a special case of a factorial design. The blocking variable is used to control for a secondary source of variance and serves as an independent variable.
10. A repeated-measures factorial design is a special case of a factorial design. The subjects are repeatedly measured under the levels of at least one variable (subjects-as-their-own-control) and at least one other independent groups variable is included in the design.
11. A Solomon four-group design is a combination of a before-after two-group design and a randomized two-group design. A Solomon four-group design is a factorial design.
12. A Solomon four-group design allows the estimation of the effect of the primary independent variable, the effect of before observations, the effect of the primary variable uncontaminated by a before measure, and the interaction effect.
13. A Solomon four-group design is the minimum necessary design for developmental studies of the effects of enriched or impoverished environments when pretests are possible.

SUGGESTED READING

Campbell, D. T., and Stanley, J. C. *Experimental and quasi-experimental designs for research.* Skokie, Illinois: Rand McNally, 1963.

Edwards, A. L. *Experimental design in psychological research.* (4th ed.) New York: Holt, Rinehart and Winston, 1972.

Hays, W. L. *Statistics for social scientists.* (2d ed.) New York: Holt, Rinehart and Winston, 1973.

Kerlinger, F. N. *Foundations of behavioral research.* (2d ed.) New York: Holt, Rinehart and Winston, 1973.

Kirk, R. E. *Experimental design: Procedures for the behavioral sciences.* Belmont, California: Brooks-Cole, 1968.

Lindquist, E. F. *Design and analysis of experiments in psychology and education.* Boston: Houghton-Mifflin, 1953.

Myers, J. L. *Fundamentals of experimental design.* Boston: Allyn and Bacon, 1966.

Selltiz, C., Jahoda, M., Deutsch, M., and Cook, S. W. *Research methods in social relations.* (Rev. ed.) New York: Holt, Rinehart and Winston, 1959.

Solomon, R. L. An extension of control group design. *Psychological Bulletin,* 1949, *46,* 137–150.

Solomon, R. L., and Lessac, M. S. A control group design for experimental studies of developmental process. *Psychological Bulletin,* 1968, *70,* 145–150.

CHAPTER 6
Research Involving Correlation Coefficients

The preceding three chapters have presented various experimental research designs. The designs differ in terms of the amount and types of potential secondary variance sources that are controlled, as well as in the number of independent variables manipulated. The experimenter attempts to control all sources of variance except the specific one (or few, in multiple treatment designs) that is being investigated. The purpose of the research is to determine if the manipulated independent variable (or variables) is related to the dependent variable. There are other types of research in which the independent variables are not manipulated by the researcher but vary naturally (naturalistic research, discussed in Chapter 2). If the independent variables are *not controlled* by the experimenter, then the researcher may determine that the independent and dependent variables are related; however, the researcher cannot conclude that the variation in the dependent variable is caused by the independent variables.

Causal inferences require that two events occur closely in time (**temporal contiguity**). If kicking an auto tire is closely followed by pain in the foot, then a person would be likely to draw a cause-effect conclusion about the kicking and the pain. However, close temporal contiguity, while necessary, is not a sufficient condition for inferring cause and effect. If a person 100 miles away stuck a pin in a doll's foot at the same time that the tire was kicked, then some people might conclude that the pin-sticking had caused the pain in the tire-kicker's foot. A skeptic might claim that such a conclusion was ridiculous. The skeptic would say that there usually should be a close **spatial contiguity** (nearness in space) between cause and effect and, furthermore, that only a limited number of events can cause other events (and sticking a pin in a doll is not a reasonable potential cause of pain in the tire-kicker's foot). In summary, (1) temporal contiguity is a *necessary but not sufficient basis* for drawing causal inferences because many events are temporally contiguous but otherwise unrelated and because, with insufficient means of observation, certain events appear to be separated in time but are actually causally related (for example, the effect of German measles during pregnancy on human embryos). (2) Spatial contiguity is supportive; however, it is *neither a necessary nor sufficient basis* for causal inference because many apparently spatially unrelated events are causally related and because many spatially close events are not causally related. (3) Not all events in the world are assumed to be caused by all other events in the world (the assumption of *finite causation*).

In order to arrive at a causal inference, a researcher needs to have control of the variables in an experiment so that the effects of the temporal (and spatial) relationship between independent and dependent variables can be carefully assessed. Further, most of the reasonable potential causal variables will be controlled (usually by holding constant) so that the effects of only a few potential causal (independent) variables can be examined in one study. In contrast, a naturalistic study does not allow such extensive control and, therefore, causal inferences from naturalistic studies are very tenuous. A naïve researcher may draw false causal inferences from a naturalistic study, and even a sophisticated researcher may be drawn in fruitless pursuits by the results of naturalistic observation. For example, the conclusion that the sex object of an adult bird is determined by the newly hatched bird's attachment to and following of a moving object located near the bird (imprinting) is misleading because in fact the bird will probably mate with its own kind, no matter what it is "imprinted" on. Naturalistic observation does indicate a great deal of interesting areas to be examined more closely with experimental research techniques.

A statistical measure frequently used in correlational, naturalistic studies is the correlation coefficient. Correlation coefficients (described below) may also be involved in experimental research. Experimental research may involve calculating correlation coefficients in order to determine if matching or randomized-blocks designs should be used; correlation coefficients may be used as the dependent vari-

Causation

able in an experimental study; measures of reliability or validity involve calculating correlation coefficients; and a correlation coefficient may be used to describe numerically the magnitude of relationship between the independent and dependent variables in an experimental study.

CORRELATION COEFFICIENTS

A correlation coefficient describes the degree and direction of relationship between two variables in numerical form. The Pearson Product Moment Correlation Coefficient (r) is the most frequently used measure of correlation. (See Section II, Unit D6.) Other coefficients approximate the Pearson r. The numerical value of a correlation ranges between +1.00 and −1.00. If there is no relationship between the variables, the value of r is zero. As the relationship between the two variables increases,

Numerical Value of r

the value of r increases from zero to plus or minus one. The *numerical value* of r describes the *strength* of the relationship between the two variables, and the *sign* describes the *direction*. A correlation can be graphically portrayed by mapping the data points onto a scatter-plot (Chapter 7). Each data point represents a pair of scores

Sign of r

on two variables. Each pair of scores is related in some way. The usual case in psychology involves two different measures of a subject's behavior. The values of each measure are arbitrarily assigned to the ordinate and abscissa of the scatter-plot. If one of the measures represents an independent variable, the independent variable is assigned to the abscissa.

A perfect correlation is depicted in Figure 6.1. The correlation is positive; large scores on measure X are associated with large scores on measure Y, and small scores on measure X are associated with small scores on measure Y. Each point in the graph represents the score of one subject on measure X and the score of the same subject on measure Y.

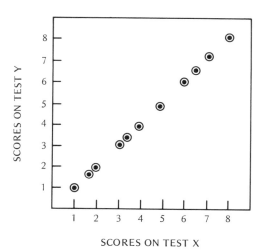

Fig. 6.1. Scatter-plot of ordered pairs where the correlation is perfect and positive ($r = +1.00$).

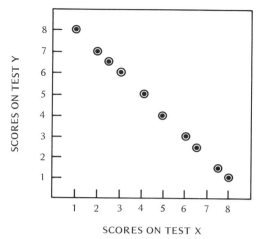

Fig. 6.2. Scatter-plot of ordered pairs where the correlation is perfect and negative ($r = -1.00$).

A perfect correlation is also portrayed in Figure 6.2. The correlation in Figure 6.2 is negative; large scores on measure X are associated with small scores on measure Y, and small scores on measure X are associated with large scores on measure Y. Again, each point represents the score of one subject on measures X and Y. A zero correlation is presented in Figure 6.3. If there is a perfect correlation between two measures, you know a subject's score on the second measure when you know his score on the first measure. If there is a zero correlation between two measures, knowledge of a subject's score on one measure gives you no information about his score on the second measure.

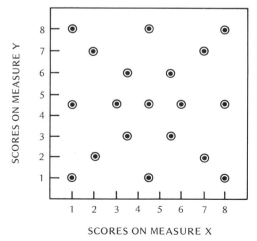

Fig. 6.3. Scatter-plot of ordered pairs where the correlation is zero ($r = 0.00$).

The **sign** of r is related to the general trend of the plotted points in the graphs. A generally downward trend from left to right yields a negative value of r; a generally upward trend from left to right yields a positive value of r. The general trend is represented by a *straight* line drawn to be as close as possible to all of the points (line of best fit). Other considerations being equal, the scatter-plot with the most widely dispersed points yields the smaller value of r. Thus, the value of r for Figure 6.4 is less than the value of r for Figure 6.5 (The formula for calculating a Pearson r is presented in Section Two, Unit D6.)

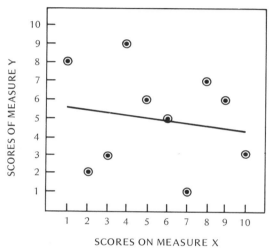

Fig. 6.4.   Scatter-plot of ordered pairs where r is equal to -0.15. The straight line in the figure is the line of best fit.

In the experimental example involving the relationship between the amount of beer consumed and handball-playing ability (Chapter 2), it would have been possible to summarize the observed relationship by calculating r between the two measures ($r = 1.00$). Although in this example the calculation is the same, when a coefficient is used to describe a relationship involving an *experimentally manipulated independent variable* and a dependent variable, it is called a **regression coefficient** (Hays, 1973). Although this seems like a trivial distinction, it is important, since a regression coefficient describes a causal relationship while a correlation coefficient does not establish causation. Since we have experimentally manipulated one of the variables and have observed the resulting changes in the other, we can tell which variable caused the change in the other. The regression coefficient gives us a basis for predicting values of the dependent variable from values of the independent variable (the regression coefficient is the slope of the best-fit line).

A more common application of correlation coefficients is to describe the relationship between two nonmanipulated variables. The correlation coefficient can be used to describe the relationship between any two variables. As long as the measures can be logically paired, a correlation coefficient summarizes the relationship.

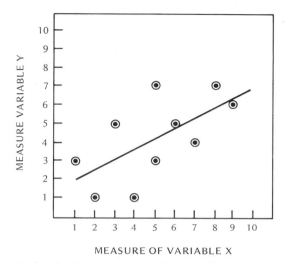

Fig. 6.5. Scatter-plot of ordered pairs where *r* is equal to 0.64. The straight line is the line of best fit.

The usual examples involve variables such as grades paired with IQ, reading speed paired with scores on a comprehension test, scores on an extroversion-introversion scale paired with leadership tendencies, and so on. It is also legitimate to use the correlation coefficient to describe the relationship between grades and height, reading speed and ability to throw a baseball, and the score on the introversion-extroversion scale and the total number of spots obtained when the person throws two dice. In all of these examples, the pairing occurs because both measures are taken on the same person (for example, one person's score on extroversion-introversion and the same person's leadership tendencies measure).

There are two important factors that are easily overlooked when using the correlation coefficient. The first is that *r* is also appropriate to describe *lack of correlation* ($r = 0$). The second is that a high correlation indicates that the two variables are related, but says nothing about *why* they are related. Unless causality is established by the experimental design used, a correlational relationship should not be used to infer causality, no matter how plausible it appears. As an example, a high correlation between IQ and grades is often cited as evidence for intelligence leading to good school performance. It is also possible, however, to suggest that students who have learned good study habits also have learned the facts and skills to do well on an IQ test. In this case it is probable that both the measures of IQ and grades are caused by a common third variable. The fact remains that the correlation only indicates that there is a relationship and not that the relationship is causal.

The concept of correlation between measures was introduced in Chapter 4 where related-groups designs are discussed. In related-groups designs certain sources of secondary variance are controlled in one of three ways: (1) the same subjects are used in two or more experimental groups (repeated measures or subjects as their own control); (2) the subjects in two groups are matched on one or more criterion variables (such as match-by-correlated-criterion design); or (3) groups, but not individual subjects, are matched on one or more criterion variables (such as randomized-blocks designs). In studies using these designs, correlation coefficients may or may not be calculated; however, the designs all involve the assumption that either there is a substantial correlation between two performance measures of a subject or there is a substantial correlation between the behavioral measures of two matched subjects or two matched groups.

STUDIES USING CORRELATION COEFFICIENTS

Descriptive (Naturalistic) Research   As indicated, correlation coefficients are used in several types of research. The following subsections present a few examples of these types.

A researcher may measure two variables and summarize the relationship between the measures with a correlation coefficient. The scores on variable X are paired in some way with the scores on variable Y. For example, you may correlate two measures of the subjects' behavior, the number of pages in term papers with the grades on the papers, or the number of trees on campuses with the academic standing of the colleges. Correlation coefficients may be used to describe the correlation between any two kinds of measures where the scores may be logically paired.

In part of a study, Leibowitz (1968) gave male undergraduates two self-report questionnaires: the Buss-Durkee Hostility Inventory and the Marlowe-Crowne Social Desirability Scale. A high total-score on the first questionnaire indicates a high level of "hostility" and high "aggressive" tendencies. A high score on the second questionnaire indicates a high "need for approval" and "need for social acceptability." The correlation between the two sets of measures was negative and moderately high ($r = -0.68$). Thus students with a high need for social approval were unlikely to exhibit high hostility-aggression scores.

Certain variables can be evaluated only in correlational studies. For example, the personality traits and sociological characteristics associated with suicide cannot be studied with the experimental approach. After a person commits suicide, the researcher looks at historical records of the person's life *(ex post facto)*. Sainsbury and Barraclough (1968) found that the suicide rates in 1959 of foreign-born United States citizens correlated highly ($r = 0.87$) with the suicide rates of their countries of birth. Given the suicide rates of their native lands, you can predict which of two immigrants is more likely to commit suicide (for example, an Austrian immigrant is more likely to commit suicide than a person from Mexico).

In a naturalistic field study, Glass, Cohen, and Singer (1973) examined the relationship between urban environmental noise and the dependent variables of auditory discrimination ability and reading achievement. They found that noise level from a heavily traveled Manhattan expressway was loudest on the first floor of an apartment building and decreased as one moved higher in the building. Previous laboratory research had indicated that exposure to excessive, unpredictable noise adversely affected performance efficiency. Using floor level as the measure of relatively constant exposure to excessive noise and using standard auditory discrimination tests, they found a significant positive relationship between the two variables for those elementary schoolchildren who had lived in the apartment building for four or more years. (Significance of r is discussed later in the chapter.) The children living on the lower floors performed the poorest on the discrimination tests. The researchers expected that impaired auditory discrimination ability might negatively affect reading ability. The lower-floor children (who had lived there for four or more years) also performed poorly on standard measures of reading ability (significant positive correlation). Even when socioeconomic factors were controlled (the upper apartments were more expensive), the relationship with auditory discrimination remained unchanged and the relationship with reading ability decreased but was still in the same direction. Living in modern cities with high noise levels may have appreciable costs.

The study cited in Chapter 2 (Rodin and Rodin, 1972) established a correlation between student ratings of the teaching effectiveness of assistant instructors (subjective measure) and performance (objective measure) on a set of 40 paradigm calculus problems (essentially the grade-determining tests for the class). The correlation between the objective and subjective measures was equal to -0.75. The graphed relationship between the two measures is presented in Figure 6.6. Gessner (1973) also constructed a study of the relationship between student ratings of instructors and student performance on an examination. In the study, the 10 instructors were all involved in teaching parts of a single one-semester basic science

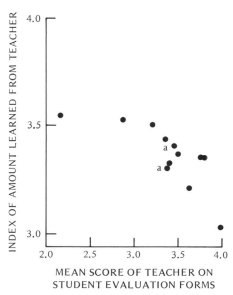

Fig. 6.6. Relationship between objective and subjective criteria of good teaching ($r = -.75$). The points labeled a are for two sections taught by the same instructor. (Data from Rodin, M., and Rodin, B., Student evaluations of teachers, *Science*, Vol. 177, pp. 1164–1166, 29 September 1972. Copyright 1972 by the American Association for the Advancement of Science.)

course for 119 sophomore premedical students. There were 23 subject areas in the course (each instructor taught one or more of these areas) and 78 of the students rated each subject area on a three-point scale (good, satisfactory, and unsatisfactory) in terms of (1) content and organization and (2) instructor's presentation. The students' learning was measured by the multiple-choice National Medical Board Examination given five weeks after the end of the class and by three departmental examinations (used for grading purposes).

The correlation between class performance on the national examination and student ratings of content and organization was +0.77 and the correlation between national examination scores and student ratings of presentation was +0.69. The scatter-plot of the scores for the 0.77 correlation is presented in Figure 6.7.

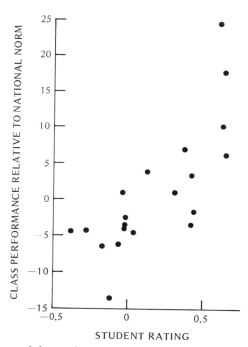

Fig. 6.7. Scatter diagram of class performance on a national normative examination in 20 subject areas of a course and of the student ratings of the content and organization of instruction in these subject areas ($r = 0.77$). (Data from Gessner, P. K., Evaluation of instruction, *Science*, Vol. 180, pp. 566–574, 11 May 1973. Copyright 1973 by the American Association for the Advancement of Science.)

The correlations between performance on the departmental grading examinations and student ratings of content and organization ($r = 0.11$) and student rating of presentation ($r = 0.17$) were very low. The discrepancy between the results of the two teacher evaluation studies may arise from the many procedural differences between the two studies. The discrepancy indicates that correlational studies should be carefully evaluated before important decisions and/or generalizations are made.

Control of Secondary Variance   Matching designs and randomized-blocks designs are discussed in Chapters 4 and 5. Matching subjects on a criterion (secondary) variable requires that the criterion variable be correlated with the dependent variable. Similarly, matching groups in blocks (randomized-blocks design) requires that the blocking variable be correlated with the dependent variable. If the correlation between the two variables is negligible, then a matching procedure is a waste of time. One way to find out if matching is useful is to sample randomly a group of subjects from the population and collect measures on the matching and dependent variables from each subject. Given a high positive or negative correlation between the two measures, you know that some form of matching will be useful.

   Correlation as a Dependent Variable   The effect of an independent variable on the *relationship* between two dependent variables may be of interest to an experimenter. In this case, the correlation between the two dependent variables can be treated as a dependent variable. (See Jones, 1968.) For example, an experimenter may wish to measure the effect of an audience on the subjects' task performance. The task involves placing pegs in a pegboard, and the experimenter records the number placed in a one-minute period. The experimenter uses a before-after two-group design. All subjects are given a one-minute before measure of peg-placing ability while isolated. Control subjects are then given a second isolated performance test. Experimental subjects also are given a second, one-minute test, but must perform in front of a psychology class. The observed before and after scores for each group (two dependent variables) are shown in Figure 6.8. Notice that the

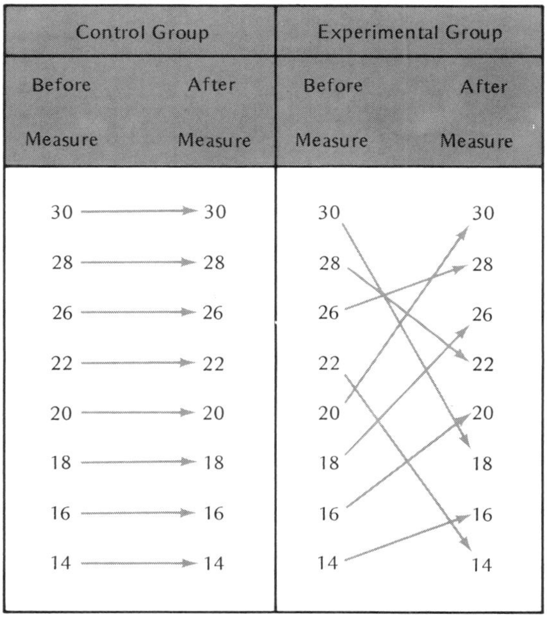

Fig. 6.8.   Hypothetical peg-placing scores of the experimental and control groups on the before and after tests. The arrows indicate each subject's two scores.

same scores occur in the before and after measures of each group. In other words, the audience did not affect the performance of the experimental group considered *as a whole.* For both groups, the average score and the variance were the same on both the before and after measures. The lines connecting the before and after scores indicate the performance of each individual subject. Thus, the control subjects scored the same on both tests ($r = 1.00$), while the presence of an audience disrupted the performance of the experimental subjects ($r = 0.45$). The scatter-plot for each group is presented in Figure 6.9.

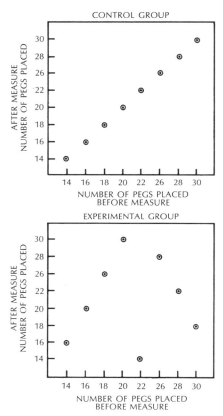

Fig. 6.9. Scatter-plots of the two dependent measures (before and after tests) of each group in the hypothetical pegboard experiment. The correlation coefficients are 1.00 and 0.45 for the control and experimental groups, respectively.

Measures of Reliability and Validity In studies that use judges (raters) to score the performance of the subjects, the researcher wants his rating (scoring) system to be reliable. That is, he wants to be confident that when he or someone else uses his scoring system, generally consistent results will be obtained. One way of checking the reliability of the rating system is to have two (or more) raters use the system. If the correlation between the two sets of ratings if fairly high, then the system is considered reliable. In their study of verbal creativity, Maier, Julius, and Thurber (1967) used two raters to score the creativity of their subjects' stories. They obtained an *inter-rater reliability coefficient* of 0.80, which they considered to be sufficiently high.

In the study (Chapter 5) about group insight and group desensitization in treating speech anxiety (Meichenbaum, Gilmore, and Fedoravicius, 1971), one of the dependent variables was a behavioral checklist of the performance of the subjects in a speech-giving situation. Two pairs of trained observers rated the presence or absence of 20 manifestations of anxiety during successive 30-second time periods for the first four minutes of each speech presentation by the subjects. The range of correlation between the ratings by the pairs of observers was +0.70 to +0.90. The average correlation (median, discussed in Chapter 8) was 0.85. The authors considered this figure to indicate the high reliability and objectivity of such measures.

When psychologists use tests such as intelligence tests, they want them to be reliable. If a test is *reliable*, a subject will receive approximately the same score each time he takes the test or an equivalent form of the test. When an applied psychologist uses a test such as an achievement test to make predictions about the *future* behavior of an individual, he wants to be fairly confident that the test is *valid*. That is, the test score should correlate with later measures of behavior. The reliability and validity of tests are described in terms of correlation coefficients. A high coefficient indicates either high reliability or high validity, depending on what variables are measured.

The Stanford-Binet Intelligence Scale is a very widely used measure of general intellectual development. The alternative-form *reliability* of the 1937 revision of the Stanford-Binet was determined by administering the two forms, L and M, of the test within one week or less to the same individuals (Terman and Merrill, 1960). Correlation coefficients were calculated for each set of paired scores. At ages $2\frac{1}{2}$ and $5\frac{1}{2}$ the reliability coefficients (correlation coefficients) ranged from 0.83 to 0.98, depending on the range of IQ scores and age range included in a sample of subjects. The older the subjects (14–18) and the lower the IQ (60–69), the higher the reliability (0.98). The correlation coefficients indicate the short-term stability of the IQ scores and the equivalence of the content of the two forms of the test. The IQ test scores are also quite stable over the elementary, high-school, and college period (Anastasi, 1968). The group test-retest correlation depends on the length of time between the two administrations of the test, for example, ten-year correlation = 0.73, one-year correlation = 0.83. The correlation between scores on an IQ test and scores on another measure of intellectual ability such as school achievement indicate the criterion-referenced *validity* of an IQ scale. The usual criterion measures include school grades, teacher ratings, or achievement test scores. The correlations between IQ scores and *concurrent criterion measures or future (predicted) criterion measures* range between 0.40 and 0.75 (Anastasi, 1968).

Measures of Magnitude of Causal Relationships   Most of the experimental research designs previously discussed involve the comparison of two or more groups of experimental subjects that are exposed to different levels of a treatment (usually including a zero level). This general paradigm is the usual one thought of when one considers a behavioral experiment. The emphasis is on the *difference* produced by the treatment condition. A statistical test determines whether or not the differences are great enough to be considered "significant." (See Chapter 10 for discussion of statistical significance.) If the experimental treatment does result in significant differences, then we infer that the treatment must have created the differences. Another way to state this is to say that there is some causal relationship between the treatment and the behavior.

Sometimes the experimenter is interested in a precise measure of the relationship between two variables. That is, instead of simply stating that the independent variable caused a difference in the measure of the dependent variable, he may wish to specify in some numerical way the extent to which different levels of the independent variable affect the observed behavior. Such a numerical description is provided by using a *linear regression coefficient.* The calculation of the regression coefficient follows the same procedure as the calculation of r when the sample standard deviations (discussed in Chapter 8) are equal. However, the standard deviations are seldom equal, so the procedure for calculating the slope of the best-fit line (discussed in Unit D6) is the usual way that regression coefficients or slopes are calculated.

Statistical Evaluation   The usual question asked about a given correlation coefficient is whether that correlation is significantly larger than zero. That is, if the population correlation is close to zero, could the sample value have been as high as it is by chance? In the Gessner (1973) study of the relationship between student evaluations of teachers and student performance on the national examinations, the correlations of 0.77 and 0.69 were both statistically significant. The probability (see Chapter 9) of these values occurring by chance was less than one in a thousand.

The concept of statistical significance is discussed in Chapter 10 and the calculation procedures for evaluating the significance of a correlation coefficient are presented in Section Two, Unit D6.

Limitations   Because the numerical notation for correlations resembles percentage figures, correlation coefficients are frequently misinterpreted. A correlation coefficient is *not a percentage figure.* You cannot interpret a correlation of 0.60 as indicating that two measures are 60 percent related. In addition, the interpretation of a given correlation coefficient depends on the sample size used to obtain the coefficient. The larger the sample size, the more reliable the coefficient. Without both the value of the coefficient and the number of observations, it is hard to tell what a coefficient means.

The most serious limitation to correlation studies is that, usually, they do not provide a basis for causal inference. A correlation coefficient describes the relationship between two sets of scores. The significant positive correlation between smoking and lung cancer leads many people to infer that smoking causes lung cancer. The fact that there is a relationship does not necessarily condemn cigarettes. As far as the coefficient is concerned, it is just as reasonable to infer that lung cancer causes smoking. The existence of a relationship between A and B does *not* allow you to make the inference that A causes B, or B causes A. The relationship itself may be caused by a third, unknown variable. It may be that hereditary or personality factors make individuals cancer prone *and* predispose them to smoke cigarettes. No matter how plausible, no causal statement should be made until an *experimental study* is conducted. That is, it must be demonstrated that controlled increases in frequency of cigarette smoking by a random sample of people leads to an increased probability of lung cancer. That has not been demonstrated. The fact remains, however, that nonsmokers are less likely to develop lung cancer.

Comments   To further illustrate the problem of causality, we list a few of the statements containing correlational information used by Clifton (1958) in his tongue-in-cheek essay entitled "The Dread Tomato Addiction."

1. Ninety-two point four percent of juvenile delinquents have eaten tomatoes.
3. Informers reliably inform that of all known American Communists, ninety-two point three percent have eaten tomatoes.
5. Those who object to singling out specific groups for statistical proof, require measurements within a total. Of those people born before the year 1800, regardless of race, color, creed or caste, and known to have eaten tomatoes, there has been one hundred percent mortality.
6. In spite of their dread addiction, a few tomato eaters born between 1800 and 1850 still manage to survive, but the clinical picture is poor—their bones are brittle, their movements feeble, their skin seamed and wrinkled, their eyesight failing, hair falling, and frequently they have lost all their teeth.

REVIEW

The correlation coefficient is often regarded with suspicion and distaste by experimental psychologists. As was done several times in this chapter, examples can be given showing the misapplication and misuses of the numerical value of the correlation coefficient. The inability to infer causality and the lack of need for careful control-group-type experimental designs, both make the correlation coefficient a dishonored statistic in some experimental psychology laboratories.

In spite of the passive avoidance, and in some cases active hostility, by researchers, the very power and generality of the correlation coefficient have kept it in the experimenter's research toolbox, albeit sometimes well hidden. It would be a mistake simply to dismiss research involving the correlation coefficient as being irrelevant or unscientific, for the numbers yielded by the calculation of the correlation coefficient are as sound as the data that lead to the numbers, and the misuse or the disadvantage lies in the interpretation. Even if the individual is biased against the correlation coefficient in research applications, understanding the concept is a necessity because of the importance of the concept of reliability and validity.

SUMMARY

1. Temporal contiguity is a necessary but not sufficient basis for a causal inference. Spatial contiguity is a presumptive, but neither necessary nor sufficient basis. It is assumed that every event has a limited number of causes.
2. Naturalistic research does not allow the degree of certainty about causal inferences that

is allowed by experimental research. Naturalistic research does disclose interesting, potentially causal relationships.

3. Correlation coefficients numerically describe the relationship between two measures of behavior. The Pearson r describes the degree and direction of relationship. The value of r varies from -1.00 to $+1.00$.

4. A positive, direct relationship is graphically depicted by an upward trend. A negative, inverse relationship is graphically depicted by a downward trend.

5. A regression coefficient is used to describe the degree and direction of relationship between experimentally manipulated independent and dependent variables.

6. Descriptive research (naturalistic) studies are concerned with describing the relationship between two measures of behavior.

7. In order for matching to be useful, the correlation between the matching and dependent variables must be nontrivial.

8. A correlation coefficient between dependent variables can also be used as a dependent variable in research.

9. Reliability and validity are described in terms of correlation coefficients. Inter-rater reliability and test reliability occur when an individual gets approximately the same score each time he is rated or takes a test, or takes alternate forms of a test. If a test score does a good job of predicting a future behavior, then the test has high predictive validity. If a test score correlates highly with another measure of the same or similar behavior, then the test has high criterion-referenced validity.

10. Regression coefficients may be used to measure the magnitude of the significant relationship between an experimentally manipulated independent variable and a dependent variable.

11. Correlation does not mean the same thing as percentage. Correlation does not necessarily imply causation.

SUGGESTED READING

Edwards, A. L. *Experimental design in psychological research.* (4th ed.) New York: Holt, Rinehart and Winston, 1972.

Edwards, A. L. *Statistical methods.* (3d ed.) New York: Holt, Rinehart and Winston, 1973.

Hays, W. *Statistics for the social sciences.* (2d ed.) New York: Holt, Rinehart and Winston, 1973.

Guilford, J. P. *Fundamental statistics in psychology and education.* (4th ed.) New York: McGraw-Hill, 1965.

Jones, M. B. Correlation as a dependent variable. *Psychological Bulletin,* 1968, *70,* 69–72.

McNemar, Q. *Psychological statistics.* (4th ed.) New York: Wiley, 1969.

Snedecor, G. W., and Cochrane, W. B. *Statistical methods.* (6th ed.) Ames, Iowa: Iowa State University Press, 1967.

Winer, B. J. *Statistical principles in experimental design.* (2d ed.) New York: McGraw-Hill, 1971.

CHAPTER 7
Summarizing and Graphically Presenting Data

After the last subject has completed the procedure of an experiment, the researcher is confronted with a collection of raw data. *Raw data* are the dependent measures recorded in the experiment. (For grammar purists, data is the plural form of the singular datum [from Latin], thus "data are" is grammatically correct.) The novice researcher usually is very unsure of what to do with the data. Raw data may not appear to be directly applicable to a research question. In order for the researcher to make meaningful statements about raw data, they must be organized, summarized, and analyzed in reference to the experimental hypotheses.

There are many ways of organizing and summarizing the data. A commonly stated, general suggestion is that the researcher should try several ways of organizing the data and see which way gives the clearest picture of the relationship between the independent and dependent variables. The art of choosing which is "the clearest" is one of the more interesting aspects of statistical manipulation of the data.

SUMMARIZING THE DATA

Lists of Data

Scores from different groups can be compared by listing them in adjacent columns. Table 7.1 gives such a comparison between the species preferences of male and female experimenters. Inspection of the table shows that there is a difference between the males and females in terms of their preference.

TABLE 7.1. A List of the Responses of 11 Males and 10 Females to the Question: "Would You Rather Work with Cats or Dogs?"

Male	Female
dog	dog
dog	cat
cat	dog
dog	cat
dog	cat
dog	dog
dog	cat
dog	cat
dog	cat
cat	cat
dog	

Frequency Tables

The information in Table 7.1 can be presented in less space by using a frequency table as illustrated in Table 7.2. The data are mapped onto a 2×2 matrix (a table consisting of two rows and two columns) with the columns denoting the sex of the subjects, and the rows indicating species preference. The numbers in each cell represent the number of subjects providing data corresponding to the row and column of that cell.

TABLE 7.2. A Frequency Table (Matrix) of the Responses of Males and Females to the Question: "Would You Rather Work with Cats or Dogs?"

	Male	Female
dog	9	3
cat	2	7

A frequency table may be made up with any size matrix as long as the categories along any dimension are arranged so that each score can be located in the appropriate cell without ambiguity. Frequency tables are usually preferred over lists, because the same information is conveyed in briefer and more direct form.

Ordered List

Raw scores are more meaningful when they are arranged in an ordered list. For example, Table 7.3 lists the scores obtained in a learning experiment. The subjects were required to memorize a list of nonsense syllables. The scores represent the number of syllables correctly recalled by each subject. Such information as the highest score, the lowest score, and the fact that there are no wide gaps in the distribution is seen immediately in an ordered list.

TABLE 7.3. Ordered Scores from a Learning Experiment.

49	30	23	15
44	29	23	14
43	29	23	13
40	29	22	12
39	29	22	11
39	28	21	10
38	28	21	9
37	27	19	7
36	26	18	5
34	26	17	1
33	26	17	
33	25	16	
33	25		
32	24		
31	24		

Frequency Distributions

An ordered list is inappropriate and cumbersome for large masses of data. Rather than listing each datum, some procedure should be employed to summarize the main features of the data. A frequency distribution shows the number of cases falling within each class interval or range of scores. To summarize the scores from an experiment, the numerical scores are usually divided into 10 to 15 class intervals. **Class intervals** are arbitrary divisions of the data into groups of scores. Suppose we want 10 intervals in a frequency distribution of the scores in Table 7.3. The numbers from one to 49 can be divided into 10 equal intervals by assigning five numbers to each interval. For example, the numbers 1, 2, 3, 4, and 5 are assigned to the first interval; 6, 7, 8, 9, and 10 to the second; and so on until the highest number is assigned. When the data are integers, the intervals are described in integers. In the example, the intervals are: 1–5, 6–10, . . ., 45–50. The scores can then be tallied and summed for each interval. (See Table 7.4.)

The interval 1–5 has an apparent upper limit of five, and the next interval 6–10 has an apparent lower limit of six. The **apparent limits** of a class interval are the highest and lowest scores of the interval. The **real limits** of a class interval are defined as one-half of the smallest measurement unit above the highest score and one-half of the unit below the lowest score. The distinction between apparent and real limits is illustrated in Figure 7.1. The **apparent width** of the interval 21–25 is four $(25 - 21 = 4)$. The **real width** of the interval 21–25 is five $(25.5 - 20.5 = 5)$ as determined by the real limits of the intervals.

TABLE 7.4. A Frequency Distribution of the Data Shown in Table 7.3.

Class Intervals	Tally Marks	Frequency (f)	Midpoint of Each Interval
46–50	I	1	48
41–45	II	2	43
36–40	IIII I	6	38
31–35	IIII I	6	33
26–30	IIII IIII I	11	28
21–25	IIII IIII I	11	23
16–20	IIII	5	18
11–15	IIII	5	13
6–10	III	3	8
1–5	II	2	3

It is convenient to have a real class-interval width that is an odd number (for example, $3, 5, 7, \ldots$). This will guarantee that the midpoint will be an integer. In our example, the interval 20.5–25.5 is five units in width with a midpoint of 23. We assume that the midpoint of each interval is the best *single value* to represent all the values in that interval. After we have constructed a frequency distribution, we may wish to present the data in graphical form.

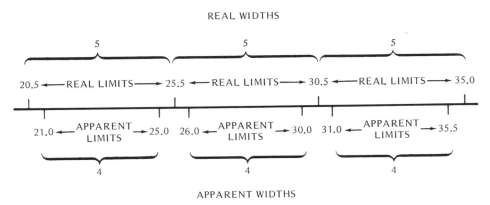

Fig. 7.1. An illustration of the relationship between real and apparent class-interval limits.

GRAPHICAL PRESENTATION

A Histogram

A histogram or bar graph is probably the easiest way to present data graphically. The graph is built around the X (class intervals) and Y (frequency) axes. A histogram derived from the data in Table 7.4 is shown in Figure 7.2.

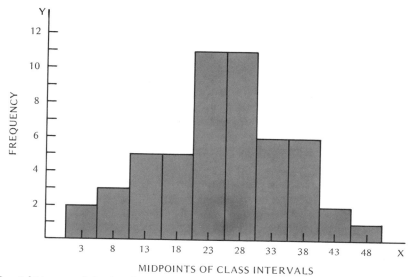

Fig. 7.2. A histogram of the data from Table 7.4. The real limits of each class interval determine the edge of each bar.

The central tendency of the distribution is easily seen in Figure 7.2. That is, the scores tend to pile up in the middle of the distribution. (The different central tendency statistics will be discussed in Chapter 8.) The height of each bar represents the frequency of the scores in that interval, and the bar width represents the real width of each class. Since the edge of each bar is determined by a real limit, there are no gaps between adjacent bars. Instead of frequencies, percentages may be labeled on the ordinate (Y axis) by dividing the frequency in each bar by the total frequency of all of the bars, (that is, interval 1–5 = 3.8 percent = ²⁄₅₂).

Bar graphs can be used deceitfully. If the bars change widths as well as heights while representing a single factor such as frequency or percentage of a measure of behavior, then they can be easily misleading. Also, if the ordinate does not begin at zero, then the relative meaning of the heights of the bars is difficult to determine. The use of such tactics to deceive the reader of graphs is amusingly described by Huff (1954).

Frequency Polygon

A frequency polygon is another method of graphically portraying data. The abscissa and ordinate are labeled as in the histogram; the midpoint scores are plotted on the X axis and frequency or percentage scores are plotted on the Y axis. A frequency polygon of the data in Table 7.4 is shown in Figure 7.3. The midpoints of each adjacent bar are connected by a solid line. A frequency polygon indicates the general shape of a distribution. In many psychological experiments, it is important to compare the data with a hypothetical distribution called the normal distribution or

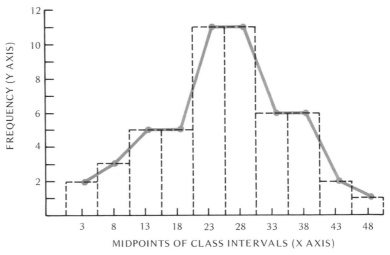

Fig. 7.3. A frequency polygon of data from Table 7.4.

"bell-shaped" curve. A normal curve is a theoretical distribution of a tremendously large amount of data (Chapter 8). A major feature of the normal distribution is that it is symmetrical; that is, there are an equal number of high and low scores in the distribution. By drawing a frequency polygon, we can estimate whether data tend to be normally distributed or skewed. By **skewed,** we mean that there are more scores on one end of the distribution than the other. (See Figures 7.4 and 7.5.) Also, by using a frequency polygon, we can determine if the distribution is flat or peaked. (See Figure 7.6.) The flatness or peakedness of a curve is called **kurtosis.** In Figure 7-6, Curve A is called leptokurtic (peaked), B is mesokurtic (normal), and C is platykurtic (flat).

Scatter-Plots

A histogram and a frequency polygon graphically summarize the distribution of the data along one dimension. They are the graphic counterparts to an ordered list and a frequency distribution. A scatter-plot, on the other hand, provides a graphic description of the relationship between *two* variables. The tabular analogy to a scatter-plot is a frequency table (Table 7.2), where one variable is represented by the rows and the other variable is represented by the columns of the table. It is possible to map one variable on the X axis and the other on the Y axis of a graph. By plotting the pairs of scores on a graph, we have a visual representation of a relationship. Frequency, percentage, errors, number of correct responses, or any other measure of the dependent variable is plotted on the ordinate; and the levels of the independent variable such as trials, drug level, age, or time are plotted on the abscissa. There are exceptions to the statements above, but, generally, the dependent variable is plotted on the Y axis and the independent variable is plotted on the X axis.

Fig. 7.4. Frequency polygon skewed left or negatively.

Fig. 7.5. Frequency polygon skewed right or positively. While most of the scores are clustered at the left, a few stragglers "pull" the curve toward the right.

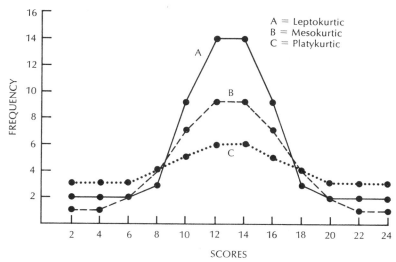

Fig. 7.6. Three frequency polygons varying in kurtosis.

Drug companies hire people to inspect pills visually on a moving belt and remove the defective pills. Figure 7.7 illustrates a scatter-plot of data from an industrial psychologist's study of the relationship between belt speed and accuracy of detection of defective pills. The independent variable is belt speed, and the dependent variable is the number of correct detections. The position of each dot on the graph precisely locates an ordered pair with respect to the independent and dependent variables. (Ties, two scores having the same value, must be approximated by placing two dots bracketing their correct position.) The pattern formed by the data points in a scatter-plot is the relationship between the independent and dependent variables.

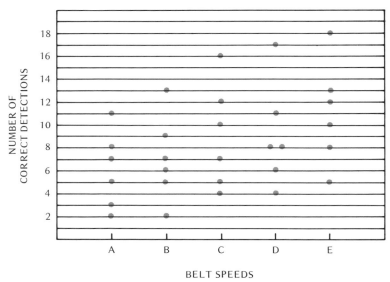

Fig. 7.7. A scatter-plot of the defective pill detection data. Each dot represents the score of a single subject.

Line Graphs

The relationship between an independent and dependent variable is graphically approximated by a line graph. A line graph summarizes the relationship between two variables in terms of the average scores under each level of the independent variable. In other words, a line graph is a *concise* (rather than *precise*) description of the relationship between two variables.

Figure 7.8 shows a line graph derived from the scatter-plot data in Figure 7.7. Each point on the line represents the average score of each treatment group.

A learning curve frequently shows the *trend* of the average performance of a group across learning trials. Such a curve is presented in Figure 7.9. The curve in Figure 7.9 starts at the lower left corner and rises to the upper right corner.

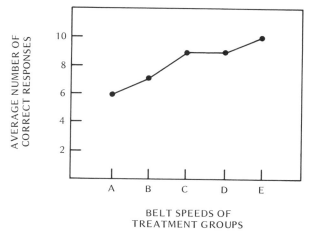

Fig. 7.8. A performance curve derived from the data in Figure 7.7. Each point is the average score of the six subjects in each group.

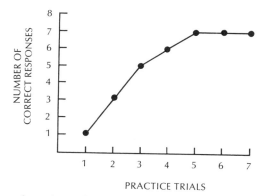

Fig. 7.9. A negatively accelerated growth curve.

Figure 7.9 illustrates a negatively accelerated growth curve. That is, the number of correct responses increases rapidly for the first few trials, but slows as the number of trials increases. Figure 7.10 shows a negatively accelerated decay curve. It is based on the same data as Figure 7.9, however, the dependent variable is the number of *errors* instead of the number of correct responses.

Figure 7.11 illustrates examples of positively accelerating growth (curve A), and positively accelerating decay (curve B). In positively accelerating curves, the behavior changes slowly at first and then changes faster as the number of trials increases. The steepest part of a positively accelerated curve is where the greatest rate of change of behavior occurs. It is possible to get various combinations of positive and negative growth and decay curves. Some of these curves are called sig-

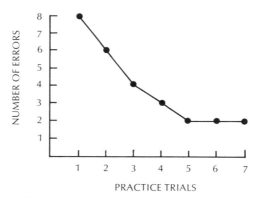

Fig. 7.10.   A negatively accelerated decay curve.

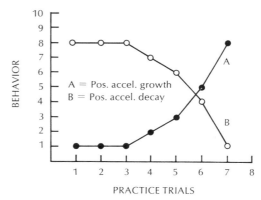

Fig. 7.11.   Positively accelerated curves.

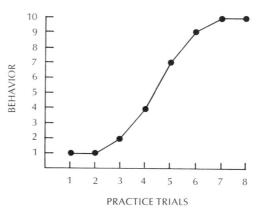

Fig. 7.12.   An S-shaped curve.

moidal or S-shaped curves. An S-shaped curve is shown in Figure 7.12. The S-shaped curve indicates that the behavior starts off slowly, then accelerates, then changes to a more stable rate after a period of time.

When there is a zero line on the ordinate, and both axes of the line graph are in proportion, the line graph provides a very simple, clear picture of the relationship between the independent and dependent variables. However, if one eliminates the zero line (chops off the bottom of the graph) and expands or contracts the Y axis relative to the X axis, he can imply just about any relationship he wishes. That is, the line graph is also capable of deceiving (Huff, 1954). The use of deceptive graphs is mainly encountered in advertising and politics. For example, during the energy shortage of the summer of 1973 in the United States, certain corporations engaged in advertising campaigns designed to convince the American public that conservationists were the root cause of the energy crisis. In a four-page advertisement in the June 4, 1973 issue of *Newsweek* (Vol. 81, No. 3, pp. 55–58), the American Gas Association presented the two line graphs of Figure 7.13. At a casual glance, the two seem to imply that the demand for natural gas was in immediate danger of exhausting the total available supply. A closer look yields the information that one graph is a projection of *future* demand (the abscissa begins in 1970 and ends in 1986) while the other graph depicts the *past* number of wells drilled (the abscissa begins in 1956 and ends in 1971). Further the ordinate of the demand graph begins at 15 quadrillion BTU and the wells-drilled ordinate begins at 20 thousand. In short, not only do the two graphs barely overlap in time (abscissa), but also the bottom of each graph has been cut-off. Very little information can be gained from comparing the two sets of information when the graphs are properly drawn. To quote the old adage: "Statistics don't lie, but liars use statistics." Fortunately, legitimate researchers do not knowingly play such games.

Line graphs are frequently used in behavior modification studies to indicate the course and results of treatment. For example, Christophersen, Arnold, Hill, and Quillitch (1972) set up a token reinforcement program to be used by parents to modify the problem behavior of their children. The children were required to earn points in order to "buy" basic privileges (such as watching television) as well as special rewards (such as movies or picnics). They earned points by performing typical household chores and lost points (were "fined") for engaging in disruptive, problem behavior (such as bickering or whining). Figure 7.14 presents one of 14 graphs presented in the research report. It is obvious that the 10-point fine had a dramatic effect on the "jumping on furniture" behavior of the girl.

In Chapter 2, the concept of interaction was introduced. In the Kleinke, et al. (1973) study, the effect of the percentage of time the girls spent gazing at the subjects depended on the attractiveness of the girls. In Chapter 5, another example of interaction was presented. Kamin and Schaub (1963) found that the effect of the extinction conditioned stimulus intensity on the conditioned emotional response depended on the acquisition level of conditioned stimulus intensity. As indicated in Chapter 5, an interaction is most clearly comprehended when presented in a graph.

Misuse of Line Graphs

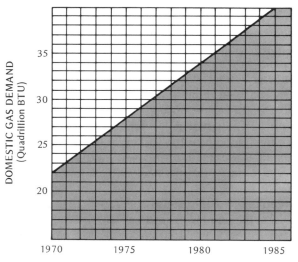

Source: U.S. Bureau of Mines

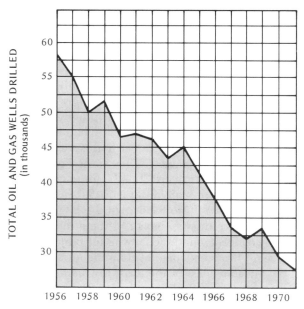

Source: American Petroleum Institute

Fig. 7.13. An example of the misleading use of line graphs. The advertisement appeared in *Newsweek*, June 4, 1973.

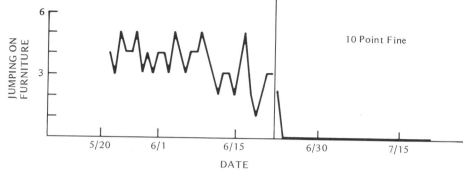

Fig. 7.14. Effects of 10-point fine on the social behavior of an 8-year-old, mildly retarded girl. The fine was introduced between June 15 and June 30; the record before the fine was the frequency of jumping on furniture when no punishment was used; after the fine was introduced the negative behavior ceased. (Graph from Christophersen, et al., *Journal of Applied Behavior Analysis,* 1972, Vol. 5, p. 491. Copyright 1972 by the Society for the Experimental Analysis of Behavior, Inc.)

Turn back for a moment to Figure 5.2. Notice that the two levels of one independent variable, the levels of acquisition CS (strong and weak), are plotted on the X axis (abscissa). The distance between strong and weak on the X axis is arbitrary, but they are set far enough apart so that the reader can see that there is a difference. Second, notice that the dependent variable measure, the magnitude of the CER, is plotted on the Y axis (ordinate). The other independent variable, the level of extinction noise CS, is plotted in the body of the graph. The two lines represent the effect of one independent variable on the other independent variable in terms of the dependent variable. It is important to remember that the *dependent* variable goes on the Y axis, one independent variable goes on the X axis, and the other independent variable goes in the body of the graph.

  Interaction

A three-variable interaction is graphically represented by four lines (assuming two levels of each variable): two lines for variable B, two for variable C, with variable A on the abscissa. (See Figure 7.15.)

Figure 7.15 is a concise, complicated way of showing a three-way interaction. Another way is to show two separate figures where two independent variables (A and B) are illustrated first under one level of the third independent variable (C_1) and then under the second level of the third independent variable (C_2). Figures 7.16*(a)* and 7.16*(b)* illustrate an alternative way of showing a three-way interaction.

Notice that the three-way interaction graphs conform to the same rules of construction as a two-way interaction: dependent variable on the Y axis, one independent variable on the X axis, and one independent variable in the body of the graph. The only difference is that the third independent variable (C) requires two graphs to show it. If C had three levels, then three graphs would be required, one for C_1, one for C_2, and one for C_3.

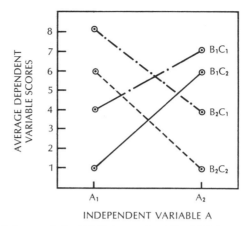

Fig. 7.15. A hypothetical three-variable (ABC) interaction. The ABC interaction is that the effect of variable B depends on the levels of variables C and A. The interaction is indicated by the four nonparallel lines.

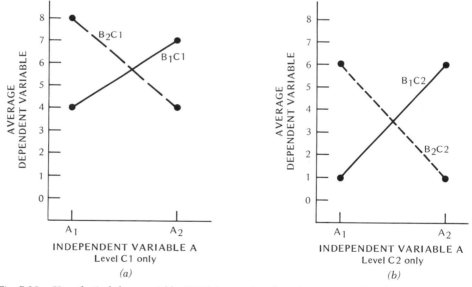

Fig. 7.16. Hypothetical three-variable (ABC) interaction plotted on two graphs. The graphs illustrate that the effect of variable B depends on the different levels of variables A and C. The ABC interaction is indicated by the fact that the pattern of the crossed lines differs between the two graphs.

Straight Lines and Slopes   Two sets of ordered pairs (X_1, Y_1) and (X_2, Y_2) are depicted in Figure 7.17. A line, L, is drawn through the two ordered pairs. In order to determine the slope of line L, a vertical line is dropped from the point (X_2, Y_2) to the X axis; and a horizontal line is drawn through the point (X_1, Y_1) and extended until it intersects the vertical line. The distances ΔY and ΔX are given by the following statements: $\Delta Y = Y_2 - Y_1$ and $\Delta X = X_2 - X_1$. The symbol Δ

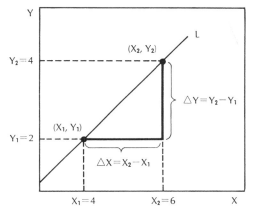

Fig. 7.17. Example of a straight line L with a slope $b = \Delta Y / \Delta X = (Y_2 - Y_1)/(X_2 - X_1) = 1$.

indicates the distance between two values of a variable. The ratio of ΔY to ΔX, $\Delta Y \div \Delta X = (Y_2 - Y_1) \div (X_2 - X_1)$, is equal to the **slope** *(b)* of the line L. That is, $b = (Y_2 - Y_1) \div (X_2 - X_1)$. The slope indicates how the variable Y changes with respect to X. In behavioral terms, the slope represents the rate at which the dependent variable (behavior) changes with respect to the independent variable (treatment): the steeper the slope, the greater the rate of change in the behavior. The values of X and Y in Figure 7.17 are $X_1 = 4$, $X_2 = 6$, $Y_1 = 2$, $Y_2 = 4$. Then $b = (4 - 2)/(6 - 4) = \frac{2}{2} = 1$. The slope of one indicates that one unit of increase on the X axis is associated with an increase of one unit on the Y axis. If $X_1 = 4$, $X_2 = 6$, $Y_1 = 4$, $Y_2 = 8$, the $b = (8 - 4)/(6 - 4) = \frac{4}{2} = 2$.

In Figure 7.18, a slope of two indicates that the dependent variable measure is increasing twice as fast as the independent variable measure. In the two

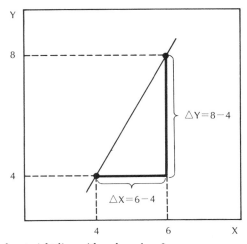

Fig. 7.18. An example of a straight line with a slope $b = 2$.

preceding examples, suppose the straight lines represent two different learning curves. The second example with a slope of two indicates the rate of learning was twice as fast as in the first case (slope of one). The slopes just mentioned were all positive; the lines ran from the lower left to the upper right of the graph. A slope may also have a negative sign. A negatively sloped line runs from the upper left to the lower right. An example is shown in Figure 7.19. The ordered pairs are (X_1, Y_1) and (X_2, Y_2). In Figure 7.19, $\Delta Y = Y_2 - Y_1 = 1 - 2 = -1$, and $\Delta X = X_2 - X_1 = 2 - 1 = 1$. The value of $b = \Delta Y / \Delta X = -1/1 = -1$. The concept of a negative slope is similar to the concept of a negative correlation coefficient. In both cases, as the value of the independent variable *increases*, the value of the dependent variable *decreases*.

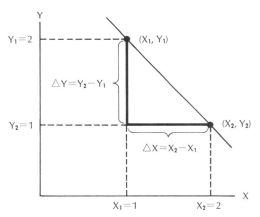

Fig. 7.19.   An example of a straight line with a negative slope ($b = -1$).

The concept of slope will be used in Section Two, Unit D to test statistically whether a straight-line relationship exists between the independent and dependent variables. The slope of curved lines may also be computed, but the procedure will not be discussed.

Logarithms

A number multiplied by itself may be symbolized as n•n or n(n) or n^2 (for example, $2^2 = 2(2) = 4$). The last symbol (n^2) is referred to as an example of a power or exponential function. A number raised to a positive integral power (exponent) simply denotes the product of several equal numbers. For example, $2^3 = 2•2•2 = 8$, where the positive integral power or exponent is 3. *Every* positive number can be expressed as some power of 10. For example, 100 is 10^2, 10 is 10^1, and 39 is $10^{1.5911}$. The **common logarithm** of any number is the exponent to which 10 must be raised to produce the number. Since 100 is equal to 10^2, the logarithm of 100 is 2 (log 100 = 2). Most numbers are not expressable as even powers of 10; therefore, most logarithms are indicated by an integer (the "characteristic") and a decimal value (the "mantissa"). Most tables of logarithms indicate the mantissas to four, five, or six places although the number is theoretically endless. The logarithm mantissa is located by finding a number in the margins of a table of common logarithms and reading the value from the body of the table. The logarithm characteristic is determined by the location of the decimal point in the number as indicated in Table 7.5.

TABLE 7.5. Examples of Characteristics, Mantissas, and Common Logarithms of Positive Integers.

Number	Characteristic	Mantissa	Complete Logarithm
0.03	−2	.47712	−2.47712
0.30	−1	.47712	−1.47712
3.00	0	.47712	0.47712
30.00	1	.47712	1.47712
300.00	2	.47712	2.47712
3000.00	3	.47712	3.47712

Logarithm scales have a number of interesting characteristics. If you add the logarithms of two numbers, the sum is the logarithm of the product of the two numbers. Thus, you accomplish the multiplication process by addition. Division is similarly accomplished by subtracting the logarithms. Calculation on a slide rule actually involves the addition of distances on a logarithm scale. Frequently, the data in a research report are transformed from the original raw data into logarithms. Such a transformation is usually done in order to make the data fit some requirement of a particular statistical test.

Logarithms are primarily of interest in the research area known as psychophysics. Psychophysics is that area of psychology that deals with the detection, recognization, discrimination, and scaling of sensory events. One method of scaling sensations (psychological measurement) is called the "direct method of scaling." For example, when using such a method in scaling coffee odors, the experimenter may present a standard intensity of the odor of coffee and tell the subject to consider that odor to have a scale value of "10." The experimenter then presents an irregular series of intensities of the odor of coffee (more and less intense than the standard) and instructs the subject to assign each odor intensity a number proportional to its apparent (psychological) intensity. The data from a series of subjects is averaged to generate the average relationship between the physical measure of intensity of the odor and the psychological measure of the intensity of the odor. According to S. S. Stevens (1958), the relationship between the psychological measure and physical measure for a certain class of phenomena is a power function in the form $\Psi = ks^n$, where Ψ refers to the psychological sensation, k is a constant of proportionality, S is the measure of the physical stimulus, and the value of the exponent, n, is a function of the particular kind of stimulus experienced (for example, coffee odor).

When Steven's psychophysical law correctly fits the data, a plot of the psychological scale as a function of physical values yields a curved line on plain graph paper (Figure 7.20) and a straight line on log-log coordinate paper (Figure 7.21). In the

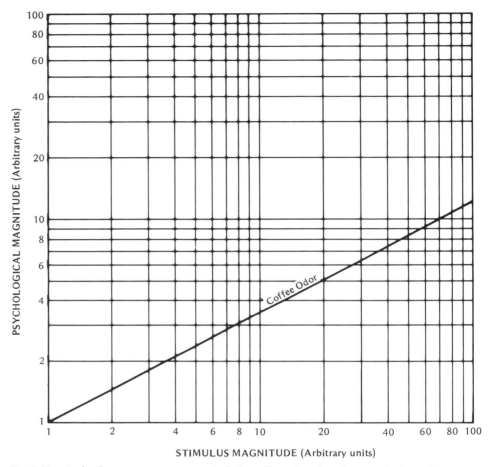

Fig. 7.20.   Scale of apparent sensory magnitude for coffee odors plotted on standard graph paper.

case of coffee odors, the value of n is about 0.55 (Sheridan, 1971) and n is the value of the slope of the line graphed on log-log graph paper (Figure 7.21).

The plot of the data on standard graph paper (Figure 7.20) does not clearly indicate if Steven's theory is supported or not. However, if the plot of the data on log-log paper closely approximates a straight line, then one can see that the theory is supported.

REVIEW

If the behavioral data are measured in numerical form, the researcher has two choices for presenting the data. He can choose to present them in some type of tabular presentation, or use a more pictorial presentation by one of the graphic methods.

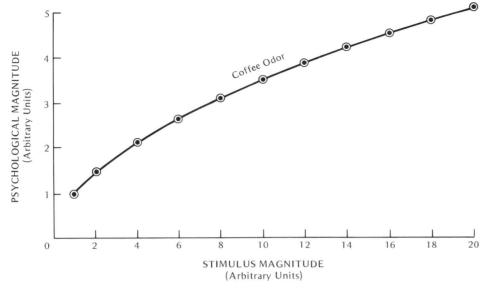

Fig. 7.21. Scale of apparent sensory magnitude for coffee odors plotted on log-log coordinate graph paper. The slope of the line is 0.55, which is the exponent of the power function relating psychological sensation to physical stimulus magnitude.

With some rare exceptions, tables and graphs are equally capable of presenting the information from the data. The choice between the two methods falls to the preference of the researcher. Some people can think and understand the data better in a table, and others rely on the pictorial presentation of the graph. If the student finds that he is either a tabular thinker or a graphic thinker, it is well to note that it is possible to translate the information presented in one mode to the other with a little work with pen and pencil.

   The discussion on logarithms in the latter portion of this chapter has a rather peculiar status, for many researchers will never need to use log scales, and consequently the information is superfluous. If, on the other hand, the student's research interest leads him into areas where logs are used, the effort spent to understand them is more than justified; it is mandatory.

SUMMARY

1. Raw data may be presented in lists or frequency tables. A frequency table is more economical than a list.
2. Raw data may be presented in ordered lists or frequency distributions. A frequency distribution is used with large masses of data and consists of arbitrary divisions of the data into class intervals.
3. The apparent limits of a class interval are the highest and lowest numbers of the interval. The real limits of an interval are one-half of the smallest unit above the highest number and one-half of the unit below the lowest number of the interval. The midpoint of a class interval is assumed to be the most representative score for that interval.

4. A histogram is a graphical presentation of a frequency distribution. A frequency polygon consists of lines connecting the midpoints of the class intervals. Frequency polygons may be skewed or approximately normal in shape. Frequency polygons may be flat or peaked (kurtosis) compared with a normal curve.

5. The relationship between two measures may be displayed in a scatter-plot. Usually, the dependent variable is plotted on the Y axis and the independent variable is plotted on the X axis.

6. A line graph summarizes the relationship between two variables. The average dependent variable measure for each level of the independent variable is plotted in a line graph. The trend of behavior is indicated by a line graph.

7. If the relationship between two measures is approximately linear, then the slope of a straight line drawn through the data summarizes the relationship in terms of one number. The slope is defined as the ratio of the change in the dependent measure (Y) to the change in the independent measure (X). Slopes can be either positive or negative.

8. The common logarithm of any number is the exponent to which 10 must be raised to produce the number. On log-log graph paper, the X and Y axes are both expressed in logarithmic units. If the relationship between the two variables is a power function of the form $Y = kX^n$, then the log-log graph of the relationship forms a straight line.

SUGGESTED READING

Amos, J. R., Brown, F. L., and Mink, O. G. *Statistical concepts. A basic program.* New York: Harper & Row, 1965.

Blommers, P., and Lindquist, E. F. *Elementary statistical methods in psychology and education.* Boston: Houghton Mifflin, 1960.

Bradley, J. I., and McClelland, J. N. *Basic statistical concepts. A self-instructional text.* Chicago: Scott, Foresman, & Co., 1963.

Courts, F. A. *Psychological statistics.* Homewood, Illinois: Dorsey, 1966.

Edwards, A. L. *Statistical methods.* (3d ed.) New York: Holt, Rinehart and Winston, 1973.

Huff, D. *How to lie with statistics.* New York: Norton, 1954.

Kurtz, K. H. *Foundations of psychological research.* Boston: Allyn and Bacon, 1965.

Spence, J. T., Underwood, B. J., Duncan, C. P., and Cotton, J. W. *Elementary statistics.* (2d ed.) New York: Appleton, 1968.

CHAPTER 8
Scales of Measurement and Descriptive Statistics

In several of the previous chapters we have used example data from experiments. Usually these data were presented in numerical form, and the reader probably had no trouble interpreting those numbers. Implicit to most empirical research is the ability to quantify the observations into a number scale. Many of the experimental controls discussed in previous chapters are aimed at the problem of obtaining accurate numerical measures of the dependent variable.

Numbers are advantageous in that they quickly transmit information. Large masses of data may be summarized in one or two numbers. Such descriptive statistics are sometimes superior to graphical methods for presenting the results of an experiment. We have all been exposed to years of learning relationships among numbers and it is relatively easy to generalize these relationships when the numbers represent empirical events.

Numbers can be misinterpreted. Our mathematical facility with numbers may cause us to make certain conclusions that are not appropriate to the data. Children beginning to learn arithmetic may add all of the digits in their telephone numbers and be delighted or dismayed to find that their sum is higher or lower than their friends'. Such manipulations serve as amusing games, but do not yield useful information. Numbers have a variety of meanings, depending upon how they are related to the empirical observations. The experimental psychologist must be sure that the manipulations and interpretations he applies to numerical data are appropriate and not simply meaningless games.

MEASUREMENT

Measurement is the assignment of symbols to events according to some set of rules. The symbols are usually numbers and the rules are normally contained within an established mathematical system. The rules of measurement may involve the direct translation of height, weight, and age in terms of inches, pounds, and years. Other rules may be more arbitrary, such as the government's assignment of voting rights to anyone over 18. (A similar example is the slogan "Never trust anyone over 30.") In either case, an arbitrary rule is established and, based on the date of birth, individuals can be mapped into the set of symbols O (old) and Y (young). The two classes O and Y are mutually exclusive and account for all members of the sample. The resultant set of pairs of people and symbols constitutes a measurement of "oldness."

If different criteria are applied to the same event, different numerical values will result. In the example above, the choice of the critical point between "old" and "young" may differ (particularly with the age of the experimenter), but the measurement is not ambiguous once a criterion is established. Given the appropriate set of rules, anything may be measured.

Assume that we are at an automobile race, and we have a program that lists the driver's name along with the number on the car he is driving. As each car crosses the finish line, we note the order of finish. Thus, we write a "1" beside the winning driver's name, a "2" beside the second place finisher, and so on until all drivers are assigned a number. A companion, however, glances at his wristwatch and notes the time each car crosses the finish line. We now find that we have three different numbers assigned to each driver (car number, rank of finish, and time of finish), and each number system yields different amounts of information concerning the automobile race.

The choice of the "correct" set of measurement rules depends on the information wanted about the event. The casual spectator may be interested in identifying the driver involved when something interesting is happening. An avid racing fan may not be happy unless he is equipped with two stopwatches and a "time to speed" conversion chart based on the length of the track.

Measurement varies from simple to complex, depending on the rules. The concept, **levels of measurement,** refers to the variation in complexity of rules.

Potentially, there are an infinite number of levels of measurement (Coombs, et al., 1954). We will focus on four levels, which lead to four scales of measurement: nominal, ordinal, interval, and ratio. A **measurement scale** consists of an operational definition of the events to be measured and the rules specifying the level of measurement.

Scales of Measurement

Nominal Scales   The simplest level of measurement is called nominal measurement. The nominal level rules specify that the total sample must be partitioned into at least two sets. All of the elements of a set are assigned the same symbol, and no two sets are assigned the same symbol (Guilford, 1965). Thus, nominal measurement consists in *naming* discriminable classes of events.

The assignment of people to the classes, male or female, is an example of nominal measurement. If the classes are assigned numbers, the numbers are only labels. For example, in the National Football League, all quarterbacks are assigned jersey numbers between 1 and 19, and all offensive ends are assigned jersey numbers between 80 and 89. In this case, the numbers serve only to label the two classes, quarterbacks and ends. In the auto-racing example, the program supplied a nominal scale of measurement. Each car was identified by a different number that identified each driver. The fact that the numbers can be added or compared with one another indicates nothing about the driver's skill, ability, or performance.

Ordinal Scales   The rules applying to nominal measurement also apply to ordinal measurement with one additional rule. The subsets partitioned from the total sample must be rank-ordered on some dimension. If we have three subsets: a, b, and c, and o stands for operation; then the relationship between them must be: if a o b and b o c, then a o c. Any operation with the subsets that satisfies the above relationship provides us with ordinal measurement. For example, the operation could be greater than, less than, or older than. If a is older than b, and b is older than c, then a must be older than c.

The person who records the first, second, third, . . . finishers in the race is using an ordinal level of measurement. Notice that the ordinal scale is also nominal; that is, it is possible to identify a driver as "the *guy* who finished first." In addition, ordinal scale numbers give us a basis for comparison between classifications. The smaller the number, the faster that driver must have gone. It does not, however, tell us how far apart two successive finishers were.

Interval Scales   The rules of the ordinal level, with the addition of one more rule, define the interval level of measurement. At the interval level, we have ordered subsets or classes with equal intervals between classes. In other words, numerically equal differences between rank values represent equal distances on the measurement dimension.

When self-concept scales are administered, one way of comparing scores between individuals is to count the number of units above or below the average (normative) score on the scale. The difference between two and three units above the norm is assumed to be equal to the difference between five and six units above the norm. Or, when using the calendar as a time measure, the difference between 1800 and 1850 is equal (in number of years) to the difference between 1900 and 1950. The interval level of measurement was achieved by the person who recorded the time of finish for each driver. The interval scale contains ordinal information in that the earliest driver took first place, the next, second, and so on. (By definition, the interval scale must include nominal and ordinal information.) The interval scale gives additional information in that it is possible to determine how far apart any two finishers were. By subtracting one driver's time from another's, it is possible to compare the differences between when they finished.

Ratio Scales The rules of the interval level, with the addition of one more rule define the ratio level of measurement. At the ratio level, we have an absolute or natural (nonarbitrary) zero point that has an empirical referent. If a measurement is zero on a ratio scale, then the measured object or being has none of the attribute being measured. Ratio scales include number (numerosity) and length, for example. When we measure number of errors in a rat maze, six errors is twice as many as three errors, since no errors at all is an absolute zero point. (The rat cannot have less than zero errors.) Similarly, time to complete a race or any task recorded from start to finish yields a ratio scale.

PURPOSES OF DESCRIPTIVE MEASURES

After an experimenter has measured the dependent variable, he must arrange the data in such a way that they are meaningful. If the number of observations is small, he may choose to present the individual data points in tabular or graphic form. As the sample size becomes larger, however, such a presentation becomes unwieldy. Data from a large sample, such as the United States population census, is overwhelming without some kind of shorthand method of describing the essential features of the data. There are four common types of descriptive statistical measures: measures of central tendency, measures of variability, measures of individual comparison, and measures of relationship.

An easily understood method of summarizing many scores is to report the value of a "typical" or "average" score. In most frequency distributions, there is a tendency for the scores to cluster around the middle values of the distribution rather than the ends. A value that would be most representative of all of the measurements would most likely come from the central part of the distribution. **Measures of central tendency** describe the "most typical" values of the distribution of scores.

Measures of central tendency vary in their descriptive value according to the amount of variation or scatter in the summarized scores. It is quite possible to have two distributions with the same typical score and yet differ greatly because one set of scores clusters tightly together, while the other is widely scattered. **Measures of variability** describe the dispersion or variation in the scores. When used appropriately, a measure of central tendency and a measure of variability summarize the major features of a large sample distribution.

In certain situations, we need to compare the performance of two individuals on some measure or compare an individual's performance with that of the group. For example, as Blommers and Lindquist (1960, p. 67) state, ". . . a single score such as is derived from most educational and psychological tests has little, if any absolute significance—that is, it is not capable of meaningful interpretation when considered alone." **Measures of individual position** are used in comparing the performance of an individual with other measures of performance.

All of the descriptive statistics mentioned above involve a group of scores collected along a single variable. In other words, we have been concerned with a single distribution. Occasionally, the concern is with the relationship between two different distributions. We may decide that grade point average (GPA) is related to hours spent in the library. We then measure each variable for a large number of students; the resulting pairs of GPAs and hours represent the observed relationship. The relationship can be numerically summarized by a single number called a **measure of relationship** or correlation.

Measures of Central Tendency

Mode   A mode (Mo) of a frequency distribution of scores is a score with a frequency that is large in relation to neighboring scores. Suppose that a spelling test is given to a 20-pupil fourth-grade class. The resulting scores on the hypothetical test are presented in Table 8.1. The mode for the distribution in Table 8.1 is 17, since that is the score with the highest frequency.

TABLE 8.1. Tabular Presentation of a Hypothetical Frequency Distribution.

Scores (number correct)	11	12	13	14	15	16	17	18	19	20
Frequency (numbers of students)	0	0	0	2	4	4	5	3	2	0

Occasionally, there will be two points in a frequency distribution where the frequencies will be relatively large. In such cases, there will be two modes (a bimodal distribution). The two modes need not have the same frequency. It is also possible to have more than two modes in a distribution. For example, the results of the spelling test might have been distributed as in Table 8.2, in which case, the three modes are 13, 16, and 20.

TABLE 8.2. Tabular Presentation of a Trimodal Distribution.

Scores	11	12	13	14	15	16	17	18	19	20
Frequency	1	0	5	0	0	4	1	1	2	6

The greatest value of a mode is simplicity of calculation. There are several limitations to using a mode as a measure of central tendency. First, in the case of multimodal distributions, the determination of which high frequency points are modes is somewhat arbitrary. Second, the mode is more sensitive to *sampling fluctuations* than any other measure of central tendency. That is, if the spelling test

Limitations of Mode

were repeated, it might lead to a different mode or modes. Third, when the frequency distribution is grouped (Chapter 7), the use of different class intervals may lead to different modes for the same data. As a consequence of these limitations, the mode is seldom used in psychology as a measure of central tendency.

Median The median (Mdn) of a distribution is defined as the midpoint (50 percent point) of that distribution. That is, half of the scores are greater and half are less than the median. For a frequency distribution, the median may be determined by arranging the scores in order and determining the value of the middle score for an odd number of subjects, or the value that lies midway between the two middle scores for an even number of subjects.[1] In the examples presented in Tables 8.1 and 8.2, both medians are 16.5 (the midpoint between 16 and 17).

In some distributions, there are tied scores around the midpoint (Table 8.3).

TABLE 8.3. Hypothetical Frequency Distribution with Ties.

Scores	3	4	5	6	7	8	9	10	11	12
Frequency	1	2	3	2	3	3	3	2	3	2

In such a case, the calculation of the median requires the use of the arbitrary rule that the discrete value of a single score represents the midpoint of an interval of length one. For example, the score value 8 represents the midpoint of the interval with real limits of 7.5 to 8.5. In the example presented in Table 8.3, the midpoint of the distribution lies somewhere in the interval between 7.5 and 8.5, since there are eleven scores below 8 and ten above. Since the median is defined as the midpoint, we could decide that the median is 8.0. However, such a conclusion conflicts with the above definition, since there are unequal frequencies above and below the score of 8. In order to reduce the discrepancy, we decide that the value of the median is really 7.83. We obtained this figure by dividing the interval 7.5–8.5 into thirds. Three people received a score of 8, each accounting for one-third of the interval. (See Figure 8.1.) By counting one of the scores as below the median and the other two as above, we meet the criterion of 12 scores above and 12 scores below the

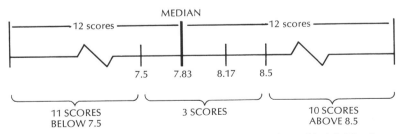

Fig. 8.1. Determination of the median for the distribution presented in Table 8.3. The three scores between 7.5 and 8.5 each occupy one-third of the interval.

---

[1] See McNemar (1969), p. 15, for the procedure used in calculating the median for grouped distributions.

median. The median is therefore located one-third of the way into the interval ($7.5 + \frac{1}{3} = 7.83$). Calculation of the median usually is not so complicated.

The median is less subject to sampling fluctuation than the mode. Also, the median is not affected by the values of the scores at either end of the distribution. For example, two distributions might have equal medians when the lowest score in one distribution is 11 and the other is 14. (See Tables 8.1 and 8.2.)

There are three disadvantages of the median as a measure of central tendency. First, the calculation of the median in the case of grouped or tied distributions is complicated and can be confusing. Second, two quite dissimilar distributions can have equal medians, which may foster erroneous conclusions. Third, the median, as an ordinal statistic, does not allow algebraic manipulation. For example, if we determined the medians for two distributions and combine the data into a single distribution, we cannot calculate the median of the new distribution by averaging the medians of the original two.

Mean   The arithmetic mean $\overline{Y}$ of a distribution is equivalent to what is commonly called the "average." The **arithmetic mean** is defined as the algebraic sum of the scores divided by the number of scores. If there are any negative scores, the negative signs are taken into account when the scores are added together. Symbolically,

$$\overline{Y} = \frac{\sum Y}{N} \qquad (8.a)$$

where Y equals each individual score value, N equals the total number of scores, and Σ (summation sign) indicates that *all* N scores must be added together. The rules for handling summation signs are contained in Appendix A. To calculate the mean of the scores in Table 8.1, the 20 scores are added to yield a sum of 329 and then the sum is divided by the N of 20 to yield a mean of 16.45. Unlike the median and mode, the value of the mean depends on the value of every score in the distribution.

The exact arithmetic definition of the mean provides a number of important implications. First, if a constant amount is added to each of the scores in a distribution, then the mean of this new distribution is equal to the original mean plus the added constant. If each of the scores is multiplied by a constant, then the mean of the new distribution is equal to the mean of the original distribution multiplied by that constant. If a set of subgroups contain the same number of scores, then the mean of the combined subgroups is equal to the mean of the subgroup means. Finally, if we subtract the mean from each score in the distribution, we obtain a set of differences. Then if we add the differences, the resulting sum equals zero.

Another advantage of the mean is that, for approximately normal distributions, the mean is least subject to sampling fluctuations. The mean is the most frequently used measure of central tendency in psychology. One reason is that most inferential statistics involve comparing means.

When you have an extremely skewed distribution, the median is perferred to

Advantages of Median

Limitations of Median

Advantages of Mean

the mean, because the value of the mean is affected by extreme scores. Table 8.4 provides a comparison of the three measures for three sets of scores.

TABLE 8.4. Measures of Central Tendency for Hypothetical Data.

		Measures		
		Mode	*Median*	*Mean*
	Table 8.1	17	16.5	16.45
Data	*Table 8.2*	13, 16, 20	16.5	16.65
	Table 8.3	None	7.83	7.75

Measures of Variability

Number of Subsets It is possible to give some indication of variation with nominal data by identifying the number of subsets used to measure the scores. For example, let's assume that a political candidate won 49 percent of the votes cast. It could make a great deal of difference to him if two or 16 candidates were running for the office. Number of subsets is so crude a measure that it is almost noninformative.

Range The range (R) is defined as the difference between the smallest and largest scores in a distribution. That is,

$$R = Y_H - Y_L \qquad (8.b)$$

where Y_H is the *upper real limit* and Y_L is the *lower real limit*. For example, in Table 8.1, $R = 19.5 - 13.5 = 6$. The range is determined by only two points in the distribution. The main advantage is simplicity of calculation; however, R is a weak measure that tells us only the maximum possible difference between the scores in a distribution.

Variance The variance (S^2) is defined as the average squared deviation from the sample mean. That is, each score is subtracted from the mean, the difference (deviation) is squared, the squared differences are summed, and the total is divided by the number of scores. The calculational formula for the variance is derived from the definition. The calculational formula for the variance is:

$$S^2 = \frac{1}{N^2} \left[N \Sigma Y^2 - (\Sigma Y)^2 \right] \qquad (8.c)$$

The calculation of S^2 should proceed according to the following steps: (The calculations are presented for the data in Table 8.1, which are repeated in Table 8.5.)

1. Sum all the scores

$$\left[(\Sigma Y) = 329 \right]$$

2. Square the total sum of the scores

$$\left[(\Sigma Y)^2 = (329)^2 = 108{,}241 \right]$$

3. Square all of the individual scores

$$(Y^2)$$

4. Sum the squared scores

$$\left[(\Sigma Y^2) = 5455\right]$$

5. Multiply the result of step 4 by N

$$\left[N(\Sigma Y^2) = (20)(5455) = 109,100\right]$$

6. Subtract the result of step 2 from the result of step 5

$$\left[N\Sigma Y^2 - (\Sigma Y)^2\right] = 109,100 - 108,241 = 859$$

7. Divide the result of step 6 by N^2 to find S^2

$$\left[S^2 = 859/400 = 2.15\right]$$

TABLE 8.5. **Frequency Distribution from Table 8.1. Organized for the Calculation of S^2.**

Scores	Frequency			
Y	f	fY	Y^2	fY^2
14	2	28	196	392
15	4	60	225	900
16	4	64	256	1024
17	5	85	289	1445
18	3	54	324	972
19	2	38	361	722
Sums:	20	329		5455

Since the variance is an algebraic quantity (as is the mean), the variance of the combination of two distributions can be determined by averaging the variance of both.[2] Also, adding or subtracting a constant amount from each score in the sample does not change the value of S^2. And, when each score is multiplied or divided by a positive constant (C), the new variance is equal to C^2S^2 or S^2/C^2, respectively. The variance is the major statistic used in the field of inferential statistics (Chapter 10) and is the most frequently used measure of variability.

A disadvantage of S^2 is that its value is not expressed in the same unit of measurement as the set of scores. For example, if the measurement unit of the set of scores is errors, then the value of the variance is expressed in square errors. The term square error is meaningless.

Standard Deviation   In order to have a measure that is expressed in the units of the sample distribution, the square root of the variance is extracted. The standard deviation (S) is defined as the square root of the variance ($S = \sqrt{S^2}$). For purely descriptive purposes, the most frequently used measure of variability is the standard deviation. Table 8.6 presents a comparison of the three measures for three sets of scores.

[2] When determining the combined variance of two or more unequal distributions, the number of subjects in each distribution must be taken into account. [See McNemar (1969), p. 24.]

TABLE 8.6. Measures of Variability for Hypothetical Data.

		Measures			
		Number of Subsets	Range	Variance	Standard Deviation
	Table 8.1	6	6	2.15	1.5
Data	Table 8.2	7	10	9.03	3.0
	Table 8.3	10	10	6.83	2.6

When descriptive statistics are used to describe the characteristics of a distribution, both a measure of central tendency and the corresponding measure of variation are presented. Consequently, the mode and number of subsets, the median and the range, and the mean and standard deviation are usually presented together. Given these two distribution characteristics, a reader can quickly grasp some of the major features of the distribution. If the sample size is large $(N > 30)$ and the data are at least an interval scale of measurement, some very precise statements can be made. Figure 8.2 illustrates the major features of the normal curve in terms of standard deviation units. The normal curve is a theoretical distribution that should result if an infinitely large sample of randomly distributed scores were collected. Thus,

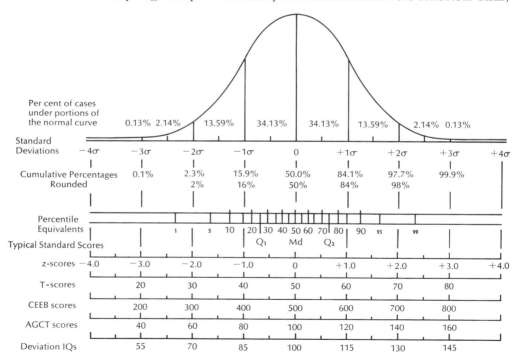

Fig. 8.2. The major characteristics of a normal distribution in terms of standard deviations, percentiles, and selected standard scores. A T score = 10z + 50. CEEB stands for College Entrance Examination Board tests. AGCT stands for the Army General Classification Test.

the characteristics of the normal curve are only approximated by a finite sample. In many cases, however, the approximation is sufficiently close with samples greater than 30 that the normal curve can be used to interpret the statistics. For example, if we collect examination scores from a class of 400 students and find that the distribution appears normal with a mean score of 84 and the standard deviation of 15, we can conclude that approximately 68 percent (256 students) scored between 69 and 99 on the exam.

Measures of Individual Position

Uniqueness Measures of individual position describe the position of an individual score within the distribution of a group of scores. If the scale of measurement is nominal, the corresponding individual position measure may be described as uniqueness. Thus, the statement that a person is the only one with a 16-foot alligator in his swimming pool provides some information about the person. Occasionally, the important factor is that the individual position is shared by many other individuals (more people choose Brand X than any other brand).

Ranks If we have ordinal measurement and wish to compare the performance of one subject with that of the total sample, we can use the rank of the individual's score. The rank of a score is its location when all the scores are arranged in order of magnitude. The direction of rank ordering must be specified. For example, a score with a rank of six is the sixth highest or lowest score in the distribution.

Percentile Ranks Obviously, the meaning of rank value depends on the number of scores in a distribution. A test score with a rank of six has a different meaning in a class of seven students than in a class of 50 students. Percentile rank provides more information about the relative position of the individual within the sample. The percentile rank indicates the position of a score in terms of the percentage of the sample that had smaller scores.

In a sample of 10 subjects, a rank of third is the 30th percentile rank. Occasionally, we must use the arbitrary rule previously discussed in the computation of the median. For example, in determining the percentile rank of the point or score of 16 in Table 8.1, we observe that 30 percent of the scores lie below 16 and 50 percent above. Therefore, the percentile rank of 16 is equal to 40; the midpoint between 30 percent and 50 percent. The median has the percentile rank of 50 percent in all distributions.

Standard Scores A standard score is a score defined in terms of the mean and standard deviation of the distribution. The most commonly used type of standard scores is called relative deviates or z scores. A z score is defined as the deviation of a score from the sample mean, divided by the standard deviation. Symbolically:

$$z = \frac{Y - \bar{Y}}{S} \tag{8.d}$$

where Y is an individual score. For example, if $\bar{Y} = 10$ and $S = 2$, a score of 5 would yield a z of $(5 - 10)/2 = -5/2 = -2.5$.

Any z score distribution has the following properties: (1) the mean of the distribution is zero, (2) the algebraic sum of the z scores is zero, (3) the variance and standard deviation of the distribution are equal to one, and (4) the sum of the squared z scores equals N (the number of scores).

The other standard scores listed in Figure 8.2 are basically z scores that have been transformed into other numerical values. Thus, the IQ measure is a distribution where $\overline{Y} = 100$ and $S = 15$. With this information, a person with a measured IQ of 120 should be able to conclude that he is within the top 10 percent of IQ scores.

The z scores are pure or abstract numbers. The quality of abstractness is the chief value of standard scores. Pure numbers can be directly compared. For example, a person's z score on a test of one ability such as typing speed may be directly compared with his z score on a test of another ability such as spelling accuracy. Positive z values indicate a person scored above the mean, and negative z scores indicate he scored below the mean.

Measures of Relationship

Correlation coefficients describe the degree of relationship between two variables in numerical form. (See Chapter 6.) There are many different correlational statistics. The calculational formulas for the Pearson and Spearman coefficients are presented in Section Two, Unit D6.

CHOICE OF DESCRIPTIVE STATISTIC

As was the case in choosing a level of measurement, the choice of the most appropriate statistic depends on the information the experimenter wishes to summarize. In most cases, the information is related to the measurement scale that describes the data. That is, there is a descriptive statistic that is usually best suited for each scale of measurement. Table 8.7 summarizes the normal choice of a descriptive statistic according to the purpose and the level of measurement. The table presents several important pieces of information. Recall that, as we move from nominal to ordinal to interval to ratio scales of measurement, the amount of information in the numerical scores increases. Stated another way, the interval scale is more powerful than the ordinal or nominal scales. Similarly the statistics for each measure becomes more powerful as we go up each column in Table 8.7.

It is possible, however, to compute a statistic that implies more than the information available. Much like the child misinterpreting the sum of telephone digits, the choice of a statistic that exceeds the power of the data is not descriptive, but misleading. Therefore, usually one should not apply any statistic in Table 8.7 below the row in which it is listed: for example, do not use a median with nominal data.

It is acceptable, and sometimes advisable, to use some other statistic than the one listed. Because the interval scale contains both nominal and ordinal information, both nominal and ordinal level statistics may be applied to interval data. In other words, it *is* appropriate to apply a statistic *above* its position in Table 8.7. (For example, the median is appropriate with interval data.) All of the interval level statistics

TABLE 8.7. Selected Descriptive Statistics Presented in Terms of Levels of Measurement and Purpose of Measure.

Level of Measurement	Purpose of Measure			
	Central Tendency	Variability	Individual Position	Relationship
Interval and Ratio	Mean	Variance Standard Deviation	Standard Scores	Pearson Product Moment Correlation Coefficient
Ordinal	Median	Range	Ranks Percentile Ranks	Rank Correlation Coefficient
Nominal	Mode	Number of Classes	Uniqueness	

can be used with the ratio level of measurement. The use of a less powerful statistic means that some of the information in the scores is ignored. Thus, an ordinal statistic ignores the distance between the scores given in a interval scale.

REVIEW

The important information in this chapter is summarized in Table 8.7. If you can read and understand the table, and define each of the terms presented in the table, you have the concepts that justified the chapter.

SUMMARY

1. Measurement is defined as the assignment of symbols to events according to rules. The rules are arbitrary; the choice of a set of rules depends on the purpose of the measures. The rules vary in complexity; each level of complexity leads to a level of measurement.
2. A measurement scale consists of a set of rules (level) of measurement and an operational definition of events to be measured.
3. Nominal level measurement consists of naming discrete classes of events. Ordinal level measurement consists of naming discrete classes with the classes ranked in order. Interval level measurement consists of ordinal measurement with equal distances (intervals) between discrete classes. Ratio level measurement consists of interval measurement with a nonarbitrary zero point.
4. Measures of central tendency provide a single representative score for a distribution. Measures of variability describe the extent of difference between the scores in a distribution. Measures of individual position are used to locate one subject's score with reference to the rest of the scores in a distribution. Measures of relationship describe the degree of correlation between two sets of scores.
5. The modes of a distribution are the outstanding scores (high frequency) of the distribution. The mode is not a reliable measure of central tendency.
6. The median is the midpoint of a distribution. The definition applies even if there are

ties asymmetrically located around the middle of the distribution. The median is more reliable than the mode and is not affected by straggling scores in the tails of a distribution.

7. The arithmetic mean is the algebraic sum of the scores divided by the number of scores in the distribution. A number of algebraic operations are possible with means. For almost any large sample and/or approximately normal distribution, the mean is the most reliable measure of central tendency of the measures presented here.

8. The number of subsets of scores is a crude measure of variability. The range is the difference between the upper real limit of the largest score and the lower real limit of the smallest score. Neither measure is very useful.

9. The variance is the average squared deviation from a sample mean. The mean and variance are algebraic measures. The standard deviation is the square root of the variance. As compared to the variance, the standard deviation has the advantage of being expressed in terms of the same unit of measurement as the subjects' scores.

10. An infrequently used measure of individual position is uniqueness; a unique class is one with only one class member. Ranks are ordinal measures of individual position. Percentile ranks indicate the position of a score in terms of the percentage of smaller scores.

11. A z score is defined as the difference between a given score and the mean of the distribution, divided by the standard deviation of the distribution. A standard score such as a z score is not stated in terms of any measurement unit.

12. The level and purpose of a measure partially determines the choice of a descriptive statistic. While nominal measures can be used with an interval scale, interval measures should not be used with a nominal scale.

SUGGESTED READING

Blommers, P., and Lindquist, E. F. *Elementary statistical methods in psychology and education.* Boston: Houghton Mifflin, 1960.

Carlborg, F. W. *Introduction to statistics.* Glenview, Illinois: Scott, Foresman and Co., 1968.

Coombs, C. H. *A theory of data.* New York: Wiley, 1964.

Coombs, C. H., Raiffa, H., and Thrall, R. M. Some views on mathematical models and measurement theory. *Psychological Review,* 1954, *61,* 132–144.

Edwards, A. L. *Statistical methods.* (3d ed.) New York: Holt, Rinehart and Winston, 1973.

Guilford, J. P. *Fundamental statistics in psychology and education.* (4th ed.) New York: McGraw-Hill, 1965.

Kerlinger, F. N. *Foundations of behavioral research.* (2d ed.) New York: Holt, Rinehart and Winston, 1973.

Kurtz, K. H. *Foundations of psychological research.* Boston: Allyn and Bacon, 1965.

Spence, J. T., Underwood, B. J., Duncan, C. P., and Cotton, J. W. *Elementary statistics.* New York: Appleton, 1968.

Stevens, S. S. *Handbook of experimental psychology.* New York: Wiley, 1951.

Stevens, S. S. Measurement, statistics, and the schemapiric view. *Science,* 1968, *161,* 849–856.

CHAPTER 9
Probability

A college student collected data of the number of four-year-old children who knew the "right" answer to a question about which of two rows of buttons was larger: the row of six that were spread out over a 12-inch line or the row of six that was bunched up in a three-inch line. Three children said both rows had the same number of buttons. Five children said that the row that was spread out had more buttons than the bunched-up row. The college student calculated that 37.5 percent of the children knew the right answer. Does that percentage support the hypothesis that most four-year-old children *do not* have a concept of conservation of number (knowing that the two rows have the same *number* of buttons)? The student must decide.

Once a set of data has been collected and described, an experimenter is concerned with interpreting the data. He has two questions to examine. First, are the experimental hypotheses supported by the data, and, second, can he generalize his conclusions to the population sampled? If the data obviously support or refute his predictions, then the first question is answered. If the data seem to fit his predictions but there is room for doubt, the experimenter must decide if the results really support the prediction or if they just happen by chance to have occurred in a way that fits the prediction. (Sometimes he may decide that he can make no decision.) When he makes a decision, he states the probability that the decision is erroneous.

The inferences (conclusions and generalizations) an experimenter makes from his data are probabilistic inferences. The field of inferential statistics, which is discussed in the next chapter, is concerned with the process of making decisions (inferences) on the basis of probability. Therefore, this chapter introduces some basic terms and concepts of probability as a foundation for the following chapter.

EMPIRICAL PROBABILITY

We frequently make statements such as: "It is likely to rain tomorrow," "I probably forgot to feed the cat," or "The chances are I won't make it to class next Friday." Such subjective statements indicate the common usage of probability concepts. Most everyday statements about the likelihood that something will happen or has happened are based on "common sense" or our subjective intuitions. While *subjective* probability statements are, to some extent, based on empirical observation, they do not have to be. *Empirical* or *a posteriori* probability must be based on empirical observations. All of the possible observed outcomes are classified, and the number of outcomes in each class (event) are counted. The **relative frequency** of a class (event) is the number of outcomes in the class divided by the total number of outcomes.

Suppose a man is observed to have a solid gold band on the third finger of his left hand. We could *infer* that he is probably married, but we are not certain. In other words, on the basis of incomplete information, we can subjectively estimate the probability that he belongs to the class of married males. Our subjective estimate may be: "There is a 95 percent chance that he is married."

To determine the empirical probability of men with gold rings being married, a sample of men with gold bands must be observed. If we were to collect a random sample of 100 men with gold rings, we might find that 85 of them were actually married. That is:

$$p\left(\begin{matrix}\text{married \&}\\\text{gold bands}\end{matrix}\right) = \frac{\text{\# gold bands \& married}}{\begin{matrix}\text{\# gold bands \& married +}\\\text{gold bands and not married}\end{matrix}}$$

$$p = \frac{85}{85 + 15} \tag{9.a}$$

Thus, p(married & gold band) = 0.85, or the relative frequency (proportion) of men with gold bands that are married is 85/100.

Our definition of **empirical probability** is:

$$p(A) = \frac{\text{set of A outcomes}}{(\text{set of A outcomes}) + (\text{set of not A outcomes})}$$

or

$$p(A) = \frac{\text{set of A outcomes}}{\text{total \# of outcomes}} \tag{9.b}$$

where p stands for probability, and an outcome is an operationally defined observation.

In the empirical probability model, a number of conditions must be met. (1) Each outcome (observation) in the sample must be counted only once. In the example, the observation of each man contributes only one outcome to the calculation of $p(A)$. (2) The classes of outcomes must be *exhaustive*. That is, every outcome must be placed in a class, and the classes must account for all the outcomes. In the example, each man in the sample was classed as being married or not married, and all 100 men were so recorded. (3) Each outcome must have a probability of occurrence that is equal to or greater than zero, but not greater than 1.0 [$1.0 \geq p(\text{an outcome}) \geq 0.0$]. (4) The sum of all the probabilities of outcomes must equal 1.0. That is, if we add the probabilities of all the outcomes, the sum will equal one [$\Sigma p(\text{outcomes}) = 1.0$]. (The sum of subjective probabilities does not have to equal one.) (5) If the classes are exhaustive and mutually exclusive, then the sum of the probabilities of each class must equal 1.0. The classes are *mutually exclusive* if an outcome can be recorded in one and only one class. In terms of the example, a man can be recorded as either married or not married. Thus, the classes, married and not married, are mutually exclusive and exhaustive, and the sum of the probabilities of both classes equals 1.0 [$p(\text{married}) + p(\text{not married}) = {}^{85}\!/_{100} + {}^{15}\!/_{100} = 1.0$]. If a set of observations satisfies these conditions, then the use of the term "empirical probability" and the operations of empirical probability with that set of observations is legitimate.

PROBABILITY OPERATIONS

In the remainder of the chapter, several different descriptive methods are used to illustrate probability concepts. The essential concept of probability is simple and the student should not let the relative complexity of the illustrations interfere with the understanding of the basic idea of probability. It would be easy for us to state authoritatively how to apply probability operations in a research setting without attempting to illuminate the underlying logic. Several "cookbook" research manuals do not attempt to explain the logic. However, the effort of learning the basic logic gives the researcher the freedom to make intelligent decisions in research situations that do not happen to be included as examples in a manual.

The group of all possible outcomes of a sample is called a sample space. Each possible outcome in the sample space is a sample point. As indicated in Figure 9.1,

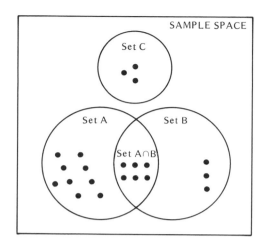

Fig. 9.1 Set A = students who have taken experimental psychology (yes on question one). Set B = students who have taken psychological statistics (yes on question two). Set C = students who have taken neither statistics nor experimental psychology (no on both questions one and two). Set A∩B = students who have taken both experimental psychology and statistics (yes on both questions one and two). Sample space = students who have taken statistics and/or experimental psychology, and students who have taken neither course.

the sample space is the set of all possible outcomes and it is made up of classes (sets of outcomes) of observation. These classes are called **events.** In Figure 9.1, sets A, B, C and A ∩ B are events. Suppose we have the sample space illustrated in Figure 9.1. The outcomes represent psychology majors. Each student in the sample space was first asked if he had taken experimental psychology (question one), then he was asked if he had taken statistics (question two). The answers were recorded as yes (Y) or no (N). The four possible answers to the questions can be listed in a table (Table 9.1).

TABLE 9.1. The Possible Answers to the Two Questions.

		Question One (Experimental Psychology)	
		(Yes) Y_1	*(No)* N_1
Question Two	*(Yes)* Y_2	$Y_1 \ Y_2$	$N_1 \ Y_2$
(Statistics)	*(No)* N_2	$Y_1 \ N_2$	$N_1 \ N_2$

Tree Diagrams   The possible answers to the two questions can also be listed via a tree diagram (Figure 9.2). Tree diagrams are often a useful way of determining the possible events in a sample space. The events in Figure 9.2 are the same events listed in Table 9.1. The events may be found in a tree diagram by starting at "start" and following each "branch" of the tree.

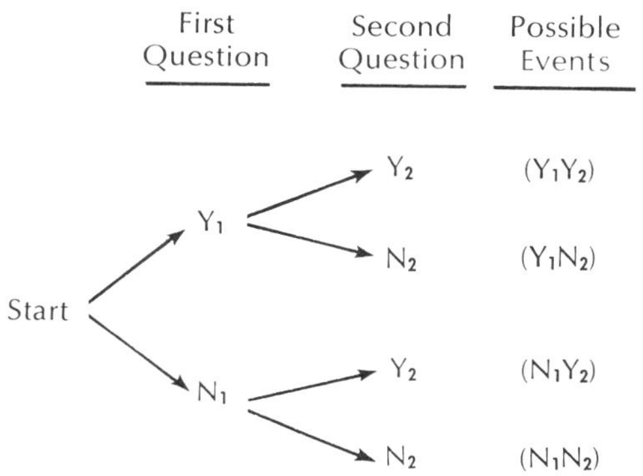

First Question	Second Question	Possible Events

Start
Y₁ → Y₂ → (Y₁Y₂)
Y₁ → N₂ → (Y₁N₂)
N₁ → Y₂ → (N₁Y₂)
N₁ → N₂ → (N₁N₂)

Fig. 9.2. A tree diagram illustrating the possible events of the two questions asked each student, when each question required a yes (Y) or no (N) answer.

Before discussing the example further, we will digress to explore some operations involving sets. There are two basic set operations called intersection and union. By **operation,** we mean the manipulation of something in a set or sets. In arithmetic we add, subtract, multiply, and divide numbers, but we "intersect" and "union" sets (Kerlinger, 1973). An **intersection** of sets is an overlapping of the elements of two or more sets and is represented by the symbol ∩. Suppose, for example, we have the following sets: A = {1, 2, 3, 4, 5} and B = {3, 4, 5, 6, 7}. These two sets can be represented by the Venn diagram in Figure 9.3. The rectangular figure is labeled as the sample space. In this case the sample space is all the numbers from one to seven. The circle to the left represents set A and the other, set B. The overlap or intersection of the two sets is shaded and is given by the term A∩B = {3, 4, 5}. This is read A *and* B = the set containing 3, 4, and 5. The intersection A∩B and set A and set B are subsets of the sample space.

Set Operations

Venn Diagrams

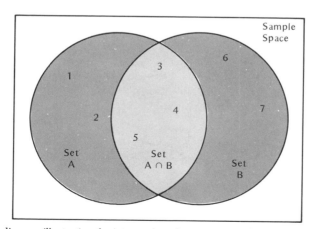

Fig. 9.3. A Venn diagram illustrating the intersection of two sets, A and B.

The **union** of two sets A and B is written A∪B and is the set which contains all members of A and all members of B. If A = {1, 2, 3, 4, 5} and B = {3, 4, 5, 6, 7}, then A∪B = {1, 2, 3, 4, 5, 6, 7}. This is read the set containing set A *or* set B *or* the intersection (set A∩B) = {1, 2, 3, 4, 5, 6, 7}.

Returning to the psychology students example, since 21 students were questioned, each combination of answers occurs several times. Each outcome or sample point in Figure 9.1 represents the combined responses of each student to the questions, and each outcome occurs in one of three sets (sets A, B, or C) or a fourth set, the intersection of sets A and B (set A∩B) in Figure 9.1. Those nine outcomes in set A but not in set A∩B are Y_1N_2 students; those three in set B but not in set A∩B are N_1Y_2 students; those six in set A∩B are Y_1Y_2 students; and those three in set C are N_1N_2 students. These are the four possible outcomes in Figure 9.2.

The problem becomes more complex as we increase the number of possible outcomes. Suppose, for example, we wanted to find the number of possible outcomes obtainable by flipping three coins in sequence. We can use the tree diagram technique, as illustrated in Figure 9.4. From Figure 9.4, we can see that the sample space of possible outcomes consists of {H_1, H_2, H_3}, (H_1, H_2, T_3), . . . , (T_1, T_2, T_3)}. In Figure 9.4, there are eight possible outcomes from flipping three coins. We can determine the outcomes by following the branches of the tree diagram. These eight outcomes are listed in the right-hand column of the figure.

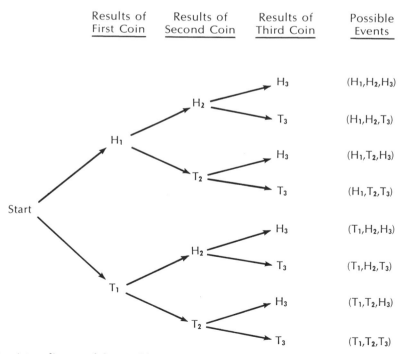

Results of First Coin	Results of Second Coin	Results of Third Coin	Possible Events

Fig. 9.4. A tree diagram of the possible outcomes of flipping three coins.

The Addition Rule

The probability of set A is determined by enumerating the number of outcomes in set A and the total number of outcomes. Thus, in Figure 9.1, $p(A) = {}^{15}\!/_{21}$ or the proportion of yes answers to question one (have taken experimental psychology) is equal to $5/7$. Similarly, $p(B) = {}^{9}\!/_{21}$, $p(C) = {}^{3}\!/_{21}$, and $p(A \cup B \cup C) = {}^{21}\!/_{21}$. The probability of the intersection of sets A and B ($A \cap B$) can also be determined by counting, for example, $p(A \cap B) = {}^{6}\!/_{21}$.

Given a pair of *mutually exclusive* sets, the probability that either *one* of the sets (the union) will occur is obtained by adding the probabilities of each separate set. Thus, $p(A \cup C) = p(A) + p(C)$. In terms of the psychology majors example, $p(A \cup C) = p(A) + p(C) = {}^{15}\!/_{21} + {}^{3}\!/_{21} = {}^{18}\!/_{21}$. Thus, the probability that a student will have either taken experimental psychology (A) *or* taken neither experimental psychology nor statistics (C) is ${}^{18}\!/_{21}$. Note, sets A and C are mutually exclusive, because a student cannot be a member of both subsets. Another way to describe mutually exclusive sets is to say that the intersection of two mutually exclusive sets ($A \cap C$) is empty or contains no elements.

The addition rule is a general rule for determining the probability of the *union* of two or more events ($A \cup B$). The **addition rule** is: To find the probability of the union, add the probabilities of the events comprising the union and subtract the probability of their intersection. For a union of two events, the addition rule in equation form is:

$$p(A \cup B) = p(A) + p(B) - p(A \cap B) \tag{9.c}$$

Returning to the psychology majors example,

$$p(A \cup B) = {}^{15}\!/_{21} + {}^{9}\!/_{21} - {}^{6}\!/_{21} = {}^{18}\!/_{21}$$

Thus, the probability that a student will have either taken experimental psychology, statistics, or both is ${}^{18}\!/_{21}$. In Equation 9.c, $p(A \cap B)$ must be subtracted because the outcomes of $A \cap B$ were counted twice (once in A and once in B). If $p(A \cap B)$ had *not* been subtracted, then we would have found that $p(A \cup B)$ in the example was ${}^{24}\!/_{21}$. This is an *impossible* result, because the conditions of empirical probability specify that the probability of any event cannot exceed 1.0.

The sample space of the outcomes in Figure 9.4 (coins) contains several possible sets of outcomes (events). Suppose we wanted to find the probability of getting the event, one head and two tails, when we flip three coins. That particular event is $\{(H_1, T_2, T_3), (T_1, H_2, T_3), (T_1, T_2, H_3)\}$. Notice that the event is composed of the fourth, sixth, and seventh outcomes in Figure 9.4. The probability of this event is found by using the addition rule. Thus, the probability of getting one head and two tails is, $p(H, T, T) = {}^{1}\!/_{8} + {}^{1}\!/_{8} + {}^{1}\!/_{8} - 0 = {}^{3}\!/_{8}$, since $p(H_1, T_2, T_3) = p(T_1, H_2, T_3) = (T_1, T_2, H_3) = {}^{1}\!/_{8}$. Note that all of the results of three flips are *mutually exclusive* and therefore, the probability of their intersection is equal to zero.

The Multiplication Rule for Independent Events

Two or more outcomes or events are **independent** if the probability of the occurrence of any one of them is in no way influenced by the occurrence of any other outcome or event. It would appear that two events are independent if they are mutually exclusive. However, mutually exclusive events are dependent; if we flip a *single* coin and it comes up heads, we know it is not tails and these two events are dependent and mutually exclusive. It is reasonable to say that if a tail is obtained with a flip of *one* coin, that outcome should not affect the probability of heads on a toss of *another* coin. Therefore, the outcomes of tossing two coins are independent. Given a set of independent outcomes or events, the probability that they will all occur is obtained by the multiplication rule. The multiplication rule for independent events is that the probability of occurrence of independent events is equal to the product of their separate probabilities. In equation form, the multiplication rule for independent events is:

$$p(X \cap Y) = p(X)p(Y) \tag{9.d}$$

In English, equation 9.d states that the probability of the occurrence of events X and Y is equal to the product of their probabilities.

In terms of the coin-toss example (Figure 9.4.), the occurrence of a head on the flip of a coin is independent of the occurrence of a head on the flip of either of the other two coins. Assuming that $p(H) = \frac{1}{2}$ for each case, the probability of obtaining three heads from flipping three coins is $p(H_1, H_2, H_3) = p(H_1) \, p(H_2) \, p(H_3) = (\frac{1}{2})(\frac{1}{2})(\frac{1}{2}) = \frac{1}{8}$.

A slightly more complex problem involves the tossing of two unbiased dice. A result of one toss of two dice is the sum of the spots showing on the top face of the two dice. Each die can have six possible outcomes {1, 2, 3, 4, 5, 6}. In Figure 9.5, the 36 possible outcomes of tossing two dice are presented in a six-by-six matrix. In the matrix, the margins represent the six possible outcomes on each die. Thus, if the first die shows three dots, and the other shows four dots, then the sum is seven. The sum of seven is located in the matrix by finding the point of intersection of the three-dot column for the first die and the four-dot row for the second die.

The probability of each sample point in the outcome sample space is $\frac{1}{36}$, since the sum of probabilities of all of the sample points must equal one. Since each die has six faces, the probability of getting any particular face on one die is $\frac{1}{6}$. The outcomes of one die are independent of the outcomes of the other die. Therefore, the probability of a two on the first die and a five on the second is $p(2 \cap 5) = (\frac{1}{6})(\frac{1}{6}) = \frac{1}{36}$.

The probability of getting any given sum (for example, the compound event "7") on a roll of two dice may be calculated by using the addition rule. Since each event is mutually exclusive, (that is, 1 and 6 are different from 2 and 5) by using the addition rule, the probability of getting a sum of seven on a single roll of two dice is $p(6,1 \cup 5,2 \cup 4,3 \cup 3,4 \cup 2,5 \cup 1,6) = (\frac{1}{36}) + (\frac{1}{36}) + (\frac{1}{36}) + (\frac{1}{36}) + (\frac{1}{36}) + (\frac{1}{36}) - 0 = \frac{6}{36}$. The same result may be obtained by enumerating the number of

Outcomes of First Die

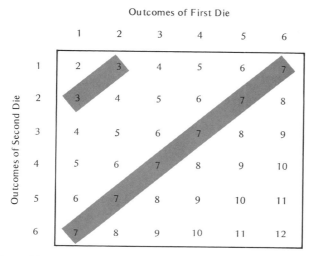

Fig. 9.5. The 36 possible outcome sums of the pips (spots) on two dice. The margins of the matrix present the six numbers of dots on the six faces of each die. The shaded numbers are the six ways to get a sum of seven and the two ways to get a sum of three.

outcomes of the event, "seven," and dividing the observed frequency by the total number of outcomes. Thus, there are six "sevens" in the matrix and 36 total outcomes and $p(7) = \frac{6}{36}$. Similarly, $p(3) = \frac{2}{36}$ and so on.

Conditional Probability

On occasion we know that one event has already occurred. In that case when determining the probability of another event we use the knowledge we already have. For example, if we know that a student has said yes to question two (statistics), we use that knowledge in determining the probability that the student will say yes to question one (experimental psychology). The effect of knowing the answer to question two and being concerned only about the probability of saying yes to question one, *limits the sample space* in Figure 9.1 to sets A and B (experimental psychology and statistics). The probability that a student will say yes to question one given that he has said yes to question two is found by counting to be $\frac{6}{9}$. The same value may be found from the original sample space of 21 points by using Equation 9.e. Equation 9.e is the definition of **conditional probability** $[p\mathrm{A|B})]$:

$$p(A|B) = \frac{p(A \cap B)}{p(B)} \qquad (9.e)$$

In the equation $p(A|B)$ is read, "the conditional probability of A *given that* B has occurred," and $p(A|B)$ is equal to the probability of the intersection of A and B $(A \cap B)$ divided by the probability of B. To use Formula 9.e. $p(B)$ must be greater than zero. Returning to the psychology majors example, $p(A|B) = \frac{6}{21} \div \frac{9}{21} = \frac{6}{9}$, which is the same answer found by enumeration.

The conditional probability of B given that A has occurred is $p(B|A) = p(B \cap A) \div p(A)$. In terms of the psychology majors, $p(B|A) = \%_{21} \div {}^{15}\!/_{21} = \%_{15}$. Thus, $p(A|B)$ is not necessarily equal to $p(B|A)$.

The Multiplication Rule

The previously introduced multiplication rule was limited to independent events The multiplication rule presented in Equation 9.f applies to independent *or* dependent events.

$$p(A \cap B) = p(A)\,p(B|A) = p(B)\,p(A|B) \qquad (9.f)$$

Equation 9.f is read, "the probability of the intersection of two events is equal to the *product* of the probability of one event and the *conditional* probability of the other event." In terms of the psychology students example, recall that $p(A) = {}^{15}\!/_{21}$ and $p(B|A) = \%_{15}$, therefore, by Equation 9.f., $p(A \cap B) = ({}^{15}\!/_{21})(\%_{15}) = \%_{21}$. Similarly, $p(B) = \%_{21}$ and $p(A|B) = \%_9$ so that $p(A \cap B) = (\%_{21})\,(\%_9) = \%_{21}$, which is the same result as obtained by enumeration. Formula 9.f was derived from Formula 9.e. If two events are independent, then $p(B|A) = p(B)$ so that Equation 9.f reduces to $p(A \cap B) = p(A)p(B)$ (which is Equation 9.d). Since, in the psychology majors example, the occurrence of A (yes to question one—experimental psychology) is not independent of the occurrence of B (yes to question two—statistics), the conditional probability of event (A) given that the other event (B) has occurred does not equal the probability of event (A). That is, $p(A|B) \neq p(A)$, since $p(A|B) = \%_9$ and $p(A) = {}^{15}\!/_{21}$.

Combinations

The number of ways of grouping a set of elements is called the number of possible combinations of the elements. Obviously, the number of possible combinations depends on the total number of elements and the number of groups that are possible. A **combination** is defined as an unordered subset of elements (an event).

In other words, a combination is a set that can be made by including all or part of a given collection of objects without taking account of the *order* of the objects For example, if we have a universe of three objects {X, Y, Z} we can make one combination of all three objects {XYZ}; three combinations of two of the objects, {(XY), (XZ), (ZY)}; three combinations of one of the objects, {(X), (Y), (Z)}; and one combination of none of the objects { }.

The total number of objects in a sample space is denoted as n, and the number of objects in a subset as r. By enumeration, we can determine the number of distinct combinations (C) of n things taken r at a time. For example, if there are $n = 4$ people in a room, then we can make one combination of $r = 0$ of the people, four different combinations of $r = 1$ persons each, six different combinations of $r = 2$ persons at a time, four different combinations of $r = 3$ people at a time, and one combination of $r = 4$ people. Figure 9.6 pictorially summarizes all of the combinations of four people. Table 9.2 enumerates the number of combinations possible for

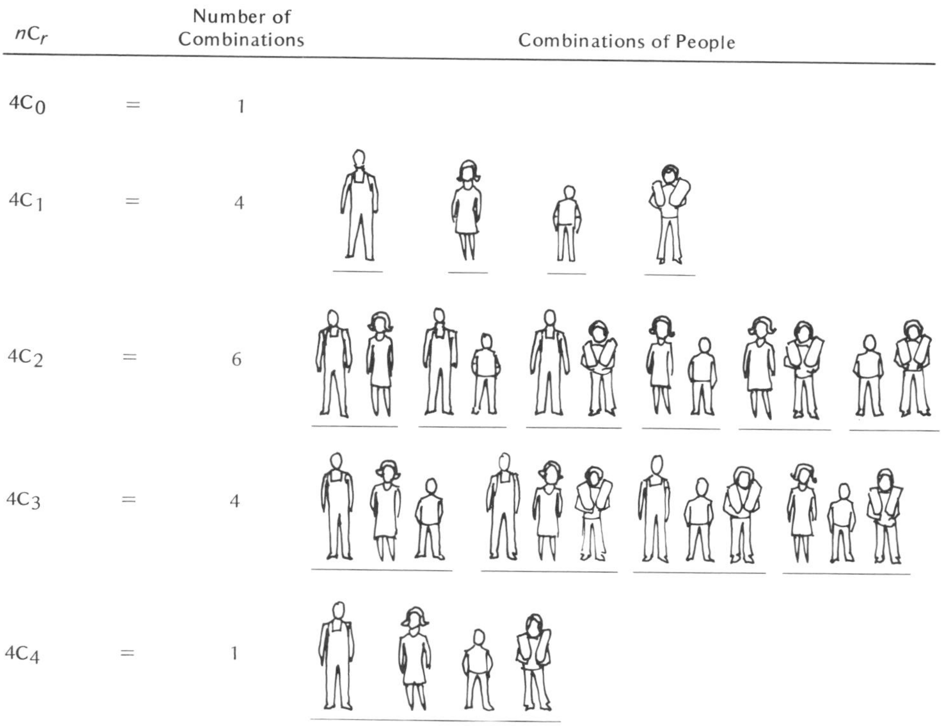

nC_r		Number of Combinations	Combinations of People
$4C_0$	=	1	
$4C_1$	=	4	
$4C_2$	=	6	
$4C_3$	=	4	
$4C_4$	=	1	

Fig. 9.6. The possible combinations of four people taken 0, 1, 2, 3, or 4 at a time.

zero to five objects. Notice that row $n = 4$ in Table 9.2 has the same sequence of digits $(1, 4, 6, 4, 1)$ as the people combined in Figure 9.6.

TABLE 9.2. The Number of Possible Combinations (C) of n Things Grouped r at a Time.

n (Total number of objects)	r (Number of Objects in Each Set)					
	0	1	2	3	4	5
0	1					
1	1	1				
2	1	2	1			
3	1	3	3	1		
4	1	4	6	4	1	
5	1	5	10	10	5	1

The numbers in Table 9.2 may be obtained by enumeration of all the combinations as in the case of $n = 4$, but this method is laborious and subject to error. Pascal's Triangle (Table 9.3) provides a shortcut method for determining the numbers in Table 9.2. Spacing from the number "1" in the top row of Table 9.3, put a "1" a half-space to the right and a "1" a half-space to the left in the second row.

TABLE 9.3 Pascal's Triangle for n = 1 through 10.

n																						Total Number of Events (Combination in a sample space)
0											1											1
1										1		1										2
2									1		2		1									4
3								1		3		3		1								8
4							1		4		6		4		1							16
5						1		5		10		10		5		1						32
6					1		6		15		20		15		6		1					64
7				1		7		21		35		35		21		7		1				128
8			1		8		28		56		70		56		28		8		1			256
9		1		9		36		84		126		126		84		36		9		1		512
10	1		10		45		120		210		252		210		120		45		10		1	1024

The sides of the triangle are continued as "1"s. Any digit in the middle of a row of the triangle is the sum of the two digits bracketing its space in the preceding row. For example, in the $n = 4$ row, the digits are 1,4,6,4,1. Each "4" is the sum of the "1" and "3" in the $n = 3$ row. Similarly, the "6" is the sum of (and bracketed by) the two "3"s in the preceding row.

The number of combinations is easy to determine with Pascal's Triangle when n is small. The determination of C can also be accomplished with Equation 9.g:

$$nCr = \frac{n!}{r!(n-r)!} \tag{9.g}$$

In the equation, nCr is the number of distinct combinations of n things taken r at a time, $n!$ is n factorial, $r!$ is r factorial, and $(n-r)!$ means subtract r from n and determine the factorial of the difference. The factorial sign (!) means that you write down all of the positive integers from one to n (or r) in order. Then multiply those integers. For example, $6! = 1 \times 2 \times 3 \times 4 \times 5 \times 6 = 720$. If $n = 6$ and $r = 3$, then $(n - r)! = (6 - 3)! = 3! = 1 \times 2 \times 3 = 6$. Applying formula 9.g to the numbers:

$$6C3 = \frac{6!}{3!3!} = \frac{720}{(6)(6)} = 20$$

The answer (20) agrees with the middle digit in the $n = 6$ row of Pascal's Triangle. Note that $6! = 6 \times 5 \times 4 \times 3!$ so that 3! could have been canceled from the numerator and denominator of the equation yielding $(6 \times 5 \times 4) \div (3 \times 2 \times 1) = 20$. When using the formula, zero factorial $(0!) =$ one factorial $(1!) =$ one (since division by zero is impossible). Also, the notation for the number of combinations can be written in several different ways, thus nCr = CN,r = $\binom{n}{r}$ = C_r^n = $C(n,r)$. The combinations formula is used in the determination of bionomial probabilities.

THE BINOMIAL
PROBABILITY DISTRIBUTION

An urn contains 30 white balls and 10 red balls intermixed together. (See Figure 9.7.) If we were to reach into the urn (without looking) and pull out a single ball, then the empirical probability that the ball will be red $p(R)$ is $^{10}\!/\!_{40}$ = $\frac{1}{4}$ and the probability that the ball will be white $p(W)$ is $^{30}\!/\!_{40}$ = $\frac{3}{4}$. Suppose we take out a ball, after looking at the ball we return it to the urn, and we repeat the observation three times. (The ball is returned to the urn and mixed thoroughly each time so that the probability of red remains $\frac{1}{4}$ and $p(W)$ remains $\frac{3}{4}$.)

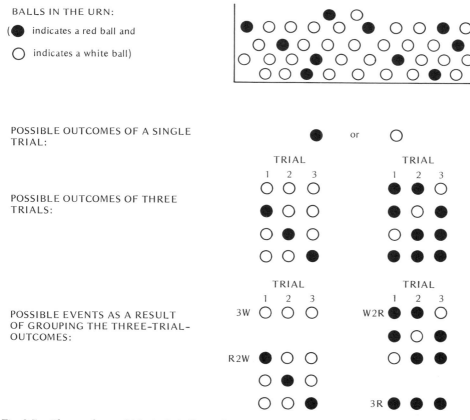

Fig. 9.7.   The urn from which single balls are drawn with replacement on each trial; the possible outcomes of a single trial; the possible outcomes of three trials; and the possible events as a result of grouping the three-trial-outcomes into four groups (events).

Each observation of a ball is called an outcome or *trial*, and on each trial only one of two results is possible, R (red ball) or W (white ball), so they are mutu-

TABLE 9.4. Possible Events and Number of Ways Each Event May Occur in the Urn Example.

Events	Number of Ways (Frequency) of Occurrence
3R	1
W2R	3
R2W	3
3W	1

ally exclusive outcomes. Since only two results are possible, each trial is called a **binomial** (two-number) trial. The possible outcomes of the three binomial trials are (R, R, R), (R, R, W), (R, W, R), (W, R, R), (R, W, W), (W, R, W), (W, W, R), or (W, W, W). The trial outcomes may be grouped into four different events: (3R), (W,2R), (R,2W), and (3W). The number of combinations or ways to get each event may be obtained by the combinations formula (Equation 9.g) or the digits in row $n = 3$ of Pascal's Triangle or the tree diagram in Figure 9.4 (using color in place of coin faces). The probability of drawing 0, 1, 2, or 3 red balls in three draws from the urn may now be determined. The probabilities of R and W are given by the make-up of the urn. The number of ways of occurrence of each event is given by calculation, triangle table, or enumeration. If each outcome *were* equally likely (number of red balls equals number of white balls) or in other symbols, $p(R) = p(W)$, then the probability would be the number of ways each event may occur (number of combinations) divided by the total number of ways of getting the events. In such a case, the probability of drawing three red balls would be $\frac{1}{8}$, because there is a total of eight possible outcomes. Similarly, the probability of getting the event W2R would be $\frac{1}{8} + \frac{1}{8} + \frac{1}{8} = \frac{3}{8}$. Note that the probability of any *particular* W2R outcome (that is, white first, then two reds) is $\frac{1}{8}$ just as in the case of 3R.

In the example originally posed, however, $p(R)$ does *not* equal $p(W)$ and some way must be found to take into account that information. From the multiplication rule (Equation 9.d) we know that the probability of the intersection of two outcomes is equal to the product of the probabilities of each outcome when the outcomes are independent.

Therefore, $p(R \cap R \cap R) = p(R)p(R)p(R) = \frac{1}{4} \times \frac{1}{4} \times \frac{1}{4} = (\frac{1}{4})^3$. Similarly, $p(W \cap W \cap W) = (\frac{3}{4})^3$, $p(R \cap W \cap W) = \frac{1}{4}(\frac{3}{4})^2$, and $p(W \cap R \cap R) = \frac{3}{4}(\frac{1}{4})^2$. Now we must add in the previously obtained information about the number of ways of occurrence of each event. According to Equation 9.c, the probability of the union of two or more outcomes is obtained by adding the probabilities of the separate outcomes making up the event. Thus, $p[(R \cap W \cap W) \cup (W \cap R \cap W) \cup (W \cap W \cap R)] = p(R \cap W \cap W) + p(W \cap R \cap W) + p(W \cap W \cap R)$. Since the outcomes are mutually exclusive, we do not subtract the probability of their intersection. Since $p(R \cap W \cap W) = p(W \cap R \cap W) = p(W \cap W \cap R)$, the solution is, $p(R2W) = 3(\frac{1}{4})(\frac{3}{4})^2$. Similarly, $p(W2R) = 3(\frac{1}{4})^2(\frac{3}{4})$, $p(3R) = 1(\frac{1}{4})^3$, and $p(3W) = 1(\frac{3}{4})^3$. These results are summarized in Table 9.5.

TABLE 9.5. The Possible Events, Their Frequency of Occurrence, the Probability of Occurrence of Each Outcome, and the Probability of Occurrence of Each Event in the Urn Example.

Event	Frequency	Outcome Probability	Event Probability
3R	1	$(\frac{1}{4})^3$	$1(\frac{1}{4})^3 = \frac{1}{64}$
W2R	3	$(\frac{3}{4})\ (\frac{1}{4})^2$	$3(\frac{3}{4})\ (\frac{1}{4})^2 = \frac{9}{64}$
R2W	3	$(\frac{1}{4})\ (\frac{3}{4})^2$	$3(\frac{1}{4})\ (\frac{3}{4})^2 = \frac{27}{64}$
3W	1	$(\frac{3}{4})^3$	$1(\frac{3}{4})^3 = \frac{27}{64}$

Using the addition and multiplication rules to find the probability of occurrence of each event can be quite time consuming. The probabilities may also be found by using formula 9.h, which is a shorthand summary of the application of the addition and multiplication rules.

$$nCrp^{r}q^{n-r} \qquad (9.\text{h})$$

In formula 9.h, nCr is the combinations formula that gives the number of ways of obtaining groups of size r with n objects, p^r stands for the probability of a color that occurs r times, and q^{n-r} stands for the probability of the other color that occurs $n-r$ times.

In terms of Formula 9.h, $nCr\ p^r\ q^{n-r} = 3C3\ p^3\ q^0 = 1\ p^3 = 1\ (\frac{1}{4})^3$, which is also the previously observed answer for the probability of getting three red balls $p(3R)$. Since $p(3R) = \frac{1}{64}$, we are not very likely to draw three red balls from the urn with only three trials. Suppose someone bet you $10.00 to your $1.00 that you could not reach into the urn and pick out three red balls (without looking). Would you take the bet? You should not, because, on the average, you would win $10.00 only once in 64 trials, while the other person would win $1.00, 63 out of 64 times.

A Research Example

In many experiments, the dependent variables are measured on a binomial scale yielding binomial data. Examples of binomial data include, yes-no answers on tests, true-false questions, left-right in a T-maze, male-female, go no-go choices, and so on. In each case, the data is recorded as falling into one of two mutually exclusive and exhaustive categories.

An observer notes that a group of 10 grade-school boys frequently play "follow the leader." Occasionally, the game involves fairly risky behavior such as walking on top of high concrete walls. The observer has noted that an apparently random one-half of the group will "chicken-out" on any given occasion. One day he observes the boys playing the game in front of an audience of other grade-school children (both boys and girls). The question is, will the group of boys be "braver" when the audience is present? The observer notes that eight of the boys do successfully walk along a high, thin wall, while two do not attempt it. Assuming that the prior observation of 50 percent nonattempts is correct, the probability of the new observation is found with Formula 9.h. Thus, $nCr\ p^r\ q^{n-r} = 10C8(\frac{1}{2})^2(\frac{1}{2})^8 = \frac{45}{1024}$, where p is the probability of attempting and q is the probability of not attempting the wall.

The numbers 45 and 1024 may also be obtained from Pascal's Triangle. The obtained result, $^{45}/_{1024} \approx 0.04$ is the probability of the exact outcome of eight boys attempting and two not attempting when p (attempt) $= 0.5$. The decision the observer must make is whether the audience has affected the boys' behavior. The probability obtained via Formula 9.h is used in the decision process as discussed in Chapter 10. The probability figure is used as a basis for deciding if the audience made the boys "braver." Chapter 10 describes how probabilities are used in making decisions.

REVIEW

The application of probability principles to research problems is actually fairly simple. If the student can intuitively grasp the concept that it is theoretically possible to list all of the potential outcomes of an experiment, and that some of the outcomes are fairly common and that others will occur only rarely, he has the basic principles presented in this chapter. Unfortunately, when evaluating an experiment, we cannot use such loose phrases as "common" and "rare," but have to present a precise numerical value estimate for an outcome. Most of the complicated materials in this chapter are involved with showing how this numerical precision is obtained.

SUMMARY

1. Inferential statistics is the subfield of statistics concerned with the process of making generalizations on the basis of empirical probability.
2. Subjective probability statements may or may not be based on observation. Subjective probabilities do not have to sum to 1.0. Empirical *(a posteriori)* probability must be based on empirical observation. These observations are the relative frequency of occurrence of finite events. The empirical probability of A = set of A outcomes divided by the total number of outcomes.
3. The rules of the empirical probability model include the following: (1) each observation must be singly counted, (2) the outcome classes (events) are exhaustive, (3) each outcome has a finite probability equal to or greater than zero, but less than one, (4) the sum of all probabilities of the outcomes must equal 1.0, and (5) if the classes are mutually exclusive and exhaustive, the sum of the probabilities of the classes must equal 1.0.
4. The set of all possible outcomes of observation is called a sample space. Each outcome in the sample space is called a sample point. Each set of outcomes is called an event. The possible outcomes and events may be portrayed in a Venn diagram. The possible outcomes and events may be listed in tabular form or in a tree diagram.
5. The addition rule is a means of determining the probability of the union of outcomes or events $(X \cup W)$. The addition rule states that the probabilities of the component events are added, and the probability of their intersection $(X \cap W)$ is subtracted.
6. The multiplication rule for independent events is a means of determining the probability of occurrence of an intersection $(X \cap W)$ when the events are independent. Independence here means that the occurrence of one event in no way influences the occurrence of the other event. The multiplication rule for independent events or outcomes is: $p(A \cap B) = p(A) \ p(B)$.

7. The conditional probability of an outcome or event, given that another event Y has occurred $[p(X|Y)]$ is equal to the probability of the intersection $[p(X \cap Y)]$ divided by the probability of Y $[p(Y)]$.
8. The general multiplication rule (for independent and dependent outcomes or events) is: $p(A \cap B) = p(A)\ p(B|A)$.
9. The number of ways of grouping (unordered) sets of objects is called the number of possible combinations of the objects. Pascal's Triangle may be used to determine the number of possible combinations (C) of n things taken in sets of r at a time. The number of combinations may be determined by the formula, $nCr = n! \div r!\ (n-r)!$ where n is the total number of objects and r is the size of a subject. $0! = 1.0$.
10. A binomial trial is an observation where only two outcomes are possible. The formula $nCr\ p^r\ q^{n-r}$ is a quick way to determining the probability of occurrence of binomial events.

SUGGESTED READING

Alder, H. L., and Roessler, E. B. *Introduction to probability and statistics.* (3d ed.) San Francisco: Freeman, 1964.

Carlborg, F. W. *Introduction to statistics.* Glenview, Illinois: Scott, Foresman, 1968.

Edwards, A. L. *Statistical methods.* (3d ed.) New York: Holt, Rinehart and Winston, 1973.

Hays, W. L. *Statistics for the social sciences.* (2d ed.) New York: Holt, Rinehart and Winston, 1973.

Mosteller, F., Rourke, R. E. K., and Thomas, G. B., Jr. *Probability with statistical applications.* Reading, Mass.: Addison-Wesley, 1961.

Stilson, D. W. *Probability and statistics in psychological research and theory.* San Francisco: Holden-Day, 1966.

Walker, H. M., and Lev, J. *Statistical inference.* New York: Holt, Rinehart and Winston, 1953.

Weaver, W. *Lady luck: The theory of probability.* Garden City, N.Y.: Doubleday, 1963.

CHAPTER 10
Inferential Statistics

At the beginning of Chapter 9, the student who studied the hypothesis that four-year-old children do not have a concept of conservation of number was left with a decision problem. The student's problem is an illustration of the general inferential statistics problem of hypothesis testing. The researcher must decide whether the observed results really support or only appear to support the prediction. The student will again be left with his problem until some basic concepts involved in the statistical model of hypothesis testing are introduced.

Inferential and descriptive statistics are valuable tools to the behavioral researcher. Graphical methods and descriptive statistics provide a means of concisely organizing and summarizing the data from a group of subjects in some capsule form. An important function of most experiments is that the observed behavior is a sample of the behavior of a larger group than only those subjects seen in the laboratory. The ability to **generalize** the experimental observations to estimate the characteristics of a population is absolutely necessary to any behavioral science. Inferential statistics provide methods for estimating the relationship between population *parameters,* from the behavior data *(statistics)* observed in an experiment.

HYPOTHESIS TESTING

Suppose that a student scored 62 on an exam but forgot which of two exams the score came from. Assume that he has the mean and standard deviation for each exam. For exam A, $\bar{Y} = 53$ and $S = 3$, and for exam B, $\bar{Y} = 75$ and $S = 5$. It is rather important to the student to know which of the two test distributions apply to the interpretation of his grade, since his grade will be extremely high in one case and low in the other. His best conclusion, given this information, is that his test score came from exam B. The score of 62 is exactly three standard deviation units above the mean of group A, and only about two and one-half standard deviation units below the mean of exam B scores. In other words, the score (62) was more likely to have come from exam B than from exam A, even though the test score was numerically nearer the mean of test A. This is not to say that the alternative explanation cannot be true; it is *more probable* that the given score came from exam B. Because he knows the characteristics of the two possible populations the score came from, the student can make an inference concerning which population most likely yielded a given score. In other words, the student tested the hypothesis that his score came from one of two distributions and made the decision that it probably came from a specific one.

   Now let us examine the plight of another student who is concerned with making a similar decision, but he only has the parameters of test A ($\bar{Y} = 53$ and $S = 3$). Assume that this student also has a score of 62. How can he make a decision when he does not know the parameters of one of the distributions? The only thing he can do is to base his decision on the information available from test A. The score of 62 is three standard deviations above the mean of test A. If the distribution of test scores is approximately normal, then by examining the information in Figure 8.2 the student finds that a score three or more standard deviations above the mean will occur only .13 percent of the time. In other words, the score of 62 is very unlikely to have come from the test A distribution assuming the population distribution is normal. Even though he does not know the mean and standard deviation of test B, it seems likely that the test score came from test B.

   If the students did not have the parameters of either of the exams, they could obtain estimates by sampling the test scores of other students in the class (who managed to keep their test A and B scores without confusing them). The same process could then be applied to determine the most likely population for the observed test score.

   The above examples describe a reasoning process similar to the procedure for drawing inferences from behavioral data. In the randomized two-group design (Chapter 4), the experimenter collects scores from the experimental group and scores from the control group. The experimenter is faced with the decision as to whether the manipulations of the independent variable had any effect on the observed behavior. If the treatment had no effect, the experimenter is essentially comparing two samples from a common population. If, on the other hand, the treatment did have some effect, the populations are now different for each group and the scores of the treatment group should have some consistent difference introduced as a result of the treatment. The problem becomes one of determing if the observed difference between the groups is likely or unlikely to have been drawn by chance from a common population of dependent scores.

**Inferential
Statistical Tests**

Inferential statistical tests compare the observed difference between the sample statistics (for example, sample means) with some estimate of the likely differences if the samples had been drawn from the same population. If the observed difference is too great, the experimenter concludes that there was a real difference between the two samples. That is, the two samples must have been drawn from different populations (treatment and nontreatment) reflecting the action of the independent variable.

Although the logic is similar to the examples discussed above with exam scores, the decision procedure has become more formalized in experimental psychology.

Experimental Hypothesis

The experimental hypothesis (H_1) usually predicts a difference between the behavior of groups. Since the groups are usually exposed to different levels of a treatment, the experimental hypothesis is the prediction the experimenter expects to support with his data.

Null Hypothesis

The null hypothesis (H_0) is usually a statement of "no difference." That is, the null hypothesis states that the experimenter expects to find no real difference between the two sets of scores. The null hypothesis is used for two reasons in making inferences from research data. First it describes the only useful population the experimenter can estimate. By assuming (as is stated by the null hypothesis) that *both* sets of scores are samples from the same population, the experimenter can use the data from *both* samples to estimate the parameters of the population. He can then compare the difference between the observed scores with the differences he would expect if the null hypothesis were true. If the differences are so great that they are unlikely to be only sampling differences, the experimenter rejects the null hypothesis and concludes that the two samples were drawn from two different populations (treatment one and treatment two). By rejecting the null hypothesis, the experimenter concludes the experimental hypothesis (sometimes called the alternative hypothesis) that there is a real difference between the two groups is supported.

The second reason for stating H_0 is that the logic of statistical tests requires that we use a null hypothesis. The easiest way, in terms of logical analysis, to support a proposition is to reject or "fail to find support" for the negative or opposite form of the proposition. The proposition that "all ravens are black" can most easily be supported by finding no support for either "no ravens are black" or "all ravens are not black." These last two statements are null hypotheses. If the data lead to the rejection of the null hypothesis, then the experimental hypothesis is *supported* but not "proven."

Types of Error

The student who knew the parameters of only one exam decided that his score must have come from the other exam. The hypothesis that his score came from the known distribution served as his H_0. The observed score was so improbable that he decided that the score must have come from some other distribution. The decision was based on a probability statement. It is possible that the wrong decision was made; however, the student chose the most likely alternative.

There are two kinds of wrong decisions (errors) which might be made in an experiment. The experimenter may accept H_1 when H_0 is really true. This type of error is called a **Type I error**. A **Type II error** is accepting H_0 when H_1 is really true. (See Table 10.1.) In most experiments, only the distribution specified by the null hypothesis can be estimated. Thus, the probability of a Type I error can be specified by the experimenter, since he can estimate the parameters of the null distribution.

TABLE 10.1. Type I and Type II Decision Errors.

		Experimenter's Decision	
		H_0 Correct (Accept H_0)	H_1 Correct (Accept H_1)
Reality	H_0 Correct	No Error	Type I Error
	H_1 Correct	Type II Error	No Error

The probability for a Type I error is identified by the Greek letter alpha (α) and represents the probability of rejecting the null hypothesis.

The probability for a Type II error is identified by the Greek letter beta (β). Beta can be specified only if the experimenter knows the population parameters for *both* distributions. Since most psychology experiments are concerned with finding out whether there are two distributions, irrespective of their specific characteristics, β is seldom specifiable in behavioral research.

The probability for Type I error (α) is always specified *by the experimenter* before an experiment begins, and it reflects how confident the experimenter wants to be in his decision making. The smaller the value of α, the less the chance of a Type I error. Alpha is often called the *level of significance*. In most psychological research, an α of 0.05 or less is used. When $\alpha = 0.05$, this means that the experimenter is willing to risk the rejection of the null hypothesis, when it is true, five times out of 100 (Type I error). When $\alpha = 0.01$, the experimenter is willing to reject the null hypothesis falsely one time out of 100.

Level of Significance

The student in Chapter 9 who studied children's concepts of conservation of number was testing the hypothesis that most four-year-old children do not have the concept. If we define "most" as meaning "more than 50 percent," then the experimental hypothesis is that less than 50 percent of the responses will be "correct" answers. The null hypothesis of no support for the experimental hypothesis is that 50 percent or more of the responses will be "correct" responses.

Region of Rejection

The null hypothesis may specify, for example, that there is no difference between the mean performance of two groups (H_0 is $\overline{Y}_1 = \overline{Y}_2$). On the basis of the H_0, the distribution of possible differences between two means is specified. The standard deviations of the two groups' scores may be combined into one estimate of the standard deviation of the entire sample (still assuming H_0 is true). (See Unit D4 for details of the procedure.) The combined estimate is used to calculate the distribution of possible differences between group means. Since H_0 specifies "no difference," the distribution of possible differences has a mean of zero. The probabilities of the various possible differences between the two means are determined.

The **region of rejection** consists of those outcomes ($\overline{Y}_1 - \overline{Y}_2$) whose probabilities are very small under H_0. The region of rejection is a subset of the total number of possible outcomes (sample space). The size of the region of rejection is determined by alpha. If $\alpha = 0.04$, then four percent of the possible outcomes are in the region of rejection. If the actual outcome of an experiment (observed difference between means) is within the region of rejection, then the H_0 is rejected. That is, H_0 may be rejected because the probability of the obtained outcome is unlikely on the basis of H_0 [$p(\overline{Y}_1 - \overline{Y}_2) < \alpha$].

One-Tailed and Two-Tailed Tests   If an experimental hypothesis strongly predicts the *direction* of the difference between two means, medians, or proportions, then H_1 constitutes a *one-tailed* or *directional* prediction. For example, suppose we have a strong suspicion that a coin will come up heads more frequently than tails ("biased toward heads"). The H_1 is p (H) $> p$(T), or p(H) > 0.5, when H stands for heads and T stands for tails. The H_0 is p(H) $= p$(T) $= 0.5$. The null hypothesis is that the coin is a "true" or unbiased coin. The level of significance is arbitrarily set at 0.0625 ($\alpha = 0.0625$). The possible outcomes of flipping the coin seven times can be listed in a bar graph (Figure 10.1). The frequencies listed in Figure 10.1 are taken from Pascal's triangle (Chapter 9). There are 128 possible outcomes and those outcomes under H_0 may be classed in terms of the number of heads. In seven tosses of a coin, there can be 0, 1, 2, . . ., 7 heads observed (as noted in Figure 10.1). Note that the H_0 distribution can be specified before the coin is actually flipped. Since α was specified as 0.0625, there are $0.0625 \times 128 = 8$ outcomes in the region of rejection. Since H_1 is directional [p(H) $> p$(T)], the region of rejection is at the right side of Figure 10.1. There are seven ways to get six heads and one tail (T6H) by flipping a coin seven times, and there is one way to get seven heads (7H). Since the region of rejection consists of the eight most extreme outcomes in the predicted direction, the region of rejection includes all of the ways to get the events (T6H) and (7H). The region of rejection is denoted by R in Figure 10.1. The region of rejection is called a *one-tailed region* because R includes only one tail of the bar graph. The statistical test is called a *one-tailed test,* because the region of rejection as

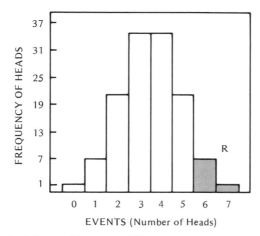

Fig. 10.1. A bar graph of the possible events of flipping a coin seven times. R is the one-tailed region of rejection for $\alpha = 0.0625$.

specified by H_0 and H_1 is one-tailed. R contains that subset of outcomes that are unlikely ($p = 0.0625$) on the basis of H_0. If the coins were flipped seven times and the observed number of heads was either six or seven, we would be able to reject H_0.

Suppose that we just suspected that the coin was biased, but we do not know if it favors heads or tails. The experimental hypothesis would be that the probability of heads does not equal the probability of tails ($p(H) \neq p(T) \neq 0.5$). The null hypothesis would be the same as before ($p(H) = p(T) = 0.5$). In this case, H_1 does not indicate direction, so it is called a *two-tailed hypothesis*. The region of rejection is split into two parts for a two-tailed hypothesis. The two-tailed regions of rejection (R_1 and R_2) are illustrated in Figure 10.2. We are using the same level of significance as be-

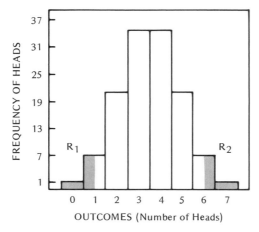

Fig. 10.2. A bar graph of the possible outcomes of flipping a coin seven times. R_1 and R_2 are the two-tailed regions of rejection for $\alpha = 0.0625$.

fore ($\alpha = 0.0625$), therefore, the eight outcomes $[(0.0625 \times 128) = 8]$ in the total region of rejection are split into two subsets of four outcomes $[p(\text{R}_1) = p(\text{R}_2) = \frac{0.0625}{2} = 0.0312]$. If we obtained a very high or very low number of heads when the coin was flipped seven times, we would reject H_0. Note that the four outcomes in the left-hand tail of the distribution include the event (7T) and a randomly chosen three of the seven (H6T) outcomes. Similarly, the four outcomes in the right-hand tail include a randomly chosen three of the seven (T6H) outcomes.

Any observed outcome of flipping the coin will either be in the right or left tail of the distribution (since the middle (3.5) is an impossible event). The two-tailed test accounts for a smaller percentage of the right tail than the one-tailed test (if α is constant). Thus, with a two-tailed rather than one-tailed test, an outcome of flipping a coin must be more unlikely in order to reject H_0. For example, of the observed outcome was in the class (T6H) then H_0 would have been rejected by the one-tailed test. However, the same observed outcome is not as likely to lead to the rejection of H_0 in the case of the two-tailed test. That is, the actually observed outcome is unlikely to be one of the three (of seven) T6H outcomes in the region of rejection.

Example Behavioral Experiment

Suppose an experimenter performs a T-maze experiment with rats. He wants to find out if hungry rats can learn to go to the right arm of a T maze if food is available in the right arm on every trial. The opposite of learned (consistent) behavior is not learned (random, chance, inconsistent) behavior. He develops two hypotheses to account for the possible data. One hypothesis is the null hypothesis (H_0), which states that the rat will not learn to go to the right or left ($p(\text{R}) = p\ (\text{L})$). In other words, H_0 states that the probability of a rat going left or right is 0.50 or chance, so that in 10 trials, we would expect an animal to go about five times to the left and five times to the right (no consistent choice, thus no learning). The one-tailed experimental hypothesis (H_1) states that the rats will learn to go to the right significantly more times than to the left $[p(\text{R}) > p(\text{L})]$. The term, *significantly,* means that the animals will go to the right so frequently that H_0 may be rejected (according to the level of significance). The level of significance α is set equal to 0.02. Again, this means that the experimenter is willing to take the risk that he will reject the null hypothesis, when in fact it is true, two times out of 100. That is, if he performed the experiment 100 times, two times out of 100 he would make a Type I error. Since he is working with a two-choice situation (binomial), the formula $n\text{C}r\ p^r q^{n-r}$ (formula 9.h from Chapter 9) is used to find the probabilities of each class of possible outcomes. Ten rats are to be run in the experiment, and the experimenter decides to give each rat four trials in the T maze. He also decides to analyze only the responses on the fourth trial. Therefore, there are 10 sets of outcomes (events) that are possible. These 10 events are listed on the abscissa in Figure 10.3. Each event consists of a particular number of occurrences of right turns (and left turns). Under the null hypothesis $p(\text{R}) = p(\text{L}) = \frac{1}{2}$. The total number of possible outcomes is illustrated in Figure 10.3 as a bar graph of a frequency distribution.

Significant Results

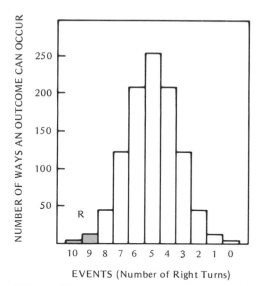

Fig. 10.3. A bar graph of the possible events (responses) to an arm of a T maze by 10 rats. The one-tailed region of rejection (R) is illustrated by dark areas in the left tail of the distribution. R is the region for $\alpha = 0.02$.

The next step is to find the subset that corresponds to the one-tailed area of rejection as defined by alpha. The probability of 10 right turns is $p^{10} = (\frac{1}{2})^{10} = \frac{1}{1024} \approx 0.001$. The probability of 9R is $10p^9q^1 = 10(\frac{1}{2})^9(\frac{1}{2}) = \frac{10}{1024} \approx 0.01$. The probability of 8R is $45p^8q^2 = 45(\frac{1}{2})^8(\frac{1}{2})^2 = \frac{45}{1024} \approx 0.04$. The first probability represents 10 right turns, the second represents nine right turns and one left, and the third represents eight right turns and two left turns. By the *addition rule* (Chapter 9), the probability of either 10R turns, 9R turns, or 8R turns $[p(10R \cup 9R \cup 8R)]$ is equal to the sum of the separate probabilities of the component events. Thus, $p(10R \cup 9R \cup 8R) \approx 0.051$.

The level of significance was set at 0.02. The probability of 10R and 9R or 8R is greater than 0.02. However, the probability of 10R or 9R is less than 0.02 $[p(10R \cup 9R) \approx 0.001 + 0.01 \approx 0.011]$. Therefore, *before the data are collected,* the experimenter knows that at least nine of the animals will have to go to the right before he can reject H_0. If 9 or 10 rats make right turns on the fourth trial, then the experimenter can reject H_0 with a probability of less than 0.02 of making a Type I error.

The experimenter has not taken into account the possibility that the rats might go to the left significantly more than to the right. Several variables might account for this behavior; for example, the rats may not like the food and may wish to avoid it. If the experimenter is interested in finding out whether the rat goes to one side significantly more than chance, but does not care which side, then his experimental hypothesis is nondirectional and a two-tailed test is used as illustrated in Figure 10.4.

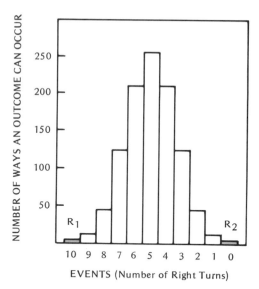

Fig. 10.4. A bar graph of the possible events (responses) to an arm of a T maze by 10 rats. The two-tailed regions of rejection (R_1 and R_2) are denoted by dark areas in both tails of the distribution. R_1 and R_2 are the regions for $\alpha = 0.02$.

The level of significance is still set at 0.02, but, in the two-tailed test, the total probability is split between the two tails of the distribution (Figure 10.4) so that $p(R_1) = p(R_2) = 0.01$. In this case, the area of rejection includes only the outcome 10 right, zero left, with an approximate probability of 0.001, and 10 left, zero right, with $p \approx 0.001$. These probabilities sum, by the addition rule, to 0.002, which is less than 0.02. However, in order to make the probability of the region of rejection close to the value of α, a randomly selected portion of the events (L9R) and (R9L) would have to be included in the region of rejection. Since such a procedure is complicated and potentially subject to charges of nonrandom selection or inadequate control of potential bias, most experimenters prefer to use those events with an associated probability close to but less than α as the definers of the region of rejection. In the present example, only the events (10R) and (10L) define the region of rejection. Thus, it makes a difference whether the experimenter uses a one-tailed or two-tailed test, since his decision in the two-tailed case would be that neither (R9L) nor (L9R) is a significant event. In general, two-tailed tests should be used unless one has strong reasons for predicting the direction of the results.

Returning to the example of the student studying children's conservation of number, the null hypothesis is that 50 percent or more of the responses will be "correct" responses. The experimental hypothesis is that less than 50 percent of the responses will be "correct." The sample size is so small (8) that seven or eight (87.5 to 100 percent) of the children must fail to give the "right" answer before the student can decide that the experimental hypothesis is correct (with $\alpha = .05$). Even if in "reality," 70 percent of all four-year-old children do not have the concept, more than 70 percent of the sample must demonstrate failure to answer correctly. That is, the probability of a Type II error is large when the sample size is small.

The binomial test is not the only method by which hypotheses are tested; however, it lays the groundwork for the next method and for the other tests described in Section Two, Units D1–D6.

ANALYSIS OF VARIANCE OF DEPENDENT MEASURES

The preceding examples have involved binomial data (nominal level of measurement, Chapter 8). However, much research data is measured at the interval level and the greater amount of information in an interval scale is used to test hypotheses. The inferential analytical technique most commonly used with interval-level data is the analysis-of-variance technique. The remainder of the chapter presents the logic of analysis of variance. An intuitive, arithmetic and pictorial approach to the logic is used in this chapter[1] while the more traditional algebraic approach is used in Unit D5 of Section Two. Regardless of the specific research design, the analytical model of the analysis of variance is constant; however, the specific details of the procedure depend on the type of research design. The following sections illustrate the analysis-of-variance procedures with four designs (multilevel, randomized blocks, factorial, and split-plot), and the same four designs are covered in Unit D5.

Multilevel Design

A study of the effects of observing models on the cooperative behavior of nursery-school children illustrates the procedure of hypothesis testing with a multiple treatment design. If children observe other children (models) taking turns at winning a simple guessing game (cooperating), they should be more likely to cooperate when they play the game. If they observe models competing, then they should be more likely to compete. To test this general modeling or imitation hypothesis, a three-group design is used with six children in each group. One group (A1) plays the game after watching the models compete; a second group (A2) plays the game without previously watching models; and a third group (A3) plays the game after watching the models cooperate. The dependent variable is the number of trials (out of 15) on which the subjects cooperate. The dependent variable measures (the data) form a ratio scale (Chapter 8). The raw data are presented in Table 10.2. The research design in this portion of the example is a *multilevel design* (Chapter 5) with 18 girls randomly assigned in groups of six to three groups. (The design of the example will be modified in subsequent sections; however, the raw data will remain the same in order to facilitate understanding of the analytic procedure.)

We are concerned with determining if the data support the modeling hypoth-

---

[1] The basis of this approach is derived from Sutcliffe (1957) and personal communication with Michael Seven (1964).

TABLE 10.2 Raw Data Modeling Experiment: Multilevel (Three-Group) Design.[a]

A1 (Competitive)	A2 (Control)	A3 (Cooperative)	Σ Y	$\overline{Y}$
GROUPS				
3	8	7	18	6
6	8	10	24	8
6	11	10	27	9
5	6	10	21	7
7	7	10	24	8
9	8	13	30	10
$\Sigma Y = 36$	48	60	144	
$\overline{Y} = 6$	8	10	Grand Mean = 8	
A_i effect: $6 - 8 = -2$	$8 - 8 = 0$	$10 - 8 = +2$		

[a] Dependent Variable is the Number of Cooperative Responses.

esis. The experimental hypothesis is that the mean cooperative response frequency for the cooperative group (A3) should be greater than the mean of the control group (A2) and the mean of the control group in turn should be greater than the mean of the competitive group (A1). Symbolically, H_1 is $\overline{Y}_3 > \overline{Y}_2 > \overline{Y}_1$. The null hypothesis is that the means should not be ranked as predicted by the experimental hypothesis (H_0 is $\overline{Y}_3 = \overline{Y}_2 = \overline{Y}_1$. The probability of a Type I error (level of significance) is set at 0.05 ($\alpha = 0.05$).

It is assumed that the children would all have behaved like the control group (within limits of error) if they had been tested *prior to* watching the models. In other words, it is expected that there was no consistent *between-groups variance* at the time of and as a result of the random assignment to the three groups (Chapter 3). Because of random error due to several possible sources including individual differences, there is variance in the scores within each of the three groups and the *within-group variance* was expected to be similar for the three groups because of the random assignment procedure. Another way of stating the experimental hypothesis is to say that after observing the models, the between-groups variance will be greatly increased while the within-group variance remains relatively stable. The null hypothesis in these terms is that the between-groups variance will remain unchanged by the experimental treatment. (H_0 is that before treatment, between-groups variance will be about zero and both between- and within-group variance will be unaffected by the treatment.)

The grand mean of the data is eight ($\overline{Y} = 8$). The **grand mean** is calculated by adding all the scores together (144) and dividing by the number of scores (18), that is, $144 \div 18 = 8$. The grand mean is the average response of all 18 children. The grand mean provides an anchor about which the three-group means vary (between-groups variance). As indicated in Table 10.2, the grand mean is calculated and then subtracted from each of the modeling group means in order to determine the effect of each treatment level on the average performance of each group. For the competitive group (A1) the grand mean was subtracted from the group mean ($6 - 8 = -2$). The value of -2 indicates that the average effect of competitive models was to decrease cooperative response frequency by two responses. Similarly, for the cooperative models group (A3) the value of +2 (10 − 8 = 2) indicates that watching the cooperative models increased the cooperative response frequency by two responses on the average.

A basic model for analyzing the raw data is that each subject's score contains several components added together. Each measure is assumed to be composed of the grand mean, the effect of the particular level of the independent variable (treatment group), and random error. Symbolically,

$$Y = (\bar{Y}) + (A_i) + (\text{error}) \tag{10.a}$$

where Y stands for any score, $\bar{Y}$ is the grand mean, and A_i refers to the effect of the treatment level from which the score is taken. The value of $\bar{Y}$ is the same for every score ($\bar{Y} = 8$) and the values of A_i were determined by substracting $\bar{Y}$ from each of the three group means (−2, 0, +2). The values of (error) are determined by subtracting the values of $\bar{Y}$ and A_i from each Y. These calculations are illustrated in the middle column of Table 10.3.

TABLE 10.3. Determination of Values of Score Components: Multilevel (Three-Group) Design.

A_1	$(Y - \bar{Y})^2$	$(Y - \bar{Y}) = y = A_i + (\text{error})$	$A_i{}^2$	$(\text{error})^2$
	25	$3 - 8 = -5 = (-2) + (-3)$	4	9
	4	$6 - 8 = -2 = (-2) + (0)$	4	0
	4	$6 - 8 = -2 = (-2) + (0)$	4	0
	9	$5 - 8 = -3 = (-2) + (-1)$	4	1
	1	$7 - 8 = -1 = (-2) + (+1)$	4	1
	1	$9 + 8 = +1 = (-2) + (+3)$	4	9
	$\Sigma = 44$	$-12 = -12 + 0$	24 +	20 = 44
A_2	$(Y - \bar{Y})^2$	$Y - \bar{Y} = y = A_i + (\text{error})$	$A_i{}^2$	$(\text{error})^2$
	0	$8 - 8 = 0 = (0) + (0)$	0	0
	0	$8 - 8 = 0 = (0) + (0)$	0	0
	9	$11 - 8 = +3 = (0) + (+3)$	0	9
	4	$6 - 8 = -2 = (0) + (-2)$	0	4
	1	$7 - 8 = -1 = (0) + (-1)$	0	1
	0	$8 - 8 = 0 = (0) + (0)$	0	0
	$\Sigma = 14$	$0 = 0 + 0$	0 +	14 = 14
A_3	$(Y - \bar{Y})^2$	$Y - \bar{Y} = y = A_i + (\text{error})$	$A_i{}^2$	$(\text{error})^2$
	1	$7 - 8 = -1 = (+2) + (-3)$	4	9
	4	$10 - 8 = +2 = (+2) + (0)$	4	0
	4	$10 - 8 = +2 = (+2) + (0)$	4	0
	4	$10 - 8 = +2 = (+2) + (0)$	4	0
	4	$10 - 8 = +2 = (+2) + (0)$	4	0
	25	$13 - 8 = +5 = (+2) + (+3)$	4	9
	$\Sigma = 42$	$12 = 12 + 0$	24 +	18 = 42
	$\Sigma\Sigma = 44 + 14 + 42 = 100$		$\Sigma = 48$ +	52 = 100

The term "analysis of variance" indicates that we are attending to the variation in scores about a mean. Subtracting the mean from each score yields a deviation score (denoted by the lower-case y in Table 10.3). Since the calculation of the mean establishes the arithmetic midpoint of a distribution of scores, it follows that the sum of all of the positive deviations from the mean would exactly cancel the sum of the negative deviations from the mean. Examination of Table 10.3 shows that the −12 deviation sum for Group A_1 is exactly offset by the +12 deviation sum for Group A_3. Similarly, the sum of all of the error deviations *within* each group is zero. (The sums of the *squared* deviation scores are not equal to zero.)

In Table 10.3 each score is analyzed into its component parts. The same analysis is illustrated pictorially in Figure 10.5. Each block in the stacks of blocks in the figure represents a cooperative response. The sequence of drawings illustrates the progression from a homogeneous group of children who all get the same score ($\overline{Y} = 8$ responses) to the inhomogeneity produced by adding random error (within-group variance), to the further inhomogeneity produced by adding the specific treatment effect to each score (between-groups variance). The blocks are shaded to show how each source of variation causes a shift of the available blocks, *not* the adding or subtracting of blocks from the total. This illustrates the previously discussed point that the sum of deviations from the mean is zero. The final variability in scores is that observed originally in the raw data. The means of the groups are ordered as predicted. The problem is to decide if the between-groups variance is so large, relative to the within-group variance (due to random error), that we can

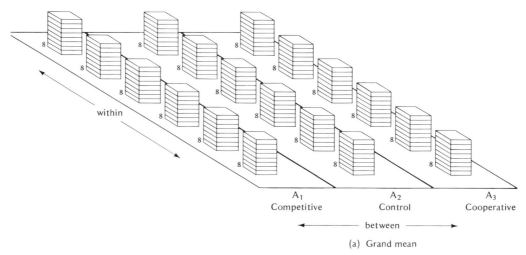

(a) Grand mean

Fig. 10.5. Physical depiction of additive model of analysis of variance for three-group multilevel design. Drawing *(a)* represents the 18 subjects with no effect of the treatment or of error — all subjects make eight (grand mean) cooperative responses. Drawing *(b)* represents the 18 subjects after the effect of random error is added to their response measure. Drawing *(c)* represents the 18 subjects after the effect of the treatment (modeling group) is added to their dependent scores — at this point the raw data of the experiment emerges.

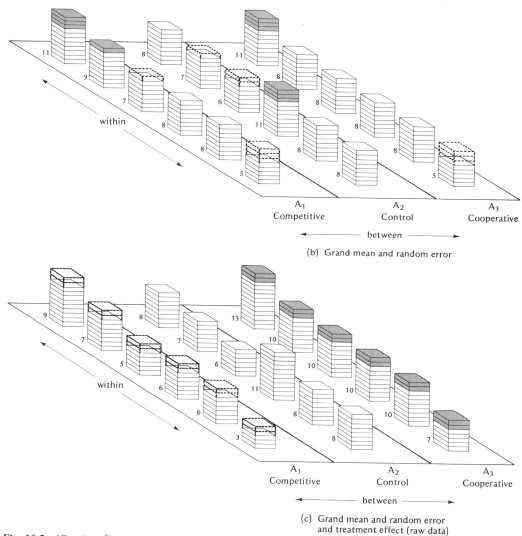

(b) Grand mean and random error

(c) Grand mean and random error
and treatment effect (raw data)

Fig. 10.5 (Continued)

conclude that the decrease of −2 and the increase of +2 responses are not due to chance, random error factors. In terms of Figure 10.5, we need to compare the number of blocks moved because of the between-groups modeling effect with the number of blocks moved because of chance (random error).

If we calculate a value for the between-groups variance and average within-group variances, we can numerically compare the two variances. The most frequently used descriptive measure of variability (Chapter 8) is the sample variance. The sample variance is the average squared deviation from the sample mean. In Table

10.3, we have calculated the values for the treatment effect (A_i, between-groups variance) and error (within-group variance) for each Y score. These values are individually squared [columns labeled $A_i{}^2$ and (error)^2] and added to yield a sum of 52 for Σ (error)^2 and 48 for Σ $(A_i)^2$. Note that the sum of the squared deviations of the Y scores about their mean is equal to 100, and 52 + 48 equals 100 so that the sum of the component parts equals the whole.

The numbers 52 and 48 represent the *sums* of the squared deviations due to each factor, while we are interested in learning the average or typical squared deviations. To find the average (mean) squared deviation we have to divide each sum by the number of deviation scores contributing to it (Chapter 8). In order to accomplish this, we must first introduce the concept of degrees of freedom. Degrees of freedom can be described as the number of scores that are free to vary. For example, if you flipped a coin 15 times and had obtained 8 heads, you know automatically that there were also 7 tails. Similarly, if you know that the total number of spots appearing on four rolls of a die was 18, and the first three tosses were 3, 5, and 6, you can also determine the number that had to appear on the fourth toss. The last number must make up the difference between the three known scores (14) and the total (18). In other words, because you know the total, the last score is "fixed" or is not free to vary. In this situation, we had three degrees of freedom (*df*). Usually, the number of *df* equals one less than the number of scores.

Degrees of Freedom

Now examine the data in the example. Since we know that the mean is 8 and that there are 18 raw scores, we also know that the sum of all the scores must equal 144 (18 × 8). This means that once 17 of the scores are given, the 18th score must make up the difference between 144 and the sum of the seventeen. Thus, the total *df* in the example is 17, (18 − 1).

The between-groups variance represents the average squared deviation of the group means around the grand mean. In our example, one group (A3) had an average deviation score of two additional responses, and a second group (A2) had an average of zero deviations from the mean. With this information we know that the third group (A1) has to have a −2 value to meet the requirement that the sum of the deviations is zero. Thus, the between-groups $df = 3 − 1 = 2$. The within-group variance represents the average squared deviation of individual scores from their group means. Since there are six subjects in each group, the *df* for each group is five. Since there are three groups, the within-group $df = 3(6 − 1) = 15$. As is the case with the component sums of squared deviations, the degrees of freedom must add up. Thus, the between *df* (2) plus the within *df* (15) equals the total *df* (17).

The concept of degrees of freedom is used in obtaining good estimates of population parameters. When sample variances are calculated according to the procedure described in Chapter 8, the value obtained is almost always smaller than the population variance. Any sample is not likely to include enough of the population's unusual or extreme scores that are needed to provide a good estimate of the population variance. That is, all of the sample scores tend to be closer to the mean than all of the population scores, and therefore the sample variance tends to be smaller than the population variance. Since we are concerned with generalizing the results of our study to the population from which the sample of 18 girls was drawn, we need an estimate of both the between-groups and within-group variance that is not biased (is a good estimate). The solution is to divide the sum of squared deviations by df. Thus, we divide 48 by 2 to yield a between-groups variance of 24. The within-group variance for group A_1 is $20 \div (6 - 1) = 20 \div 5 = 4$, A_2 is $14 \div 5 = 2.8$, and A_3 is $18 \div 5 = 3.6$. Under the assumption that each of the three within-group variance values is an estimate of a common population value (because subjects were assigned at random to the three groups), the average of the three within values is calculated $(4 + 2.8 + 3.6)/3 = 3.47$ and the value is assumed to be the *best single value* to estimate the population within-group variance.

The between-groups variance is an estimate of the within-group variance (error), plus the additional variance produced by the treatment. The null hypothesis is that the treatment variance is zero. One way to compare the two variances is to make a ratio of the between to the within. The null hypothesis of no treatment (modeling) effect leads to the prediction that the ratio should be close to 1.00 because the two estimates are both estimates of the common within-group variance. The experimental hypothesis leads to the prediction that the between-groups variance should be large relative to the within-group variance since the between-groups estimate is magnified by the treatment. Therefore, the ratio of between to within should be larger than 1.00 if H_1 is correct. R. A. Fisher developed the preceding argument and the associated mathematical theory. He developed a method of determining the probability of various values of the between/within ratio (the F ratio, subsequently named in honor of Fisher). Some values of F and their associated probabilities are listed in Section Two, Unit D5. The value of the F ratio in this example is $24 \div 3.47 = 6.92$. The probability of observing a ratio equal to or greater than 6.92 under the null hypothesis is less than 0.05 (α). Figure 10.6 illustrates how to locate the critical values of F. In the present example the critical value is 3.68; the probability of observing an F value equal to or greater than 3.68 with 2 and 15 df is equal to or less than 0.05. The obtained value of 6.92 exceeds the critical value of 3.68; therefore, under the null hypothesis the probability of obtaining the value of 6.92 by chance is less than 0.05. We can therefore conclude that observing the models did have a nonchance effect on the children's subsequent cooperative behavior. The experimental hypothesis was supported.

The results of the analysis of variance are usually summarized in tabular form (Table 10.4).

TABLE 10.4. Multilevel Design: Summary of Analysis of Variance.

Source of Variation	S.S.	df	Mean Square	F	P
Between (modeling)	48	2	24.00	6.92	<0.05
Within (error)	52	15	3.47		
Total	100	17			

In Table 10.4, *S.S.* stands for the *sum* of *squared* deviations, *df* stands for degrees of *freedom*, mean square stands for the average (*mean*) squared deviation (variance estimate), and *p* stands for *probability*.

Critical Values of $\alpha = 0.05$ of the F Ratio for Specified Values of Numerator $df(df_n)$ and Denominator $df(df_d)$

df_d \ df_n	1	2	3	4	5	6	7	8	9	10	12	15	
1	161.4	199.5	215.7	224.6	230 2	234 0	236.8	238.9	240.5	241.9	243.9	245.9	248.0
2	18.51	19.00	19.16	19.25	19.30	19.33	19.35	19.37	19.38	19.40	19.41	19.43	19.4
3	10.13	9.55	9.28	9.12	9.01	8.94	8.89	8.85	8.81	8.79	8.74	8.70	
4	7.71	6.94	6.59	6.39	6.26	6.16	6.09	6.04	6.00	5.96	5.91	5.86	
5	6.61	5.79	5.41	5.19	5.05	4.95	4.88	4.82	4.77	4.74	4.68	4	
6	5.99	5.14	4.76	4.53	4.39	4.28	4.21	4.15	4.10	4.06	4.00		
7	5.59	4.74	4.35	4.12	3.97	3.87	3.79	3.73	3.68	3.64	3.5?		
8	5.32	4.46	4.07	3.84	3.69	3.58	3.50	3.44	3.39	3.35			
9	5.12	4.26	3.86	3.63	3.48	3.37	3.29	3.23	3.18	3.14			
10	4.96	4.10	3.71	3.48	3.33	3.22	3.14	3.07	3.02				
11	4.84	3.98	3.59	3.36	3.20	3.09	3.01	2.95					
12	4.75	3.89	3.49	3.26	3.11	3.00	2.91	2.85					
13	4.67	3.81	3.41	3.18	3.03	2.92	2.83	2.?					
14	4.60	3.74	3.34	3.11	2.96	2.85	2.76						
15	4.54	3.68	3.29	3.06	2.90	2.79							
16	4.49	3.63	3.24	3.01	2.85	2.74							
17	4.45	3.59	3.20	2.96	2.81	2.?							
18	4.41	3.55	3.16	2.93	2.77								
19	4.38	3.52	3.13	2.90									
20	4.35	3.49	3.10	2.87									
21	4.32	3.47	3.07										
22	4.30	3.44	3.05										
23	4.28	3.42	3.03										
24	4.26	3.40	3.										
25	4.24	3.39											
26	4.23	3.3?											
27	4.21												
28	4.20												
29	4.1?												
30													
40													

Fig. 10.6. An illustration of how to use an F table. In the example the numerator (between-groups variance) df were 2 and the denominator (within-group variance) df were 15. Thus the critical value at $\alpha = 0.05$ is located in the table.

Randomized-Blocks Design

If each subject experiences all levels of the independent variable, then the research design is a *repeated measures* design (Chapter 5), that is a particular form of *randomized-blocks* design. (See Chapters 4 and 5.) In the study of the effects of models on cooperative behavior, each child could play the game under each of the three modeling conditions. Each child would have to start with the A_2 condition (no model) then would proceed to the randomly selected A_1 (competitive) or A_3 (cooperative) condition and finish with the remaining condition. For the purpose of the example, the raw data remain the same. Table 10.2 is now perceived with the understanding that the first row represents the three scores of *one* child under the three conditions (3, 8, 7); the remaining five rows of data points represent the scores of five more children so that now there are a total of six children in the study instead of 18. The experimental hypothesis, null hypothesis, and level of significance remain the same.

The structural model for the multilevel, randomized-groups design was that $Y = (\overline{Y}) + (A_i) + (\text{error})$. The structural model for the randomized blocks design is that $Y = (\overline{Y}) + (A_i) + (S_k) + (\text{error})$, where S_k refers to the effect of each subject averaged across the three conditions. That is, each dependent measure is composed of the sum of the grand mean, the effect of the treatment level, the effect of individual differences (differences between the six children's response tendencies), and random error. The values of $\overline{Y}$ and A_i are the same as in the preceding section ($\overline{Y} = 8$; $A_1 = -2$, $A_2 = 0$, $A_3 = +2$). The values of S_k are determined by subtracting $\overline{Y}$ from each of the six subjects' means located in the rightmost column of Table 10.2 (-2, 0, $+1$, -1, 0, $+2$). The values of (error) are determined by subtracting $\overline{Y}$, A_i, and S_k from each Y score. The inclusion of S_k in the model means that the values of (error) calculated for this design differ from the previous values of (error). These calculations are illustrated in the middle section of Table 10.5.

TABLE 10.5. Determination of Values of Score Components in Randomized-Blocks Design (Three Levels of Treatment and Six Blocks).

S_1	$(Y - \overline{Y})^2$	$(Y - \overline{Y}) = y = A_i + S_k + (error)$	A_i^2	S_k^2	$(error)^2$
	25	$3 - 8 = -5 = (-2) + (-2) + (-1)$	4	4	1
	0	$8 - 8 = 0 = (0) + (-2) + (+2)$	0	4	4
	1	$7 - 8 = -1 = (+2) + (-2) + (-1)$	4	4	1
	$\Sigma = 26$	$-6 = 0 + -6 + 0$	$8 +$	$12 +$	$6 = 26$

S_2	$(Y - \overline{Y})^2$	$(Y - \overline{Y}) = y = A_i + S_k + (error)$	A_i^2	S_k^2	$(error)^2$
	4	$6 - 8 = -2 = (-2) + (0) + (0)$	4	0	0
	0	$8 - 8 = 0 = (0) + (0) + (0)$	0	0	0
	4	$10 - 8 = +2 = (+2) + (0) + (0)$	4	0	0
	$\Sigma = 8$	$0 = 0 + 0 + 0$	$8 +$	$0 +$	$0 = 8$

S_3	$(Y - \overline{Y})^2$	$(Y - \overline{Y}) = y = A_i + S_k + (error)$	A_i^2	S_k^2	$(error)^2$
	4	$6 - 8 = -2 = (-2) + (+1) + (-1)$	4	1	1
	9	$11 - 8 = +3 = (0) + (+1) + (+2)$	0	1	4
	4	$10 - 8 = +2 = (+2) + (+1) + (-1)$	4	1	1
	$\Sigma = 17$	$3 = 0 + 3 + 0$	$8 +$	$3 +$	$6 = 17$

S_4	$(Y - \overline{Y})^2$	$(Y - \overline{Y}) = y = A_i + S_k + (error)$	A_i^2	S_k^2	$(error)^2$
	9	$5 - 8 = -3 = (-2) + (-1) + (0)$	4	1	0
	4	$6 - 8 = -2 = (0) + (-1) + (-1)$	0	1	1
	4	$10 - 8 = +2 = (+2) + (-1) + (+1)$	4	1	1
	$\Sigma = 17$	$-3 = 0 + -3 + 0$	$8 +$	$3 +$	$2 = 13$

S_5	$(Y - \overline{Y})^2$	$(Y - \overline{Y}) = y = A_i + S_k + (error)$	A_i^2	S_k^2	$(error)^2$
	1	$7 - 8 = -1 = (-2) + (0) + (+1)$	4	0	1
	1	$7 - 8 = -1 = (0) + (0) + (-1)$	0	0	1
	4	$10 - 8 = +2 = (+2) + (0) + (0)$	4	0	0
	$\Sigma = 6$	$0 = 0 + 0 + 0$	$8 +$	$0 +$	$2 = 10$

S_6	$(Y - \overline{Y})^2$	$(Y - \overline{Y}) = y = A_i + S_k + (error)$	A_i^2	S_k^2	$(error)^2$
	1	$9 - 8 = +1 = (-2) + (+2) + (+1)$	4	4	1
	0	$8 - 8 = 0 = (0) + (+2) + (-2)$	0	4	4
	25	$13 - 8 = +5 = (+2) + (+2) + (+1)$	4	4	1
	$\Sigma = 26$	$6 = 0 + 6 + 0$	$8 +$	$12 +$	$6 = 26$

$$\Sigma\Sigma = 26 + 8 + 17 + 17 + 6 + 26 = 100 \qquad \Sigma\Sigma = 48 + 30 + 22 = 100$$

In Table 10.5 each score is analyzed into its four component parts. As before, the pictorial analysis in Figure 10.7 involves the use of a block as a symbol for one cooperative response. The drawing sequence progresses from a homogeneous group of $\bar{Y} = 8$ scores to the introduction of random error (within-group variance), to the introduction of individual differences (between-blocks variance), to the introduction

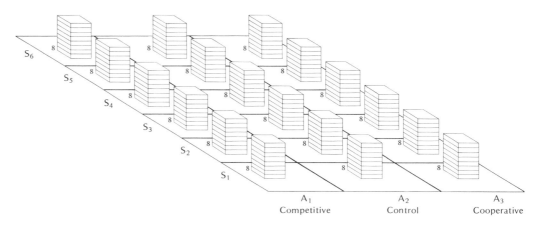

(a) Grand mean

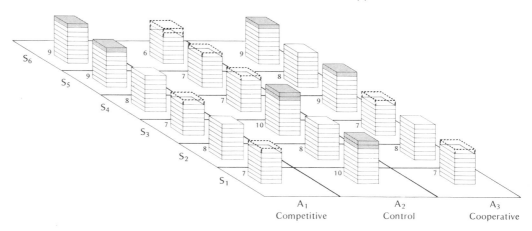

(b) Grand mean and random error

Fig. 10.7. Physical depiction of additive model of analysis of variance for randomized-block design. Drawing *(a)* represents the 6 subjects with no effect of the treatment or of error—all subjects make eight (grand mean) cooperative responses under each of three conditions. Drawing *(b)* represents the 6 sets of three scores after the effect of random error is added to each response measure. Drawing *(c)* represents the 18 scores after the blocks effect (repeated measures—subjects effect) is added to the response measure. Drawing *(d)* represents the 18 scores after the effect of the treatment (modeling group) is added to the dependent scores—at this point the raw data of the experiment emerges. (The dotted lines indicate response blocks lost and the shaded blocks indicate those added to each stack.)

of the treatment effect (between-groups variance). The final drawing is the original raw data.

In Table 10.5, the sum of squared values of the treatment effect (A_i^2) is 48; the sum of squared values of the blocks effect (S_k^2) is 30; and the sum of the squared values of the random error is 22. The df for the total variance and treatment variance were previously determined to be $18 - 1 = 17$ and $3 - 1 = 2$, respectively. The df for the blocks variance is $6 - 1 = 5$ since there are six blocks (six subjects).

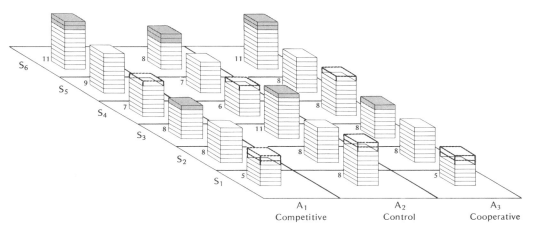

(c) Grand mean and random error
and blocks (subjects) effect

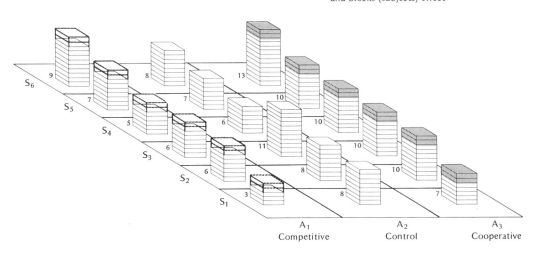

(d) Grand mean and random error
and blocks (subjects) effect
and treatment effect (raw data)

Fig. 10.7 (Continued)

The between-groups variance estimate is $48 \div 2 = 24$ as in the first example. The blocks variance estimate is $30 \div (6 - 1) = 6$. The variance due to random error is the variance remaining after the effects of the blocks and modeling treatment variables have been removed from the deviation y scores.

The df for the random error variance estimate is the number of df remaining after the df for the other two estimates have been removed from the total df available. The total $df = 17$, treatment $df = 2$, and blocks $df = 5$; therefore, the error $df = 17 - 2 - 5 = 10$. (There are 2 df for each of five of the six blocks.)

The procedure of determining the values of error in Table 10.5 is based on the variability in the ten scores that are free to vary, since the sum over all 18 scores of the A_i values, the S_k values, and the (error) values must all equal zero. Therefore, the estimate of the variance due to random error is calcuated by dividing the sum of squared (error) scores by df to yield $22 \div 10 = 2.2$.

The value of the F ratio from the modeling effect is now $24 \div 2.2 = 10.91$. Table 10.6 summarizes the analysis. The extra control included in the randomized-blocks design relative to the randomized multilevel design produced a smaller variance due to uncontrolled error sources and thus a larger F ratio. According to the table in Figure 10.6, the critical value is 4.10. The probability of obtaining an F ratio equal to or greater than 10.91 with 2 and 10 df is less than 0.05 (α). Again, we can conclude that observing the models did have a real effect on the girls' subsequent cooperative behavior. The experimental hypothesis was supported.

TABLE 10.6. Randomized Blocks Design: Summary of Analysis of Variance.

Source of Variation	S.S.	df	Mean Square	F	p
Treatment (modeling)	48	2	24.0	10.91	<.05
Blocks (subjects)	30	5	6.0		
Within (error)	22	10	2.2		
Total	100	17			

Factorial Design

If the multilevel design described in Table 10.2 is used with the addition of children of both sexes, and if the design is organized as in Table 10.7, the resulting design is a factorial design. There are two levels of the sex variable and three levels of the modeling variable and all possible combinations of the levels of sex and modeling exist as structural components of the design.

The raw data remain the same as in Table 10.2. The only design difference from the multilevel design is that the first three subjects in each modeling group column of Table 10.7 are boys and the last three are girls. The modeling experimental hypothesis, null hypothesis, and level of significance remain the same.

No large difference between the average response of the two sexes is expected. An interaction between sex and modeling conditions is also not predicted to occur. In such cases, the experimenter includes the variable (sex) as an independent variable in order to control for its possible effect on the scores and to increase the range of generalization of the modeling effect from girls to both sexes (provided that the same results occur for both sexes). The research is "exploratory" research with regard to the sex variable and the modeling by sex interaction. The data analysis will involve the examination of the sex effect and the interaction effect. Therefore, the experimenter as a matter of statistical formality will test the formal null hypotheses of no mean difference between the sexes and no difference between the average response of each sex as a function of the modeling condition (the hypothesis of no real interaction effect) against the alternative hypotheses of any sex effect and any interaction effect. The level of significance will be set at $\alpha = 0.025$ for each test. (The level of significance for the set of two hypotheses involving sex is 0.05, split equally between the two hypotheses.)

The building-blocks, structural model for the factorial design is that $Y = (\bar{Y}) + (A_i) + (B_j) + (AB_{ij}) + (\text{error})$, where B_j refers to the average effect of each sex group and AB_{ij} refers to the effect of the interaction between variables A and B. (See Chapter 5.) Thus, each dependent measure is composed of the sum of the grand mean, the effect of modeling treatment, the effect of sex group, the interaction effect, and random error. The values of $\bar{Y}$ (8) and A_i (-2, 0, $+2$) were determined in the multilevel design section. The values of B_j are determined by subtracting $\bar{Y}$ from each of the two sex group means ($7\frac{2}{3} - 8 = -\frac{1}{3}$, $8\frac{1}{3} - 8 = \frac{1}{3}$). The values of AB_{ij} are determined by subtracting $\bar{Y}$ from the cell means ($\overline{AB}_{ij}$) in Table 10.7, yielding -3, -1, $+1$, -1, $+1$, and $+3$. These AB_{ij} deviation scores are made up of three components: the A_i, B_j and AB_{ij} effects. [The (error) component is

TABLE 10.7. Raw Data of Modeling Experiment: Factorial (2 $\times$ 3) Design.[a]

			*Modeling Groups*					
	A_1 *(competitive)*		A_2 *(control)*		A_3 *(cooperative)*		ΣY	$\Sigma \bar{Y}$	B_j *effect*
	3	$\Sigma = 15$	8	$\Sigma = 27$	7	$\Sigma = 27$			
B_1 *(male)*	6	$\overline{AB}_{11} = 5$	8	$\overline{AB}_{21} = 9$	10	$\overline{AB}_{31} = 9$			
	6	$\overline{AB} - \bar{Y} = -3$	11	$\overline{AB} - \bar{Y} = +1$	10	$\overline{AB} - \bar{Y} = +1$	69	$7\frac{2}{3}$	$-\frac{1}{3}$
	5	$\Sigma = 21$	6	$\Sigma = 21$	10	$\Sigma = 33$			
B_2 *(female)*	7	$\overline{AB}_{12} = 7$	7	$\overline{AB}_{22} = 7$	10	$\overline{AB}_{23} = 11$			
	9	$\overline{AB} - \bar{Y} = -1$	8	$\overline{AB} - \bar{Y} = -1$	13	$\overline{AB} - \bar{Y} = +3$	75	$8\frac{1}{3}$	$+\frac{1}{3}$

[a] Dependent Variable is the Number of Cooperative Responses.

not present because the AB_{ij} cell means are averages of the three scores within each cell and the estimate of the within-cell (error) variance is calculated from the differences within each cell.] In order to find the AB_{ij} interaction effect the effects of B_j and A_i must be removed from each AB_{ij} deviation score. The B_j and A_i effects are subtracted from each AB_{ij} deviation score [for example, $(-3) - (-\frac{1}{3}) - (-2) = -\frac{2}{3}$, and $(+3) - (+\frac{1}{3}) - (+2) = +\frac{2}{3}$]. The resulting values of AB_{ij} for row B_1 are $-\frac{2}{3}$, $+1\frac{1}{3}$, $-\frac{2}{3}$, and for row B_2 are $+\frac{2}{3}$, $-1\frac{1}{3}$, $+\frac{2}{3}$. The values of (error) are determined by subtracting $\bar{Y}$, A_i, B_j, and AB_{ij} from each Y score. The values of (error) differ from the previous two sets of values of (error). These calculations are illustrated in the middle section of Table 10.8.

TABLE 10.8. Determination of Values of Score Components in Factorial Design (Three Levels of A and Two of B).

	$(Y-\bar{Y})^2$	$(Y-\bar{Y}) =$ $y =$ $A_i +$ $B_j +$ $AB_{ij} +(error)$	A_i^2	B_j^2	AB_{ij}^2	$(error)^2$
A_1B_1	25	$3-8 = -5 = (-2) + (-1/3) + (-2/3) + (-2)$	4	1/9	4/9	4
	4	$6-8 = -2 = (-2) + (-1/3) + (-2/3) + (+1)$	4	1/9	4/9	1
	4	$6-8 = -2 = (-2) + (-1/3) + (-2/3) + (+1)$	4	1/9	4/9	1
	$\Sigma = 33$	$-9 = -6 + -1 + -2 + 0$	$12 +$	$1/3 +$	$1\,1/3 +$	$6 = 19\,2/3$
A_1B_2	9	$5-8 = -3 = (-2) + (+1/3) + (+2/3) + (-2)$	4	1/9	4/9	4
	1	$7-8 = -1 = (-2) + (+1/3) + (+2/3) + (0)$	4	1/9	4/9	0
	1	$9-8 = +1 = (-2) + (+1/3) + (+2/3) + (+2)$	4	1/9	4/9	4
	$\Sigma = 11$	$-3 = -6 + +1 + +2 + 0$	$12 +$	$1/3 +$	$1\,1/3 +$	$8 = 21\,2/3$
A_2B_1	0	$8-8 = 0 = (0) + (-1/3) + (+1\,1/3) + (-1)$	0	1/9	16/9	1
	0	$8-8 = 0 = (0) + (-1/3) + (+1\,1/3) + (-1)$	0	1/9	16/9	1
	9	$11-8 = +3 = (0) + (-1/3) + (+1\,1/3) + (+2)$	0	1/9	16/9	4
	$\Sigma = 9$	$+3 = 0 + -1 + +4 + 0$	$0 +$	$1/3 +$	$5\,1/3 +$	$6 = 11\,2/3$
A_2B_2	4	$6-8 = -2 = (0) + (+1/3) + (-1\,1/3) + (-1)$	0	1/9	16/9	1
	1	$7-8 = -1 = (0) + (+1/3) + (-1\,1/3) + (0)$	0	1/9	16/9	0
	0	$8-8 = -0 = (0) + (+1/3) + (-1\,1/3) + (+1)$	0	1/9	16/9	1
	$\Sigma = 5$	$-3 = 0 + +1 + -4 + 0$	$0 +$	$1/3 +$	$5\,1/3 +$	$2 = 7\,2/3$
A_3B_1	1	$7-8 = -1 = (+2) + (-1/3) + (-2/3) + (-2)$	4	1/9	4/9	4
	4	$10-8 = +2 = (+2) + (-1/3) + (-2/3) + (+1)$	4	1/9	4/9	1
	4	$10-8 = +2 = (+2) + (-1/3) + (-2/3) + (+1)$	4	1/9	4/9	1
	$\Sigma = 9$	$3 = +6 + -1 + -2 + 0$	$12 +$	$1/3 +$	$1\,1/3 +$	$6 = 19\,2/3$
A_3B_2	4	$10-8 = +2 = (+2) + (+1/3) + (+2/3) + (-1)$	4	1/9	4/9	1
	4	$10-8 = +2 = (+2) + (+1/3) + (+2/3) + (-1)$	4	1/9	4/9	1
	25	$13-8 = +5 = (+2) + (+1/3) + (+2/3) + (+2)$	4	1/9	4/9	4
	$\Sigma = 33$	$9 = +6 + +1 + +2 + 0$	$12 +$	$1/3 +$	$1\,1/3 +$	$6 = 19\,2/3$
	$\Sigma\Sigma = 33 + 11 + 9 + 5 + 9 + 33 = 100$		$\Sigma = 48 +$	$2 +$	$16 +$	$34 = 100$

In Table 10.8 each score is analyzed into its five component parts. As before, the pictorial analysis in Figure 10.8 involves the use of blocks as a symbol for one cooperative response. The drawing sequence progresses from a homogeneous group of $Y = 8$ scores to the introduction of random error (within-group variance), to the interaction effect (between-groups variance), to the B (sex) effect (between-groups variance) to the A (modeling) effect (between-groups variance). The final drawing is the original raw data. (Note that the pictorial analysis may also be viewed from the bottom, Figure 10.8(e), to the top in sequence. In that case the raw data is pictorially analyzed into component building blocks rather than synthesized from the various components.)

The between-modeling-groups variance estimate is 24, as before. The between-sex-groups variance estimate is $2 \div (2 - 1) = 2$. The between-modeling-and-sex-groups interaction variance estimate is $16 \div (2) = 8$. The df for the sex effect is $2 - 1 = 1$, since there are two values of the sex variable. The df for an interaction effect is the product of the degrees of freedom for each variable involved in the interaction variance estimate. Thus, the *df* for the interaction of sex and modeling is $(2 - 1)(3 - 1) = (1)(2) = 2$. The interaction variance is the variance represented by the variability in the six cell means of the design (for example, $\overline{AB}_{11} = 5$, $\overline{AB}_{21} = 9$, and so on) with the A_i and B_j effects removed.

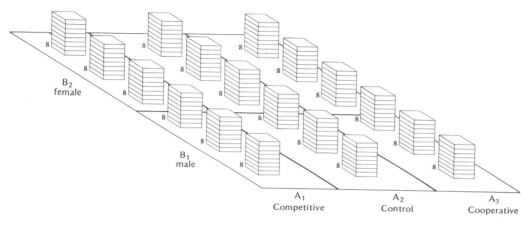

(a) Grand mean

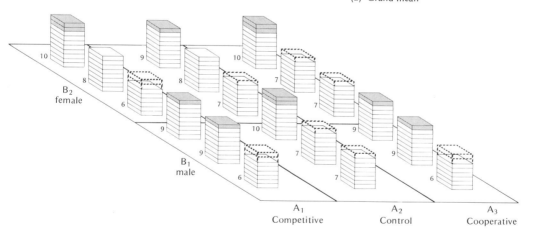

(b) Grand mean and random error

Fig. 10.8. Physical depiction of additive model of analysis of variance for factorial design with two levels of variable B and three levels of variable A. Drawing (a) represents the 18 subjects with no effect of the treatment or of error—all subjects make eight (grand mean) cooperative responses. Drawing (b) represents the 18 subjects after the effect of random error is added to their response measure. Drawing (c) represents the 18 subjects after the interaction effect ($A \times B$) is added to the response measure. Drawing (d) represents the 18 subjects after the effect of variable B (sex) is added to the scores. Drawing (e) represents the 18 subjects after the effect of variable A (modeling) is added to the scores—at this point the raw data of the experiment emerges. (Fig. 10.8 continues on pp. 176–177.)

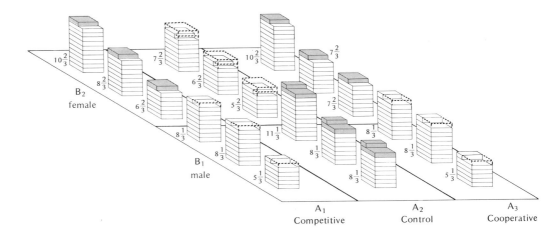

(c) Grand mean and random error
and interaction (A × B) effect

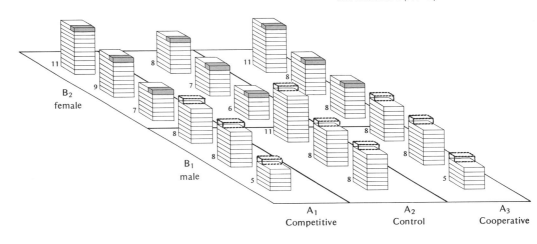

(d) Grand mean and random error
and interaction effect and
B (sex) effect

Fig. 10.8 (Continued)

The average within-groups variance can be calculated by averaging the values of the sum of squared AB_{ij} scores divided by the number of scores in each cell minus one $(3 - 1 = 2)$. The average within-groups variance may also be calculated by summing the squared AB_{ij} scores to get a sum of 34 and then dividing that sum by $6(3 - 1) = 12$ $(df = 12)$ to yield $34 \div 12 = 2.83$. [The value of six occurs because there are six cells of three scores each in the design and there are 2 df for the within (error) estimate in each cell.]

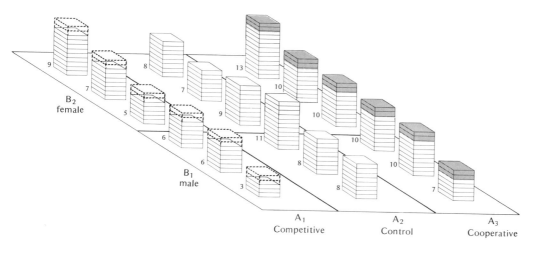

(e) Grand mean and random error
and interaction effect and B(sex)
effect and A(modeling) effect

Fig. 10.8 (Continued)

The F ratio for the modeling variable is $24 \div 2.83 = 8.48$; the F ratio for the sex effect is $2 \div 2.83 < 1.00$; the F ratio for the interaction effect was $8 \div 2.83 = 2.83$. Using the table in Figure 10.6; the probability of obtaining an F ratio equal to or greater than 8.48 with 2 and 12 df is less than α (.05). Using Table D.5.7 in Unit D5, the probability of obtaining an F ratio less than 1.00 with 1 and 12 df is much greater than 0.025. The probability of obtaining an F ratio of 2.83 or larger with 2 and 12 df is greater than α (0.025). These results are summarized in Table 10.9.

TABLE 10.9. Factorial Design: Summary of Analysis of Variance.

Source of Variation	S.S.	df	Mean Square	F	p
Treatment A (modeling)	48	2	24.00	8.48	<.05
Treatment B (sex)	2	1	2.00	—[a]	
Interaction A × B	16	2	8.00	2.83	
Within Cells (error)	34	12	2.83		
Total	100	17			

[a] Values of F less than 1.00 are indicated by a dash line.

We can therefore conclude that observing models did have a real effect on the cooperative behavior of boys and girls. The nonsignificant B (sex) effect means that there was little mean difference between boys and girls in terms of frequency of cooperative behavior. The nonsignificant A × B interaction effect means that the effects of the three modeling conditions were almost the same for both sexes, with some differences due to random error. Again, the use of a design controlling one more variable, increases the F ratio for the modeling effect because of the decrease in the average within-cell variance. We conclude that observing a model's behavior had a real effect on the cooperative behavior of both boys and girls and there was no real sex effect or interaction between sex and treatment. The experimental hypothesis was supported and shown to generalize to both sexes.

Factorial Design with Repeated Measures

If the factorial design described in Table 10.7 is used with the addition that only six children are used (three boys and three girls), with each child experiencing each level of the modeling variable, the design is a factorial design with repeated measures (sometimes called a "split-plot" design). The design is a combination of the randomized-blocks design and the factorial design. (See Chapter 5.)

The raw data remain the same. Table 10.7 is now perceived with the understanding that the first row represents the three scores of one boy under the three modeling conditions $(3, 8, 7)$ and the fourth row represents the three scores of one girl under the three conditions $(5, 6, 10)$. The modeling experimental hypothesis, null hypothesis, and level of significance remain the same. As in the case of the factorial design, the null hypotheses for the sex and sex-by-modeling interaction effects are that there will be no such effects and the level of significance will be 0.025 for each hypothesis.

TABLE 10.10. Determination of Values of Score Components in Factorial Design with Repeated Measures (Two Levels of B and Three Levels of Repeated Measure A).

	$(Y - \bar{Y}) = y =$	$A_i +$	$B_j +$	$S_k +$	$AB_{ij} +$	$(error)$	S_k^2	$(error)^2$
$A_1B_1\ \{S_1$	$3 - 8 = -5 =$	$(-2) +$	$(-1/3) +$	$(-1\frac{2}{3}) +$	$(-2/3) +$	$(-1/3)$	$25/9$	$1/9$
$\{S_2$	$6 - 8 = -2 =$	$(-2) +$	$(-1/3) +$	$(+1/3) +$	$(-2/3) +$	$(+2/3)$	$1/9$	$4/9$
$\{S_3$	$6 - 8 = -2 =$	$(-2) +$	$(-1/3) +$	$(+1\frac{1}{3}) +$	$(-2/3) +$	$(-1/3)$	$16/9$	$1/9$
$A_1B_2\ \{S_4$	$5 - 8 = -3 =$	$(-2) +$	$(+1/3) +$	$(-1\frac{1}{3}) +$	$(+2/3) +$	$(-2/3)$	$16/9$	$4/9$
$\{S_5$	$7 - 8 = -1 =$	$(-2) +$	$(+1/3) +$	$(-1/3) +$	$(+2/3) +$	$(+1/3)$	$1/9$	$1/9$
$\{S_6$	$9 - 8 = +1 =$	$(-2) +$	$(+1/3) +$	$(+1\frac{2}{3}) +$	$(+2/3) +$	$(+1/3)$	$25/9$	$1/9$
$A_2B_1\ \{S_1$	$8 - 8 = \ \ 0 =$	$(0) +$	$(-1/3) +$	$(-1\frac{2}{3}) +$	$(+1\frac{1}{3}) +$	$(+2/3)$	$25/9$	$4/9$
$\{S_2$	$8 - 8 = \ \ 0 =$	$(0) +$	$(-1/3) +$	$(+1/3) +$	$(+1\frac{1}{3}) +$	$(-1\frac{1}{3})$	$1/9$	$16/9$
$\{S_3$	$11 - 8 = +3 =$	$(0) +$	$(-1/3) +$	$(+1\frac{1}{3}) +$	$(+1\frac{1}{3}) +$	$(+2/3)$	$16/9$	$4/9$
$A_2B_2\ \{S_4$	$6 - 8 = -2 =$	$(0) +$	$(+1/3) +$	$(-1\frac{1}{3}) +$	$(-1\frac{1}{3}) +$	$(+1/3)$	$16/9$	$1/9$
$\{S_5$	$7 - 8 = -1 =$	$(0) +$	$(+1/3) +$	$(-1/3) +$	$(-1\frac{1}{3}) +$	$(+1/3)$	$1/9$	$1/9$
$\{S_6$	$8 - 8 = \ \ 0 =$	$(0) +$	$(+1/3) +$	$(+1\frac{2}{3}) +$	$(-1\frac{1}{3}) +$	$(-2/3)$	$25/9$	$4/9$
$A_3B_1\ \{S_1$	$7 - 8 = -1 =$	$(+2) +$	$(-1/3) +$	$(-1\frac{2}{3}) +$	$(-2/3) +$	$(-1/3)$	$25/9$	$1/9$
$\{S_2$	$10 - 8 = +2 =$	$(+2) +$	$(-1/3) +$	$(+1/3) +$	$(-2/3) +$	$(+2/3)$	$1/9$	$4/9$
$\{S_3$	$10 - 8 = +2 =$	$(+2) +$	$(-1/3) +$	$(+1\frac{1}{3}) +$	$(-2/3) +$	$(-1/3)$	$16/9$	$1/9$
$A_3B_2\ \{S_4$	$10 - 8 = +2 =$	$(+2) +$	$(+1/3) +$	$(-1\frac{1}{3}) +$	$(+2/3) +$	$(+1/3)$	$16/9$	$1/9$
$\{S_5$	$10 - 8 = +2 =$	$(+2) +$	$(+1/3) +$	$(-1/3) +$	$(+2/3) +$	$(-2/3)$	$1/9$	$4/9$
$\{S_6$	$13 - 8 = +5 =$	$(+2) +$	$(+1/3) +$	$(+1\frac{2}{3}) +$	$(+2/3) +$	$(+1/3)$	$25/9$	$1/9$

$$\sum A_i^2 + B_j^2 + S_k^2 + AB_{ij}^2 + (error)^2 = \sum (Y - \bar{Y})^2 \qquad \sum = 28 \qquad \sum = 6$$
$$48 + 2 + 28 + 16 + 6 = 100$$

The structural model for the factorial design with repeated measures is that any $Y = (\overline{Y}) + (B_j) + (S_k) + (A_i) + (AB_{ij}) + (error)$. Each measure is composed of the sum of the grand mean $(\overline{Y})$, the sex effect (B_j), the blocks (individual differences between subjects) effect (S_k), the modeling effect (A_i), the sex-by-modeling interaction effect (AB_{ij}), and random error.

The values of $\overline{Y}$, B_j, A_i, and AB_{ij} were determined in the three preceding sections. The values of S_k have to be calculated again because in the randomized-blocks design the values of S_k were calculated without including a B_j component in the design. The values of (error) are different from the preceding estimates of error effects because the effects of subjects, the interaction, and so forth have been removed from the estimate of error. The values of (error) are the values left after all other sources of variation have been subtracted from each score. The calculations are illustrated in the middle section of Table 10.10.

In Table 10.10 each score is analyzed into its six component parts. The pictorial analysis in Figure 10.9 is a building-block analogy of the analysis of variance. As before, each block in a stack of blocks is a symbol of a cooperative response. The drawings progress from a homogeneous group of $\overline{Y} = 8$ scores to the introduction of random error (within variance), to the introduction of the $A \times B$ interaction effect (between-treatment combinations variance), to the introduction of subject effects

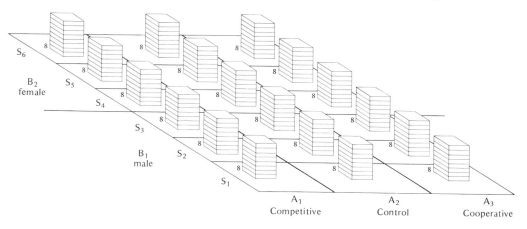

(a) Grand mean

Fig. 10.9. Physical depiction of additive model of analysis of variance for factorial design with repeated measures (split-plot) with two levels of variable B and three levels of variable A (repeated measures variable). Drawing *(a)* represents the 6 subjects with no effect of the treatment or of error—all subjects make three sets of eight (grand mean) cooperative responses. Drawing *(b)* represents the 6 subjects after the effect of random error is added to their response measures. Drawing *(c)* represents the 18 scores after the interaction effect (A × B) is added to the response measure. Drawing *(d)* represents the 18 scores after the blocks effect (subjects effect) is added to the response measure. Drawing *(e)* represents the 18 scores after the effect of variable B (sex) is added to the scores. Drawing *(f)* represents the 18 scores after the effect of variable A (modeling) is added to the scores—at this point the raw data of the experiment emerges. (Fig. 10.9 continues on pp. 180–181.)

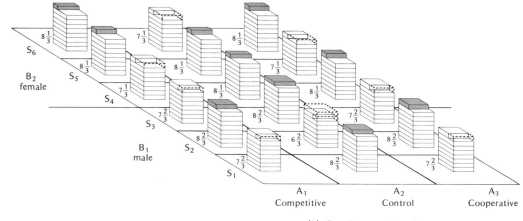

(b) Grand mean and random error

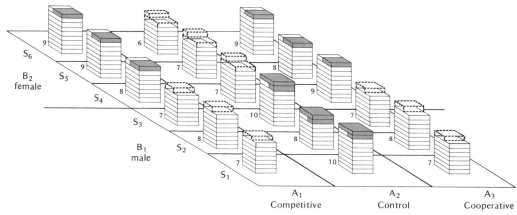

(c) Grand mean and random error
and interaction (A × B) effect

(d) Grand mean and random error
and interaction effect and
blocks (subjects) effect

Fig. 10.9 (Continued)

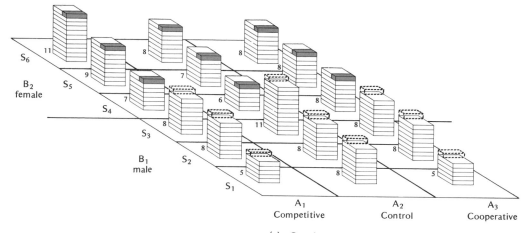

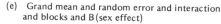

(e) Grand mean and random error and interaction and blocks and B (sex effect)

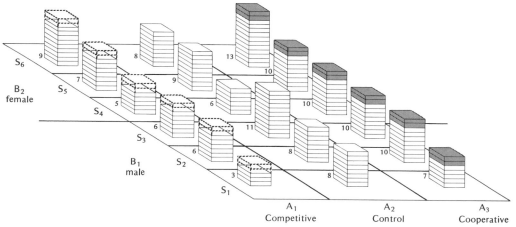

(f) Grand mean and random error and interaction and blocks and B (sex) and A (modeling) (raw data)

Fig. 10.9 (Continued)

(between-blocks variance), to the introduction of the sex effect (between-sex-groups variance), to the introduction of the modeling treatment effect (between-groups variance). The final drawing [Figure 10.9(f)] is the original raw data. [Starting from (f) and reading to (a) Figure 10.9 illustrates the step-by-step decomposition (analysis) of the raw data into its component parts.]

In the preceding sections the between-groups variance estimates of variables A, B, and the interaction $A \times B$ were determined to be 24, 2, and 8, respectively. The sum of squared values of the blocks effect (S_k^2) is 28. The df for the blocks effect is $2 (3 - 1) = 4$, because there are two sets of blocks of three subjects each (one set for each sex). The between-blocks variance is $28 \div 4 = 7.0$. The variance due to random error is the variance remaining between the Y scores after the effects of all other sources of variance have been removed. The sum of squared error values $(error)^2$ is 6. The variance estimate due to random error is $6 \div 8 = 0.75$. There is a total of 17 df; the sex effect accounts for 1 df, the blocks (subjects) effect accounts

181

for 4 df, the modeling effect accounts for 2 df, and the sex-by-modeling interaction effect accounts for 2 df. That leaves 8 df for the within (error) estimate.

In the F ratio for the sex effect, the numerator is the between-sex-groups variance and the denominator is the between-blocks variance. The subjects are grouped into boys and girls and the sex (B) variance is the measure of the difference between the boy mean and the girl mean. The measure of the average variance within the boys' group and within the girls' group is the blocks variance estimate (the variability between subjects after the sex effect is removed). The value of the F ratio for the sex effect with 1 and 4 df is less than 1.00. The probability of an F ratio equal to or greater than 1.00 is 0.50, which is much larger than 0.025 (α).

The F ratio for the modeling effect is $24 \div 0.75 = 32.0$. Using the table in Figure 10.6, the probability of an F ratio equal to or larger than 32 with 2 and 8 df is less than 0.05. The F ratio for the modeling-by-sex interaction is $8 \div 0.75 = 10.67$. Using Table D.5.7, the probability of an F ratio equal to or larger than 10.67 with 2 and 8 df is less than 0.025. This significant interaction effect is depicted in Figure 10.10.

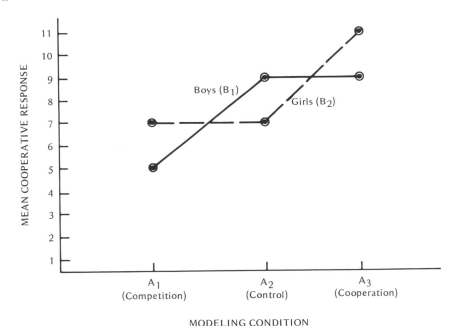

Fig. 10.10.   Line graph of the modeling-by-sex interaction in the factorial design with repeated measures version of the cooperation modeling experiment.

By examining Figure 10.10 we can see that the boys were more competitive than the girls under the competitive models condition, but the girls were more co-operative than the boys under the cooperative modeling condition. The boys were not affected by the cooperative modeling (no difference from the boys' control mean) and the girls were not affected by the competitive modeling condition (no difference from the girls' control mean). There is no real (significant) overall sex effect (boys' and girls' mean cooperative responses were nearly equal). However, there is a real modeling effect and the effect of modeling does depend on the sex of the children. The results are summarized in Table 10.11.

TABLE 10.11. Split-Plot Design: Summary of Analysis of Variance.

Source of Variation	S.S.	df	M.S.	F	p
Sex (B)	2	1	2.00	—	
Blocks (S-subjects)	28	4	7.00		
Modeling (A)	48	2	24.00	32.00	<.05
Sex X Modeling (A × B)	16	2	8.00	10.67	<.05
Within (error)	6	8	0.75		
Total	100	17			

The factorial design with repeated measures controls for more variables than any of the three preceding designs. Since the between-subjects block variance is not small, and the sex-by-modeling condition interaction variance is also not small, the complexity of the design is justified. That is, individual differences and the interaction accounted for a significant proportion of the variance not accounted for by the modeling variable.

The analysis of variance is a useful statistical technique for a number of research designs in addition to those illustrated in the chapter. Often, however, the analysis of variance does not fit a particular research design. There are a number of other inferential statistical tests available. Section Two, Units D1 to D6, present some of the more commonly used tests.

A common feature of statistical hypothesis testing is that the null hypothesis is used to establish an expected (chance) outcome or distribution of outcomes for the data. The actually observed data is compared with the outcome expected on the basis of the null. If the observed (for example, between-groups variance) is sufficiently different from the expected (for example, within-groups variance), the researcher can conclude that the null is probably incorrect. The probability of error (level of significance) and null hypothesis concepts have the same general meaning in all statistical tests.

REVIEW

Rumors to the contrary notwithstanding, research is *not* statistics. The application of inferential statistics gives the researcher a powerful tool for making decisions concerning his data. Understanding the principles behind this application considerably increases the researcher's ability to use the tool wisely. Perhaps an oversimplified version of the highlights of the chapter will help the student who is turned off by statistics. All behavior researchers are confronted with the problem of interpretation of their data. Is the difference that they observe between experimental scores and control scores a real difference, or is it just an accident by the assignment of subjects? There are times when the data are so obvious that statistics are unnecessary.

For example, if we hypothesize that the treatment condition should enhance the scores of the subjects, and we find that the experimental group scores are actually inferior, it does not take statistics to tell us that the treatment conditions did not do what we predicted. Similarly, if the experimental subjects perform three or four times better than *any* of the control subjects, then statistics only confirm our conviction that the treatment had an effect on behavior. Inferential statistics gives us the chance to draw the line precisely between these two extremes when it is more difficult to be sure about the conclusions.

All statistics share some common features, although the calculations and assumptions are different. All statistics look at one part of the data and generate some prediction of what kind of chance differences should be expected between the experimental and control observations. In the analysis of variance example in this chapter, we utilize the within-group variance to calculate our expectation about how two or more groups ought to differ from one another under the assumption of no treatment effect. This is the null hypothesis. Given the null hypothesis, and the calculation of the within-group variance, it is then possible to calculate the distribution of between-groups variances that would occur with no treatment. In the analysis of variance, we simply divide the within-group variance estimate into the actual difference observed in the experiment. If the difference is substantially greater than what would be expected under the null hypothesis, we then conclude that there was a real effect because of the treatment. The use of different levels of alpha error and of one- and two-tail tests are details to help the experimenter get the most out of his data, but the real question that is asked with inferential statistics is "How likely were my results to have occurred by chance alone?"

SUMMARY

1. Hypothesis testing consists of examining the obtained data to see which of two hypotheses it seems most likely to fit. An experimenter must determine if an observed difference between experimental groups is likely or unlikely on the basis of chance.
2. A null hypothesis (H_0) is a negation of an experimental hypothesis (H_1). Usually H_0 is a statement of no difference. A null hypothesis is used for two reasons: (1) it is used to specify a population in which the parameters may be estimated from sample statistics, and (2) an easy way to support a proposition is to fail to find support for its negative.
3. The two kinds of errors that may be made in testing hypotheses are (1) the Type I error, accepting H_1 when H_0 is correct, and (2) the Type II error, not rejecting H_0 when H_1 is correct. The probability of a Type I error is labeled α (the level of significance). The size of α is set by the experimenter.
4. The region of rejection is those outcomes whose probabilities are very small under H_0. A one-tailed test is a statistical test where H_1 is directional so that the region of rejection is entirely in one tail of the distribution of possible outcomes. A two-tailed test occurs when H_1 does not specify direction so that the regions of rejection occur in both tails of the outcome distribution.
5. In the analysis of variance technique the null hypothesis is that the between-groups variance will not differ very much from the within-group variance. The experimental hypoth-

esis is that the between-groups variance will be larger than the within-group variance. The F ratio is a ratio of the between-groups variance to the within-group variance. The basic structural model of the data that is assumed in the analysis of variance technique is that the data is composed of building blocks of sources of variance that sum to yield the raw data scores. The specific components in the structural model for each analysis depend on the nature of the research design.

SUGGESTED READING

Edwards, A. L. *Statistical methods.* (3d ed.) New York: Holt, Rinehart and Winston, 1973.

Hays, W. L. *Statistics for the social sciences* (2d ed.) New York: Holt, Rinehart and Winston, 1973.

Kirk, R. E. *Experimental design: Procedures for the behavioral sciences.* Belmont, Calif.: Brooks/Cole, 1968.

McNemar, Q. *Psychological statistics.* (4th ed.) New York: Wiley, 1969.

Steger, J. A. (Ed.) *Readings in statistics for the behavioral scientist.* New York: Holt, Rinehart and Winston, 1971.

Walker, H. M., and Lev, J. *Statistical inference.* New York: Holt, Rinehart and Winston, 1953.

CHAPTER 11
Pragmatic Issues

The preceding chapters have been primarily concerned with the philosophical issues involving the research process. That is to say, we have been dealing for the most part with generalized problems that permeate all research efforts. Obviously, the strategies adopted by the researcher to deal with these problems have a significant effect on the experiment he will conduct. However, there is another category of problems that are at least as important: no matter how sophisticated the research design, the experimenter is constrained by the resources he has available for the actual collection of data. Almost any experimenter will admit that he could have improved his project if he had been able to find more: time, subjects, money, equipment, access to a computer, and so on. It does not matter if the researcher is a nationally recognized scientist or a freshman college student; the experiment is often determined by what *can* be done more than what *ought to* be done. This chapter addresses itself to some of the problems that must be considered in getting the project off the drawing board and into the real world.

SPECIES CHOICE

There are approximately 1,250,000 animal species left on Earth. About ten species have been extensively studied by psychologists. The ten include flatworms, goldfish, pigeons, mice, rats, cats, dogs, rhesus monkeys, chimpanzees, and human beings. This number of studied species is appallingly large or small depending on your bias as to whether psychology should understand human behavior or all behavior. Irrespective of that issue, however, the selection of subjects is important to the success of the experiment.

Animals—Theoretical Factors

There are two basic reasons why a researcher is involved in observing animal behavior. In some cases, the animal species presents a unique means of investigating a universal behavioral trait, and thus gives a clue to understanding human behavior. The other reason for studying animal behavior is that the animal or the behavior is intrinsically interesting. Although the choice of a species is often a matter of circumstance and not consciously considered by the researcher, some illustrative discussion may make the reader aware of the process.

The theory of evolution is based primarily on the acquisition of behaviors and structures necessary to the continued survival of the evolving species. Inherent in this view is the idea that the "more advanced" species share a common basis with species lower on the scale. If we are interested in the study of one of these lower, common traits, it is sometimes advantageous to study it in a species where it may not be overridden by newer developments. For example, the foundation for the behavior modification techniques now extensively applied to humans was established in Skinner's laboratory using rats and pigeons.

Cross Species Generalization

Drug companies invest substantial amounts of money in animal research before releasing a new compound for use by human beings. Similarly, psychological experiments on animals are giving us information on the potentially harmful and helpful effects of certain environments. Harlow's (1962, 1969) studies on early socialization in monkeys, Calhoun's (1962) studies on overcrowding in rat colonies, Held and Hein's (1963) investigation of the effects of early sensory-motor experience on cats, and the wide variety of studies indicating the superiority of animals raised in an enriched early environment (such as Krech, Rosenzweig, and Bennett, 1962) have far-reaching implications for the human condition.

In addition to providing a substitute for human beings in some research programs (particularly when the experiment involves conditions that cannot be ethically employed with humans, such as brain surgery), animals occasionally provide a unique combination of circumstances for research. For example, the fruit fly combines a rapid breeding rate, an unusually small number of chromosomes, and a unique situation where the chromosomes are enlarged enough to be directly observed. All of these factors give clues about the hereditary transmission of traits. Although human chromosomes are far more numerous and complex, so that such direct observation has not been achieved, the rules for genetic transmission in the fruit fly are equally applicable in human genetics.

Other animal species offer other unique traits that provide rich research opportunities. The nerve cells in the squid are giant-size compared with those found in a human being. Experiments on this relatively easily observed cell have yielded much information concerning the functioning of nervous systems. The normally neat, geometric pattern of a spider web is converted into a chaotic, almost random pattern when the spider is given a fly dosed with LSD. Whether the disruption of the normal web spinning is due to bizarre perceptual effects as reported by humans, or represents a general disruption of the spider's system, the web spinning provides an easily observed indicator of deviation from normal. Hibernating animals provide interesting possibilities for a comparison between hibernation and normal sleep, as well as the effects of passage of time (in the active and passive state) on phenomena such as learning and memory.

It would be a mistake to justify all animal behavioral research in terms of its direct application to understanding more about human behavior. Many animal species have behavior capabilities that are interesting for their own sake. The echolocating ability in bats in avoiding trees and catching moths is well documented. The similar ability of the dolphin is not only interesting, but has been put to practical use in training dolphins to locate objects under water.

There is a large group of researchers who observe and write about animal behavior simply "because it is there." Most of these animal books are a direct off-shoot of the efforts of a naturalist who has chosen to do a careful study of that particular species. The months spent in careful observation may be necessary to meet the criteria of science, but the fact that such books are profitable shows that the interest is shared by the public. Walt Disney Enterprises have also found animal behavior to be profitable, both in nature and in whimsy.

Sometimes the efforts of the naturalist are expanded to apply to human behavior even when that was not his original intent. The work of the European ethologists began as the careful observation of common species in their normal environment. From this work came such terms as "innate behavior patterns," "pecking orders" (and the corresponding "Alpha animal"), and "territoriality." Now there are a number of books written by such authors as Desmond Morris, Robert Ardrey, and others that basically argue that man is equally locked into certain innate behavior patterns and that the explanation for much of man's behavior lies in understanding the genetic heritage passed on by our Darwinian ancestors.

Animals—Practical Factors

There are also a number of very practical reasons for using animals in a behavioral experiment instead of only people. A major factor is that it is possible to establish considerable control over the heredity of experimental laboratory animals. The experimenter can obtain "maze-bright" or "maze-dull" animals from commercial suppliers. Based on the work by Tryon (1940), special strains of laboratory rats have been bred through several generations specifically for their learning ability in a particular maze situation. The "maze-bright" animals are from ancestral stock all of which learned a standard maze task very quickly. Correspondingly, the "maze-dull" animals derived from slow-performing ancestors. Thus, the experimenter can specify the abilities of his subjects depending on the type of maze study he wishes to run. For example, if he wishes to study learning phenomena, he may specify "maze-dull" so that the learning process can be extended for better observation. If, on the other hand, he is not interested in learning but wishes to study how a task is remembered, then he might shorten his training time by using "maze-bright" animals. (It is interesting to note that "maze-dull" and "maze-bright" animals do not differ in tasks other than mazes and do not differ in other kinds of mazes, Searle, 1949.)

Since animal species such as mice and rats have faster reproduction rates and individuals mature relatively rapidly, the effects of heredity and maturation are more conveniently studied in animals. Multiple births also provide opportunities to test simultaneously several individuals with common genetic characteristics and/or identical early environments up to the time of testing.

Animals provide an obvious and unique contribution to behavioral research. There is a class of experiments that cannot be ethically conducted using human subjects. The effects of certain drugs, destruction of certain regions of the brain, extreme environmental stresses, or testing on a prolonged time scale (years) in a restricted environment cannot be determined using human subjects. One of the major reasons the rat is found so frequently in laboratories is because of its fantastic degree of tolerance to surgical insult.

Probably more important to many behavioral researchers is the opportunity to exercise almost complete control over environmental factors. This cannot be accomplished in most human studies. Experience between laboratory sessions can be manipulated according to the design of the experimenter. Animals can be raised from birth in a specified environment, either as part of a specific research effort, or as a means of standardizing the animals in a colony. Even dietary supplements or deficiencies are utilized as a part of animal research.

As stated at the beginning of this chapter, the history of experimental psychology has consisted mainly of the study of ten species. Of these, rats, pigeons, and college students have made the largest contribution to our knowledge of behavior. A great deal is known about the morphology and behavior of these animals. The background of available knowledge promotes the use of these species in preference to other animals. Most frequently, these animals are used in graduate and undergraduate curricula. Consequently, each new scientist builds up a repertoire of research skills and knowledge in terms of one or two species. This means that the selection of any new species should be carefully considered in terms of the contribution of the new species compared with the behavioral information base we already have.

Laboratory animals all share one important virtue: they are available on demand. People are not so dependable. A relatively large colony of small animals such as rats, mice, chickens, or pigeons may be inexpensively maintained. In the case of a large, or ongoing, research effort, the problem of obtaining additional subjects for comparable study is often easier with animals.

Human Beings

The case for using human subjects in psychological research can be stated very succinctly. If you are interested in explaining human behavior, then use human research subjects whenever possible. Obviously, there are a large number of behavioral phenomean that are uniquely human. Human subjects are best suited for research into language and abstract reasoning (although animal subjects have been used successfully in some instances). A case can be made for observing the lower behavioral functions in human subjects as well. If we follow the phylogenetic scale type of argument, the behavior humans share with lower animals has been superseded by newer, higher functions. Undoubtedly, some of the lower functions have been altered and/or replaced in the evolutionary process. Thus, to evaluate appropriately the role of these lower functions in human behavior, perhaps the human being is the only appropriate research subject.

Human subjects are superior to animal subjects for a number of practical reasons. The experimenter does not have to worry about the daily operations of maintaining a research colony. Human subjects can be given specific directions as to what to do (and what *not* to do) in the experimental situation. In the case of some problem-solving tasks, human subjects can be instructed to limit themselves to certain modes of attack for the sake of the experiment. Humans can be told to push a button, or pull a knob, or even hold still for the sake of the recording instruments; animals can be most uncooperative in these aspects of an experiment.

The verbal report of human subjects can provide valuable insight into the process being studied, or may point out weaknesses in the procedures being used. The alert investigator can use this information to improve his research project.

EQUIPMENT CHOICE

The equipment used in early experimental laboratories led critics to apply the term "brass instrument psychology" to the developing behavioral science. Today's experimental psychologist is more likely to order stainless steel, plastic, or electronic devices for his laboratory. However, equipment is still a major factor in the behavioral research process.

Advantages

Although it is possible to conduct behavioral research without experimental apparatus, equipment has definite advantages. (1) A mechanical response-measuring device is more likely to be reliable and free from bias than observations made without mechanical aids. (2) Equipment often allows the collection of a greater quantity of data than could be accomplished without equipment. For example, several machines may be used to detect and record different aspects of behavior simultaneously. (3) Some behavior is so complex and/or rapid that an experimenter cannot accurately record it during the experiment. Audio and video tape recorders allow an experimenter to record behavior during the experiment and later replay the recording for tabulating the responses. (4) It is sometimes possible to detect and measure with a mechanical device behavior that may not be directly observable to the experimenter. Emotional responses such as those measured by the polygraph, or lie detector, can normally be measured only with the aid of special detection devices. (5) Equipment may be necessary when the data-collection process involves prolonged periods of observation. Apparatus may be used to free the experimenter from repetitious portions of the data collection process. The experimenter may utilize the released time to observe more carefully the subject's behavior, examine the data for unexpected trends, or otherwise strengthen the overall research process.

Disadvantages

Occasionally the use of equipment has disadvantages. (1) Equipment failure is a particularly serious problem in mechanized behavioral research. If the failure is not immediately discovered, the experimenter may be collecting inaccurate data without realizing it. Total failure is usually recognized quickly, but the apparatus may slowly go out of adjustment, so that the measures change gradually over a period of time. Electronic devices drift from the nominal adjustment points, and even mechanical devices are subject to wear. (2) Equipment may provide secondary variables in the experimental situation. Children can become so engrossed with manipulating the levers of a novel device that they will ignore the experimental task. An animal that has had its tail pinched in the door of a maze may alter its behavior in the maze. In either case, the results of the experiment might have been different had the apparatus been designed differently. (3) Subjects can learn to take advantage of features of the experimental apparatus. The click of a counter can alert an animal and act as a reinforcer, the scratch of a pen or pencil can tell a human subject if his response was right or wrong. An experiment designed to provide well-exercised rats by letting them eat only when they have run in an exercise wheel may produce a very fat, lazy rat who has learned how to spin an empty wheel with a flip of the paw. (4) Available equipment may dictate the course of behavioral experiments, which can be either an advantage or a disadvantage, depending on the circumstances. Several well-known behavioral researchers have parlayed new laboratory equipment into a research trend, because of the ideas produced by using the device. On the other hand, researchers may fail to follow promising research ideas suggested by data because the available apparatus cannot be applied to the phenomena. Another version of this "apparatus myopia" results when the researcher fails to consider alternative ways to measure a certain behavior. The accepted way to measure reaction time involves accurate electric stop-clocks and stimulus and response detecting devices. A "sophisticated" experimenter may decide that he cannot use reaction time as an experimental variable because he does not have a reaction timer. An imaginative researcher may realize that reaction time can be measured by asking a subject to catch a yardstick dropped between his thumb and

Apparatus Myopia

forefinger. The data may be recorded as the number of inches the stick fell, or can be translated into milliseconds if desired. (5) Equipment is usually expensive. This can be translated into dollars if it is purchased from a commercial supplier or into hours if the researcher decides to design and build his own apparatus. Equipment must also be maintained and/or modified in order to keep its value in the laboratory. Trouble shooting and calibrating existing equipment may become a major preoccupation of the laboratory worker.

Sources of Information on Equipment

A researcher has two ways he can acquire apparatus for his laboratory; he can purchase a manufactured device from a commercial supplier, or he can outline a description of the desired device and have it constructed or construct it himself. Commercial suppliers provide catalogues with descriptions of the devices they sell. For the person interested in purchasing a specific item of equipment, *buyer's guides* provide a list of the manufacturers and suppliers of different kinds of equipment. Usually, a guide is organized by the function served by the equipment, so it can be used to locate most of the sources of equipment for any specific research application. The special instrumentation issue of *American Psychologist* [J. B. Sidowski and S. Ross (Eds.), 1969] includes a buyer's guide for psychologists. *Science* magazine publishes an *Annual guide to scientific instruments* (Sommer, 1972).

Custom-built equipment ranges from elaborate units that are designed specifically for a research program to home-built devices made of cardboard and glue. There are a number of sources that provide plans and/or specifications for laboratory apparatus. The equipment section of any research report in a journal provides a description of the apparatus used. In addition, several behavioral research journals publish apparatus notes that provide information on new devices developed in behavioral laboratories. The journal *Behavioral Research Methods and Instrumentation* publishes articles dealing with technological developments in psychology. The March 1969 issue of *American Psychologist* provides a special section on the uses of instrumentation in psychology. The reader who wishes to find a more thorough and technical discussion of laboratory equipment may find Sidowski's *Experimental methods and instrumentation in psychology* to be a valuable source. Zucker's *Electronic circuits for the behavioral and biomedical sciences* (1969) and Malmstadt, Enke, and Toren's *Electronics for scientists* (1963) provide a similar function for electronic devices.

RELEVANCE OF PROCEDURE

Up to this chapter, the discussion of research designs has been based on rather abstract and esoteric criteria. Another important consideration is the relevance of the observed data once the research is conducted. Recently, behavioral research has been criticized because of the unnatural environment created in the laboratory setting. It has been argued that subjects who know they are in an experiment behave differently than they do in the real world. Stop and consider how you would respond if you were a subject in a "panic" type of experiment. Your answer on a questionnaire or even your performance in a contrived situation would probably be different from the behavior we all know can occur in a real burning building.

In our attempts to eliminate sources of extraneous variance, we also may be limiting the possible behavior of the subjects so that we are merely plugging the subjects into the situation as sources of response. Occasionally subjects react to the perceived limitations by deliberately exceeding the limits of the experiment. Questionnaires often elicit additional responses over the simple choice offered by the experimenter. It is interesting to note that the acceptable treatment of these "aberrant" responses is to reject them from the sample since they do not fit in the tabulation categories.

Animal subjects also show an almost perverse tendency to flaunt the "rules" of the experiment. Whether it is jumping out of the apparatus instead of running the appropriate path, discovering a way to spin the exercise wheel without running, or shorting out the shock grid by urinating or defecating on the bars, "aberrant" subjects are also the problem of the researcher who uses animals ("rat-runners"). The usual procedure is to design a better model apparatus to deprive the animal of these unwanted behaviors (after eliminating the "unscorable" data). One cannot help but speculate on the possibility that our constraints on extraneous behavior might also be limiting the primary variable. Simply as a hypothetical possibility, inedible nesting material may protect the deprivation schedule, but edible material may result in a more natural nest, which in turn may significantly affect maternal or other behaviors. Although control of extraneous variance is a major part of research design, the unconstrained measure of the primary variance is the reason for the research.

Even in research situations where there is a minimum of constraint on behavior, the mere act of observation can adversely affect the behavior of interest. Some subjects will deliberately alter an experiment for a variety of reasons: boredom, resentment of the simplicity of the task, the challenge of "outfoxing" the experimenter, or even personal vendetta. However, subjects can also generate novel behavior simply because they know they are being observed. Subjects become aware of behavioral alternatives that they would not normally use if they were not being observed. Unfortunately, the change may occur even when the subject wishes to cooperate. It is about the same as trying to determine your own eyeblink rate; if you count it yourself you will probably not blink at a natural rate. You may ask a friend to do the counting, but as long as you know there is a count going on, you will blink differently.

The obvious solution in the eyeblink problem is to ask a friend to count your eyeblinks at some time when you are unaware that the count is being taken. Similarly, there is a group of psychologists that believes observing the behavior while it is naturally occurring is a better method of learning about behavior (Willems and Raush, 1969; Proshansky, Ittelson, and Rivlin, 1970). Naturalistic observation (Chapter 2) still has the problem of the subject becoming aware of being observed. Webb, et al. (1966), have suggested a number of imaginative data-collection procedures that minimize subject reaction (unobtrusive measures, Chapter 2).

Experimental Rigor Versus Sterility

The strict experimental psychologist may protest that naturalistic observation lacks control and scientific rigor while the naturalistic observer claims that the laboratory is sterile and irrelevant. Instead of adding any fuel to this potential fire, it should be noted that both views are both right and wrong. Experiments like the study of obedience by Milgram (1963) and the model prison study by Zimbardo (1973) both show a frightening side of human behavior precisely measured in a laboratory setting. Similarly the careful observation of animal behavior by European ethologists like Eibl-Eibesfeldt (1970), Tinbergen (1951), and von Frisch (1950) meet very strict scientific requirements. The answer to the "rightness" or "wrongness" of any procedure is answered by the demands of the research question.

EXPERIMENTER EFFECT

There are obvious sources of secondary variance in the characteristics of the experimenter. A person who is afraid of rats will probably treat the animals differently from one who kept small animals as pets, and the animals will behave differently as a result. The personality characteristic of the experimenter can affect the attitude and performance of the subjects in his research. Whether this is due to the long-run characteristics (traits) of the experimenter or just to his having a "bad day," it is a source of error. This kind of experimenter effect is not particularly disturbing. It does mean that two different researchers may not get identical data, but relatively standard control procedures could be introduced to minimize this effect.

Experimenter Bias

A far more serious source of error is the possibility that the experimenter cannot be an unbiased observer and that his bias affects the outcome of the research. Rosenthal (1966) has emphasized the problem of experimenter bias in behavioral research.

An example of the experimenter bias effect is provided by Rosenthal and Lawson (1964). A group of undergraduate students worked with 12 rats over a period of two months. Half of the experimenters were told that their six rats were "maze bright" and the other half of the students got "maze-dull" rats. The rats were actually a random sample from the colony. The rats were given seven learning tasks. On five of the tasks there were no significant differences between the scores of the two groups. On two of the tasks, stimulus generalization and stimulus discrimination, the "maze-bright" animals learned faster than the "maze-dull" rats. These differences may be due to: (1) the physical interaction between the experimenters and animals (for example, handling procedures); (2) the scoring procedures (for example, cheating by either group); or (3) unintended communication between the experimenters and animals (for example, accidental cueing of the correct response).

Barber and Silver (1968) have questioned Rosenthal's conclusions about the experimenter bias effect. These criticisms range from the suggestion that the students who conducted the research deliberately cheated (in the example just cited, possibly the students felt they had to get the "right results" for the grade in the class), to faulty analysis of the data by Rosenthal himself. The fact that there is a controversy over the experimenter effect illustrates the importance of the problem. If experimenter bias is a strong factor in all experiments, then it becomes almost impossible to conduct an experiment that is free of it. From the first idea to the write-up of the data, all of the research decisions both formal and informal must be examined and closely controlled. If bias cannot be eliminated and cannot be measured, then it subverts the entire research process.

Rosenthal and others have suggested possible ways to control for experimenter bias. At one extreme is to sample experimenters randomly to conduct a given research project. Another suggestion is to mechanize all procedures and remove the human element contributed by the experimenter. Here, once again, practicality becomes the decision criterion. We are not willing to give up all behavioral research because the researcher can affect the results. Our choice is to be aware of the possibility of our bias influencing the results and guard against it as efficiently as we can.

ETHICAL ISSUES

Popular magazines frequently publish articles informing the public about scientific research. Occasionally one of these articles is of an exposé nature. These exposés suggest that scientists have wandered into an area that the writers consider inappropriate. Of particular recent concern has been the issue of "invasion of privacy" by psychologists (A.P.A., 1965). Another recent public issue has been the unscrupulous misuse and ill-treatment of animal subjects.

The fact that a scientist must examine his data in an impartial and unemotional manner does not mean that his relationship to society is similarly restricted. There are certain topics and research techniques that are not appropriate to experimental research. While a value judgment concerning the nature of collected data is inappropriate, value judgments about the methods by which the data were collected are relevant.

Any statement concerning ethical standards in research somehow sounds like a restrictive code designed to impede the progress of science. However, such a statement is often based on sound, logical research practices. For example, the guidelines for minimum standards in housing experimental animals assures the experimenter that he will be observing the behavior of healthy animals. For a more complete statement, see the booklet entitled *Ethical standards for psychologists* (A.P.A., 1963).

General Research Ethics

Progress in science is enhanced by the public nature of the data. A major savings in time and effort is accomplished by utilizing the data from observations made in other laboratories. A basic assumption of both preceding statements is that the data are carefully and accurately recorded. If the original observations were made haphazardly or inaccurately, the entire structure based on those observations may collapse like a house of cards. Before offering data to the scientific community, the researcher should be absolutely certain that his observations are accurate.

In addition to conscientiously collecting the data, a researcher must be absolutely honest in describing his observation procedures. Accidents and unexpected contingencies often occur in the middle of an experiment. Some of these accidents may make an experimenter appear foolish. If, however, the accidents had any possible effect on the scores obtained in the research, they should be faithfully reported.

Most research projects are the result of continuing dynamic processes of exchanging ideas with colleagues. Seldom is the research project entirely a one-man project. If any of the features of a research project are the result of suggestions or ideas from other individuals, they should be given credit for it.

Ethics in Animal Research

Most states have laws regulating the use of animals in scientific research. These laws are primarily intended for medical research facilities and include standards for administering anesthesia, surgical procedures, and postoperative recovery. Because of the wording of most of these laws, they also apply to animal colonies used in behavioral research. Thus minimum standards for maintaining animals are prescribed by law.

Legal requirements should not be the basis for good care of an animal colony. On purely pragmatic grounds, the colony is maintained to supply animals for research projects. Animals that are sick, or in pain, do not make good subjects in behavioral research. Fearful animals are much more likely to bite the researcher as well as behave abnormally in the research situation. Animals stressed by overcrowding or improper diet are more subject to disease and abnormal behavior. A colony of animals kept in prime condition is necessary to a research program.

For most animal researchers, not even the practical reasons are necessary for good colony care. Most individuals are interested in the welfare of their animals because they like them. It is the rare researcher who deliberately mistreats the animals in his care, although unfortunate incidents too often occur because of inattention or lack of foresight. The following suggestions illustrate some of the problems that take the fun out of conducting animal research and result in the charge of cruelty to animals.

Any condition that contributes to the untimely death or unnecessary discomfort of an animal can be considered cruelty. Filthy cages and unclean colony quarters are an invitation to infection and disease (for the researchers as well as the animals). Cages that are too small may seriously impair the physical condition of the animals. Overcrowded cages can result in death or injury due to the battles that may result. With some wild species, leaving two individuals in the same cage will automatically result in the death of the loser in the power struggle. Inadequate food or water supply or infrequent monitoring of same can result in starved animals. New cages and new animals must be monitored carefully during the initial period, as the animal sometimes cannot reach the food that appears to be in abundance. (One author discovered that a squirrel's nose is shorter than that of a rat and the squirrel could not eat out of the food hopper in a rat cage.) A more common example is a clogged delivery tube on a water bottle, or the attachment of the bottle to the cage at an angle so that the water cannot flow through the tube.

Assuming that the animals are being maintained successfully in the colony, a new set of problems may be introduced by the requirements of the experiment. Food deprivation (the most common method of manipulating motivation in an experiment) provides a case in point. The deprivation schedule should not be so extreme as to endanger the survival of the animal. If the schedule requires a daily feeding period, care must be taken to see that the period is not cut short and sufficient food is available during the period. The feeding period for food-deprived animals may be ineffective if water is not also available, if several animals are expected to eat simultaneously from a single feeder, or if a different kind of food from the regular laboratory diet is used. Rats can conveniently tolerate a 24-hour deprivation of food and even accidentally skipping one day will not be fatal. Other animal species are not always so hardy. In most animal species, water deprivation is more stringent than the equivalent in food, and water deprivation almost invariably includes food deprivation, since the animal cannot swallow the usual amount of food without water.

The other major motivational variable in animal research is the use of punishment (such as electric shock). Obviously the shock must be uncomfortable in order to be effective, but precautions should be taken to see that the shock level is appropriate at all times. Accidental extreme shocks caused by someone changing the controls between experimental sessions are preventable. Extremely painful shock may completely disrupt the animal's behavior without allowing it to learn the desired response. In addition to the charge of cruelty, animals subjected to high shock levels are just plain nasty to handle!

Occasionally an experimenter wishes to impose an extremely stressful condition on an animal deliberately. For instance, there are some studies that use survival rate as the measure of the dependent variable. Such research should be conducted only if the data are unavailable by other approaches. The decision concerning the justifiability of such research must be made in terms of the profits to be gained and the costs to be incurred. If you choose to run an experiment involving an extreme stress situation for animals, you may become the example of why behavioral research should be sharply curtailed. Be prepared to justify your research on both scientific and humanitarian grounds.

If the research requires that the animals be sacrificed as a part of the research design, obviously the most painless and humane methods should be employed. Humane killing procedures are an integral part of the animal colony procedures. (See Section Two, Unit A.) The possibility of cruelty during the killing process is so obvious, that it is a relatively rare problem. Unfortunately, not all killing methods are totally effective. Thus, special precautions should be taken to ensure that the animal is indeed dead before disposing of the carcass.

Ethics in Human Research

The rights of the individual have become a major issue in many social contexts within the past few years. As an example of the increased concern with this problem, the Surgeon General of the United States issued a directive (identified as Policy and Procedure Order 129, dated July 1, 1966) to the Public Health Service, Division of Research Grants on the subject: "Investigations involving human subjects, including clinical research: requirements for review to insure the rights and welfare of the individuals." To put it simply, even the federal government will not financially support research that infringes on the rights and welfare of human subjects, occasional scandals notwithstanding.

Exploitation of individuals or groups of individuals is unethical. An individual's right to privacy must be respected for legal as well as moral reasons. It is not acceptable to force all members of a group such as a college class to be subjects in a research project. The use of social pressures to take part in research should be carefully considered from a moral viewpoint. Coerced subjects may cause a researcher considerable problems including consciously or unconsciously distorting the data.

Another serious problem is that of protecting the rights of a subject within the structure of research. The data collected in behavioral research should be considered *privileged communication*. Individuals should not be able to utilize the observations of a subject for purposes other than the experiment. Particularly relevant is the case where one of the measures consists of a personality test, and some other person wishes to use the score to evaluate the individual subjects. The best way to avoid this kind of problem is to establish the anonymity of a subject as soon as possible.

Informed Consent

The use of personality tests in behavioral research involves another aspect of subjects' rights. It may be argued that the measurement of personality traits constitutes an invasion of a person's privacy (A.P.A., 1965). In this case, subjects must be given the opportunity to refuse to serve in an experiment, or they must give permission for an experimenter to use their scores. The usual interpretation is that, if a subject voluntarily participated in an experiment, he implicitly gave permission for the data to be used anonymously.

A frequent technique in human experiments is to conceal or disguise the real purpose of the experiment. The subjects are supplied with some kind of misinformation that distracts the subjects from the real intent of the research. The reasons behind deception depend on the research purpose.

Debriefing

Advocates of the use of deception justify it by pointing out that the subjects are informed of the real intent of the experiment before leaving the experimental situation. Thus, the effects of the misinformation are established for a limited time in a laboratory setting, and the situation is corrected as soon as possible. The effect on the subjects, however, is to make them very wary of experimental psychologists in subsequent interactions. Although subterfuge yields very interesting research data, it should be used sparingly because of its negative "public image."

A final problem is the investigation of the behavior of human subjects under stress. Some experiments are concerned with behavior at the extremes of psychological or physical endurance. Other experiments may expose the subject to a short-term stress, such as a simulated emergency, or a traumatic social interaction. While the data from this type of study may be quite informative, the beginning researcher *should avoid it*. There are too many things that can potentially go wrong to risk any possible damage to the subjects. Even for established professional researchers, this type of research is of questionable value.

The American Psychological Association has published a monograph (1973) on the topic of ethical considerations in the conduct of research on human subjects. The monograph contains an extensive discussion (104 pages) of the above and related issues.

REVIEW

The issues in this chapter, rather than being the "how" and "why" of experimental designs, are addressed more to the question of "so what?" The choice of animal species, the method of selecting and treating human subjects, the selection of which equipment to use, and the use of certain experimental settings, all may have a significant impact on the observed behavior, irrespective of the research design. The factors discussed in this chapter are by no means exhaustive of the problems that will be encountered by the behavioral researcher. They are mentioned primarily to give some feeling of the problems that might occur. This chapter should be read as a discussion of the *kinds* of problems that might be encountered, rather than a list of the problems that *will* be encountered.

Although all of the categories of the problems discussed are important, particular attention should be paid to the problem of the experimenter effect and to the discussion of ethical issues in behavioral research. These two issues have received a considerable amount of attention in recent professional journals.

SUMMARY

1. Selection of species of subjects is made because either the species is particularly suited for the investigation of a particular trait shared by other species or the animal's behavior is intrinsically interesting.
2. The practical reasons for selecting animals for a research study include: (1) better control of heredity and faster reproduction rates, (2) better control of the environment during maturation, (3) ethical limitations on research with human beings, (4) greater control of the total environment. (5) In the history of the discipline, a body of knowledge about a few species has been established and the knowledge can be used to assist the design of research on those species. And (6) animals are frequently more available than human beings.
3. Human beings are best suited for research on primarily human characteristics, such as language and abstract reasoning. And, human beings are occasionally easier to manipulate for a particular research purpose, for example, imagining a scene or thinking of addition problems.
4. The advantages of experimental equipment include: (1) reliability and freedom from observer bias, (2) efficiency, (3) speed of observation and recording, (4) subtle measurement, and (5) insusceptability to fatigue.
5. The potential disadvantages of research equipment include: (1) unnoticed equipment failure, (2) the distracting aspects of the equipment, (3) possible sources of secondary variance provided by the equipment, (4) "apparatus myopia," and (5) the expense involved in obtaining and maintaining the equipment.

6. The struggle to control sources of extraneous (secondary) variance may lead to research that does not generalize to any "real-life" situation. The mere fact of being observed may affect the subjects' behavior.

7. The characteristics of and expectations of the experimenter (experimenter bias) may affect the behavior of the subjects or the way the data is recorded in an experiment. The researcher must keep these possibilities in mind while designing a research project.

8. A researcher is ethically bound to describe his observation procedures honestly and make as accurate observations as possible.

9. For legal, ethical, and scientific reasons, the animals used in research must be kept in the best possible condition. Research requiring the use of extreme stress with animals should be conducted only if the research question is important and if there is no other way to answer the question.

10. Ethical principles in research with human beings include: (1) informing the subjects of the conditions of the experiment that might influence willingness to participate, (2) ensuring the participant's understanding of the reasons for concealment or deception if it is necessary (this includes explaining the purpose after the subject has completed his participation). (3) The potential subject must be guaranteed the freedom to decline to participate, (4) the researcher must honor all promises and commitments he has made to his subjects, (5) the experimenter must protect his subjects from the possibility of physical and mental discomfort or danger; it is recommended that novice researchers avoid using stressful situations with human beings. And (6) the researcher must maintain the confidentiality of information about the research participants.

SUGGESTED READING

American Psychological Association, Ad Hoc Committee on Ethical Standards in Psychological Research. *Ethical principles in the conduct of research with human participants*, Washington, D.C.: A.P.A., 1973.

American Psychological Association, Council of Editors. Congress and social science. *American Psychologist*, 1967, *22*, 877–1041.

American Psychological Association, Council of Editors. *Ethical standards of psychologists.* Washington, D.C.: A.P.A., 1963.

American Psychological Association, Council of Editors. Testing and public policy. *American Psychologist*, 1965, *20*, 857–993.

American Psychological Association, Committee on Precautions in Animal Experimentation. *Rules regarding animals.* Washington, D.C.: A.P.A., 1949.

Animal Welfare Institute. *Basic care of experimental animals.* (Rev. ed.) New York: Animal Welfare Institute, 1965.

Ardrey, R. *The territorial imperative.* New York: Dell, 1966.

Ardrey, R. *The social contract.* New York: Dell, 1970.

Barber, T. X., and Silver, M. J. Fact, fiction and the experimenter effect. *Psychological Bulletin Monographs*, 1968, *70*, 1–29.

Barber, T. X., and Silver, M. J. Pitfalls in data analysis and interpretations. A reply to Rosenthal. *Psychology Bulletin Monographs*, 1968, *70*, 48–62.

Barnett, S. A. *The rat. A study in behavior.* Chicago: Aldine, 1963.

Baumrind, D. Some thoughts on ethics of research: After reading Milgram's "Behavioral study of obedience." *American Psychologist*, 1964, *19*, 421–423.

Breland, K., and Breland, M. *Animal behavior.* New York: Macmillan, 1966.

Calhoun, J. B. Population density and social pathology. *Scientific American,* 1962, *206* (2), 139–148.

Castaneda, A., and Fahel, L. S. The relationship between the psychological investigator and the public schools. *American Psychologist,* 1961, *16,* 201–203.

Committee on Revision of Guide for Laboratory Animals. *Guide for laboratory animal facilities and care.* (3d rev. ed.) Institute of Laboratory Animal Resources. National Research Council. United States Department of Health, Education, and Welfare. Bethesda, Md.: National Institutes of Health, 1968, Public Health Service Publication Number 1024.

Denny, M. R., and Ratner, S. C. *Comparative psychology; Research in animal behavior.* (Rev. ed.) Homewood, Ill.: Dorsey, 1970.

Eibl-Eibesfeldt, I. *Ethology: The biology of behavior.* New York: Holt, Rinehart and Winston, 1970.

Harlow, H. F. The heterosexual affectional system in monkeys. *American Psychologist,* 1962, *17,* 1–9.

Harlow, H. F. Age-mate or peer affectional systems. In D. S. Lehrman, R. A. Hinde, and E. Shaw (Eds.), *Advances in the study of behavior,* Vol. 2, New York: Academic Press, 1969.

Held, R., and Hein, A. Movement-produced stimulation in the development of visual guided behavior. *Journal of Comparative and Physiological Psychology,* 1963, *56,* 872–876.

Jung, J. *The experimenter's dilemma.* New York: Harper & Row, 1971.

Katz, M. M. Ethical issues in the use of human subjects in psychopharmacologic research. *American Psychologist,* 1967, *22,* 360–363.

Kelman, H. C. Human use of human subjects: The problem of deception in social psychological experiments. *Psychological Bulletin,* 1967, *67,* 1–11.

Krech, D., Rosenzweig, M., and Bennett, E. Relations between brain chemistry and problem solving among rats in enriched and impoverished environments. *Journal of Comparative and Physiological Psychology,* 1962, *55,* 801–807.

Langer, E. Human experimentation: New York verdict affirms patient's rights. *Science,* 1966, *151,* 663–666.

Lorenz, K. *King Solomon's ring.* New York: Crowell, 1952.

Maier, N. R. F., and Schneirla, T. C. *Principles of animal psychology.* New York: Dover, 1964.

Malmstadt, H. V., Enke, C. G. and Toren, E. C., Jr., *Electronics for scientists.* New York: W. A. Benjamin, 1963.

Milgram, S. Behavioral study of obedience. *Journal of Abnormal and Social Psychology,* 1963, *67,* 371–378.

Milgram, S. Issues in the study of obedience: A reply to Baumrind. *American Psychologist,* 1964, *19,* 848–852.

Miller, S. E., and Rokeach, M. Psychology experiments without subjects' consent. Letters in *Science,* 1966, *152,* 15.

Morris, D. *The naked ape.* New York: McGraw-Hill, 1967.

Mullen, F. A. The school as a psychological laboratory. *American Psychologist,* 1959, *14,* 53–56.

Munn, N. L. *Handbook for psychological research in the rat.* Boston: Houghton Mifflin, 1950.

Mussen, P. H. (Ed.) *Handbook of research methods in child development.* New York: Wiley, 1960.

Proshansky, H. M., Ittelson, W. H., and Rivlin, L. G. *Environmental Psychology.* New York: Holt, Rinehart and Winston, 1970.

Rogers, C. R., and Skinner, B. F. Some issues concerning the control of human behavior: A symposium. *Science,* 1956, *124,* 1057–1066.

Rosenthal, R. *Experimenter effects in behavioral research.* New York: Appleton, 1966.

Rosenthal, R., and Lawson, R. A. Longitudinal study of the effects of experimenter bias on the operant learning of laboratory rats. *Journal of Psychiatric Research,* 1964, *2,* 61–72.

Ruch, F. L. Personality: Public or private. *Psychology Today,* 1967, *1* (6), 46, 58–61.

Scott, W. A., and Wertheimer, M. *Introduction to psychological research.* New York: Wiley, 1962.

Searle, L. V. The organization of hereditary maze-brightness and maze-dullness. *Genetic Psychology Monographs,* 1949, *39,* 279–325.

Sidowski, J. B. (Ed.) *Experimental methods and instrumentation in psychology.* New York: McGraw-Hill, 1966.

Sidowski, J. B., and Ross, S. (Eds.) Instrumentation in psychology. Special issue of *American Psychologist,* 1969, *24,* 185–384.

Smith, M. B. Conflicting values affecting behavioral research with children. *American Psychologist,* 1967, *22,* 377–382.

Sommer, R. G. Guide to scientific instruments. Special edition of *Science,* 1972, *178A.*

Stricker, L. J. The true deceiver. *Psychological Bulletin,* 1967, *68,* 13–20.

Tinbergen, N. *The study of instinct.* New York: Oxford, 1951.

Tryon, R. C. Genetic differences in maze learning in rats. *Yearbook of the National Society for the Study of Education,* 1940, *39,* 111–119.

von Frisch, K. *Bees—their vision, chemical senses and language.* New York: Cornell University Press, 1950.

Webb, E. J., Campbell, D. T., Schwartz, R. D., and Sechrest, F. *Unobtrusive measures: Nonreactive research in the social sciences.* Chicago: Rand McNally, 1966.

Willems, E. P., and Rausch, H. L. *Naturalistic viewpoints in psychological research.* New York: Holt, Rinehart and Winston, 1969.

Zimbardo, P. G. The Stanford prison experiment. Paper and film presented at the Western Psychological Association annual convention, Anaheim, 1973.

Zucker, M. H. *Electronic circuits for the behavioral and biomedical sciences: A reference book of useful solid state circuits.* San Francisco: Freeman, 1969.

CHAPTER 12
Research Proposals and Reports

Whether a proposal is concerned with a psychology class experiment or a large government grant, the proposal serves as a model for the entire experiment. This chapter is concerned with practical problems that an individual encounters in the course of selecting a research project and the details of writing a research proposal and final report.

FINDING A TOPIC

Initially, a student may be unable to find researchable ideas. More experienced individuals realize that the most difficult aspect of the research process is to *limit* the number of ideas to be empirically tested. As a researcher reads a research report, questions occur, such as: "I wonder how that relates to . . . ?" or "What if the experimenter had . . . ?" Each of these questions can lead to a potential research project. However, many such ideas are forgotten as the reader encounters newer material. Unless a researcher can jog his memory, the ideas may be lost.

There are a number of ways to recover a research idea. For example, one may return to the original article and try to rediscover the idea. Articles may be read the first time with the express purpose of developing and remembering researchable ideas. However, to the newcomer, reading for research ideas interferes with understanding the article.

A person may find an idea logbook helpful in recording research ideas. An **idea logbook** contains ideas briefly noted as they occur while reading. A logbook provides a permanent record of potential research topics that may be evaluated at a more convenient time. If an individual has established and maintained an idea logbook, the problem of choosing a research topic becomes one of selecting the most interesting questions.

Unfortunately, many students must conduct a research project before they have collected a set of ideas. They need a promising source of instant ideas. Such students should read a number of general references, jotting down ideas as they occur. Almost any introductory psychology textbook is a gold mine of researchable ideas. If the person's interests are restricted to a specific research area, concentrating on the relevant chapters in an introductory text or reading a book about that area should expose many research possibilities.

Reviewing Psychology Literature

As an individual becomes acquainted with an area, he relies more on primary sources that communicate new developments to people involved in research. Journals such as *Psychological Review,* and *Psychological Reports* publish articles concerned with theories and theoretical issues in psychology. *Behavioral Science* provides a similar function for all behavioral disciplines. Theoretical articles are rich sources for research ideas.

There are a few publications that include research from a broad spectrum of psychological areas. The editors of these journals try to select articles that are contemporary and stimulating. These articles provide good raw material for research ideas. *Psychology Today* attempts to keep its readers informed of recent developments throughout the area of psychology. *Scientific American* serves a similar function for all scientific fields. Both publications usually present background research as well as new findings.

Psychonomic Science and its replacement, the *Bulletin of the Psychonomic Society,* publishes brief (two pages) research reports from all areas of psychology. *Science* magazine provides a similar service for those interested in all fields of science. Both of these publications sample the latest empirical discoveries. Articles in these journals are characterized by a short time period between submission and publication.

For the student interested in generating research hypotheses, any of the above publications should suit his purpose. In addition, there are a large number of professional journals (Figure 12.1) devoted to publishing research in specific areas of behavior. The articles published in these journals are often so technical that the reader must have some prior acquaintance with the field (especially terminology) in order to understand and evaluate the articles. These sources provide empirical data for understanding an area or expose the reader to novel experimental techniques. If an individual has some background in an area, these publications also provide a rich source for research ideas.

Alternative Methods of Finding Topics

A literature search is not the only way to generate research hypotheses. Listening to someone give a lecture on a topic can lead to research possibilities. If possible, involving the lecturer in an informal discussion may be even more productive. An alert student will find that a "rap session" with other interested students may expose many research possibilities.

SELECTING THE TOPIC

Assuming that a student has succeeded in locating a few research possibilities, his task then becomes one of evaluating and selecting the most promising topics. He should ask himself the question, "Would this experiment be a waste of my time?"

The initial step in the selection process is to examine each question and develop tentative research proposals. After forming a tentative research proposal, the researcher should evaluate the proposal. Reading the research reports of investigators working in the same area may reveal a better method for collecting the data and indicate potential secondary and error variables.

Bibliographic Publications

There are three publications that are published for the person seeking research articles in limited behavioral areas. These references provide relevant and sometimes comprehensive bibliographic sources for research articles in a specific area. *Psychological Bulletin* contains articles that summarize and integrate the research findings on specific research topics. The *Annual Review of Psychology* provides a similar service, emphasizing research that has been published within the past three to four years. *Psychological Abstracts* presents abstracts of articles published in many journals, catalogued according to the topic of investigation.

Current Contents (Behavioral, Social, and Management Sciences edition) is a weekly publication that lists the table of contents for a large number of behavioral science journals. The publishers of *Current Contents* also offer a special service that lists all article titles containing certain key terms.

Personal Communication and Reprints

If a person has done considerable work in a research area of interest, it is often profitable to contact him directly. While their supply lasts, people who have published research articles are quite willing to send article reprints (copies) to anyone

Journal	Animal Psychology	Human Psychology	Theory and Systems	Research Technology and Statistics	Perception and Sensation	Motivation and Emotion	Learning and Thinking	Physiological Psychology	Pharmacology	Genetics	Developmental and Child Psychology	Educational Psychology	Social Psychology	Personality	Mental Retardation	Clinical Psychology
American Journal of Clinical Hypnosis		■	■		■									■		■
American Journal of Mental Deficiency		■		■							■	■			■	■
American Journal of Ortho-psychiatry	■	■						■			■	■	■			■
American Journal of Psychiatry, The		■						■	■		■			■	■	■
American Journal of Psychology, The	■	■	■		■	■	■	■					■	■		
American Psychologist	■	■	■	■	■	■	■	■	■	■	■	■	■	■	■	■
American Scientist	■	■	■		■	■	■	■	■	■						
American Statistical Association Journal				■												
Amercian Statistician				■								■				
Animal Behavior	■		■		■	■	■	■		■						
Animal Learning and Behavior	■				■	■	■	■								
Annual Review of Physiology	■				■	■		■	■	■						
Annual Review of Psychology	■	■	■	■	■	■	■	■	■	■	■	■	■	■	■	■
Archives of General Psychiatry	■	■		■		■		■	■		■		■			■
Australian Journal of Psychology	■	■	■	■	■	■	■	■			■	■	■	■	■	■
Behavioral Science		■	■	■	■	■	■	■			■		■	■		■
Behavior	■		■		■	■	■	■		■						
Behavior Research and Therapy	■		■				■				■			■		■
Behavior Research Methods and Instrumentation	■	■		■												
Biometrics				■												
Biometrika				■												
British Journal of Educational Psychology		■					■				■	■		■	■	
British Journal of Medical Psychology		■									■		■	■		■
British Journal of Psychiatry		■				■		■			■					■
British Journal of Psychology	■	■	■		■	■	■	■			■	■	■	■		
Bulletin of the Psychonomic Society	■	■		■	■	■	■	■								
Canadian Journal of Psychology	■	■	■	■	■	■	■	■		■	■		■	■		
Canadian Psychologist	■	■	■	■	■	■	■	■				■	■	■	■	■
Child Development		■		■	■	■	■	■		■	■	■	■	■	■	
Developmental Psychology	■	■	■	■	■	■	■	■		■	■	■	■	■	■	■

Fig. 12.1. A partial listing of professional journals publishing psychological research. The column headings present an approximate guide to the usual contents of a journal.

	Animal Psychology	Human Psychology	Theory and Systems	Research Technology and Statistics	Perception and Sensation	Motivation and Emotion	Learning and Thinking	Physiological Psychology	Pharmacology	Genetics	Developmental and Child Psychology	Educational Psychology	Social Psychology	Personality	Mental Retardation	Clinical Psychology
Developmental Psychobiology	■	■	■	■	■	■	■	■	■	■	■			■	■	■
Dissertation Abstracts	■	■	■	■	■	■	■	■	■	■	■	■	■	■	■	■
Educational and Psychological Measurement			■	■							■	■	■	■		
Genetic Psychology Monographs	■	■						■		■	■	■		■		■
Journal of Abnormal Psychology		■	■	■		■	■	■			■	■	■	■	■	■
Journal of Acoustical Society of America	■	■		■	■			■								
Journal of Autism and Childhood Schizophrenia	■	■				■	■	■		■	■	■	■	■	■	■
Journal of Applied Psychology		■		■	■	■	■					■	■	■		■
Journal of Applied Behavior Analysis		■				■	■				■	■	■		■	■
Journal of Auditory Research	■	■		■	■			■								
Journal of Biological Psychology	■				■	■	■	■	■	■						
Journal of Child Psychology and Psychiatry		■	■	■		■	■	■			■	■	■	■	■	■
Journal of Clinical Psychology		■	■	■								■	■	■	■	■
Journal of Comparative and Physiological Psychology	■	■		■	■	■	■	■	■	■						
Journal of Consulting Psychology		■	■	■							■	■	■	■	■	■
Journal of Consulting and Clinical Psychology		■	■	■		■					■	■	■	■	■	■
Journal of Educational Measurment			■	■								■				
Journal of Educational Psychology		■	■	■	■	■	■				■	■	■	■	■	■
Journal of Experimental Child Psychology		■	■	■	■	■	■				■	■	■	■	■	■
Journal of Experimental Psychology	■	■	■	■	■	■	■	■								
Journal of Experimental Research in Personality		■	■	■		■	■	■			■	■	■	■		■
Journal of Experimental Social Psychology		■	■	■		■	■				■		■	■		
Journal of General Psychology	■	■	■	■	■	■	■	■	■	■						
Journal of Genetic Psychology	■	■	■							■	■	■				
Journal of Mathematical Psychology	■	■	■	■	■	■	■									
Journal of Mental Deficiency Research	■			■			■	■	■	■		■		■	■	

Fig. 12.1 (Continued)

	Animal Psychology	Human Psychology	Theory and Systems	Research Technology and Statistics	Perception and Sensation	Motivation and Emotion	Learning and Thinking	Physiological Psychology	Pharmacology	Genetics	Developmental and Child Psychology	Educational Psychology	Social Psychology	Personality	Mental Retardation	Clinical Psychology
Journal of Personality		■		■				■			■		■	■		
Journal of Personality and Social Psychology	■	■		■							■		■	■		
Journal of Social Psychology, The		■									■		■	■		
Journal of the Experimental Analysis of Behavior	■	■		■			■	■			■					
Journal of the Optical Society of America	■	■			■							■				
Journal of Verbal Learning and Verbal Behavior		■		■			■				■					
Memory and Cognition		■		■	■		■				■	■	■			
Perception and Psychophysics		■		■	■						■		■			■
Perceptual and Motor Skills		■		■	■		■				■	■	■			■
Physiology and Behavior	■	■					■	■	■							■
Physiological Psychology	■	■		■	■			■								
Psychological Abstracts	■	■	■	■	■	■	■	■	■	■	■	■	■	■	■	■
Psychological Bulletin	■	■	■	■	■	■	■	■	■	■	■	■	■	■	■	■
Psychological Record	■	■	■	■	■	■	■	■			■	■	■	■	■	■
Psychological Reports	■	■	■	■	■	■	■	■			■	■	■	■	■	■
Psychological Review	■	■	■	■	■	■	■	■			■	■	■	■	■	■
Psychology Today	■	■	■		■	■	■	■	■	■	■	■	■	■	■	■
Psychometrika		■		■								■		■		
Psychonomic Science	■	■		■	■	■	■	■	■		■		■			■
Psychopharmacologica	■	■				■		■	■							
Psychophysiology	■	■		■	■	■		■				■				■
Quarterly Journal of Experimental Psychology	■	■		■	■		■									
Review of Educational Research		■	■	■	■	■	■				■	■	■	■	■	■
Scandinavian Journal of Psychology	■	■	■	■	■	■	■	■			■	■	■	■	■	■
Science	■	■	■		■	■	■	■	■	■	■		■	■	■	■
Scientific American	■	■	■		■	■	■	■	■	■	■		■	■	■	■
The Journal of Psychology	■	■	■		■	■	■	■			■	■	■	■	■	■
The Journal of Social Issues		■									■	■	■	■	■	■

Fig. 12.1 (Continued)

requesting them. Research insights often involve utilizing a method employed in an apparently unrelated field. Thus, students should maintain an interest in developments in a variety of disciplines.

MEETING LIMITATIONS

A tentative research design will usually be modified during the evaluation process. Assuming a proposed experiment appears meaningful, it should be examined in terms of feasibility. That is, can the problem be successfully attacked within the limitations of available facilities?

To the student, limited facilities can become a major factor in the design of his experiment. One of the most important, yet least often considered limitations is the *time* necessary to conduct the research. Completing a relatively small research project is more valuable than leaving a more comprehensive effort hanging because of lack of time. Sufficient time must be allotted to set up the experimental conditions, collect the data, and analyze and write-up the collected data. Also, time should be set aside for "mulling-over" the research results prior to the preparation of the final report.

Another limitation is obtaining the necessary *equipment* for the experiment. (See Unit C.) Some colleges have behavioral research equipment available for student use. Students are often ingenious in designing and building experimental apparatus. Home-built apparatus is less expensive and often better suited to the particular research problem; however, it is more likely to malfunction in the middle of the experiment than a commerical unit. If buying or building is out of the question, it is sometimes possible to borrow equipment long enough to gather the data.

A final limitation is associated with the type of *subjects* used in the experiment. (See Units A and B.) Animal subjects must be acquired, housed, and cared for. All experimental animals should be given the best possible care for two reasons. First, healthy animals are more likely to generate valid behavioral data than unhealthy animals, and second, the student should avoid violating the standards established by state law and local humane societies. Human subjects may require payment, are often less convenient than other animals, and are frequently undependable.

EVALUATING COST AND UTILITY OF ANTICIPATED DATA

The final decision to conduct an experiment should be based on a very simple rule: *Will the utility of the expected data justify the cost required to collect it?* Sometimes a magnificent expenditure of time and money may result in trivial conclusions. In this case, the experimenter should consider more profitable uses for the time spent in the laboratory. On the other hand, the anticipated results may look so promising that the expense is justifiable.

Evaluating the utility of anticipated data is a highly subjective process. The same research conclusion may generate different degrees of enthusiasm in different investigators.

Pilot Studies

Sometimes it is wise to look at a sample of the dependent variable measures to estimate their utility. An abbreviated experiment utilizing a few subjects (a **pilot study**) may be used to estimate the research results. An additional advantage of a pilot study is that it often reveals the need for additional control procedures. A pilot study allows the experimenter to make an evaluation of his potential data before investing significant amounts of time and/or money in the laboratory.

FORMAL PROPOSAL

If an experimenter concludes that his research plans are acceptable, he should prepare a formal research proposal. A research proposal is a written statement of the procedures the experimenter intends to follow. Most of the procedures should have evolved in the research evaluation process. However, stating them in written form forces the experimenter to face any remaining ambiguities. A thorough and well-organized research proposal represents considerable effort on the part of the experimenter and is an important step in the process of translating an abstract idea into empirical observations. Because of the intrinsic value of a research proposal, and because it is often required by individuals who must evaluate the research, a suggested form for written research proposals is presented.

Except for the discussion of previous research and background theories, a research proposal is written in future tense. The following outline is presented in formal outline style. An actual research proposal is not written in outline form (for example, the I, A breakdown is not included); rather, it is written in narrative form.

Sample Outline of a Research Proposal

I. Introduction

The first part of a proposal introduces the general context of a research problem. Relevant theoretical and empirical developments are mentioned along with some indication of why the experimenter feels the research should be conducted. References to background research are cited in the introduction.

II. Statement of the Problem

A. Conceptual hypotheses

A **conceptual hypothesis** is a brief general statement of the expected relationship between the independent and dependent variables. A conceptual hypothesis is derived from an experimenter's model, background research, and/or relevant theories. The terms within a conceptual hypothesis are *not* explicitly defined in terms of operational definitions.

B. Identifications or coordinating definitions

In order to develop an experimental hypothesis, each concept in a conceptual hypothesis must be operationally defined.

C. Independent and dependent variables

The levels of the independent and dependent variables must be labeled and operationally defined.

D. Experimental hypothesis

In terms of the identifications and the specification of the independent and dependent variables, an experimental hypothesis is explicitly stated. Each term and measure in an experimental hypothesis must be explicitly stated in terms of experimental manipulations.

III. Method

A. Subjects

The method of selection, the number, and the relevant descriptive characteristics of the subjects are described.

B. Design and method of assignment of subjects

The specific type of research design to be used is stated and clearly illustrated. The method of assigning subjects to treatment is specified.

C. Equipment

The equipment to be used in a study is described. The equipment includes such things as mazes, paper and pencil tests, response recorders, or stimulus pictures.

D. Procedure

The order of the events of a proposed experiment are described. A description of procedures includes such things as where the subjects are contacted, how they are pretrained, or when they are exposed to a treatment. Sometimes a description of the experiment as seen by a subject is the clearest way to describe the procedure.

E. Control of secondary and error variance

The relevant, potential sources of secondary and error variance are specified and the procedures used to control these sources are described.

IV. Proposed Data Analysis

A. Measures of the dependent variable

From the operational definition of a dependent variable, a researcher specifies precisely how behavior is measured and recorded in a study.

B. Statistical tests

An experimenter briefly indicates how the experimental data will be organized in the final report. An experimenter should also specify how he will statistically evaluate the data.

V. References

When citing previous research and theories within the text of a proposal, the author's names and date of publication are presented ["Jones (1969) said . . ."]. At the end of a proposal, the cited references are listed in alphabetical order by the authors' last names. The reference style suggested by the American Psychological Association is presented later in this chapter.

Example Research Proposal

Hess (1965) suggested that people with dilated pupils will appear more attractive than people without dilated pupils, other variables being equal. Stass and Willis (1967) found that male college students were more likely to choose a girl with dilated pupils as a partner for an experiment than a girl without dilated pupils. Hess (1965) also suggested that a picture with artificially enlarged pupils would be more attractive than a picture of the same person, but with the pupils artifically reduced in size from the normal. There is a need for a well-controlled study of the effect of retouching the pupils in a photograph on preference behavior.

The conceptual hypothesis is that dilated pupils are more attractive to people than undilated pupils. The independent variable will be the amount of dilation of the pupils of the eyes in a retouched photograph. The two levels of the independent variable will be no dilation (normal pupil size) and 30 percent dilation (the diameters of the pupils in a picture will be increased by 30 percent). The dependent variable will be the frequency of preference for retouched and unretouched photographs.

The experimental hypothesis is that undergraduate, male, college students will more frequently indicate as most attractive a photograph of a girl with 30 percent enlarged pupils (retouched) in preference to a photograph of a girl with normal pupils (unretouched).

Method Thirty male, undergraduate college students will be randomly selected from the sophomore class of X college. All 30 subjects will scale (before measure) eight photographs of different females in terms of attractiveness. For each subject, the two photographs that are ranked four and five will be used for the after observation. The research design will be a randomized, before-after, two-group design. The 30 subjects will be randomly assigned to two treatment groups of 15 subjects each. The after measure for Group One will consist of choosing between the fourth- and fifth-ranked pictures with the pupils dilated in the fifth-ranked photograph. For Group One, the fifth-ranked photograph will be retouched rather than the fourth-ranked photograph; thus, the secondary variable of original attractiveness is conservatively arranged. The second group will choose between the two photographs, with the fourth-ranked photograph retouched.

The experimenter will select eight photographs that appear to him to be about equivalent in attractiveness. Each photograph will be the same size (4 inches by 5 inches) and will consist of a face-on shot of a girl's head. Three copies of each photograph will be made. One copy of each photograph will be retouched so that the pupils are increased in diameter by 30 percent.

Each subject will rank the eight photographs from first (most attractive) to eighth (least attractive). The before ranking will take place on Day One. Approximately ten minutes will be alloted for each subject to rank the photographs. Since each individual will scale (rank) the photographs while alone, scaling will require five hours (six subjects per hour) of the experimenter's time. The subjects will be asked to return on Day Two at randomly assigned intervals. On the second day, each subject will be asked individually to indicate which of the two photographs previously ranked four and five is most attractive. About three minutes will be alloted for each subject, requiring one and one-half hours of the experimenter's time.

The secondary variable of attractiveness will be minimized by selecting adjacently ranked pictures for each subject and *conservatively arranged* by retouching the fifth-ranked photograph for Group One. If the subjects in Group One prefer the fifth- to the fourth-ranked photograph on the second day, that will show strong support for the experimental hypothesis, since it will indicate a shift in preference. Alternation of responses is frequently encountered in studies of behavior (Harlow, 1959). Alternation of preference would consist of ranking two photographs as fourth and fifth on Day One and reversing their ranks on Day Two. Group Two is included as a control for alternation. If the subjects in Groups One *and* Two prefer the retouched photographs on Day Two, then neither alternation nor repetition of the previous rankings could account for the observed data.

Eight photographs will be used for scaling, and the after measures will take place one day after scaling. Both of these procedures are designed to decrease the likelihood of remembering the before rank-order of the two middle-ranked photographs. Group pressure will be eliminated by having the subjects rank and choose while alone. One copy of each photograph will be used on Day One, and the remaining two copies will be used on Day Two. The use of new copies on Day Two will eliminate the effect of smudging or other marks that may be placed on the photographs on Day One.

Data Analysis Individually, all subjects will indicate which of the two photographs (retouched or not) they think is the most attractive on the second day. In each group, the number of students choosing each rank will be recorded. The data will be presented in tabular form. The table will be a 2×2 matrix with the before ranks as the two values on one axis and the two groups as the two values on the second axis of the table. The number of subjects in each group choosing each type of photograph will be the data in each cell of the table.

TABLE 12.1. Proposed Photo Preference Data Display.

	Experimental Groups		
	One Fifth-Ranked Retouched	*Two* Fourth-Ranked Retouched	
Fourth-Ranked Photo			
Fifth-Ranked Photo			
Number of Subjects	15	15	30

The experimental hypothesis predicts that for Group One, the subjects will prefer the retouched, fifth-ranked photograph; and for Group Two, the subjects will prefer the retouched, fourth-ranked photograph. The data will be analyzed with the one-tailed χ^2 test for two independent samples. The level of significance (α) will be equal to 0.025.

Harlow, H. F. Learning set and error factor theory. In Koch, S. (Ed.) *Psychology: A study of a science.* Vol. 2. New York: McGraw-Hill, 1959, pp. 492–537.

Hess, E. H. Attitude and pupil size. *Scientific American,* 1965, *212,* 46–54.

Stass, J. W., and Willis, F. N., Jr. Eye contact, pupil dilation, and personal preference. *Psychonomic Science,* 1967, 7, 375–76.

Comments

Williams (1966) and Allen (1960) indicate the most frequently encountered problem with research proposals that are submitted for government grants. Some of these problems are: (1) an inadequately defined experimental hypothesis, (2) an experimental hypothesis incapable of being directly tested by research, (3) an inadequate research design, (4) a lack of sufficient control of relevant secondary variables, and (5) a generally unclear proposal.

If a research proposal is done well, data collection consists of following the written procedures. (An experienced researcher does not prepare a complete research proposal for all studies conducted; however, beginners are required to prepare proposals.) An experimenter should always be alert for any unusual or unexpected behavior that may occur in the course of an experiment. Pursuing accidental phenomena sometimes leads to more interesting findings than adhering to a research design. The term **serendipity** refers to recognizing the potential importance of an unexpected observation and following up that observation. Serendipity is particularly valuable in uncovering previously undocumented behavioral events (Skinner, 1956). Many experimenters find their names perpetuated in psychology because they were alert enough to "accidentally discover" a new phenomenon (for example, Asch, Land, Olds, Skinner, and Pavlov).

The proposal acts as the specific step-by-step guide for the research. The actual experiment, if guided by the carefully constructed proposal, should run smoothly. The next step is putting down on paper the essence of the experiment in written form—the research report. The research report is not difficult if the proposal was well done.

THE RESEARCH REPORT

While working secretly and alone, individuals such as Leonardo da Vinci and Gregor Mendel made brilliant gains in knowledge. Such achievements do not constitute *scientific* knowledge unless the research is reported so that it may be verified. Eventually, the research of da Vinci and Mendel was publicized, and some of their results were incorporated into organized bodies of scientific knowledge.

The printing press was developed just prior to the rapid expansion of knowledge in a number of sciences such as physics and chemistry. The printing press can be considered a major development in scientific equipment. Books and scientific journals provide a permanent record of observations and hypotheses. As compared to personal communication, these records rapidly and precisely transmit information to a large number of people. The free exchange of information provided by printed records is necessary to the growth and development of the sciences.

Advantages of Publication

The transmission of information enhances scientific progress in several ways. Research publications occasionally indicate *blind alleys* or fruitless approaches to a research problem that may be avoided by subsequent experimenters. Publication of research also reduces the likelihood of needless repetitions or *redundancy* if the publications are read. As indicated, the chief purpose of research publications is that they allow the possibility of *verification* and add to the systematic *body of knowledge* of a science. The results of experiments at one laboratory are used to supplement or clarify the results of experiments at another laboratory.

Methodological innovations (equipment and/or procedural) are described in research reports. Research publications also serve a *historical* function. Human beings place a high value on identifying who was the first person to accomplish something. The date of first publication serves as an official historical record in science.

GENERAL CRITERIA
FOR A RESEARCH REPORT

Research data can be communicated in a variety of ways, ranging from a term paper to a research article in a professional journal. Whatever the vehicle of communication, the researcher should adhere to certain general guidelines in reporting his research. First, the information contained in a report must be *accurate.* Reporting erroneous research data not only nullifies the time and effort spent in the laboratory, but can have major consequences for other researchers who accept the report as valid. (For example, see Libby, 1968.)

A second general characteristic of a research report is that it be *complete* enough to allow verification. In addition, as research on a specific behavior progresses, more details concerning the experimental conditions are found to be relevant. If an earlier experiment is described in sufficient detail, the data can be re-examined in the light of new developments.

A third characteristic is that a research report be *concise.* Those reports which are brief and concise are more likely to be read.

The attempt to be concise seems contrary to the goals of accuracy and completeness. That is, one way to describe an experiment accurately and completely is to pour sentences into the research paper until everything is covered. It is doubtful that a reader will be willing to wade through all of the verbiage. However, a well-organized report can be compact without sacrificing the other communication goals.

A research report should be *readable.* Readability is the least important criterion of a research report. The other criteria place severe restrictions on literary freedom. However, within these limitations, an author should try to write *for the* reader rather than simply documenting facts. The unrestricted and undefined use of jargon violates readability and may violate the criteria of accuracy and completeness.

Writing a research report is not an easy task. In fact, the task of writing reports consumes a substantial part of an experimenter's time. To assist both authors and readers, a standard form for a psychology research article has evolved. The form allows reports to be read rapidly and efficiently.

Suggested Form for a Research Report

Title   A title indicates the general problem area and includes some clue about the research method. Such titles as: "Memory transfer through cannibalism in Planarians" (McConnell, 1962) or "Pupil size as related to interest value of visual stimuli" (Hess and Polt, 1960) allow the reader to discern quickly whether the article is of interest to him. Clever or catchy titles such as: "The snark was a boojum" (Beach, 1949) or "Pigeons in a pelican" (Skinner, 1960), do not convey much information, but are likely to be read because of the reputation of the authors.

Abstract   A brief abstract (approximately 100 words) of the report immediately follows the title. The abstract has two functions: (1) to give additional content cues to assist in the selection of articles to read, and (2) to provide a concise summary of the articles to aid in reading. An abstract provides the following information:

(1) the kind of problem investigated;
(2) the subjects used;
(3) the name of the apparatus used;
(4) an indication of the experimental procedure;
(5) a statement of the major results; and
(6) (if space permits) the major conclusions drawn from the research.

An example of an abstract is found in the article by Warkany and Takacs (1968) entitled "Lysergic acid diethylamide (LSD): No teratogenicity in rats."

> Abstract: Lysergic acid diethylamide (LSD) in doses of 1.5 to 300 micrograms was given to 55 pregnant rats during periods of organogenesis and on the 4th or 5th day of pregnancy to 34 rats. Examination of the resultant 887 young for congenital defects showed no greater frequency than in controls. These experiments failed to prove that LSD is teratogenic in rats.

Another example of an abstract is found in the article by Heinemann, Chase, and Mandell (1968) entitled: "Discriminative control of 'attention.'"

> Abstract: Three pigeons were trained to discriminate between two tones differing in frequency in the presence of light of one color (A), and not to discriminate between the tones in the presence of light of another color (B). Generalization functions that were determined in the presence of light A showed control of behavior by the frequency of the tone; those determined in the presence of light B did not.

A limited use of technical terminology is recommended in an abstract because of the space limitations that must be met.

Introduction   The purpose of an introduction is to present a general conception of the problem in its broadest context, to narrow the area to the limited issues involved in the specific problem, and, finally, to state precisely the hypotheses tested. This progression involves an analysis of previous research, a discussion of alternative theories, and a concise summary of the present state of knowledge.

These topics may be organized in various ways. A logical pattern is:

1. Begin with the broadest conception of the problem.
2. Discuss the origin of the problem and the conceptual hypothesis.
3. Indicate the relevant theories.
4. Describe important previous studies.
5. Give a careful and precise summary of the present state of knowledge in the area of the problem, noting the most important studies.
6. Show how the present study evolved from the previous knowledge in the area.

A clear, concise statement of the problem under investigation should follow the introductory material. The statement should include the experimental hypotheses being tested and the necessary identifications relating the hypotheses to empirical events. If the experimenter prepared a research proposal, the introductory material may be taken directly from the proposal.

Method   A well-written method section allows the reader to replicate the experimental conditions. *All* of the relevant details of the procedure must be described. A suggested sequence of topics is:

1. *Subjects.* Describe the relevant characteristics of the sampling population; tell how the subjects were selected for the experiment and assigned to the experimental conditions.
2. *Apparatus.* Detailed descriptions should be provided, including drawings if necessary.
3. *Procedure.* Describe the research design; provide a step-by-step description of what happened to the subjects; if necessary, include a description of procedures followed when unanticipated events occurred in the experiment.

Results   The results section clearly describes the data obtained in an experiment. The description should be complete enough to allow the reader to examine the data in any way he wishes. A suggested format is:

1. Describe and/or summarize the data. Tables, figures, and/or descriptive statistics may be used. A table of all of the measures of each subject may be placed in the appendix if it is too cumbersome for the results section.
2. Analyze the data in terms of the experimental hypotheses. Name and present the calculational values of any statistical tests. Present the probability levels obtained.
3. If observed, any interesting results not related to the experimental hypotheses may be described.
4. Following the presentation of results, the results are interpreted in the following section.

Discussion   In the discussion section, the experimenter interprets and evaluates the results of his research. The preceding sections are concerned with the clear and accurate transmission of empirical observations. The discussion section allows the experimenter to select, emphasize, and interpret his findings in a way he feels is most informative. A suggested organization is as follows:

1. Discuss the results of the experiment in relationship to the alternative and/or conflicting theories and hypotheses presented in the introduction. Summarize the present state of knowledge with the addition of the data for the new experiment.
2. Discuss the implications for further theorizing and research.

For brief research projects, the results and discussion sections are frequently combined.

References   All reference sources that were used should be listed in the reference section at the end of a report. Accurate and complete citations are an acknowledgement of the assistance provided by other individuals as well as an aid to a reader who may wish to pursue the topic more thoroughly. Citations in the text are made by giving the author's last name with the date of publication in parentheses. For example, "Ratesaljevich (1969) said something." References are listed in alphabetical order according to the first author's last name and the date of publication. The references listed below follow the American Psychological Association's approved form (A.P.A., 1967) and may be used as a guide for preparing a research report. Some specific examples are:

Barron, F. *Creative person and creative process.* New York: Holt, Rinehart and Winston, 1969.
Ferster, C. B. The autistic child. *Psychology Today,* 1968, 2(6), 34–37, 61.
Heinemann, E. G., Chase, S., and Mandell, C. Discriminative control of "attention." *Science,* 1968, *160,* 553–554.
Koch, S. (Ed.) *Sensory, perceptual, and physiological formulations.* Vol. 1. *Psychology: A study of a science.* New York: McGraw-Hill, 1959.
Sarbin, T. R. The scientific status of the mental illness metaphor. In S. C. Plog and R. B. Edgerton (Eds.), *Changing perspectives in mental illness.* New York: Holt, Rinehart and Winston, 1969.
Siegel, S. *Nonparametric statistics.* New York: McGraw-Hill, 1956.
Warkany, J., and Takacs, E. Lysergic acid diethylamide (LSD): No teratogenicity in rats. *Science,* 1968, *159,* 731–732.

Appendix   If the research report is extensive, it is occasionally necessary to include additional relevant material in an appendix. Nothing in the appendix should be necessary to understanding the material in the text of the report. The appendix may include such material as extensive tables of raw data, descriptions of the construction and/or operating procedures for special equipment, or verbatim instructions to the subjects.

Supplementary Comments

Abrupt changes in tense ("All subjects were seated in a comfortable chair, given the paper and pencil test, and *are* dismissed when finished.") tend to distract the reader. Similarly, the use of ambiguous pronouns interferes with the communication process. ("The experimenter allowed each subject to continue until *he* became tired.") Many of these basic mistakes may be corrected if an early draft of the report is given to another person to criticize.

As a general rule, all research reports are written in the third person. ("The experimenter read the instructions to the subject" rather than "I then read the instructions.") Most people find that the third person helps to maintain the desired attitude of impersonal involvement, while the use of "I" or "we" is too personal. In terms of communication, either form is effective; however, the latter can lead to opinion statements more easily than the former. When possible, both third and first person should be avoided (for example, "The instructions were read to the subjects.").

Another general characteristic of research reports is the use of abbreviations. If a term is used frequently in the report, the complete term is used the first time and an abbreviation replaces the term in subsequent instances. The introduction of an abbreviation is accomplished by a parenthetical example after the first use of the word. For instance: "The experimenter (E) allowed each subject (S) 10 minutes to complete the paired associate list (PA list). Ten minutes after completing the PA list, each S was then given a mild shock." An abbreviated term is often underlined in the text each time it is used. However, some journals do not require the underlining of abbreviations.

Footnotes are avoided if possible. Technical writing involves a greater use of commas than other forms of writing. Numbers less than 10 are spelled out except for numbers in a series, dates, scores, percents, and units of measurement. And all numbers should be spelled out when they begin a sentence.

The research report form suggested above is one that will meet most research publication requirements from a term paper to a professional journal article. More detailed information concerning specific questions of writing style may be found in the *Publication Manual of the American Psychological Association* (1967) or Turabian (1955).

Occasionally the publication medium places additional or alternative restrictions on a research report. When preparing a research report for a specific journal, the author is advised to consult the publication policy statement of that journal, or examine the articles in a recent issue. Similarly, class research reports may be required to meet certain criteria not covered in the general form.

REVIEW

The material in this chapter serves a two-fold function. The obvious intent in the context of the chapter is to lay down the rules for writing a good report as the end product of the student's behavioral research efforts. To this end, the suggested outlines for the proposal and research report provide a checklist for the student to use to avoid missing significant details in his written work.

The suggested style and arrangement for the research write-up is the model used in professional journal research publications. Consequently, this chapter also provides an excellent introduction to the ways to read professional journal articles and to obtain the maximum information from them. If the student takes the time to study the format presented here, he will find it will enhance his ability to locate the exact information he needs when he is reading a professional article.

SUMMARY

1. There are several potential sources of research topics. These sources include: published articles, general references such as introductory textbooks, listening to lectures, and discussions with other students.
2. There are a large number of psychological research journals. Some of these publications are devoted to new developments; some cover a broad spectrum of areas; and some are devoted to specific areas of research.
3. The evaluation of a proposed research project involves reading the relevant research on the topic; and examining the feasibility of the research in terms of time, equipment, and type of subject required.
4. A pilot study is a small, inexpensive, prerun of an experiment. A pilot study is used to estimate the potential value of a more complete study and to examine the effectiveness of the proposed control procedures.
5. A research proposal is a formal, written statement of the plan for an experiment. A proposal includes: a statement of the problem, the method to be used, the proposed data analysis, and the references.
6. The advantages of publication include: (1) avoiding blind alleys, (2) reducing the probability of needless redundancy, (3) allowing the possibility of verification, (4) adding to the body of knowledge of a science, (5) describing methodological innovations, and (6) providing an historical record.
7. The general criteria for a research report include: (1) accuracy of information, (2) completeness of information, (3) conciseness of information, (4) readability.
8. The suggested form of a research report includes: title, abstract, introduction, description of method, presentation of results, discussion of results, references, and appendixes.
9. Elements of style include: (1) avoiding abrupt tense changes, (2) avoiding the use of the first person (or any person), (3) the use of abbreviation, and (4) avoidance of footnotes.

SUGGESTED READING

Allen, E. M. Why are research grant applications disapproved? *Science*, 1960, *132*, 1532–1534.

American Psychological Association, Council of Editors. *Publication manual of the American Psychological Association.* Washington, D.C.: A.P.A., 1967.

Payne, L. V. *The lively art of writing.* New York: Follett, 1965.

Turabian, K. L. *A manual for the writers of term papers, theses, and dissertations.* Chicago: University of Chicago Press, 1955.

Williams, S. R. *The ingredients of a successful research grant application.* Bethesda, Maryland: Office of Research and Development, Division of Chronic Diseases, National Institutes of Health, 1966.

INTRODUCTION   This section addresses itself to some of the practical problems of conducting research. The material is included to provide a creative base on which the student may construct solutions to problems encountered in a project. A researcher is confronted with the choice of procedures, apparatus, and statistical tests in order to make his research idea work. The discussion here is kept brief since entire volumes have been written on the topics in each unit. We have limited ourselves to some of the basic information needed to run a research project. In addition, some of the more commonly used inferential statistical techniques are described in outline fashion. The student may find our treatment inadequate for his needs so the following list of references is included.

General

Anderson, B. *The psychology experiment: An introduction to the scientific method.* (2d ed.) Belmont, Calif.: Wadsworth, 1971.

Bell, J. E. *A guide to library research in psychology.* Dubuque, Iowa: William C. Brown, 1971.

Candland, D. K. *Psychology: The experimental approach.* New York: McGraw-Hill, 1968.

Kling, J., and Riggs, L. (Eds.) *Woodworth/Schlosberg's experimental psychology.* (3d ed.) New York: Holt, Rinehart and Winston, 1971.

Koch, S. (Ed.) *Psychology: A study of a science.* (6 vols.) New York: McGraw-Hill, 1959–1963.

McGuigan, F. *Experimental psychology: A methodological approach.* (2d ed.) Englewood Cliffs, N.J.: Prentice-Hall, 1968.

Osgood, C. E. *Method and theory in experimental psychology.* New York: Oxford University Press, 1953.

Runkel, P. J., and McGrath, J. E. *Research on human behavior.* New York: Holt, Rinehart and Winston, 1972.

Sheridan, C. L. *Fundamentals of experimental psychology.* New York: Holt, Rinehart and Winston, 1971.

Sidowski, J. B. (Ed.) *Experimental methods and instrumentation in psychology.* New York: McGraw-Hill, 1966.

Stevens, S. S. *Handbook of experimental psychology.* New York: Wiley, 1951.

Underwood, B. J. *Experimental psychology.* (2d ed.) New York: Appleton, 1966.

Comparative

Denny, M. R., and Ratner, S. C. *Comparative psychology: Research in animal behavior.* (Rev. ed.) Homewood, Ill.: Dorsey, 1970.

Dethier, V., and Stellar, E. *Animal behavior.* (3d ed.) Englewood Cliffs, N.J.: Prentice-Hall, 1969.

Gay, W. I. (Ed.) *Methods of animal experimentation.* (3 vols.) New York: Academic Press, 1968.

Maier, N. R. F., and Schneirla, T. C. *Principles of animal psychology.* New York: Dover, 1964.

Maier, R., and Maier, B. *Comparative animal behavior.* Belmont, Calif.: Brooks/Cole, 1970.

McGill, T. E. (Ed.) *Readings in animal behavior.* New York: Holt, Rinehart and Winston, 1965.

Sluckin, W. *Imprinting and early learning.* Chicago: Aldine, 1965.

Waters, R. H., Rethlingshafer, D. A., and Caldwell, W. E. *Principles of comparative psychology.* New York: McGraw-Hill, 1960.

Developmental and Cognition

Ausubel, D., and Sullivan, E. *Theories and problems of child development.* (2d ed.) New York: Grune & Stratton, 1970.

Bandura, A., and Walters, R. *Social learning and personality development.* New York: Holt, Rinehart and Winston, 1963.

Bruner, J. S., Olver, R. R., Greenfield, P. M., Hornsby, J. R., Kenney, H. J., Maccoby, M., Modiano, N., Mosher, F. A., Olson, D. R., Potter, M. C., Reich, L. C., and Sonstroem, A. M. *Studies in cognitive growth.* New York: Wiley, 1966.

Endler, N. S., Boulter, L. R., and Osser, H. (Eds.) *Contemporary issues in developmental psychology*. New York: Holt, Rinehart and Winston, 1968.

Flavell, J. *The developmental psychology of Jean Piaget*. New York: Van Nostrand Reinhold, 1963.

Ginsberg, H., and Opper, S. *Piaget's theory of intellectual development: An introduction.* Engelwood Cliffs, N.J.: Prentice-Hall, 1969.

Hurlock, E. *Developmental psychology*. (3d ed.) New York: McGraw-Hill, 1968.

Jensen, A. R., Kagan, J. S., Hunt, J. M. V., Crone, J. F., Bereiter, C., Elkind, D., Cronbach, L. J., and Brazziel, W. F. *Environment, heredity, and intelligence*. Cambridge, Mass.: Harvard Educational Review, Reprint Series, No. 2, 1969.

Langer, J. *Theories of development*. New York: Holt, Rinehart and Winston, 1969.

Lefrancois, G. R. *Of children: An introduction to child development*. Belmont, Calif.: Wadsworth, 1973.

Mussen, P. H. (Ed.) *Handbook of research methods in child development*. New York: Wiley, 1960.

Mussen, P. H., Langer, T., and Covington, M. (Eds.) *Trends and issues in developmental psychology*. New York: Holt, Rinehart and Winston, 1969.

Reese, H., and Lipsitt, L. (Eds.) *Experimental child psychology*. New York: Academic Press, 1970.

Staats, A. W. *Learning, language, and cognition*. New York: Holt, Rinehart and Winston, 1968.

Learning

Bandura, A. *Principles of behavior modification*. New York: Holt, Rinehart and Winston, 1969.

Deese, J., and Hulse, S. H. *The psychology of learning*. (3d ed.) New York: McGraw-Hill, 1967.

Ferster, C. B., and Perrott, M. C. *Behavior principles*. New York: Appleton, 1968.

Hall, J. F. *The psychology of learning*. Philadelphia: Lippincott, 1966.

Hilgard, E. R., and Bower, G. H. *Theories of learning*. (3d ed.) New York: Appleton, 1966.

Jung, J. *Verbal learning*. New York: Holt, Rinehart and Winston, 1968.

Kimble, G. A. *Hilgard and Marquis' conditioning and learning*. New York: Appleton, 1961.

Kimble, G. A. (Ed.) *Foundations of conditioning and learning*. New York: Appleton, 1967.

Logan, F., and Wagner, A. *Reward and punishment*. Boston: Allyn and Bacon, 1965.

Motivation

Bolles, R. *Theory of motivation*. New York: Harper & Row, 1967.

Cofer, C. N., and Appley, M. H. *Motivation: Theory and research*. New York: Wiley, 1964.

Haber, R. N. (Ed.) *Current research in motivation*. New York: Holt, Rinehart and Winston, 1966.

Hall, J. F. *Psychology of motivation*. Chicago: Lippincott, 1961.

Troland, L. *The fundamentals of human motivation*. New York: Hafner, 1967.

Vernon, M. *Human motivation*. New York: Cambridge University Press, 1969.

Naturalistic Observation

Proshansky, H. M., Ittelson, W. H., and Rivlin, L. G. *Environmental psychology*. New York: Holt, Rinehart and Winston, 1970.

Stokes, A. W. (Ed.) *Animal behavior in laboratory and field*. San Francisco: Freeman, 1968.

Thorpe, W. H. *Learning and instinct in animals.* (2d ed.) London: Methuen, 1963.

Webb, E. J., Campbell, D. T., Schwartz, R. D., and Sechrest, L. *Unobtrusive measures: Nonreactive research in the social sciences.* Skokie, Illinois: Rand McNally, 1966.

Willems, E., and Raush, H. (Eds.) *Naturalistic viewpoint in psychological research.* New York: Holt, Rinehart and Winston, 1969.

Wright, H. *Recording and analyzing child behavior.* New York: Harper & Row, 1967.

Sensory and Perception

Cornsweet, T. *Visual perception.* New York: Academic Press, 1970.

Corso, J. F. *The experimental psychology of sensory behavior.* Holt, Rinehart and Winston, 1967.

Day, R. *Human perception.* New York: Wiley, 1969.

Dember, W. N. *The psychology of perception.* New York: Holt, Rinehart and Winston, 1960.

Forgus, R. H. *Perception: The basic process in cognitive development.* New York: McGraw-Hill, 1966.

Geldard, F. A. *The human senses.* (2d ed.) New York: Wiley, 1972.

Gibson, E. *Principles of perceptual learning and development.* New York: Appleton, 1969.

Gibson, J. J. *The senses considered as perceptual systems.* Boston: Houghton Mifflin, 1966.

Gregory, R. *Eye and brain: The psychology of seeing.* New York: McGraw-Hill, 1966.

Gregory, R. *The intelligent eye.* New York: McGraw-Hill, 1970.

Haber, R. N. (Ed.) *Contemporary theory and research in perception.* New York: Holt, Rinehart and Winston, 1968.

Haber, R. N., and Hershenson, M. *The psychology of visual perception.* New York: Holt, Rinehart and Winston, 1973.

Murch, G. *Visual and auditory perception.* Indianapolis, Ind.: Bobbs-Merrill, 1973.

Stevens, S. S. Problems and methods of psychophysics. *Psychological Bulletin,* 1958, *55,* 177–196.

von Békésky, G. *Sensory inhibition.* Princeton, N.J.: Princeton University Press, 1967.

Social

Brown, R. *Social psychology.* New York: Free Press, 1965.

Eisenberg, J. F., and Dillon, W. S. *Man and beast: Comparative social behavior.* Washington, D.C.: Smithsonian Institution Press, 1971.

Gergen, K., and Marlowe, D. *Personality and social behavior.* Reading, Mass.: Addison-Wesley, 1970.

Hollander, E. P. *Principles and methods of social psychology.* New York: Oxford University Press, 1967.

Lindesmith, A., and Strauss, A. *Social psychology.* (3d ed.) New York: Holt, Rinehart and Winston, 1968.

Lindzey, G., and Aronson, E. (Eds.) *Handbook of social psychology.* (Rev. ed.) (5 vols.) Cambridge, Mass.: Addison-Wesley, 1967–1969.

McGinnies, E. *Social behavior: A functional analysis.* Boston: Houghton Mifflin, 1970.

Mills, J. (Ed.) *Experimental social psychology.* New York: Macmillan, 1969.

Selltiz, C., Jahoda, M., Deutsch, M., and Cook, S. W. *Research methods in social relations.* (Rev. ed.) New York: Holt, Rinehart and Winston, 1959.

Tests and Questionnaires

Anastasi, A. *Psychological testing.* (3d ed.) New York: Macmillan, 1968.

Buros, O. K. *The sixth mental measurements yearbook.* Highland Park, N.J.: Gryphon Press, 1965.

Edwards, A. *The measurement of personality traits by scales and inventories.* New York: Holt, Rinehart and Winston, 1970.

Kerlinger, F. N. *Foundations of behavioral research.* (2d ed.) New York: Holt, Rinehart and Winston, 1973.

Nunnally, J. *Introduction to psychological measurement.* (2d ed.) New York: McGraw-Hill, 1970.

Oppenheim, A. *Questionnaire design and attitude measurement.* New York: Basic Books, 1966.

UNIT A
Experimental Procedures for Animals

As indicated in Chapter 11, animal behavioral research is undertaken for a variety of reasons. There are a number of research procedures that can be profitably applied in laboratory experiments. There is an increasing interest in observing the ongoing behavior of a species in order to determine what the animal can and does do on its own. And there are a number of researchers who apply laboratory based techniques in natural settings or contrived naturalistic settings (Chapter 2).

The following material represents a biased set of examples of research procedures used with animals. The examples are not exhaustive in any of the subareas of animal research included, and not all possible areas of animal research are mentioned. Rather, the selection includes those areas in which the text authors have some interest and/or experience (the bias mentioned above).

OBTAINING SUBJECTS

Selecting appropriate research animals requires knowledge of the morphology and behavior of the different species available. Certain animal species are particularly suited to a particular research problem. The fact that planaria can be cut in half and that each half will regenerate a whole animal allows interesting possibilities in determining the physiological location of learning and memory. The additional fact that planaria will "cannibalize" chopped up bits of other planaria provides the opportunity for a chemical transfer of learning. (See Section Three, Topic 14, "The Memory Molecule.") If cannibals who have eaten animals trained on a task then perform better on the same task, there is a possibility that the learned task is somehow transferred in the consumed tissue.

Bee colonies are often considered good subjects for the study of social behavior. However, the ability of the common honeybee to detect and orient according to the polarizing orientation in the sky (Frisch, 1950) or the fact that Italian honeybees can orient themselves along the lines of force in an A.C. magnetic field (Caldwell and Russo, 1968) make these animals useful for more than the study of social behavior. The fabled "march to the sea" of huge populations of lemmings would indicate that this is an animal very similar to the rat in that both are extremely subject to the stress of overcrowding. Thus, lemmings might make ideal subjects for studies of population density.

Knowledge of the species will also prevent foolish research mistakes. One of the reasons little behavioral research has been conducted on snakes is the fact that snakes can go for a month without food and will exist quite well on only one meal a week. It is difficult to use food deprivation as a motivator for snakes. Similarly, desert mammals such as the kangaroo rat (and to a lesser extent the gerbil and hamster) are very efficient in their use of water; therefore, water-deprivation schedules are not very effective. However, care must be taken in generalizing about desert animals, for desert wood rats store succulent plants as a water reservoir and will die if placed on a strict 24-hour water-deprivation schedule.

In some ways, the common laboratory rat is a singularly unsuitable animal for the behavioral laboratory. Although a majority of the experiments require that the animal make some sort of response to visual cues, rats are not a primarily visual animal. In addition, many students use colored stimuli in their research without realizing that the rat is color blind. Color-blind species (which are predominantly nocturnal) can be observed under subdued red light, since the receptors in their eyes are not sensitive to that region of the spectrum. Thus, it is possible to observe the behavior of animals "in the dark" by using color receptors of the human eye that can see in the red. One disadvantage of this phenomenon is that many discrimination studies require that the rat determine if a light is on or off. If the discrimination apparatus happens to be equipped with a red discrimination light, the sensing becomes very difficult for the subject (rat) although easily seen by the experimenter.

A major determinant of species choice is the *cost* of the subjects. When evaluating a research proposal, a researcher must consider the initial cost of subjects and the cost of maintaining the subjects. Chimpanzees are interesting research animals, but the initial cost is more than $2000 per animal, and maintenance costs are also high. A researcher may find day-old cockerel chicks at five cents a head more appropriate to his budget.

Commercial animal suppliers are the usual sources for research animals. These suppliers advertise in journals such as *Science,* and the managers of research colonies can provide the names of their suppliers. Poultry can be obtained at chicken hatcheries or through large mail-order houses. If a college is located near a farming area, poultry may also be bought directly from farms. If the research project is acceptable, it may be possible to work with animals at a zoo. Small numbers of subjects can be purchased from pet stores. However, a researcher has no control of the past history of animals obtained from pounds or pet stores. Naturalistic observations of wild animals are possible, but experimental studies of wild animals are usually beyond the economic and time resources of the beginning student. One can try trapping wild animals. However, we do not recommend that untrained students attempt wild trapping. Our main objection is that wild animals potentially carry various "bugs" that can be fatal to human beings (for example, rabies, bubonic plague, tularemia, or Rocky Mountain spotted fever).

The biology, pharmacology, zoology, physiology, or psychology departments at a college may maintain animal colonies. A student *may* be able to obtain a small number of research animals from these colonies. First check with the instructor of the introductory research course to find out the appropriate channels for obtaining animals for student research.

The following section provides material supplementary to that in Chapter 11.

TREATMENT OF SUBJECTS

Physical Environment

Animal cages and the room containing cages must be adequately ventilated. A functioning excretion-removal system must also be provided, as well as a continuously available water supply. The cages must have food containers sufficient to provide enough food for at least one day. Several companies provide balanced chow for commonly used laboratory animals. The use of exotic animals requires prior knowledge of their dietary requirements.

Temperature and humidity should also be controlled. People and laboratory rats have about the same temperature and humidity preferences, which makes rat housing simpler. Hermit tree crabs require a high level of humidity.

The animals should be checked daily to see that they are healthy and have enough food and water. Diseased animals should be separated from the other animals. When working with colonies of small animals, it is advisable in most cases to destroy diseased animals immediately.

The use of an infrahuman species requires a good deal of knowledge about the care of that species. The references at the end of this chapter list a few sources of information. In addition, laboratory food suppliers such as the Purina Company often supply manuals for animal care; and animal caretakers, laboratory technicians, or research professors in biology, zoology, physiology, and psychology should be able to provide some tips on animal care. A researcher should find out as much as he can in order to keep the animals as clean, comfortable, and healthy as possible. Incidentally, the number of animals in each cage should be a constant in any experiment unless crowding is an independent variable.

Food Deprivation

Food deprivation is frequently used as a motivation technique with laboratory animals. It is easy to confound an experiment through the use of food deprivation. For example, an inexperienced researcher may either use levels of food deprivation that have little effect on his animals, or use extremely stressful levels that may end in death. A researcher must use levels of deprivation that are appropriate to the species.

A researcher must *adapt* his animals to their particular deprivation treatments. A typical erroneous assumption is that depriving an animal (for example, a rat) of food for a single day will be sufficient to motivate the animal to work for food. Food deprivation for a single day may have a powerful effect on human beings, but it has little effect on rodents. However, 23 hours of food deprivation can be very effective if the rodents are adapted for at least 10 to 14 days to a schedule of eating only during one hour of a day. The animals gradually learn that food will be provided at a particular time of day. As the feeding time approaches, the animals will become alert and active, and they will work for food in the experimental setting.

Three ways of using food deprivation as a motivator are: (1) hourly food-deprivation schedules, (2) manipulating the amount of food provided, and (3) controlling the body weight of animals. The most frequently used *food-deprivation schedule* consists of providing an ample supply of food at the same time each day for one hour and depriving the animals for the remaining 23 hours of a day. Subjects are tested just prior to the scheduled daily feeding hour. Such a schedule serves as an adequate motivation source for rats and pigeons and is not detrimental to the animals. Smaller animals (like the shrew) cannot survive 23 hours without food, so employ deprivation carefully with an unfamiliar species. A schedule of deprivation provides an operational definition for motivation. Water must be continuously available to food-deprived animals, particularly during the feeding period, since most laboratory chow is dry. A food-deprivation schedule is convenient for an experimenter, since he can precisely schedule the time of his experiment, as well as the daily time at which he will have to feed his subjects.

If only one subject is maintained in a cage, then an experimenter can provide only a *specified amount* of food during each day. The amount of food is defined in terms of weight or volume, and the daily caloric intake can be exactly specified.

Manipulating the amount of food is convenient, since an experimenter will not have to return to remove food from each cage at the end of a specified time. Of course, a researcher must know approximately how much food is necessary to keep an animal hungry, but not debilitated. Since the necessary amount varies with the species and chronological age, the procedure of providing a specified amount of food is seldom used.

A third food-deprivation method is to adjust the amount of available food so that a subject's *body weight* is maintained at some arbitrary percentage of normal. The most frequently used figure for laboratory rats is 80 percent of normal body weight. Subjects are weighed daily until reliable measures of average body weight are obtained. Then food deprivation is gradually introduced until the subjects reach the 80 percent point. Throughout the experiment all subjects are weighed daily and provided with more or less food to maintain the required percentage. The body-weight procedure is the most precise of the three methods, because the deprivation procedures are fitted to each individual subject. In the other two methods, a large, fat subject is less affected by the deprivation procedure than a small, thin subject. However, the body-weight procedure is the most time consuming of the three procedures. Ehrenfreund (1960) has devised a set of rodent cages that automatically weigh each subject and automatically dispense the required amount of food to maintain the required percentage of body weight. One additional problem with the body-weight method is that, if young animals are used, the body-weight figures must be adjusted for normal increases in weight due to physical growth.

Adaptation

The purpose of adaptation procedures is to eliminate specific fears of extremely novel procedures and equipment, and to minimize the level of anxiety of each subject. Any procedure that is likely to aid in producing comfortable, alert subjects should be employed. For example, if subjects are put in new living cages for the research, then they should be allowed a few days to adapt to the cages before behavior measurement begins. Individual subjects can be identified by tagging, by ear clipping, or by moving and housing them in individual cages.

Most studies of animal behavior require researchers to *handle* the subjects as part of the procedure. Of course, certain species are not usually handled (for example, adult rhesus monkeys, piranha, and rattlesnakes), and all wild-trapped subjects should *never* be handled without gloves. Some companies manufacture armored gloves for use in handling animals. However, with small laboratory-raised animals such as rodents, we suggest that the most comfortable procedure for the animals is to not use gloves when handling them. Naïve subjects must be adapted to handling ("tamed" or "gentled"). For example, laboratory rats benefit from at least 10 days of handling for a few minutes each day. Incidentally, if a person is bitten by a laboratory-bred and reared animal, then a tetanus shot is recommended, because such bites are usually puncture wounds. Other treatment is normally not required, although check with local health laws, as some locales require that *all* animal bites be reported. When bitten by a wild-trapped animal, try to keep the animal alive and isolated, and immediately notify the Public Health Service and see a medical doctor.

Subjects should also be adapted to experimental equipment and procedures. The standard procedure, when mazes are used, is to allow subjects a limited amount of time to explore the maze prior to training and testing. Animals are adapted to Skinner boxes and are "magazine trained" before testing. Magazine training consists of adapting a subject to the noise of a food delivery mechanism as well as letting it find out where food is delivered.

Termination

When obtaining animals, a researcher should consider how he is going to dispose of the animals at the end of the experiment. Termination is an unpleasant task, particularly to novice researchers who frequently become attached to particular subjects. Naturalistic observers do not have such problems, because they just leave the subjects after completing the research.

Sometimes you may be able to give subjects away as pets or keep a few as your own pets. Depending on the nature of your research, animals may be recycled into the colony for other research projects. Physiological and pharmacological studies often do not require completely naïve subjects. Some of your subjects may be used as breeding stock. Wild species can sometimes be returned to their natural environment, provided they have not been confined in the laboratory so long they might no longer survive in the wild. If all else fails, then the subjects must be sacrificed. There is a variety of procedures for humanely killing laboratory animals. Ether or chloroform may be used in a tightly closed container, provided the animal's skin does not come in contact with the liquid as it can cause painful burns. If there is a tank of carbon dioxide available, this also painlessly kills the animals in a container, without involving the risk of also gasing the experimenter or involving him in an explosion of volatile fumes. An injection of an overdose of an anesthetic provides a very clean and humane way of sacrificing an animal, provided, of course, that the needle is sharp and the experimenter experienced in the means of administration. Most laboratories have a standard procedure for killing and disposing of used animals.

EXPERIMENTAL PROCEDURES

Most psychologists have adopted an analytical approach to the study of behavior. That is, a behavioral sequence is analyzed into components. These components are labeled in terms of explanatory constructs, such as motivation, sensation, perception, innate behavior, learning, and cognition. Thus, some aspects of behavior are consider to be primarily motivational, some perceptual, and so on.

A specific research procedure may emphasize one component by manipulating the antecedent conditions (independent variables) that presumably contribute to a component of behavior. If a research effort is aimed at one of the behavioral components, for example perception, *all* of the other components serve as possible secondary variables in the observed scores.

To illustrate some of the procedural decisions made during the design of an experiment, suppose an experimenter wished to determine if dogs have color vision. The first question might be which colors to use as stimuli in the experiment. Because the experimenter wishes only to demonstrate that dogs can tell the difference between different colors, the simplest procedure would be to have the dogs discriminate between two distinct colors. An initial choice of distinctness might be to choose two colors that are complementary, that is, located opposite one another on a color wheel. Red and green seem very appropriate until one considers the fact that even some human subjects are red-green color blind, that is, they cannot discriminate between reds and greens, although they can identify colors in the rest of the spectrum. The other class of partial color blindness is yellow-blue (also complementary colors). It might seem wiser to select one color from one system, say red, and the other color from another system, say blue. Thus, if dogs are partially color blind, they will still be able to discriminate between the hues in the experiment.

The next problem might be to establish how the dogs are to indicate they can make the discrimination. Choice behavior seems most appropriate to this research question; one of the discrimination devices that presents the subject with both stimuli and allows it to select one of them is used. For the dogs, the experimenter may choose to confront the animal with two doors, one red and the other blue. The doors are hinged at the top so that the animal can walk through the chosen door.

The next problem is the method of stimulus presentation. The doors could be painted red and blue, although the animals pushing against a painted surface might eventually alter the apparent color of the doors. Since the experimenter wishes to emphasize the independent variable, one solution would be to have the doors be the only visible objects in an otherwise dark room. Thus, the experimenter may choose to have the doors made of translucent plastic with colored light projectors placed behind the doors transluminating the doors for the subjects.

So far, a dog is in a darkened room with two illuminated doors confronting it. Unless the dog is afraid of the dark, or until there is something more attractive on the other side of the doors, the dog will not push through either door, much less one with a specific color. Motivation can be manipulated in several different ways. The dog could be food or water deprived for a period of time prior to the experiment, and food or water might be made available behind one of the doors. Another possibility would be to wire the floor of the darkened room with a shock grid and lock one of the doors. Thus, the dog should learn to go to the color that is unlocked in order to escape the noxious stimulus. The experimenter may feel, however, that either deprivation or shock introduces an element of stress into the experiment that may interfere with performance. He chooses to place the dog in the room, walk behind the two doors, and call the dog by whistling to it. When the dog discovers the unlocked door, the performance is reinforced by petting and praising the animal.

If the two doors are always the same color, and the same door is unlocked each time, the dog may learn to go through the unlocked door without paying any attention to the color. He could learn to choose the right or left of the two doors, whichever is appropriate. To control for position learning, the experimenter could switch the color projectors every trial. Unfortunately, dogs can learn to alternate a left-right choice if the situation demands it. Various stimulus presentation or ordering sequences have been developed to control for position learning (Gellerman, 1933; and Fellows, 1967). One way to avoid position learning is to change the projectors randomly.

Position Learning

Even if the dog learns to select the "red" door (which is unlocked) each time, the experimenter cannot be sure that it is due to color vision. There could be a spot or wrinkle on one of the color filters so that the animal could learn to attend to this secondary cue. A particularly troublesome secondary variable in color vision research involves other dimensions of the color stimulus. Color perception is affected by three psychological *attributes:* (1) hue, which corresponds to the physical wavelength of the stimulus; (2) saturation or purity, which corresponds to the physical complexity of the stimulus (saturated colors are "intense" colors while unsaturated colors are pastels or faded colors); and (3) brightness, which corresponds to the physical intensity of the light source.

Control for a spot or wrinkle on the filter could be accomplished by utilizing several different filters for the same hue. Thus, the spot would be used only part of the time. Brightness, however, presents a major problem to our experimenter. If the red stimulus appears brighter to the dogs, even a color-blind animal could learn to choose the red door. It does little good to have humans adjust the brightness of the projectors until the red and blue appear to be the same brightness, since the sensitivity characteristics of the human eye may not correspond to those for the dog. The same problem prevents the use of a light meter as the reference device. The only thing the experimenter can do is to make the brightness dimension an irrelevant one for the discrimination task. The experimenter must make up a series of red filters, all exactly the same color, but all varying in brightness. A similar series of identical hue blue filters must also be prepared. By randomly pairing the colors that differ in brightness, the animal is confronted with a brightness cue that is unrelated to the discrimination task. Color is the only cue that is relevant to the location of the unlocked door. If the dogs have color vision, they must use it in order to perform above a chance level on the discrimination task.

The experiment, which involves dogs selecting a red or a blue illuminated door in order to receive attention and praise from the experimenter, requires that the unlocked door always be a certain color, the right-left position of the colors be randomized, and that the brightness of the colors also be randomized. It should be noted that the procedure is still not free from potential secondary variables. For example, if the experimenter inadvertantly positions himself nearer the correct door when calling the dog, the animal may learn to choose the side where the call is coming from, which may be interpreted as a color response.

The sample procedure is only one of many possible procedures for investigating color vision in dogs. Different stimulus cues, different tasks, and different response measures including physiological measures of cell responses in the retinae of the eyes could be used with equal justification. This is not to imply that the decision to use a certain procedure is to be taken lightly. A color vision experiment using different procedures might draw conclusions that support or refute the conclusions of the example experiment. When the data are in agreement, multiple procedures demonstrate the generality of the observed phenomena. When the data are in disagreement, the difference may reflect an inconsistency in the phenomena, or it may reflect a difference in the experimental methodology.

Perceptual Antecedent Variables

There are three basic questions asked in studies of animal perceptual abilities: (1) Can the animal detect a stimulus; or, if it can, what are the minimum stimulus characteristics necessary for detection? (2) Can the animal discriminate between two stimuli that differ in some way? (3) To what extent does the animal perceive similarities (generalize) between different stimuli?

Detection Detection studies require the animal to learn a response when a stimulus occurs and not to respond when the stimulus is absent. The procedure is to begin with a stimulus level that the experimenter is sure the animal can easily perceive. After the animal has learned to respond appropriately to the stimulus, the stimulus intensity may be gradually reduced until the animal's response level does not change when the stimulus is on or off. The minimum intensity stimulus that is reliably responded to by the animal defines the absolute perceptual threshold for that animal.

Physiological psychologists utilize the detection type of experiment by presenting the stimulus to a sense organ and measuring for the response in the appropriate part of the nerve or brain. Other researchers may teach the animal a special response that serves as an indicator of perception of the cue stimulus. Thus, it is possible to utilize the naturally occurring response pattern in the animal, which often makes the experiment easier to conduct. After a spider has spun a web, it usually retires to some corner of the web and waits for a fly to blunder into the sticky net. The spider detects the presence of the fly by feeling the vibrations in the web. Children may tease the spider by tossing blades of grass into the web, but behavioral scientists can introduce a measured vibration to the web and determine the minimum motion detectable to the spider. Another example of detection behavior can be found in the placement of piano wires across the mouth of a bat cave. Since none of the bats collide with the wire, the bat's echolocating system must be capable of detecting and avoiding the thin wires. By calibrating the diameter of the wires, one could potentially reduce the size of the wire to the point that the bat could no longer detect it.

Discrimination   Perceptual discrimination studies are exemplified by the color vision experiment involving dogs. The animal is trained to respond to one of two or more stimuli by selective reinforcement of the "correct" response. If the animal successfully learns the task, and sources of secondary variance have been controlled, the animal must be able to detect the difference between the stimuli. Measurement of the *differential threshold* involves an additional manipulation where one or both of the stimuli are gradually changed to resemble the other stimulus. The point at which the stimuli become so similar that the animal cannot reliably choose the appropriate stimulus defines the differential threshold for the animal.

Threshold

Workers in Liddell's (1954) laboratory noted an interesting by-product of the discrimination procedure. In attempting to measure the discrimination ability of sheep to choose a circle instead of an ellipse, they used a strong shock punishment for incorrect responses. The animals quickly learned to select the appropriate stimulus to avoid the shock. Then, the ellipse was made more and more circular until the animal was no longer capable of making the necessary discrimination. Under this procedure, the sheep's performance rapidly deteriorated and consisted of random responses with frantic attempts to escape the entire situation. Even returning to an easy pair of stimuli did not improve the sheep's performance. Liddell called this behavior *"experimental neurosis"* and found several analogies to the behavior of human neurotics.

Generalization   Generalization studies train the animal to respond to a certain stimulus and then measure the strength of the learned response to other stimuli differing in their similarity to the training cue. For example, Pavlov found that dogs classically conditioned to salivate to a specific tone would also salivate to a different tone. The greater the difference between the test tone and the training tone, the less the magnitude of the salivation response. Generalization procedures are also used when the experimenter wishes to obtain some measure of the perceived similarity between several objects. The greater the generalized response, the greater the perceived similarity.

Motivational Antecedent Variables

There are four general types of motivational antecedent variables. These are deprivation, noxious stimulation, incentive manipulation, and change from preferred levels of stimulation. The types are not necessarily mutually exclusive.

Deprivation   The organisms are not allowed to engage in a particular type of activity for a period of time. As previously indicated, consumatory behaviors such as food or water consumption are the most commonly studied behaviors. Another deprivation condition involves depriving an organism of specific sensory activities such as vision. Alternatively, the subject may be deprived of the opportunity for specific motor activities such as sexual behavior or general motor activities such as locomotion.

Deprivation has the distinct advantage of specifying the nature of the goal object. The onset of the deprivation is established by removing the object (or activity) from the subject. The strength of the resulting motivation can usually be expressed by stating the time of deprivation: the greater the deprivation time, the stronger the motivation, within limits. Deprivation schedules also possess the real advantage that the animal can be run in the experiment at a specified motivational level by scheduling the experiment relative to the deprivation schedule.

Noxious Stimulation   There are certain forms of stimulation that a given species will actively avoid. When it is reliably demonstrated that organisms will avoid commerce with a particular form of external stimulus, that stimulus is called an **aversive** or **noxious stimulus.** Electric shock, of sufficient magnitude, will serve as a noxious stimulus for rats and college students. Small, enclosed spaces serve as noxious stimuli for a particular subset of people. Pictures of nude women serve as noxious stimuli for another subset of people. The threat of punishment serves as a noxious stimulus for dogs and children.

The advantage of noxious stimulation is that one does not have to contend with deprivation schedules, which can be inconvenient. Electric shock is the most common noxious stimulus used in the laboratory and can be easily adjusted to increase or decrease the motivational level in the experiment. Electric shock also has a number of disadvantages. The most obvious is that very high levels can be lethal to the subject. The same shock level may not be equally aversive to all subjects. There is the possibility that different animals have different pain tolerances, but also the amount of shock differs with the physical differences between animals, degree of contact with the grid, and so on. If a constant current shock generator is not used, the shock level can change rather markedly for a single rat during a single session, since nervous rats perspire on their feet and urinate on the grid, both of which conduct the current from the shock grid more efficiently. If the shock is adjusted to be really aversive, the animals want to avoid it and anything associated with it including the experimenter. Thus, shocked animals are more emotional and less amenable to easy handling.

Incentive Manipulation   The occurrence of incentives, rewards, or reinforcers serves to increase the probability of a response. These three terms are often used interchangeably. However, *incentives* and *rewards* are sometimes limited to physical objects such as candies. The term **reinforcer** is occasionally denoted as the most general term including rewards, incentives, and nonphysical events such as the promise of a future reward or removal of a noxious stimulus. The incentive value of an event for a particular type of organism may be innately determined (for example, rats' preference for sweet tastes or the effect of intracranial self-stimulation) or learned (for example, the reward value for most humans of pieces of silver, or the reinforcing value of "Good Boy!" to a trained dog).

Incentive manipulation involves adjusting the amount of reward given the subject for performance. The usual practice is to use incentive manipulation in conjunction with deprivation schedules. Although it seems obvious that an animal will be more highly motivated for a larger reward than a small one, most experimenters only think of manipulating the deprivation schedule in motivation studies. In some instances, a suitable reward substance can be found that enhances the behavior of nondeprived animals. Monkeys have been known to solve puzzles in order to solve more puzzles (Harlow, Harlow, and Meyer, 1950).

Preferred Levels of Stimulation   All organisms have momentary preferences for certain levels of stimulation. These preferred levels vary with (1) the species, (2) the sensory modality, (3) the long-term history of the organism, (4) the short-term history of the organism, and (5) the immediate environmental situation. For example, when given the opportunity, rats and cats will exhibit characteristic daily activity cycles. Rats will press a bar in order to maintain a particular level of illumination. Snakes and dogs will work to maintain a preferred level of temperature. People will attempt to maintain a preferred level of auditory stimulation.

Extreme changes from the level of stimulation to which the organism has been adapted will usually serve as an aversive stimulus for that organism. However, small changes will normally serve as a reinforcer for an organism. Thus, monkeys will work to perceive an unusual event such as a moving model train (Butler, 1954). Rats will run straight-alley mazes to encounter black and white pictures (May and Beauchamp, 1969). Children will press a button in order to look at novel drawings (Cantor and Cantor, 1964).

Learning Antecedent Variables

Probably more man (and rat) hours have been spent in the psychology laboratory dealing with problems of learning than any other area of psychology. When an area of investigation has many investigators and many different theoretical orientations, the terminology in that area is not standardized. This problem is particularly true in the area of learning. The reader is cautioned to determine the author's meaning for a particular term, since it might vary substantially from the reader's own definition for the term. Even the definition for the term learning is subject to some disagreement. Generally speaking, **learning** is the result of experience. A more formal definition might be: any long-term change in the behavior of an intact organism due to prior experience with the environment. The important part of the definition is that the behavior is altered. It is also to be noted that the alteration does *not* result from maturational factors, short-term drug effects, or environmentally induced physical injury.

Classical Conditioning   Pavlov's famous experiments involving the pairing of a bell and food in order to condition the flow of saliva in dogs is the usual illustration of classical conditioning.

Several terms must be introduced in the discussion of classical conditioning. The unconditioned stimulus (UCS) is defined as any stimulus that elicits a consistent reflex when presented to the organism. The unconditioned response (UCR) is the reflex the organism gives to the UCS. The conditioned stimulus (CS) is any stimulus that does not elicit the UCR at the onset of the experiment. In classical conditioning, the CS and the UCS are presented to the organism in close proximity, and the CS "acquires" the ability to elicit the UCR. Pavlov rang a bell (CS) each time the dog was about to be fed (UCS). The food caused the dog to salivate (UCR) and after pairing the CS and UCS for a number of trials, Pavlov found that the dog would salivate when the bell was rung without the food.

The methodology of classical conditioning does not allow the animal much choice in terms of responding. The UCR is a response that occurs whenever the experimenter presents the UCS; that is, the animal's behavior is under direct control of the experimenter. If the CS and UCS are paired often enough, the CS will elicit the desired response. In other words, the CS substitutes for the UCS.

Classical conditioning may be used to examine problems in learning such as generalization and discrimination, retention, magnitude of reinforcement, temporal relationship between the CS and UCS, secondary reinforcement, and other basic problems in learning. The Russian psychologists have emphasized classical conditioning to a much greater extent than have the American psychologists. The Russian results indicate that the range of conditionable responses may extend to specific visceral responses (both initiation and inhibition) and even so far as to conditioning the clotting of blood (Razran, 1965).

Operant Conditioning The name of B. F. Skinner has become almost synonymous with the operant conditioning technique. The best example of operant conditioning may be found by using a *Skinner box.* Operant conditioning is also called **instrumental learning,** because the animal is instrumental in obtaining the reinforcement. The reinforcement is given only after a certain response is emitted by the animal. If the animal "chooses" not to give the response, the experimenter cannot give the reinforcement. Thus, the animal has considerable control in the operant conditioning situation.

Almost any trained animal act, where the animals perform some kind of trick or stunt, exemplifies operant conditioning. The trainer reinforces the behavior he wishes the animal to exhibit, and the animal learns to perform for the reward. Human beings are exposed daily to operant learning. Vending machines. weekly salaries, course grades, approval of peers are all examples of reinforcing events for which humans will learn the appropriate operant responses. Indeed, we all may live in little Skinner boxes inside bigger Skinner boxes, inside bigger. . . .

Operant conditioning is usually used as a means of investigating the effects of certain independent variables on a learned response. In other words, operant conditioning serves as a vehicle for obtaining the measure of the dependent variable. It is possible, however, to utilize the principles of effective operant training to enhance the training process for the organism. The many "programmed textbooks" represent an attempt to utilize the principles of effective operant conditioning in a practical application. The proliferation of "teaching machines" demonstrates a similar application.

In addition, it is possible to use operant techniques to test the behavioral limits of the organism. There are several instances of students teaching a rat a long and complicated sequence of tasks to obtain a food reinforcement. A rat that can open a door, turn on the light, climb a ladder, and walk across a tight wire to get a pellet of food seems to be more "intelligent" than a rat that merely presses a bar or runs a straight alley. However, the learning principles involved are similar and the complex behavior may be explained in terms of combinations of the simpler tasks.

Unless you specifically wish to observe the uncontaminated learning process in operant conditioning, it is usually most efficient to *shape* the organism's behavior during the initial trials. In the case of the bar-pressing response in the Skinner box, the experimenter can enhance the learning process by reinforcing successive approximations to the desired behavior. The first thing the animal must learn is the location of the food cup. This is done by leaving one or two food pellets in the cup and allowing the animal to discover and eat them. The next time the animal investigates the food cup, the experimenter should drop in another pellet of food. The animal then learns that the food cup gets refilled and learns the sound of the food delivery mechanism when this occurs. This sound soon acquires some of the reinforcing properties of the food, which helps in the training process. After the animal is returning to the food cup each time he hears the food delivery mechanism, the experimenter must shape his behavior toward the bar. The experimenter first reinforces any movement toward the bar. Soon he reinforces the animal only when there is an obvious and direct movement toward the bar. Eventually the animal places its paw on or near the bar before the experimenter gives the food pellet. Finally, the animal presses the bar, and the desired response is established. Unless some kind of shaping procedure is applied to the animal, a surprising variety of responses can intercede between the bar presses.

Mazes Mazes, discrimination boxes, puzzle boxes, and jumping stands all represent a peculiar type of operant conditioning device. The animal must learn the appropriate sequence of responses to attain the goal. The responses might be learning the correct pathway in a complex maze, or it might be learning to identify the correct stimulus on a door. Instead of pressing a bar to have food delivered, the animal learns to move to food.

The advantage of the maze-type device is that the experimenter can observe and quantify the number and types of errors during the learning process. The ability to divide the learning process into identifiable trials is very useful to the measurement of the dependent variables.

Social Behavior

To an increasing extent, psychologists are becoming interested in the interactive behavior between two or more animals of the same species. Some of this research involves the nonmanipulative but controlled observation of naturally occurring social phenomena and some entails elaborate manipulations of the antecedent variables. Rather than try to fit this rapidly growing area of research into a framework of antecedent variable procedures, the following section describes a few examples of the major behavioral areas of interest.

The study of the natural social interactive behavior of animals represents a significant shift in emphasis in American experimental psychology. Rather than the preoccupation with acquisition of unnatural or novel behavior by an individual,

Shaping through Successive Approximation

the emphasis is shifting to the study of behaviors that are useful to species. Much of this type of research represents a subtle shift in the assumptions about behavior. By talking about behavior common to all individuals of a species, the notion of inherited behavior traits or skills is reintroducing itself. The concept of *instinct* was rejected in the 1920s as a nonfunctional term in understanding behavior; the alternative but similar concept of *"species specific behavior"* is being introduced as a useful concept now.

Maternal Behavior   All facets of the process of rearing the young provide rich possibilities for the behavioral scientist. From the mother's behavior during the birth of the young to weaning and separation from the young, there are a number of interesting problems. Hess (1959) studied the phenomenon of "imprinting." The term **imprinting** refers to the tendency of baby animals to follow moving objects such as their mothers. This tendency is particularly characteristic of ducks and geese. Dilger (1962) has compared the nest-building behaviors of closely related strains of lovebirds. Primate care and protection of the young has been studied in the laboratory by Harlow (1959) and in the wild by van Lawick-Goodall (1967) and Washburn and DeVore (1961). Harlow (1962) and his students have also investigated the effect of different types of maternal behavior on the babies themselves.

Sexual Behavior   Courtship and display behavior during mating has been observed and recorded in a wide variety of species: Stickleback fish (Tinbergen, 1953), gulls and ducks (Lorenz, 1958), rats (Beach, 1965), dogs (Beach, 1968), and chimpanzees (van Lawick-Goodall, 1967). Beach (1965) has also conducted extensive research on the effects of hormones and environmental conditions on the sexual behavior of several species.

Social Hierarchies   Researchers have discovered a number of mechanisms by which animals of a species maintain order with a minimum of physical injury. The discovery that individuals of a species establish and strongly defend territories provides an interesting source of behavioral data as well as a source of speculation on human preoccupation with property ownership. If the individual is in his own territory, he can usually evict any intruder; however, if he strays into another's territory he becomes the loser.

Another rich area is the social interactions within a flock or herd of animals in a common territory. There is usually a well-established "pecking order" in barnyard chickens where the top animal can peck all others, a second chicken is subservient only to the top chicken, and so on down the line to the bottom chicken who flees from everybody. Similar "pecking orders" can be observed in other species of birds, some reptiles, and even in primates. Behavioral scientists are learning much about the mechanisms that determine the pecking order both in terms of the total interactions in a community and the characteristics of animals that assume specific positions in the order. Of particular interest is the nature of the "alpha" or top animal in the social order. Even in species that usually interact by territory, if members of this species are confined in a limited space (such as a laboratory cage), pecking orders may be established. It seems possible that this could affect the behavior of the animals in the experimental situation, even if the animals are run individually.

SUMMARY

1. Selection of animal species requires knowledge of the morphology and behavior of the species being studied. Certain animals are especially suited for certain types of research, and some are particularly unsatisfactory.
2. The common laboratory rat presents some distinct limitations as well as advantages (Chapter 11) as a behavioral study species.
3. Sources of animal subjects include: commercial suppliers, research animal colonies, zoos, farms, pet stores, and wild trapping.
4. Food deprivation must be appropriate to the species (and the individual animal) and all subjects should be adapted to the deprivation treatment.
5. Food deprivation can be achieved through: (1) controlling the daily schedule of food and deprivation, (2) controlling the total amount of food available, or (3) controlling the body weight of the animals.
6. Animals are adapted to the experimenter, the research equipment, their living cages, and the research procedures.
7. Some experimental animals can be recycled as subjects, pets, or breeding stock, but humane killing procedures are the usual method of terminating animal subjects.
8. When an experiment is concerned primarily with one component of behavior, all other possible components provide potential sources of secondary variance. The dog–color–vision example illustrates this point.
9. The color-vision example indicated the following sources of secondary variance: color-weakness, type of response measuring equipment, stimulus presentation equipment, motivation source, position learning, unintended perceptual cues, other dimensions of the stimulus (brightness and saturation), and unintended experimenter cues.
10. The study of perceptual abilities requires the answers to three basic problems: (1) What are the stimulus characteristics necessary for detection? (2) Is discrimination possible? and (3) What generalization occurs?
11. The four general types of motivational antecedent variables are: (1) deprivation, (2) noxious stimulation, (3) incentive manipulation, and (4) change from preference levels.
12. Classical conditioning involves the pairing of a conditioned stimulus (CS) with an unconditioned stimulus (UCS) in order to obtain a conditioned response. In classical conditioning the animal has little control over the experimental situation.
13. In operant conditioning, the animal has comparatively greater control of the situation. Operant conditioning consists in providing an animal with the opportunity to earn a reward for some specific behavior. In most operant conditioning studies, the correct response is shaped by the experimenter, and after a stable rate of responding occurs, the independent variable is introduced.
14. The natural occurring social interactions between members of the same species are a rich source of behavioral data. Specific social behaviors of interest to researchers include: maternal behavior, sexual behavior, and social hierarchies.

SUGGESTED READING

American Psychological Association, Committee on Precautions in Animal Experimentation. *Rules regarding animals.* Washington, D.C.: A.P.A., 1949.

Animal Welfare Institute. *Basic care of experimental animals.* (Rev. ed.) New York: Animal Welfare Institute, 1965.

Barnett, S. A. *The rat: A study in behavior.* Chicago: Aldine, 1963.

Beach, F. A. *Sex and behavior.* New York: Wiley, 1965.

Beach, F. A. Coital behavior in dogs. III. Effects of early isolation on mating in males. *Behavior,* 1968, *30,* 218–238.

Breland, K., and Breland, M. *Animal behavior.* New York: Macmillan, 1966.

Butler, R. A. Incentive conditions which influence visual exploration. *Journal of Experimental Psychology,* 1954, *48,* 19–23.

Caldwell, W. E., and Russo, F. An exploratory study of the effects of an A.C. magnetic field upon the behavior of the Italian honeybee *(Apid Millifica). The Journal of Genetic Psychology,* 1968, *113,* 233–252.

Cantor, G. N., and Cantor, J. H. Observing behavior in children as a function of stimulus novelty. *Child Development,* 1964, *35,* 119–128.

Committee on Revision of Guide for Laboratory Animals. *Guide for laboratory animal facilities and care.* (3d rev. ed.) Institute of Laboratory Animal Resources. National Research Council. United States Department of Health, Education, and Welfare. Bethesda, Md.: National Institutes of Health, 1968, Public Health Service Publication Number 1024.

Denny, M. R., and Ratner, S. C. *Comparative psychology: Research in animal behavior.* (Rev. ed.) Homewood, Ill.: Dorsey, 1970.

Dilger, W. C. The behavior of lovebirds. *Scientific American,* 1962, *206,* 88–98.

Eisenberg, J. F., and Dillon, W. S. *Man and Beast: Comparative social behavior.* Washington, D.C.: Smithsonian Institution Press, 1971.

Fellows, B. J. Chance stimulus sequences for discrimination tasks. *Psychological Bulletin,* 1967, *67,* 87–92.

Gellermann, L. W. Chance orders of alternating stimuli in visual discrimination experiments. *Journal of Genetic Psychology,* 1933, *42,* 206–208.

Harlow, H. F. Love in infant monkeys. *Scientific American,* 1959, *200*(6), 68–74.

Harlow, H. F. The heterosexual affectional system in monkeys. *American Psychologist,* 1962, *17,* 1–9.

Harlow, H..F., Harlow, M. K. and Meyer, D. R. Learning motivated by a manipulation drive. *Journal of Experimental Psychology,* 1950, *40,* 228–234.

Hess, E. H. Imprinting, *Science,* 1959, *130,* 133–141.

Lawick-Goodall, J. van. Mother-offspring relationship in free ranging chimpanzees. In D. Morris (Ed.), *Primate Ethology.* London: Weidenfeld and Nicolson, 1967.

Liddell, H. S. Conditioning and emotions. *Scientific American,* 1954, *190*(1), 48–57.

Lorenz, K. The evolution of behavior. *Scientific American,* 1958, *199,* 67–78.

Lorenz, K. *King Solomon's ring.* New York: Crowell, 1952.

Maier, N. R. F., and Schneirla, T. C. *Principles of animal psychology.* New York: Dover, 1964.

May, R. B., and Beauchamp, K. L. Stimulus change, previous experience and extinction. *Journal of Comparative and Physiological Psychology,* 1969, *68,* 607–610.

Munn, N. L. *Handbook of psychological research in the rat.* Boston: Houghton Mifflin, 1950.

Razran, G. Russian physiologists' psychology and American experimental psychology. *Psychological Bulletin*, 1965, *63*, 42–64.

Rheingold, H. L. (Ed.) *Maternal behavior in mammals.* New York: Wiley, 1963.

Sidowski, J. B. (Ed.) *Experimental methods in instrumentation in psychology.* New York: McGraw-Hill, 1966.

Tinbergen, N. *Social behavior in animals.* London: Methuen, 1953.

von Frisch, K. *Bees, their vision, chemical senses and language.* New York: Ithaca, 1950.

Washburn, S. L., and DeVore, I. The social life of baboons. *Scientific American*, 1961, *204*(6), 62–71.

UNIT B
Experimental Procedures
with Human Subjects

Two continuing issues regarding human behavioral experimentation have received recent emphasis. The first issue is the question of whether the subjects' behavior in a laboratory experiment is a real reflection of the behavior of the human population outside the laboratory. Is the experiment giving us an insight into general behavioral phenomena, or only into the way human beings behave when they are being observed? The second issue is whether the experimental subjects are adequately protected from the whims and schemes imposed by the experimenter. Are experimental subjects treated as anonymous sources of behavior or are they treated as real people? Is the experimenter free to lie to the subjects in order to create the atmosphere needed for the research, and/or are some situations so potentially harmful that otherwise legitimate scientific curiosity must be constrained? In his book, *The experimenter's dilemma,* Jung (1971) addresses himself to these problems in considerable detail.

VALIDITY OF DATA

Several potential, secondary variance sources affect the issue of generalizing from the behavior observed in an experiment to real-world behavior. The sampling procedure employed by the experimenter may bias the results. *Sampling bias* can occur because the experimenter selects from a limited or otherwise inappropriate population (which is the usual criticism of generalizing from college students to all human adults). A more insidious source of sampling bias is that people who volunteer to be research subjects are different in some ways from nonvolunteers (Bell, 1962). Thus, the experimenter must be aware of the potential bias in the method of obtaining subjects so that the results are not invalidated.

Sampling Bias

As a matter of realistic appraisal there is no way a researcher can actually get an exactly representative sample of the entire human population. Thus, any sampling procedure employed is some compromise from the ideal. The researcher should be aware of this and select from the procedures practically available to minimize the degree of nonrepresentativeness. If there are significant sampling problems, the researcher should be honest in evaluating the generality of the results.

Invalid human data may result from the effects of the peculiar environment provided in a laboratory setting. People who know they are being observed are more conscious of their own behavior. Many subjects (especially psychology students) spend more time trying to decipher the experimental design than they do working on the specific research task. If the experiment involves novel equipment, then the fascination of novel switches, knobs, sounds, and movement may interfere with the behavior. Even the wording of the instructions to the subjects has been shown to affect the observed research data.

Laboratory Bias

Once again, there is no way to eliminate completely the artificiality of a laboratory setting for all research projects. Sometimes, moving the study outside of the laboratory to a natural setting minimizes the restricting impact of the research. Allowing time for subjects to adapt to the laboratory is another way to reduce the impact. Honesty with the subjects as to the experimenter's intent and procedure may prevent the subjects from trying to "outguess" the experimenter. If the experimenter is aware of the problem he can incorporate research procedures to minimize the effect of the laboratory setting.

As discussed in Chapter 11, the experimenter can inadvertently affect the behavior of the subjects. For example, telling the subjects what the experimenter is really doing is a potential problem, for that information might cause the subjects to perform better or worse because of the researcher's expectations. The problem of experimenter expectations may form a basis for invalidating all behavioral research. Here again, awareness and preventive procedures are the necessary compromise from the ideal. There is no way to design out the possibility of experimenter bias in all behavioral research.

Experimenter Bias

RIGHTS OF SUBJECTS

If behavioral scientists were only interested in commonplace, everyday behavior, then research would be a relatively simple process. The behavioral researcher, however, is often interested in seeing what behavior occurs in unusual situations, such as behavior during emergencies, certain drug-induced states, fatigue, or other stressful situations. Since we know that behavior under stress due to natural occurrences such as theater fires, earthquakes, floods, or robbery is different from the usual, nonstress-related behavior, the ability to create stressful situations in the laboratory could provide valuable information. But is it fair to the subjects, however short the duration of the stress?

The question of the rights of human subjects in experimentation has received much attention recently. One of the outstanding examples of violation of the rights of subjects ostensibly in the cause of science is the infamous Tuskegee study of the 1930s, where black males known to be infected with syphilis were specifically not treated for the disease in order to ascertain the full effects of the disease. This study, along with some of the "medical experiments" conducted in Nazi concentration camps may have provided useful information; however, the cost in terms of human suffering was far greater than the gain.

Behavioral research usually does not have the spectacular potential of medical research in terms of disease and disfigurement; however, psychological damage may be fully as inhumane even though the ugliness is not so visible. Experiments that induce a subject apparently to electrocute a fellow subject might lead to permanent change in the subject's self-concept even after he learns that it was all a test. Falsifying test scores so that the subject is led to believe that he is a potential homosexual, psychopath, or mental incompetent might trigger very interesting behavior that the subject might never have displayed—ever! Even the simple knowledge that he had been duped, irrespective of the actual nature of the deception, might significantly increase the distrustfulness of the individual. The television program "Candid Camera," filming unsuspecting people in potentially funny situations created for the program, altered the American public's evaluation of aberrant situations for several years. Whenever an odd event occurred, people began to look for the hidden camera.

As indicated in Chapter 11, the fact that subjects in an experiment are real people and have important rights is being recognized with more force all the time. The federal government requires strict protection of the rights of the subjects in any research involving human subjects. Guidelines are provided and review committees must monitor federally funded research and research conducted at institutions receiving federal funds, to insure adherence to the guidelines. The use of physical or psychological stress is discouraged. Even deception is to be avoided unless it is absolutely necessary to the research. If subjects are deceived, thorough *debriefing* services must be provided. Subjects are also protected from procedures that are basically an invasion of their privacy. Questionnaires or interviews that bring into question the subjects' moral or ethical behavior are discouraged. Similarly, asking for intimate details about relationships and feelings involving relatives or associates is considered to violate the subject's rights as a person and the subjects must be guaranteed the opportunity not to answer such questions.

Obviously, the researcher can advise the subjects of these rights and seek their informed consent to waive some of these rights. Protective measures such as guaranteeing anonymity when the information does not need to be attached to each individual is also a way to collect data without violating the subject's rights. The fact remains, however, that more than ever before, the experimenter must also consider his research in the light of the impact on the individual integrity of his subjects. In keeping with this newly emphasized responsibility of researchers, the American Psychological Association has released a new set of guidelines for protecting the rights of subjects in psychological experiments (American Psychological Association, 1973).

Informed Consent

OBTAINING SUBJECTS

A researcher defines the subset of those people in his vicinity that will constitute his sampling population. The defined subset will consist of people who can be grouped according to organismic variables such as sex, ethnic origin, vocation, or church affiliation. A defined sampling population may not take account of several potential grouping variables. For example, the population of all freshman students at a particular college includes the variables of sex, socioeconomic level, and ethnic group. When sampling from *that* population, the experimenter must make certain that the variables do not influence his sampling procedure. The researcher must decide whether to collect subjects *individually* or in *intact groups*. In order to obtain a representative sample from his population the researcher should randomly choose names from the entire list of freshmen, and speak to each person individually. If, on the other hand, he can reasonably assume that one or two freshman courses contain representative samples of the entire freshman class, then the researcher can save time by soliciting students from those intact groups.

General Techniques

Several techniques can be used when soliciting subjects individually or in intact groups. No matter what the situation, a researcher must *sell* a potential subject on the idea of taking part in a study. Usually, the subjects are asked to provide their time and effort for little payoff.

When the subjects are initially reached, a researcher explains the general purpose of the study and why the particular subjects were selected. *Do not lie* to a potential subject. If the study requires misleading instructions or procedures, then do not detail these procedures.

No matter what a study is about, the subjects' *anonymity* outside the study *must be guaranteed*. The subjects must be assured that no one other than the experi-

Confidentiality   menter will know how they performed. In a research study, a researcher is not concerned with "finding out" anything about a particular individual. In some way, a researcher must convey the idea that he wants to make a general conclusion about a population of people, not the individual subjects. If subjects generate interesting behavior in the experimental situation, personal identifying traits should be deleted when discussing the behavior.

An introductory description of a study should make participation sound interesting. In most studies, the only payoff the subject receives is the chance to do something unusual. Appeals in terms of "doing your bit for science" have been used too frequently and lead people not to participate in a study. Instead, emphasize any part of the procedure that would most likely be interesting to the population sampled.

When subjects must report at some time other than the initial contact period, sign-up sheets are used. A sheet lists the researcher's name, clearly directs the subject to the exact research location, indicates the time and date of participation, and offers a choice of meeting times. If behavioral observation will take place several days after the initial contact, a sign-up sheet should require the subjects to list their telephone numbers and mailing addresses. Once a person has indicated that he will participate, a researcher mails a postcard one or two days prior to the designated participation date. A reminder postcard contains the name of the researcher, the location of the meeting place, and the name of the study. Among college students, about two-thirds of those people who sign up for a study are likely to appear at the proper time. After failure to appear, a researcher can try phoning a delinquent subject and rescheduling the meeting date. *It is most important* that the researcher shows up at the meeting place on time. Prospective subjects get very angry when stood up. If a researcher cannot make a scheduled meeting, he should call the subjects beforehand and reschedule a meeting time.

A researcher *may* offer to let the subjects know about the results of the research. In the case of intact groups, a researcher can indicate when he will meet with the group. In the case of individually contacted people, a researcher can promise to mail them a summary of the research. The feedback is a simple description of the study and the general results in layman's language. Unless a very small number of subjects participates, individual feedback in the form of conferences with each subject should not be promised.

When individual subjects are randomly selected, every effort should be made to ensure that they participate in the study. Failure to obtain participation restricts the effects of the randomization procedure. In other words, the sample is biased. Sometimes, no matter what a researcher does, he cannot convince a subject to participate. The number of such failures is recorded and included in the final report of a study. Also, record the number of subjects that signed up for a study but could not participate. Similarly, when questionnaires are mailed to people, on the average, about one-third of the questionnaires will be returned. The number mailed out and the number returned are included in a final report.

Contacting Subjects Individually

If the defined sampling population includes strangers that a researcher normally would not meet, then he should provide advance notice to the potential subjects. A typed letter of introduction includes the researcher's academic affiliation, the researcher's status, briefly describes the research project, how the individual was selected, and notifies the potential subject that the researcher will phone to schedule an interview. When an interview takes place, the general techniques previously listed are followed. In addition, a potential subject must be convinced that the researcher is competent and serious, and the researcher must clearly indicate that he is not trying to sell a product. Trying to convince a subject that he will be helping you out sometimes works, and some subjects respond to implied prestige. If a subject wants to be paid for his time, and if you have the funds available, then a promise of payment sometimes works. However, the promise of money works better with indigent college students than with other groups.

Contacting Subjects in Intact Groups

Most researchers sample from intact groups such as college classes, church groups, PTA meetings, and so on. Such sampling is efficient because the introductory appeal is made to an entire group at one time, and feedback at the end of the experiment is provided to the entire group. If a group is clearly defined, such as a fraternity or a church, then the anonymity of the group, as well as the individuals, must be guaranteed. If the research does not require a laboratory, then, occasionally, the experiment can immediately follow the introductory appeal.

If the subjects must go to a laboratory, then sign-up sheets are used. In addition to sign-up sheets, the researcher may provide a small card for each subject to take with him. The card includes a space for the subject to record the time of his appointment.

When dealing with college students, a researcher should schedule more subjects than he needs. When any sizable group is scheduled, you can count on some of the subjects not showing up when expected.

Opportunity to escape from participation must be provided for those people who are unwilling to participate. To decrease the incidence of escape, social pressure may be used. Social pressure may consist of calling for a show of hands of those who are willing to participate. Stooges or shills are used to facilitate social pressure, but such procedures raise ethical questions. Captive audiences such as introductory psychology classes provide a large supply of subjects, but the use of these audiences raises additional ethical problems.

Intact groups have at least one person in a position of leadership or authority. Primary schools, factories, or public institutions have several authority figures that stand between a researcher and a potential subject pool. Starting at the topmost authority position, an investigator must present his appeal for subjects. Appeals must be geared to authority positions, and thus change as the researcher moves down the line of command. The techniques used in approaching an individual subject can be modified for use with authority figures. An authority figure is more likely to be helpful if the research appears to be interesting and potentially useful to him or his people. A research proposal including the use of shock or stress with nursery-school children is unlikely to get past a school's director and teachers. Research that examines a new way of teaching geometric concepts is likely to appear meaningful to school personnel. The undergraduate students of one of the authors have conducted more than 100 studies in public schools and nursery schools. The author has received letters from school principals thanking him for sending the students to the schools and asking that more be sent. In all these cases, the research could not be considered potentially dangerous to the subjects, and the research provided a welcome, short break in routine for the children, as well as occasionally useful information for the teachers.

A researcher must check on the state laws pertaining to research. Some states regulate certain kinds of research, particularly with human subjects. For example, in California, written permission from the parents or legal guardians of children in grades 5 through 12 must be obtained prior to administering any questionnaire concerning the personal beliefs or practices of a child or his parents in the areas of sex, family life, morality, or religion.

Castaneda and Fahel (1961) and Mullen (1959) discuss procedures for establishing research programs in public schools. Do not rely on school teachers to select the subjects for an experiment. Teachers will not select children at random. Rather, they select children to impress the experimenter or to find out more about particular children.

A researcher may subtly enlist the aid of an authority figure in approaching subordinate authorities and the actual subjects. For example, a researcher may ask what aspect of his research is most likely to be interesting to the potential subjects. College instructors do not like to have strangers come in and take class time for their research. However, college professors can usually be persuaded to let a researcher ask for volunteers. A psychology professor may even let a researcher use an entire class period for research, provided that the research has educational value and is interesting to the class.

Unusual Intact Groups

Prisons, drug-addict hospitals, mental hospitals, and detention homes provide potential captive samples of socially deviant subjects. We recommend that introductory students do not attempt to deal with these groups unless they are already working in such a public institution. Dealing with these subjects and their authority figures presents problems that sometimes cannot be handled by a novice. In some cases, the problems cannot be handled by expert researchers. Similarly, the research study of social problems such as homosexuality, alcoholism, or drug addiction involves a tremendous array of ethical, legal, and measurement problems. The novice should stay away from these areas, unless the project is directed by an experienced and competent researcher.

TREATMENT OF SUBJECTS

A researcher should play the role of a subject in order to get an estimate of a subject's personal reaction to the research procedure. Then the researcher can use that estimate to aid him in maintaining rapport with each subject. As with infrahuman subjects, a researcher, within the limits of his research design, should strive to make his subjects as comfortable and calm as possible.

Children

Adaptation to an experimenter may be even more important with children than other types of subjects. Unless children are adapted to an experimenter, he will have difficulty in getting them to "play his game" voluntarily, (particularly if they must be left alone in the experimental room, Sharpe, 1951). With nursery-school and kindergarten children, a researcher should spend several days at a school letting the children get used to seeing him around. During the adaptation period, a researcher should try to talk with each child for at least a few minutes.

The research room should be as free from distracting stimuli as possible. As Stevenson and Wright (1966, p. 581) point out: "The child's attention is often diverted from the experimental task by his exploration of the apparatus and the experimental room, and it appears that almost any stimulus change may serve further to reinforce such activity." Children should be allowed to explore the experimental setting prior to the onset of the experiment. Such adaptation increases the likelihood of their attending to the important changes involved in the research.

The comprehension of verbal instructions is a major problem. As Bijou and Baer (1960, p. 166) indicate: "If successful, this is undoubtedly an efficient technique. Too often, however, the experimenter may find that he promoted misunderstanding in the child by only the use of verbal instruction." Particular care should be taken to use very elementary terms. Asking a child if he has understood your instructions is fruitless. A young child will usually nod his head and say "yes" whether or not he comprehends what you are saying. In general, each child should be pretested to see if he understands the instructions. When using children in a school setting, another major problem is controlling communication between the subjects between experimental sessions. A researcher can tell children to keep their experiences secret. And, he can obtain a measure of communication by asking each child prior to testing whether he knows anything about the experiment. However, in school settings, one should avoid research where prior communication may be detrimental.

In summary, to ensure that a child understands what is required of him, the experimenter should develop a series of adaptation and pretesting procedures. The use of standardized verbal instructions, contrary to the purpose of such instructions, will often increase rather than decrease the individual differences within an experiment. Rather, the experimenter should fit instructions and pretraining procedures to the individual subject.

There are several reasons for not using rewards with children. Parents and/or school officials may prefer that children not be given rewards (either tokens or foods). If the task is inherently interesting to the subject, then rewards are unnecessary and may distract the subject. However, if the task is repetitive, time consuming, or boring (for example, bar pressing) the use of rewards is necessary.

Candy as a reward for children leads to more problems than it is worth. Bijou and Sturges (1959) present a list of token rewards that have been shown to be reinforcing for children. If possible, the reward value of a token should be determined by pilot studies. Infants as well as older children respond positively to mild surprises or novelty. For example, Bower (1966) successfully used "peek-a-boo" with infants. Social reinforcers such as talking with the experimenter can also be used to motivate performance. The use of the phrase "Let's go play a game" is based on the idea that "game-playing" is reinforcing to children.

In general, the use of punishment should be avoided. In children, the effect of punishment is to increase the variance of the dependent measures. In any young animal, the use of punishment may terminate responding, produce varied emotional responses, or produce confusion.

Finally, if the procedures are brief and intrinsically interesting to a child, he will pay attention throughout the experiment. However, if a task is repetitious and boring, a child is apt to stare out a window or even get up and leave. A general rule of thumb is that for children under 10, a half-hour should be the *maximum* time for an experimental session.

Termination

After completion of data collection, an experimenter should thank each subject for his participation. If a researcher has promised feedback, then he should specify exactly when the feedback will be provided. In the case of small children, a suggestion that the research was "fun" is usually appropriate along with some comment about how well the child did.

If adult subjects were subjected to pain, deception, or stress of any kind, then an experimenter is obligated to explain why these procedures were necessary, relate the procedure to the research purpose, and in a variety of ways, provide an opportunity for subjects to dissipate their anxiety and/or displeasure. If deception is used with small children, Smith (1967) recommends that disclosure of the deception may not be desirable. We strongly recommend that novice researchers *not* use unpleasant procedures with any type of subject.

EXPERIMENTAL PROCEDURES

As in Unit A, the following materials are a sample of techniques used in research with human subjects. The choice of techniques to be included was determined by the experiences and/or interests of the authors.

The procedures used with animal subjects (Unit A) can also be appropriate for the measurement of human behavior, particularly in the case of experiments with young children. Human subjects also respond to a number of experimental procedures not available to the animal experimenter. Human subjects understand verbal instructions; thus, the subject can be told about certain aspects of the experiment rather than having to discover them by trial and error. Similarly, special conditions or behavioral restrictions can be verbally introduced into the experiment. In addition to the freedom gained in manipulating antecedent conditions, the verbal ability of the subject allows the experimenter to collect a new type of behavior, namely the verbal reports of the subject.

Verbal reports of subjects have been useful dependent variable measures since psychology "became" a science in 1879 at Wundt's laboratory in Leipzig, Germany. Wundt founded a school of thought called Structuralism, which relied on the use of "introspection." **Introspection** is the generic term for a method of studying stimuli, which relies upon the subjective report of the subject's sensations, images, and feelings. The structuralists were criticized by many psychologists, because the introspective method did not adhere to two of the criteria of science, namely, that an experiment be public and repeatable. How, then, is the verbal report of a subject in a perception experiment different from the data of the introspectionists? The resolution of this problem is that the perceiver in an experiment can provide a verbal report that is *correlated* with the physical dimensions of the stimulus (Haber, 1968). When a verbal response is correlated with the physical measure of the stimulus or with some behavioral characteristic such as a neural response, then the verbal response is no longer purely introspective, but a legitimate (public and repeatable) response measure. According to Haber, "Introspective responses should be objected to only when they are elicited under free conditions and not tied down to specific stimulus and response conditions" (Haber, 1968, p. 4).

Natsoulas (1968) has presented information on two categories of perceptual reports: (1) phenomenal reports that are informative about perceptual experience and (2) cognitive reports that tell the experimenter something about how the subject identifies and describes the stimulus objects presented to him (introspection). The former category yields information such as Steven's (1958) use of subjective magnitude estimates of stimuli in a direct manner to infer the magnitude of a subject's perception. Cognitive reports are thought to be determined by the degree of sensory excitation in the subject. For example, Swets (1961) in his theory of signal detectability, treated a subject's "yes" response as indicating a belief by the subject that a signal had occurred on that trial.

Perception Antecedent Conditions

An **afterimage** may be produced by having a subject focus on a flashbulb as it is discharged. The intensity of a visual afterimage may be measured by asking the subject to scale or rate several afterimages verbally on the basis of their intensity prior to the experiment. After a practice period, the subject should be able to scale afterimages into categories such as strong, moderate, or weak. His subsequent responses in the experiment would be consistent and allow the experimenter to measure the strength of response.

One variable of interest to the experimenter is the number of changes observed in the afterimage. Of particular interest are the number of changes in the color of the afterimage (**flight of colors**). That is, the experimenter could ask the subject to delineate whether the afterimage was red, pink, green, azure, and so on. Prior training on identification of colors and their changes will facilitate the measurement of color changes. Color changes may correspond to chemical changes on the retina or may correspond to differential neural firing in higher cortical areas so that precise measurement is imperative. By accurately counting the response changes in the perception of color, the experimenter may approximate physiological changes.

The duration of an afterimage, as well as the duration of each color perceived during the afterimage, may be important. Each time period may be measured by the experimenter by measuring the time between indicated changes by the subject. The sum of these time scores would yield the total time of the afterimage. This procedure would necessarily involve several time devices and fast work by the experimenter. Each duration of a particular color might yield further information about chemical changes on the retina or about neural firing in high cortical centers.

When asking a subject to scale an afterimage, be careful to maintain constant observation conditions. If the room lights are flashed on and off, the image becomes stronger, and can be so "driven" for unusually long periods of time. Similarly, if the subject blinks his eyes, the image is enhanced.

A somewhat similar perceptual phenomenon is known as the **autokinetic effect.** If a small pinpoint of light is presented in an otherwise dark environment, most subjects perceive a distinct drift or motion to the light over time. If the eye lacks a point of reference in determining the stationary nature of the light, it apparently cannot do so. It would appear that the movement results from the unconscious natural movements of the eye. The measure of the direction and extent of the apparent movement must come from the verbal report of the subjects. Investigating the conditions that affect the extent of the illusion might give information about the operation of the visual perceptual system.

Another example of an investigatable illusion is the discovery of a **haptic (touch) illusion** by Cormack (1973). If a coin is held on edge between the thumb and forefinger of one hand and spun end-over-end by the thumb and forefinger of the other hand, the coin feels longer to the turning hand. Cormack found that size of the coin and rate of turning changed the extent of the illusion. Here again, verbal report must be the dependent variable, since the extent of the illusion is estimated by the subjects.

Threshold Measurement   The study of the relationship between the physical characteristics of the stimulus and the response characteristics of the perceiver is called **psychophysics.** The relationship was one of the earliest behavioral problems to be studied in the laboratory. As was the case with animal perceptual studies, one of the major concerns is with accurate measurement.

In most psychophysical experiments, the experimenter determines the level at which a subject detects a stimulus 50 percent of the time. The 50 percent level is called the **threshold** for a particular sensory modality. In order for an experimenter to determine a subject's threshold, the subject must indicate whether or not he detects the stimulus. There are two response indication methods commonly used in psychophysics. First, there is the **yes-no method** where the experimenter asks the subject, "Did you detect the stimulus?" and the subject responds either "yes" or "no." The second type of indication is obtained by the **forced-choice method.** In the forced-choice method, the stimulus occurs in one of several alternative positions in a display, or during one of the several time intervals. On each trial, the subject must indicate in which position or time interval he feels that the stimulus occurred. In the forced-choice method, the subject must not only detect the stimulus, but must indicate where or when he saw it.

Generally speaking, the yes-no method requires less time in an experimental setting than the forced-choice method. The yes-no method requires shorter time intervals per trial, which is an advantage, since rapid measurements of thresholds are less subject to changes in the subject's sensitivity over time. The yes-no response requires that the experimenter believe the subject's report, while the forced-choice method requires the subject to convince the experimenter. It has been found that the forced-choice method yields lower threshold values than the yes-no method (Blackwell, 1953). Sometimes, however, highly motivated subjects generate spuriously low thresholds in the yes-no method (Dember, 1960). If the subject says "yes" each time, then his threshold will measure lower than it should. In order to compensate for this "maximizing strategy," many experimenters insert **blank trials** into the regular trials. There is no stimulus present during a blank trial. An honest subject will say "no" to these blank trials more often than not. If a subject knows about the blank trials, he will give less *"false alarms,"* but it may increase his number of *"misses."* Consequently, the yes-no method seems to be influenced by more spurious factors than the forced-choice method.

In the **method of limits,** the experimenter consistently increases or decreases the physical measure of the stimulus until a change in response is noted. For example, suppose that the experimenter wants to determine an auditory threshold. He chooses an initial auditory stimulus that is below threshold and increases the intensity by very small increments until the subject says he hears it. Then the experimenter chooses a stimulus above threshold and decreases its intensity until the subject indicates that he cannot hear it. The experimenter repeats both the ascending and descending procedures many times. In the above example, we have combined the method of limits with the yes-no method.

The method of limits has advantages and disadvantages. The major disadvantage is that subjects, after several ascending and descending trials, tend to anticipate the following trial. This tendency decreases the accuracy of the threshold estimate. Another tendency is that subjects who have said "yes" on several trials tend to say "yes" on the following trial *(response perseveration).* Still another disadvantage is *response alternation.* This is the tendency for a subject to change his response. These two tendencies may cancel each other out, but are still potential sources of error. The forced-choice method tends to limit the influence of perseveration and alternation, but is incompatible with the assumptions basic to the method of limits (Dember, 1960, p. 39). Therefore, this combination cannot be used. One further source of error in the method of limits is the tendency for one stimulus to affect the perception of another. This is called the *adaptation-level effect.* For example, if a descending series starts very far above the threshold, there is a tendency for the threshold to be high. On the other hand, if a series starts very low, the obtained threshold will be lowered. The adaptation level effect can be controlled by randomly varying the starting points for both ascending and descending series. The method of limits combined with the yes-no method is most widely used in psychophysics.

Cornsweet (1962) has combined the yes-no method and method of limits in what is known as the **staircase method.** In this procedure, the stimulus is started well above (or below) threshold and then is adjusted in small increments toward threshold while the subject reports "yes" or "no" as to whether he perceives the stimulus. When the subject's report changes, the direction of the stimulus change is reversed. Several increasing and decreasing cycles are used for an experiment. The result is a relatively narrow band of stimulus intensities that received both yes and no responses in various frequencies. The threshold is the 50 percent point in this band.

Although adaptation level, response perseveration, and response alternation all could be active in the staircase method, all are minimized and/or balanced in such a way that this is a relatively efficient method for obtaining an absolute threshold.

Another stimulus presentation method is the **method of constant stimuli.** In this method, the experimenter selects several stimuli (usually about five) that he thinks are likely to surround the subject's threshold. These stimuli are then each presented to the subject about 50 times in random order. The stimulus yielding a frequency of "yes" responses closest to 50 percent is used as the best estimate of threshold. Blackwell, however, has found that grouping the stimuli in blocks of ten and presenting a particular stimulus on ten successive trials yields more stable results than does randomization (Dember, 1960). The major disadvantage to the method of constant stimuli is that it does not provide a quick and easy method of finding thresholds. If time is not important, the method of constant stimuli is superior to the method of limits. The constant stimulus method is less subject to perseveration and alternation; consequently, the threshold measures derived are more stable.

Classical psychophysical methods assume that the receptor system is completely accurate. That is, if the signal is of a certain strength, it will be above the threshold for perception, and if the signal is below that strength, it will not be perceived. Swets (1961) suggests that this is an erroneous assumption. He compares the sensory receptor to a radio receiver that must detect the radio signal emanating from the broadcast station in a background of interference from similar electrical events (such as radio ignition, electric shavers, and so on) as well as the electrical events spontaneously generated in the circuitry of the radio itself. Swets calls the broadcast *signal* and the interference *noise.* Basically, then, in a threshold experiment, the subject must identify when there is a signal present mixed with noise, and when he perceives only noise.

In both situations the receptor is active, although the activity contributed by the noise varies randomly over time. Thus the subject must discriminate between some activity (noise) and greater activity (signal plus noise). Remember, however, that the noise activity level changes randomly from one moment to the next. Thus the problem becomes complicated when the signal is weak enough that there is no clear separation over the normal variation in the noise. In the threshold situation where one is using minimum signals, sometimes the noise level alone will be greater than the signal-plus-noise condition. Since the subject can only work from total activity level, he must arbitrarily set some criterion level, anything above which he calls "signal" and below which he calls "noise" even though he will occasionally be incorrect in each call. This **response criterion** is the basis on which the subject performs in the experiment and represents his "threshold" in that experiment. Notice that this is a rather radical change from the classic concept of threshold, but it also accounts for some of the apparent inconsistencies in threshold experiments.

The **signal-detection method** is designed to enable the experimenter to estimate independently both the sensory capacity (sensitivity) for the detection of signals and the response criterion of the observer. Response criterion refers to the basis for making a "yes" or "no" decision about sensory input. The existence of false alarms in a sensory threshold experiment (reporting a signal when, in fact, it has not occurred) suggests that the "threshold" depends partly upon the sensitivity of the observer's sensory processes and partly on his response criterion. The basic aim of the signal-detection method is to separate the response criterion of a subject from his actual sensitivity. A person's response criterion can be estimated by the relative frequency of false alarms. The criterion may be changed by manipulation of the *a priori* probability of signal presentation. Suppose, for example, that you give a subject 200 trials. A near threshold signal is randomly presented during 100 of the trials, and during the other 100 trials, no signal occurs. Therefore, the *a priori* probability of signal is $0.50[p(SN) = .50]$. The fictitious data obtained are shown in Table B.1.

Quadrant (a) in Table B.1 states that 60 percent of the time the subject correctly detected a signal (hits) and quadrant (b) shows that 25 percent of the time the subject made false alarms. If we had used an *a priori* signal probability of $p(SN) = .90$, we might have obtained the data shown in Table B.2. The signal strength is the same as in Table B.1.

TABLE B.1. Fictitious Data to Illustrate the Relative Frequencies (Proportions) of Yes and No Responses in a Signal Detection Experiment with p (SN) = .50.

		Stimulus	
		On	Off
Response	Yes	(a) 0.60	(b) 0.25
	No	(c) 0.40	(d) 0.75

TABLE B.2. Fictitious Data in a Signal Detection Experiment with p (SN) = 0.90.

		Stimulus	
		On	Off
Responses	Yes	0.97	0.72
	No	0.03	0.28

Notice that as the hit rate increased, so did the false-alarm rate. The detection rate can also be changed by paying the subject for hits and/or charging him for false alarms.

Sensory Scaling Methods Human beings do not spend most of their time perceiving stimulation that hovers around their sensory thresholds. Rather, they perceive stimuli that are supra-threshold, and it is the function of sensory and perception psychologists to understand the measurement techniques for these stimuli. The magnitudes of sensations are not directly measurable in the same way as physical quantities. The following methods are available for sensory scaling.

In **magnitude estimation,** the subject is asked to estimate sensory input in terms of a numerical scale. For example, if an experimenter is interested in scaling the brightness of a light, he might ask the subject to estimate the brightness of the light on a scale from 1 to 10, with 1 being the least bright and 10 being the brightest possible light.

Another method of measuring psychological attributes is the **method of fractionation.** In this method, the subject chooses or adjusts one stimulus so that the subjective magnitude is some fraction of another stimulus. That is, a subject may be asked to adjust one stimulus so that it looks "half as bright" as a standard stimulus. This method usually yields large response variability and consequently the amount of measurement error should be specified (Boynton, 1968).

A third scaling technique is the **equal-sense distance method.** Here, a subject arranges three or more stimuli so that their subjective distances are equal. This method yields an interval scale of measurement. This method enables the experimenter to say that there is as much difference between stimuli 1 and 2 as between 3 and 4.

Motivational Antecedent Variables

Several motivational variables are available to an experimenter when human subjects are used in an experiment.

Physiological Measures Both the polygraph (lie detector) and the electroencephalograph (brain-wave recorder) provide a means of measuring degree of *arousal* or *emotion* in the human subject. Several specific changes are known to correlate with various motivational states in the subject. Physiological measures may be used as a direct measure of a dependent motivational response, or they may be used to select or identify subjects with certain motivational characteristics as an independent (organismic) variable in an experiment.

Measures of Personality   Certain personality tests are presumed to measure the contemporary motivational state of the organism. For example, the Taylor Manifest Anxiety Scale is used to *classify* people into two groups, "high" and "low" anxiety. Projective tests are also used to *classify* people in terms of motivational states. For example, variations of the Thematic Apperception Test (TAT) are used to measure achievement motivation (McClelland, et al., 1953) and affiliation motivation (Atkinson, 1958).

The use of personality tests is often questioned because the reliability and validity of paper and pencil tests have infrequently been examined. In addition, much of the research involving the personality test technique has been solely concerned with the correlation between various test measures. Comparatively little research on the antecedents of the test scores has been conducted. Exceptions to these statements include the research of McClelland and Atkinson.

Social Pressure   "Man is a gregarious animal." Statements such as this imply that man is a social organism with certain inherent tendencies towards interactions with other persons. As such, there must be certain motives found in human beings that relate to their interactions with others. Consequently, many human motivation studies involve the manipulation of the interaction conditions between two or more individuals. Asch's discovery (1951) that college students could be manipulated into making errors on a simple length of line identification task illustrates the effect of social pressure. Students who could normally identify the length of lines correctly, tended to name a wrong line if everyone else in the group had already chosen the wrong line. Some of the subjects who followed the majority choice stated that they "called them as they saw them," which leads to the conclusion that even the perception of the lines was altered by the action of others.

Antecedent Variables in Learning

The development of language in the human species provides an ideal method for the investigation of learning in the laboratory. We can ask subjects to study verbal material under controlled laboratory conditions. Verbal material presents the subjects with a type of learning problem with which they are already familiar. Verbal material may be easily and inexpensively produced for use in experiments. Although it is possible to have subjects learn verbal discourse in a laboratory setting, the usual method is to provide the subject with a problem of learning a number of discrete verbal elements.

Verbal Material   The elements used in a verbal learning study may be categorized into three basic categories: words, nonsense syllables, and numbers. The experimenter may have the subject learn any or all of these categories in a single experiment.

Words used in an experiment usually consist of common nouns or adjectives, such as boat, star, rope; or heavy, funny, and so on. Not all words within a category are equally easy to learn however, since a list of nouns like logoryph, paraonym, and zamarra would be a more difficult list of words to learn. The problem of difficulty of the individual elements is a significant one in most verbal learning studies.

The example above gives several possible interpretations of "difficulty." One interpretation would be the length of each word determined by the number of letters. The difficult words also contain an unusual number of rare letters, such as v, z, and y. Another indicant of difficulty is the amount of letter overlap between items in the same list. And, difficulty of pronunciation may be a relevant criterion.

The most important determiner of difficulty in words is the *meaningfulness* of the word. The terms xylophone or pneumonia seem to fit the above identifications for difficulty, yet would provide little problem for most subjects. The difference occurs because the latter terms have already been learned in association with a specific object or concept. These terms are meaningful to the subject. If the experimenter plans to use a list of words in a verbal learning experiment, he should consider some sort of control for meaningfulness in the items he selects. Thorndike and Lorge (1944) provide a list of 10,000 words that are ranked in terms of their frequency of occurrence in the English language. Selecting all of the items from the same general frequency category allows the experimenter to equalize the difficulty of the items. The relative frequency of the words selected allows the experimenter to manipulate the difficulty of learning the task.

The difficulty of the task may also be manipulated by changing the length of the list of items to be learned. If less than seven or eight items are used, most subjects will learn the list on the first learning trial. A list of 20 items is common in verbal learning studies, although it is often wise to test the difficulty of any particular list on a few pilot subjects to be sure it fits your research requirements.

The first verbal learning experiments by Ebbinghaus (1885) were conducted using nonsense syllables. Ebbinghaus wished to find learning material that was similar to the learning of words, but which avoided the learning already associated with meaningful words. Ebbinghaus developed the **nonsense syllable,** which usually consists of a three-letter trigram made up of a consonant, a vowel, and a consonant (CVC). The resulting "word" allows the experimenter to present a list of "meaningless" verbal material that may be learned. Examples of nonsense syllables are KUQ, XOC, and ZIF. Unfortunately, terms as DOG, CAT, and MAP may also be generated as "nonsense" syllables. Even if real-word trigrams are eliminated, trigrams such as ROP, BIZ, or TEX hardly qualify as being "nonsense." Thus, trigrams vary in their meaningfulness. Glaze (1928), Noble (1961), and Underwood and Schulz (1960) have scaled trigrams according to some measure of meaningfulness (frequency, pronounceability, and so on). These lists may be used to select items of equal difficulty and to manipulate the degree of difficulty of the task.

Numbers are highly discriminable elements for verbal learning studies. The usual method when numbers are used in a verbal learning study is to select the numbers 0–9 or 1–99. Battig and Spera (1962) have listed the numbers from 1 to 100 in terms of their meaningfulness to subjects.

Verbal Learning Paradigms   The most frequently used experimental paradigm in verbal learning studies involves learning the association between two elements in a list of materials. The **paired-associate** task consists of exposing a subject to both elements of a pair. For instance, say that you showed a subject the following three pairs: star–5, boat–8, and rope–3. On the next trial, you show the subject only the words, star, boat, rope; and the subject is to respond with the number that was paired with each word. The trials where the subject is shown both elements of the pair are termed **learning trials.** The trials on which the subject must try to give the right response are called **test trials** and the general method is called the **recall method.** Separating learning and test trials allows an experimenter to determine the status of each item in the list after each exposure to the pair.

Another way to present material is to show the word (stimulus element) and then show the word paired with the appropriate response element. On subsequent trials, the subject must say the appropriate response before it is shown to him. The method is called the **paired-anticipation** method and has the advantages of giving the subject immediate positive or negative reinforcement for his guesses. It also requires half the number of trials to accomplish the same level of learning as the separate learn and test trial method.

In **serial learning,** a list of verbal items is presented to a subject. After a specified amount of study, the list is hidden from the subject, and he must attempt to reproduce, in order, the list of items. Recall may involve writing the items on a sheet of paper or verbally naming the items. If the list was not reproduced correctly, the list is given to the subject again and the process is repeated until the list is learned.

Serial lists of words can also be presented with an anticipation type of learning by showing the list of items to the subject, one at a time. When a subject sees the first item, he must respond with the second, when the second appears, he must call out the third and when the third item is shown, he must anticipate the fourth, and so on. **Serial anticipation** provides immediate reinforcement for the subject's responses and also allows a subject to learn the list as a whole instead of being restricted to the stimulus-response associations required in the paired-associate method.

A third type of verbal task is that of learning the **discrimination** between two elements of verbal material, and identifying the correct one. For this method, a subject is exposed to two (or more) words, and must respond with one of them. The cue to the correct response may be: (1) learned by rote ("ball" is correct and "coal" is wrong), (2) each discrimination may be related by some principle (whichever word starts with "b"), or (3) it may be a certain sequence of responses (right, right, left, left, and so on). The learning in a verbal discrimination experiment and that involved in animal discrimination studies is similar.

Concept Formation   The study of the development of logical thought in children provides another illustration of the problems of verbal report. Currently, a considerable number of psychologists are investigating the age at which children acquire certain concepts and the way in which the concepts are acquired. Stimulated by the theory and research of Piaget (reported in Flavell, 1963), many experiments present conservation problems to children.

One of the conservation problems is called *conservation of continuous quantity* or "conservation of liquid mass." The classic study consists of: (1) presenting two equal-sized beakers (A and B) to a child and telling him to pour the same amount of colored water into each beaker; (2) pouring the water from one beaker (A) into a differently shaped beaker (C); and (3) asking the child if there is still the same amount of water in the two beakers (B and C). (See Figure B.1.) If the third beaker (C) is wider than the other beakers, a child below about six or seven will usually say that there is less water in C, because the water level is lower. If beaker C is narrower than the other beakers, the child will usually say that there is more water in C, because the water level is higher. Thus, a four- or five-year-old child seems unable to understand that the amount of water is the same (conserved) no matter what the shape of the container.

There are two serious problems of interpretation and procedure involved in evaluating the classic study. *First,* the child must understand the terms of the observer, and the observer must understand the *language* of the child. If either person in the study does not understand the other, then the study is meaningless. For example, if the child does not know what the observer means by the term "same," then his answers may constitute passive agreement with the observer. That is, if the child says "yes, the two beakers (A and B) have the same amount of water," and "yes, the two beakers (B and C) have the same amount of water," and if the child is confused about the term "same," then probably (as noted in Chapter 11) the child is just being agreeable.

A *second,* related problem is the distinction between *identity* and *equivalence.* If a child has an appreciation for the concept "same," he may reliably indicate that the amount of water in the first two beakers (A and B) is the same and that the amount of water in beakers B and C is not the same. He may mean that the amount of water does not appear to be the same (nonequivalent) or, because there are two containers (B and C), the two waters are not the same (nonidentical). Even if a child answers the second question correctly (beakers B and C contain the same amount of water), we are not sure whether he means that the amounts of water are equivalent *or* that the *water* is the same (identical) liquid in both beakers.

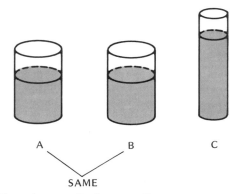

Fig. B.1.   Beakers A and B are the same. Beaker C is taller and thinner but contains the same **amount** of water as A and B.

How can an experimenter determine whether a child understands the concept of conservation of volume across transformations in the shape of containers? That is, how may an experimenter determine that a child can reliably and correctly apply the concept? The language problem and the identity-equivalence interpretation problem must be eliminated. There have been a number of attempts to handle one or both of the problems. No attempt has been completely satisfactory, but they indicate how such problems are attacked by research psychologists.

Nair (1966) conducted a study specifically aimed at controlling for the identity-equivalence problem. The children were pretested with the classic problem and then given a plastic "lake" (box) and wooden duck who "owned" the water in the lake. Each child was told to move his duck and his duck's water to a larger container. The children were asked if there was just as much, more, or not as much water in the new lake as the old. In addition, they were asked if the *same* water was contained in the new lake.

The results were that all the children who said there was the same amount of water in the lakes (conservation, equivalence) also said it was the same water (identity). Many children, however, answered correctly that it was the same water, but did not recognize the conservation of liquid mass (equivalence). About one-third of those children who were nonconserving on the pretest remained nonconservers throughout the study. However, the remaining two-thirds seemed to learn conservation during the study and exhibited the correct conservation responses at the end of the study. Thus, identity was correctly used by the conservers, but not all of the nonconservers. Also, the procedures employed in the study seemed to shape some children's awareness of the distinction between identity and equivalence.

One reason why a child may not be able to separate identity and equivalence is that the child may focus on only one perceptual attribute of the "lakes." That is, a child may look only at the height of the water in a beaker or lake. Frank (1966) conducted a study of the effect of concealing the water from a child so as to reduce the likelihood of focusing on only one aspect of the situation. The water was poured from a standard beaker into a beaker that was equal or wider than the standard. A *screen* was placed between the beakers and the child so that he could see the water being poured, but not the height of the water in the beakers. The children were then asked to predict the height of the water in the new beakers and to say whether or not the new beakers contained the same amount of water as the first beaker.

The results were that the screen forced most of the children to consider that the identical water was present in the standard and comparison beakers. The children were given the classic problem as a pretest and a posttest (after the screening experience). There was a considerable increase in the proportion of five-, six-, and seven-year-olds who gave conservation answers on the posttest as compared to the pretest. The four-year-old children made the right kinds of predictions during the screening portion of the study, but reverted to nonconservation on the posttest. Thus, the perceptual characteristics of the containers appear very seductive to the four-year-olds. These two experiments seem to support the idea of Bruner, et al.

(1966) that a working knowledge of identity is crucial to acquiring the concept of conservation.

Attacking the language problem, Silverman and Schneider (1968) used a "nonverbal" method of testing conservation of volume. The children were presented with jars of candy, where the two jars were the same size and one obviously had less candy (M & M's) in it. Then, the lesser amount was poured into a taller, thinner jar and the child was told to choose which jar he wished to have. In terms of age trends, the results were similar to those previously obtained; the major point of the study was that one aspect of the language problem was eliminated. However, the child was still required to be able to understand the experimenter's language.

One way to avoid the language problem is to pretrain each child on the terms and ideas that are crucial to the tests. Kingsley and Hall (1967) found that such training requires a considerable amout of time spent with each child. Their results indicate that when the children received training on the concepts of conservation of weight and length, the training seemed to generalize to conservation of mass or substance. The generalization test is important, because the effects of training should generalize beyond the tools used in the training period.

SUMMARY

1. An important issue in human research is the validity of data collected in the laboratory in terms of generalizing to real-life situations.
2. Behavior in the laboratory can be affected by sampling error, laboratory artifacts, and experimenter effects.
3. The rights of the human subjects in any experiment must be protected. Excess stress and invasion of privacy are two of the important areas of subject rights.
4. Human beings may be sampled individually or from intact groups.
5. The general techniques for sampling human beings include: (1) politely selling the subjects on participating in an experiment, (2) not lying to the subjects, (3) guaranteeing anonymity, (4) making participation sound interesting, (5) providing sign-up sheets when necessary, and (6) offering feedback on the results of the research.
6. When getting in touch with subjects individually, a researcher warns potential subjects that he is coming and tries to convince them that he is competent.
7. When sampling from intact groups, the anonymity of the group is assured, and an opportunity to escape is provided. The approval of the authority figures (gatekeepers) of an intact group must be secured prior to meeting the group.
8. Unusual intact groups should not be approached by novice researchers.
9. Children are adapted to the experimenter and his equipment. Verbal instructions with children are often as useless as verbal instructions with infrahuman subjects. Candy should not be used as a reward for children in an experiment. Punishment should also not be used.
10. Introspective reports are not acceptable because they are not public or repeatable. However, when a verbal report is correlated with either physical events or other behavioral events, the verbal report becomes useful. The flight of colors, the autokinetic effect, and the haptic illusion examples indicate ways that verbal reports may be measured and how reliability may be increased.

11. Psychophysics is the study of the relationship between the physical measures of a stimulus and measure of behavior. The threshold is defined as the point at which a stimulus is detected 50 percent of the time. The two response methods used in psychophysics are the yes-no and forced-choice methods.
12. The stimulus presentation methods include (1) the method of limits, (2) the staircase method, (3) the method of constant stimuli, and (3) the signal-detection method.
13. Signal-detection theory includes consideration of the noninformative noise in addition to the signal, as well as the response criterion of the perceiver.
14. Sensory scaling methods include relative magnitude estimation, the method of fractionation, and equal-sense distance method.
15. Physiological measures and measures of personality may be used to class people according to some organismic motivational variable. Social pressure can be contrived to manipulate the motivational level of human subjects.
16. The verbal material used in human learning studies includes (1) words, (2) nonsense syllables, and (3) numbers. Words and nonsense syllables vary in difficulty and meaningfulness. Words and numbers differ in familiarity.
17. Problems involved in conservation concept attainment studies include: (1) language understanding and (2) separating identity and equivalence.

SUGGESTED READING

American Psychological Association, Ad Hoc Committee on Ethical Standards in Psychological Research. *Ethical principles in the conduct of research with human participants,* Washington, D.C.: American Psychological Association, 1973.

Asch, S. E. Effects of group pressure upon the modification and distortion of judgments. In E. E. Maccoby, T. M. Newcomb, and E. L. Hartley (Eds.), *Readings in social psychology.* New York: Holt, Rinehart and Winston, 1951.

Atkinson, J. W. (Ed.) *Motives in fantasy, action, and society.* New York: Van Nostrand, 1958.

Battig, W. F., and Spera, A. J. Rated association values of numbers from 0–100. *Journal of Verbal Learning and Verbal Behavior,* 1962, *1,* 200–202.

Bell, C. R. Personality characteristics of volunteers for psychological studies. *British Journal of Social and Clinical Psychology,* 1962, *1,* 81–95.

Bijou, S. W., and Baer, D. M. The laboratory-experimental study of child behavior. In P. H. Mussen (Ed.), *Handbook of research methods in child development.* New York: Wiley, 1960.

Bijou, S. W., and Sturges, P. T. Positive reinforcers for experimental study with children—consumables and manipulatables. *Child Development,* 1959, *30,* 151–170.

Blackwell, H. R. *Psychological thresholds: Experimental studies of methods of measurement.* Ann Arbor: University of Michigan Press (Eng. Res. Bull. No. 36), 1953.

Bower, T. G. R. The visual world of infants. *Scientific American,* 1966, *215* (6), 80–92.

Bruner, J. S., Olver, R. R., Greenfeld, P. M., Hornsby, J. R., Kenney, H. F., Maccoby, M., Modiano, N., Mosher, F. A., Olson, D. R., Potter, M. C., Reich, L. C., and Sonstroem, A. M. *Studies in cognitive growth.* New York: Wiley, 1966.

Castaneda, A., and Fahel, L. S. The relationship between the psychological investigator and the public schools. *American Psychologist,* 1961, *16,* 201–203.

Cormack, R. H. Haptic Illusion: Apparent elongation of a disc rotated between the fingers. *Science,* 1973, *179,* 590–592.

Cornsweet, T. N. The staircase-method in psychophysics. *American Journal of Psychology,* 1962, *75,* 485–491.

Dember, W. N. *The psychology of perception.* New York: Holt, Rinehart and Winston, 1960.

Ebbinghaus, H. *Uber das gedachtnis: Untersuchungen zur experimentellen psychologie.* Leipzig: Dunker and Humblot, 1885 (translated as *Memory: A contribution to experimental psychology,* by H. A. Ruger and C. E. Bussenius). New York: Teachers College, Columbia University, 1913.

Flavell, J. H. *The developmental psychology of Jean Piaget.* Princeton, N.J.: Van Nostrand, 1963.

Frank, F. Untitled and unpublished research. Reported in Bruner, et. al. *Studies in cognitive growth,* New York: Wiley, 1966, 193–202.

Glaze, J. A. The association value of nonsense syllables. *Journal of Genetic Psychology,* 1928, *35,* 255–267.

Haber, R. N. (Ed.) *Contemporary theory and research in perception.* New York: Holt, Rinehart and Winston, 1968.

Jung, J. *The experimenter's dilemma.* New York: Harper & Row, 1971.

Kingsley, R. C., and Hall, V. C. Training conservation through the use of learning sets. *Child Development,* 1967, *38,* 1111–1126.

McClelland, D. C., Atkinson, J. W., Clark, R. A., and Lowell, E. L. *The achievement motive.* New York: Appleton, 1953.

Mullen, F. A. The school as a psychological laboratory. *American Psychologist,* 1959, *14,* 53–56.

Nair, P. Untitled and unpublished research. Reported in Bruner, et al. *Studies in cognitive growth.* New York: Wiley, 1966, 187–192.

Natsoulas, T. Interpreting perceptual reports. *Psychological Bulletin,* 1968, *70,* 575–591.

Noble, C. E. Measurement of association value (a), rated associations (a'), and scaled meaningfulness (m') for the 2100 CVC combinations of the English language. *Psychological Reports,* 1961, *8,* 487–521.

Runkel, P. J., and McGrath, J. E. *Research on human behavior: A systematic guide to method.* New York: Holt, Rinehart and Winston, 1972.

Silverman, I., and Schneider, D. S. A study of the development of conservation by a nonverbal method. *The Journal of Genetic Psychology,* 1968, *112,* 287–291.

Smith, M. B. Conflicting values affecting behavioral research with children. *American Psychologist,* 1967, *22,* 377–382.

Stevenson, H. W., and Wright, J. C. Child psychology. In J. B. Sidowski (Ed.), *Experimental methods and instrumentation in psychology.* New York: McGraw-Hill, 1966.

Swets, J. A. Is there a sensory threshold? *Science,* 1961, *134,* 168–177.

Thorndike, E. L., and Lorge, I. *The teacher's wordbook of 30,000 words.* New York: Teacher's College, 1944.

Underwood, B. J., and Schulz, R. W. *Meaningfulness and verbal learning.* Chicago: Lippincott, 1960.

UNIT C
Research Equipment

A list of all of the apparatus used in psychology would be both long and redundant, since different names are often applied to equipment with overlapping features. Different equipment may share common components used in different behavioral applications, and, conversely, different hardware components may be used to accomplish the same end. Rather than try to list all of the combinations that have been used in meeting specific research specifications, we have chosen to list and identify component devices that often have been found useful in psychology laboratories. The list is organized according to the major function served by the device, and specific examples are provided under each heading. By combining the listed devices, a student can "custom-build" an apparatus for his research requirements.

The list provides a sample of different ways to accomplish specific research functions. The discription of individual devices is deliberately general in nature. Because the list is a very basic description of laboratory devices, the student should be able to home-build many of the devices with material readily available to him.

ENVIRONMENTAL CONTROL

Stimulus Restriction

Many experiments are conducted with a subject in an **isolation booth** or a **test chamber** during the data-collection process. If the experimenter is concerned with the control of auditory stimuli, a **soundproof room** may be used. Soundproofing may be necessary if the experiment involves very low levels of auditory stimulation. An analogous device for visual studies may be found in the use of a photographic darkroom. For some research applications, an entire room need not be involved. **Ear plugs** or **blindfolds** may effectively isolate subjects from unwanted external stimuli. For some auditory studies, a pair of over-the-ear **headphones** simultaneously provides the experimental stimulus and occludes extraneous sounds.

Effective auditory isolation may also be accomplished by using a **white-noise generator.** White noise randomly varies in both frequency and intensity (a sort of soft hissing sound like that heard on a short-wave radio tuned between stations). Sometimes, a radio may be used to drown out extraneous sounds.

Response Restriction

An experimenter may wish to channel the behavior of a subject so that observed responses are relevant to the research hypotheses. Cages or boxes may be used to keep animal subjects from leaving the experimental area. **Mazes** of all types restrict the animal to a certain set of available pathways to be traversed during the experiment. Occasionally, an animal may be mounted in a harness or some other **restraining device** that allows almost no movement during the experiment. An effective restraining device for some human perception experiments involves having the subject bite down on a wax block that is firmly mounted to a frame. The wax impression of the teeth prevents unwanted head movement.

REINFORCEMENT DEVICES

Particularly in the study of learning, some type of reward must be provided the subject for performance of a task. There are a number of different **dispensers** available to deliver a reinforcement mechanically. The dispenser may be activated by the experimenter when he observes a correct response, or it may be connected to a response-recording device and operate automatically. Most experiments with infra-human species use primary reinforcers, such as food or water. Also, animals placed in a chilled environment will learn a task in order to turn on a heating device. Most human experiments do not involve primary reinforcement, although M & M candy dispensers are occasionally used in research involving children. Humans will work

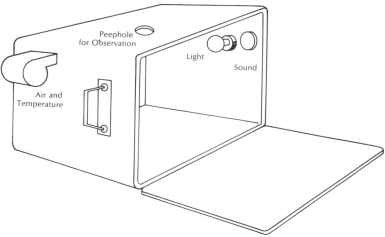

Fig. C.1.   Stimulus Restriction.

for secondary reinforcers. For example, children will learn a task for a reward of a small toy, while adults may find a coin dispenser more to their liking.

Dispensers are not the only way to provide reinforcement to a subject. Many learning experiments may provide some kind of feedback cue that identifies the response as "right" or "wrong." The behavior of a person, in or out of the laboratory, can be manipulated through the judicious use of verbal reinforcement (Greenspoon,

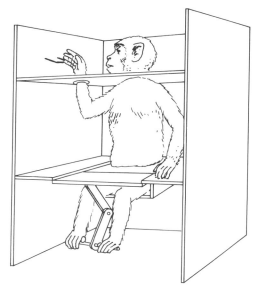

Fig. C.2.   Restraining Device.

1955). By selectively manipulating verbal replies, an experimenter can effectively guide the verbal behavior of another person.

In some cases, an experimenter may be interested in punishing subjects whenever a wrong response occurs. Although there are studies that bombard animals with loud sounds or blasts of air for a wrong response, the most frequent punishment situation involves the use of an electric shock. There are a number of **electric shock sources** that may be connected to a shock grid built into the floor of the cage, the chair of the subject, or directly to the subject, and may be activated whenever an undesired response occurs.

A recently developed technique involves the delivery of a small electric shock to the brain of an animal via wires surgically implanted in the skull of the animal. Depending upon the stimulus and the location of the electrode, electric shock to the brain (ESB) may be either pleasurable or punishing to the animal. Thus, it may be used as a replacement for food, water, or punishment.

STIMULUS GENERATING EQUIPMENT

There are a large number of specialized devices available for manipulating or presenting stimuli to subjects in an experiment.

Vision

Most sensory research involves visual displays. When visual stimuli consist of photographs, drawings, inkblots, words, or nonsense syllables, they may be presented on a sheet of paper or a deck of cards. A **memory drum** presents a sequence of stimuli printed or drawn on a sheet of paper by showing the paper through a screen with a window in it, and advancing the paper one step at a time past the window.

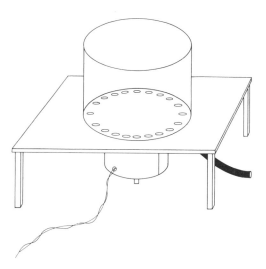

Fig. C.3. Dispenser.

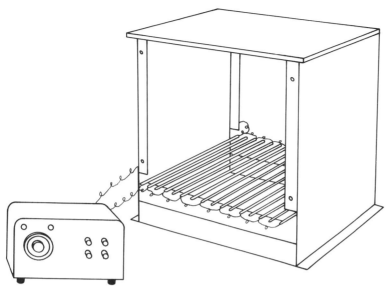

Fig. C.4.   Electric Shock Source.

If a camera shutter is mounted to the lens of a projector, it can be made into a flash projector or **tachistoscope.** Camera shutters may be purchased from most camera shops, and they accurately control the length of stimulus exposure over several intervals. An inexpensive version may consist of a card with a certain size slot cut into it. If the card is held in front of the projector and dropped, the stimulus will be projected onto the screen only during the time the slot is passing through the light beam. Tachistoscopes are often used in target identification tasks. The brightness of the projector bulb, the distance and angle the subject and projector are from the screen, the nature of the screen, the degree of room illumination, as well as exposure time all affect the visibility of a flashed target stimulus. Anyone who has looked at a photographer's flashbulb as it fires knows that a brief, intense light stimulus may be used to produce visual afterimages. A tachistoscopic projector, when aimed at a subject, will also produce afterimages.

A **ganzfeld** is a homogeneously illuminated field. In a ganzfeld, the visual field has no "target." Rather, it seems as if one is seeing dense fog. A colored ganzfeld has the peculiar quality of rapidly disappearing, that is, the color vision adapts very quickly. When the light is abruptly changed to white, the subjects report seeing a negative afterimage color. Several methods of producing a ganzfeld have been used in research, but an effective and inexpensive technique involves placing half of a ping-pong ball over the (open) eyes of the subject. As long as there is no brand name or seam available to serve as a target, the desired homogeneous field is effective, and manipulations of the brightness or hue may be accomplished by adjusting the external light transluminating the pingpong ball.

Several devices have been developed for the laboratory study of color vision.

Isochromatic plates are numbers or patterns made of small dots varying in color and/or brightness as a test for color blindness. A **monochrometer** is a light projector that may be adjusted to deliver a narrow portion of the visible spectrum for precise color vision research. A projector with **color filters** is a less expensive, less precise version of the same device. A **color mixer** allows the subject or experimenter to adjust the mixture of three or more colors (usually the primary colors) to match a target color. Color mixers may consist of several projectors casting superimposed filtered beams onto the same screen, or it may be a multicolored, sectored disk mounted on the shaft of an electric motor. The spinning-disk (Benham's top) technique may also be used to demonstrate subjective color from a black and white disc with one of the patterns shown on this page. In addition, a spinning disk can be used to demonstrate the phenomenon of "Mach bands" where shades of gray yield rings (light or dark bands) at the border, because of the contrast between adjacent brightnesses (shades).

The phenomenon of depth perception has been extensively studied. Various depth chambers have been employed where the subject is to estimate the distance between himself and several objects, or he is to adjust a movable object so that it is the same distance as some target object. A **visual cliff** has been frequently used in testing visual depth perception in infrahuman species. A subject is placed on a solid, horizontal plate of glass, and a visually "solid" material is placed at various depths below the surface of the glass. The subject is then confronted with a solid basis for physical support, but visually, he may appear to be floating several feet above the nearest surface. Some animals avoid the "visually deep" side of the apparatus.

Motor Learning

In order to investigate perceptual-motor learning, a **mirror drawing device** requires that the subject trace a pathway with a pencil he can see only in a mirror. Another way to alter the "visual world" is to have a subject wear special glasses with lenses that distort light rays in certain ways. One technique is to use **prism glasses** adjusted so that everything appears to be to one side of where it would normally be. Thus, a subject finds that he tends to miss any objects he wishes to touch, because he reaches toward the displaced image rather than the true location. A more extreme example of altered visual input is found in special glasses that turn the subject's visual world upside-down. Subjects usually successfully adjust to the altered situation, some more quickly than others. All report, however, that they must readjust when the goggles are taken off, since everything now appears distorted in the opposite direction.

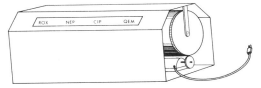

Fig. C.5. Memory Drum.

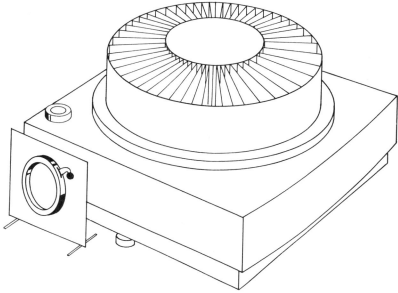

Fig. C.6.   Slide Projector Used as a Tachistoscope.

Hearing

Almost any noise-making device can be used in some kind of auditory research. Metal clickers, buzzers, whistles, and bells are only a few of the possibilities for sound localization research. In addition to asking a subject to locate the source of the sound, a researcher may have the subject utilize the reflection of the sounds to navigate without visual cues (for example, the echolocation observed in bats). If a relatively pure tone is required for an experiment, a tuning fork is a workable device. For most auditory research involving pure tones, an electronic **audio signal generator** is used because it may be precisely adjusted to different levels of frequency and intensity.

A **tape recorder** may be used to present a wide variety of auditory stimuli and, as with visual projectors, a programmed sequence of stimuli. Recent developments in high-fidelity sound equipment make a tape recorder an adequate choice for almost any research involving sounds. A **delayed auditory feedback device** alters the auditory world of a subject much as the prism goggles alter the visual world. The device is usually a special tape recording unit that records the subject's voice, stores it for a short period of time, and then plays it back to the subject. Certain tape recorders are equipped with an extra playback head to allow monitoring of input. These recorders may be used to provide delayed auditory feedback. At certain delay intervals, subjects often find it difficult to complete a simple sentence. They stammer, repeat themselves, and sometimes report difficulty maintaining a thought trend because of the disruption caused by their own voices. Delayed visual

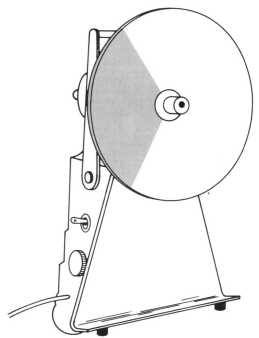

Fig. C.7.   Spinning Disk.

feedback has been accomplished through the use of special television videotape devices, with similar behavioral disruption.

Other Senses

Research involving the sense of touch usually requires precise control of the pressure of a stimulus. An **aesthesiometer** is a series of thin fibers (**von Frey hairs**), calibrated in thickness. When each fiber is applied to the surface of the skin, it exerts only so much pressure before it starts to bend. Thus, it is possible to determine the sensitivity of the touch receptors by noting the minimum pressure reliably detected by the subject. Another touch device is the two-point aesthesiometer that allows the measurement of the minimum discriminable distance between two points touched on the skin. When used at very low levels, a shock device may serve as an appropriate stimulator for skin perception research. Careful control of temperature may be accomplished with expensive thermoregulatory devices; however, a heating plate, several buckets of water, and an accurate thermometer are often adequate for an experiment on temperature sensation in the hands. The experimenter may wish to have a subject estimate the weight of visually identical objects. Such objects can be easily produced by buying a number of identical capped containers (drugstore capsule containers work very well), painting the inside surface so that they are opaque, then filling each container with sand until the desired weight is attained.

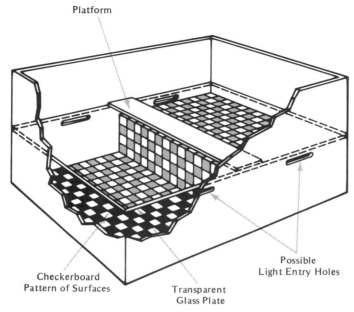

Platform

Checkerboard
Pattern of Surfaces

Transparent
Glass Plate

Possible
Light Entry Holes

Fig. C.8. Visual Cliff.

The senses of taste and smell present special problems of precise control of the stimulus characteristics. A review of the devices and techniques used in experimenting on these and other senses may be found in von Békésy's (1967) *Sensory inhibition.*

MEASURING DEVICES

When the physical dimensions of a stimulus must be stated, a mechanical device is often used as the measuring instrument. The brightness of a light may be specified in terms of foot-candles by using a **light meter.** The hue of a light can be specified in terms of wavelength or spectral distribution by using a **spectrophotometer.** Sound intensity may be expressed in decibel units with a **decibel meter,** and pitch may be designated in terms of frequency as measured by a **frequency analyzer.** A thermometer provides a measure of temperature, and an ammeter may be used to specify the current of the electric shock given the subject.

Null Devices

In experiments where the characteristics of the stimulus are important, precise definitions are essential. There are a number of stimulus-measuring devices that use a biological receptor as the detection device, and the behavior of the organism as the measure. Most of these devices involve the subject matching the stimulus with a standard stimulus, thus the term null (no difference) device. For example,

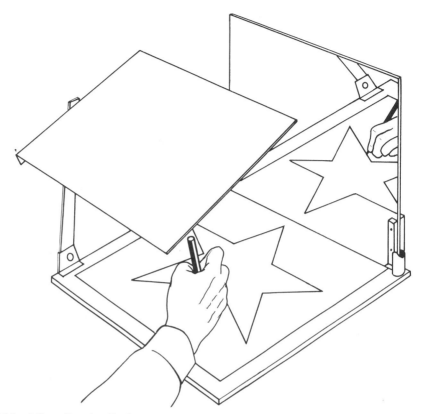

Fig. C.9.   Mirror Drawing Device.

two stimuli may be adjusted to equal brightness by training an animal to choose the brighter or dimmer of two stimuli, and then adjusting the stimuli until the animal can no longer discriminate between the two. A special example of this approach is found in the use of an **illuminometer** to measure brightness. The researcher looks at the target in question through a device that presents a "standard stimulus" for comparison purposes. By adjusting the comparison stimulus until it matches the characteristics of the target, the researcher can describe the target in terms of the adjusted characteristics of the standard stimulus. A similar technique for specifying surface color can be accomplished by using a **Munsell color book.** The Munsell color chips are similar to the sample paint chips supplied by paint stores, except that they are arranged in a book according to hue and saturation. By naming the characteristics of the closest matching sample, it is possible to provide an unambiguous statement of these dimensions to anyone who has access to a Munsell book. If a stimulus is a musical tone, the tone may be defined by identifying the characteristics of the closest matching piano note or tuning fork.

A novel application of the use of a biological organism in quantification is the

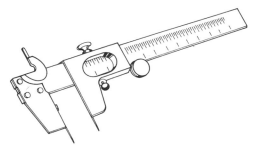

Fig. C.10.   Two-Point Aesthesiometer.

development of a device that allows the quantification of pain stimuli. A **warm-spot device** involves focusing a variable spot of warm light on the subject's forehead as he is experiencing a constant pain stimulus. By gradually increasing the intensity of the spot until the subject reports that it is no longer "warm," but now feels "hot" one can quantify the degree of pain as the intensity of the warm spot at the point of subjective change. In other words, the more intense the pain, the warmer the spot must be before the subject reports it as hot.

RESPONSE MEASUREMENT

Response measurement consists of two basic functions: the detection of a response and the recording of the detected response. Mechanical detection devices are sensing mechanisms that usually generate an electrical signal when a certain event occurs. Recording devices provide a permanent record of the detection signals. A response may be measured in one of three basic dimensions: the number of times the response occurred (**frequency**), the length of time the response occurred (**duration**), or the amplitude (**intensity**) of the response. Measurement devices may be used in two categories, and some measures seem to fit equally well into either of two categories depending on the interpretation. Therefore, the following discussion

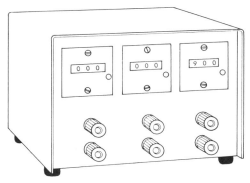

Fig. C.11.   Electric Counter.

of response measuring devices is arranged arbitrarily in terms of the categorical function served by the device.

Some devices such as an audio tape recorder, a moving-picture camera, or a video tape recorder, measure and record some of the subject's behavior in an experiment. An experimenter can replay the recording at his convenience to tabulate the various response dimensions he wishes to measure.

Frequency Recording

Frequency data may be interpreted in two ways: the number and the rate (number of responses per unit time) of response occurrences. If a frequency-recording device includes some measurement of the passage of time, rate information is simultaneously recorded. The number of times a specific response occurred during the experiment may be recorded in a number of ways. The experimenter may observe the subject's behavior and tabulate a running frequency count of different classes of behavior by marking on a tally sheet. A mechanical equivalent to a tally sheet is a **counter.** A counter may be manipulated by the observer-experimenter, or it may be connected to a response-detection device so that the counter automatically advances at each response. Counters may be activated mechanically or electrically; they may be reset to start counting at zero or they may start with the last number recorded. They may display the count by a pattern of lights or a variety of numerical displays. The experimenter should be sure that his counters are capable of accurately registering the fastest response rates that will occur in the experiment. Response rate can be obtained from a counter by recording the displayed number at the end of each time period. A printing counter may be programmed to print the count on adding-machine paper tape at specified time intervals.

Graphic recorders also allow the automatic collection of frequency data. Most graphic recorders use a roll of paper that is moved past a pen at a constant speed. The pen moves according to incoming electrical signals, usually reflecting the subject's behavior in an experiment. The resulting graph has two major axes. Time

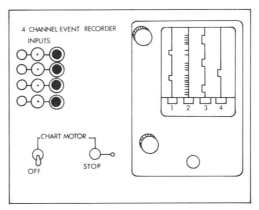

Fig. C.12.   Four-Channel Event Recorder.

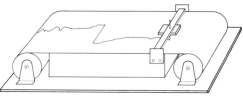

Fig. C.13. Cumulative Recorder.

is indicated in one direction (usually the X axis), and behavior is recorded in the other (Y axis) direction. The pen of an **event recorder** moves whenever an event (such as a certain response) occurs. The pen acts as an "on-off" indicator; that is, the pen is either in the "off" (no response) position or in the "on" (response) position. The number of responses is reflected by the number of pen deflections on the record. Time samples can be drawn by noting the response record in different sections of the chart. Most event recorders can record several channels of information simultaneously. That is, several different pens, each recording separate events, can be combined on a single paper record. Thus, it is quite possible to record the bar-pressing behavior of the animal, whether the room lights are on or off, whether the experimenter is in the room or out, and so on, on the same graphic record.

A special type of event recorder is a **cumulative recorder.** With a cumulative recorder, the pen is moved a certain distance across the paper each time the response occurs. The resulting record looks like a series of little steps, each step indicating a response. Thus, if the chart is arranged so that time is recorded from left to right, a fast series of responses will appear as a steep line moving upward and to the right. If the animal stops responding, the line becomes horizontal, indicating only the passage of time without any responses. Intermediate response rates are shown as intermediate slope lines. Other information, such as the occurrence of a reinforcement, can be recorded by a pen acting as an event recorder. Most cumulative recorders also have a "snapback" feature where the pen automatically returns to its starting position when it has moved all the way across the recording-paper. Thus, the height of the cumulative curve is theoretically limitless, allowing the experimenter to record large numbers of responses without having to reset the recorder.

Frequency Detection

Response-detection devices for frequency data may be roughly classified into two general categories: those which must be directly manipulated by a subject and those which detect ongoing behavior. **Manipulanda** are any devices that must be manipulated by the subject. The best-known instance of a manipulanda device is the bar found in a Skinner box. A Skinner box (or operant conditioning box) is a test chamber in which the operation of the manipulanda device (usually a depressable bar) by the subject activates a reinforcing device in addition to registering on a graphic recorder. Animals may have to depress a bar, peck at a small window, or open a door to indicate their responses in the experiment. Human subjects may have

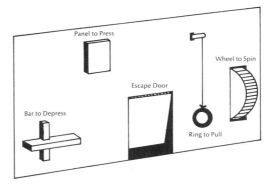

Fig. C.14.   Manipulanda.

to press a button, move a lever, or turn a knob. All of these devices may be connected to a frequency recorder to measure the number of times the specific response occurs.

There are a number of remote detection devices available that do not require direct manipulation by the subject. A **photoelectric device** consists of a light source and a receiver unit sensitive to light. Whenever an object breaks the light beam between the source and the receiver, a switch is closed. A photoelectric unit can be obtained that is sensitive in the infrared region so that the light beam need not be visible to the subject.

Electronic amplifiers may be used to detect a variety of responses without interfering with the ongoing behavior of the subject. For example, an amplifier can be used with an antenna wire in the floor of a maze to detect an animal's passage near that point. The amplifier will respond to changes in the electromagnetic field near the antenna, and the disruption caused by the animal can be amplified to close a switch. A less sensitive device is a **drinkometer** where the contact of the animal's tongue with the drinking tube may be recorded because of the minute electrical current flowing with each contact. A rat drinks an approximately constant volume of fluid per tongue lick, so the amount and rate of water consumed may be directly recorded from a counter connected to the drinkometer. Another amplifier device is the **voice-operated relay.** A microphone detects any sounds emitted by the subject and the resulting electrical activity is amplified until an electrically operated switch (relay) is activated. With this device, the experimenter can count any sounds created by the subject, or he can use the device to turn on some other apparatus automatically when the sound occurs.

Remote detection devices are particularly useful if the experimenter is interested in recording an animal's activity in an **activity box.** An animal can be placed in an enclosure that is crisscrossed with multiple photoelectric devices, or with multiple amplifier antennae embedded in the floor. The more active the animal, the more activity recorded by the devices. Activity could also be measured by placing sensitive switches under different sections of the floor so that the weight of a moving animal activates the switches. Another possibility would be to suspend a cage on springs with sensitive devices attached to the cage so that any jiggling caused by the animal would be detected. A "squirrel cage" or **running wheel** can be equipped with a counter so that the number of wheel turns can be recorded. There are also a number of different **exploration mazes** that have clearly marked compartments (sometimes squares painted onto the floor of an open field) so that the observer-experimenter can tabulate the number of different compartments traversed by the animal. Exploration mazes may be used to measure the activity of the subject in terms of the total number of compartments entered or the exploration of the subject in terms of the number of *new* compartments entered.

There are a number of manual dexterity tasks that may be used to measure the accuracy, coordination, or speed with which a person may accomplish a specific task. These tasks may range from transfering small objects with tweezers, sorting nuts and bolts into different bins, fabricating a specific object out of parts, or fitting square pegs into round holes. Measurement often consists of recording the number of items correctly manipulated within a certain length of time.

Duration Detection and Recording

Duration measuring devices give information concerning the time characteristics of the response. In addition to measures of the time length (duration) of each response, duration measures include the time between introduction to the apparatus until the first response occurs (response latency) and the length of time between two responses (inter-response interval).

A hand held **stopwatch** may be used by an observer-experimenter to obtain duration measures of the response. There are a wide range of electrically operated stopclocks that may be connected to any response detection device. Sometimes, an

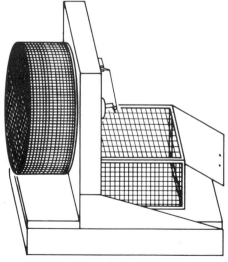

Fig. C.15.   Running Wheel.

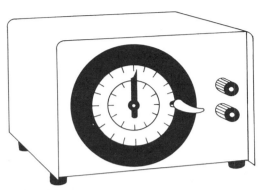

Fig. C.16.   Electric Stopwatch or Timer.

experimenter may be interested in the duration information available from one device. For example, the experimenter may be interested in the length of time the animal holds down the bar in a Skinner box. Running time is the length of time it takes an animal to run from one end of a maze to the other end. Running time may be recorded by photocell controlled clocks. Light beams are placed at each end of a maze and the passage of an animal through the beams starts and stops a clock.

Most graphic event recorders record time as one dimension of a display. Consequently, by measuring the length of the line indicating that the event occurred, it is possible to determine the duration of the event. By measuring the length of the "no event" line, various latency measures may be obtained. Thus, both frequency and duration information is available from an event recorder, depending on how the measure is examined.

A number of devices may be combined to form a reaction timing device. The basic function of a **reaction timer** is to present a subject with a signal (such as a light); provide some kind of response detector device (such as a switch); and measure time lapse between the signal and response.

Some devices measure discrimination time by providing several lights and switches for a subject; the subject must give the correct response according to the stimulus condition. If the required response is complicated, the device may give

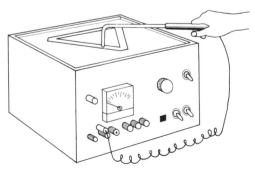

Fig. C.17.   Pursuit Rotor.

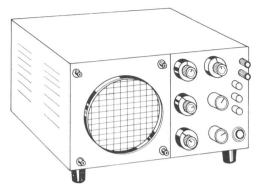

Fig. C.18.   Oscilloscope.

two reaction time measures: time to start the response and time to response completion. Reaction timers have been especially popular in evaluating the effects of stressful conditions or drugs on motor performance.

A **pursuit rotor** presents a moving target that a subject must attempt to follow with a stylus or probe. The response is usually measured in terms of time on and off target, which reflects the accuracy of the subject's tracking efforts. A simple pursuit rotor consists of attaching a dime on top of a record turntable. The subject must try to keep a pencil point on the coin as the turntable revolves. More elaborate devices allow automatic timing of the on and off target time, variable speed and direction control of the turntable, and more complicated orbital patterns of the target.

Intensity Detection and Recording

Intensity measures provide information concerning the strength or magnitude of the response. Response intensity may be directly measured by analog devices, or indirectly measured by adjusting the situation so that an increasing response magnitude is required to make a response.

Analog devices provide a direct numerical reading of magnitude of response. Occasionally, an experimenter reads the numerical indication on the instrument and records the number on a data sheet; however, the usual situation is to use a transducer connected to an oscillograph. A **transducer** is any device that converts one type of energy into another. For example, the force the animal uses to press a bar may be converted by a strain gauge into electrical signals. There are a number of different oscillographs available that record the characteristics of incoming electrical signals. A relatively common device is the **oscilloscope,** which provides a visual display of the signal as a moving spot of light on a screen. Permanent records of an oscilloscope trace may be obtained by photographing the screen.

Oscillographs are basically similar to graphic event recorders, except that oscillographs provide more information about a response. Most physiological response recording involves measuring the amplitude of a response. Thus, a **polygraph** (lie detector) utilizes pens that sweep back and forth across the paper accord-

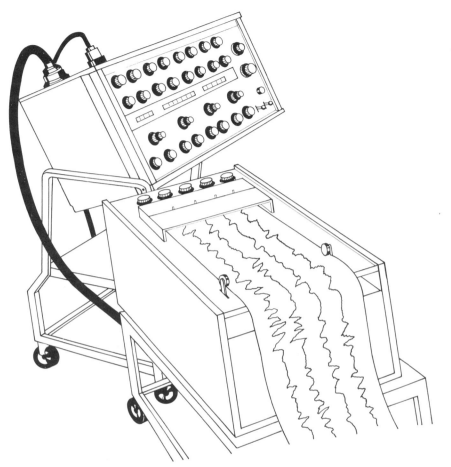

Fig. C.19. Polygraph.

ing to the size of the response. An oscillograph allows measurement of all response characteristics (frequency, duration, and intensity) provided the response-detection device and the recorder are calibrated.

The recording of heart rate, blood pressure, breathing rate, skin resistance, eye movements, pupil size, or brain waves require special detection devices. **Biosensors** are devices that directly measure ongoing physiological activity. A machine that measures the galvanic skin response (GSR) records the electrical resistance across the surface of the skin due to sweat-gland activity. Brain waves (electroencephalograms or EEG) and electrocardiograms (EKG) are amplified records of electrical fields generated by the cells in the brain and heart, respectively.

Other physiological responses are detected indirectly by special devices. **A plethysmograph** detects heart rate by mechanically transducing arterial changes in pressure, or phototransducing changes in the amount of light reflected back by the changing volume of blood under the skin. Breathing may be detected by a **strain** gauge attached to a strap around the chest. A **pupilometer** is a device that is strapped to the head of a subject with an optical device aimed at his eye. The optical device detects any change in the size of the pupil. Degree of interest may be measured by recording pupil size.

The strength of voluntary responses can sometimes be directly measured. For example, it is possible to place a strain gauge on the bar of a Skinner box to record how hard the animal presses on the lever. The speed at which an animal runs in a maze is used as a reflection of the strength of the maze-running task. In animal research, it is often the practice to measure the strength of the behavior by indirect means. An **obstruction device** places some sort of adjustable barrier between an animal and some goal. The largest barrier the animal will traverse provides a measure of the strength of the response. The barrier may be a physical barrier that must be climbed over, gnawed through, or moved aside. Other obstruction devices may involve a shock grid to be crossed or exposure to a noxious stimulus in order to attain the goal. The lever in a Skinner box can serve as an obstruction device if weights are added to the lever, making it harder to manipulate.

The usual concept of an intensity-recording device involves mechanical devices like those described above. Tests and questionnaires also serve the function of measuring the strength of the subject's response along some dimension. If the test consists of a number of questions about a given topic, the total score attained on the test reflects the subject's behavior on that topic. Tests that are designed to measure intelligence, achievement, or aptitude all attempt to provide a numerical measure of the subject's performance in that particular class of skills.

Tests and Questionnaires

Questionnaires are a frequently used method of measuring the strength of attitudes and opinions. A large number of statements about a topic, such as prejudice, are compiled and the subject is asked to check the statements he feels are true. In the simplest case, counting the number of statements marked may indicate the strength of the attitude. In more subtle situations, negative responses to some statements may reflect positive attitudes toward the dimension of interest, so scoring becomes more complicated.

For the beginning researcher established questionnaires present an attractive method of measuring attitudes. The creation of a reliable and valid test is a difficult skill and the beginning student is advised to utilize the efforts of professionals if the opportunity is available. In many cases, however, the research problem may be of a very local nature (such as attitudes toward a situation on a specific campus) so that the researcher has no published instrument that would be appropriate. In such a case, the responses of subjects on a rating scale provide a useful basis for obtaining a numerical comparison. A rating scale usually involves a line divided into segments with labels identifying each end of the scale. A subject is told to place a mark on the line that corresponds to his attitudinal position. For example, a study on attitudes toward grades might have the items shown in Figure C.20. The usual practice is to divide the line into an odd number of segments so that the subject has an easily identified neutral point between the two extreme positions. Some researchers prefer to label all of the intermediate steps, instead of only identifying the extremes. If the numbers are carefully arranged, it is possible to summarize the data by

Grades are a good estimate of a student's ability.

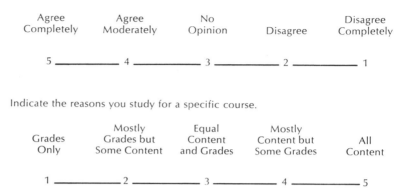

Indicate the reasons you study for a specific course.

Fig. C.20.   Two examples of Likert-type five-point scale items to measure attitudes toward grades.

cumulating the scores on each item. A low score on the attitude study (Figure C.20) would indicate a general disapproval of grades, and a high score would indicate general approval.

Two special rating techniques are the Q-sort and the semantic differential. In the **Q-sort** technique, a subject is given a number of cards with statements written on them. He is also shown a number of boxes with different labels on them. His task is to sort the cards into the appropriate boxes according to how he feels about the statements on the cards. For example, the cards may read: "I enjoy meeting people"; "I dislike large crowds"; "I am sometimes afraid I am failing"; "I would never knowingly break a law"; and so on. The boxes may be labeled: "Describes me perfectly"; "Somewhat like me"; "Neutral"; "Not likely to be me"; and "Never in my lifetime." By evaluating the distribution of cards after a subject has sorted them into the boxes, the experimenter may draw some conclusion about the subject's self-concept. A **semantic differential** involves a rating scale concerned with the subject's perception

Rating Scales

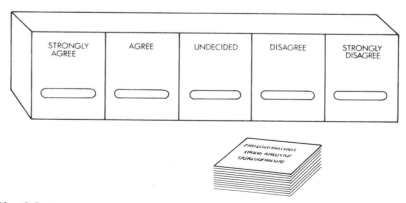

Fig. C.21.   Q-Sort.

of the meaning of words, or attitudes toward things, people, or concepts. A subject is usually asked to rate a word or statement on a number of different dimensions, such as hard-soft, warm-cool, flexible-rigid, light-dark, happy-sad. A semantic differential may be used to compare a subject's interpretation of different words by comparing the differential responses to each word, or may be used to compare differences between different subjects (such as children and adults) in their interpretation of the same word.

Choice-Preference

Response measurement can be accomplished by confronting a subject with a choice point where the subject may make one of two or more responses. The experimenter records which response is made. In simple discrimination devices, the subject must learn to give the correct response when a certain cue is presented and must learn not to respond when the cue is absent. In a **shuttle box,** an animal may move between two compartments. When the cue (either a light or a sound) is turned on, the subject must move to the other compartment or receive an electric shock.

A more complicated example of discrimination learning involves an animal learning to respond appropriately to two or more different cues. A Skinner box may have two different bars with the correct response indicated by a light cue. Similarly, the shuttle box becomes a complex discrimination device if a certain cue identifies a specific compartment as "safe."

A frequently used discrimination device is the **T-maze,** so named because it is a T-shaped alley maze. The start box is located at the base of the T, and there are two goal boxes located at the end of each arm. After leaving the start box, the animal is confronted with a choice point. The usual procedure is to place the reward in only one of the goal boxes. The animal must learn to locate the reward according to the cues provided.

Another apparatus is the **discrimination box,** which presents the animal with a choice of two or more doors. Entry through only one of the doors leads to reinforcement. Discrimination cues are usually placed on the doors, and the doors are hinged so that an animal can easily push through them. A **Lashley jumping stand**

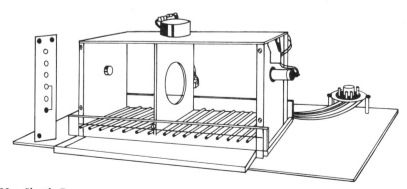

Fig. C.22. Shuttle Box.

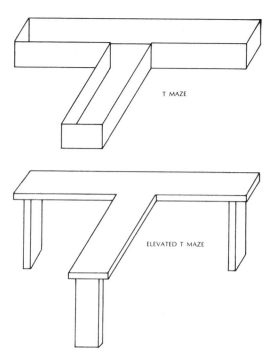

Fig. C.23. T-Maze.

presents the animal with the same task as the discrimination box except that the animal is placed on a platform and is made to jump to the correct door. If the choice is correct, the door opens onto a platform. If the choice is incorrect, the animal collides with the locked door and then drops into a net or, possiblly, a tank of water. The jumping stand introduces a punishment for an incorrect choice, a technique that can be added to other discrimination devices if desired.

Discrimination devices may be cascaded to create multiple discrimination problems for the subject. A Skinner box may be automatically programmed to change the stimulus cues (and the electrical connections leading from the bars) so that an animal must then respond according to a new cue situation. Multiple unit mazes present the animal with a sequence of choice points that must be successfully traversed to reach the goal box. The incorrect choice in a multiple unit maze usually leads to a "blind" alley, while the correct choice leads to the next choice point. They

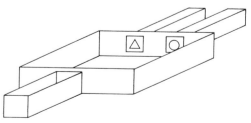

Fig. C.24. Discrimination Box.

may be arranged in a linear pattern where the subject must learn a certain sequence of right-left responses, or they may consist of interlocked paths, only one of which leads to the goal box.

All of the learning and discrimination devices used in animal research can be adapted to human applications. The usual procedure for investigating human maze learning is to reduce the scale of the maze. The maze pathway is reproduced on a sheet of paper, and the subject traces his route using his finger tip or a pencil. A problem with a **printed maze** is that the subjects can visually explore alternative pathways without moving the pencil from the choice point. A **finger maze** is a maze path that is embossed onto or engraved into a flat surface. The subject is blindfolded and must trace the pathway channel with his fingertip.

A **memory drum** allows the experimenter to make up verbal mazes for human subjects. The subjects must select the correct word from several presented on a line. The next line identifies the correct word, and the machine moves on to on the next "choice point." Thus, the subject is confronted with a series of choice points analogous to the rat in the multiple unit maze.

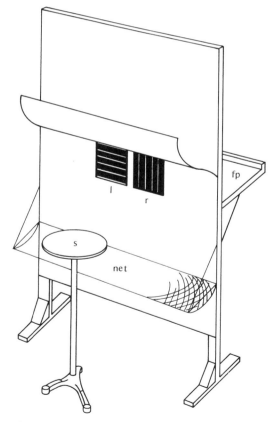

Fig. C.25.   Lashley Jumping Stand. Rat stands on s and jumps to 1 or r, which opens if a correct choice is made and the subject climbs onto the food platform (fp). Otherwise, he falls to net n.

Miscellaneous Devices

There are a number of perceptual phenomena that have been investigated. These phenomena have been found to differ according to the past experience of the subject, different levels of stress, or even personality differences between subjects. Consequently, these phenomena are often used as measures of the behavioral effects of a variety of independent variables.

Visual Phenomena

The **flicker-fusion apparatus** is a device that presents the subject with a flashing light that can be adjusted to different flash rates. At a certain rate, depending on the situation, the light no longer flickers but appears to be a steady but dimmer light. The **phi-phenomenon device** presents the subject with two lights that flash alternately. At certain flash rates, a subject reports that he no longer sees two separate lights, but a single light moving back-and-forth from one position to the other. The **autokinetic effect** is obtained by exposing the subject to a pinpoint light source in a darkroom. Even though the light is stationary, the subjects often report that the light appears to move and float about the room. The direction and magnitude of the apparent motion varies with the observer and the observation conditions. A **rod-frame apparatus** provides the subject with an illuminated rod he is to adjust to a vertical position. The experimenter can adjust the angle of an illuminated frame that surrounds the rod. Since the apparatus is used in a darkroom, it is possible to determine how much the subject is influenced by the frame in his perception of verticality.

Problem-solving behavior and social processes are often too complex to fit into simple response categories. Research into these behavioral areas often involves specialized techniques and recording devices for data collection. The following discussion illustrates a few of the devices that have been used.

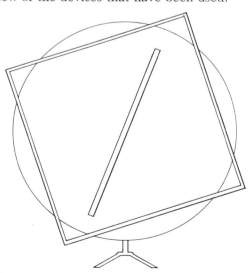

Fig. C.26.   Rod-Frame Apparatus.

There are a large number of **pencil and paper tests** that present a subject with hypothetical problems and allow space for the subject to note his response. The advantage of a paper and pencil test is that you can ask a subject to project his behavior into a hypothetical situation without having to create the situation. The disadvantage is that a subject might behave differently in the real situation.

The study of problem-solving behavior need not use only hypothetical examples as a source of problems. There are a number of problems that can be presented directly to the subject. Monkeys may be presented with **puzzle boxes** that require that a number of latches, bolts, and hasps must be undone before they can be opened. Other infrahuman tasks may require animals to learn to detour around a transparent obstruction placed between them and the goal object. The usual example is to place a glass wall between a hungry animal and a full food container. The problem is solved if the animal turns away from the container long enough to walk around the end of the glass wall.

Laboratory problems for human subjects come in a wide variety of types. Any well-supplied toy store sells a number of **games** for individuals that may serve as the basis for problem solving in the laboratory. Games requiring two or more players allow the observation of competitive behavior in human beings. Psychologists have found that games have a number of advantages in the laboratory. They may create an artificial situation that resembles a naturally occurring situation. The rules of a game may be established so that certain types of behavior can be emphasized or minimized. In addition, games can be arranged in such a way that the data-collection process is a naturally occurring part of the procedure. For example, an experimenter may require that subjects communicate by using notes rather than talking to one another. The notes can then be collected for subsequent analysis. The major problem with game research is that the games are artificial and the behavior of the subject may be the same.

PROGRAMMING EQUIPMENT

Automation appears to be the trend in the laboratory as well as in everyday living. Several manufacturers offer individual programming modules, each of which can be combined with other modules to accomplish the programming requirements of experiments. Most laboratories are equipped with electromechanical devices, that is, switches that literally open or close an electrical circuit by making or breaking contacts in the circuit. Problems with electromechanical devices are that they are subject to mechanical wear and breakage, they are comparatively slow, and they require a relatively large amount of power to operate. The present trend is to solid-state semiconductors, which are smaller, faster, more efficient, and more reliable than their earlier counterparts. The development of printed circuits means that relatively complicated solid-state programming circuits will be available at nominal cost in the near future.

The laboratory that has both types of devices may encounter problems trying to mix the two types in a single control circuit. The speed of solid-state circuits may cause them to respond to brief transient signals created in the electrome-chanical devices. For example, when electrical contacts in a switch come together, they may bounce on initial contact. The solid-state devices will respond to each im-pulse caused by the bouncing contacts.

The important feature of any solid state programming device is that it re-leases an electrical impulse (output signal) only under certain circumstances. An AND gate releases an impulse only when *both* of two inputs are activated. By con-necting one input to a light circuit and the other to a manipulanda, the output to a reinforcing mechanism will only occur when the bar is pressed when a light is on. A similar device (OR gate) can be set to respond when one event occurs *or* another event occurs. It is also possible to stop a signal when certain input characteristics are met. In this case, the devices are called NAND (Not AND) gates and NOR (Not OR) gates. A NOR gate might be used if the experimenter wanted to turn *off* a tone stimulus if the subject pressed a bar *or* pulled a string.

Counting mechanisms may be connected into an electrical circuit so that the output signal occurs only when a certain pattern of input signals has occurred. For example, a flip-flop (or its electromechanical equivalent, a latching relay) changes its output signal only when the input signals alternate. A flip-flop may be used if an experimenter wants an animal to turn a light on with one lever and to turn it off with another lever. If the animal presses the "on" lever, the flip-flop switches on the light. If the animal continues to press the "on" lever, the flip-flop remains in the same position and the light stays on. Only when the "off" lever is pressed will the device switch to the other position and the light will turn off. One kind of control counter can be constructed by cascading a number of flip-flop devices together so that the final output signal occurs only after a specified number of input signals have occurred. Partial reinforcement schedules requiring that an animal press a lever a specified number of times before the reinforcing mechanism is activated are easily established with a control counter.

Control timers release the output signal after a preset time interval has elapsed. An interval timer is started by some trigger signal, runs for a specified period of time, and then the output signal occurs. Most interval times have a manual or automatic reset feature so that they can be recycled to repeat the interval when the next input signal occurs. Interval timers are useful when some delay must be introduced between two events in an experimental sequence. One example would be to introduce a delay period between a response and reinforcement.

Some control timers measure the specified time interval, automatically reset and repeat the measurement, reset and repeat, and so on. Such a repeat timer pro-vides a train of pulses that occur at equal time intervals. If the experiment requires a repetitious cycle of events where careful timing of the cycle is necessary, the re-peat timer provides the initiating impulse for each cycle.

Interval timers can be connected together so that the output from one starts the other, and vice versa. The resulting repeat cycle timer provides a sequence of alternating short and long time intervals. A repeat cycle timer is especially valuable in time-sample research. The recording device can be turned on during the short time interval and turned off during the long period. It is possible to obtain five-minute samples of the subject's behavior every hour, or any other sample-nonsample sequence necessary for the research. More complicated repeat cycles can be created by using more than two timers in the circuit.

Complicated control cycles are usually accomplished by using some form of a variable programmer. A **variable programmer** can be adjusted (or programmed) so that the output signals all occur at different time intervals. The simplest programmer device is a disk mounted on a constant speed motor. The switch lever is positioned so that is rides on the edge of the disk which is rotated on the motor. The experimenter can cut notches into the edge of the disk so that the switch lever drops into each notch, causing the circuit to open or close. By measuring the rotational speed of the motor and the circumference of the disk, the distance between adjacent notches can be translated into a time interval.

A similar device is a film programmer, which has a motion picture projector sprocket mounted on a constant speed motor. The sprocket draws the film past a switch that rides on the film. A hole punched into the film with a paper punch is translated by the switch into the necessary electrical signal. The advantage of a film programmer is that the length of the program is almost limitless. In addition, the film may be easily changed for a new program. Measuring the distance along the film for the placement of the holes is also simpler than cutting notches in a disk.

Modern business machines and some computers utilize a paper tape that can be used to program a sequence of events. The tape may contain up to eight rows of holes that can be punched into it. Each row represents a separate channel, so eight different events may be simultaneously controlled with this device. (The number of output channels can be greater than this if the information in two or more rows is combined.) The holes may be programmed into the tape by a tape punch, which has an eight-key keyboard similar to a typewriter keyboard. The holes are then read by a tape reader, which converts the punched holes into electrical signals that are then fed out to the output devices. The basic tape reader is a counting device; that is, the reader progresses from one step on the tape to another whenever an input signal occurs. Thus, the input signals can be an animal's response, and the output signals a number of different stimulus events. Each time an animal presses the lever, a different stimulus may occur according to which row has a hole punched into it. If a repeat timer is used to feed into the tape reader, it can be effectively converted into a multichannel variable interval control timer.

SUMMARY

1. The advantages of equipment are: (1) it is more reliable and free from bias than an observer, (2) more data can be collected, (3) multiple measures can be simultaneously recorded, (4) previously unobservable behavior may be recorded, and (5) equipment will record continuously over prolonged data-collection periods.

2. The disadvantages of equipment are: (1) the device may fail or go out of adjustment, (2) apparatus may provide a source of secondary variance, (3) subjects may learn to take advantage of equipment characteristics, (4) available devices may dictate the course of research, and (5) equipment is expensive.

3. Stimulus restriction devices isolate the subject from potential secondary sources of variance.

4. Reinforcement devices deliver reward or punishment to the subject.

5. Stimulus-generating equipment consists of specialized devices for manipulating or presenting stimuli to subjects.

6. Stimulus measuring devices are used to specify the characteristics of the stimuli in the experiment. Stimulus measuring devices fall into two general categories: (1) null devices, which provide the characteristics of a matching stimulus, and (2) mechanical devices, which transduce the stimulus intensity into some numerical readout.

7. Behavior can be measured in one of three basic dimensions: (1) frequency, (2) duration, and (3) intensity.

8. Response recording devices may be divided into two categories: (1) response-detection devices, which usually convert the response into an electrical signal, and (2) recording devices that permanently record the electrical signals.

SUGGESTED READING

Sommer, R. G. (Ed.) Guide to scientific instruments. Special edition of *Science*, 1972, 178A.

Sidowski, J. B. (Ed.) *Experimental methods and instrumentation in psychology.* New York: McGraw-Hill, 1966.

Sidowski, J. B., and Ross, S. (Eds.) Instrumentation in psychology. Special issue of *American Psychologist*, 1969, 24, 185–384.

Zucker, M. H. *Electronic circuits for the behavioral and biomedical sciences: A reference book of useful solid state circuits.* San Francisco: Freeman, 1969.

UNIT D
Statistical Tests

INTRODUCTION

The following six units present a series of inferential statistical tests. Each test is presented in "cookbook" fashion. That is, only the bare essentials necessary for calculating each statistic are outlined. The student would profit by reviewing Chapter 9 and Chapter 10 before attempting to apply any of the tests in Units D1–D6. These units will not take the place of a statistics course. The statistical tools are presented for the student who has not had a course in statistics.

The selection of the appropriate test depends on the level of measurement and the type of research design. Table D1.1 is a matrix of the tests in terms of measurement level and experimental design. There are many tests other than those listed in Table D1.1. The researcher whose data do not fit the tests in Units D1–D6

TABLE D1.1. Matrix of Tests. A Test Can Be Used with the Level of Response Measurement Indicated (Rows) and All Greater Levels.

Measurement Level	*Research Design (Sets of Scores)*				
	One-Group Designs (One Set of Scores)	*Related Two-Group Designs* (Two Related Sets of Scores)	*Independent Two-Group Designs* (Two Independent Sets of Scores)	*Multilevel and Factorial Designs* (Multiple Sets of Scores)	*Correlation Coefficients*
Nominal	Binomial Unit D1 One-Group χ^2 Unit D2	Significance of changes χ^2 Unit D2	Two independent groups χ^2 Unit D2	r independent groups χ^2 Unit D2	
Ordinal		Sign test Unit D1	Median χ^2 Unit D2 Wilcoxon-Mann-Whitney Test Unit D3		r_s Unit D6
Interval or Ratio		Randomized Blocks ANOVA[a] Unit D5 t test for related scores Unit D4	Multilevel ANOVA Unit D5 Two independent samples t test Unit D4	ANOVA Unit D5	r Unit D6

[a] ANOVA is standard abbreviation for Analysis of Variance.

should consult one of the texts listed at the end of those units or one of the following texts: Edwards, 1973; Lindquist, 1953; Levy, 1968; Lewis, 1960; Meyers, 1966; or Winer, 1971.

UNIT D1
Binomial and Sign Tests

Both the binomial and sign tests are concerned with binomial (binary) data. Binary data consist of events classified into two exhaustive categories (for example, male-female, true-false answers to a test, or left-right in a T-maze). The binomial test is used with a single set of scores measured on at least a nominal scale. The sign test is used with two sets of related scores measured on at least an ordinal scale.

THE BINOMIAL TEST

The binomial test is used with a one-group design. The dependent measure is the classification of scores into two discrete categories. For example, we may ask a group of people to describe themselves as "liberal" or "conservative" in terms of political philosophy.

Logic and Method

The freqency of subjects within one of the categories may be divided by the total frequency (frequency in both categories) to obtain the proportion (P) within that category. Since the sum of the two proportions must be one, the proportion in one category is arbitrarily labeled P and the proportion in the other category is labeled $1 - P$. The values of P and $1 - P$ are fixed for a given population and measurement scale. However, random samples from that population are not likely to yield an observed P that is exactly the same as the population parameter. For example, if there are exactly 2000 males and 2000 females in a village, a random sample of 120 people may yield 66 males (55 percent). The difference between the sample 55 percent and the population 50 percent is due to chance.

Frequency Data Only

Pascal's Triangle and the formula for the binomial test are presented in Chapter 9. We may use these tools to specify the sampling distribution of the proportions we might observe with random samples from a binomial population. The null hypothesis (H_0) for a binomial experiment specifies the population value of P (and $1 - P$). In such an experiment, we wish to know if the difference between the *observed* P and the *population* P is likely on the basis of chance. If there is no difference between the observed statistic and the population parameter, then there is no need for a statistical test. If there is a difference between the observed P and the population parameter, then the binomial test is used to decide the likelihood that the difference is due to chance.

Calculational Example of a One-Tailed Test   Suppose that someone claims that most of the faculty at a community college are conservative in terms of political philosophy. Since we have no prior information about their philosophies, we might expect that about half of the faculty are conservative and half are liberal. That is, H_0 specifies that the P of conservatives $= 0.50$ and the proportion of liberals $(1 - P) = 0.50$. The alternative hypothesis (H_1) is that P conservative is greater than one-half $(P > 0.50)$.

We randomly sample 16 of the faculty members and ask them to anonymously indicate their political philosophy as either liberal or conservative. Since the data are binomial and H_1 is directional, we use a one-tailed binomial test. We arbitrarily set $\alpha = 0.10$. If the probability of the observed proportion and all greater proportions is less than α, then we reject H_0. H_1 states that P will be greater than one-half. Thus, the region of rejection consists of the 10 percent of all possible values of P that contain the largest values of P (conservative).

Eleven of the 16 faculty members indicate that they are political conservatives. Table D1.4 presents the cumulative binomial probabilities of various outcomes (r) for given sample sizes (N). Table D1.4 is limited to the case where H_0 specifies that $P = \frac{1}{2}$. The columns of Table D1.4 are labeled as values of x where $x = r$ or $N - r$, whichever is *smallest*. Our observed value of r is 11 and $N = 16$. Therefore, $x = N - r = 5$. We locate the number at the point where the $N = 16$ row and the $x = 5$ column intersect. The number is 0.105 which is the one-tailed probability (p) of an obtained proportion of $\frac{11}{16}$ or greater $(\frac{12}{16}, \frac{13}{16}$, and so on). (Note that the decimal points have been omitted from the table.) Since the observed $p = 0.105$ and $\alpha = 0.10$, we cannot reject the null hypothesis. We conclude that, on the basis of the observed sample, the proportion of conservatives is not significantly greater than 0.5.

Calculational Example of a Two-Tailed Binomial Test   A housemother at a college fraternity receives a report from the Dean of Students that her charges have been doing too much drinking during the week. The housemother becomes rather disturbed at this possibility and decides to test the Dean's hypothesis. Being an ex-statistics major from a large eastern university, she randomly selects Thursday night for her experiment. She manages to obtain the assistance of the president of the fraternity who acts as her data collector. He selects a sample of 12 men at random from those that enter the house between the hours of 11:00 P.M. and 2:30 A.M. on Thursday night. He asks each member of the sample to answer "yes" or "no" to the question, "Have you been drinking?" The null hypothesis is that the proportion of "yes" responses is 0.50 $(P = 0.50)$, and the proportion of "no" responses is also 0.50 $(1 - P = 0.50)$. Her alternative hypothesis (H_1) is that the proportion of "yes" responses is not 0.50 $(P \neq 0.50)$. Since H_1 does not specify direction, she uses a two-tailed binomial test. The housemother wants to minimize the probability of a Type I error, so she sets $\alpha = 0.03$. Since she has a two-tailed test, the region of rejection is split in half so that the rejection region consists of 0.015 of the outcomes at each end of the sampling distribution specified by H_0 (that is, $\frac{0.03}{2} = 0.015$).

Only one out of the 12 men sampled was drinking that night. According to Table D1.4, the probability of obtaining one out of 12 by chance is 0.006 (double the probability for a one-tailed test). The housemother, on the basis of the data collected, can reject the null hypothesis, since the probability of the obtained data is less than α. Since less than half of the sample were found to be drinking, and since the null is rejected, she concludes that less than half of the fraternity is drinking during the week. If two students had said "yes," she would not have been able to reject H_0 [p ($r \le 2$) = 0.038].

Instead of using the tabled value in Table D1.4, the housemother could have used Equation D1a. Equation D1a presents the general expression for the probability (p) of any binomial outcome (r) for any value of the proportion specified by H_0 (P) and any size sample (N).

$$p(r;P,N) = \frac{N!}{r!(N-r)!} \, P^r (1-P)^{N-r} \tag{D1a}$$

The exclamation point (!) after N, r, and $(N - r)$ in the formula is the *factorial sign* discussed in Chapter 9. Substituting in the values of the housemother's experiment we find:

$$p\left(r = 1; P = \frac{1}{2}, N = 12\right) = \frac{12!}{1!(12-1)!} \cdot \left[\left(\frac{1}{2}\right)^1 \left(1 - \frac{1}{2}\right)^{12-1}\right],$$

$$= \frac{12}{1}\left(\frac{1}{2}\right)^1 \left(\frac{1}{2}\right)^{11},$$

$$= 12\left(\frac{1}{2}\right)^{12},$$

$$= \frac{12}{2^{12}},$$

$$= \frac{12}{4096},$$

$$p\left(r = 1; P = \frac{1}{2}, N = 12\right) = 0.0029.$$

Since she was concerned with the probability of the observed outcome and all more extreme outcomes in the same direction, we also compute the probability when $r = 0$ (no "yes" answers). Substituting the appropriate values into Equation D1a, we find:

$$p\left(r = 0; \mathrm{P} = \frac{1}{2}, \mathrm{N} = 12\right) = \frac{12!}{0!\,(12-0)!} \left[\left(\frac{1}{2}\right)^0 \left(1 - \frac{1}{2}\right)^{12-0}\right],$$

$$= \frac{12}{12}\left(\frac{1}{2}\right)^{12},$$

$$= \frac{1}{2^{12}},$$

$$= \frac{1}{4096},$$

$$p\left(r = 0; \mathrm{P} = \frac{1}{2}, \mathrm{N} = 12\right) = 0.0002.$$

Adding the values of p when $r = 0$, and $r = 1$, we find that the rounded-off value of $p = 0.003$, which is the same as the value (one-tailed) in Table D1.4. Since the housemother had a two-tailed test, we double the obtained value of p ($2 \times 0.003 = 0.006$) to account for the two most extreme values in the direction opposite to the observed r ($r = 11$ and $r = 12$). Thus, the calculated probability ($p = 0.006$) is the p for the set of four r values (0, 1, 11, 12) at both extremes of the H_0 distribution.

Equation D1a is presented because Table D1.4 provides the value of p only when H_0 specifies that $\mathrm{P} = \frac{1}{2}$ (and $1 - \mathrm{P} = \frac{1}{2}$). For values of P that differ from $\frac{1}{2}$, the equation *must* be used to determine p.

The largest tabled value of N is 25. If N is greater than about 12, the calculations on the basis of Equation D1a become unwieldy. If an appropriate computer program is not available, the binomial test is used only for relatively small values of N.

THE SIGN TEST

The sign test is a variation of the binomial test. The sign test is used with a one-group before-after design or with a two-matched-groups design. The measurement scale is either ordinal or interval. Thus, we have two sets of at least ordinal scores that are paired (related) in some way. For example, we may hypothesize that achievement test scores (for example, Graduate Record Examination scores) can be increased by specific training. We can pretest one group of students; give them a two-week cram course; and then obtain an after measure of their test scores.

Logic and Method

The data of interest is the *difference* between the paired scores. In the sign test, it is the *sign* of the related differences that is evaluated.

The null hypothesis (H_0) specifies that the two sample sets of scores were randomly sampled from the same universal set or population. Therefore, any differences between the two sets of scores are due to chance sampling, and the signs of about half of the differences should be positive and half negative. Symbolically, H_0 specifies that $p\ (Y_{A1} > Y_{B1}) = p\ (Y_{A1} < Y_{B1}) = \frac{1}{2}$, where Y_A is the score of one member of each pair (or the after measure of a subject) and Y_B is the score of the other member of the matched pair (or the before measure of a subject). Alternatively, H_0 specifies that p (positive difference) $= p$ (negative difference) $=$ one-half.

We obtain two sets of scores and subtract one set of scores from the other. It does not matter if we subtract set A from set B or set B from set A, as long as we are consistent. If there are any *tied scores*, the difference is zero and the pair is discarded. (See pair C in Table D1.2.)

Calculational Example of a One-Tailed Test   We decide to determine the effects of specific training on achievement test scores of a sample of 13 students. We obtain their before measures on one form of the achievement test. Then six weeks later, they are given a two-week cram course. At the end of the course, we obtain their after scores on an equivalent form of the achievement test. The experimental hypothesis (H_1) is that the after scores will be *greater than* the before scores ($H_1 = Y_A > Y_B$). In terms of the sign test, the number of positive scores will be greater than the number of negative scores ($Y_A - Y_B$). We arbitrarily set $\alpha = 0.08$.

The data are displayed in Table D1.2. The tied score is discarded, so $N = 12$. Nine scores are positive and three are negative. Under H_0, the P of positive scores $=$ the P of negative scores. Using Table D1.4 with $x = 3$ ($x = 12 - 9$ or 9, whichever is smaller) and $N = 12$, we find $p(r) = 0.073$. Since the obtained p is less than α, we can reject H_0. Therefore, we conclude that for our sample the cram course did lead to improved achievement test scores, assuming that nothing else that happened to the subjects in the two months between the tests influenced their scores. With this assumption, we can generalize the results of the experiment to the population sampled.

TABLE D1.2. Before and After Achievement Test Scores of a Group of 13 Students. All Subjects Received Two Weeks of Training between the Two Measures.

| | *Achievement Test Scores* | | |
	After Measure Set A	Before Measure Set B	Sign of Difference
Subjects			
A	633	614	+
B	632	612	+
C	643	643	0
D	633	615	+
E	617	638	−
F	634	646	−
G	622	611	+
H	644	618	+
I	628	614	+
J	618	606	+
K	626	634	−
L	629	615	+
M	639	626	+

Calculational Example of a Two-Tailed Sign Test   An experimenter may hypothesize that complex stimuli are reinforcing to animals. He obtains 10 pairs of female guinea pigs. Each pair comes from the same litter. He decides to use a three-finger (three-choice) maze to test the conceptual hypothesis. (See Figure D1.A.) The arms of the maze are equipped with removable wall inserts. Each arm can have medium gray walls; all white walls; or random, black and white, dotted walls.

WALL INSERTS

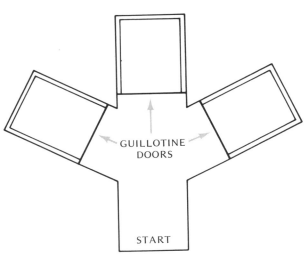

Fig. D1.A.   A three-choice (three-finger) maze. Each arm of the maze contains removable wall inserts.

The experimenter randomly assigns one member of each pair of pigs to Group A and the other member to Group B. The subjects in Group A are given 24 choice trials in the maze with one arm containing the dotted walls and two arms containing the gray walls. The placement of the dotted wall insert is randomized so that each arm contains the dot pattern about eight times. The subjects in Group B are given 24 trials in the maze with two arms containing gray walls and one arm containing the white walls. The placement of the white wall insert is randomized between trials. The difference between the white wall and the two gray walls is designated as a "low complexity" change. The difference between the dot pattern and the two gray walls is designated as a "high complexity" change.

The experimenter predicts that the animals in Group A will more frequently choose the dot pattern than the gray walls, and the animals in Group B will more frequently choose the white wall rather than the two gray walls. The experimenter also predicts that the number of choices of the "high complexity" arm (Group A) will be different from the number of choices of the "low complexity" arm (Group B).

The dependent measure is the number of choices of the "different" (spatially complex) arm for each group. The hypothetical data are presented in Table D1.3.

The scores for *each* group can be analyzed by a one-tailed binomial test. The experimenter predicts that the number of choices of the complex arm for each group would be greater than the number of choices of the other two arms. The choice data can be categorized into two sets of scores for each group; those subjects who made more than eight choices of the complex arm and those who made eight or less choices of the complex arm. Under H_0, the number of choices of the complex arm should be, by chance, about eight ($\frac{1}{3}$ of 24). Stated another way, under H_0, of those animals that show a preference for one arm, one-third will choose the complex arm more than eight times. The alternative hypotheses are that the number of choices of the complex arm will be greater than eight. Therefore, for both groups, H_1 specifies that more than one-third of the animals will make more than eight choices of the complex arm. The experimenter arbitrarily sets α at 0.01.

For Group A, eight pigs made more than eight choices of the complex arm. From Formula D1a we obtain the one-tailed binomial probability of eight or more choices is approximately equal to 0.001 [$p(r \geq 8; P = \frac{1}{3}, N = 10) \approx 0.001$]. For Group B, six pigs made more than eight choices of the complex arm. The one-tailed binomial probability of six or more choices of the complex arm is approximately equal to 0.006 [$p(r \geq 6; P = \frac{1}{3}, N = 10 \approx 0.006$]. Thus, for both groups, the observed p is less than α and the experimenter rejects H_0. For both groups, the observed frequency of choice of the complex arm is greater than would be expected on the basis of chance.

The experimenter's third prediction was that the number of choices of the complex arm by the two groups would differ. He arbitrarily set $\alpha = 0.10$ for this prediction. H_0 is $P(+) = P(-) = \frac{1}{2}$ and H_1 is $P(+) \neq P(-) \neq \frac{1}{2}$. The observed number of positive signs (r) is seven. Since a matched pair of subjects got the same score, that pair is discarded from the data analysis ($N = 9$). H_1 does not specify the direction of the difference between the two groups. Therefore, a two-tailed sign test is used to analyze the data. Using Table D1.4, the two-tailed probability of seven or more positive differences is 0.18 [$p(r \geq 7; P = \frac{1}{2}, N = 9) = 0.18$]. Since the obtained p is greater than α, the experimenter cannot reject H_0. Therefore, he concludes that there was no significant difference between the choice behavior of groups A (high complexity) and B (low complexity).

TABLE D1.3. The Number of Choices of the Complex Arm by the Guinea Pigs in 24 Trials.

Matched Pairs	Group A (High Complexity)	Group B (Low Complexity)	Sign of Difference
A	18	14	+
B	13	15	−
C	16	8	+
D	10	9	+
E	14	6	+
F	8	5	+
G	6	5	+
H	22	20	+
I	12	12	0
J	9	10	−

ADVANTAGES AND LIMITATIONS

When H_0 specifies $P = \frac{1}{2}$, both the binomial and sign tests are easy to use, because of Table D1.4. To use the binomial test, each score must be independent of each other score, and to use the sign test, each pair of scores must be independent of each other pair of scores. Data in any scale of measurement may be analyzed with the binomial test, so long as only one set of scores is involved. The scale of measurement must be at least ordinal to use the sign test. The probability of the obtained outcome for both tests is difficult to compute when large values of N are involved. Information provided by a level of measurement higher than the nominal level is ignored in the binomial test. Information provided by a level of measurement higher than the ordinal level is ignored by the sign test. (All differences between the paired scores are treated as equivalent.) If the measurement scale allows a comparison of the magnitude of the difference between paired scores, (interval level), then an experimenter should consider using the t test (Unit D4) instead of the sign test.

TABLE D1.4. Cumulative Probabilities of Observed x for a Given N in the Binomial and Sign Tests.[a]

NX	0	1	2	3	4	5	6	7	8	9	10	11	12	13	14	15
5	031	188	500	812	969	°										
6	016	109	344	656	891	984	°									
7	008	062	227	500	773	938	992	°								
8	004	035	145	363	637	855	965	996	°							
9	002	020	090	254	500	746	910	980	998	°						
10	001	011	055	172	377	623	828	945	989	999	°					
11		006	033	113	274	500	726	887	967	994	°	°				
12		003	019	073	194	387	613	806	927	981	997	°	°			
13		002	011	046	133	291	500	709	867	954	989	998	°	°		
14		001	006	029	090	212	395	605	788	910	971	994	999	°	°	
15			004	018	059	151	304	500	696	849	941	982	996	°	°	°
16			002	011	038	105	227	402	598	773	895	962	989	998	°	°
17			001	006	025	072	166	315	500	685	834	928	975	994	999	°
18			001	004	015	048	119	240	407	593	760	881	952	985	996	999
19				002	010	032	084	180	324	500	676	820	916	968	990	998
20				001	006	021	058	132	252	412	588	748	868	942	979	994
21				001	004	013	039	095	192	332	500	668	808	905	961	987
22					002	008	026	067	143	262	416	584	738	857	933	974
23					001	005	017	047	105	202	339	500	661	798	895	953
24					001	003	011	032	076	154	271	419	581	729	846	924
25						002	007	022	054	115	212	345	500	655	788	885

[a]The value of x = r or N − r, whichever is smallest. The table contains one-tailed probabilities under H_0 when $P = Q = .5$. Double the tabled probability values for a two-tailed test. Decimal points are omitted to save space.

° 1.0 or approximately 1.0

(From *Statistical Inference* by Helen M. Walker and Joseph Lev. Copyright 1953 by Holt, Rinehart and Winston, Inc. Reproduced by permission of Holt, Rinehart and Winston, Inc.)

REFERENCES

Further discussion of the sign test may be found in Guilford (1965, pp. 253–255); Runyon and Haber (1967); Siegel (1956, pp. 68–75); and Walker and Lev (1953, pp. 430–432).

UNIT D2
χ^2 Tests

There are several different tests which use the χ^2 (chi square) distribution as a basis for statistical decisions. The three most common include: (1) the one-group test, (2) the independent two-group test, and (3) the related two-group test. In all cases, a χ^2 test is used to answer the question: Is there a significant (nonchance) relationship between two or more variables?

THE ONE-GROUP TEST

The one-group test is used to determine the significance of the correspondence between a set of sample proportions and a set of theoretical proportions. That is, we collect data from a single sample and see if it is distributed as some theory suggests it should be. The two variables involved in such a study are (1) the response categories (nominal or greater level of measurement) and (2) the behavior of the subjects—the *frequency* with which they fall into the categories.

Logic and Method

The χ^2 test is a test of the significance of the differences between the *observed frequencies* (number of subjects) and the *expected frequencies* falling in each category. In the one-group χ^2 test, the null hypothesis states the proportion of subjects *expected* to fall in each category. When we know the size of the group, we can determine the expected frequencies by multiplying the expected proportions by the total sample size. Given a set of expected and observed frequencies, the χ^2 test is used to determine if the observed differences between frequencies in each category are likely to have occurred if the null hypothesis is true.

Frequency Data Only

The null hypothesis is tested with the following formula:

$$\chi^2 = \Sigma \left[\frac{(0 - E)^2}{E} \right]$$

(D2a)

where O is the observed frequency in each category, and E is the expected frequency in each category, and Σ indicates that the squared differences divided by E for *each* category should be summed across *all* categories. Note that the difference for each category must be squared and then divided by the expected frequency for *that* category. If the differences between the observed and expected frequencies are small, then the resulting value for χ^2 will be small. The larger the difference between the two sets of frequencies, the larger will be the value of χ^2. In general, as the value of χ^2 increases, the likelihood of support for the null hypothesis decreases. To determine the significance of the computed value of χ^2, it is compared with the tabled values in Table D2.5. The table presents the probabilities for *critical values* of χ^2. For example, in the first row (one *df*) with the null assumed to be true, one would expect to obtain a value of χ^2 equal to or greater than 1.64 two times out of ten. In other words, if the null is true, and with ten random samples of different subjects, by chance we would expect to calculate two values of χ^2 greater than 1.64.

Degrees of Freedom

Because χ^2 is the sum of the comparisons in all categories, the χ^2 distribution changes with the number of categories. Thus, we must compare our data with the *appropriate* χ^2 distribution according to the number of degrees of freedom (*df*). The number of *df* is determined by the number of categories or classes involved in a study. The *df* for the one-group χ^2 is equal to k − 1, where k stands for the total number of categories used. That is,

$$df = k - 1 \tag{D2b}$$

If we have 20 people and two categories (for example, "yes" and "no" responses to a questionnaire), then if 10 people answer "yes," we know that the remaining 10 answered "no" and we have one *df*. With three categories and a fixed number of people sampled, as soon as we know the frequencies in two categories, we know the frequency in the third category. Thus, with three categories, there are only two categories "free to vary" (2 *df*). With less than 30 *df*, you must use the correct theoretical distribution when evaluating a set of sample data. This means that you must enter the χ^2 table in the appropriate row (with the appropriate number of *df*). Beyond 30 *df*, there is very little change in the critical values of χ^2.

Calculational Example   Most Americans are familiar with the adage "Southerners prefer bourbon." Since it is a hypothesis about human behavior, we decide to test it. The identification for "Southerners" is college males from Southern college fraternities. The operational definition of "preference" is the fraternities' number of bottles of a type of liquor consumed per academic year. We randomly select one fraternity from each of 60 randomly chosen Southern four-year colleges and universities. The identification for liquor type is the description of the alcoholic beverage by the distiller. Three types of liquor are compared: bourbon whiskey, blended

TABLE D2.1. Hypothetical Frequency of Whiskey Choice.

Whiskey			
Blended	Scotch	Bourbon	Total
(E = 20) 10	(E = 20) 20	(E = 20) 30	60 (Σ E) 60 (Σ O)

whiskey, and Scotch whiskey. The null hypothesis is that there will be an equal number of choices of each type of whiskey. The alternative hypothesis is that there will be more bottles of bourbon consumed. Only the most frequently consumed type of whiskey is recorded for each fraternity. Alpha is set at the 0.05 level. Assume that the data presented in Table D2.1 was collected. Applying Formula D2a to the data in Table D2.1 we find,

$$\chi^2 = \frac{(10-20)^2}{20} + \frac{(20-20)^2}{20} + \frac{(30-20)^2}{20} \; ,$$

$$= \frac{100}{20} + 0 + \frac{100}{20}$$

$$\chi^2 = 10 \; .$$

We have two df since k (number of categories) $= 3$. Since we have a directional prediction, we use a one-tailed test. Turning to Table D2.5, we locate the number where the two-df row and the one-tailed 0.05 column intersect. The one-tailed critical value of χ^2 at the 0.05 level with two df is 4.60. Since our obtained value of χ^2 exceeds 4.60, the data do not support the null hypothesis. The hypothetical data significantly support the experimental hypothesis. We conclude that, with our identifications and measurements, the adage is empirically supported (assuming price is irrelevant).

Supplementary Note   The null hypothesis does not have to specify a rectangular distribution (equal proportions under each category). The null hypothesis may specify any kind of distribution. For example, McNemar (1969, pp. 267–271) presents an explanation of the use of the one-group χ^2 test where the null distribution is normal.

THE INDEPENDENT TWO-GROUP TEST

The independent two-group test is used to determine the significance of the behavioral differences between two independent groups of subjects. We may have two or more response categories. We want to know if two groups of subjects significantly differ in terms of the proportion of each group falling in each category. The three variables involved in such a study are (1) the response categories (nominal or greater level of measurement), (2) the two independent groups of subjects (independent variable), and (3) the behavior of the subjects—the *frequency* with which they fall into the categories.

Logic and Method

The logic of the two-group test is the same as that of the one-group test. The methods differ slightly. In the independent two-group test, the data are arranged in a two-by-k matrix or contingency table. That is, we know that we will have two rows (the two groups of subjects) and at least two columns (k = the response categories) of data. (See Table D2.2.)

The calculation of the expected frequencies (E) is not as easy as in the one-group case. The null hypothesis most commonly states that the groups variable (rows) and response category variable (columns) are independent of each other. If the rows and columns are independent, then the probability of any subject falling into any cell of the contingency table is determined by the multiplication rule for independent events (Chapter 9). The probability of a *row* is equal to the number of subjects in the group divided by the total number of subjects. The probability of a *column* is equal to the total number of responses in *that* column divided by the total number of subjects. Since we can only have *one response per subject,* these probabilities are always less than or equal to one. We multiply the probability of a row by the probability of a column in order to find the probability that any subject will fall into the cell consisting of the intersection of that row and that column. Since the E are frequencies, we must multiply the above probability of the cell by the total number of subjects in order to obtain the expected frequency for that cell. In practice, this is much simpler than it sounds. (See the calculational example.)

Only One Response per Subject

The *degrees of freedom* (*df*) for the independent two-group test is determined by the formula

$$df = (r - 1)(k - 1) \qquad \text{(D2c)}$$

where r is the number of rows and k is the number of columns in the data matrix. In a two-by-two contingency table, there is only one *df* $[(2 - 1)(2 - 1) = 1]$. With a fixed number of subjects in each group, and with a given total number of responses in each category, as soon as the frequency in one cell of a two-by-two matrix is known, the frequencies in the remaining three cells are known. Since $(r - 1)$ always equals one in the two-independent-samples test, the *df* for the two-group test simplifies to $(k - 1)$.

Calculational Example

Suppose that we develop the hypothesis that college students can play roles with no training. In order to test this idea, we randomly divide a group of 90 college students into two groups. One group is told that they are to consider themselves

TABLE D2.2. Hypothetical Ratings of a Single Cartoon.

Student Groups		Response Categories			
		Not Funny	Mildly Amusing	Funny	Σ
	"Guards"	(E = 10) 0	(E = 20) 20	(E = 30) 40	60
	"Flowers"	(E = 5) 15	(E = 10) 10	(E = 15) 5	30
	Σ	15	30	45	90

as guards on a prison chain gang. The other group is told that they are to consider themselves as completely peace-loving "flower children." We predict that there will be a difference in the responses of the two groups to examples of sadistic behavior. Both groups are shown a single cartoon depicting a woman beating a snake with a heavy club. The snake's balloon reads, "It's nice to be needed." The students are told to rate the cartoon on a three point scale: "not funny," "mildly amusing," and "funny." We arbitrarily set alpha at the 0.01 level. The null hypothesis is that there will be no significant difference between the responses of the two groups of students. Assume that we obtained the data presented in Table D2.2. The expected value for the first cell (the intersection of the first row and first column) is determined by multiplying the sum for the first column (15) by the ratio of the sum of the first row and the total ($^{60}/_{90}$). That is, $E = 15 \times {}^{60}/_{90} = 10$. The preceding equation is equal to the probability of the first row ($^{60}/_{90}$) multiplied by the probability of the first column ($^{15}/_{90}$) with the results multiplied by the total (90). That is $^{15}/_{90} \times {}^{60}/_{90} \times 90 = 15 \times {}^{60}/_{90} = 10$. Thus, to determine the expected frequency in any cell of an r × k contingency table, you multiply the marginal sum of that cell's column by the ratio of the marginal sum of that cell's row and the total sum.

Applying Formula D2a to the data in Table D2.2 we find,

$$\chi^2 = \frac{-10^2}{10} + \frac{0^2}{20} + \frac{+10^2}{30} + \frac{-10^2}{5} + \frac{0^2}{10} + \frac{+10^2}{15},$$

$$\chi^2 = 10 + 0 + 3^1/_3 + 20 + 0 + 6^2/_3,$$

$$\chi^2 = 40.$$

There are two *df*, because k = 3. Since we did not make a directional prediction, we use a two-tailed test. The *critical value* of a two-tailed χ^2 at the .01 level with two *df* is 9.21. Since the obtained value of χ^2 exceeds the critical value we reject the null hypothesis and conclude that the data supports the experimental hypothesis. Finally, we conclude that the data, with the given identifications and procedures, supports the conceptual hypothesis.

Supplementary Note The independent two-group χ^2 test can be easily generalized to the r-independent-groups test. That is, one can apply the method and logic directly to the case where there are more than two groups of subjects.

The χ^2 test may be used to determine the significance of the difference between two groups measured at the ordinal level (for example, rank scores on a test of learning speed). The two sets of scores are pooled and the *median* of the combined scores is determined. Then, the two groups are each divided into two categories: (1) the number of subjects within a group that ranked above the combined median, and (2) the number of subjects within the group that did not rank above the combined median. The resulting data are presented in a two-by-two contingency table with the two groups as the rows and the two categories (above and not above the median) as the columns. Then, the χ^2 formula is applied. Such an application of χ^2 is sometimes called a *median* χ^2 test.

THE RELATED TWO-GROUP TEST

The related two-group χ^2 test is used with a "subjects as their own control" or "repeated measures" design. That is, there are two measures at the nominal or greater level of the behavior of each subject. Such a design might be a "before-after" design in which each subject is categorized or ranked before and after the introduction of some treatment (Chapter 4). This χ^2 test is sometimes called the "McNemar test for the significance of changes" (Siegel, 1956).

Logic and Method

The data are arranged in a two-by-two contingency table. The general form of the table is presented in Table D2.3. The "no" and "yes" indicate the different responses.

Cells A and D contain those subjects that changed their responses. The B and C cells contain those individuals whose measure did not change. The *sum* of A and D is the total number of people that changed. The null hypothesis (H_0) is that half of these cases would change in one direction and half in the other. Since we are interested in only two cells, the usual χ^2 formula becomes,

$$\chi^2 = \frac{(|A - D| - 1)^2}{A + D} \tag{D2d}$$

where $|A - D|$ indicates that the sign of the difference between A and D is to be ignored. That is, if the difference between A and D is negative, ignore the negative sign and reduce the obtained difference by 1 before squaring. The *df* is always 1, since there are only two cells of interest. As before, use Table D2.5 to evaluate the significance of the obtained value.

Calculational Example

Suppose that a psychology professor has the theory that freshmen college students generally view psychology positively. Furthermore, he hypothesizes that this positive emotional connotation decreases with exposure to the more statistical

TABLE D2.3. General Form of Two-by-Two Table for Significance of Changes χ^2 Test.

		After	
		No	Yes
Before	Yes	A	B
	No	C	D

aspects of psychology. He decides to test his hypothesis with one of his introductory classes of 40 students. First, he obtains a measure of each student's general attitude toward psychology during the first week of the course. He devotes the entire second week to a series of lectures on descriptive and inferential statistics. At the beginning of the third week, he obtains a second measure of each student's general attitude. The null hypothesis is that of those students who change their attitude, one-half will change in the positive direction and one-half in the negative. He sets alpha at the 0.05 level. Suppose that the data in Table D2.4 were obtained.

Applying Formula D2d he finds that,

$$\chi^2 = \frac{(|4 - 16| - 1)^2}{16 + 4},$$

$$\chi^2 = \frac{(11)^2}{20},$$

$$\chi^2 = 6.05.$$

There is one df. The tabled value of a one-tailed χ^2 at the 0.05 level with one $df = 2.71$. Since the obtained value of χ^2 exceeds 2.71, and the difference is in the predicted direction, he rejects H_0. He concludes that his conceptual hypothesis is supported by the data.

Supplementary Note   If the expected frequency is less than 5 [$E = \frac{1}{2}(A + D)$], the sign test should be used in place of the related two-groups χ^2 test.

ADVANTAGES AND LIMITATIONS

The major advantage of the χ^2 tests is that they are frequently the only tests available for analyzing frequency data arranged in categories (nominal level of measurement). A secondary advantage of the χ^2 tests is that they are comparatively easy to compute.

TABLE D2.4. The Hypothetical Responses of a Class to a Questionnaire on Their Attitudes toward "Psychology."

		After	
		Positive	Negative
	Negative	A 4	B 10
Before			
	Positive	C 10	D 16

There are three major limitations or restrictions to the use of χ^2 tests. First, the data points *must be independent* of each other. In practice this means that you can have *only one* response from each subject involved in the computation of χ^2. Thus, if there are several measures of each subject in an experiment, only one score (such as the rank of the mean of the subject's scores) can be used in χ^2 test.   Second, the data points *must be in frequency form*. The most common way that this is achieved is by tallying the number of subjects that fall in a cell of a contingency table. Finally, the expected values for any cell of a contingency *must not be too small*. This restriction varies with the type of test: one-group, independent two-group, or related two-group.

One-Group Test   When the *df* equal one (the number of categories, $k = 2$), all of the E must be equal to or greater than 5. When the *df* are greater than one ($k > 2$), no more than 20 percent of the E can be less than five and no E can be less than one. When $k > 2$, the categories can sometimes be meaningfully combined in order to satisfy the restriction on the size of E.

Independent Two-Group Test   In the case of the two-by-two contingency table, if the total sample size (N) is greater than 40, there are no restrictions on the size of E. If N is between 20 and 40, all of the E must be equal to or greater than 5. If N is less than about 20, the Fisher exact test (Siegel, 1956) should be used instead of χ^2. In the two-by-two χ^2 test, calculation Formula D2e should be used for a more accurate calculation of χ^2.

$$\chi^2 = \frac{N\left(|AD - BC| - \dfrac{N}{2}\right)^2}{(A + B)(C + D)(A + C)(B + D)} \tag{D2e}$$

where N is the total sample size; A, B, C, and D are the frequencies in the four quadrants of the two-by-two table; and $\left(|AD - BC|\dfrac{N}{2}\right)$ indicates that the absolute value of the difference (ignoring the sign of the difference) should be reduced by $\dfrac{N}{2}$.

When there are more than two categories ($k > 2$), no more than 20 percent of the E can be less than five and no E can be less than one. As before, it may be possible to combine categories *meaningfully* in order to meet this restriction. That is, the combined categories must make sensible groups.

Related Two-Group Test   As previously indicated, if the expected frequency $[\frac{1}{2}(A + D)]$ is less than five, the sign test should be used.

REFERENCES

More extensive discussion of the various χ^2 tests is contained in Cochran (1952 and 1954); Edwards (1973, pp. 130–148); Lewis and Burke (1949); McNemar (1969, pp. 245–275); Mood and Graybill (1963, pp. 226–227, 308–319, and

412–413); Siegel (1956, pp. 42–47, 63–67, 104–116, and 175–184); and Walker and Lev (1953, pp. 81–108, 130–135, and 183–184).

Table D2.5. Table of χ^2.

Degrees [a] of Freedom df	one-tail p = .25 two-tail p = .50	.15 .30	.10 .20	.05 .10	.025 .05	.01 .02	.005 .01
1	.455	1.074	1.642	2.706	3.841	5.412	6.635
2	1.386	2.408	3.219	4.605	5.991	7.824	9.210
3	2.366	3.665	4.642	6.251	7.815	9.837	11.341
4	3.357	4.878	5.989	7.779	9.488	11.668	13.277
5	4.351	6.064	7.289	9.236	11.070	13.388	15.086
6	5.348	7.231	8.558	10.645	12.592	15.033	16.812
7	6.346	8.383	9.803	12.017	14.067	16.622	18.475
8	7.344	9.524	11.030	13.362	15.507	18.168	20.090
9	8.343	10.656	12.242	14.684	16.919	19.679	21.666
10	9.342	11.781	13.442	15.987	18.307	21.161	23.209
11	10.341	12.899	14.631	17.275	19.675	22.618	24.725
12	11.340	14.011	15.812	18.549	21.026	24.054	26.217
13	12.340	15.119	16.985	19.812	22.362	25.472	27.688
14	13.339	16.222	18.151	21.064	23.685	26.873	29.141
15	14.339	17.322	19.311	22.307	24.996	28.259	30.578
16	15.338	18.418	20.465	23.542	26.296	29.633	32.000
17	16.338	19.511	21.615	24.769	27.587	30.995	33.409
18	17.338	20.601	22.760	25.989	28,869	32.346	34.805
19	18.338	21.689	23.900	27.204	30.144	33.687	36.191
20	19.337	22.775	25.038	28.412	31.410	35.020	37.566
21	20.337	23.858	26.171	29.615	32.671	36.343	38.932
22	21.337	24.939	27.301	30.813	33.924	37.659	40.289
23	22.337	26.018	28.429	32.007	35.172	38.968	41.638
24	23.337	27.096	29.553	33.196	36.415	40.270	42.980
25	24.337	28.172	30.675	34.382	37.652	41.566	44.314
26	25.336	29.246	31.795	35.563	38.885	42.856	45.642
27	26.336	30.319	32.912	36.741	40.113	44.140	46.963
28	27.336	31.391	34.027	37.916	41.337	45.419	48.278
29	28.336	32.461	35.139	39.087	42.557	46.693	49.588
30	29.336	33.530	36.250	40.256	43.773	47.962	50.892

[a] For different values of df, the table contains one- and two-tailed critical values of χ^2 under H_0. For values of df greater than 30, the expression $\sqrt{2\chi^2} - \sqrt{2(df) - 1}$ may be used as a normal deviate (z) with unit standard error.

(Table D2.5 is abridged from Table III of Fisher: *Statistical Methods for Research Workers*, published by Oliver & Boyd Ltd., Edinburgh, and by permission of the author and publishers.)

The Wilcoxon-Mann-Whitney test is used with an independent two-group design. The dependent variable must be measured at least at an ordinal level. The test combines the Wilcoxon test for small samples of equal size, and the Mann-Whitney test for samples of unequal size.

Logic and Method

The test is used to decide whether the scores of the two independent groups differ significantly. The null hypothesis (H_0) is that the independent variable has no differential effect on the two groups. Thus, the two groups represent two random samples from the same population, and, if H_0 is true, the two sets of scores should differ only by chance. The alternative hypothesis (H_1) is that the experimental treatment produced a nonchance difference between the two groups. For example, an experimenter may hypothesize that hypnosis may be used to increase retention of verbal material. One group of subjects (A) would learn the material under hypnosis, and the other group (B) would learn the material while not under hypnosis. H_0 would be that the probability of any score (a) from group A being larger than any score (b) from group B is one-half. That is, $p\ (a > b) = p\ (b > a) = \frac{1}{2}$. H_1 would be $p\ (a > b) \neq p\ (b > a) \neq \frac{1}{2}$; a two-tailed hypothesis with no direction stated.

The scores from the two groups are combined and ranked into *one* ordered series. The *smallest* score of the combined groups receives a rank of 1, and the largest score receives the highest rank. If there are N_1 subjects in one group and N_2 subjects in the other group, then the highest rank is $N_1 + N_2$. Two scores of the same size are given the *average* of the two ranks. For example, if the fourth and fifth scores are the same, then they each receive the rank of $4\frac{1}{2}$ (the average of ranks 4 and 5).

Alternatively, the researcher may conservatively arrange (see Chapter 2) the tied data so that the tied scores are ranked in the way that is *least* favorable to the experimental hypothesis and most favorable to the null. The experimental hypothesis is that group A would have larger retention scores than Group B. If a score from Group A is equal to (tied with) a score from Group B, then the conservative arrangement would be to give the smaller rank to the score from Group A. The sum of the *ranks* of the *smallest* sample (N_1) is called T ($T = \Sigma$ ranks of N_1). If the two groups are the same size, it does not matter which one is labeled N_1.

Since the two groups may be of different sizes, the null hypothesis becomes the following: the ratio of T to the sum of ranks for the larger sample (N_2) should be approximately equal to the ratio of N_1 to N_2. H_1 becomes this: the ratio of T to Σ ranks N_2 should not be equal to the ratio of N_1 and N_2. If T is sufficiently larger or smaller than expected on the basis of N_1/N_2, then we can reject H_0. If we ranked the scores with the largest score getting a rank of 1, then the sum of the ranks for N_1

would be T'. The formula, $T' = N_1(N_1 + N_2 + 1) - T$, saves us the trouble of re-ranking and resumming the numbers. Table D3.6 is based on using T or T', *whichever is smaller*. In summary, (1) determine the value of T for the *smaller sample*, (2) using the formula, determine the value T', and (3) use whichever is *smallest*, T or T', in locating the tabled probability. T' is always calculated in order to be sure that we have the smallest sum of ranks.

Calculational Example with Unequal Sample Sizes (N's)

Suppose the experimenter tests the hypnosis hypothesis on college freshmen. He obtains one sample of $N_1 = 10$, and another sample of $N_2 = 12$. Group A (N_1) is hypnotized and given the same instructions as group B (N_2), which is not hypnotized. The dependent variable is the number of nonsense syllables recalled by both groups one day later. Arbitrarily, α is set at 0.10. The hypothetical data are presented in Table D3.1.

Table D3.1. Recall Scores of Each Subject in the Hypnosis Experiment.

Group A (hypnotized):	25, 40, 34, 26, 46, 45, 34, 28, 40, 31.
Group B (not-hypnotized):	20, 24, 31, 34, 23, 20, 19, 15, 24, 28, 19, 21.

All $N_1 + N_2 = 22$ scores are ordered from smallest to largest and ranks are assigned to the scores. (See Table D3.2.) *Tied scores*, whether within a group or between the two groups, are given the average of their ranks. For example, in Table D3.2, there are three scores of 34, and each score is given the rank of 17, because that is the average of the ranks of 16, 17, and 18. Next, the observations from the smaller sample are underlined and their *ranks* are summed. That is, $10 + 11 + 12\frac{1}{2} + 14\frac{1}{2} + 17 + 17 + 19\frac{1}{2} + 19\frac{1}{2} + 21 + 22 = 164 = T$.

From the obtained T value, $T' = 10(10 + 12 + 1) - 164 = 66$. Since T' is less than T, its value is used with Table D3.6. The tabled values in Table D3.6 are the *critical* values for given sample sizes N_1 and N_2 and for a given α. To use the table, we find the set of four numbers where the column (N_1) and row (N_2) intersect. In order, from top to bottom, the four numbers are the critical values of the smaller of T or T', for α equal to 0.20, 0.10, 0.05, and 0.01 (two-tailed). If

TABLE D3.2. Recall Scores of the Hypnosis Experiment Combined and Ranked.

Scores:	15,	19,	19,	20,	20,	21,	23,	24,
Ranks:	1,	$2\frac{1}{2}$,	$2\frac{1}{2}$,	$4\frac{1}{2}$,	$4\frac{1}{2}$,	6,	7,	$8\frac{1}{2}$,
Scores continued:	24,	25,	26,	28,	28,	31,	31,	
Ranks continued:	$8\frac{1}{2}$,	10,	11,	$12\frac{1}{2}$,	$12\frac{1}{2}$,	$14\frac{1}{2}$,	$14\frac{1}{2}$,	
Scores continued:	34,	34,	34,	40,	40,	45,	46	
Ranks continued:	17,	17,	17,	$19\frac{1}{2}$,	$19\frac{1}{2}$,	21,	22	

the observed T (or T') is *equal to or less than* the tabled critical value for a given α level, then the H_0 is rejected. For a *one-tailed* test, the values of α in the left-hand column of the table are halved.

In the hypnosis experiment, α was set at 0.10. Since $N_1 = 10$ and $N_2 = 12$, and since H_1 is two-tailed, the critical value is 89. The obtained value of T' was 66. Therefore, H_0 is rejected and the experimenter concludes that hypnosis did affect recall of nonsense syllables. Assuming that the two groups were randomly sampled from the population of freshmen students, he can generalize the conclusion to that population.

Calculational Example with Equal Sample Sizes ($N_1 = N_2$)

Suppose an experimenter hypothesizes that rapid breathing lowers reaction time. Ten subjects are randomly sampled and randomly assigned to two groups of five subjects each. Group I is told to breathe normally during the test, and Group II is told to breathe rapidly. The dependent variable is the subjects' reaction time (button press) to a visual signal. The scores are measured to the nearest millisecond. H_0 is that the ratio of T to Σ ranks N_2 will be approximately equal to N_1/N_2 (1.0). Since a high score equals a slow reaction time, H_1 is that the ratio of T (Σ of ranks of Group II) to Σ ranks N_2 (Group I) will be less than N_1/N_2. The level of α is arbitrarily set at 0.025. The data in Table D3.3 is obtained. The scores in Table D3.3 are combined and ranked. (See Table D3.4.)

TABLE D3.3. Reaction Time in Milliseconds for 10 Subjects.

Group I:	8,	10,	15,	7,	20;
Group II:	5,	4,	3,	9,	6.

The scores from Group II are underlined, and their corresponding ranks are summed to obtain T. $T = 1 + 2 + 3 + 4 + 7 = 17$. $T' = 5(5 + 5 + 1) - 17 = 38$. Since T is smaller than T', the value of T is compared to the critical value in Table D3.6. With $N_1 = N_2 = 5$, and $\alpha = 0.025$, the one-tailed critical value of T is 17. H_0 is rejected, since the obtained T value is equal to the critical value. The experimenter concludes that rapid breathing did significantly decrease reaction time.

TABLE D3.4. Combined and Ranked Data from Table D3.3.

Scores:	3,	4,	5,	6,	7,	8,	9,	10,	15,	20;
Ranks:	1,	2,	3,	4,	5,	6,	7,	8	9,	10.

Large Values of N_1 and N_2   When the value of N_2 exceeds 20, then Table D3.6 cannot be used. When the value of N_1 exceeds 2 and the value of N_2 exceeds

20 ($N_1 > 2$, $N_2 > 20$), then Equation D3a can be used to determine the critical values of T. The calculated critical value is called $\tilde{T}$.

$$\tilde{T} = N_1 (N_1 + N_2 + 1)/2 - z \sqrt{N_1 N_2 (N_1 + N_2 + 1)/12} \qquad \text{(D3a)}$$

The two-tailed critical values ($\tilde{T}$) can be obtained for different levels of α by substituting in the appropriate values of z. The values of z are the points locating areas of the normal curve (Figure 8.2); selected values of z are presented in Table D3.5. Formula D3a provides a good approximation to the exact critical values. For a one-tailed hypothesis, the values of α are halved. For example, the two-tailed value of z to substitute in Formula D3a with $\alpha = 0.05$ is 1.96 and the one-tailed value of z with $\alpha = 0.025$ is 1.96.

TABLE D3.5. Two-Tailed Value of z for Levels of α.

$\alpha =$	0.20	0.10	0.05	0.02	0.01
$z =$	1.28	1.64	1.96	2.33	2.58

ADVANTAGES AND LIMITATIONS

When two independent, randomly sampled groups of subjects are measured at the ordinal level, the Wilcoxon-Mann-Whitney test is a comparatively simple test to use. Tied scores between subjects within a group have no effect on the value of T (or T'). Tied scores *between groups* tend to decrease the value of T, thus spuriously increasing the likelihood of rejecting H_0. One way to decrease the effect of ties between groups is to assign ties the least favorable ranks instead of the average rank. That is, the rank of tied scores is assigned so as to *increase* the value of T (or T', whichever is smaller). This conservative procedure tends to decrease the likelihood of rejecting H_0. Usually, the effect of between-groups ties is negligible. Unless a quite *large* proportion of between-groups ties occurs, the conservative procedure need not be used. The Wilcoxon-Mann-Whitney test is useful when certain assumptions about the sampling distribution do not seem feasible. For example, the *t* test (Unit D4) is based on the assumption that two independent groups are randomly sampled from normally distributed populations. As compared to the median χ^2 test (Unit D2), the Wilcoxon-Mann-Whitney uses all of the information provided by ordinal measurement.

REFERENCES

For further discussion see Kruskal and Wallis (1952) and Tate and Clelland (1957, pp. 89–91).

TABLE D3.6. Critical Values of T in the Wilcoxon-Mann-Whitney Sum of Ranks Test.[a]

Values of T or T', whichever Is Smaller, Significant at the 20, 10, 5, and 1 Percent Levels[b]

N_2	α																				
		1	2	3	4	5	6	7	8	9	10	11	12	13	14	15	16	17	18	19	20
																					N_1 (Smaller Sample)
3	.20		3	7																	
	.10			6																	
	.05																				
	.01				(4)																
4	.20		3	7	13																
	.10			6	11																
	.05				10																
	.01					(5)															
5	.20		4	8	14	20															
	.10		3	7	12	19															
	.05			6	11	17															
	.01					15	(6)															
6	.20		4	9	15	22	30														
	.10		3	8	13	20	28														
	.05			7	12	18	26														
	.01				10	16	23	(7)														
7	.20		4	10	16	23	32	41													
	.10		3	8	14	21	29	39													
	.05			7	13	20	27	36													
	.01				10	16	24	32	(8)													
8	.20		5	11	17	25	34	44	55												
	.10		4	9	15	23	31	41	41												
	.05		3	8	14	21	29	38	49												
	.01				11	17	25	34	43	(9)												
9	.20	1	5	11	19	27	36	46	53	70											
	.10		4	9	16	24	33	43	54	66											
	.05		3	8	14	22	31	40	51	62											
	.01			6	11	18	26	35	45	56	(10)											

TABLE D3.6. Critical Values of T in the Wilcoxon-Mann-Whitney Sum of Ranks Test. [a] **(continued)**

n_2	α	1	2	3	4	5	6	7	8	9	10	(11)	(12)	(13)	(14)	(15)	(16)	(17)
10	.20	1	6	12	20	28	38	49	60	73	87							
	.10		4	10	17	26	35	45	56	69	82							
	.05		3	9	15	23	32	42	53	65	78							
	.01			6	12	19	27	37	47	58	71							
11	.20	1	6	13	21	30	40	51	63	76	91	106						
	.10		4	11	18	27	37	47	59	72	86	100						
	.05		3	9	16	24	34	44	55	68	87	96						
	.01			6	12	20	28	38	49	61	73	87						
12	.20	1	7	14	22	32	42	54	66	80	94	110	127					
	.10		5	11	19	28	38	49	62	75	89	104	120					
	.05		4	10	17	26	35	46	58	71	84	99	115					
	.01			7	13	21	30	40	51	63	76	90	105					
13	.20	1	7	15	23	33	44	56	69	83	98	114	131	149				
	.10		5	12	20	30	40	52	64	78	92	108	125	142				
	.05		4	10	18	27	37	48	60	73	88	103	119	136				
	.01			7	14	22	31	41	53	65	79	93	109	125				
14	.20	1	7	16	25	35	46	59	72	86	102	118	136	154	174			
	.10		5	13	21	31	42	54	67	81	96	112	129	147	166			
	.05		4	11	19	28	38	50	62	76	91	106	123	141	160			
	.01			7	14	22	32	43	54	67	81	96	112	129	147			
15	.20	1	8	16	26	37	48	61	75	90	106	123	141	159	179	200		
	.10		6	13	22	33	44	56	69	84	99	116	133	152	171	192		
	.05		4	11	20	29	40	52	65	79	94	110	127	145	164	184		
	.01			8	15	23	33	44	56	69	84	99	115	133	151	171		
16	.20	1	8	17	27	38	50	64	78	93	109	127	145	165	185	206	229	
	.10		6	14	24	34	46	58	72	87	103	120	138	156	176	197	219	
	.05		4	12	21	30	42	54	67	82	97	113	131	150	169	190	211	
	.01			8	15	24	34	46	58	72	86	102	119	136	155	175	196	(17)

TABLE D3.6. Critical Values of T in the Wilcoxon-Mann-Whitney Sum of Ranks Test.[a] (continued)

Values of T or T', whichever Is Smaller, Significant at the 20, 10, 5, and 1 Percent Levels[b]

N_1 (Smaller Sample)

N_2	α		2	3	4	5	6	7	8	9	10	11	12	13	14	15	16	17	18	19	20
17	.20	(1)	9	18	28	40	52	66	81	97	113	131	150	170	190	212	235	259			
	.10		6	15	25	35	47	61	75	90	106	123	142	161	182	203	225	249			
	.05		5	12	21	32	43	56	70	84	100	117	135	154	174	195	217	240			
	.01			8	16	25	36	47	60	74	89	105	122	140	159	180	201	223	(18)		
18	.20	(1)	9	19	30	42	55	69	84	100	117	135	155	175	196	218	242	266	291		
	.10		7	15	26	37	49	63	77	93	110	127	146	166	187	208	231	255	280		
	.05		5	13	22	33	45	58	72	87	103	121	139	158	179	200	222	246	270		
	.01			8	16	26	37	49	62	76	92	108	125	144	163	184	206	228	252	(19)	
19	.20	(2)	10	20	31	43	57	71	87	103	121	139	159	180	202	224	248	273	299	325	
	.10	(1)	7	16	27	38	51	65	80	96	113	131	150	171	192	214	237	262	287	313	
	.05		5	13	23	34	46	60	74	90	107	124	143	163	182	205	228	252	277	303	
	.01		3	9	17	27	38	50	64	78	94	111	129	147	168	189	210	234	258	283	(20)
20	.20	(2)	10	21	32	45	59	74	90	107	125	144	164	185	207	230	255	280	306	333	361
	.10	(1)	7	17	28	40	53	67	83	99	117	135	155	175	197	220	243	268	294	320	348
	.05		5	14	24	35	48	62	77	93	110	128	147	167	188	210	234	258	283	309	337
	.01		3	9	18	28	39	52	66	81	97	114	132	151	172	193	215	239	263	289	315

[a] The table contains two-tailed critical values of T under H_0. The given value of α is halved for a one-tailed test. When $N_1 > 2$ and $N_2 > 20$, approximate critical values of T ($\tilde{T}$) are given by: $T = N_1(N_1 + N_2 + 1)/2 - z\sqrt{N_1 N_2(N_1 + N_2 + 1)/12}$, where z is 1.28 for α = .20, 1.64 for α = .10, 1.96 for α = .05, and 2.58 for α = .01.

[b] Computed from Donavon Auble's *Extended Tables of the Mann-Whitney Statistic.* Bloomington: Indiana University Institute of Educational Research, 1953. (Table D3.6 is reprinted with permission of The Interstate Printers & Publishers, Inc., from Table L, p. 137, M. W. Tate and R. C. Clelland, *Non-Parametric and Short-Cut Statistics,* 1957.)

The *t* tests are used with matched or independent two-group designs. The dependent variable must be measured at the interval level. The *t* test for independent groups is used to test whether the scores of two groups differ on the basis of chance. The *t* test for related groups is used to test whether the scores of two matched groups or two measures of a single group (before-after design) differ on the basis of chance. Both tests involve the use of the standard error of the difference between means.

Standard Error

A set of subjects is sampled from a population, and the subjects are measured on some variable. The procedure is repeated several times, and the arithmetic mean of each sample is calculated.

The obtained distribution of means is called the *sampling distribution of means*. If the samples for each experiment were randomly sampled from the same population, then the means of each sample are random samples from the population. The mean of the sampling distribution (mean of means or *grand mean*, $\overline{Y}_G$) and the standard deviation of the means may be calculated. The standard deviation of the sampling distribution is called the *standard error of the means* ($S_{\bar{y}}$).

Suppose we obtain five random samples from a population. The hypothetical means of each sample are presented in Table D4.1.

TABLE D4.1. Sampling Distribution from N = Five Means.

$\overline{Y}$	$(\overline{Y} = \overline{Y}_G)$	$(\overline{Y} = \overline{Y}_G)^2$
5	2	4
4	1	1
3	0	0
2	-1	1
1	-2	4
$\Sigma = 15$	$\Sigma = 0$	$\Sigma = 10$

The grand mean of the sampling distribution is $\overline{Y}_G = \Sigma\overline{Y}/N = 15/5 = 3.0$. The variance of the sampling distribution is $S^2 = \Sigma(\overline{Y}-\overline{Y}_G)^2/N = 10/5 = 2.0$. The square root of the variance (S^2) yields the standard error for the five sample means. Thus, $S_{\bar{y}} = \sqrt{2} = 1.4$. The standard error ($S_{\bar{y}}$) describes the variability of the sample means about $\overline{Y}_G$. With random samples, $S_{\bar{y}}$ is due to chance factors.

Usually, an experimenter does not repeatedly sample a population. Rather, he randomly samples one set of subjects from the population. If he uses a two-group design, then he randomly assigns the subjects of his sample to the two groups. Following the administration of an experimental treatment, he obtains the dependent scores for the two groups. If he uses an interval measurement scale, he may calculate the mean ($\overline{Y}$) for each group. The difference between the two $\overline{Y}$s is presumably due to the independent variable. In order to decide whether the observed difference $(\overline{Y}_1 - \overline{Y}_2)$ is due to the independent variable or chance factors, he must be able to compare the difference to some estimate of the expected variance of randomly sampled means from the population.

The measure of the expected differences between randomly sampled means is obtained from the standard error of the means $(S_{\overline{y}})$. Since the experimenter did not repeatedly sample from the population, he must use some statistic to *estimate* $S_{\overline{y}}$. The value of $S_{\overline{y}}$ is estimated by the square root of the unbiased variance of the sample divided by the square root of N (Equation D4 a).

Estimate of Standard Error of Means

$$S_{\overline{y}} = \sqrt{\frac{s^2}{N}} = \frac{s}{\sqrt{N}} \tag{D4a}$$

Unbiased Estimate of Variance

If a distribution of scores is generally bell-shaped, a small sample of scores is likely to underestimate the standard deviation of the distribution. That is, because extreme scores are relatively infrequent, they are less likely to appear in the sample. Consequently, a sample will probably have a narrower distribution. To partially correct for the inaccuracy caused by the smallness of the sample, an *unbiased estimate* of the variance of the population may obtained by using the formula

$$s^2 = \frac{\Sigma (Y - \overline{Y})^2}{N - 1} \tag{D4b}$$

where $\Sigma(Y = \overline{Y})^2$ is the sum of squared deviation scores of the sample distribution, N is the number of scores in the sample, and s^2 is the estimate of the variance of the population sampled. Note the difference between the formula for the unbiased estimate of the variance and the formula for a sample variance (Formula 8.c in Chapter 8) is the divisor of $N - 1$ instead of N. The effect of subtracting 1 from N diminishes with increasing sample size which reflects the increasing accuracy of large sample estimates.

The experimenter has two groups with a mean and variance for each group. An estimate of the standard error of the *difference* between two means is provided by combining the unbiased variances for each group $(s_1{}^2$ and $s_2{}^2)$. The unbiased variance can be combined into one estimate by Formula D4c.

$$s_c^2 = \frac{\Sigma (Y_1 - \overline{Y}_1)^2 + \Sigma (Y_2 - \overline{Y}_2)^2}{N_1 + N_2 - 2} \tag{D4c}$$

$s_c{}^2$ is the *combined unbiased estimate* of the population variance where Y_1, $\overline{Y}_1$, N_1 refer to Group One and Y_2, $\overline{Y}_2$, N_2 refer to Group Two.

The standard error of the difference between two means $(S\overline{Y}_1 - \overline{Y}_2)$ is estimated by

Standard Error of Difference between Means

$$S_{\overline{y}_1 - \overline{y}_2} = \sqrt{s_c^2 \left(\frac{1}{N_1} + \frac{1}{N_2}\right)} \tag{D4d}$$

where N_1 is the number of subjects in Group One and N_2 is the number of subjects in Group Two. The mean of the distribution of differences between randomly sampled means is zero.

THE *t* TEST FOR INDEPENDENT TWO-GROUP DESIGNS

Logic and Method

The independent *t* test is used to decide whether the difference between the means of two independent groups is likely on the basis of chance. The null hypothesis (H_o) is that the independent variable has no consistent effect on the behavior of the two groups of subjects. The difference between two $\overline{Y}$s randomly sampled from the same population should, on the average, be equal to zero. Thus, $H_0 : \overline{Y}_1 - \overline{Y}_2 = 0$. The experimental hypothesis (H_1) is that the difference between the means is not zero ($H_1 : \overline{Y}_1 - \overline{Y}_2 \neq 0$).

The *t* ratio is defined as the ratio of the observed difference between the means minus the expected difference, divided by the standard error of the difference.

$$t = \frac{(\overline{Y}_1 - \overline{Y}_2) - 0}{S_{\overline{y}_1 - \overline{y}_2}} \qquad \text{(D4e)}$$

Thus, the *t* ratio provides a comparison of the difference between observed and expected variance (differences) to the estimate of chance variance. For a given value of $S_{\overline{Y}_1 - \overline{Y}_2}$, the larger the value of the numerator in Equation D4e the larger the value of *t*. For a given value of N_1 and N_2, as the value of *t* increases, the probability of rejecting H_0 increases. Thus, all other things being equal, the greater the difference between the two means, the greater the likelihood of rejecting H_0 and accepting H_1.

The calculational formula for the independent *t* is derived from Equations D4c, D4d, and D4e.

$$t = \frac{\overline{Y}_1 - \overline{Y}_2}{\sqrt{\left[\dfrac{N_1 \sum Y_1{}^2 - (\sum Y_1)^2}{N_1}\right] + \left[\dfrac{N_2 \sum Y_2{}^2 - (\sum Y_2)^2}{N_2}\right]}{N_1 + N_2 - 2} \left[\dfrac{1}{N_1} + \dfrac{1}{N_2}\right]} \qquad \text{(D4f)}$$

where: $\overline{Y}_1$ = mean of Group One; N_1 = size of Group One; ΣY_1 = sum of squared scores of Group One; and $(\Sigma Y_1)^2$ = square of the sum of the scores of Group One. Similarly, the subscript 2 refers to Group Two.

A calculated value of *t* is compared with the *critical values* listed in Table D4.4. The left-hand column of Table D4.4 is labeled *df*. The *degrees of freedom* (*df*) for an independent two-sample test are the total number of subjects minus two ($df = N_1 + N_2 - 2$). For a one- or two-tailed test, a given value of *df*, and a given value of α, the critical values of t are specified in Table D4.4. If an obtained value of t is *equal to or greater than* the tabled critical value, then H_o may be rejected.

Calculational Example

Suppose an experimenter hypothesized that the chemical magnesium pemoline (MgPe) would facilitate discrimination learning in cats. He randomly samples one group of 10 and one group of 11 male subjects of the same age. The experimenter assumes that the average learning ability, level of activity, and so on, for the two groups are approximately equal. The experimental group ($N_1 = 10$) is given an injection of MgPe and the control group ($N_2 = 11$) an injection of a placebo (carboxymethylcellulose). The dependent measure is the number of correct responses out of 20 discrimination trials. Arbitrarily, $\alpha = 0.001$. The scores for each subject are presented in Table D4.2.

TABLE D4.2. Discrimination Learning Scores of Two Independent Groups of Cats.

Subject	Score (Y_1)	$Y_1{}^2$	Subject	Score (Y_1)	$Y_1{}^2$
A	10	100	K	6	36
B	8	64	L	7	49
C	12	144	M	10	100
D	13	169	N	9	81
E	9	81	O	6	36
F	12	1·44	P	7	49
G	14	196	Q	9	81
H	12	144	R	10	100
I	10	100	S	8	64
J	10	100	T	9	81
			U	8	64

$N_1 = 10 \qquad \Sigma Y_1 = 110 \qquad \Sigma Y_1{}^2 = 1242 \qquad N_2 = 11 \qquad \Sigma Y_2 = 89 \qquad \Sigma Y_2{}^2 = 741$

$\overline{Y}_1 = \Sigma Y_1 / N_1 = 11 \qquad\qquad\qquad \overline{Y}_2 = \Sigma Y_2 / N_2 = 8.1$

First, the scores (Y_1) and the square of each score $(Y_1{}^2)$ are listed. Then, as indicated in Table D4.2, each column is summed to provide the values of N, ΣY, and ΣY^2 for each group. Then the means of each group are calculated. When all these steps are completed, then the information is substituted into Equation D4f. Note that $\Sigma Y_1{}^2$ (1242) is *not* the same as $(\Sigma Y_1)^2$ $(110)^2$.

$$t = \frac{11.0 - 8.1}{\sqrt{\dfrac{\left[\dfrac{(10)(1242) - (110)^2}{10}\right] + \left[\dfrac{(11)(741) - (89)^2}{11}\right]}{10 + 11 - 2}\left[\dfrac{1}{10} + \dfrac{1}{11}\right]}}$$

To solve the equation for t, the following steps are followed:

(1) Complete the operations required by the parentheses, (), in the denominator. For example (10) (1242) = 12420, (11) (741) = 8151, $(110)^2 = 12100$, $(89)^2 = 7921$.
   The denominator of the t equation thus reduces to:

$$\sqrt{\dfrac{\left[\dfrac{12420 - 12100}{10}\right] + \left[\dfrac{8151 - 7921}{11}\right]}{10 + 11 - 2}\left[\dfrac{1}{10} + \dfrac{1}{11}\right]}$$

(2) Complete the subtraction and addition within each set of brackets, []. For example, $12420 - 12100 = 320$, $8151 - 7921 = 230$, $1/10 + 1/11 = 21/110$. The *t* denominator is reduced to:

$$\sqrt{\dfrac{[320/10] + [230/11]}{10 + 11 - 2}\left[\dfrac{21}{110}\right]}$$

(3) Complete the division within each bracket, and the addition, subtraction required. For example, $320/10 = 32$, $230/11 = 20.9$, $10 + 11 - 2 = 19$, $21/110 = 0.19$. The *t* denominator is reduced to:

$$\sqrt{\left[\dfrac{32 + 20.9}{19}\right](0.19)}$$

(4) Complete the addition and division within the brackets. For example,

$$32 + 20.9 = 52.9, \quad 52.9 \div 19 \approx 2.78$$

The *t* denominator becomes:

$$\sqrt{2.78\,(0.19)}$$

(5) Complete the multiplication and compute the required square root. For example,

$$2.78 \times 0.19 \approx 0.53, \quad \sqrt{0.53} \approx 0.73.$$

Thus the denominator of the *t* ratio $(S_{\overline{Y}_1} - \overline{Y}_2)$ is 0.73.

(6) The subtraction required in the numerator of the *t* ratio is completed. For example, $11.0 - 8.1 = 2.9$.

Therefore, the *t* ratio becomes:

$$t = 2.9/0.73 \approx 3.97.$$

Since the experimenter predicted that $\overline{Y}_1 > \overline{Y}_2$, he uses a one-tailed test. The *df* $= 10 + 11 - 2 = 19$, and $\alpha = .001$. The critical value in Table D4.4 is 3.579. Since the obtained value of t (3.97) exceeds 3.579, H_0 is rejected ($t = 3.97$, $df = 19$, one-tailed $p < 0.001$). Therefore, the experimenter concludes that MgPe does significantly facilitate discrimination learning in cats.

THE *t* TEST FOR TWO RELATED GROUPS

The second *t* test is used with matched-group designs or repeated measures designs (before-after, one-group). In such designs, the *pairs* of scores are correlated in some way. (See Chapter 6.) The *t* test for related scores takes into account the correlation between paired measures in calculating the value of the standard error of the mean.

Logic and Method

The related *t* test is used to decide if the difference between the means of two related groups is likely on the basis of chance. The difference between two means $(\overline{Y}_1 - \overline{Y}_2)$ is equal to the mean of the differences between the paired scores $(\overline{Y}_D)$. That is, $\overline{Y}_D = \overline{Y}_1 - \overline{Y}_2$. The null hypothesis is that the independent variable has no consistent effect on the behavior of the two groups of subjects. Thus, H_0 is $\overline{Y}_D = 0$. The experimental hypothesis is that the difference between the means is not zero $(H_1 : \overline{Y}_D \neq 0)$.

The *t* ratio is defined as the ratio of the observed $\overline{Y}_D$ minus the expected $\overline{Y}_D$, (based on H_0), divided by the standard error of the differences.

$$t = \frac{\overline{Y}_D - 0}{S_D} \tag{D4g}$$

For a given value of S_D, the larger the value of the numerator $(\overline{Y}_D - 0)$, the larger the value of *t*. All else being equal, the greater the difference between the scores of the two groups, the greater the likelihood of rejecting H_0 and accepting H_1.

The standard error of the mean difference is based on the variance of the difference between the *paired scores*. Formula D4h defines the standard error of the mean difference (S_D).

$$S_D = \sqrt{\frac{\Sigma (D_i - \overline{D})^2}{N(N-1)}} \tag{D4h}$$

In Formula D4h, N is the number of *paired scores,* D_i is the difference between any pair of scores, and $\overline{D}$ is the average difference between paired scores $(\overline{D} = Y_D)$.

The calculational formula for the related *t* is derived from Equations D4g and D4h. The calculational formula is presented in Equation D4i,

$$t = \frac{\overline{Y}_D}{\sqrt{\left[\frac{N \Sigma D^2 - (\Sigma D)^2}{N}\right]\left[\frac{1}{N(N-1)}\right]}} \tag{D4i}$$

In Formula D4i, $\overline{Y}_D$ = mean of the difference scores; N = the number of paired scores; ΣD^2 = the sum of the squared difference scores; and $(\Sigma D)^2$ = the square of the sum of the difference scores.

A calculated value of t is compared with the *critical values* listed in Table D4.4. The number of *degrees of freedom* equals the number of difference scores minus one ($df = N - 1$). If the obtained t value is *equal to or greater than* the critical value, then H_0 may be rejected.

Calculational Example

Suppose a high-school counselor thinks that anxiety-producing instructions will affect the achievement test scores of students. On the basis of IQ scores, the counselor obtains 10 matched pairs of subjects (matched by correlated criterion). The students are all enrolled in college preparatory programs. One member of each pair is randomly assigned to Group A and the other to Group B. The two groups are placed in separate, but similar rooms. Just before taking the achievement test, Group B is told that the test is a college entrance examination and will directly affect their chances of getting into college. Supposedly, the instructions will arouse anxiety in the students in Group B. Group A is told that the test is a practice test to help them discover which areas they should study in order to improve their chances of getting into college.

The counselor is not sure whether anxiety will increase or decrease the treatment scores. Thus, H_1 is two-tailed. The counselor arbitrarily sets $\alpha = 0.05$. The dependent variable is the performance of the two groups on the achievement test (measured as percentile scores). The counselor assumes that the test provides an interval scale. The counselor obtains the data shown in Table D4.3.

First the scores of each group are listed. Then the scores of one group are subtracted from the scores of the other and the differences (D_1) and (D_1^2) are listed. (It does not really matter which group is subtracted from which, so long as you are consistent and remember which way you subtracted.) As indicated in Table D4.3, the D_1 and D_1^2 columns are summed. The sum of each group's scores provides a

TABLE D4.3. Scores on Achievement Test for Matched Subjects.

Pair of Subjects	Scores of Group A	Scores of Group B	Difference between Paired Scores $D_i = (Y_1 - Y_2)$	D_i^2
A	90	87	3	9
B	88	89	−1	1
C	93	91	2	4
D	94	92	2	4
E	88	86	2	4
F	87	84	3	9
G	89	90	−1	1
H	92	89	3	9
I	93	87	6	36
J	85	88	−3	9
$N = 10$	$\Sigma \bar{Y}_A = 899$ $\bar{Y}_A = 89.9$	$\Sigma \bar{Y}_B = 883$ $\bar{Y}_B = 88.3$	$\Sigma D = 16$ $\bar{Y}_D = 1.6$	$\Sigma D^2 = 86$

check on the subtraction procedures, since the difference between the two groups' sums must equal the sum of the differences. (The means of each group do *not* have to be calculated for the *t* test.) When these steps are complete, the information is substituted into Equation D4i:

$$t = \frac{1.6}{\sqrt{\left[\frac{10\,(86) - (16)^2}{10}\right]\left[\frac{1}{10\,(10 - 1)}\right]}}$$

To solve the equation for *t*, the following steps are followed:

(1) Complete the operations required by the parentheses, (), in the denominator. For example,

$$(10)\,(86) = 860,\,(16)^2 = 256,$$
$$(10 - 1) = 9,\quad 10\,(9) = 90.$$

The demoninator of the *t* equation then is reduced to:

$$\sqrt{\left[\frac{860 - 256}{10}\right]\left[\frac{1}{90}\right]}$$

(2) Complete the subtraction and division within each set of brackets []. For example, $860 - 256 = 604$,

$$\frac{604}{10} = 60.4;\frac{1}{90} = 0.011.$$

The *t* denominator is reduced to:

$$\sqrt{(60.4)\,(0.011)}$$

(3) Complete the multiplication within the square root (radical) sign and compute the square root. For example,

$$(60.4) \times (0.011) = 0.66,$$

$$\sqrt{0.66} \approx 0.81.$$

Thus, the denominator of the *t* ratio (S_D) is 0.81.

(4) The *t* ratio becomes,

$$t = \frac{1.6}{0.81} \approx 1.98.$$

The $df = N - 1 = 9$ (*pairs* of scores) and the two-tailed $\alpha = 0.05$. The critical value in Table D4.4 is 2.262. Since the obtained value of t (1.98) is less than the critical value, H_0 cannot be rejected ($t = 1.98$, $df = 9$, two-tailed $p > 0.05$). Therefore, the counselor concludes that the "anxiety-provoking instructions" did *not* have any significant differential effect on his subjects.

ADVANTAGES AND LIMITATIONS

While complicated to compute, the *t* tests take advantage of all of the information presented by interval measurement to test differences between the means of two groups. The *t* tests are limited to comparing the means of only two groups. An experimenter may use multiple *t* tests to test the difference between any two groups in a multilevel or factorial experiment. The alpha level is inflated in a multiple *t* test; thus, multiple comparison tests are usually preferred for multiple group comparisons. Multiple comparison tests (Kirk, 1968) are based on the logic of the *t* test and are specifically designed for multiple group comparisons.

The independent two-group *t* test *demands* that the two groups are independent, random samples from a population. The assumptions of independence and randomness are met if the groups are randomly sampled, and if subjects are randomly assigned to the two groups.

Independent Random Sampling

In order for the sample standard deviation to be a good estimate of the standard error of the mean, the population should be normally distributed. However, the assumption of normality of the population distribution is relatively unimportant, particularly if N_1 and N_2 are both greater than about 25 (Boneau, 1960).

In order for the two sample standard deviations to be combined into one estimate of the standard error of the mean, the populations from which both samples were derived should have approximately equal variances. Again, the assumption of equal population variance is relatively unimportant if the sample sizes are equal and both at least equal to 25 (Boneau, 1960). In general, if the sample sizes of the two groups are equal ($N_1 = N_2$), then as the sample size increases, extreme violations of the assumptions of normality and equal population variance have little effect on *t*. Slight differences in sample size have little effect as long as the smallest N is fairly large.

The related two-group *t* test *demands* that each pair of subjects is randomly assigned to the two treatment groups. The assumptions of normality and equal population variance also apply to the related *t* test. As was the case with the independent *t* test, the assumptions are not very important with a fairly large number of pairs ($N > 25$).

Random Assignment

The related *t* test is based on the differences between the scores of paired subjects. The difference scores are used in order to eliminate the correlation between the paired scores. Each pair contributes only one score (D) to the analysis. The use of only one score for each pair of subjects reduces the number of degrees of freedom (*df*) for the *t* test. If you look at Table D4.4, you will note that the critical values of *t* increase as the *df* decrease. The use of the *related t* test with *independent* groups would lead to more frequent failures to reject H_0 when H_0 is false (Type II errors). Thus, the two sets of scores must be correlated in order to use the related *t* test legitimately. In addition, the correlation between the two groups should *not*

TABLE D4.4. Upper Percentage Points of the t Distribution.[a]

df	one-tailed p = 0.4 two-tailed p = 0.8	0.25 0.5	0.1 0.2	0.05 0.1	0.025 0.05	0.01 0.02	0.005 0.01	0.001 0.002
1	0.325	1.000	3.078	6.314	12.706	31.821	63.657	318.31
2	.289	0.816	1.886	2.920	4.303	6.965	9.925	22.326
3	.277	.765	1.638	2.353	3.182	4.541	5.841	10.213
4	.271	.741	1.533	2.132	2.776	3.747	4.604	7.173
5	0.267	0.727	1.476	2.015	2.571	3.365	4.032	5.893
6	.265	.718	1.440	1.943	2.447	3.143	3.707	5.208
7	.263	.711	1.415	1.895	2.365	2.998	3.499	4.785
8	.262	.706	1.397	1.860	2.306	2.896	3.355	4.501
9	.261	.703	1.383	1.833	2.262	2.821	3.250	4.297
10	0.260	0.700	1.372	1.812	2.228	2.764	3.169	4.144
11	.260	.697	1.363	1.796	2.201	2.718	3.106	4.025
12	.259	.695	1.356	1.782	2.179	2.681	3.055	3.930
13	.259	.694	1.350	1.771	2.160	2.650	3.012	3.852
14	.258	.692	1.345	1.761	2.145	2.624	2.977	3.787
15	0.258	0.691	1.341	1.753	2.131	2.602	2.947	3.733
16	.258	.690	1.337	1.746	2.120	2.583	2.921	3.686
17	.257	.689	1.333	1.740	2.110	2.567	2.898	3.646
18	.257	.688	1.330	1.734	2.101	2.552	2.878	3.610
19	.257	.688	1.328	1.729	2.093	2.539	2.861	3.579
20	0.257	0.687	1.325	1.725	2.086	2.528	2.845	3.552
21	.257	.686	1.323	1.721	2.080	2.518	2.831	3.527
22	.256	.686	1.321	1.717	2.074	2.508	2.819	3.505
23	.256	.685	1.319	1.714	2.069	2.500	2.807	3.485
24	.256	.685	1.318	1.711	2.064	2.492	2.797	3.467
25	0.256	0.684	1.316	1.708	2.060	2.485	2.787	3.450
26	.256	.684	1.315	1.706	2.056	2.479	2.779	3.435
27	.256	.684	1.314	1.703	2.052	2.473	2.771	3.421
28	.256	.683	1.313	1.701	2.048	2.467	2.763	3.408
29	.256	.683	1.311	1.699	2.045	2.462	2.756	3.396
30	0.256	0.683	1.310	1.697	2.042	2.457	2.750	3.385
40	.255	.681	1.303	1.684	2.021	2.423	2.704	3.307
60	.254	.679	1.296	1.671	2.000	2.390	2.660	3.232
120	.254	.677	1.289	1.658	1.980	2.358	2.617	3.160
∞	.253	.674	1.282	1.645	1.960	2.326	2.576	3.909

[a]For different values of *df*, the table contains one- and two-tailed critical values of *t* under H_0. (Table D4.4. is abridged from Table 12 of the *Biometrika Tables for Statisticians*, Vol. 1 (ed. 1), edited by E. S. Pearson and H. O. Hartley. Reproduced here with the kind permission of E. S. Pearson and the trustees of *Biometrika*.)

be small. The correlation between the two groups must be large enough to offset the loss of *df* associated with using the related *t* test.

With both tests, as the sample size increases, the standard deviation of the mean or mean differences becomes a better estimate of the standard error of the sampling distribution of means or mean differences. Also, as the sample size increases, the likelihood of detecting a small difference between means increases.

The *F* test (Unit D5) may also be used to test the significance of differences between the means of two groups (independent two-group design or related two-group design). The calculated value of F equals t^2 in those two cases.

REFERENCES

For further discussion of the *t* test and the underlying assumptions, see Alder and Roessler (1964, pp. 123–140); Edwards (1973, pp. 56–74); Hays (1973, pp. 389–431); or Walker and Lev (1953, pp. 145–160).

UNiC D5
Analysis of Variance

In Chapter 10, the analysis-of-variance technique for analyzing interval level data was discussed. The statistical test used in the analysis of variance is the *F* test. The *F* test may be used with two or more (multilevel) independent groups designs, with two or more (randomized blocks) related groups designs, and with factorial designs involving either randomized, independent groups, or combinations of independent and related groups (repeated measure factorial, split-plot designs).

LOGIC AND METHOD

Multilevel Design

The logic of analysis of variance was presented in Chapter 10. In contrast to the tabular and pictorial presentation of the analysis-of-variance technique in Chapter 10, the present material briefly outlines the technique in an algebraic fashion. The order of presentation here will be the same as the order in Chapter 10, beginning with the multilevel design. The example data of Chapter 10 will also be used here. Table D5.1 repeats the data of Table 10.2.

The structural model for the multilevel design is that any girl's Y score is composed of the sum of three parts: $Y = (\overline{Y}) + (A_i) + (error)$. The symbol $\overline{Y}$ stands for the grand mean or average score of all 18 subjects; A_i represents the effect of a particular level of the A independent variable, and (error) stands for the effect of random error on a particular score. The effect of various levels of the modeling condition (A_i) produces the *between-groups variance* (variation in the means of the A_i levels), and the effect of random error within each A group produces the *within-*

TABLE D5.1. Raw Data of Modeling Experiment (Dependent Variable is the Number of Cooperative Responses) Multilevel (Three-Group) Design.

	Groups			
A1 (Competitive)	*A2* (Control)	*A3* (Cooperative)	$\overset{i}{\Sigma Y}$	$\bar{Y}_k$
3	8	7	18	6
6	8	10	24	8
6	11	10	27	9
5	6	10	21	7
7	7	10	24	8
9	8	13	30	10
$\overset{k}{\Sigma Y} = 36$	48	60	144	
$\bar{Y}_i = 6$	8	10	Grand Mean = 8	

group variance. The *F* ratio is defined as the ratio of between-groups variance to within-group variance.

The calculation of the between and within variance requires first that the *sums of squares* associated with the total set of scores, the between-group means, and the within-group scores be calculated. The formula for the total sum of squares (abbreviated Total SS) is:

$$\text{Total SS} = \sum Y^2 - \frac{(\sum Y)^2}{N} \qquad \text{(D5a)}$$

where ΣY^2 is the sum of all 18 scores squared, $(\Sigma Y)^2$ is the *square of the sum* of the 18 scores, and N is the number of scores (18).

The formula for the between-groups (treatment) sum of squares (abbreviated Treatment SS) is:

$$\text{Treatment SS} = \overset{i}{\sum} \frac{(\overset{k}{\Sigma}Y)^2}{N_k} - \frac{(\sum Y)^2}{N} \qquad \text{(D5b)}$$

where $(\overset{k}{\Sigma}Y)^2$ is the *square of the sum* of the six scores in a treatment group, N_k is the number of scores in a treatment group ($N_k = 6$), $(\overset{k}{\Sigma}Y)^2 \div N$ is defined for Equation D5a and the results of $(\overset{k}{\Sigma}Y)^2 \div N_k$ are summed across the three groups (three treatment levels) before subtracting the value of $(\Sigma Y)^2 \div N$.

The formula for the within-groups (within-treatment) sum of squares is:

$$\text{Within Subjects SS} = \overset{i}{\sum} \left[\overset{k}{\sum} Y^2 - \frac{(\overset{k}{\Sigma}Y)^2}{N_k} \right] - \frac{(\sum Y)^2}{N} \qquad \text{(D5c)}$$

where $\overset{k}{\Sigma}Y^2$ is the sum of the squared scores within a treatment group, $(\overset{k}{\Sigma}Y)^2$ is the square of the sums of scores within a group (the summation sign outside the brackets means the arithmetic operations are carried out for each treatment group and the results summed across the treatment groups as indicated in Appendix A), and $(\Sigma Y)^2 \div N$ is defined in Equation D5a. There is a simpler equation for the value of Within Subjects SS, which is algebraically equivalent to Equation D5c. The simple formula for the within-groups (within-treatment) sum of squares (abbreviated Within Subjects SS) is:

$$\text{Within Subjects SS} = (\text{Total SS}) - (\text{Treatment SS}) \qquad \text{(D5d)}$$

Squaring each of the 18 scores and summing the squares yields $\Sigma Y^2 = 1252$. Substituting the values of Table D5.1 into Equation D5a:

$$\text{Total SS} = 1252 - \frac{(144)^2}{18}$$

$$= 1252 - \frac{(20,736)}{18},$$

$$= 1252 - 1152,$$

$$\text{Total SS} = 100.$$

Substituting the values of Table D5.1 into equation D5b:

$$\text{Treatment SS} = \left[\frac{36^2}{6} + \frac{48^2}{6} + \frac{60^2}{6} \right] - \frac{144^2}{18},$$

$$= \left[\frac{1296}{6} + \frac{2304}{6} + \frac{3600}{6} \right] - 1152,$$

$$= (216 + 384 + 600) - 1152,$$

$$= 1200 - 1152,$$

$$\text{Treatment SS} = 48.$$

Substituting the above calculated values into Equation D5d:

$$\text{Within Subjects SS} = 100 - 48,$$

$$\text{Within Subjects SS} = 52.$$

The between and within variances are equal to the between and within sums of squares divided by the appropriate degrees of freedom (df). In general, the de-

Degrees of Freedom

grees of freedom for each variance term are equal to one less than the number of squared sums or scores upon which each variance is based (ignoring the square of the sum of all the scores). Thus, in the calculations of the Treatment SS, three squared sums were involved ($36^2, 48^2, 60^2$), so there are $3 - 1 = 2$ df for the Treatment SS. Similarly, in the case of the Total SS, there were 18 squared scores (each datum point) so there are $18 - 1 = 17$ df for the Total SS. For the Within Subjects SS, there were $3(6 - 1) = 15$ df. That is, there were three treatment groups in which there were six subjects each, so that there were six squared scores for each treatment group. The simple df formula parallel to equation D5d is Within Subjects df = Total df − Treatment df, so that the df for the Within Subjects SS is $17 - 2 = 15$.

Mean Square

The between and within variances are also called "mean squares." Treatment mean square (variance) is $48 \div 2 = 24$. The within-group variance (Within Subjects mean square) is $52 \div 15 = 3.47$.

The F test of the modeling treatment effect is the ratio of the between-groups variance to the within-group variance. The null hypothesis is that there is no treatment effect; that the three treatment groups were sampled from the same population and, therefore, the means of the three treatment groups differ only by chance. Thus, the expected variance between the three treatment means is approximately zero. The between-groups variance (Treatment mean square) is an estimate of the variance due to random error plus the variance due to the modeling treatment. The within-group variance (Within Subjects mean square) is an estimate of the variance due to random error. If there is no real treatment effect (the null hypothesis is correct), then the F ratio should be close to 1.0. The experimental hypothesis is that the modeling conditions do have a real effect on the cooperative behavior of nursery-school girls. If the experimental hypothesis is correct, the F ratio should be greater than 1.0 (the numerator should be larger than the denominator).

The F ratio for the multilevel design was: $F = 24 \div 3.47 = 6.92$ with 2 df for the numerator and 15 df for the denominator. These calculations are summarized in Table D5.2.

Critical Values of F

The value of F is compared with the critical value of F in Table D5.7. The values in the table are the values for each combination of numerator and denominator df and several levels of α. The level of significance in the modeling study was set at 0.05. The critical value for $\alpha = 0.05$, $df = 2, 15$ is 3.68. As indicated in Table D5.2, the probability of an F ratio as large or larger than 6.92 is less than α. Therefore, we can conclude that the modeling treatment had a nonchance effect on the cooperative behavior of the children. There is a real difference between at least one

TABLE D5.2. Summary Table of Analysis of Variance For Multilevel Design.

Source of Variation	SS	df	Mean Square	F	p
Treatment	48	2	24.00	6.92	< .05
Within Subjects	52	15	3.47		
Total	100	17			

pair of the means of the treatment groups. The experimenter would normally apply a multiple comparison test (Kirk, 1968) in order to find which means did and did not significantly differ. It is possible that in the modeling experiment the competitive and cooperative modeling group means differ significantly from each other, but neither group's mean differed significantly from the control group's mean. The significant F test, where there are more than two treatment groups, does not indicate which means are significantly different; it only indicates that there are some significant differences between means.

Multiple Comparisons   One type of multiple comparison can be used when the researcher has made specific predictions about the relative size of specific pairs of means. The t test is used to determine if the difference between the two means is not likely to be due to chance. The researcher has previously chosen α to be a specific value (for example, $\alpha = 0.10$). The level of α is chosen for the entire set of means, not just a specific pair. If the researcher applied the t test to *all possible pairs* of means in a multilevel design, then the probability of at least one Type I error would be greater than α. The probability of at least one Type I error equals one minus the probability of no Type I errors. The probability of no Type I error equals (by the multiplication rule of Chapter 10) the probability of no Type I error for one comparison of two means multiplied by the probability of no Type I error for another comparison, multiplied by the probability for the next, multiplied, and so on. In symbolic form:

p(at least one Type I error) $= 1 - [\text{p(no Type I)} \cap \text{p(no Type I)} \cap . . . \cap \text{p(no Type I)}]$,
p(at least one Type I) $= 1 - [1 - \alpha \cap 1 - \alpha \cap . . . \cap 1 - \alpha]$,
p(at least one Type I) $= 1 - (1 - \alpha)^k$,

where k is the number of comparisons of pairs of means. For example, if $\alpha = 0.10$ and if that value of α were used for the t test of all ten possible comparisons of means (k $= 10$) when there are five group means in a five-group multilevel design ($_5C_2 = 10$), then the probability of *at least one* Type I error equals $1 - (1 - 0.10)^{10} = 1 - (.90)^{10} = 0.65$. Thus, there is a probability of 0.65 that at least one Type I error will occur among the 10 t tests. The solution to the problem of maintaining the probability of Type I error at the stated level of α is to divide the value of α by the number of multiple comparison tests to be made. Thus, if k $= 10$ and $\alpha = 0.10$, $\alpha \div k = 0.01$ is the significance level for *any one* comparison of two means. In that case $1 - (1 - .01)^{10} = 0.10$, which is the stated level of α for the entire experiment (entire set of 10 comparisons of five means).

In the case of the modeling experiment, $\alpha = 0.05$ and k $= 3$ because there are three means and $_3C_2 = 3$ possible combinations (comparisons) of the three means taken in pairs. Suppose that the researcher had predicted that the mean of the cooperation group would be greater than the mean of the control group and the mean of the control group was predicted to be larger than the mean of the competition group ($\bar{Y}$ cooperation $> \bar{Y}$ control $> \bar{Y}$ competition) in terms of the number of cooperative responses made. Dividing α by k we have $.05 \div 3 = 0.017$. If we

Setting
α

used 0.017 as the level of significance for each of the three t tests, the overall probability of a Type I error would be $1 - (1 - .017)^3 = 0.05$. However, the tabled values of t (Table D4.4) do not contain a value of $\alpha = 0.017$. The closest tabled value of α is 0.02 for a two-tailed test or 0.01 for a one-tailed test. Since the predictions are one-tailed, the value of 0.01 is used for the t tests. This is a conservative procedure since α for all three t tests will be $1 - (1 - .01)^3 = 0.03$ instead of 0.05. The independent two-group t test (Unit D4) is applied to the three pairs of means. The value of the Within Subjects Mean Square is equal to the average value (across the three possible pairs of groups) of

$$\frac{\left[\Sigma \, Y_1{}^2 - (\Sigma \, Y_1)^2 \right] + \left[\Sigma \, Y_2{}^2 - (\Sigma \, Y_2)^2 \right]}{N_1 + N_2 - 2}$$

where Y_1 and Y_2 are first the cooperative and control groups, then the cooperative and the competitive groups, and finally the control and competitive groups.

That is, the value of Within Subjects Mean Square is the best single estimate of variance due to random error. Therefore, Within Subjects Mean Square (M. S. Within Subjects) is substituted in Equation D4f to yield:

$$t = \frac{\overline{Y}_1 - \overline{Y}_2}{\sqrt{\text{M. S. Within Subjects} \left(\dfrac{1}{N_1} + \dfrac{1}{N_2} \right)}}. \tag{D5e}$$

The difference between two pairs of means is 2 ($\overline{Y}$ cooperative $- \overline{Y}$ control and $\overline{Y}$ control $- \overline{Y}$ competitive) and the difference is 4 in the last possible pair ($\overline{Y}$ cooperative $- \overline{Y}$ competitive). The value of the t denominator is $\sqrt{3.47 \, (2/6)} = 1.08$ in all three cases. Therefore, the resultant t values are:

cooperative *vs.* control $t = 1.85, df = 10, p > .01$;
cooperative *vs.* competitive $t = 3.70, df = 10, p < .01$;
control *vs.* competitive $t = 1.85, df = 10, p > .01$.

The significant t for the comparison between the cooperative and competitive group means indicated that the statistical significance of the F value was due to the difference between those two group means. The prediction that they would differ was supported, but the two other predictions regarding the differences between the control group mean and the means of the other two groups were not supported.

Randomized-Blocks Design

If each girl experiences each of the three modeling conditions, then the research design is a *repeated measures* design (Chapter 5), which is also a particular form of randomized-blocks design (Chapters 4 and 10). Each child would first play the game under the control condition (no model) and then under the other two conditions (competition and cooperation modeling) in random order. The data in Table D5.1 remain the same, except that the data points represent the three scores from each of six girls.

The structural model for the randomized-blocks design is $Y = (\bar{Y}) + (A_i) + (S_k) + (error)$, where S_k refers to the average performance of each subject across the three modeling conditions.

The .calculational formulas and values for the Total SS and Treatment SS remain the same (Equations D5a and D5b). The sum of squares for between blocks (between subjects) is calculated from the sums at the right-hand margin of Table D5.1. The calculational formula is:

$$\text{Blocks SS} = \overset{k}{\underset{i}{\sum}} \frac{(\overset{i}{\sum} Y)^2}{N_i} - \frac{(\sum Y)^2}{N} \tag{D5f}$$

where $\overset{i}{\sum} Y$ is the sum of scores for each block (subject), N_i is the number of scores for each block (subject), and $(\sum Y)^2 \div N$ is defined in Equation D5a.

The calculational formula for the residual within-subjects variance (random error variance) is

$$\text{Within Subjects SS} = (\text{Total SS}) - (\text{Treatment SS}) - (\text{Blocks SS}) \tag{D5g}$$

Substituting in the values from Table D5.1,

$$\begin{aligned}
\text{Blocks SS} &= \left[\frac{18^2}{3} + \frac{24^2}{3} + \frac{27^2}{3} + \frac{21^2}{3} + \frac{24^2}{3} + \frac{30^2}{3} \right] - 1152, \\
&= \left[\frac{324}{3} + \frac{576}{3} + \frac{729}{3} + \frac{441}{3} + \frac{576}{3} + \frac{900}{3} \right] - 1152, \\
&= (108 + 192 + 243 + 147 + 192 + 300) - 1152, \\
\text{Blocks SS} &= 1182 - 1152 = 30.
\end{aligned}$$

$$\text{Within Subjects SS} = 100 - 48 - 30 = 22.$$

There are $6 - 1 = 5$ df for Blocks and $17 - 2 - 5 = 10$ df for Within Subjects. The Blocks Mean Square (Blocks M.S.) equals Blocks SS $\div$ Blocks $df = 30 \div 5 = 6$. The Within Subjects Mean Square equals Within Subjects $\div$ Within $df = 22 \div 10 = 2.2$. The F ratio for treatment is equal to the Treatment M.S. $\div$ Within Subjects M.S. $= 24 \div 2.2 = 10.91$. These calculations are summarized in Table D5.3.

TABLE D5.3. Summary Table of Analysis of Variance: Randomized-Blocks Design.

Source of Variation	SS	df	Mean Square	F	p
Treatment	48	2	24.00	10.91	$< .05$
Blocks	30	5	6.00		
Within Subjects	22	10	2.20		
Total	100	17			

Again, the conclusion is that the modeling treatment had a real differential effect on the children's behavior. However, the F ratio does not tell where the source of significance lies.

The multiple comparison techniques used with the multilevel design may also be used with the randomized-blocks design. In both cases, a strong reason for a one-tailed directional prediction must be available *before* the data is collected. Equation D5e is used with the same mean differences as before; however, the denominator changed, since M.S. Within Subjects is now 2.2. The value of the t denominator in all three cases is $\sqrt{2.2 \, (\%)} = \sqrt{.73} = 0.85$. The resulting values of t are:

cooperative *vs.* control $t = 2.35, df = 5, p > .01$;
cooperative *vs.* competitive $t = 4.70, df = 5, p < .01$;
control *vs.* competitive $t = 2.35, df = 5, p > .01$.

The df are 5 for each comparison because the randomized-blocks design is a related groups design (same subjects under each pair of levels of the modeling treatment). The calculation of Within Subjects M.S. takes into account the correlation between repeated scores, and each t test is calculated from six pairs of scores so $df = 6 - 1 = 5$.

These results are the same as in the multilevel design; the "cooperative" group of girls were significantly more cooperative than the competitively modeled group. The control group did not significantly differ from either of the other two groups.

Factorial Design

Table D5.4. repeats the data of Table 10.5. Children of both sexes are used so that a sex variable is added to the multilevel design of Table D5.1. All possible combinations of levels of sex and modeling conditions are included so the design is a factorial design (Chapter 5).

The level of significance for the modeling effect is 0.05. The level of significance for each of the two effects involving sex (sex effect and modeling by sex interaction effect) is $0.05 \div 2 = 0.025$.

The structural model for the factorial design is $Y = (\bar{Y}) + (A_i) + (B_j) + (AB_{ij}) + (error)$, where B_j refers to the sex groups and AB_{ij} refers to the interaction between sex and modeling conditions. The Total SS and modeling Treatment SS

TABLE D5.4. Raw Data of Modeling Experiment: Factorial (2 × 3) Design.

Modeling Groups

	A_1 (Competitive)	A_2 (Control)	A_3 (Cooperative)	$\overset{i}{\Sigma}$
B_1 (Male)	3	8	7	18
	6	8	10	24
	6	11	10	27
	$\overset{k}{\Sigma} = 15$	$\overset{k}{\Sigma} = 27$	$\overset{k}{\Sigma} = 27$	$\overset{i\ k}{\Sigma\Sigma} = 69$
B_2 (Female)	5	6	10	21
	7	7	10	24
	9	8	13	30
	$\overset{k}{\Sigma} = 21$	$\overset{k}{\Sigma}= 21$	$\overset{k}{\Sigma} = 33$	$\overset{i\ k}{\Sigma\Sigma} = 75$
	$\overset{j\ k}{\Sigma\Sigma} = 36$	$\overset{j\ k}{\Sigma\Sigma}= 48$	$\overset{j\ k}{\Sigma\Sigma} = 60$	$\overset{i\ j\ k}{\Sigma\Sigma\Sigma} =144$

(now called Modeling SS) are calculated the same way as in the multilevel design. The formula for the between-sex-groups sum of squares (abbreviated Sex SS) is:

$$\text{Sex SS} = \overset{j}{\Sigma} \frac{(\overset{i\ k}{\Sigma\Sigma}Y)^2}{N_{ik}} - \frac{(\Sigma Y)^2}{N} \qquad \text{(D5h)}$$

where the $(\overset{i\ k}{\Sigma\Sigma}Y)^2$ is the *square of the sum* of all nine scores in each sex group, and N_{ik} is the number of scores in each sex group (9).

The Sex by Modeling Interaction SS is:

$$\text{Sex by Modeling SS} = \overset{i}{\Sigma}\overset{j}{\Sigma} \left[\frac{(\overset{k}{\Sigma}Y)^2}{N_k} \right] - \frac{(\Sigma Y)^2}{N} - (\text{Modeling SS}) - (\text{Sex SS}) \qquad \text{(D5i)}$$

where $(\overset{k}{\Sigma}Y)$ stands for the sum of all scores in any single cell of the design, which is then squared and divided by N_k, the number of subjects in each cell of the design (3). The Within Subjects SS is calculated as before. The value of Sex SS is:

$$\text{Sex SS} = \left[\frac{75^2}{9} + \frac{69^2}{9} \right] - \frac{144^2}{18},$$

$$= \left[\frac{5626}{9} + \frac{4761}{9} \right] - 1152,$$

$$= (625 + 529) - 1152,$$

$$\text{Sex SS} = 1154 - 1152 = 2.$$

$$\text{Sex by Modeling SS} = \left[\frac{15^2}{3} + \frac{21^2}{3} + \frac{27^2}{3} + \frac{21^2}{3} + \frac{27^2}{3} + \frac{33^2}{3} \right] - 1152 - 2 - 48,$$

$$= \left[\frac{225 + 441 + 729 + 441 + 729 + 1089}{3} \right] - 1202,$$

Sex by Modeling SS $= 1218 - 1202 = 16$.

Within Subjects SS $= 100 - 48 - 2 - 16 = 34$.

The df for Sex is $2 - 1 = 1$, for Sex by Treatment is $(3 - 1)(2 - 1) = 2$ and for Within Subjects SS $= 17 - 2 - 1 - 2 = 12$. The Treatment M.S. is the same as before; Sex M.S. $= 2 \div 1 = 2$; Sex by Modeling M.S. $= 16 \div 2 = 8$; Within Subjects M.S. $= 34 \div 12 = 2.83$. These calculations are summarized in Table D.5.5.

TABLE D5.5. Summary Table of Analysis of Variance: Factorial Design.

Source of Variation	SS	df	Mean Square	F	p
Modeling	48	2	24.00	8.48	$< .05$
Sex	2	1	2.00	—	$> .025$
Sex by Modeling	16	2	8.00	2.83	$> .025$
Within Subjects	34	12	2.83		
Total	100	17			

Multiple Comparisons

The multiple comparison technique used with the multilevel design may be applied to the modeling variable. The one-tailed predictions were $\bar{Y}$ cooperative $> \bar{Y}$ control $> \bar{Y}$ competitive. Equation D5e is used with the same mean differences in the numerator as before; however, the denominator is different, since Within Subjects M.S. is now 2.83. The value of the t denominator in all three comparisons of the means is $\sqrt{2.83 \, (\%)} = \sqrt{.94} = 0.97$. The resulting values of t are:

cooperative *vs.* control $t = 2.06, df = 10, p > .01$;
cooperative *vs.* competitive $t = 4.12, df = 10, p < .01$;
control *vs.* competitive $t = 2.06, df = 10, p > .01$.

The same conclusion about modeling drawn before pertains here. In addition, there is no sex effect and no interaction with sex. Contrary to the experimenter's intuitive expectation, sex of child had no effect on the cooperative behavior. The lack of an interaction with sex indicates that the modeling treatment generalized to both sexes, not just girls. The experimenter did not have any *a priori* predictions about the sex effect and the sex-by-treatment interaction effect. Since these effects were both not statistically significant, the experimenter *does not* apply a multiple comparison test to the data.

Factorial Design with Repeated Measures

If each subject experiences each of the three modeling conditions (repeated measures) and the design is the factorial design discussed in the preceding section, then the design is a factorial design with repeated measures or a split-plot design (Chapters 5 and 10). The data in Table D5.4 remain the same except that the data points represent the three scores for each of six children. As in the case of the factorial design, the experimenter makes no prediction about the sex effect or sex-by-modeling group interaction effect. The null hypothesis is that there are no such effects; the researcher is exploring the sex effect to see if there is any relationship.

The structural model for the factorial design with repeated measures is $Y = (\bar{Y}) + (A_i) + (B_j) + (AB_{ij}) + (S_k) + (error)$, where S_k refers to the between-subjects mean differences. The Total SS, Modeling SS, Sex SS, Sex-by-Modeling SS are calculated as in the case of the factorial design. The formula for the between-subjects sum of squares (abbreviated Between Subjects SS) is:

$$\text{Between Subjects SS} = \sum^{j} \sum^{k} \frac{(\overset{i}{\sum} Y)^2}{N_i} - \frac{(\sum Y)^2}{N} - (\text{Sex SS}) \qquad \text{(D5j)}$$

where $\overset{i}{\sum}Y$ is the sum of the three repeated scores for each subject, squared and divided by N_i, which is the number of repeated measures (number of levels of A_i since the subjects experience all levels of A_i).

The value of Between Subjects SS is different from the previously calculated value of Blocks SS because the effect of sex is removed from the Blocks SS to yield the Between Subjects SS.

$$\text{Within Subjects SS} = (\text{Total SS}) - (\text{Modeling SS}) - (\text{Sex SS}) -$$

$$(\text{Between Subjects SS}) - (\text{Sex by Modeling SS}). \qquad \text{(D5k)}$$

Applying the formula to the data in Table D.5.4,

$$\text{Between Subjects SS} = \left[\frac{18^2}{3} + \frac{24^2}{3} + \frac{27^2}{3} + \frac{21^2}{3} + \frac{24^2}{3} + \frac{30^2}{3} \right] - 1152 - 2,$$

$$= 1182 - 1152 - 2 = 28.$$

$$\text{Within Subjects SS} = 100 - 48 - 2 - 28 - 16 = 6.$$

The *df* for Between Subjects is $2(3 - 1) = 4$; that is, there are two *df* for Between Subjects within each sex group. The *df* for Within Subjects is $17 - 1 - 4 - 2 - 2 = 8$. After dividing each SS term by the appropriate *df*, the resulting values are displayed in Table D5.6.

TABLE D5.6. Summary Table of Analysis of Variance; Factorial Design with Repeated Measures.

Source of Variation	SS	df	Mean Square	F	p
Sex	2	1	2.00	—	> .025
Between Subjects	28	4	7.00		
Modeling	48	2	24.00	32.00	< .05
Sex by Modeling	16	2	8.00	10.67	< .025
Within Subjects	6	8	0.75		
Total	100	17			

As in the preceding section the level of significance was set at 0.025 for each of the two "sex" effects and at 0.05 for the modeling effect. The F ratio for Sex is equal to Sex Mean Square ÷ Between Subjects M.S. The Between Subjects variance estimate represents the variance in average scores of the six subjects that is not accounted for by the difference between the sexes (residual random error). The Sex variance estimate represents the variance due to random error for all six subjects plus the variance due to the difference between the average response of each sex. The F ratio for the modeling effect involves Modeling M.S. divided by Within Subjects M.S. The F ratio for the Sex by Modeling interaction involves Sex-by-Modeling M.S. divided by Within Subjects M.S.

There is no significant Sex effect (when F is less than 1.0; the traditional practice is to indicate this with a horizontal dark line in a summary table). The Modeling effect is significant at $\alpha = 0.05$, as before. Also the Sex-by-Modeling effect is significant at $\alpha = 0.025$ (from Table D5.7). The significant interaction can be seen in Figure 10.10. The effect of modeling depended on the sex of subject, even though there was no overall conditions sex difference in cooperation.

Multiple Comparisons

The multiple comparison technique used with the randomized-blocks design may also be used with the modeling variable in the factorial design with repeated measures. As before, the df for each comparison is six pairs of scores minus one equals five df. Equation D5e is used with the same numerators as before, but the value of the denominator is $\sqrt{0.75 \, (2/6)} = \sqrt{0.25} = 0.50$. The resulting values of t are:

cooperative *vs.* control $t = 4.0, df = 5, p < .01$;
cooperative *vs.* competitive $t = 8.0, df = 5, p < .01$;
control *vs.* competitive $t = 4.0, df = 5, p < .01$.

In contrast to the results of the multilevel, randomized-blocks, and factorial analyses of variance, all predicted differences between pairs of means were statistically significant in the factorial design with repeated measures. The use of subjects as their own control (repeated measures), and the inclusion of sex in the design as an independent variable, controlled for a great amount of secondary and error variance. The estimate of variance due to random error decreased from 3.5 to 0.75. At the same time that the size of Within Subjects SS decreased, the df for the estimate also decreased from 15 to 8. However, the loss in *df* was more than compensated for by the decrease in size of Within Subjects SS. That is, the Sex-by-Modeling interaction source of variation and the variation due to average performance of each subject across repeated measures accounted for a large portion of the total variance. The researcher can conclude that the three groups all responded as predicted and that all three groups were significantly different from each other.

The Sex-by-Modeling interaction was also significant. However, the researcher had no strong reason for predicting the nature of the interaction prior to the experiment. Therefore, the multiple comparison technique using *t* tests is *not* appropriate for the $_6C_2 = 15$ possible comparisons between the six mean cooperation scores in the six cells of the design (cooperative boys, cooperative girls, control boys, and so on). There are multiple comparison tests for this kind of data; Kirk (1968) has the best integrated presentation of these tests.

There are many, many possible designs and combinations of designs for which the analysis-of-variance techniques and multivariate analysis-of-variance techniques (for the case of more than two kinds of dependent measures from each subject or, alternatively, in the case of more than two dependent measures of one kind from each subject) have been developed. These techniques are frequently encountered in advanced statistical analysis or advanced research design courses.

ADVANTAGES AND LIMITATIONS

Like the *t* tests, the analysis of variance utilizes all of the information in interval measurement to test differences between the means of two or more groups. The analysis of variance may be used with independent groups and related groups designs and is particularly appropriate to factorial designs or any design involving more than one independent variable.

The analysis-of-variance technique *demands* that the estimates of between-groups and within-group variance be independent estimates. In theory, the demand means that the scores must be randomly sampled from a normally distributed population of scores. In practice the *F* distribution is relatively unaffected by moderate departures from population distribution normality.

The analysis of variance *demands* that the "random errors" be random and independent within each treatment level and across treatment groups. If subjects are randomly assigned to the levels of the independent variable and if other (secondary) sources of variance are controlled, these errors will be random and independent.

A basic assumption of analysis of variance is that any score is the sum of the various effects involved in the linear model for each design.

The various estimates of random error variance are averaged to yield the Within Subjects estimate of random error variance. That procedure is legitimate on the assumption that all within-group sources of variance are estimates of a common population error variance. In effect, this means that it is assumed that the error variance within each group is homogeneous (S^2 error$_1$ = S^2 error$_2$ = S^2 error$_3$, and

TABLE D5.7. Probabilities of Values of the F Ratio for Specified Values of α, Numerator df (v_1) and Denominator df (v_2)

$$\alpha = 0.05$$

v_2 \ v_1	1	2	3	4	5	6	7	8	9	10	12	15	20	24	30	40	60	120	∞
1	161.4	199.5	215.7	224.6	230.2	234.0	236.8	238.9	240.5	241.9	243.9	245.9	248.0	249.1	250.1	251.1	252.2	253.3	254.3
2	18.51	19.00	19.16	19.25	19.30	19.33	19.35	19.37	19.38	19.40	19.41	19.43	19.45	19.45	19.46	19.47	19.48	19.49	19.50
3	10.13	9.55	9.28	9.12	9.01	8.94	8.89	8.85	8.81	8.79	8.74	8.70	8.66	8.64	8.62	8.59	8.57	8.55	8.53
4	7.71	6.94	6.59	6.39	6.26	6.16	6.09	6.04	6.00	5.96	5.91	5.86	5.80	5.77	5.75	5.72	5.69	5.66	5.63
5	6.61	5.79	5.41	5.19	5.05	4.95	4.88	4.82	4.77	4.74	4.68	4.62	4.56	4.53	4.50	4.46	4.43	4.40	4.36
6	5.99	5.14	4.76	4.53	4.39	4.28	4.21	4.15	4.10	4.06	4.00	3.94	3.87	3.84	3.81	3.77	3.74	3.70	3.67
7	5.59	4.74	4.35	4.12	3.97	3.87	3.79	3.73	3.68	3.64	3.57	3.51	3.44	3.41	3.38	3.34	3.30	3.27	3.23
8	5.32	4.46	4.07	3.84	3.69	3.58	3.50	3.44	3.39	3.35	3.28	3.22	3.15	3.12	3.08	3.04	3.01	2.97	2.93
9	5.12	4.26	3.86	3.63	3.48	3.37	3.29	3.23	3.18	3.14	3.07	3.01	2.94	2.90	2.86	2.83	2.79	2.75	2.71
10	4.96	4.10	3.71	3.48	3.33	3.22	3.14	3.07	3.02	2.98	2.91	2.85	2.77	2.74	2.70	2.66	2.62	2.58	2.54
11	4.84	3.98	3.59	3.36	3.20	3.09	3.01	2.95	2.90	2.85	2.79	2.72	2.65	2.61	2.57	2.53	2.49	2.45	2.40
12	4.75	3.89	3.49	3.26	3.11	3.00	2.91	2.85	2.80	2.75	2.69	2.62	2.54	2.51	2.47	2.43	2.38	2.34	2.30
13	4.67	3.81	3.41	3.18	3.03	2.92	2.83	2.77	2.71	2.67	2.60	2.53	2.46	2.42	2.38	2.34	2.30	2.25	2.21
14	4.60	3.74	3.34	3.11	2.96	2.85	2.76	2.70	2.65	2.60	2.53	2.46	2.39	2.35	2.31	2.27	2.22	2.18	2.13
15	4.54	3.68	3.29	3.06	2.90	2.79	2.71	2.64	2.59	2.54	2.48	2.40	2.33	2.29	2.25	2.20	2.16	2.11	2.07
16	4.49	3.63	3.24	3.01	2.85	2.74	2.66	2.59	2.54	2.49	2.42	2.35	2.28	2.24	2.19	2.15	2.11	2.06	2.01
17	4.45	3.59	3.20	2.96	2.81	2.70	2.61	2.55	2.49	2.45	2.38	2.31	2.23	2.19	2.15	2.10	2.06	2.01	1.96
18	4.41	3.55	3.16	2.93	2.77	2.66	2.58	2.51	2.46	2.41	2.34	2.27	2.19	2.15	2.11	2.06	2.02	1.97	1.92
19	4.38	3.52	3.13	2.90	2.74	2.63	2.54	2.48	2.42	2.38	2.31	2.23	2.16	2.11	2.07	2.03	1.98	1.93	1.88
20	4.35	3.49	3.10	2.87	2.71	2.60	2.51	2.45	2.39	2.35	2.28	2.20	2.12	2.08	2.04	1.99	1.95	1.90	1.84
21	4.32	3.47	3.07	2.84	2.68	2.57	2.49	2.42	2.37	2.32	2.25	2.18	2.10	2.05	2.01	1.96	1.92	1.87	1.81
22	4.30	3.44	3.05	2.82	2.66	2.55	2.46	2.40	2.34	2.30	2.23	2.15	2.07	2.03	1.98	1.94	1.89	1.84	1.78
23	4.28	3.42	3.03	2.80	2.64	2.53	2.44	2.37	2.32	2.27	2.20	2.13	2.05	2.01	1.96	1.91	1.86	1.81	1.76
24	4.26	3.40	3.01	2.78	2.62	2.51	2.42	2.36	2.30	2.25	2.18	2.11	2.03	1.98	1.94	1.89	1.84	1.79	1.73
25	4.24	3.39	2.99	2.76	2.60	2.49	2.40	2.34	2.28	2.24	2.16	2.09	2.01	1.96	1.92	1.87	1.82	1.77	1.71
26	4.23	3.37	2.98	2.74	2.59	2.47	2.39	2.32	2.27	2.22	2.15	2.07	1.99	1.95	1.90	1.85	1.80	1.75	1.69
27	4.21	3.35	2.96	2.73	2.57	2.46	2.37	2.31	2.25	2.20	2.13	2.06	1.97	1.93	1.88	1.84	1.79	1.73	1.67
28	4.20	3.34	2.95	2.71	2.56	2.45	2.36	2.29	2.24	2.19	2.12	2.04	1.96	1.91	1.87	1.82	1.77	1.71	1.65
29	4.18	3.33	2.93	2.70	2.55	2.43	2.35	2.28	2.22	2.18	2.10	2.03	1.94	1.90	1.85	1.81	1.75	1.70	1.64
30	4.17	3.32	2.92	2.69	2.53	2.42	2.33	2.27	2.21	2.16	2.09	2.01	1.93	1.89	1.84	1.79	1.74	1.68	1.62
40	4.08	3.23	2.84	2.61	2.45	2.34	2.25	2.18	2.12	2.08	2.00	1.92	1.84	1.79	1.74	1.69	1.64	1.58	1.51
60	4.00	3.15	2.76	2.53	2.37	2.25	2.17	2.10	2.04	1.99	1.92	1.84	1.75	1.70	1.65	1.59	1.53	1.47	1.39
120	3.92	3.07	2.68	2.45	2.29	2.17	2.09	2.02	1.96	1.91	1.83	1.75	1.66	1.61	1.55	1.50	1.43	1.35	1.25
∞	3.84	3.00	2.60	2.37	2.21	2.10	2.01	1.94	1.88	1.83	1.75	1.67	1.57	1.52	1.46	1.39	1.32	1.22	1.00

TABLE D5.7. Probabilities of Values of the F Ratio for Specified Values of α, Numerator df (v_1) and Denominator df (v_2) (Continued)

$$\alpha = 0.025$$

v_1 →	∞	120	60	40	30	24	20	15	12	10	9	8	7	6	5	4	3	2	1	← v_2
	1018	1014	1010	1006	1001	997.2	993.1	984.9	976.7	968.6	963.3	956.7	948.2	937.1	921.8	899.6	864.2	799.5	647.8	1
	39.50	39.49	39.48	39.47	39.46	39.46	39.45	39.43	39.41	39.40	39.39	39.37	39.36	39.33	39.30	39.25	39.17	39.00	38.51	2
	13.90	13.95	13.99	14.04	14.08	14.12	14.17	14.25	14.34	14.42	14.47	14.54	14.62	14.73	14.88	15.10	15.44	16.04	17.44	3
	8.26	8.31	8.36	8.41	8.46	8.51	8.56	8.66	8.75	8.84	8.90	8.98	9.07	9.20	9.36	9.60	9.98	10.65	12.22	4
	6.02	6.07	6.12	6.18	6.23	6.28	6.33	6.43	6.52	6.62	6.68	6.76	6.85	6.98	7.15	7.39	7.76	8.43	10.01	5
	4.85	4.90	4.96	5.01	5.07	5.12	5.17	5.27	5.37	5.46	5.52	5.60	5.70	5.82	5.99	6.23	6.60	7.26	8.81	6
	4.14	4.20	4.25	4.31	4.36	4.42	4.47	4.57	4.67	4.76	4.82	4.90	4.99	5.12	5.29	5.52	5.89	6.54	8.07	7
	3.67	3.73	3.78	3.84	3.89	3.95	4.00	4.10	4.20	4.30	4.36	4.43	4.53	4.65	4.82	5.05	5.42	6.06	7.57	8
	3.33	3.39	3.45	3.51	3.56	3.61	3.67	3.77	3.87	3.96	4.03	4.10	4.20	4.32	4.48	4.72	5.08	5.71	7.21	9
	3.08	3.14	3.20	3.26	3.31	3.37	3.42	3.52	3.62	3.72	3.78	3.85	3.95	4.07	4.24	4.47	4.83	5.46	6.94	10
	2.88	2.94	3.00	3.06	3.12	3.17	3.23	3.33	3.43	3.53	3.59	3.66	3.76	3.88	4.04	4.28	4.63	5.26	6.72	11
	2.72	2.79	2.85	2.91	2.96	3.02	3.07	3.18	3.28	3.37	3.44	3.51	3.61	3.73	3.89	4.12	4.47	5.10	6.55	12
	2.60	2.66	2.72	2.78	2.84	2.89	2.95	3.05	3.15	3.25	3.31	3.39	3.48	3.60	3.77	4.00	4.35	4.97	6.41	13
	2.49	2.55	2.61	2.67	2.73	2.79	2.84	2.95	3.05	3.15	3.21	3.29	3.38	3.50	3.66	3.89	4.24	4.86	6.30	14
	2.40	2.46	2.52	2.59	2.64	2.70	2.76	2.86	2.96	3.06	3.12	3.20	3.29	3.41	3.58	3.80	4.15	4.77	6.20	15
	2.32	2.38	2.45	2.51	2.57	2.63	2.68	2.79	2.89	2.99	3.05	3.12	3.22	3.34	3.50	3.73	4.08	4.69	6.12	16
	2.25	2.32	2.38	2.44	2.50	2.56	2.62	2.72	2.82	2.92	2.98	3.06	3.16	3.28	3.44	3.66	4.01	4.62	6.04	17
	2.19	2.26	2.32	2.38	2.44	2.50	2.56	2.67	2.77	2.87	2.93	3.01	3.10	3.22	3.38	3.61	3.95	4.56	5.98	18
	2.13	2.20	2.27	2.33	2.39	2.45	2.51	2.62	2.72	2.82	2.88	2.96	3.05	3.17	3.33	3.56	3.90	4.51	5.92	19
	2.09	2.16	2.22	2.29	2.35	2.41	2.46	2.57	2.68	2.77	2.84	2.91	3.01	3.13	3.29	3.51	3.86	4.46	5.87	20
	2.04	2.11	2.18	2.25	2.31	2.37	2.42	2.53	2.64	2.73	2.80	2.87	2.97	3.09	3.25	3.48	3.82	4.42	5.83	21
	2.00	2.08	2.14	2.21	2.27	2.33	2.39	2.50	2.60	2.70	2.76	2.84	2.93	3.05	3.22	3.44	3.78	4.38	5.79	22
	1.97	2.04	2.11	2.18	2.24	2.30	2.36	2.47	2.57	2.67	2.73	2.81	2.90	3.02	3.18	3.41	3.75	4.35	5.75	23
	1.94	2.01	2.08	2.15	2.21	2.27	2.33	2.44	2.54	2.64	2.70	2.78	2.87	2.99	3.15	3.38	3.72	4.32	5.72	24
	1.91	1.98	2.05	2.12	2.18	2.24	2.30	2.41	2.51	2.61	2.68	2.75	2.85	2.97	3.13	3.35	3.69	4.29	5.69	25
	1.88	1.95	2.03	2.09	2.16	2.22	2.28	2.39	2.49	2.59	2.65	2.73	2.82	2.94	3.10	3.33	3.67	4.27	5.66	26
	1.85	1.93	2.00	2.07	2.13	2.19	2.25	2.36	2.47	2.57	2.63	2.71	2.80	2.92	3.08	3.31	3.65	4.24	5.63	27
	1.83	1.91	1.98	2.05	2.11	2.17	2.23	2.34	2.45	2.55	2.61	2.69	2.78	2.90	3.06	3.29	3.63	4.22	5.61	28
	1.81	1.89	1.96	2.03	2.09	2.15	2.21	2.32	2.43	2.53	2.59	2.67	2.76	2.88	3.04	3.27	3.61	4.20	5.59	29
	1.79	1.87	1.94	2.01	2.07	2.14	2.20	2.31	2.41	2.51	2.57	2.65	2.75	2.87	3.03	3.25	3.59	4.18	5.57	30
	1.64	1.72	1.80	1.88	1.94	2.01	2.07	2.18	2.29	2.39	2.45	2.53	2.62	2.74	2.90	3.13	3.46	4.05	5.42	40
	1.48	1.58	1.67	1.74	1.82	1.88	1.94	2.06	2.17	2.27	2.33	2.41	2.51	2.63	2.79	3.01	3.34	3.93	5.29	60
	1.31	1.43	1.53	1.61	1.69	1.76	1.82	1.94	2.05	2.16	2.22	2.30	2.39	2.52	2.67	2.89	3.23	3.80	5.15	120
	1.00	1.27	1.39	1.48	1.57	1.64	1.71	1.83	1.94	2.05	2.11	2.19	2.29	2.41	2.57	2.79	3.12	3.69	5.02	∞

TABLE D5.7. Probabilities of Values of the F Ratio for Specified Values of α, Numerator df (v_1) and Denominator df (v_2) (Continued)

$$\alpha = 0.01$$

v_2 \ v_1	1	2	3	4	5	6	7	8	9	10	12	15	20	24	30	40	60	120	∞
1	4052	4999.5	5403	5625	5764	5859	5928	5982	6022	6056	6106	6157	6209	6235	6261	6287	6313	6339	6366
2	98.50	99.00	99.17	99.25	99.30	99.33	99.36	99.37	99.39	99.40	99.42	99.43	99.45	99.46	99.47	99.47	99.48	99.49	99.50
3	34.12	30.82	29.46	28.71	28.24	27.91	27.67	27.49	27.35	27.23	27.05	26.87	26.69	26.60	26.50	26.41	26.32	26.22	26.13
4	21.20	18.00	16.69	15.98	15.52	15.21	14.98	14.80	14.66	14.55	14.37	14.20	14.02	13.93	13.84	13.75	13.65	13.56	13.46
5	16.26	13.27	12.06	11.39	10.97	10.67	10.46	10.29	10.16	10.05	9.89	9.72	9.55	9.47	9.38	9.29	9.20	9.11	9.02
6	13.75	10.92	9.78	9.15	8.75	8.47	8.26	8.10	7.98	7.87	7.72	7.56	7.40	7.31	7.23	7.14	7.06	6.97	6.88
7	12.25	9.55	8.45	7.85	7.46	7.19	6.99	6.84	6.72	6.62	6.47	6.31	6.16	6.07	5.99	5.91	5.82	5.74	5.65
8	11.26	8.65	7.59	7.01	6.63	6.37	6.18	6.03	5.91	5.81	5.67	5.52	5.36	5.28	5.20	5.12	5.03	4.95	4.86
9	10.56	8.02	6.99	6.42	6.06	5.80	5.61	5.47	5.35	5.26	5.11	4.96	4.81	4.73	4.65	4.57	4.48	4.40	4.31
10	10.04	7.56	6.55	5.99	5.64	5.39	5.20	5.06	4.94	4.85	4.71	4.56	4.41	4.33	4.25	4.17	4.08	4.00	3.91
11	9.65	7.21	6.22	5.67	5.32	5.07	4.89	4.74	4.63	4.54	4.40	4.25	4.10	4.02	3.94	3.86	3.78	3.69	3.60
12	9.33	6.93	5.95	5.41	5.06	4.82	4.64	4.50	4.39	4.30	4.16	4.01	3.86	3.78	3.70	3.62	3.54	3.45	3.36
13	9.07	6.70	5.74	5.21	4.86	4.62	4.44	4.30	4.19	4.10	3.96	3.82	3.66	3.59	3.51	3.43	3.34	3.25	3.17
14	8.86	6.51	5.56	5.04	4.69	4.46	4.28	4.14	4.03	3.94	3.80	3.66	3.51	3.43	3.35	3.27	3.18	3.09	3.00
15	8.68	6.36	5.42	4.89	4.56	4.32	4.14	4.00	3.89	3.80	3.67	3.52	3.37	3.29	3.21	3.13	3.05	2.96	2.87
16	8.53	6.23	5.29	4.77	4.44	4.20	4.03	3.89	3.78	3.69	3.55	3.41	3.26	3.18	3.10	3.02	2.93	2.84	2.75
17	8.40	6.11	5.18	4.67	4.34	4.10	3.93	3.79	3.68	3.59	3.46	3.31	3.16	3.08	3.00	2.92	2.83	2.75	2.65
18	8.29	6.01	5.09	4.58	4.25	4.01	3.84	3.71	3.60	3.51	3.37	3.23	3.08	3.00	2.92	2.84	2.75	2.66	2.57
19	8.18	5.93	5.01	4.50	4.17	3.94	3.77	3.63	3.52	3.43	3.30	3.15	3.00	2.92	2.84	2.76	2.67	2.58	2.49
20	8.10	5.85	4.94	4.43	4.10	3.87	3.70	3.56	3.46	3.37	3.23	3.09	2.94	2.86	2.78	2.69	2.61	2.52	2.42
21	8.02	5.78	4.87	4.37	4.04	3.81	3.64	3.51	3.40	3.31	3.17	3.03	2.88	2.80	2.72	2.64	2.55	2.46	2.36
22	7.95	5.72	4.82	4.31	3.99	3.76	3.59	3.45	3.35	3.26	3.12	2.98	2.83	2.75	2.67	2.58	2.50	2.40	2.31
23	7.88	5.66	4.76	4.26	3.94	3.71	3.54	3.41	3.30	3.21	3.07	2.93	2.78	2.70	2.62	2.54	2.45	2.35	2.26
24	7.82	5.61	4.72	4.22	3.90	3.67	3.50	3.36	3.26	3.17	3.03	2.89	2.74	2.66	2.58	2.49	2.40	2.31	2.21
25	7.77	5.57	4.68	4.18	3.85	3.63	3.46	3.32	3.22	3.13	2.99	2.85	2.70	2.62	2.54	2.45	2.36	2.27	2.17
26	7.72	5.53	4.64	4.14	3.82	3.59	3.42	3.29	3.18	3.09	2.96	2.81	2.66	2.58	2.50	2.42	2.33	2.23	2.13
27	7.68	5.49	4.60	4.11	3.78	3.56	3.39	3.26	3.15	3.06	2.93	2.78	2.63	2.55	2.47	2.38	2.29	2.20	2.10
28	7.64	5.45	4.57	4.07	3.75	3.53	3.36	3.23	3.12	3.03	2.90	2.75	2.60	2.52	2.44	2.35	2.26	2.17	2.06
29	7.60	5.42	4.54	4.04	3.73	3.50	3.33	3.20	3.09	3.00	2.87	2.73	2.57	2.49	2.41	2.33	2.23	2.14	2.03
30	7.56	5.39	4.51	4.02	3.70	3.47	3.30	3.17	3.07	2.98	2.84	2.70	2.55	2.47	2.39	2.30	2.21	2.11	2.01
40	7.31	5.18	4.31	3.83	3.51	3.29	3.12	2.99	2.89	2.80	2.66	2.52	2.37	2.29	2.20	2.11	2.02	1.92	1.80
60	7.08	4.98	4.13	3.65	3.34	3.12	2.95	2.82	2.72	2.63	2.50	2.35	2.20	2.12	2.03	1.94	1.84	1.73	1.60
120	6.85	4.79	3.95	3.48	3.17	2.96	2.79	2.66	2.56	2.47	2.34	2.19	2.03	1.95	1.86	1.76	1.66	1.53	1.38
∞	6.63	4.61	3.78	3.32	3.02	2.80	2.64	2.51	2.41	2.32	2.18	2.04	1.88	1.79	1.70	1.59	1.47	1.32	1.00

so on). The actual calculated values of each estimate will seldom be precisely equal. When the sample sizes for each group vary greatly, *and* the actual values of S^2 error also vary greatly, then it is possible that the probabilities for the F ratio obtained from the F table are erroneous. When the sample sizes are equal, then there is probably little reason to suspect the obtained probabilities.

REFERENCES

More complete examinations of the analysis-of-variance techniques are provided by Edwards (1972, pp. 115–324); Edwards (1973, pp. 95–130, 215–235); Hays (1973, pp. 443–615); Kirk (1968); Myers (1966); and Winer (1971).

UNiT D 6
Product-Moment and Rank-Order Correlation Coefficients

THE PEARSON COEFFICIENT

The Pearson product-moment correlation coefficient (r) is an index of the degree of *linear* relationship between two variables measured at the interval level. Several individuals are sampled and two measures are obtained from each individual. To determine the extent to which the two measures are related, a single statistic (r) may be computed. (See Chapter 6 for interpretation of values of r.)

Formulas

The Pearson r is defined as the ratio of the covariance of X and Y and the geometric mean of the unbiased variances of X and Y. That is,

$$r = \frac{\sum xy/N - 1}{\sqrt{\left(\frac{\sum x^2}{N-1}\right)\left(\frac{\sum y^2}{N-1}\right)}} \tag{D6a}$$

In Formula D6a, $x = X - \bar{X}$, $y = Y - \bar{Y}$, and $N =$ sample size (number of *pairs* of scores). By multiplying both numerator and denominator by $N - 1$, we arrive at another common definitional formula,

$$r = \frac{\sum xy}{\sqrt{(\sum x^2)(\sum y^2)}} \tag{D6b}$$

By substituting the calculational formulas for the terms in Equation D6b, we arrive at the *calculational formula* for *r*,

$$r = \frac{\Sigma XY - \dfrac{\Sigma X \Sigma Y}{N}}{\sqrt{\left[\Sigma X^2 - \dfrac{(\Sigma X)^2}{N}\right]\left[\Sigma Y^2 - \dfrac{(\Sigma Y)^2}{N}\right]}} \tag{D6c}$$

In Formula D6c, ΣXY is the sum of the products of the *paired* X and Y scores. Usually, this means that each person's score on one measure (X) is multiplied by his score on the other measure (Y).

Calculational Example   Suppose that a paper-and-pencil test of cooperativeness is given to a sample of 25 students. The students also serve as subjects in a study of cooperative behavior. The study consists of a two-person game in which each subject tries to win the most money. The two people playing the game each have a choice of pushing one of two buttons on each trial. The payoff matrix is presented in Table D6.1.

For example, if A punches "2" and B punches "1," then A loses 50¢ and B wins 50¢. The only way that they can both win in the long run (20 trials) is for both of them to punch "2." They cannot verbally communicate.

A measure of "cooperation" is the frequency with which a student presses button number 2. We can determine the correlation between the two measures of "cooperation." The hypothetical data are presented in Table D6.2. Applying Formula D6c to the data of Table D6.2, we find that:

$$r = \frac{\Sigma XY - \dfrac{\Sigma X \Sigma Y}{N}}{\sqrt{\left[\Sigma X^2 - \dfrac{(\Sigma X)^2}{N}\right]\left[\Sigma Y^2 - \dfrac{(\Sigma Y)^2}{N}\right]}},$$

$$r = \frac{2757 - \dfrac{(289)(224)}{25}}{\sqrt{\left[3697 - \dfrac{(289)^2}{25}\right]\left[2354 - \dfrac{(224)^2}{25}\right]}},$$

$$r = \frac{2757 - 2589.4}{\sqrt{(356.2)(347.0)}},$$

$$r = \frac{167.6}{351.6},$$

$$r = 0.48 .$$

TABLE D6.1. Payoff Matrix for a Two-Person Game (the Numbers 1 and 2 Represent the Two Buttons).

		If Player B Chooses	
		1	2
And Player A Chooses	1	Both Lose 20¢	B Pays A 50¢
	2	50¢ A Pays B	20¢ Both Win

Thus, the correlation between the two measures is 0.48. The two measures are moderately, positively correlated. The value of r indicates that, while somewhat related, the two tests are primarily measuring different characteristics.

Advantages and Limitations

One feature of the Pearson correlation coefficient is that the X scores and the Y scores need not be on the same measurement scale. The calculation process converts the X and Y values to standard scores.

TABLE D6.2. Results of Example Experiment on Cooperation.

Subject #	Cooperativeness Test Score (X)	Cooperation Study Score (Y)	X^2	Y^2	XY
1	10	6	100	36	60
2	12	8	144	64	96
3	16	14	256	196	224
4	7	9	49	81	63
5	8	10	64	100	80
6	10	7	100	49	70
7	14	6	196	36	84
8	20	12	400	144	240
9	13	11	169	121	143
10	11	15	121	225	165
11	10	3	100	9	30
12	9	8	81	64	72
13	11	10	121	100	110
14	8	4	64	16	32
15	10	5	100	25	50
16	16	13	256	169	208
17	8	11	64	121	88
18	7	2	49	4	14
19	6	10	36	100	60
20	12	16	144	256	192
21	18	12	324	144	216
22	17	13	289	169	221
23	15	8	225	64	120
24	14	6	196	36	84
25	7	5	49	25	35
$\Sigma =$	289	224	3697	2354	2757

Another characteristic of the Pearson r is that it reflects the *linear* (straight-line) *relationship* between the two variables being correlated. As the scores deviate more and more from the straight line of best fit, the correlation coefficient decreases toward $r = 0.00$. A correlation coefficient of 0.00 indicates that there is no overall linear trend to the data; in other words, there is no linear relationship between the values of the X and Y variables.

Because the correlation coefficient reflects deviations from a straight line, any nonlinear relationship will yield a lower correlation coefficient. There is a statistic called the *correlation ratio* (Edwards, 1967, pp. 136–142), which indicates curvilinear relationships between two sets of scores. All applications of the Pearson r require the assumption that the relationship being measured is basically linear in nature.

In addition to providing a short-hand expression for summarizing the direction and degree of relationship between two variables, the correlation coefficient provides the basis for a number of further interpretations. (See McNemar, 1967, pp. 129–153.) The correlation coefficient may be statistically tested for *significance* to determine whether or not the observed relationship is due to random factors. Once the relationship between two variables is determined, values of one variable may be *predicted* from corresponding values of the other variable. The correlation coefficient allows an experimenter to state the *accuracy of his predictions* by specifying the confidence limits of his prediction. If the correlated scores represent the independent and dependent variables in an experiment, the correlation coefficient allows the experimenter to state what *proportion of the variance* in the dependent variable is due to variation of the independent variable.

Significance of r

If the subjects are randomly sampled from a population, then one is usually concerned with deciding whether the two variables are correlated in the population. That is, one tests the null hypothesis that the population correlation coefficient is zero. The significance of r can be tested with the t test. Thus,

$$t = \frac{r}{\sqrt{1 - r^2}} (\sqrt{N - 2}) \tag{D6d}$$

where $df = N - 2$. The obtained value of r in the cooperation example was 0.38. Applying Formula D6d we find,

$$t = \frac{0.48}{\sqrt{1 - 0.48^2}} (\sqrt{25 - 2}),$$

$$t = \frac{0.48}{\sqrt{0.77}} (\sqrt{23}),$$

$$t = 2.62.$$

With 23 *df*, and assuming $\alpha = 0.05$, the two-tailed *critical* value of $t = 2.07$ (Table D4.4). Since the obtained value of t does exceed the tabled critical value, we conclude that the two variables are associated in the population. That is, the population correlation coefficient is greater than zero. Since the value of r for the same example exceeded 0.41, then the obtained value of t exceeded the tabled critical value. In such a case we conclude that the two variables were positively associated in the population. We know the size of the population correlation coefficient; we just do not know that it is greater than zero in the population.

Goodness of Fit

The t test of the significance of r is very similar to the t test used to test how well a straight line fits a set of plotted data points. The concept of the slope (b) of a straight line was discussed in Chapter 7. The method of determining the value of b is presented in this section.

Most frequently the data from an experiment do not fall exactly on a straight line. However, the data points sometimes do seem to approximate a straight line, and, in such a case, the experimenter would like to know precisely how well a straight line fits the data. In other words, the experimenter wants to know the goodness of fit of a straight line to the data.

Fitting a Straight Line   Suppose a therapist is working with electively mute, autistic children. All of the children occasionally mutter unintelligible sounds, and the therapist wishes to increase the frequency of these sounds. He hopes to eventually have the children speak intelligible words, but first must get them to vocalize on command. The therapist hypothesizes that, if the children are food deprived and food reinforced for making sounds, their rates of vocalizing will be increased. He predicts that the rate of vocalization will increase linearly with the amount of food reinforcement. He manipulates the amount of food reinforcement given five autistic children. After one week of training, the number of vocalizations in a single five minute period are recorded. The data are presented in Table D6.3.

TABLE D6.3. Amount of Food Reinforcement and Number of Verbalizations of Five Autistic Children.

I Children	II Amount of Food Reinforcement in Grams X	III Number of Verbalizations per Five Minute Period Y	IV Deviations from Means		V Squared Devia- tions		VI Cross Products
			x	y	x^2	y^2	xy
A	1	2	-6	-3	36	9	18
B	4	3	-3	-2	9	4	6
C	7	4	0	-1	0	1	0
D	10	7	3	2	9	4	6
E	13	9	6	4	36	16	24
Sum $(\Sigma) = 35$ Mean $= 7$		25 5	0	0	90	34	54

The data points are presented in Figure D6.A. Each data point represents the value (X) of the independent variable assigned to a child and the dependent score (Y) of that child.

In order to fit a straight line through the data points in Figure D6.A the slope of the line of best fit must be calculated. The calculation proceeds according to the following steps:

(1) Subtract the mean of the X scores (Column II) from each X score ($x = X - \bar{X}$). These deviation scores (difference scores) are recorded in column IV of Table D6.3.
(2) Similarly, the mean of the Y scores (Column III) is subtracted from each Y score ($y = Y - \bar{Y}$). These deviation scores are also recorded in column IV of Table D6.3.
(3) The deviation scores (x and y) are squared and recorded in column V of Table D6.3.
(4) The corresponding x and y scores for each child are multiplied to provide the cross products (xy) recorded in column VI. For example, the child A had an x score of −6 and a y score of −3. The cross-product of −6 and −3 is 18, which is the first score in column VI.
(5) The sums of the squared deviation scores (x^2 and y^2) are determined. In the example, $\Sigma x^2 = 90$ and $\Sigma y^2 = 34$. The sum of the crossed products is also determined. In the example, $\Sigma xy = 54$.

In Figure D6.A, the straight line the therapist is interested in is the line that represents a prediction of a Y score from the value of an X score. That is, the therapist is interested in predicting the vocalizations of the children (Y) as a function of

Slope   magnitude of food reinforcement (X). The formula for the value of the slope (b) of the straight line relating Y to X is:

$$b_{y.x} = \Sigma xy / \Sigma x^2 \tag{D6e}$$

where $b_{y.x}$ is the slope of y on x, Σxy is the sum of cross products, and Σx^2 is the sum of squared x deviation scores.

(6) Substituting the values of Σxy and Σx^2 in Formula D6e, the results are: $b_{y.x} = {}^{54}\!/_{90} = 0.60$.

In order to draw the straight line, the equation for a straight line must be used. In the example, the equation is called the *sample regression equation of Y on X* and is

$$\hat{Y} = \bar{Y} + b_{y.x}(X - \bar{X}) \tag{D6f}$$

where $\hat{Y}$ is an estimated value of Y given the mean of the Y scores, the value of $b_{y.x}$, and a given X deviation score ($x = X - \bar{X}$). The estimated Y values ($\hat{Y}$) are the points on the straight line that the therapist fits to his data. If Equation D6f is used, the straight line fit to the data is called the *line of best fit*. Using Equation D6f, the

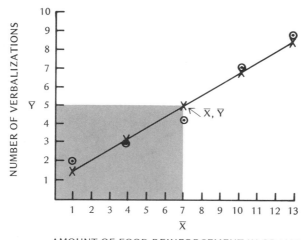

Fig. D6.A.   A graph of the data points provided in Columns II and III of Table D6.3. Each of the five circled points represents the score of a single child. The crossmarks on the straight line represent the five estimated values of Y.

straight line in Figure D6.A was drawn. The value of $\bar{Y}$ is 5, the value of $\bar{X}$ is 7, and the value of $b_{y.x}$ is 0.60. Substituting these values in Equation D6f, we have $\hat{Y} = 5 + 0.60\ (X - 7)$. Algebraically, the equation may be simplified to $\hat{Y} = 0.8 + 0.60(X)$. Now, the values of X may be substituted into the equation to provide the points on the best fit straight line. Thus, when $X = 1$, $\hat{Y} = 1.4$, where $X = 4$, $\hat{Y} = 3.2$, and so forth, as indicated in Table D6.4 and Figure D6.A.

   Test of Fit   Since the line of best fit is now determined, the therapist may examine the line to see precisely how good a fit he has. The original values of X and Y are repeated in Table D6.4. The estimated values, $\hat{Y}$, are also presented in Table D6.4 along with the differences (deviations) between the estimated values and the

TABLE D6.4. Calculated Values of $\hat{Y}$ and Deviations from Actual Scores ($d_{y.x} = Y - \hat{Y}$).

Amount of Food Reinforcement in grams X	Actual Number of Verbalizations Y	Estimated Number of Verbalizations $\hat{Y}$	Deviations $Y - \hat{Y} = d_{y.x}$	Squared Deviations $d_{y.x}^2$
1	2	1.4	.6	.36
4	3	3.2	$-$ .2	.04
7	4	5.0	$-$ 1.0	1.00
10	7	6.8	.2	.04
13	9	8.6	.4	.16

$$\Sigma d_{y.x} = 0.0 \quad \Sigma d_{y.x}^2 = 1.60$$

actually obtained values $(Y - \hat{Y})$. These deviations are labeled $d_{y.x}$. Finally, the deviations are squared $(d_{y.x}^2)$ and the sum of the squared deviations is calculated $(\Sigma d_{y.x}^2)$. For the therapist's data, the sum of the squared deviations is $\Sigma d_{y.x}^2 = 1.60$. The $\Sigma d_{y.x}^2$ represents the amount of squared error when fitting a straight line to the data points.

The therapist's hypothesis (H_1) is that the frequency of verbalization will increase linearly with the amount of food reinforcement. His null hypothesis (H_0) is that the independent and dependent variables are *not* linearly related. Thus, the two-tailed H_1 is $b_{y.x}$ is greater than or less than zero and the relation is linear, and H_0 is $b_{y.x}$ is zero and the relationship is not linear. The therapist sets $\alpha = 0.01$. In order to test H_0, the therapist needs some unbiased estimate of the population variance of the deviations from the best fit straight line.

The estimate is:

$$s_{y.x}^2 = \Sigma d_{y.x}^2 / (N - 2)$$

where N is the number of paired X and Y scores. The estimated variance of the deviations from the best fit line is used in the calculation of the standard deviation of the slope $b_{y.x}$. The formula for the standard deviation of the slope is:

$$s_{b_{y.x}} = \sqrt{s_{y.x}^2 / \Sigma x^2} \tag{D6g}$$

In the autistic child example, $\Sigma d_{y.x}^2 = 1.60$, $N = 5$, and $\Sigma x^2 = 90$. Substituting these values in Equation D6g, the therapist found that,

$$s_{b_{y.x}} = \sqrt{\frac{1.60/3}{90}},$$

$$s_{b_{y.x}} = \sqrt{\frac{0.53}{90}},$$

$$s_{b_{y.x}} = \sqrt{0.006},$$

$$s_{b_{y.x}} = 0.078.$$

The t test of H_0 is:

$$t = b_{y.x} / s_{b_{y.x}} \tag{D6h}$$

The value of $b_{y.x}$ in the autistic child example was 0.60 and the value of $S_{b_{y.x}}$ was 0.078. Substituting these figures in Equation D6h, the calculated value of t is t

$= {}^{0.60}/_{0.078} = 7.69$. The degrees of freedom for this t test are $df = N - 2$. In terms of the example, $df = 5 - 2 = 3$. The critical values of t are presented in Table D4.4. The level of significance was set at 0.01 ($\alpha = 0.01$) and H_1 was a two-tailed prediction. The two-tailed critical value of t with $\alpha = 0.01$ and $df = 3$ is 5.84 (Table D4.4). Since the calculated value of t exceeds 5.84, H_0 may be rejected ($t = 7.69$, $df = 3$, $p < .01$). The therapist concludes that the deviations from the straight line of best fit are due to chance and that there is a positive linear relationship between the amount of food reinforcement and frequency or rate of vocalization.

Degrees of Freedom

Note that this t test is a test of two hypotheses at once. That is, the t test is a test of the *goodness of fit* of a straight line to the data points and a test of the null hypothesis that the *population slope is zero*. When the t is significant (H_0 may be rejected), then both the goodness of fit and nonzero slope hypothesis are supported. Thus, the therapist can conclude that, in the population sampled, there is a positive linear relationship between amount of reinforcement and amount of vocalization. However, when a calculated t is not significant, either the population slope is about zero (population r is zero), or the population relationship between the independent and dependent variables is not linear, or both parts of H_0 may be correct.

Ambiguity of Nonsignificant Test

THE SPEARMAN COEFFICIENT

The Spearman rank-order correlation coefficient (r_s) is an index of the relationship between two variables measured at the ordinal level. The coefficient, r_s, is an approximation to the Pearson r. The r_s is used in place of r under the condition that the data is measured at only the ordinal level. For example, a group of engineers might be ranked in terms of their creativity and then ranked again in terms of their technical competence. In this case, we would use r_s to determine the degree of association between the two measures. If only one of the measures is at the ordinal level, we can use r_s by converting the interval scores to ranks. This is done by ranking the interval scores from highest to lowest.

Logic and Method

Suppose that we have two judges rank a sample of librarians on their degree of repressed hostility. We wish to know the degree of agreement between the two sets of ranks (two judges). The ranks of the first judge are denoted as $X_1, X_2, \ldots, X_N$ and the ranks of the second judge are labeled $Y_1, Y_2, \ldots, Y_N$. N is the number of librarians sampled.

The correlation between the two sets of paired ranks would be perfect if $X_i = Y_i$ for all N cases. Thus, the difference between the paired ranks ($D_i = X_i - Y_i$) is an indication of the correlation between the two measures. The larger the values of D_i, the less the correlation between the two measures. The squared values of D_i are used as an indication of the magnitude of association, because the negative and positive values of D_i would tend to cancel each other.

$$D_i{}^2 = (X_i - Y_i)^2 \qquad \text{(D6i)}$$

It can be shown (Edwards, 1973) that the calculational formula for r_s is derived from the formula for the Pearson r. The *calculational formula* for r_s is:

$$r_s = 1 - \frac{6\sum D_i{}^2}{N^3 - N} \qquad \text{(D6j)}$$

where r_s is the rank order correlation, $\sum D_1{}^2$ is the sum of all the squared differences between paired ranks, and N equals the number of paired ranks.

Calculational Example Suppose that a group of mothers were given an interest inventory. The scores were expressed in terms of percentage of interest in homemaking activities. In addition, these mothers were ranked in terms of the degree of authoritarianism observed in parent-child interactions. The researcher wished to know the degree of relationship between the two measures. The fictitious data are presented in Table D6.5.

In Table D6.5, the percentage scores were converted to ranks. Given the D_i in Table D6.5 we calculate the value of r_s with Formula D6j.

$$r_s = 1 - \left[\frac{6\sum D_i{}^2}{(11)^3 - 11} \right],$$

$$r_s = 1 - \frac{6(94)}{1320},$$

$$r_s = 0.57.$$

TABLE D6.5. Scores on Interest Inventory and Rank Order of Authoritarianism.

Mother	Interest Inventory Percentage Scores	Interest Inventory Scores Converted to Ranks	Authoritarianism Rank	D_i	$D_i{}^2$
A	20	4	7	-3	9
B	25	5	5	0	0
C	10	2	4	-2	4
D	30	6	8	-2	4
E	40	8	2	6	36
F	65	11	6	5	25
G	45	9	11	-2	4
H	35	7	9	-2	4
I	15	3	1	2	4
J	50	10	10	0	0
K	5	1	3	-2	4

N = 11 $\qquad \Sigma = 94$

The observed coefficient of correlation (r_s) between homemaking interest and authoritarianism for these 11 people is 0.57. Thus, there is a moderate positive relationship between the two measures.

Tied Observations

Frequently, two or more subjects will have the same score on a single variable. Tied scores *between* two measures are not important. If observations on one measure are tied at a given rank, the subjects should be assigned the *average* of the tied scores. (See Table D6.6.) If the proportion of ties is small, r_s is little affected. If there is a *large* proportion of ties, then the calculational formula must be corrected for ties. The calculation formula for r_s corrected for ties is:

$$r_s = \frac{\Sigma x_c^2 + \Sigma y_c^2 - \Sigma D_i^2}{2\sqrt{\Sigma x_c^2 \Sigma y_c^2}} \tag{D6k}$$

In the calculation formula corrected for ties; $\Sigma x_c^2 = (N^3 - N)/12 - \Sigma C$, and $\Sigma y_c^2 = (N^3 - N)/12 - \Sigma C$. C is obtained by the formula:

$$C = \frac{t^3 - t}{12} \tag{D6l}$$

where t represents the number of scores tied at a given rank. C is summed across all groups of tied ranks to provide ΣC.

Computational Example with Ties Suppose that we have 10 nursery school children who are ranked by their teacher in terms of creativity. We also measure the amount of time each child spends looking at a novel picture. The time scores are converted to ranks. We wish to determine the degree of association between the two sets of ranks. Assume that the data in Table D6.6 were obtained.

TABLE D6.6. Ranking of 10 Children on Creativity and Response to Novelty.

Children	Time Spent Looking at Novel Picture		Rank of Time Scores X	Creativity Rank Y	D_i	D_i^2
A	30 sec.		1	3	−2	4
B	16 sec.	Ties	2.5	6	−3.5	12¼
C	16 sec.	← →	2.5	5	−2.5	6¼
D	9 sec.		4	1	3	9
E	8 sec.		5	2	3	9
F	5 sec.		7	8	−1	1
G	5 sec.	Ties	7	10	−3	9
H	5 sec.	← →	7	4	3	9
I	3 sec.		9	9	0	0
J	2 sec.		10	6	4	16
N = 10					$\Sigma D_i^2 = 75.5$	

Since half of the time scores are tied, the formula incorporating a correction for ties is used to calculate r_s. We find the values of Σx_c^2 and Σy_c^2. For the x scores, we have a set of two tied scores and another set of three tied scores.

$$\Sigma x_c^2 = \left(\frac{(10)^3 - 10}{12}\right) - \left(\frac{2^3 - 2}{12} + \frac{3^3 - 3}{12}\right),$$

$$\Sigma x_c^2 = 82.5 - (0.5 + 2),$$

$$\Sigma x_c^2 = 80.0.$$

Since there are no tied Y scores,

$$\Sigma y_c^2 = \frac{10^3 - 10}{12} - (0),$$

$$\Sigma y_c^2 = 82.5.$$

Adding up the squares of the D_i in Table D6.6, we obtain $\Sigma D_i^2 = 75.5$. Substituting this value in Formula D6k, we find:

$$r_s = \frac{80.0 + 82.5 - 75.5}{2\sqrt{(80.0)(82.5)}},$$

$$r_s = \frac{87.0}{2(81.2)},$$

$$r_s = +0.54.$$

Thus, for the 10 children, the correlation between the measures of creativity and curiosity is $+0.54$, which is a moderate, positive correlation.

Test of the Significance of r_s

So far, we have been concerned only with the descriptive use of r_s. That is, the value of r_s has been used to describe the relationship obtained in the given sample. If the subjects were randomly sampled from a population, it is possible to test the hypothesis that the two variables are significantly associated in the population. That is, we test the null hypothesis that the two variables are *not associated* in the population ($H_0 : r_s = 0$).

Small N   When there are no ties, the H_0 sampling distribution of r_s can be specified. If the two variables are independent (H_0 is true), for a given rank order of the X scores, any ranking of the Y scores is just as likely as any other order. For N randomly sampled subjects, there are N! possible rankings of the X scores that may occur with a given Y rank order. The probability of the occurrence of any one ranking of the X scores is $1/N!$. For each possible ranking of the X scores, there is an associated value of r_s. The probability of the occurrence of any value of r_s is proportional to the number of possible rankings that yield that value. Table D6.7 is a table of selected *critical* values of r_s for values of N from 4 to 10. The probabilities of the table are one-tailed. If an observed value of r_s is *equal to or greater than* the critical value for a given N, then we conclude that r_s is significant (one-tailed) at the p level indicated in the table. That is, H_0 can be rejected. For example, the obtained value of r_s in the study of children's creativity and curiosity was 0.54. Assume that we had predicted a positive value of r_s prior to collecting the data. For an N of 10, an r_s of 0.54 is significant at less than the 0.06 level. If α had been arbitrarily set at 0.06, we would conclude that there is a significant correlation between the two measures in the population of nursery-school children sampled. By rejecting H_0, we reject the hypothesis that r_s for the population is zero. We cannot be certain, however, that the sample r_s exactly describes the population parameter.

Large N   When N is greater than 10, we may test the significance of r_s by:

$$t = r_s \sqrt{\frac{N-2}{1 - r_s^2}} \tag{D6m}$$

where $df = N - 2$. We compute the value of t and enter the t table (Table D4.4.) with the appropriate df. For example, the calculated value of r_s in the case of the mothers ranked on authoritarianism and homemaking interests was 0.57. The calculated value of t is:

$$t = 0.57 \sqrt{\frac{11-2}{1 - (0.57)^2}},$$

$$t = 0.57\,(3.65),$$
$$t = 2.08.$$

Since $N = 11$, $df = 11 - 2 = 9$. *Assume* that we had predicted a positive association between the two variables as ranked. Assume that α had been set at the 0.05 level and that the mothers were a random sample from a population. Then, we observe that the table one-tailed value of t for 9 df at the 0.05 level is 1.85. Since the calculated value of t is greater than 1.83, we observe that the data do not support the null hypothesis. We can conclude that the measures of authoritarianism and homemaking interests are positively associated in the population sampled.

REFERENCES

The Pearson r is discussed in much greater detail in Edwards (1973, Chapters 11 and 12), Hays (1973, Chapters 15 and 16), McNemar (1969, Chapters 8, 9, 10, and 11), and Walker and Lev (1953, Chapters 10 and 13). The t test for goodness

TABLE D6.7. Values of the Rank Correlation Coefficient r_s at Selected Significance Points. [a]

N	r_s	p
4	1.000	.0417
5	1.000	.0083
5	.900	.0417
5	.800	.0667
5	.700	.1167
6	.943	.0083
6	.886	.0167
6	.829	.0292
6	.771	.0514
6	.657	.0875
7	.857	.0119
7	.786	.0240
7	.750	.0331
7	.714	.0440
7	.679	.0548
7	.643	.0694
7	.571	.1000
8	.810	.0108
8	.738	.0224
8	.690	.0331
8	.643	.0469
8	.619	.0550
8	.595	.0639
8	.524	.0956
9	.767	.0106
9	.700	.0210
9	.650	.0323
9	.617	.0417
9	.583	.0528
9	.550	.0656
9	.467	.1058
10	.733	.0100
10	.661	.0210
10	.612	.0324
10	.576	.0432
10	.552	.0515
10	.527	.0609
10	.442	.1021

[a]The table presents one-tailed probabilities of critical values of r_s for different values of N (the number of pairs of scores) under H_0.
(Values of r_s were computed from Table IV of E. G. Olds, Distributions of sums of squares of rank differences for small numbers of individuals. *Annals of Mathematical Statistics*, 1938, 9, 133–148, by permission of the author and the editors of the *Annals of Mathematical Statistics*.)

of fit is discussed in Edwards (1973, Chapter 12), and in Hays (1973, Chapter 15).

Further discussion of the Spearman correlation coefficient may be found in Edwards (1967; pp. 133–136, 342–344, 364–366); Hays (1973; pp. 788–792); Kendall (1948); McNemar (1969; pp. 232–234); Siegel (1956; pp. 202–213); Spearman (1904); and Walker and Lev (1953; pp. 278–283).

SECTION THREE

RESEARCH TOPICS

INTRODUCTION   The research methods presented in Sections One and Two may be employed in *any* area of psychology. In the present section, samples of research topics of current interest in psychology are presented. The first three topics are social psychology research; the next five are sensation and perception research; and the last nine are learning and motivation research topics. The number of topics selected per area represents the backgrounds and interests of the text's authors. Each topic presents theoretical notions, a brief review of the literature, and suggests an experiment to perform. The student should use parts of Sections One and Two for help in designing, conducting, and analyzing the research. It is strongly suggested that the student refer to the references at the end of each topic for further information.

tOPiC 1
The "Risky Shift" Phenomenon

The risky shift phenomenon is the tendency for people in groups to be willing to take greater risks than they ordinarily would by themselves. Suppose that a group of people was asked to discuss a topic of national interest. A group (individually or collectively) ultimately would make a decision that would be more risky than if they had not had the discussion.

Wallach and Kogan (1965) conducted an experiment on the risky shift phenomenon. They used 360 college students (180 male and 180 female). The students met in groups of five each to discuss topics such as whether a severely ill heart patient should risk an operation that could cure him (or kill him) or to resign himself to a dull and inactive life. Another topic concerns a chess player and the problem of whether he should stake his reputation on a risky play in a tournament.

There were three experimental conditions in the experiment (multilevel design). The first group (condition 1) held a group discussion on the problems and was asked to arrive at a consensus. The second group (condition 2) was not allowed to discuss the topics, but rather, each member had to announce his opinion repeatedly until all opinions were unanimous. The group was told that they would have to make repeated announcements until all announced opinions were the same. Finally, a third group (condition 3) held group discussion, but no attempt was made by the group to come to a collective decision. Members of the third group made all their decisions individually and privately.

RESULTS OF THE STUDY

Under conditions 1 and 3, where discussion had taken place, the risky shift occurred whether the individuals had come to agree (condition 1) or not (condition 3). That is, the groups that held group discussions tended to take a risky position. In sharp contrast, the second group (condition 2), which had not discussed the problems together, did not shift in the direction of taking a risk. Apparently, the group discussion is the important factor in the risky shift. Information about the opinions of other members (which was present in all groups), and social pressure to conform (not present in group 3) were not the key factors in the shift. Wallach and Kogan attributed their results to the fact that, during the discussion periods, the group members came to feel that the responsibility for any possible failure (that is, the heart patient dying or the chess player losing his reputation) was spread among the members of the group. Consequently, they could all "share" in the blame. That is, they felt freer to take more risk in the group than they would be themselves.

You are to design an experiment to test the idea that group discussion facilitates risk behavior in groups. The need to control for group conformity pressure, concensus instructions, and knowledge of others' opinions requires a multiple treatment design (Chapter 5).

SUGGESTED READING

Bem, D. J., Wallach, M. A., and Kogan, N. Group decision making under risk of aversive consequences. *Journal of Personality and Social Psychology,* 1965, *1,* 453–460.

Lamm, H. Will an observer advise higher risk-taking after hearing a discussion of the decision problem? *Journal of Personality and Social Psychology,* 1967, *6,* 467–471.

Madaras, G. R., and Bem, D. J. Risk and conservatism in group decision-making. *Journal of Experimental Social Psychology,* 1968, *4,* 350–365.

Teger, A. I., and Pruitt, D. G. Components of group risk taking. *Journal of Experimental Social Psychology,* 1967, *3,* 189–205.

Wallach, M. A., and Kogan, N. The roles of information, discussion, and consensus in group risk taking. *Journal of Experimental Social Psychology,* 1965, *1,* 1–19.

Wallach, M. A., Kogan, N., and Bem, D. J. Group influence on individual risk-taking. *Journal of Abnormal and Social Psychology,* 1962, *65,* 75–86.

Wallach, M. A., Kogan, N., and Burt, R. B. Are risk takers more persuasive than conservatives in group discussion? *Journal of Experimental Social Psychology,* 1968, *4,* 76–88.

Wallach, M. A., and Wing, C. W., Jr. Is risk a value? *Journal of Personality and Social Psychology,* 1968, 9, 101–106.

Zajonc, R. B., Wolosin, R. J., Wolosin, M. A., and Sherman, S. J. Individual and group risk-taking in a two-choice situation. *Journal of Experimental Social Psychology,* 1968, *4,* 89–106.

tOPiC 2
Competition, Threat, and Interpersonal Accommodation

Kelley (1968) provides a review of the research on interpersonal accommodation. The subjects in these studies usually play a two person (dyad) game. The games present a problem for the players to solve, and the solution consists of an *accommodation* such that the players act so as to achieve each other's goals as well as their own goals.

The games are frequently described in terms of a two-dimensional matrix. A simple game is presented in matrix form in Unit D6 of Section Two (Table D6.1). The two players (subjects) are typically given two choices and the possible outcomes (four combinations of the two choices) are listed in the matrix. Another example of a game matrix is presented in Figure 2.A. The type of game depicted in Figure 2.A is called an interdependent game or conflict of interest game. In such a game there is no simple solution (as there is in Table D6.1) in which both players consis-

Player A

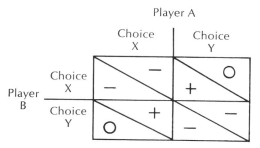

Fig. 2.A.   An example of a two-person interdependence game (after Kelley, 1968). If both players choose the same response (X, X or Y, Y) then they both lose. If player A chooses X and B chooses Y, then A wins. If player A chooses Y and B chooses X, then B wins. The accommodation solution is for both to take turns winning.

tently make a single choice. Rather, in Figure 2.A, the players should both avoid the mutually negative outcomes and take turns winning so that both will get the maximum gain. With complete information about the game, unrestricted communication between the players, and a number of trials to learn how the game works, the players should soon achieve accommodation (taking turns). To make the problem interesting, social psychologists have introduced handicaps for the players. One of these handicaps is to provide full information to the players, but allow only limited communication.

THE TRUCKING GAME

Deutsch and Krauss (1960) invented a clever game situation that corresponds to the game in Figure 2.A. The pairs of subjects (dyads) were the managers of competing trucking companies (Acme and Bolt.) Each player had one truck which carried cargo from one location (start) to another (end). There was a single lane road that provided the shortest route from "start" to "end" for both players. Only one truck at a time could travel this route. Both the Acme and Bolt companies had their own alternate routes which were long winding roads that required considerably more time to traverse than the one-lane road. Each completed trip was worth sixty cents minus operating expenses. The operating expenses consisted of a time charge of one cent a second. Thus, if Acme got a load to "end" within thirty seconds, that player earned thirty cents (60¢ − 30¢ = 30¢). The players were working for imaginary money (poker chips) and were told that they would not actually get their earnings when the game was over. (See Figure 2.B.)

The road-bed and trucks were represented by counters and switches on individual control panels. Each subject could control route choice, and the forward and backward "motion" of her truck. Each subject knew the position of her own truck, but did *not* know the position of the other player's truck except when they met (were blocked) somewhere on the one-lane route. Each dyad made 20 hauls (trials) with their trucks, starting each trial at the same time.

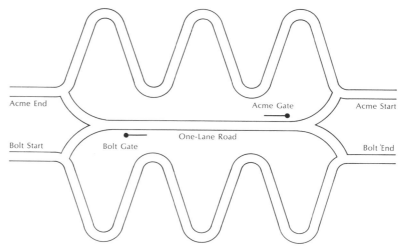

Fig. 2.B. The Trucking Game.

Sixteen pairs of telephone company girls were used as subjects in the study. Under the *standard condition* (as described above) the subjects quickly learned accommodation. They took turns driving on the one-lane road.

Deutsch and Krauss manipulated the variable of "threat." Threat was defined as, ". . . the expression of an intention to do something detrimental to the interests of another" (1960, p. 182). In terms of the trucking game, the threat consisted of closing a gate on the one-lane road, which blocked the other truck from getting through to its goal. Under the standard condition, neither girl had a gate. Under the *unilateral threat condition*, one girl had a gate. Under the *bilateral threat condition*, both girls had a gate (multilevel design).

The results were that most dyads made money (about two dollars) under the standard condition, somewhat less money was made under the unilateral threat condition, and the average *loss* under the bilateral threat condition was about nine dollars.

Deutsch and Krauss interpreted the results as indicating that a means of threat and retaliation interfered with mutual accommodation. They indicated that under the bilateral threat condition (two gates), the girls frequently said things such as "I've lost so much now that I'll be damned if I'll give in." Such comments and the losses sustained indicated that the girls were actively competing with each other rather than cooperating.

Borah (1963) criticized the competition interpretation of the Deutsch and Krauss study. Borah repeated the trucking game experiment with pawns instead of the original electronic apparatus. He found the same kind of results as Deutsch and Krauss. However, he concluded that, in both the no-threat (standard) situation and the bilateral threat situation, there is very little competition as measured by the amount of time spent in a stand-off on the one-lane route. The average stand-off time was about the same for both conditions. He concluded that the bilateral threat condition produced only a greater use of the costly alternative routes because the subjects could not seem to achieve accommodation.

INCENTIVE EFFECTS

The incentives used in the Deutsch and Krauss study were probably insignificant (small amounts of imaginary money). Gallo (1966) repeated the study using a main blackboard display of the highways and small, hand-held blackboards for each member of a dyad. The undergraduate female subjects simultaneously indicated their truck movements on the small blackboards and the outcomes of their decisions were presented on the wall blackboard. Two groups of 16 pairs of subjects were used (randomized two-group design). One group worked for real money. The subjects in the real money group could possibly make as much as sixteen dollars in the twenty trials. The other group worked for the same amount of imaginary money. The costs and payoffs were the same, but the imaginary money group knew that they would not be able to keep the money earned. Gallo found that, under the bilateral threat condition, the real money dyads earned an average of almost ten dollars, which they were allowed to keep. However, under the same two gate (bilateral threat) condition, the imaginary money dyad *lost* an average of almost thirty-nine dollars over the twenty trials. Under the standard, no-threat condition, both the real money dyads and imaginary money dyads made an average gain of about ten dollars over the twenty trials.

Shomer, Davis, and Kelley (1966) found that if there were alternative routes (long, costly highways) the bilateral threat condition had a detrimental effect on only the first few trials. They also examined the effect of a "threat" and "fine" condition. Each member of a dyad could signal a threat (light) that if the second member of the dyad did not let him through, he would request that the experimenter levy a 20¢ fine on the second player. A control group did not have the "threat" and "fine" lights available. They found that there was little difference in the average joint profit of the two groups. There was an insignificant tendency for the threat-fine group to earn more money.

To summarize, "threats" may, but do not necessarily, have a disruptive effect on the accommodation processes. High positive incentives (Gallo, 1966) seem to facilitate accommodation, and low positive incentives (Deutsch and Krauss, 1960) seem to interfere with accommodation. However, Daniels (1967) has found that the effects of high positive incentives depend on other elements of the game. If double-crosses and exploitation are possible, high positive incentives may disrupt accommodation.

Design an experiment to examine either the effects of varying degrees of threat, varying incentives, or both on accommodation in a conflict of interest problem. If both degree of threat and amount of incentive are included, then a factorial design (Chapter 5) would probably be most appropriate.

SUGGESTED READING

Borah, L. A., Jr. The effects of threat in bargaining: Critical and experimental analyses. *Journal of Abnormal and Social Psychology,* 1963, *66,* 37–44.

Daniels, V. Communication, incentive, and structural variables in interpersonal exchange and negotiation. *Journal of Experimental Social Psychology,* 1967, *3,* 47–74.

Deutsch, M. and Krauss, R. M. The effect of threat upon interpersonal bargaining. *Journal of Abnormal and Social Psychology,* 1960, *61,* 181–189.

Gallo, P. S., Jr. The effects of increased incentives upon the use of threat in bargaining. *Journal of Personality and Social Psychology,* 1966, *4,* 14–20.

Kelley, H. H. Experimental studies of threats in interpersonal negotiations. *Journal of Conflict Resolution,* 1965, *9,* 79–105.

Kelley, H. H. Interpersonal accommodation. *American Psychologist,* 1968, *23,* 399-410.

Kelley, H. H., Candry, J. C., Jr., Dahlke, A. E., and Hill, A. H. Collective behavior in a simulated panic situation. *Journal of Experimental Social Psychology,* 1965, *1,* 20–54.

Shomer, R. W., Davis, A. H., and Kelley, H. H. Threats and the development of coordination: Further studies of the Deutsch and Krauss trucking game. *Journal of Personality and Social Psychology,* 1966, *4,* 119–126.

tOPiC 3
Nonverbal Attitude Communication

The participants in a conversation verbally communicate their attitudes about a topic and, occasionally, about each other. In addition, they *nonverbally* communicate their attitudes about the topic and, particularly, their attitudes about each other. Posture, physical closeness, eye contact, facial expression, and vocal intonation all significantly contribute to the total amount of information presented. Mehrabian (1968a) suggests that the total impact of a statement is conveyed much more by facial expression and vocal tone than by the verbal content of the statement.

The importance of nonverbal indices of information has been recognized intuitively by successful courtesans for centuries. The psychoanalysts and other therapists have written about the necessity of attending to these cues in therapy sessions as well as everyday life. Recently, Mehrabian (1967, 1968a, b, c) has conducted a series of experiments designed to determine the relative importance of various nonverbal indices in conveying attitudes.

RESEARCH PROCEDURES

Several different procedures are available for the study of nonverbal communication. As indicated in Table 3.A, three environmental situations are possible: real-life (candid) conversations, staged conversations designed to simulate real life, and laboratory situations with no attempt to simulate real life. Four kinds of "conversation" are possible: candid (real) conversations, "talks" or lectures (monologues), staged conversations run at least partially according to a script, and "imaginary" conversations with one person talking to an inanimate object. Three methods of presentation may be used: live performance, film or TV, or photographs. The subject can have two kinds of task: determining the attitude of someone else (decode) or attempting to portray (role play) a particular attitude (encode). Finally, the experimenter can choose to have the audio portion of a conversation (verbal and vocal cues) included or eliminated either by not using sound recordings, or by not having

TABLE 3.A. Potential Research Procedures.

Mode of Presen-tation	Exper. Subjects Task	Environmental Situation								
		Candid (Real Life) Conversation		Staged ("Real Life") Conversation				Lab. (No "Real Life") Conversation		
		Candid	"Talk"	Candid	Script	Talk	Imaginary	Script	Talk	Imaginary
Live Perform.	Decode								●	
	Encode	⨯	⨯	⨯						●
Film or TV	Decode									
	Encode	⨯	⨯	⨯						
Photo	Decode									●
	Encode	⨯	⨯	⨯						

any words actually spoken. The cross-hatched squares in Table 3.A are impossible combinations. All noncross-hatched squares are potentially possible. The squares with dots in them are the particular combinations that have been used by Mehrabian (1967, 1968b, c). The laboratory situation (no attempt at imitation of a real-life situation) is the most likely choice for research because it is cheap and control of variables is best accomplished in a laboratory setting. However, the results of research in such a setting may not be generalizable to a real life setting. Of course, it is extremely difficult to attempt to use candid conversations in a real-life setting because of the great lack of control and other problems such as the rights to privacy of the participants in a candid conversation (Chapter 11 and Unit B).

INDEPENDENT AND
DEPENDENT VARIABLES

A large number of different independent and dependent variables may be manipulated in a research study of nonverbal communication. The potential variables may serve as either independent or dependent variables depending on the subjects' task (encoding or decoding). The main categories of nonverbal communication cues include: (1) vocal cues, intonation of voice as in sarcasm or surprise; (2) facial cues, for example, eyebrow position; (3) physical distance between communicators with actual touch as a special subcategory; (4) body movements, for example, gestures; (5) orientation and posture cues; (6) organismic cues, for example, status, sex, and age differences between communicators. Orientation and posture cues include: immediacy of head orientation (direct or turned away); immediacy of body (shoulder) and leg orientation; eye contact; openness of arms and legs; angle of inclination of trunk (forward or backward lean); degree of relaxation—tension of hands, legs, and trunk; head tilt; and seated or standing position. Attitude measures include: positive-negative, pleasant-unpleasant, and like-dislike. These attitude measures may refer to one or all of the participants in a conversation or to the ideas involved in the conversation.

Mehrabian (1967) has organized most of the preceding nonverbal communication orientation variables under the construct *immediacy*. For example, immediacy of head orientation refers to the percentage of time that a communicator is looking at the person he is talking to. Immediacy of angle of body inclination refers to the degree of inclination toward the person being addressed.

Mehrabian (1967) found that head orientation and the interaction between head and body orientation had a significant effect on the subjects' inferences about a speaker's attitude towards them. The subjects thought that the speaker had a more positive attitude toward them when the speaker directly faced the subject. The interaction indicated that a direct (immediate) head and body orientation produced the greatest feeling of positive attitude. Direct body orientation, but a turned away (nonimmediate) head orientation produced the least feeling of positive attitude. However, when the subjects made judgments about the degree of positive attitude of a speaker toward another person, the judgments were significantly influenced only by head orientation.

Mehrabian (1968b) in a series of photograph decoding experiments, found that greater relaxation, leaning toward the spoken-to person, and shorter distance between communicators all facilitate judgment of a positive attitude toward the person being addressed. Openness of posture and body orientation interacted with other variables. In an encoding experiment, male communicators used eye contact, shorter distance, and absence of arms-akimbo to convey positive attitudes. Female communicators used the absence of arms-akimbo, shorter distance and arm openness to convey positive attitudes.

Mehrabian (1968c), using the encoding procedures, found that eye contact was a decreasing function of degree of dislike toward an addressee (person talked to) and an increasing function of degree of unfamiliarity with an addressee. He also found that distance was a decreasing linear function of attitude, and that shoulder orientation was the major body orientation cue. Male communicators exhibited less body relaxation and greater vigilance (shoulder orientation and eye contact) toward intensely disliked males. When males addressed females, intense dislike was communicated through a high degree of relaxation. When females communicated with either male or female addressees, intense dislike was communicated through relaxation of posture.

There are, obviously, a great number of combinations of procedures and variables that have yet to be formally examined. The research of Mehrabian indicates some interesting preliminary findings that need to be replicated. Design a study of the effect of any of the suggested variables (and combinations of variables) on nonverbal attitude communication. If one-way viewing mirrors and cameras are not available it may be possible to use a "peep-hole" scoring system. If the experimental conditions may be effectively counterbalanced, then a repeated measures multilevel design (Chapter 5) might be most appropriate.

SUGGESTED READING

Mehrabian, A. Orientation behaviors and nonverbal attitude communication. *The Journal of Communication*, 1967, *17*, 324–332.

Mehrabian, A. Communication without words. *Psychology Today,* 1968, *2* (4), 53–55.(a)

Mehrabian, A. Inference of attitudes from the posture, orientation, and distance of a communicator. *Journal of Consulting and Clinical Psychology*, 1968, *32*, 296–308.(b)

Mehrabian, A. Relationship of attitude to seated posture, orientation, and distance. *Journal of Personality and Social Psychology*, 1968, *10*, 26–30.(c)

tOPiC 4
The Moon Illusion

When the moon is near the horizon, it appears much larger than when it is directly overhead. The moon does not change in size, and the retinal image of the horizon moon is no larger than the retinal image of the moon overhead. The moon illusion has fascinated scientists for centuries (Holway and Boring, 1940). One explanation of the illusion is the apparent-distance hypothesis, which states that the horizon moon is seen in relation to its background (for example, houses, trees, and so on), and the background provides distance cues so that the horizon moon appears farther away than the overhead moon. (See Figure 4.A.) When two objects form equal retinal images, and one of the objects seems farther away than the other, the apparently farther object (horizon moon) must be larger than the apparently nearer object (overhead moon) (Rock and Kaufman, 1962). It is possible to test the apparent-distance hypothesis in a laboratory. By adjusting objects of the same and different distances from the observer, one can determine the perceptual effects of the size and distance variables.

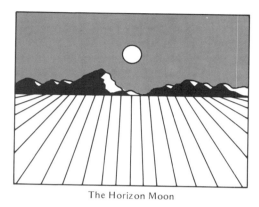

The Horizon Moon

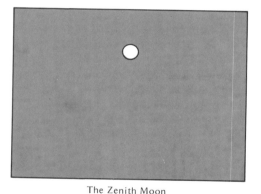

The Zenith Moon

Fig. 4.A.   The Moon Illusion.

THE VESTIBULAR HYPOTHESIS

Another theoretical approach to explain the moon illusion was advanced by Wood, Zinkus, and Mountjoy (1968) and Zinkus and Mountjoy (1969). They feel that the moon illusion can, at least in part, be attributed to changes in vestibular stimulation (body position cues). They noted that changes in head position or orientation (resulting in changes in vestibular stimulation) affect visual perception. Thor and Wood (1968) indicated that, when an overhead target was viewed, it was judged to be smaller and farther away than a target of the same size and distance on a horizontal plane. Wood et al. (1968) allowed subjects to manipulate the distance of equal-size targets placed in different planes of space in a totally darkened room (thus reducing the effects of the surroundings). The subjects adjusted the distance of either the overhead or horizontal stimulus so that the two seemed to be equally distant. They found that subjects consistently judged the overhead stimulus to be smaller than the horizontal stimulus even though the stimuli were of equal size and, originally, at an equal distance from the observer. Their results appear to make the Rock and Kaufman (1962) explanation insufficient, since the effects of terrain, the flattened sky effect, and other explanations that attribute the cause of the moon illusion entirely to factors outside the organism were controlled. The apparent-distance hypothesis seems to have less credibility in explaining the results of the Wood et al. (1968) experiment, since a change in head and eye position causing a corresponding alteration of vestibular impulses to the optic cortex was the only variable manipulated.

Design an experiment to test the apparent distance hypothesis and the vestibular change hypothesis. One possibility would be to rotate the head in a vertical plane and rotate the head in a horizontal plane while varying body position. Also, one might test the effect of both distance cues and vestibular cues simultaneously, in which case a factorial design (Chapter 5) should be most efficient.

SUGGESTED READING

Holway, D. H., and Boring, E. G. The moon illusion and the angle of regard. *American Journal of Psychology*, 1940, *53*, 109–116.

Rock, I., and Kaufmann, L. The moon Illusion. II. *Science*, 1962, *136*, 1023–1031.

Thor, D. H., and Wood, R. J. The moon illusion. Paper presented at the meeting of the Midwest Psychological Association, Chicago, May 1968.

Wood, R. J., Zinkus, P. W., and Mountjoy, P. T. The vestibular hypothesis of the moon illusion. *Psychonomic Science*, 1968, *11*, 356.

Zinkus, P. W., and Mountjoy, P. T. The effect of head position on size discrimination. *Psychonomic Science*, 1969, *14*, 80.

TOPIC 5
Comparative Depth Perception

Since 1957, there has been a large number of studies in depth perception using the visual cliff technique. (See Walk et al., 1957; Gibson and Walk, 1960; Walk and Gibson, 1961; and Walk, 1965.) The technique can be used with any animal that can walk or crawl. Some of the types of visual behavior that can be studied using a visual cliff include pattern preference, texture discrimination, and absolute brightness thresholds for depth discrimination. In addition, the age at which depth discrimination develops in different species has been studied with the visual cliff.

THE VISUAL CLIFF APPARATUS

A visual cliff is an apparatus containing two surfaces, one that appears close to and one that appears farther from the organism (Figure 5.A). A sheet of glass is placed parallel to and above the two surfaces. Thus, the animal is always physically sup-

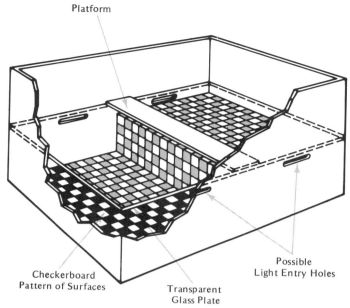

Platform

Checkerboard
Pattern of Surfaces

Transparent
Glass Plate

Possible
Light Entry Holes

Fig. 5.A. A model of the visual cliff that can be used with animals such as kittens, rabbits, and skunks,
Lights may be mounted under the center platform, in the side walls under the glass, or the surfaces may
be translucent and lighted from below. The dimensions of the cliff depend on the animal to be used.

ported on both sides of the visual cliff, but one side looks deep. A platform is centered on top of the glass. In most studies, the organism is given the choice of descending from the center platform to one of two surfaces. One of the surfaces is located flush beneath one-half of the glass. The other surface is placed at some distance below the other half of the glass. If the organism moves off the center platform, it can choose to step onto the "deep side" (distant surface) or "shallow side" (close surface). One form of the apparatus is illustrated in Figure 5.A. Other forms are presented in Walk and Gibson, 1961.

The sheet of glass controls for some nonvisual cues. In the *physical cliff* (a cliff without the glass), an animal may use echolocation (sound reflection cues) to detect depth. The visual cliff eliminates differential sound cues. The physical cliff may also be dangerous to an animal if the "deep side" is very deep. The visual cliff eliminates the danger problem. Odor cues can be controlled in the visual cliff by washing the glass between animals. The visual cliff is usually used with small animals (for example, chicks) so that the optical field may be approximately equal on both sides. For example, a checkerboard pattern may be placed on both sides of the cliff. Very small squares are placed on the shallow side, and the squares are made large enough on the deep side so that, from the center platform, the pattern appears to be continuous. In addition, the level of illumination can be equated for the two sides. The illumination may be measured with a light meter or small portions of each side may be visually compared to see if they are equally bright.

Tactual (touch) cues can be eliminated by raising the center platform high enough above the glass so that the organism cannot touch the glass before descending. The use of under-lighting with translucent surfaces eliminates the reflection of light off the glass surface. Adult human beings can use reflection cues to detect depth. However, it is not yet known whether other organisms use reflection cues. In any case, reflection cues may be eliminated so that they do not confound the interpretation of an experiment.

COMPARATIVE VISUAL DOMINANCE

The dependence of various species on visual cues *(visual dominance)* or tactual cues (*tactual* or *haptic dominance*) can be compared using the visual cliff technique. The deep side of the visual cliff provides *physical support* without *optical support*, while the shallow side provides both physical and optical support for an animal. An organism's response to being placed on the deep or shallow side can be used as a measure of visual dominance. If an animal makes an avoidance response (moving toward the shallow side) when placed on the deep side, then he is considered visually dominant. Tactually dominant animals should not show the avoidance response and may explore the entire glass sheet of the cliff (which offers continuous tactual support). Walk (1965) and Schiffman (1968a) found that chicks are optically dominant, and both hooded and albino rats are tactually dominant. It is unclear whether kittens are visually dominant (Walk, 1965). Some types of rabbits, dogs, and goats are visually dominant (Walk, 1965; Walk and Gibson, 1961).

You are to design an experiment to test and compare the reaction to apparent depth (visual dominance) of at least two species (randomized two-group design, Chapter 4). Your design and procedure should control for all cues other than tactual and visual cues. The development of visual dominance in animals that have been shown to be visually dominant might also be investigated by varying the chronological age and experience of the subjects, in which case a Solomon four-group design might be used (Chapter 5).

SUGGESTED READING

Gibson, E. J., and Walk, R. D. The "visual cliff." *Scientific American,* 1960, *202,* 64–71.

Lore, R., Kam, B., and Newby, V. Visual and nonvisual depth avoidance in young and adult rats. *Journal of Comparative and Physiological Psychology,* 1967, *64,* 525–528.

Schiffman, H. R. Physical support with and without optical support: Reaction to apparent depth by chicks and rats. *Science,* 1968, *159,* 892–894.

Schiffman, H. R. Texture preference in the domestic chick. *Journal of Comparative and Physiological Psychology,* 1968, *66,* 540–541.

Walk, R. D. The study of visual depth and distance perception in animals. In D. S. Lehrman, R. A. Hinde, and E. Shaw (Eds.), *Advances in the study of behavior.* New York: Academic Press, 1965.

Walk, R. D. Monocular compared to binocular depth perception in human infants. *Science,* 1968, *162,* 473–475.

Walk, R. D., and Bond, E. K. Deficit in depth perception of 90-day-old dark-reared rats.

Psychonomic Science, 1968, *10,* 383–84.

Walk, R. D., and Gibson, E. J. A comparative and analytical study of visual depth perception. *Psychological Monographs,* 1961, *75,* 1–44.

Walk, R. D., Gibson, E. J., and Tighe, T. J. Behavior of light- and dark-reared rats on a visual cliff. *Science,* 1957, *126,* 80–81.

τopic 6
Verbal Transformation
and "Stabilized" Auditory Images

An auditory stimulus becomes "stabilized" by repeating a word or sound at a constant rate over an extended period of time. The words tend to undergo perceptual changes during that time. Words may be constantly repeated by using a continuous tape loop on a tape recorder. The term stabilized means that the stimulus is presented in such a way so as to prevent the usual kinds of change in stimulus input.

Auditory stabilization and visual stabilization are similar. Heckenmueller (1965) has reviewed the basic methodological and theoretical aspects of visual stabilization. In general, stabilized images have been studied primarily in the *visual* modality by restricting eye movements. Early studies of stabilization relied upon a contact lens method of compensating for eye movements and stabilizing a retinal image. A microlamp projector was attached to a contact lens and fitted to the subject's eye. An image was projected by this device onto the retina so that eye movements had little or no effect upon the locus of the projected image on the retina. When eye movements are controlled, the perception of the projected image is altered. That is, when a pattern is stabilized on the retina, the perception of the pattern may disappear in whole or in part (Ditchburn and Pritchard, 1956). When the perception of the pattern fragments, the pattern breaks up into nonrandom segments the most characteristic of which are straight lines (Evans, Longden, Newman, and Pay, 1967). For example, a pattern such as a circle with an inscribed cross will typically lose either the vertical or horizontal bar or the whole cross, or occasionally, the whole circle leaving the cross intact. Regeneration of the pattern occurs from time to time when some change in stimulation is detected by the observer. The contact lens method was not entirely satisfactory, because there is a certain amount of slippage of the contact lens on the cornea (Barlow, 1963). A more satisfactory method has been developed by Evans and Drage (1967). Evans flashed a very bright light of short duration through a projector containing a stimulus slide and created a very stable entopic afterimage. Heckenmueller (1965) maintains that the stopping of involuntary eye movement is essential to produce a stable retina image. Evans et al. (1967) maintain that the essence of the phenomenon is not so much the restriction of movement on the retina, but rather a lack of significant *change* in the nature of the stimulus input. Cornsweet (1956) found results that suggest that change in stimulation is one factor involved in maintaining perception of an image. Matheson (1967) found that changes in auditory stimulation affect the duration of entoptic visual afterimages.

AUDITORY STABILIZATION

The effect of stabilizing an auditory stimulus (a word) is noticed by the observer when the auditory stimulus undergoes illusory changes called verbal transformations. These verbal transformations may range from a perception of a word that rhymes with the actual stimulus to extreme phonetic distortions (Warren, 1968). Evans and Kitson (1967) have studied auditory "stabilized" images. They felt that the invariance (lack of change) in the auditory stimulus input produces a form of failure of auditory perception. For example, if a word is repeated aloud to oneself a number of times, it soon loses meaning.

Warren (1968) found that, while visual illusions occur with only some stimulus configurations, verbal transformations (illusory changes associated with auditory stimulus stabilization) occur with all words. He concluded that stabilized auditory images undergo more perceptual change than do stabilized visual images. Furthermore, he states that distortion of auditory input (when stabilized) is an inverse function of phonetic complexity. That is, as phonetic complexity increases, distortions tend to become less. This finding is comparable to visual data presented by Pritchard (1961). Pritchard found that the length of time a target remains visible is a direct function of the complexity of the target. Apparently there are gross similarities between the functioning of the two sensory modalities.

Design an experiment to study the effects of auditory stabilization on the perception of words. The phonetic complexity, meaningfulness, and/or familiarity of the words might be manipulated. A repeated measures design (Chapter 3) might be used to be efficient in terms of number of subjects.

SUGGESTED READING

Barlow, H. B. Slippage of contact lenses and other artifacts in relation to fading and regeneration of supposedly stable retinal images. *Quarterly Journal of Experimental Psychology,* 1963, *15,* 36–51.

Cornsweet, T. N. Determination of the stimuli for involuntary drifts and saccadic eye movements. *Journal of the Optical Society of America,* 1956, *46,* 987–993.

Ditchburn, R. W., and Pritchard, R. M. Stabilized interference fringes on the retina. *Nature,* 1956, *177,* 434.

Evans, C. R. *Prolonged after-images employed as a technique for retinal stabilization: Some further studies of pattern perception and some theoretical considerations.* National Physical Laboratory: Autonomics Division, Teddington, Middlesex, England, 1966.

Evans, C. R., and Drage, D. J. *Some notes on apparatus used to produce a prolonged after-image for studies of perfect retinal stabilization.* National Physical Laboratory: Autonomics Division, Teddington, Middlesex, England, 1967.

Heckenmueller, E. G. Stabilization of the retinal image: A review of method, effects, and theory. *Psychological Bulletin,* 1965, *63,* 157–169.

Matheson, D. W. Facilitation of visual afterimages with auditory stimulation. Unpublished doctoral dissertation, Claremont Graduate School, 1967.

Pritchard, R. M. Stabilized images on the retina. *Scientific American,* 1961, *204* (6), 72–78.

Warren, R. M. Verbal transformation effect and auditory perceptual mechanisms. *Psychological Bulletin,* 1968, *70,* 261–270.

tOPiC 7
Signal Detection and Psychophysics

A sonar operator watches a visual display and listens to his headset in a submarine. His job is to detect signals reflected off of enemy ships. In order for the sonar operator to do his job, he must be sensitive to the stimulus input. The fact that some signals are not detectable suggests that some lower limit of sensitivity exists that depends upon signal energy. This lower limit is called the "absolute threshold" and is a point on an energy scale below which we do not detect a stimulus, and above which we do (Mueller, 1965). Operationally, the absolute threshold is defined as the intensity of a stimulus to which the observer responds, "Yes, I detect it" on 50 percent of the stimulus presentations (Egan and Clarke, 1966). Thus, the threshold value is measured on an energy scale (for example, sound pressure levels or foot-candles of illumination) and is defined by the behavior of the observer. For example, one could change the stimulus by twisting a dial controlling the physical intensity of a stimulus until the observer reported, "Yes I detect it" and then record the number from the energy scale on the dial. The recorded number would be the threshold of detection for that stimulus.

The detection of signals is of great interest to the experimental psychologist who studies sensory processes. For over one hundred years, sensory psychologists have been measuring the signal energy required for a stimulus to be just detectable. The task falls into the domain of experimental psychology called psychophysics (Unit B), which is concerned with finding relationships between the physical environment and man's response to that environment (Boring, 1942; Woodworth and Schlosberg, 1954).

Classical psychophysical methods (Unit B) have been used in the attempt to find and measure *the* "absolute" threshold for most of the senses, and these methods have had difficulty in specifying *the* threshold (Swets, 1961). Too often, experimenters found that the measured threshold would change from trial to trial or that the same stimulus would not elicit a "Yes, I detect it" response on successive trials (Egan and Clarke, 1966).

THE THEORY OF SIGNAL DETECTABILITY

Recently, several experimental psychologists have taken exception to the concept of the "absolute" threshold and have offered an alternative theory of detection behavior. The theory is called "The Theory of Signal Detectability" (TSD). The theory stresses the importance of motivation and expectancy of the observer and their joint effect upon detection. By motivation, we mean the effect that a *payoff* or *cost* has on making a decision. The payoff and cost are contingent upon the type of response the observer makes. For example, in a *"Yes-No"* situation, the subject must say either, "Yes, I detect it," or "No, I do not detect it," during a trial. The signal may not be present during the trial. Therefore, there are four possible outcomes in such a situation; these are shown in Figure 7.A.

Of interest to the TSD are two of the four outcomes. These are the correct

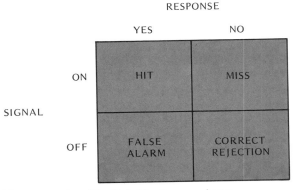

Fig. 7.A.   The possible outcomes in a "Yes-No" detection experiment.

detection (hits) and the error of saying, "Yes," when in fact the signal has not occurred (false alarms). Ideally, a subject should say, "Yes, I detect it," only when he actually hears or sees the signal. The probability of such a response is dependent on the strength of the signal. That is, the stronger the signal, the higher the probability for detecting it. Sometimes, however, a subject will report detecting a signal when, in fact, no signal occurred. What kinds of variables could cause an observer to make such a false alarm? The theory suggests two variables that influence detection. The first is called *expectancy,* which is defined in terms of the expectations a subject will develop during an experiment. If a subject hears or sees nothing for five or ten trials, he might be tempted to say, "Yes" even though he hears no signal (Galanter, 1962, p. 101). If an observer comes to expect a signal almost every time, his false alarm rate will be higher than if he did not expect the signal as often. If the expectancy for a signal was quite low, we might see an increase in the frequency of "no" responses. Apparently, the "threshold" can be altered without making a change in the signal energy, which means that a "threshold" is not absolute.

A second variable that affects detection behavior is the *payoff.* The payoff is determined by the value of correctly detecting a signal and the cost of not detecting or falsely detecting a signal. These conditions affect the *motivation* of the observer. Suppose, for example, that our sonar man received $10.00 (payoff) every time he correctly detected a signal (a hit or correct rejection) and lost $5.00 (cost) every time he made a false alarm or miss. The payoff-cost scheme is called an outcome structure or payoff function. This payoff function is illustrated in Figure 7.B. Suppose that the sonar man knows that he can expect a signal half of the times he looks at his visual display and listens to his headset (a trial). It would be to the sonar man's advantage to say "Yes" every time, since in the long run he would win. This amounts to lowering his criterion or "threshold." If, however, we changed the payoff matrix so that he received $5.00 for a hit, but it cost him $10.00 for a false alarm, we would see a subsequent decrease in false alarm rate and a rise in his criterion.

The theory of signal detectability accounts for variables in addition to signal

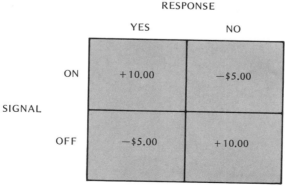

Fig. 7.B.   A payoff function for the sonar man.

strength that influence detection behavior. In summary, these variables are: (1) the subject's expectation, which depends upon the probability of signal presentation, and (2) the motives induced by the payoff function (Galanter, 1962, p. 107).

Design an experiment to test the idea that changes in the expectancy of the subject and/or changes in the payoff function result in changes in the false alarm rate. Because of great individual differences (Chapter 3) between subjects, a repeated measures design would probably be best.

SUGGESTED READING

Boring, E. G. *Sensation and perception in the history of experimental psychology.* New York: Appleton-Century-Crofts, 1942.

Egan, J. P., and Clarke, F. R. Psychophysics and signal detection. In J. B. Sidowski (Ed.), *Experimental methods and instrumentation in psychology.* New York: McGraw-Hill, 1966, 211–246.

Galanter, E. Contemporary psychophysics. In *New directions in psychology.* Vol. I. New York: Holt, Rinehart and Winston, 1962.

Mueller, C. G. *Sensory psychology.* Englewood Cliffs, N.J.: Prentice-Hall, 1965.

Swets, J. A. Is there a sensory threshold? *Science,* 1961, *134,* 168–177.

Woodworth, R. S., and Schlosberg, H. *Experimental psychology.* (Rev. ed.) New York: Holt, Rinehart and Winston, 1954.

τOPiC 8
Stimulus Contrast and Lateral Inhibition in Perception

A problem that is of concern to some experimental psychologists is the stimulation of one sensory modality and observing the subsequent effect on a response in another modality. An effect was observed anecdotally as far back as 1669, when it was noted that people who were hard of hearing were able to hear better in the light than in the dark. Apparently, visual input facilitated auditory stimulus detection. Observations such as the one just described lead to questions concerning relationships between different sensory modalities such as how are they similar, how are they different, and how do they influence each other. For example, how are the receptors in the skin like the rods and cones in the eye? How similar are the functions in the brain for tactile stimulation and visual stimulation? These questions and thousands of others are being examined.

Bach-y-Rita, Collins, Saunders, White, and Scadden (1969) are working on a problem concerning how blind people might "see" through stimulation of the skin. The substitution of one sensory modality for another is called "sensory plasticity." Bach-y-Rita et al. (1969) have designed an apparatus consisting of a television camera, a transducer (an instrument that transforms one form of energy to another) and a tactile display. (See Figure 8.A.) The TV camera takes a picture of a stimulus, and the picture is displayed tactually by means of 400 vibrating stimulators or tactors (a 20×20 matrix), which are fitted to a person's back. The matrix impresses a two-dimensional vibrating facsimile that the TV camera "sees." A basic research problem is to determine how a person learns to discriminate between various stimuli presented to the skin through the TV camera. More recently the researchers have miniaturized the system so that the tactile information is presented to a much smaller area of the stomach and the television camera is mounted on the subject's head.

STIMULUS CONTRAST

The study of the skin sense may provide many answers to applied problems. Also, we can learn much about skin sensitivity variables by conducting rather simple perceptual experiments. One variable that is of interest is *stimulus contrast*. Stimulus contrast refers to the increased apparent difference between sensations when they are presented together (Figure 8.B.) The circles inside each rectangle are physically equal in brightness. However, because of the stimulus contrast created by the background, the circle on the left appears brighter than the one on the right. Several explanations have been offered to account for this phenomenon. Granit (1955) found that the firing of one retinal cell inhibits the firing of adjacent cells. Consequently, since the circle on the right is surrounded by a light surface, retinal

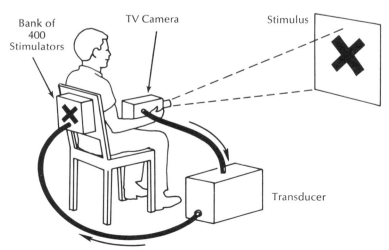

Fig. 8.A. Cutaneous image projection apparatus.

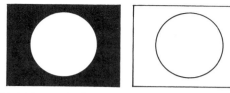

Fig. 8.B. An example of brightness stimulus contrast.

activity in the circle area might be inhibited and appear darker than the circle on the left.

Ratliff and Hartline (1959) and Ratliff, Hartline, and Miller (1963) have studied inhibition in the eye of a small crab. They found that adjacent retinal receptors exert inhibition on each other. The amount of inhibition is an inverse function of the distance between receptors and a direct function of the intensity of the stimulation. This finding is consistent with Granit's (1968). Theoretically, the effect of this *lateral inhibition* is to enhance the difference in brightness between the circle and the surrounding area.

LATERAL INHIBITION

Von Békésy (1967) suggested a neural funneling model for the visual and *skin* senses that could account for the contrast effect. Essential to the model is the assumption that the areas adjacent to the point of stimulation are inhibited, and the main stimulus is funneled into a common pathway. The funneling concept is represented in Figure 8.C and lateral inhibition in Figure 8.D. The lateral inhibition of sense organs appears to inhibit the smaller stimulus impulses, and the stimulation is funneled into a common pathway and accentuated. Therefore, the areas adjacent to the stimulated area will be inhibited. This prediction was supported by Granit (1955) and Ratliff and Hartline (1959) in the visual modality.

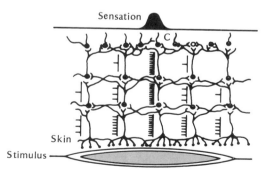

Fig. 8.C. An illustration of neural funneling. The nerve C is directly in line with the point of maximum stimulation on the skin. The nerve C is the common pathway into which surrounding stimulation is eventually funneled.

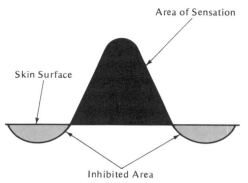

Fig. 8.D.   An illustration of lateral inhibition.

Von Békésy has studied lateral inhibition in the skin by using two point stimulation (compass tips) and varying the distance between the two points. The points are pressed against the hand of a highly trained subject, and he responds by describing the sensation in terms of one point, two points, or no sensation at all. Von Békésy (1967) found that, as he moved the two points a distance of 1.5 cm. apart, the subjects perceived a unitary pattern. (See Figure 8.E.) As the distance between the two points was increased to 2.0 cm. the sensation appeared as one point, but it felt spread out. When the distance between the two points reached 3 cm., the subjects reported perceiving two distinct points, but the subjective magnitude of the sensation decreased sharply. Notice how the sensation of two points on the skin is similar to the stimulus contrast example we used earlier. (See Figures 8.B and 8.E.) Figure 8.F illustrates the analogy. The points of stimulation on the skin correspond to the surrounding light area in Figure 8.B.

Carmon (1968) reasoned that an annular stimulus should be tactually discriminated better than a disk at the same intensity. The annular stimulus produces

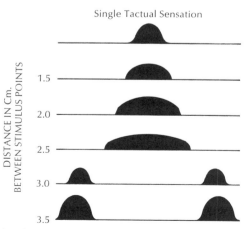

Fig. 8.E.   Subjective stimulus characteristics for various distances between stimulus points.

Skin sensation

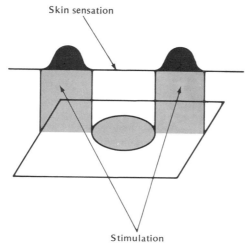

Stimulation

Fig. 8.F.   Analogical comparison of skin contrast and brightness control.

better contrast. The annular and disk stimuli are shown in Figure 8.G. Carmon argued that an annular stimulus would: (1) concentrate more intensity at the border, thereby increasing the inhibition of the surround (analogous to Figure 8.B) and (2) increase contrast, since the center would not have inhibitory effects on the border. His results supported the predictions that tactual resolution (discrimination) was better for annular stimuli than for circular. Carmon also found that resolution varied with pressure. That is, a pressure of 9.4 grams produced the best resolution at an inside diameter of 8 mm., whereas a pressure of 3.68 grams yielded best resolution at a diameter of 10 mm. Carmon's stimuli were not vibrating during the experiment. Vibration could change the parameters in the experiment. Carmon's data support the theoretical ideas of Granit, Ratliff and Hartline, and Von Békésy.

Your task is to devise an experiment to test the theoretical ideas advanced above concerning stimulus contrast. Either the visual or tactual modality may be used. The need for control for individual differences in sensitivity (Chapter 3) suggests a repeated-measures design.

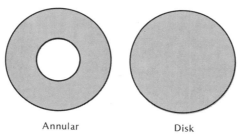

Annular   Disk

Fig. 8.G.   Examples of annular and disk stimuli.

SUGGESTED READING

Bach-y-Rita, P., Collins, C., Saunders, F., White, B., and Scadden, L. Vision substitution by tactile image projection. *Nature,* 1969, *221,* 963–964.

Beauchamp, K. L., Matheson, D. W., and Scadden, L. A. Effect of stimulus-change method on tactile-image recognition. *Perceptual and Motor Skills,* 1971, *33,* 1067–1070.

Carmon, A. Stimulus contrast in tactile resolution. *Perception and Psychophysics,* 1968, *3,* 241–245.

Granit, R. *Receptors and sensory perception.* New Haven: Yale University Press, 1955.

Granit, R. The development of retinal neuro-physiology. *Science,* 1968, *160,* 1192–1196.

Ratliff, F., and Hartline, H. K. The responses of the Limulus optic nerve fibers to patterns of illumination on the receptor mosaic. *Journal of General Physiology,* 1959, *42,* 1241–1255.

Ratliff, F., Hartline, H. K., and Miller, W. H. Spatial and temporal aspects of retinal inhibitory interaction. *Journal of the Optical Society of America,* 1963, *53,* 110–120.

Von Bêkesy, G. *Sensory inhibition.* Princeton: Princeton University Press, 1967.

τOPiC 9
Fear and Alcoholic State

Casual observation supports the notion that alcohol can substantially alter the behavior of an individual. A frequent statement is that alcohol "releases inhibitions" in the person's behavior. That is, the person does things he might avoid doing if he were sober. Such universal explanations seem hard pressed when one considers the wide variety of behaviors that may be observed in different individuals when they are inebriated.

Most laboratory studies of the effect of alcohol have concentrated on the slowing of reaction time or the impairment of problem-solving abilities when the subject is administered measured doses of alcohol. Masserman and Yum (1946) conducted research into some of the psychological effects of alcohol intoxication in cats. They trained the cats to open a food box for a food reward. After the cats had learned to obtain the food reward, an electric shock or an air blast was introduced as the cat approached the food box. When the noxious stimulus was strong enough, the cats refused to approach the food box to obtain the food reward. When the cats were administered alcohol, they resumed their food-getting behavior (see Figure 9.A). As described here the research design was a one-group before-after design (Chapter 3).

FEAR REDUCTION HYPOTHESIS

The usual explanation for the change in the cat's behavior is that the alcohol somehow decreases the impact of the punishment in the approach-avoidance situation. The cat's senses may have been so dulled by the alcohol that the noxious stimulus was not as painful as when the animal was sober. Another possibility is that their sensory systems were functioning properly, but that their brains did not perceive the incoming information as sharply. The usual terminology for this type of explanation is that the alcohol reduces the fear resulting from the noxious stimulus. The inebriated animal is not as fearful of the noxious stimulus so it successfully makes its way to the food. Learning theorists prefer to think of the fear as a negative reinforcement that leads to the extinction of the food box approach behavior. Psychoanalytically oriented psychologists prefer to describe the fear as an inhibiting factor that prevents the expression of the food-getting behavior. In either case, the alcohol attenuates the effect of the noxious stimulus without an appreciable effect on the approach response.

DISCRIMINATION HYPOTHESIS

Conger (1951) tested the differential effect of alcohol by measuring how hard lab rats pulled on a harness to obtain a reward or to avoid a shock. Animals were tested while drunk and sober. Conger concluded that alcohol changed the strength of the avoidance response without altering the approach behavior. In a portion of his research, Conger observed that rats could be trained to approach food when sober and to avoid food when inebriated, and vice versa. In other words, the animals

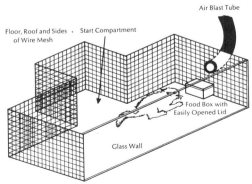

Fig. 9.A. Cat choice apparatus used in approach-avoidance conflict study.

were able to discriminate between the two states and adjust their behavior accordingly (discrimination hypothesis).

STATE DEPENDENT HYPOTHESIS

If the two states (inebriation and sobriety) are discriminable, an alternative explanation for the different behaviors when drunk or sober may be offered. Behavior learned in one state may be supplanted by different behavior in the other state if the learning situations differed in each case. Overton (1966) suggests that a drugged and undrugged state are not only discriminable, but that learning may be *state dependent*. That is, the behavior learned in one state (sober) may not even be available to the animal in the other state (drunk). If the state dependent hypothesis is true, there would be little reason to expect continuity between the behavior of an individual when drunk and sober other than the learning experiences common to both states. The discrimination hypothesis, on the other hand, allows for some generalization between the two drug states, but explains the difference in behavior in terms of the discriminably different situation.

Kanzler (1969) observed that rats trained to give a conditioned emotional response when sober gave a much lower emotional response when drunk, as would be predicted by any of the above explanations. He also found, however, that animals trained while drunk gave a lower emotional response when sober. Since a conditioned emotional response may be considered a measure of fear, this observation would seem to support the discrimination hypothesis.

Two possible research paths are immediately available based on the above observations:

(1) collect additional evidence concerning the fear reduction versus discrimination explanation for the difference in behavior; or
(2) devise an experiment that will test the state dependent explanation without introducing generalizing factors that might blur the distinction between the two states.

SUGGESTED READING

Conger, J. J. The effects of alcohol on conflict behavior in the albino rat. *Quarterly Journal of Studies on Alcohol,* 1951, *12,* 1–29.

Kanzler, A. W. Alcohol as a discriminative stimulus in the conditioned emotional response. Unpublished doctoral dissertation, Claremont Graduate School, 1969.

Masserman, J. H., and Yum, K. S. An analysis of the influence of alcohol on experimental neurosis in cats. *Psychosomatic Medicine,* 1946, *8,* 36–52.

Overton, D. A. State-dependent learning produced by depressant and atropinelike drugs. *Psychopharmacologia,* 1966, *10,* 6–31.

TOPiC 10
Stimulus Change and Exploratory Behavior

Stimuli can be measured in terms of the relative amount of stimulus change they provide. For example, a melody played on a piano provides more auditory stimulus change over time than a single note monotonously repeated. A stimulus that is a new experience for an organism is called a novel stimulus. Organisms attending to a novel stimulus can either avoid the stimulus (through fear or boredom) or approach the stimulus (exploratory or curiosity behavior). According to the theories of Berlyne (1960), Dember and Earl (1957), Fiske and Maddi (1961), Glanzer (1958), Leuba (1955), and Walker (1964), an organism's response to stimulus change is determined jointly by the amount of perceived change within a stimulus, the immediate past history of the organism in terms of his experience of stimulus change, the psychological state of the organism (for example, anxiety), and the immediate history of interaction between the organism and the stimulus. Extremely simple (little change) or extremely complex (too much change) stimuli should produce avoidance. Moderately complex stimuli (medium amounts of change) should produce approach behavior.

A number of recent studies of the behavior of diverse species have indicated that animals will explore novel stimuli provided that the amount of stimulus change is neither too little nor too great. Some of the species studied include: fish (Russell, 1967); monkeys (Haude and Ray, 1967); rats, mice, guinea pigs, chinchillas, hamsters, and gerbils (Glickman and Hartz, 1964); calves (Beauchamp, Chapman, and Grebing, 1967); and children (Rabinowitz and Robe, 1968).

RESEARCH VARIABLES

A large number of independent and dependent variables have been examined in the study of exploratory behavior. The following is a brief, selected sketch of some of the variables recently explored. Russell (1967) presented novel objects to fish and controlled the familiarity of the fish with the test environment and the long- and short-term novelty of the novel objects. The greater the familiarity of the fish with the test situation, the more they explored the novel objects (white squares with black borders and black squares with white borders). The more experience a fish had with the novel objects, the less the fish investigated the objects. Sales (1968) allowed rats to look from a dark compartment into an adjacent, illuminated compartment. The illuminated compartment could contain nine checkerboard pattern inserts containing 2, 4, 9, 16, 25, 64, 100, 196, or 256 checks (squares). Nine independent groups of subjects (multilevel design, Chapter 5) were exposed to the nine panels. Sales found an inverted U relationship between number of squares and average inspection time per response of looking into the illuminated compartment. The panels with 9, 16, or 25 squares produced the largest average inspection time.

Franken (1967) exposed food-satiated rats to a six choice-point multiple T maze (Unit C) for two trials per day for five days (repeated measures). Between the two daily trials, different parts of the maze were changed in brightness (black to white or white to black). The animals increased their exploration of the parts of the maze that were changed. Then the subjects were food deprived and food reinforced for running the maze. During the food deprivation part of the study, the maze was not changed in brightness between trials. On the first day of food-reinforced responding, the subjects that had previously experienced brightness changes in the cul-de-sacs of the maze spent more time on the second trial in the culs than did any of the other animals. Thus, the animals seemed to be responding to the expected stimulus changes rather than the food reward. Franken et al. (1968) varied the intertrial interval for subjects run in his six choice-point, multiple T maze. He found that the effect of brightness changes on exploration decreased with increasing time between trials.

May and Beauchamp (1969) ran food-deprived animals in an I maze for a food reward (five days at four trials per day). At the end of the five days (20 trials), the food rewards were no longer presented in the maze. Instead, varying degrees of stimulus change (black and white patterns) were presented on inserts in the goal box for five more days. They found that animals that ran to a different black and white pattern on each of the four trials of a day were more resistant to extinction (kept running) than animals that received no change or experienced the same pattern on all four trials per day (multilevel, repeated measures design).

Rats exhibit a significant increase in bar-press rate over operant level if dim light onset is the reward for bar pressing. Lowe and Williams (1968) investigated the effect of plain light illumination versus patterned light illumination (12 squares of light). They found no difference in the bar-press rates under the two illumination conditions. The slight amount of difference between the two conditions did not facilitate approach behavior (bar pressing). Eacker (1967) found that the Skinner box complexity (stripes versus gray) influenced the rate of bar pressing for dim light onset. The more stimulus change in the bar-press chamber, the greater the bar-press rate. Under bright light onset, the amount of stimulus change in the chamber did not differentially affect the behavior of the subjects.

Hughes (1968) allowed rats to explore either a novel half of a box or the half that they had been confined in for one day. The animals spent more time in the novel half than the familiar half. In addition, female rats exhibited more exploration than male rats.

Haywood and Wachs (1967) forced animals to go to one arm of a Y maze for three trials and then allowed the animals a free choice on the fourth trial. The arms differed in brightness (black and white). One group was exposed to white noise (a very loud sound) just prior to the fourth trial. A second group experienced three electric shocks prior to the fourth trial. A third group did not experience any intense arousing stimulation before the choice trials (control group). The control group made a significantly greater number of choices of the previously unexplored arm (multilevel design). The intense arousing stimulation (shock and white noise) reduced the number of choices of the novel arm to chance.

Haude and Ray (1967) confined monkeys in small metal test chambers. The chambers had a window in them that was constructed so that the monkey had to stick his head into a tunnel (channel) in order to see what was in the window. In one experiment, after base line measures of window looking were taken, the rate of presentation of different color slide pictures of monkeys was varied (change every 5, 25, 625, or 3600 seconds). As the rate of presentation increased, the frequency of looking and cumulative viewing time of the monkeys increased. In a second experiment, the amount of time the monkeys were confined in the test chamber with a blank window was varied (0, 2, 4, and 8 hours). Following the periods of sensory deprivation (confinement), the animals were allowed to look at color slides of monkeys. Haude and Ray found no significant effect of deprivation time on visual exploration.

Rabinowitz and Robe (1968) presented fourth-grade children with six buttons, any one of which could be pressed on each trial. Five of the buttons turned on a single light (D). The sixth button turned on: (1) a single light (A); (2) a flickering single light (A); (3) a green or orange light (A); (4) a flickering green or orange light (A); (5) five lights (E, F, A, B, and C); (6) consistently alternating lights (F or B); (7) randomly alternating lights (F or B); (8) lights E, F, A, B, or C in that order; (9) lights E through C in random order; or (10) lights E, F, A, B, C in that order for four trials, followed with a random selection of the five lights. The children all chose the sixth button more frequently than the other five buttons over all ten conditions. Condition 10 led to the most choice of button six followed by conditions 8 and 7.

Design a study of the effects of any of the indicated variables on the exploratory behavior of animals. A great deal of work has been conducted with children (for example, May, 1963; Cantor and Cantor, 1966). However, with the exception of Berlyne's (1960) research, little has been done with adults. Most of the research requires that the subjects' immediate past experience be controlled. Thus, a before-after (Chapter 4) or repeated-measures design (Chapter 3 or 5) is used.

SUGGESTED READING

Beauchamp, K. L., Chapman, A., and Grebing, C. Response by the calf to stimulus change. *Psychonomic Science*, 1967, *9*, 125–126.

Berlyne, D. E. *Conflict, arousal, and curiosity.* New York: McGraw-Hill, 1960.

Dember, W. N., and Earl, R. W. Analysis of exploratory, manipulatory and curiosity behavior. *Psychological Review*, 1957, *64*, 91–96.

Cantor, J. H., and Cantor, G. N. Functions relating children's behavior to amount and recency of stimulus familiarization. *Journal of Experimental Psychology*, 1966, *72*, 859–863.

Eacker, J. N. Behaviorally produced illumination change: visual exploration and reinforcement facilitation. *Journal of Comparative and Physiological Psychology*, 1967, *64*, 140–145.

Fiske, D. W., and Maddi, S. R. *The functions of varied experience.* Homewood, Illinois: Dorsey, 1961.

Franken, R. E. Stimulus change, exploration, and latent learning. *Journal of Comparative and Physiological Psychology*, 1967, *64*, 301–307.

Franken, R. E., Jones, C. E. B., and Hanley, D. A. Adaptation, intertrial interval, and response to preferred and nonpreferred change. *Canadian Journal of Psychology*, 1968, *22*, 45–51.

Glanzer, M. Curiosity, exploratory drive, and stimulus satiation. *Psychological Bulletin*, 1958, *55*, 302–315.

Glickman, S. E., and Hartz, K. E. Exploratory behavior in several species of rodents. *Journal of Comparative and Physiological Psychology*, 1964, *58*, 101–104.

Haude, R. H., and Ray, O. S. Visual exploration in monkeys as a function of visual incentive duration and sensory deprivation. *Journal of Comparative and Physiological Psychology*, 1967, *64*, 332–336.

Haywood, H. C., and Wachs, T. D. Effects of arousing stimulation upon novelty preference in rats. *British Journal of Psychology*, 1967, *58*, 77–84.

Hughes, R. N. Behaviour of male and female rats with free choice of two environments differing in novelty. *Animal Behaviour*, 1968, *16*, 92–96.

Leuba, C. Toward some integration of learning theories: The concept of optimal stimulation. *Psychological Reports*, 1955, *1*, 27–33.

Lowe, G., and Williams, D. I. Light reinforcement in the rat: The effects of visual pattern and apparatus familiarization. *Animal Behaviour*, 1968, *16*, 338–341.

May, R. B. Pretest exposure, changes in pattern complexity, and choice. *Journal of Comparative and Physiological Psychology*, 1968, *66*, 139–143.

May, R. B. Stimulus selection in preschool children under conditions of free choice. *Perceptual and Motor Skills*, 1963, *16*, 203–206.

May, R. B., and Beauchamp, K. L. Stimulus change, previous experience and extinction. *Journal of Comparative and Physiological Psychology*, 1969, *68*, 607–610.

Rabinowitz, F. M., and Robe, C. V. Children's choice behavior as a function of stimulus change, complexity, relative novelty, surprise, and uncertainty. *Journal of Experimental Psychology*, 1968, *78*, 625–633.

Russell, E. M. The effect of experience of surroundings on the response of *Lebistes Reticulatus* to a strange object. *Animal Behaviour*, 1967, *15*, 586–594.

Sackett, G. P. Reward frequency and choice behavior in naïve and sophisticated monkeys and mentally retarded children. *Journal of Comparative and Physiological Psychology*, 1967, *64*, 151–153.

Sales, S. M. Stimulus complexity as a determinant of approach behaviour and inspection time in the hooded rat. *Canadian Journal of Psychology*, 1968, *22*, 11–17.

Walker, E. L. Psychological complexity as a basis for a theory of motivation and choice. In David Levine (Ed.), *Nebraska symposium on motivation*. Lincoln: University of Nebraska Press, 1964, pp. 47–95.

τOPiC 11
Observational Learning and Behavioral Contagion

Social *imitation learning* is defined to occur when the observation of the behavior of a model (M), ". . . or of expressions attributing certain behavior to M, affects O [an observer] so that O's subsequent behavior becomes more similar to the observed, or alleged, behavior of M." (Flanders, 1968, p. 316.) The study of imitative behavior is based on the idea that the observation of a model's behavior causes a change in the observer's behavior.

The social psychologists working on this topic have used several forms of reinforcement for imitative behavior. One form of reinforcement is *direct positive* reinforcement. In terms of human subjects, direct positive reinforcement usually consists of verbal reinforcement such as "Good." In terms of infrahuman subjects, direct positive reinforcement usually consists of food rewards. A second form of positive reinforcement is termed vicarious reinforcement. *Vicarious reinforcement*

(VR) consists of the observation of the model receiving a direct positive reinforcement. In terms of human subjects, VR usually consists of observing a model receive positive verbal reinforcement for some behavior. In terms of infrahuman subjects, VR usually consists of the observing animal watching a model animal receive a food reward contingent on the occurrence of a particular behavior. Nonreinforcement means that the observer does *not* receive either a positive reinforcement or a punishment for imitation.

Observational learning refers to imitation learning when the observer is either vicariously reinforced (VR) or nonreinforced for imitating. Observational learning does *not* refer to the case when an observer is directly reinforced for imitating the behavior of a model.

Miller and Dollard (1941) maintain that training with nonreinforcement does not produce imitative learning. On the other hand, Bandura and Walters (1963) suggest that training with nonreinforcement should have at least some minimal effect on imitative behavior. Subsequent research (Bandura and Menlove, 1968; and Berger, 1966) has indicated that observers trained under nonreinforcement do imitate more than control subjects who were not exposed to a model.

A related set of experiments on observational learning indicates that vicarious reinforcement is more effective than nonreinforcement training on imitation (Bandura, Grusec, and Menlove, 1967; Marlowe, Beecher, Cook, and Doob, 1964; and Marston, 1966).

OBSERVATIONAL LEARNING
VERSUS OPERANT CONDITIONING

Bandura and Walters (1963) also suggest that observational learning procedures may be more efficient than operant conditioning procedures (direct positive reinforcement). Bandura and McDonald (1963) partially examined this idea in a study of the effects of observational learning and imitation training on the moral judgments of children. A group of children between five and eleven years of age was used. An operant level measure of the moral judgment styles of the children was taken. Each child was categorized as belonging mainly to one of two types. The younger children were generally *objective* in their moral judgments. That is, the children judged the degree of "badness" of an act in terms of the amount of material damage resulting, rather than in terms of the intentionality of the actor. Most of the older children were classed as *subjective;* they tended to focus on the intention of the actor rather than the amount of material damage as a result of the act. The classification (operant level) was based on the children's responses to a series of 12 pairs of stories. One story of each pair presented a well-intentioned act which resulted in considerable material damage. The other story of each pair presented a selfishly or maliciously motivated act which resulted in minor material damage. The children were asked, "Who did the naughtier thing?"

About two weeks after the baseline measures were taken, a group of 84 children were selected from the original 165. These 84 children (equally divided between boys and girls) were either primarily subjective or primarily objective in their answers to the 12 questions. The children that were not used any more were not classifiable.

The 84 children were divided into three groups. Group I observed an adult (model) express her moral judgments (answer to the question) with 12 new pairs of stories. The model expressed an opinion that was opposite to a child's previously determined moral orientation. The model was verbally reinforced by the experimenter. The children were also given 12 new pairs of stories alternating with the model's stories. The children were also verbally reinforced for expressing a moral judgment opposite to their previous style and consistent with the model's answers. Thus, Group I was a double reinforced group (positive reinforcement for the model and the observer-child).

Group II experienced the same procedures as Group I except that the children were not reinforced for imitating the model. Thus, Group II was a VR group (the model, but *not* the child was directly reinforced). Group III was not exposed to a model. Each child was directly reinforced for making moral judgments opposite to his previous style. Thus, Group III was an operant training or direct reinforcement group. The design was a factorial design (Chapter 5) with three levels of reinforcement (Groups I to III) and two levels of the operant level classification (objective and subjective).

In general, the results were that the double reinforcement and vicarious reinforcement Groups (I and II) were not significantly different in terms of the number of responses opposite to their previous style. Both Groups I and II came to exhibit a large percentage of reversed moral judgments. However, the operant training Group (III) made less changed moral judgments than the other two groups. These results support Bandura and Walter's contention.

Marston (1966) also found that, in a verbal imitation study with undergraduate males, the VR group exhibited more imitation than a no VR group. The model in this case was a tape-recorded voice and the design was a randomized two-group design (Chapter 4). The subjects were required to say words on signal, and the experimenter reinforced all words that could be classed as weapons. The experimenter told the subjects that he was working with two subjects at a time. In the vicarious reinforcement situation, he said "good" when the tape-recorded voice said a weapon word. The tape-recorded voice increased its presentation of weapon words over the training trials, whether or not it was reinforced. The VR group had a higher mean proportion of weapons responses and a faster rate of learning than the no VR group.

Another set of related experiments are concerned with "behavioral contagion." Behavioral contagion (Wheeler, 1966) refers to the imitation of a model when neither the model nor the observer is reinforced. For example, Wheeler and Caggiula (1966) found that adult male subjects exhibited strong verbal aggression toward a target person only when the target person stated unconventional social beliefs *and* a model made a strong verbal attack on the target person. If the model did not attack the target person, then the observer did not. Also, VR had no effect on the observer's behavior when VR consisted of the target person changing his expressed opinion as a result of the model's attack.

Design an experiment on either observational learning or behavioral contagion. The subjects may be humans or other animals. The effect of vicarious reward and direct positive reward on either form of imitation might be investigated.

SUGGESTED READING

Bandura, A., Grusec, J. E., and Menlove, F. L. Some social determinants of self-monitoring reinforcement systems. *Journal of Personality and Social Psychology*, 1967, *5*, 449–455.

Bandura, A., and Menlove, F. L. Factors determining vicarious extinction of avoidance behavior through symbolic modeling. *Journal of Personality and Social Psychology*, 1968, *8*, 99–108.

Bandura, A., and McDonald, F. J. Influence of social reinforcement and the behavior of models in shaping children's moral judgments. *Journal of Abnormal and Social Psychology*, 1963, *67*, 274–281.

Bandura, A., and Walters, R. H. *Social learning and personality development.* New York: Holt, Rinehart and Winston, 1963.

Berger, S. M. Observer practice and learning during exposure to a model. *Journal of Personality and Social Psychology*, 1966, *3*, 696–701.

Flanders, J. P. A review of research on imitative behavior. *Psychological Bulletin*, 1968, *69*, 316–337.

Marlowe, D., Beecher, R. S., Cook, J. B., and Doob, A. N. The approval motive, vicarious reinforcement, and verbal conditioning. *Perceptual and Motor Skills*, 1964, *19*, 523–530.

Marston, A. R. Determinants of the effects of vicarious reinforcement. *Journal of Experimental Psychology*, 1966, *71*, 550–558.

Miller, N. E., and Dollard, J. *Social learning and imitation.* New Haven: Yale University Press, 1941.

Wheeler, L. Toward a theory of behavioral contagion. *Psychological Review*, 1966, *73*, 179–192.

Wheeler, L., and Caggiula, A. R. The contagion of aggression. *Journal of Experimental Social Psychology*, 1966, *2*, 1–10.

ᴛOPIC 12
Errorless Learning

A typical discrimination task requires the subject to learn to approach only one of two different stimuli. The usual procedure is to confront the subject with both stimuli (and two potential responses) and to reward only the appropriate response. Such a discrimination task may occur in a two-choice maze, a discrimination box, or a Skinner box with two bars (Unit C). In most discrimination tasks, the subject first responds randomly to the two stimuli, making many initial errors. As the training proceeds, the subject learns to make the response that is reinforced and not make the unrewarded response. Thus, by a process of *trial and error*, the subject learns the discrimination.

The nature of discrimination behavior has a number of interesting features. The subject will occasionally relapse and make error responses. Animals that make many errors in the task often display marked emotional behavior in the testing situation. If the positive and negative stimuli are arranged along a continuum, the subject responds maximally to a stimulus near the positive stimulus but displaced *away from* the negative stimulus value.

FADING-IN TRAINING

Terrace (1963a) devised a method of discrimination learning that eliminated almost all error responses. Using pigeons, Terrace presented a brightly illuminated positive stimulus with a very dimly illuminated negative stimulus. The pigeons' tendency to peck at the brighter target was reinforced with food. As the training progressed, the negative stimulus was made gradually brighter ("fading in"). Eventually, the two targets were equally illuminated, and the pigeon continued to peck only at the reinforced key. Thus, discrimination learning occurred with few or no error responses (Figure 12.A).

Since they did not respond to the incorrect stimulus, pigeons that learned the discrimination task without error showed superior learning to animals trained under the usual procedure. Errorless animals also show less emotional behavior in the situation, possibly as a result of the lack of frustration involved with errors. In addition, observation of the generalization gradient shows that there is no "peak shift." That is, the animals respond maximally to the positive stimulus rather than

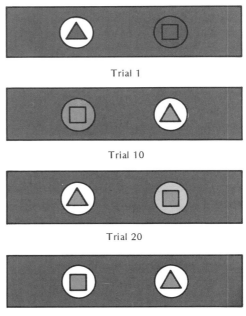

Trial 1

Trial 10

Trial 20

Trial 30

Fig. 12.A.   Stimulus Fading.

shifting away from the negative stimulus. Thus, errorless learning appears to be more efficient than conventional discrimination procedures.

Terrace (1963b) has found that it is possible to teach a difficult discrimination task to pigeons by using the errorless learning procedure. First, the animals are taught a simple discrimination task. When the discrimination is well established, the difficult stimuli are gradually superimposed on the learned stimuli. In time, the difficult stimuli will completely replace the easy stimuli and the animals will have responded only to the positive stimulus. The animals will have learned a difficult discrimination without making an error.

Hilgard and Bower (1966) point out that the errorless learning phenomenon may offer a practical way to arrange optimum learning conditions. Theoretical explanations of its effectiveness have not been fully developed.

Two possible research plans might be developed about errorless learning. First, Terrace's procedure has been very effective with pigeons in a Skinner box. Other animals and other tasks might equally profit from the procedure. Second, the process of fading in the negative stimulus is not the only way to accomplish errorless performance. Other possibilities include presenting the negative stimulus with no response key during the initial trials. A more intriguing possibility might be to build a device that could rapidly reverse the two stimuli. If the animal begins a response to the incorrect stimulus, the correct-incorrect designations could be switched so that the completed response is to the correct stimulus. For comparison purposes, a two-group design (Chapter 4) might be used with one group trained under standard conditions.

SUGGESTED READING

Ferster, C. B., and Perrott, M. C. *Behavior principles.* New York: Appleton, 1968.

Hilgard, E. R., and Bower, G. H. *Theories of learning.* New York: Appleton, 1966.

Terrace, H. S. Discrimination learning with and without "errors." *Journal of Experimental Analysis of Behavior,* 1963, 6, 1–27.(a)

Terrace, H. S. Errorless transfer of a discrimination across two continua. *Journal of Experimental Analysis of Behavior,* 1963, 6, 223–232.(b)

Terrace, H. S. Discrimination learning and inhibition. *Science,* 1966, *154,* 1677–1680.

τOPiC 13
The Effects of Embryonic Drug Stimulation on Later Behavior

Psychologists generally agree that the early experience of all animals has a marked effect on later behavior. One source of information about the effects of early experience is related to the phenomenon called imprinting (Sluckin, 1965). **Imprinting** is defined as very rapid learning of a following response that occurs in some animals during a critical early stage of development. Imprinting has been observed mostly in birds, although other animals such as fish, sheep, deer, and buffalo have been imprinted (Hess, 1959). Infant birds, especially ducklings and goslings, have been observed following objects other than their mothers (Figure 13.A). There appears to be a *critical period* during the early development of a bird in which the bird learns to follow its own mother. The critical period for Mallard ducklings (that is, the period for maximum imprinting) has been found to be between 13 and 16 hours after hatching. Hess (1959) points out that the possibility of imprinting terminates

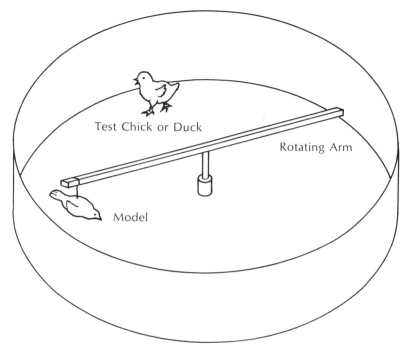

Fig. 13.A. Imprinting Apparatus.

with the onset of fear. That is, when an animal develops a fear response (the end of the critical period) imprintability ceases. Instead of following a strange object, an animal that is old enough to show fear will avoid the strange object.

FEAR-REDUCING DRUGS

The effects of fear-reducing drugs on the imprintability of birds have been studied. Certain potential fear-reducing drugs are: (1) chlorpromazine, (2) meprobamate, and (3) nembutol. Chlorpromazine is a synthetic tranquilizer drug commonly used to treat psychotic reactions in people. It acts as a sedative and reduces anxiety and fear reactions. Meprobamate (marked as "Miltown" or "Equanil") is another tranquilizer drug. It acts as a general muscle relaxant and has a "taming" effect on most animals. Nembutol is a barbiturate. It is a general nonvolatile anesthetic. In small doses it has a calming effect on behavior and generally inhibits certain central nervous systems functions.

With respect to the effects of drugs on imprinting, meprobamate, if given during the critical period, makes imprinting impossible. However, it does not interfere with the effects of imprinting if used after imprinting has taken place. Chlorpromazine allows a high degree of imprinting during the critical period or after imprinting has taken place. Nembutol generally reduces imprintability except when given after imprinting has taken place. Hess (1959) suggests that, since meprobamate and nembutol are muscle relaxants, the afferent neural impulses (motor feedback) originating from following behavior may be inhibited, nullifying the imprinting experience. Chlorpromazine is not a muscle relaxant, so the motor feedback is probably not inhibited, and thus imprinting can take place.

Drugs have always been used *after* the birds had hatched from the egg. One might consider what the effects of certain drugs might be if given to the embryo *before* hatching. The effects on imprinting and the critical period could both be studied (Coleman, 1969).

MAGNESIUM PEMOLINE

One drug that is of current interest to psychologists is magnesium pemoline (MgPe). MgPe is a mild central nervous system stimulant and is packaged under the name "Cylert." Glasky and Simon (1966) found that MgPe stimulates RNA production in the brain, and predicted that the drug would enhance learning. Plotnikoff (1966) found that MgPe enhanced learning of a conditioned avoidance response in rats. Thompson and Knudson (1968) found that rats injected with MgPe required fewer trials to reach criterion on an avoidance task. Filby and Frank (1968) found that MgPe facilitated avoidance performance. Chase and Rescorla (1968), however, found that MgPe failed to facilitate learning of an active avoidance discrimination in rats. They felt that the drug, being a stimulant, disrupted learning. Generally, however, the results seem to indicate that MgPe facilitates avoidance learning. What about other forms of learning? An interesting problem would be to determine the effects of MgPe administered prior to hatching on imprinting behavior in ducks. If MgPe facilitates learning, we might expect Mallard ducklings to imprint earlier (that is, earlier than the 13–16 hour critical period) or we might expect imprinting to be more complete than if the drug is not used.

The administration of the drug to the egg is relatively simple. One selects a fertilized duck egg that is to hatch in about five days. A small hole is punched in the shell at the small end of the egg, and the drug can be carefully placed inside the shell with a hypodermic needle. The hole is immediately sealed with paraffin to prevent dehydration. The egg is returned to the incubator for the remainder of the incubation period. When the egg hatches, the imprinting test can be made and the effects of MgPe on later behavior can be assessed. Generally speaking, the effects of any drug can be tested by this method. For example, common household drugs such as aspirin, vitamins, antibiotics, or even alcohol can be administered by the above method, and the effect on subsequent behavior can be assessed. The dosage of certain drugs can be determined from the available literature. The dosage of other drugs must be determined by pilot studies.

The task is to investigate the effects of some drug on imprinting in birds. The drugs should be administered to the embryo before the bird hatches, and appropriate control procedures should be used. Fertile eggs are often difficult to obtain during the winter months, so careful planning of the time schedule for the experiment is necessary. Also, the experimenter should expect occasional physical abnormalities in newly hatched birds, whether or not a drug is administered. Usually, this type of research requires a randomized two-group (Chapter 4) or multilevel (Chapter 5) design.

SUGGESTED READING

Chase, T. C., and Rescorla, R. A. The effect of magnesium pemoline on learning an active avoidance-passive avoidance discrimination. *Psychonomic Science*, 1968, *10*, 87–88.

Coleman, C. The effects of embryonic drug stimulation with Methylphenidate on imprinting of chicks. Unpublished research. University of the Pacific, 1969.

Filby, Y., and Frank, L. Magnesium pemoline: Effects on drl performance. *Psychonomic Science*, 1968, *10*, 265–266.

Glasky, A. J., and Simon, L. N. Magnesium pemoline: enhancement of brain RNA polymerases. *Science*, 1966, *151*, 702–703.

Gottlieb, G. Prenatal behavior of birds. *Quarterly Review of Biology*, 1968, *43*, 148–174.

Hess, E. H. Imprinting. *Science*, 1959, *130*, 133–141.

Orzack, M. H., Taylor, C. L., and Kornetsky, C. A research report on the anti-fatigue effects of magnesium pemoline. *Psychopharmacologia*, 1968, *13*, 413–417.

Plotnikoff, N. Magnesium pemoline: Enhancement of learning and memory of a conditioned avoidance response. *Science*, 1966, *151*, 703–704.

Sluckin, W. *Imprinting and early learning*. Chicago: Aldine, 1965.

Thompson, R. W., and Knudson, G. R. Magnesium pemoline: Facilitation of one way and two way avoidance learning. *Psychonomic Science*, 1968, *11*, 155.

Yuwiler, A., Greenough, W., and Geller, E. Biochemical and behavioral effects of magnesium pemoline. *Psychopharmacologia*, 1968, *13*, 174–180.

TOPIC 14
The Memory Molecule

A great deal of interest has been expressed in the suggestion that learning and memory are accomplished in the nervous system by means of a chemical change inside the nerve cell. The work of Hurwitz and Furth (1962) demonstrated that all of an individual's genetic characteristics are encoded and stored by the chemical deoxyriboneucleic acid (DNA). Although DNA never leaves the nucleus of the cell, it produces a chemical copy of itself that is capable of approaching and directing the activity of portions of the cell. This chemical "messenger" belongs to a family of chemicals called riboneucleic acid (RNA), which differs slightly from DNA in terms of actual chemical makeup, but is capable of similar information encoding functions. Hyden and Egybazi (1963) suggested that RNA is complex enough and in the right location to serve as the "memory molecule." They demonstrated that if rats are trained on a "tight wire" task, nerve cells in the balancing areas of the brain show changes in RNA content. Injections of substances that are known to block the production of RNA result in failure to learn or remember a task (Agranoff, 1967).

INGESTION AND INJECTION OF RNA

One of the most spectacular demonstrations in support of the RNA hypothesis is found in McConnell's cannibal planaria studies. Several studies have shown that planaria (a small primitive flatworm found in ponds and streams) can learn a conditioned response to a light being turned on, if the light is paired with a strong electric shock for a number of trials. If these planaria are then ground with a mortar and pestle and fed to a group of naïve planaria, these "cannibals" learn the task much faster than naïve animals that do not eat trained planaria. McConnell (1966) argues that the better performance reflects the "learning" accomplished by ingesting the appropriate memory molecule. He generalizes this finding to a typical human learning situation by suggesting the use of "professor-burgers."

A similar improvement in learning performance is claimed to occur when RNA, extracted from the brains of rats that have learned a maze, is injected into the brains of naïve animals (Jacobson, et al., 1965). That is, the RNA from trained animals is supposed to aid significantly the learning of untrained animals. However, there is substantial contradictory evidence (Byrne, et al., 1966; Luttges, et al., 1966).

It has been noted that facilitation of learning performance by ingestion of

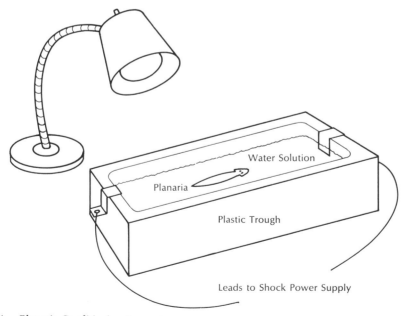

Water Solution

Planaria

Plastic Trough

Leads to Shock Power Supply

Fig. 14.A.   Planaria Conditioning Apparatus.

"prelearned" RNA is not necessarily support for the idea of a specific memory molecule appropriate to that task. It may be that *any* diet that is enriched in the compounds comprising RNA would facilitate RNA production in the cell. The cell may use the injected or ingested raw material to produce its own appropriate RNA molecule more quickly. Evidence supporting this notion is found in the fact that injecting RNA from the brains of rats who learned to run to the black arm of a "T-maze" facilitates the injected animals' learning to run to the white side. The recipient animals exhibited faster learning of the response opposite to that learned by the donor animals.

Hartry, Keith-Lee and Morton (1964) suggested that the improved performance of the cannibal planaria is a function of the increased "handling" these animals received during the feeding process and is independent of the compound ingested. They found that noncannibals that were handled in the same way as the cannibals also showed better learning performance than naïve planaria.

Design an experiment using planaria to test McConnell's specific memory molecule hypothesis. The effects of handling and enriched diets should be controlled. Since number of subjects is usually not a problem, a complex factorial design (Chapter 5) would probably be best.

SUGGESTED READING

Agranoff, B. W. Memory and protein synthesis. *Scientific American,* 1967, *216* (6), 115–122.
Byrne, W. L., et al. Memory transfer. *Science,* 1966, *153,* 658–659.
Hartry, A. L., and Keith-Lee, P. Learning in cannibal planaria. *Science,* 1963, *150,* 1038.
Hartry, A. L., Keith-Lee, P., and Morton, W. D. "Planaria: Memory transfer through cannibalism" re-examined. *Science,* 1964, *146,* 274–275.
Hurwitz, J., and Furth, J. J. Messenger RNA. *Scientific American,* 1962, *206* (2), 41–49.
Hyden, H., and Egybazi, E. Glial RNA changes during a learning experiment in rats. *Proceedings National Academy of Science,* 1963, *49,* 618–24.
Jacobson, A. L., Babich, F. R., Bubash, S., and Jacobson, A. Differential-approach tendencies produced by injection of riboneucleic acid from trained rats. *Science,* 1965, *150,* 636–37.
Luttges, M., Johnson, T., Buck, C., Holland, J., and McGaugh, J. An examination of "transfer of learning" by nucleic acid. *Science,* 1966, *151,* 834–837.
McConnell, J. V. Comparative physiology: Learning in invertebrates. *Annual Review of Physiology,* 1966, *28,* 107–36.

tOPiC 15
Intradimensional and Extradimensional Concept Shifts

A subject is presented with several stimuli (for example, card drawings) that vary in several dimensions (for example, brightness and shape) and each dimension has at least two cues (for example, shape: circle or square; brightness: black or white). For example, each card can contain a drawing with one of two shapes and one of two brightnesses. (See upper half of Figure 15.A.) The subject's task is to identify which dimension is relevant as predetermined by the experimenter, and the subject must find out which cue of the relevant dimension is the "correct" or positive cue. Usually, the experimenter presents two cards from a set and indicates that one of the two cards is a positive (correct) instance of the concept. For example, the experimenter may present a card with a white square on it and a card with a black circle on it. In this case, the experimenter may have decided that the concept is "all white cards." Thus, the *relevant dimension* is brightness and the *correct cue* is

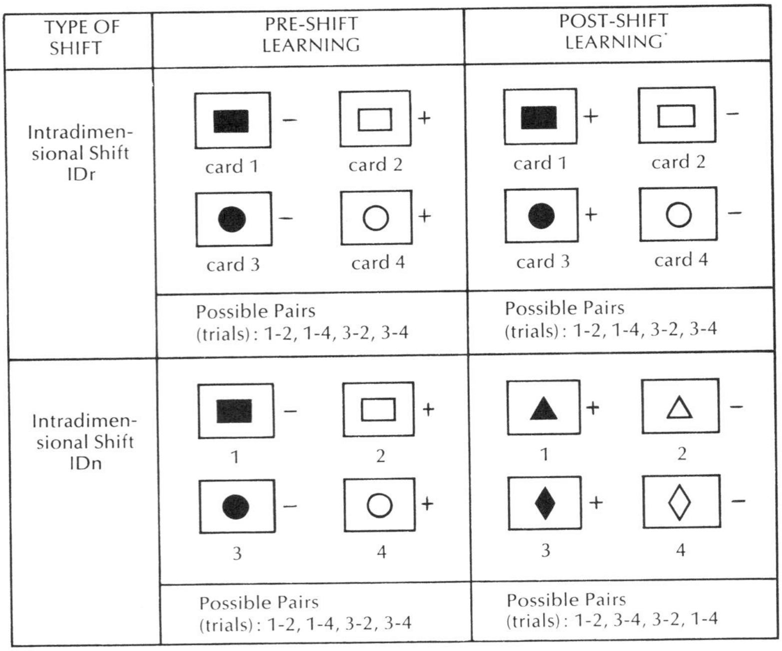

TYPE OF SHIFT	PRE-SHIFT LEARNING	POST-SHIFT LEARNING
Intradimensional Shift IDr	card 1 (black square, −) card 2 (white square, +) card 3 (black circle, −) card 4 (white circle, +)	card 1 (black square, +) card 2 (white square, −) card 3 (black circle, +) card 4 (white circle, −)
	Possible Pairs (trials): 1-2, 1-4, 3-2, 3-4	Possible Pairs (trials): 1-2, 1-4, 3-2, 3-4
Intradimensional Shift IDn	1 (black square, −) 2 (white square, +) 3 (black circle, −) 4 (white circle, +)	1 (black triangle, +) 2 (white triangle, −) 3 (black diamond, +) 4 (white diamond, −)
	Possible Pairs (trials): 1-2, 1-4, 3-2, 3-4	Possible Pairs (trials): 1-2, 3-4, 3-2, 1-4

Fig. 15.A. Simple examples of two types of intradimensional shifts. The IDr shift is called a "reversal shift." In the IDr shift the relevant dimension and cues remain the same between pre- and postshift learning, but the correct cue is shifted (reversed) from white + to black +. In the IDn (new cues) shift the relevant dimension remains the same between pre- and postshift learning, but new cues are introduced for postshift learning (triangles and diamonds) and the correct cue is shifted (white + to black +). Modified from Wolff, 1967.

white. The irrelevant dimension would be shape. If the subject chooses the white square, the experimenter says "yes" or "correct." After the first pair, the subject is presented with another pair and the trials are continued until all possible pairs of one negative and one positive card have been presented at least once. Each time the subject chooses a card with a white shape (either circle or square), the experimenter says "yes" and each time the subject chooses a card with a black shape, the experimenter says "no" or "incorrect." Such a learning task is called a *concept identification learning* task. The trials are continued until the subject indicates that he has identified the concept.

A *concept shift learning* task consists of a concept identification learning task in which at some point (usually without the subject's foreknowledge) the "correct" cues are changed or "shifted." For example, the correct cue might be shifted from white to black so that, for the first part of the task (preshift learning), the experimenter reinforces all white choices and then without warning he reinforces all black choices (postshift learning). Since the relevant dimension is still brightness, the shift from white to black is called an *intradimensional shift* (relevant dimension is constant, but the correct cue is shifted). (See Figure 15.A.)

As another example, the correct cue might be shifted from white to square so that during preshift learning the experimenter reinforces all white choices, and during postshift learning he reinforces all choices of a card with a square on it. In such a case, the relevant dimension is shifted (brightness to shape) so that a shift from white to square is called an *extradimensional shift* (the relevant dimension and, necessarily, the correct cue is shifted). (See Figure 15.B.)

One procedure frequently used with college students is the Wisconsin Card Sorting Task (WCST). The subject is given a pack of 64 cards that vary in color (red, green, yellow, and blue), form (triangles, stars, crosses, and circles), and number (one, two, three, or four figures per card). Four "stimulus" cards are presented. The stimulus cards contain (a) one red triangle, (b) two green stars, (c) three yellow crosses, and (d) four blue circles. The subject must sort the pack of 64 cards into four piles under stimulus cards a through d. For example, when shape is the relevant dimension, the cards containing triangles are piled under a, stars under b, and so forth. With an EDcv type of extradimensional shift, during preshift learning shape may be relevant and then under postshift learning color might be relevant. During postshift learning, the subject must learn to sort the cards with all red cards under a, green cards under b, and so forth.

THEORIES

Two general theories of shift learning have been offered: Kendler and Kendler (1962) and Zeaman and House (1963). Both of these theories are briefly described in Wolff, 1967.

The Kendlers have proposed a two-stage model in which the associations between stimuli and responses are assumed to be mediated by implicit (internal) responses. An external stimulus is assumed to generate an implicit response (such as a verbal label for the stimulus) that provides an internal stimulus that is in turn associated with the overt response of choosing the stimulus; or the internal response acts directly as a cue for the consequent overt response. According to the Kendlers' two-stage theory, any type of extradimensional shift (ED) should be harder to learn than an intradimensional, reversal shift (IDr). ED shifts should be harder to learn than IDr shifts because there are a greater number of implicit-overt stimulus response associations involved in ED shifts than in an IDr shift. For example, in a single IDr shift (Figure 15.A) a subject might implicitly label the correct response in preshift learning as "brightness important, white-right and black-wrong." When presented with cards 1 and 2, the external stimuli (black squares and white squares) are associated with the implicit labels, which in turn are associated with the overt response of choosing the white square and avoiding the black square. During postshift learning, the preceding associations must be extinguished and the new implicit label "brightness important, black-right and white-wrong" would be associated with the correct response. In a simple EDcv shift (Figure 15.B), a subject might develop the same implicit label during preshift learning. During postshift learning, the previous associations must be extinguished and a new dimension must be identified

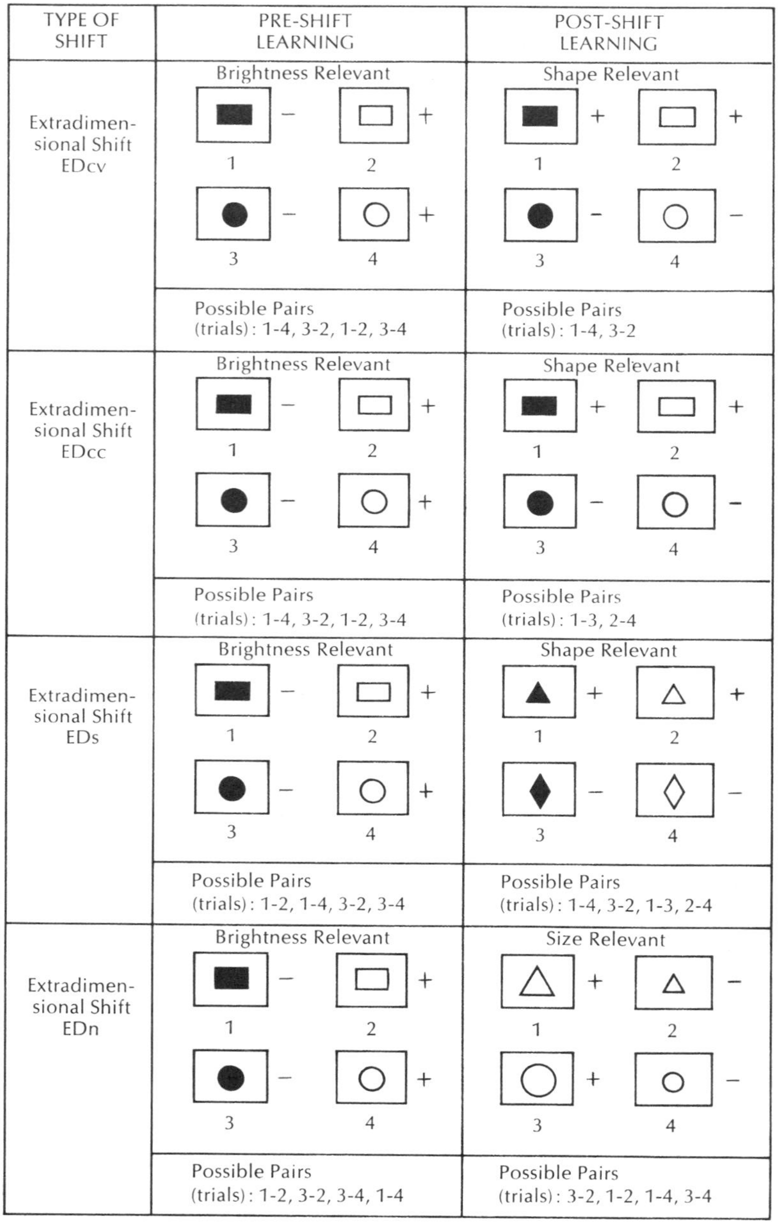

TYPE OF SHIFT	PRE-SHIFT LEARNING	POST-SHIFT LEARNING
Extradimensional Shift EDcv	Brightness Relevant	Shape Relevant
	Possible Pairs (trials): 1-4, 3-2, 1-2, 3-4	Possible Pairs (trials): 1-4, 3-2
Extradimensional Shift EDcc	Brightness Relevant	Shape Relevant
	Possible Pairs (trials): 1-4, 3-2, 1-2, 3-4	Possible Pairs (trials): 1-3, 2-4
Extradimensional Shift EDs	Brightness Relevant	Shape Relevant
	Possible Pairs (trials): 1-2, 1-4, 3-2, 3-4	Possible Pairs (trials): 1-4, 3-2, 1-3, 2-4
Extradimensional Shift EDn	Brightness Relevant	Size Relevant
	Possible Pairs (trials): 1-2, 3-2, 3-4, 1-4	Possible Pairs (trials): 3-2, 1-2, 1-4, 3-4

Fig. 15.B. Simple examples of four types of extradimensional shifts. In the EDcv and EDcc shifts, the cues (circles and squares) remain the same throughout pre- and postshift learning but the relevant dimension shifts (brightness to shape) so that the "correct" cues shift from white to square. The difference between the EDcv and EDcc shifts is that in the EDcv shift the originally relevant dimension (brightness) varies on each trial while in the EDcc shift the originally relevant dimension is constant on each trial

(shape), a new correct cue must be identified (square), new implicit responses developed for the newly correct cues must be formed, and new associations must be developed. In the IDr shift, only a reversal of the correct cue is learned postshift. In the EDcv shift, a change of dimension and cues is involved, each with new implicit responses.

The Kendlers also state that the two-stage theory fits the behavior of college students, but not young children (under about five years of age) or infrahuman subjects. The behavior of animals and young children can be described with a one-stage model in which each physical stimulus (cue) is associated directly with an overt response. The Kendlers suggest that, from nursery-school age on, children are more likely to behave according to the two-stage theory because they are more likely to use verbal mediators. The one-stage model implies that ED shifts of any type would be easier to learn than IDr shifts and about as difficult as IDn shifts. Thus, animals and young children should find reversal shifts (IDr) harder to learn than extradimensional shifts (ED).

Zeaman and House suggest that the subject makes a chain of two responses in concept shift learning, an attention response to the dimension involved followed by an approach response to one of the two cues of the attended dimension. Reinforcement of an approach response makes a change in the probability of attending to the dimension as well as a change in the probability of approaching the cue. Nonreinforcement similarly reduces the two probabilities. The increments due to reinforcement are different from the decrements due to nonreinforcement. Using several rules and assumptions about the original probabilities of attending to the various dimensions and cues, Zeaman and House were able to develop several hypotheses about concept shift behavior. For example, they hypothesize that intradimensional shifts (IDn) should be easier to learn than extradimensional shifts (ED) of any type. They also hypothesize that IDn shifts should be easier to learn than reversal shifts (IDr).

SUMMARY OF DATA ON AGE HYPOTHESES

The Kendlers maintain that intradimensional reversal shifts (IDr) should be easier to learn than extradimensional shifts (ED) for college students. The data (Wolff, 1967) generally support their prediction. Zeaman and House predict that IDn shifts should be learned more easily than ED shifts. Again the data from college students generally support this prediction.

The Kendlers also suggest that animals and children should learn ED shifts faster than reversal shifts (IDr). Wolff (1967) suggests that, while lower animals

---

(1-3 and 2-4). In the EDs shift, the cues are changed between pre- and postshift learning (circles and squares to triangles and diamonds) and the relevant dimension shifts (brightness to shape) so that the correct cue is triangle. In the EDn shift, a new dimension is introduced (size) and the formerly relevant dimension (brightness) is held constant (all white) for postshift learning. In addition, new cues may be introduced (triangles substituted for squares). The newly introduced dimension (size) is relevant and the new correct cue is large. Modified from Wolff, 1967.

may behave according to the model, there is no clear evidence supporting this prediction in terms of young children. Tighe and Tighe (1967) generally found that their four-year-old subjects did learn ED shifts faster than IDr shifts and that the reverse was true for their ten-year-old children. Saravo (1967) also found that four-year-old children tended to learn ED shifts faster than ID shifts when only two dimensions were involved. Saravo's seven-year-old children tended to learn ID shifts faster than ED shifts. These two studies tend to support the Kendlers' prediction. However, Blank (1967) found that IDr shifts were learned faster than EDn shifts by her five-year-old children. Blank used complex, unusual shapes instead of the usual circles and squares.

The Kendlers hypothesized that kindergarten children can be divided into two groups (slow learners and fast learners) and the slow learners should behave according to the single-stage model, while the fast learners should behave like older children (two-stage model). The problem with this hypothesis is that children may have dimensional preferences. For example, one child might like colors rather than shapes while another may prefer to attend to shapes. Thus, the "slow learners" may be only those children whose dimensional preferences interfered with their concept identification learning, and the fast learners may be those children whose dimensional preference happened to facilitate concept identification learning. Saravo (1967) seemed to provide support for the Kendlers' hypothesis. The slow learners found the ED shifts easier to learn than the ID shifts, and the fast learners found the ID shifts easier to learn than the ED shifts. However, in general the data seem neither to support nor refute the Kendlers' hypothesis.

The Kendlers hypothesized that as children grow older, they are more likely to behave according to the two-stage model. Thus, as age increases, IDr shifts should be easier to learn than ED shifts. The Saravo (1967) and Tighe and Tighe (1967) data generally support the hypothesis although there are some negative cases in these studies. Whether or not the irrelevant dimension is constant or variable seems to have an effect on this relationship. Why this should make a difference is unclear. In general, it appears that there is some slight support for the hypothesis.

OTHER VARIABLES

The effects of other variables on concept shift learning are summarized in Wolff (1967). Partial reinforcement of the previously positive dimension during the postshift learning of an extradimensional shift (ED) problem seems to slow down shift learning. Increasing the number of dimensions in a shift problem seems to have an inconsistent effect on the relationship between ED and IDr shift performance in college students. Zeaman and House have made several predictions about the relationship between intelligence and shift performance. In general, the data are inconsistent. Some studies support their prediction that normals should do better than retardates on hard visual discriminations (ID), but other studies do not support the prediction. Apparently, extradimensional shift performance is not related to intelligence.

Overtraining or overlearning on the preshift identification task seems to facilitate reversal shift learning (IDr) for adult subjects, but with children the effect of overlearning depends on the stimulus material. The relationship between degree of original training and ease of shift is very complex.

Design an experiment to study the relationship between intradimensional and extradimensional shift learning. Although most studies have involved human subjects, a number of studies have been conducted with other animals. If young children are available, the age and type of shift problem could be investigated. The effect of overlearning on extradimensional shift performance needs to be examined with college student subjects.

SUGGESTED READING

Blank, M. Effect of stimulus characteristics on dimensional shifting in kindergarten children. *Journal of Comparative and Physiological Psychology,* 1967, *64,* 522–525.

Hirayoshi, I., and Warren, J. M. Overtraining and reversal learning by experimentally naïve kittens. *Journal of Comparative and Physiological Psychology,* 1967, *64,* 507–510.

Kendler, H. H., and Kendler, T. S. Vertical and horizontal processes in problem solving. *Psychological Review,* 1962, *69,* 1–16.

Mandler, J. M. Overtraining and the use of positive and negative stimuli in reversal and transfer. *Journal of Comparative and Physiological Psychology,* 1968, *66,* 110–115.

Marquette, B. W., and Goulet, L. R. Mediated transfer in reversal and nonreversal shift paired-associate learning. *Journal of Experimental Psychology,* 1968, *76,* 89–93.

Martin, E. Short-term memory, individual differences, and shift performance in concept formation. *Journal of Experimental Psychology,* 1968, *76,* 514–520.

Rothblat, L. A., and Wilson, W. A. Jr. Intradimensional and extradimensional shifts in the monkey within and across sensory modalities. *Journal of Comparative and Physiological Psychology,* 1968, *66,* 549–553.

Saravo, A. Effect of number of variable dimensions on reversal and nonreversal shifts. *Journal of Comparative and Physiological Psychology,* 1967, *64,* 93–97.

Tighe, T. J., and Tighe, L. S. Discrimination shift performance of children as a function of age and shift procedure. *Journal of Experimental Psychology,* 1967, *74,* 466–470.

Warren, J. M. An assessment of the reversal index. *Animal Behaviour,* 1967, *15,* 493–498.

Wolff, J. L. Concept-shift and discrimination-reversal learning in humans. *Psychological Bulletin,* 1967, *68,* 369–408.

Zeaman, D., and House, B. J. The role of attention in retardate discrimination learning. In N. R. Ellis (Ed.), *Handbook of mental deficiency.* New York: McGraw-Hill, 1963, pp. 159–223.

TOPIC 16
Incentive Contrast in Instrumental Learning and Differential Conditioning

What would happen if an organism was trained with one amount of reward for a specific response and then the amount of reward was abruptly changed? If the amount was significantly decreased, the organism's behavior might be depressed, and if the amount was increased, the organism might work harder at the task. Possibly, a change from small to large reward might lead to stronger responding than that observed with a consistent larger reward. In human terms, such an increase in responding above the normal large reward level might be called an "elation effect." Similarly, a change from large to small reward might lead to weaker responding than that observed with a consistent small reward. Again, in human terms, such a decrease in responding below the normal small reward level might be called a "depression effect."

Crespi (1942) examined the above questions. He ran rats in a straight runway or I maze (Unit C) with one magnitude of reward for a number of trials. Subsequently, the subjects were shifted to either a higher or lower magnitude of reward. The rats shifted from low to high reward began to run faster than the preshift performance of the subjects that had been running for high reward. Crespi labeled the observed excessive increase in running speed an "elation effect." The rats shifted from high to low reward abruptly began to run *slower* than the preshift speed of the subjects that had been running for low reward. Crespi labeled the observed excessive decrease in running speed a "depression effect."

Because the terms "elation" and "depression" effects seem to be too anthropomorphic, contemporary experimenters refer to the overshooting or "elation" effect as "positive contrast." Also, the undershooting or "depression" effect is called "negative contrast." Positive and negative contrast effects are the two possible kinds of incentive contrast effect.

Collier and Marx (1959) varied the concentration (sweetness) of the sucrose solutions used as rewards in a Skinner box (Unit C). Three groups of rats were given eight days of magazine training (Unit A) under three concentrations (high, medium, and low) of sucrose. Following magazine training, all three groups were given 10 days of bar-press training with a medium concentration as a reward. The group shifted from low to medium bar pressed at a faster rate than the medium-medium control group (a positive contrast effect). The group shifted from high to medium bar pressed at a slower rate than the medium-medium control group (a negative contrast effect).

Bower (1961a) trained three groups of rats in *two* different straight runways (I mazes). One group (1-1) received one food pellet in both alleys. A second group (8-8) received eight food pellets in both alleys. The third group (1-8) received one pellet in one alley and eight pellets in the other. In the eight-pellet alley, the 1-8 group ran slower than the 8-8 group (no positive contrast effect). In the one-pellet alley, the 1-8 group ran faster than the 1-1 group during the early trials. However, during the later trials, the 1-8 group ran slower in the one-pellet alley than the 1-1 group (a negative contrast effect). Thus, no evidence for a positive contrast effect was found; however, some evidence for a negative contrast effect was observed.

Speer and Hill (1965) ran one group of subjects (large-small) in a T maze with a large incentive in one arm and a small incentive in the other. One control group (small-small) was run with small incentives in both arms and a second control group (large-large) was run with large incentives in both arms. On a given trial, stimuli associated with both arms of the T maze were available, but each subject was forced to go into one of the two arms. They found that large-small subjects did *not* run faster to the large incentives than the large-large subjects (no positive contrast). They also found that the large-small subjects did run slower to the small incentive than the small-small subjects (a negative contrast effect).

Fowler (1963) trained two groups of subjects in a Y maze. Both arms of the maze contained sucrose rewards and the concentrations differed between the two arms. One group (8-16) received an 8 percent solution in one arm and a 16 percent solution in the other. The other group (16-32) received a 16 percent solution in one arm and a 32 percent solution in the other. The dependent variable was the running speed in the two arms.

The study provided a test for a "nonspecific" contrast effect. The response to the 16 percent solution could be examined when it was the larger of two rewards (8-16) and when it was the smaller of two rewards (group 16-32). The subjects ran faster to the 16 percent arm when it was the larger concentration (group 8-16) than when it was the smaller concentration (group 16-32). The nonspecific contrast effect could be due to a positive contrast effect for the 8-16 group or a negative contrast effect for the 16-32 group. The research design does not allow the experimenter to determine whether the nonspecific effect is due to negative or positive contrast.

The five studies just described represent the four types of between-groups studies of contrast effects. The four types are: (1) A *successive, nondifferential* conditioning design as represented by the Crespi study. The subjects had to learn a single association between a cue and a response (running the I maze) and were exposed to different successive incentive conditions. (2) A *successive, differential* conditioning design as represented by the Collier and Marx study and the Bower study. The subjects learned two different cue-response associations (magazine training and bar pressing or running in two alleys) and were exposed to different successive incentive conditions. (3) A *simultaneous, differential, specific* effect design as represented by the Speer and Hill study. The subjects had to learn two different cue-response associations (two different arms of the T maze) and were simultaneously exposed to different incentive conditions. (4) A *simultaneous, differential, nonspecific* effect design as represented by the Fowler study. The subjects learned two different cue-response associations (two arms of a Y maze) and were simultaneously exposed to different incentive conditions. The fourth type is a variant on the third type. The names of the designs were developed by Black (1968) and Dunham (1968). All of these types refer to discrete trial learning situations.

SUMMARY OF RESEARCH RESULTS

Since the original Crespi study, the successive, nondifferential design has provided little evidence for positive contrast. Apparently, Crespi and the few other studies that did obtain evidence of positive contrast did not train the subjects long enough before the incentive shifts were made. The subsequent over-shooting observed for the upward shift groups was probably due to the expected increases in performance associated with increased training time. Studies that have controlled for the insufficient learning factor have failed to find evidence of positive contrast (Schrier, 1967).

Successive, differential studies have also failed to find evidence for positive contrast. The one exception is the Collier and Marx study. However, it is possible that in that study the differences in sucrose concentration between the three groups may have been confounded with deprivation differences due to the eight days of magazine training (Dunham and Kilps, 1969; and Dunham, 1967).

No consistent evidence for a positive contrast effect has been discovered with a simultaneous, differential, specific design. Nonspecific contrast effects have been observed with the simultaneous, differential, nonspecific designs. Since little evidence for the positive contrast effect has been observed in well controlled experiments, it appears that the observed nonspecific effect is due to negative contrast.

With some exceptions (Beery and Black, 1968), studies using any of the first three types of designs have found negative contrast effects. As indicated, the nonspecific contrast effect is assumed to be a function of the negative contrast. The shift from low to high magnitude of incentive leads to an increase in performance to the level of subjects that have been working for a high magnitude incentive. The shift from high to low magnitude of incentive leads to a decrease in performance below the level of subjects that have been working for a low magnitude incentive. In summary, negative contrast effects have been consistently observed with the *between-groups* designs (Chapter 3), but positive contrast effects have seldom been observed. It should be noted that Dunham's (1968) review indicates that positive contrast is usually found with *within-group* designs.

THEORIES OF CONTRAST EFFECTS

There have been three different types of theories involved with accounting for the contrast effects. One theory (the "absolute" theory) assumes that the behavioral effects of a given incentive depend *entirely* on the physical characteristics of the incentive. A second theory (the "relative" theory) assumes that the behavioral effects of a given incentive depend on the characteristics of the incentive as perceived by the subject and the subject's immediate previous experience with incentives in the same or similar situations. The third theory (the "modified-absolute" theory) assumes that the behavioral effects of a given incentive depend on the physical characteristics of the incentive *and* the subject's immediate previous experience with incentives in the same or similar situations. All three of the theories are concerned with quantitative but *not* qualitative shifts in incentives. The three theories are reviewed in Black (1968).

Design an experiment to test for the presence of incentive contrast effects. The magnitude of incentives might be varied in terms of weight, size, or number of units of incentive. Alternatively, the amount of delay before receiving an incentive after task completion, the percentage of reinforcement, or the rate of reinforcement might be manipulated. While laboratory rats have been most frequently used as subjects, there is no reason why other species could not be used. For example, tokens or money could be used with students.

SUGGESTED READING

Beery, R. G., and Black, R. W. Reversal of magnitude of reward in differential conditioning. *Psychological Record*, 1968, *18*, 179–183.
Black, R. W. Shifts in magnitude of rewards and contrast effects in instrumental and selective learning: A reinterpretation. *Psychological Review*, 1968, 75, 114–126.

Bower, G. H. A contrast effect in differential conditioning. *Journal of Experimental Psychology*, 1961, *62*, 196–199.

Capaldi, E. J., and Lynch, D. Repeated shifts in reward magnitude: Evidence in favor of an associational and absolute (noncontextual) interpretation. *Journal of Experimental Psychology*, 1967, 75, 226–235.

Collier, G., and Marx, M. H. Changes in performance as a function of shifts in the magnitude of reinforcement. *Journal of Experimental Psychology*, 1959, 57, 305–309.

Crespi, L. P. Quantitative variation of incentive and performance in the white rat. *American Journal of Psychology*, 1942, *55*, 467–517.

Dunham, P. J. Incentive contrast and deprivation factors in a discrete-trial bar-press situation. *Journal of Comparative and Physiological Psychology*, 1967, *64*, 485–487.

Dunham, P. J. Contrasted conditions of reinforcement: A selective critique. *Psychological Bulletin*, 1968, *69*, 295–315.

Dunham, P. J., and Kilps, B. Shifts in magnitude of reinforcement: Confounded factors or contrast effects. *Journal of Experimental Psychology*, 1969, *79*, 373–374.

Fowler, R. L., Jr. Magnitude and delay of reinforcement in spatial discrimination learning. Unpublished doctoral dissertation, University of Tennessee, 1963. Reported in Black, R. W. Shifts in magnitude of reward and contrast effects in instrumental and selective learning: A reinterpretation. *Psychological Review*, 1968, 75, 114–126.

Schrier, A. M. Effects of an upward shift in amount of reinforcer on runway performance of rats. *Journal of Comparative and Physiological Psychology*, 1967, *64*, 490–492.

Speer, N. E., and Hill, W. F. Adjustment to new reward: Simultaneous and successive contrast effects. *Journal of Experimental Psychology*, 1965, *70*, 510–519.

tOPiC 17
Verbal Learning

Every student of a foreign language is familiar with the problem of learning a new vocabulary list. The task is usually approached by first going through the list of foreign words paired with their English translation. The English words are then concealed, and the student tries to give the correct translation for each foreign word, confirming or correcting items he is not sure about. He will continue this process for several trials until all of the words are correct.

This same procedure is used by psychologists to investigate the human learning process (Unit B). The procedure is called a "paired-associate" task, since it consists of learning the association between paired items (Figure 17.A). The psychologist may use different verbal material, such as nonsense syllables, and may carefully control the length of time spent on each item, but the basic process remains the same. Unless the material is very easy, the subjects require several trials to learn any paired-associate task. They often learn several items on the first trial, but other items seem very difficult and take several trials before they are correct. If one were to graph the number of items correct on each trial, he will find that his data approximates the classic learning curve. (See Chapter 7, Figure 7.9.)

STIMULUS LETTERS	RESPONSE NUMBERS
A	6
M	18
CC	30
RR	4
STIMULUS SYLLABLES	RESPONSE SYLLABLES
RAJ	CEQ
KUC	MOZ
BIH	TAH
XIP	ZEJ

Fig. 17.A.   Paired-Associate Stimuli.

LEARNING THEORIES

Learning theorists have offered two different theories to account for the classic learning curve. Both theories agree that the items are learned once they are correctly associated by the subject, but they disagree concerning the state of learning immediately prior to that correct trial. The *incremental theory* says that each time the subject sees the two items together, the association between them becomes stronger. When enough trials have occurred that the new association is stronger than any other in the subject's repertoire, a correct response occurs on that and any subsequent trials. Thus, learning is a continuous process of strengthening the association throughout the learning trials.

According to the *all-or-none* theory, the association between each pair of items is not learned until the trial on which the subject gets it correct. When he makes the correct prediction and is reinforced by seeing the two words together, the association is formed all (100 percent) at once. Several trials are necessary to learn a list of items, because a subject must go through the "trial and error" process of saying the initial correct response for each item. Thus, a learning curve is the result of accumulating a list of associations, each individual item remaining completely unlearned until the trial when it becomes completely learned. The learning process itself is not gradual, but all or none.

ROCK'S EXPERIMENT

In order to choose between the theories, one must examine the characteristics of the association between the items *prior* to the trial on which they are considered learned. Rock (1957) designed a paired-associate experiment to make such an evaluation. He reasoned that, if the incremental theory is correct, then items that had been experienced previously by a subject should be easier to learn than items seen for the first time, since experienced items would already have some association strength; while the all-or-none position would predict that previous experience is irrelevant to the learning process. Consequently, Rock had each of two groups of subjects learn an equal-length list of paired-associate words. The control group was given a list of pairs that were repeated in random order until mastered. The experimental group started out with the same list and was required to learn in the same way, *except* that any pair that was *missed* was replaced by a new pair drawn from a pool of paired items. He found that there was no difference in rate of learning between the two groups. Rock concluded that his data lent support to the all-or-none theory for several reasons. He pointed out that the association strength being built up for the experienced items as predicted by the incremental theory would suggest an obvious difference in favor of the control group. In addition, the items missed by the experimental group would have some association strength associated with them to provide interference in subsequent pairs. Also, some of the items may have actually been learned on the trial they were replaced, so the subjects may have had to learn a "longer" list that would further slow their learning.

The most frequent criticism of Rock's study is that the replacement condition may have allowed the subjects to learn all of the "easy" items in the list and the hard ones were replaced by easier ones. If the subjects continued the process, they could eventually "select" a list of all easy items. It is not known that they did select the "easier" items; it may have happened. Although it is improbable to encounter two opposing factors exactly canceling one another, it is possible that the item selection process exactly offset the incremental learning in the constant condition. Therefore, the lack of difference in the performance of the two groups may not be contrary to the incremental theory.

Devise an experiment that will examine the incremental, all-or-none controversy and attempt to control for the item selection problem. That is, somehow the subjects should not be allowed to select the items easier to learn. The design solution has not been discovered by learning researchers. Perhaps a yoked-control design is appropriate (Chapter 4).

SUGGESTED READING

Bower, G. H. Application of a model to paired associate learning. *Psychometrica*, 1961, *26*, 255–280.

Estes, W. K. Learning theory and the new "mental chemistry." *Psychological Review*, 1960, *67*, 207–223.

Estes, W. K., Hopkins, B. L., and Crothers, E. J. All-or-none and conservation effects in the learning and retention of paired-associates. *Journal of Experimental Psychology,* 1960, *60,* 329–339.

Hilgard, E. R., and Bower, G. H. *Theories of learning.* (3d ed.) New York: Appleton, 1966.

Jones, J. E. All-or-none vs. incremental learning. *Psychological Review,* 1962, *69,* 156–160.

Lockhead, G. R. A re-evaluation of evidence of one-trial associative learning. *American Journal of Psychology,* 1961, *74,* 590–595.

Rock, I. The role of repetition in associative learning. *American Journal of Psychology,* 1957, *70,* 186–193.

Rock, I., and Heimer, W. Further evidence of one-trial associative learning. *American Journal of Psychology,* 1959, *72,* 1–16.

Underwood, B. J., and Keppel, G. One trial learning? *Journal of Verbal Learning and Verbal Behavior,* 1962, *1,* 1–13.

UNDERGRADUATE
RESEARCH PROJECTS:
EXAMPLES

INTRODUCTION The following section provides actual examples of student research. The students were all undergraduates in psychology classes between the years 1968 and 1972. Some were freshmen, others were juniors and seniors; but most were sophomores when the research was done. Most of the students had taken one elementary statistics class. The studies represent the results of a lot of sweat and worry coupled with the self-satisfaction that goes along with the successful completion of a research project. The reports were abstracted and copy edited in order to save space. The projects illustrate a wide range of complexity in research design, beginning with a N = 1 time series design and ending with a combined repeated-measures factorial and before-after three-group design.[1]

[1] If you complete an interesting project begun as part of an experimental psychology class, please send a copy of your report to K. L. Beauchamp for possible future inclusion in the text. The return of unused projects cannot be guaranteed, so do not send your original copy.

PROJECT 1
Verbal Reinforcement of Movement in a Catatonic Schizophrenic

PEGGY GIFFIN

University of the Pacific, 1969

Numerous studies have been conducted on the effects of reinforcement in conditioning appropriate behavior in severely disturbed patients (Ullmann and Krasner, 1965). The classic recent example of this effect is an experiment conducted by Isaacs, Thomas, and Goldiamond (1960). In this experiment, two catatonic schizophrenics were conditioned to verbalize. The experimenters used chewing gum as a reinforcement for a verbalization. The purpose of the present study was to determine the effect of verbal reinforcements and encouragement on motor movements in a catatonic schizophrenic.

The experimental hypothesis was that words of praise and/or encouragement spoken to a subject after movement would increase the movements over time.

METHOD[1]

Subject

One male subject, age 57, was used in the experiment. The subject had been admitted to a state hospital in 1933 and was diagnosed as a chronic catatonic schizophrenic. The patient was capable of movement, but usually sat in one position all day. He would take short walks to the toilet and bed, but aside from these movements, he would sit motionless.

Apparatus

Thirteen building blocks and a card table were used in the experiment. The experiment consisted of eight one-half-hour sessions. At each session the 13 blocks were placed on a table in front of the patient and the experimenter began to build with them. Any movement by the patient was verbally reinforced.

RESULTS AND DISCUSSION

The number of movements per half-hour session increased from two during the first session to 351 during the eighth session. The number of movements were plotted against the number of sessions and the slope of the line was calculated. The slope was tested by a t test against a slope of zero and was found to be significant ($p <$ .001).

The data indicate that verbal reinforcement is effective in modifying catatonic behavior. Because of the nature of individual patients, the specific method may not generalize to other patients. The success of this particular experiment gives rise to questions such as: Is verbal reinforcement as effective as nonverbal reinforcement? Are female experimenters more effective with male patients and would the same technique work with other patients? Only further research can answer these questions.

REFERENCES

Isaacs, W., Thomas, J., and Goldiamond, I. Application of operant conditioning to reinstate verbal behavior in psychotics. *Journal of Speech and Hearing Disorders*, 1960, *25*, 8–12.

Ullmann, L. P., and Krasner, L. *Case studies in behavior modification*. New York: Holt, Rinehart and Winston, 1965.

---

[1] Editors' note: The design is a "N = 1" time series design (Chapter 3). The experimenter has used prior reports on the subject as a baseline with which to compare the effect of verbal reinforcement. She should have collected her own baseline measurements over several days before instituting verbal reinforcement. It is possible that her presence alone (without reinforcement) would have yielded the change in movement behavior.

PROJECT 2
Tactual Perception in Deaf and Hearing Children

MARCI PHELAN

University of the Pacific, 1972

It is commonly believed that if a child is sensory deprived in one area (e.g., deaf, blind), he will exhibit greater acuity in his remaining senses. In other words, if the child is deaf, his remaining senses of sight, touch, smell, etc. will become more acute than those of the normal hearing child. The increased acuity might be due to increased organ sensitivity, greater attention paid to the other senses, or more efficient usage of the information derived from the other senses.

METHOD[1]

In the present study, 20 subjects (10 deaf and 10 hearing) between the ages of 9 and 12 participated in a tactual discrimination task.

[1] Editors' Note: The design was a static group comparison design (Chapter 4). The author indicates some of the problems of accounting for the differences observed when such a design is used.

Six styrofoam cups were covered completely with one of three different textures of sandpaper: fine, medium, or coarse. There were two cups of each type. The deaf and hearing children were presented with three cups, two were the same texture and one was different. It was hypothesized that the deaf children would be able to pick out the different one with more accuracy than the hearing children.

Each subject was tested separately. The experimenter explained to each subject before testing him (verbally to the hearing and in signs to the deaf), that there were six cups, and that they had three different textures. The subject was allowed to touch each cup and indicate that he saw which were coarse, medium, and fine. The experimenter took two fine cups and one coarse, and pointed out that one was different from the others letting the subject touch the three cups once again.

Candy was placed under the different cup while the subject watched. The subject was told that he would be blindfolded and that the cups would be mixed up. By touching, he was to find the cup that was different and pick it up. If he found the right one, he would get the candy.

The test was repeated three times with each subject, using different groups of cups each time. The groups of cups were presented in the following order: fine vs. coarse, fine vs. medium, and medium vs. coarse. The easiest discrimination problem was presented first in order to avoid discouraging the subjects.

RESULTS AND DISCUSSION

Each child could make three correct responses (3 yes), two correct responses (2 yes, 1 no), one correct response (1 yes, 2 no) or no correct response (3 no). The binomial probabilities of each event are $\frac{1}{8}$, $\frac{3}{8}$, $\frac{3}{8}$, and $\frac{1}{8}$, respectively. If the choices of 10 children were random, there would be 1.25, 3.75, 3.75, and 1.25 occurrences of 3 yes, 2 yes, 1 yes, and 0 yes, respectively. The hearing group's correct responses were 1, 4, 4, and 1, respectively. The distribution of frequencies of correct responses by the hearing group was as close to chance as possible with 10 children. The deaf children's frequencies were 6 (3 yes), 1 (2 yes), 2 (1 yes), 1 (no yes). These observed frequencies were compared to the expected frequencies using the one-group chi-square test. The calculated value of chi-square was 20.94 with 3 df. The probability of a chi-square equal to or greater than 20.94 with 3 df is less than 0.001. Therefore, the deaf-group performed significantly better than chance and the difference between the hearing and deaf group's behaviors is not likely to be due to chance.

The experimenter noticed that during the instruction period, the deaf subjects paid closer attention and were more anxious to physically enter into the "game" (they always took full advantage of the opportunity to feel the cups, while often the hearing children were reluctant to really "get in there and feel").

As a rule, the deaf children spent more time touching the cups and did not make decisions as hastily as did some of the hearing children. Two of the deaf children and one of the hearing children touched each cup briefly and then immediately responded correctly.

The deaf children have had emphasis put on visual and tactual perception in everyday situations, and have perhaps learned to use tactual information more effectively than hearing children. One problem with the procedure in the present study was that, because their instructions were received visually rather than aurally, the deaf children had to look at the experimenter during instructions. In almost every case, the experimenter had the deaf subjects' full attention. It was not possible to determine if the hearing subjects attended to the instructions to the same extent.

It can be concluded that because the deaf students were so consistently superior to the hearing students in their responses, they were able to distinguish minor tactual differences more efficiently than the hearing students. However, it is impossible to determine whether this greater ability on the part of the deaf subjects is due to a more acute development of tactual perception or just a greater ability to make better use of the tactual information than the hearing children.

If the difference is due to an ability of the deaf children to make better use of the available information, we can ask why they have this ability. It could be due to the fact that these children in their school projects (and maybe at home), are more visually and tactually oriented. For instance, in the class of subjects tested, the teacher always makes a point of having the students feel the texture of objects introduced in the classroom. When they grew plants, they felt the seeds, dirt, and leaves, which might not be emphasized in a class of hearing students.

Previous experience with games might also have influenced the results of the present study. The deaf group may have had more experience with tactual discrimination games. On the other hand, the hearing group may have had more experience with such games but treated them like a "guessing game" instead of really putting all of their effort into it. Or, if they had had much previous experience, they might take the "just another game" attitude, which would account for the fact that they did not spend as much time feeling the cups before making their choices (of course, if they couldn't detect any difference in textures, that would account for the fact that they did not take the time the deaf subjects did).

Amount of previous contact with the experimenter could have affected the performance of the subjects. The experimenter had worked with the deaf subjects, but had had only casual contact with the hearing subjects. Nevertheless, it appears that the deaf children were more accurate at detecting tactual differences than normal hearing children.

PROJECT 5
The Relationship between Color Preference as Measured on the Luscher Color Test and Personality as Measured on the Eysenck Personality Inventory Test

NANCY SMITH
University of the Pacific, 1972

Luscher (Scott, 1969) theorized that color likes and dislikes have much psychological meaning and tell a lot about a person's personality. There is a need to investigate the relationship between color preference and personality traits. It was hypothesized that undergraduate female students would prefer the color or colors which are supposed to correspond to their personality type. By knowing one score, either on a personality test or the color test, it might be possible for a researcher to predict the other one.

METHOD[1]

Twenty female, undergraduate college students were selected from South-West Hall of the University of the Pacific. All 20 subjects were given the Eysenck Per-

[1] Editors' Note: A limitation of the study is the relatively small number of Ss. Significant correlation coefficients are unlikely, particularly with personality tests, when so few subjects are used.

sonality Inventory Test to determine their personality type. The test measures two characteristics of personality types from which Eysenck says all personality traits can be derived. The two characteristics are extroversion-introversion and high-low neuroticism.

Next, the subjects were given the Luscher Color Test which consists of eight colored squares arranged on a piece of white paper. The colors used were: neutral gray, dark blue, forest green, orange-red, bright yellow, violet, brown, and black. Each color was given a number: 0, 1, 2, 3, 4, 5, 6, 7, respectively. Each subject ranked her color preference zero through seven. Both tests were given one after the other to each subject individually and then collected. The research design was a correlational design. The experimenter constructed a scatterplot of the subjects' scores and determined the Pearson product-moment correlation coefficients (r). Extroversion-introversion and high-low neuroticism were correlated separately for each color. Eight colors under each of the two personality traits made 16 correlation coefficients that were calculated.

RESULTS AND DISCUSSION

The Pearson product-moment correlation coefficients for each set of preference scores and personality test scores are contained in Table 1. All the (r) values were too small to be significant, at $\alpha= 0.05$. The values of r appear to randomly vary around a correlation of 0.00. Since the correlations were not significant, it doesn't

TABLE 1. Correlation Coefficient Results of the Study.

	Extroversion	*Neuroticism*
Gray	.29	− .01
Blue	.07	.39
Green	− .19	.31
Orange	.10	− .25
Yellow	.29	− .31
Violet	− .33	.18
Brown	− .01	− .11
Black	− .31	− .34

matter what the Luscher test predicts in terms of personality type. The highest correlation reached was .39 (blue and neuroticism) which should have been a high negative correlation according to Luscher. The results of the present study do not support the hypothesis that the two sets of scores would be related. Further research might take into consideration the possibility of choosing a personality test that would measure a larger number of personality traits.

REFERENCES

Scott, I. A. (trans. and ed.) *The Luscher color test.* New York: Random House, 1969.

PROJECT 4
The Effects of Hypnotic Induction versus High Motivation on Oral Temperature Increase

THOMAS JACKSON AND STEVEN PASHKO

University of the Pacific, 1972

(Abstract of a paper presented at the Western Psychological Association Convention, Anaheim, California, April 1973)

According to Timney and Barber (1969), hypnotic induction produces an increase in oral temperature. Barber (1970) maintains that the hypnotic state is simply a state of high motivation and that behavior observed under hypnosis can be duplicated by producing high motivation with verbal instructions. The present study was performed to compare the effects of high motivation induced by verbal instructions (as used by Barber, 1970) with the effects of hypnotic induction on oral temperature measurements.

METHOD[1]

Thirty-three subjects were randomly assigned to three groups: (1) control group—given instructions to read silently for 10 minutes, (2) high motivation group—given verbal instructions to induce motivation (these instructions included statements that the subjects could raise their oral temperature if they really tried, that previous Ss had been able to easily, and that they should really try hard), and (3) hypnotic induction group—given hand levitation suggestion (a method involving the suggestion that a hand will raise by itself; a procedure used to induce hypnosis—Hilgard, 1965). The dependent variable was oral temperature measured in degrees Farenheit to the nearest 0.1 of a degree. The procedure consisted of two temperature measures 20 minutes apart followed by the appropriate treatment and an immediate third temperature measure. During the 20-minute interval between the first two measures, all subjects read quietly to allow oral temperature to stabilize.

RESULTS

An analysis of variance was performed on the difference scores (temperature after treatment minus second temperature before treatment) for each group. There was a significant difference between groups ($F = 5.04$, $df = 2/30$, $p < .05$). Scheffe's method for multiple comparisons showed that the mean temperature increase for the hypnotic induction group was signifiantly greater than the mean increases of the high motivation and control groups ($t = 7.50$, $df = 1/10$, $p < .05$, for both comparisons). The high motivation and control group means did not differ from each other.

The data support the hypothesis that hypnotic induction facilitates oral temperature increase. They do not support the hypothesis that high motivation induced by instructions has the same effects as hypnosis.

REFERENCES

Barber, T. X. *Suggested "hypnotic" behavior: The trance paradigm vs. an alternative paradigm.* Harding, Mass.: Medfield Foundation, 1970.
Gilbert, J. E., and Barber, T. X. Effects of hypnotic induction, motivational suggestion, and level of suggestibility on cognitive performance. *The International Journal of Clinical and Experimental Hypnosis,* 1972, *20* (3), 156–168.
Hilgard, E. R. *Hypnotic susceptibility.* New York: Harcourt Brace Jovanovich, 1965.
Timney, B. M., and Barber, T. X. Hypnotic induction and oral temperature; *The International Journal of Clinical and Experimental Hypnosis,* 1969, *17* (2), 121–132.

[1] Editors' note: The design used was a multilevel design (Chapter 5). The procedure for inducing high motivation and hypnotic induction is particularly susceptible to the Rosenthal experimenter effect (Chapter 11).

PROJECT 5
How to Control Behavior in Used-Car Dealers

DON BLAKEY
University of the Pacific, 1968

According to nonscientific observation, people rely on first impressions, and in an economic relationship an individual is treated in accordance with the first impression he makes. The present study investigated the relationship between a customer's style of dress and knowledge of cars and the prices quoted by used-car salesmen. It was predicted that used-car salesmen would lower their initial price of an automobile if a customer gave the impression that he was knowledgeable about cars and would raise the price of a car if the customer gave the impression that he did not know much about cars.

METHOD[1]

Six used-car lots were chosen and one salesman was selected from each lot. There were two levels of two independent variables: (1) style of dress (a "potential cus-

[1] Editors' note: The design used was a 2×2 factorial design (Chapter 5). The problem of generalizing from six nonrandomly selected salesmen to all used-car salesmen should be recognized.

tomer" wearing slacks and a sports coat or wearing Levi's, tennis shoes and a windbreaker) and (2) knowledge of cars displayed (a "potential customer" acted very knowledgeable, or did not act knowledgeable.) Each salesman was approached and asked about a particular car by four different people representing the four possible combinations of the two levels of the independent variables (casually dressed, knowledgeable man; formally dressed, knowledgeable man; casually dressed, nonknowledgeable man; and formally dressed, nonknowledgeable man). All conversations were tape recorded with hidden recorders.

RESULTS AND DISCUSSION

The results indicated that the type of dress did not affect the price quoted for a car. Knowledge of cars was a significant variable. In every case the more knowledgeable person was quoted a lower price than the less knowledgeable person regardless of his dress. The probability of all six salesmen quoting a lower price equals 0.0156 by a one-tailed sign test.

It was assumed from the results that the final price of a car may be determined by the salesman's assessment of the customer's knowledge of cars. The salesman will set the price of a car higher than he expects to sell it for so that in the bargaining process he can take the price down. If the buyer does not bargain, the dealer makes out!

REFERENCES

Day, R. What not to look for when buying a used car. *Popular Science*, 1968, 84–87.
Jackson, C. R. *How to buy a used car.* New York: Chilton, 1965.

PROJECT 6
Embarrassment and Its Relation
to Eye Contact in a Dyadic Encounter

KAREN BARBARIO

University of the Pacific, 1972

Embarrassment is a special, short-lived, but often acute, loss of self-esteem. Man's behavior in social gatherings is markedly a pervasive desire to maintain "face" (Goffman, 1955) and people will generally go to great lengths to avoid an action or situation that might produce embarrassment.

In social situations a private awareness of a self-deficiency can also be sufficient to produce embarrassment because, apparently, such an awareness leads an individual to imagine that others perceive him as deficient (Modigliani, 1967). Self-awareness of a deficiency in social situations can be described as shyness and may lead to ungraceful action that is inhibited and guarded, or to actions that lack spontaneity. A person may find himself without anything to say, or unable to meet the gaze of another person. When he does say something, he may stumble or stammer (Sattler, 1965).

452

The embarrassed person usually is strongly motivated to conceal the fact of his arousal (Excline, Gray, and Schuette, 1965). An embarrassed person will avert his eyes and reduce the amount of eye contact (Modigliani, 1971).

The amount of mutual visual interaction between two persons varies directly with the positiveness or negativeness of the effect characterizing their relationship (Excline and Winters, 1965). During social interaction, people look each other in the eye, repeatedly but for short periods. The longer the glance, the more anxiety is aroused (Ellsworth and Carlsmith, 1968). Studies by Gibson and Pick (1963) have shown that a person can perceive with a high degree of accuracy whether or not another person is looking at him directly in the face.

The present study investigated the amount of eye contact maintained by male and female college students in a dyadic interaction (two person conversation). There were two interaction conditions; one involving embarrassing topics and one involving neutral material. Eye contact was defined as a one-to-one mutual glance in the eye line of regard. Any look in any other direction is aversion of the eyes. Embarrassing and more personal topics were defined as those dealing with sex and neutral material was defined as discussion about goals and recreation. The two levels of the independent variable of subject matter of conversation were innocuous (neutral) topics versus embarrassing topics. The dependent variable was the observed visual behavior of the subjects. The experimental hypothesis was that undergraduate, male and female, college students would look at an interviewer significantly less during a conversation consisting of personal and embarrassing questions than during a neutral conversation.

METHOD

Twenty volunteers (10 male and 10 female) from a freshman psychology course were randomly assigned to one of two treatment groups with the restriction that each group contained five males and five females.

The design that was used in this experiment was a 2×2 factorial design with two levels of sex of subject and two levels of content of questions.

A stopwatch was used to limit the length of each individual conversation and to estimate and measure the time of returned eye contact.

Procedure [1]

The experimenter (E) visited a lecture class and told the students that she was conducting a study designed to learn more about the value of face-to-face interviews as a method of obtaining information about other's opinions. E then asked for volunteers to participate in the experiment and passed around a sign-up sheet. E set up an appointment with each subject to last approximately 15 minutes; the interview

[1] Editors' note: The experimenter was simultaneously the embarrassment stimulus, conversationalist, and dependent variable measurer. The possibility for measurement error and experimenter bias is very great. Any replication must have an independent (and unbiased) observer recording the gaze behavior of the subjects.

between the E and each S was held in a lounge. At the beginning of each appointment, the S was seated on the couch while the E sat on a chair across the coffee table from the S. Each S was reminded again of the purpose of the study and told that the personal information that the E obtained would be entirely irrelevant to the study and would be discarded immediately after the data was recorded. (See Chapter 11.) The E also told each subject that she was interested in their first reactions, not a carefully thought-out synthesis, and that she wished them to say all they could about the topic to fill the time span allotted for each question.

The interview consisted of five conversations incited by the five questions posed by the E to each S. These five questions were embarrassing or innocuous, depending on the group assignment of the S. The questions were as follows:

Questions designed to maintain neutrality: (1) What did you do last summer? (2) What are your educational and/or career goals? (3) What is your favorite sport and why is it such? (4) What is your favorite TV program or movie and why? (5) What are the various things you like to do during your leisure hours?

Questions designed to provoke embarrassment: (1) What are your views on premarital sex? Why or why not would you engage in it? (2) What are your feelings on masturbation? (3) You are in a coed dorm and you get caught nude in the bathroom by someone of the opposite sex. What would you do to enhance or detract from this situation? (4) Have you ever desired to have intimate contact with a member of your same sex? If not, how would you react if someone approached you in this type of situation? (5) How would you feel and what would you do if you couldn't arouse and excite your sex partner?

Each individual conversation lasted for 2 minutes. The E attempted to direct the conversation, not actively engage in it; therefore, the E's verbalization was minimal. The E gazed continuously at the S's eyes. Since the E could not utilize an observer to record the exact amount of returned eye contact, she set up an interval scale to measure eye contact after each 2-minute conversation. This was the only way the E could efficiently measure the S's eye contact in the absence of an observer while E retained her constant eye contact. The interval scale was as follows:

(1) Minimum: S gives E three or less short glances
(2) Below Average: S looks at E less than one minute but gives more than three glances
(3) Average: S looks at E collectively for half the time (one minute)
(4) Above Average: S looks at E more than half the time but looks away more than three glances
(5) Maximum: S looks away from E three or less short glances

At the end of each complete interview, the E asked the S to not discuss the content of the interview with anybody else. The E also told S that she would inform him as to the results of the experiment when they were completely analyzed.

Control of Secondary and Error Variance

There were many sources of secondary and error variance in this experiment:

1. The E was female and there was no male conducting the same experiment to see if this factor has an influence or not. The E controlled for this by assign-

ing an equal number of men and women to each group so that the data was influenced equally.

2. Results of Excline, Gray, and Schuette (1965) showed that subjects looked at the interviewer more when listening than when speaking to her (ratio of 3:1 but E chose to lump the timing of both together. The timing was constant between and within groups.

3. Hopefully, randomization equally distributed those who did or did not like to engage in conversation but this factor was probably controlled by the simple fact that all S's were volunteers.

RESULTS AND DISCUSSION

The mean scores for each subject across the five questions were then used as data to perform an independent t-test which revealed that there was significantly less eye contact during conversations stemming from embarrassing questions than during those initiated by neutral questions. ($t = 2.98$, $df = 18$, one-tailed $p < .01$).

Regardless of type of question with the exception of question 5, the amount of returned eye contact consistently increased as the series of questions progressed. Males had a higher average amount of eye contact than females in the embarrassing conversation ($\overline{X} = 2.8$ and 1.9) while the females had a higher average amount of eye contact than males in the neutral conversation ($\overline{X} = 3.9$ and 3.2).

Gibson and Pick (1963) reported that the amount of eye contact in a dyadic interaction has a significant effect on the subject's reaction to both the situation and the other person, and that this effect depends on the verbal content of the interaction. The obtained data suggests that embarrassing topics will decrease the amount of eye contact in comparison to neutral topics.

It is interesting to note that the male subjects in the embarrassing conversations had a higher mean score than the female subjects. This supports Excline's (1963) findings of differences among men and women in the exchange of mutual glances. The fact that the present experimenter was female may play some part in these data. The experiment should be conducted again by a male to allow for comparative analysis. However, the fact that, in the neutral group, females had a higher mean score suggests something about the male's "embarrassment potential." Males tended to feel more free and confident about expressing their views on sex. It is the opinion of this experimenter that further research related to this observation is needed. There were no "minimum" scores in the neutral conversation data which suggests that the subjects felt a definite need for some degree of visual interaction with the interviewer.

REFERENCES

Ellsworth, P., and Carlsmith, J. M. Effects of eye contact and verbal content on affective response to dyadic interaction. *Journal of Personality and Social Psychology*, 1968, *10*, 15–20.

Excline, R. V. Explorations in the process of person perception: Visual interaction in relation to competition, sex, and need for affiliation. *Journal of Personality*, 1963, *31*, 1–20.

Excline, R. V., Gray, D., and Schuette, D. Visual behavior in a dyad as affected by interview content and sex of respondent. *Journal of Personality and Social Psychology*, 1965, *1*, 201–209.

Excline, R. V., and Winters, L. C. Affective relations and mutual glances in dyads. In S. S. Tomkins and C. E. Izard (Eds.), *Affect, cognition, and personality.* New York: Springer, 1965, 319–350.

Gibson, J. J., and Pick, A. D. Perception of another person's looking behavior. *American Journal of Psychology*, 1963, *76*, 386–394.

Goffman, E. On facework. *Psychiatry*, 1955, *18*, 213–231.

Modigliani, A. Embarrassment and social influence. *Dissertation Abstracts International*, 1967, *28A*, 295A.

Modigliani, A. Embarrassment, facework, and eye contact: Testing a theory of embarrassment. *Journal of Personality and Social Psychology*, 1971, *17*, 15–24.

Sattler, J. A theoretical development and clinical investigation of embarrassment. *Genetic Psychology Monographs*, 1965, *71*, 19–59.

PROJECT 7
Effects of Socioeconomic Status
on Conservation in Young Children[1]

FRIEDA FIFE AND ROBERT A. BARKER

American River College, 1972

In the fifty years since Jean Piaget began his studies of the cognitive development of children, much research has been published dealing with his concepts. Piaget has labeled various stages of development in the mental growth of children. The "operational" stage connotes mental operations, one of which is "conservation," defined as the ability to realize that certain attributes of an object remain constant even though the object changes in appearance (Pulaski, 1971).

Piaget developed many devices to test conservation in children and maintained that, in the children he tested, seven was the average age for the development of this ability. A delay of about two years in attaining the ability was reported for rural Swiss children as compared to urban children, yet Piaget maintains that the

[1] Experiment under the supervision of Dr. Wayne R. Bartz.

457

concept of conservation cannot be taught (Pulaski, 1971). Darbyshire and Reeves (1969) compared children having impaired hearing with normal children on conservation task performance and found no significant difference between these two groups, but did note a positive correlation between performance and favorable socioeconomic background.

The purpose of this study was to determine the average age of appearance of conservation concepts and thus the "operational" stage in "normal" white, American children of widely differing social class.

METHOD[2]

Subjects

"Upper middle-class" children were students attending a school located in an expensive and "exclusive" housing area of Sacramento. The "lower-class" children attended a "Title I" school in the same district. Title I schools have been designated by the Federal Government to receive special funding based upon the low economic status of the families which the school serves.

Sixty children were tested, thirty from each school. This included groups of ten children from kindergarten, first, and second grade. Ages ranged from five years four months to eight years three months. Children who had skipped or repeated a grade were excluded from the study, thus within-grade ages ranged only a few months. All subjects were randomly selected from the teacher's attendance sheet.

Procedure

On the day of testing, each child was taken individually to a testing room where the Experimenter (E) had the test apparatus set up at a child-sized table. After the Subject (S) was greeted warmly by E he was presented with Test I: two equal balls of "Play-Doh." E then established with S that the two balls of clay contained equal amounts of Play-Doh. If S said they were not equal, E then removed clay from one ball and put it on the other ball until S agreed that there was the same amount of clay in each. E then said, "I am going to roll this one into a long, pink sausage and leave the other in a ball." E then asked S if he thought there was more Play-Doh in "this one" (E held up the ball), "this one" (E held up the sausage), or if both contained the same amount. S's answer on this and the other tests was scored one point for a "same amount" answer and zero for an answer showing that S perceived a difference in amount.

[2] Editors' note: The research design was a 2 × 3 factorial design (Chapter 5) with two levels of social class and three grade levels. In any such attempt to examine Piaget's theory, one must constantly be aware of the significant role that language plays in Piaget's theory. The "same" or "not same," "equal" or "not equal" answer to the test question is almost irrelevant to Piaget. The concepts used in answering the question "why" is what he considers critical to determining the child's stage of intellectual development.

S was then given Test II, two clear twelve-ounce glass containers, one tall and thin and the other short and fat, and two piles of large, multicolored beads of ten beads each. *S* was asked to count one pile of beads into one container and one pile into the other. When *S* had placed and counted ten beads in each container, *E* said, "Now look at these containers and tell me if you think there are more beads in one and less beads in the other, or if there is the same amount of beads in both."

Test III consisted of two green tinkertoy sticks put side by side and equality of length established with *S*. *E* then said, "If I move this one like this (*E* moved one so that it extended beyond the other at one end), is one longer than the other or are they the same length?

Ten red and ten blue poker chips in a pile were presented for Test IV and *S* was asked to arrange them in rows by color. When sameness of amount had been established, *E* said "Now, if I move the red ones like this (all scattered) and the blue ones all piled up together like this, are there more red chips, less red chips, or are there the same amount of each?"

The *S*'s were led to believe that whatever answer they gave was correct and were complimented on their performance. *S*'s were then taken back to class and asked to keep what we had done a secret until everyone else was finished.

RESULTS AND DISCUSSION

Analysis of variance (school and grade variables) was significant for the two variables but not their interaction: Grade level, F $(2,54) = 8.82$, $(p < .001)$; school, F $(1,54) = 8.42$, $(p < .01)$; Grade level x school, F $(2,54) = .13$ (N.S.). Mean score differences clarify these findings: Upper middle-class children obtained means of 2.6, 3.5, and 3.8, for kindergarten, first, and second grades respectively; lower-class children's means were 1.6, 2.8, and 3.1 respectively.

Both schools showed an increase by grade in conservation scores, but the students at the wealthier school were found to function at a consistently higher level. The largest attained difference occurred at the kindergarten level. This is noteworthy for it is here that the variable of school experience is at a minimum. Thus our findings may actually conflict with Piaget's in two ways: (a) We found a difference in conservation ability between children of differing social groups within the same school district (thus it was not, in our study, an urban-rural variable); (b) in addition, we found marked conservation ability at kindergarten level, considerably earlier than Piaget suggests.

Whether such findings are due to environmental or perhaps genetic factors is not clear. If it is an environmental variable, efforts to provide an early enriched environment could operate to close the gap between performance levels of children from differing social classes. In addition, programs such as Head Start and DISTAR could in part be evaluated in terms of conservation concepts. If effective, we might expect to see a reduction in social class differences.

REFERENCES

Darbyshire, J. O., and Reeves, V. R. The use of adaptations of some of Piaget's tests with groups of children with normal and impaired hearing. *British Journal of Disorders of Communication*, 1969, *4*(2).

Pulaski, M. A. S. *Understanding Piaget: An introduction to children's cognitive development.* New York: Harper & Row, 1971.

PROJECT 8

Color Perception: The Effect of Primary Colors on Area Perception of Rectangles and Visual Comparison

ALICE BLOCHER
University of the Pacific, 1969

Rubin (1921) conducted an experiment with the colors blue and yellow using an ambiguous figure. He observed that the yellow figure appeared to move outward from the background but the blue figure seemed to move inward behind the ground. Other studies have shown that some colors appear to advance nearer than others. More specifically, colors whose dominant hues are of shorter wave-lengths (violet, blue, green) are retiring and those whose dominant hues are of longer wave-lengths (yellow, orange, red) are advancing (Luckiesh, 1965). In the present study, it was predicted that yellow and red rectangles would be perceived as largest, with blue appearing smaller. The prediction was derived on the basis of the relative effect of the colors yellow, blue, and red found in previous literature. The experimental hypothesis stated that male and female college students would most frequently perceive yellow and red forms to have a greater area than blue forms.

461

METHOD[1]

Forty subjects were randomly selected from university living groups (20 males and 20 females). Subjects were assigned to three experimental groups of 10 and a control group of 10.

The stimulus materials consisted of four sheets of $8\frac{1}{2} \times 11$ in. white bond paper on which three 1 in. $\times$ 3 in. rectangles were drawn, spaced 1 in. apart. On three sheets, the rectangles were colored: one red, one yellow, and one blue. The position of the three colored rectangles on each sheet differed for each of the three experimental groups. On the fourth sheet, the control sheet, the rectangles were not colored.

Each subject was asked which rectangle on a given sheet appeared to be largest in area, regardless of its actual measured size.

RESULTS AND DISCUSSION

In the experimental groups, 20 out of 30 subjects felt that the yellow rectangles were the largest with red and blue receiving five responses each. All of the subjects in the control group judged the rectangles equal in size. A χ^2 test shows a value of $\chi^2 = 15$ ($df = 2$) which is significant at the 0.05 level.

The hypothesis was partly supported in the case of the yellow rectangles, but not supported in the case of the red rectangles.

REFERENCES

Foss, V. *Experiments in visual perception.* Baltimore, Maryland: Penguin, 1966, pp. 7–28.

Luckiesh, M. *Visual illusions: Their causes, characteristics and applications.* New York: Dover, 1965.

Rubin, E. *Visuell Wahregenommene figuren: Studien in Psychologischer analyse.* Teil I. Berlin: Gyldendalske Boghandel, 1921.

[1] Editors' note: The experimental design was a combination of a multilevel design (Chapter 5) and a randomized two-group design (Chapter 4). The three orders of colored rectangles on a card (three groups) formed the three levels of the independent variable for the multilevel part of the design. The comparison of the control group and the average performance of the other three groups constituted the two-group design. It would have been better to have used a repeated measure design in which each subject experienced each of the three position orders of the rectangles. Also, each subject should have been asked to judge the relative size of all red, all blue, and all yellow rectangles instead of noncolored rectangles.

PROJECT 9

The Effects of Embryonic Drug Stimulation with Methylphenidate on Imprinting of Chicks

CHRISTINE COLEMAN

University of the Pacific, 1969

Young birds tend to follow moving objects that they see soon after hatching (imprinting). Under natural conditions chicks would ordinarily follow their mother, but in a controlled experiment they can be imprinted on almost any moving model. Imprinting takes place within a short period in the day or two after hatching, a period known as the "critical period." The critical period terminates with the development of fears. Studies have shown that fear-reducing drugs such as tranquilizers (muscle relaxants) decrease the speed of or eliminate imprinting (Hess, 1959). The present study attempted to determine the effects of a mild central nervous system stimulant (methylphenidate or "Ritalin") on the speed of imprinting. The experimental hypothesis was that chicks given methylphenidate one week prior to hatching would imprint significantly faster than chicks in control (no drug) groups.

METHOD[1]

Four-dozen Rhode Island Red fertile chicken eggs were incubated for 21 days. On the sixteenth day, 21 eggs were randomly selected for the experiment. Ten (experimental group) were injected with the drug methylphenidate (2.5 milligrams per chick) and seven hatched. Of the remaining 11 eggs, five were injected with a saline solution to control for injection effects (three hatched), and six were not injected (six hatched).

The apparatus consisted of a large tin can placed in the center of a circle (10-foot diameter) on the laboratory floor. The tin can was attached to a strong string looped over a pipe near the ceiling. Each chick was placed under the tin can 8 hours after hatching. An observer sat 10 feet from the can with a stop watch. The "imprinting" experimenter was next to the can. The can was lifted by the observer and the imprinter moved his hand back and forth in front of the subject in an attempt to imprint the subject on the experimenter's hand. The imprinter moved away from the can while the chick followed. The procedure was repeated for each chick every four hours for 36 hours. The dependent variable measure was the amount of time it took the chick to cross the outer edge of the circle.

RESULTS

The mean response time for the experimental group subjects (injected with methylphenidate) was 36 seconds. The mean response time was 53 seconds for the saline-injected group and 54 seconds for the noninjected control chicks. A split plot analysis of variance showed that there was no significant difference between the means of the treatment groups ($F = 2.10$, $df = 2/13$, $p > .05$). The trials effect was significant ($F = 9.21$, $df = 8$, 104, $p < .05$) indicating that imprinting did take place, since the subjects got faster at following the imprinter over the nine trials. The interaction between treatment and trials was not significant.

DISCUSSION

While the results did not support the hypothesis, it is possible that stronger dosage levels than 2.5 milligrams might support the hypothesis. Background noise in the laboratory may have caused some problems and the speckled tile of the laboratory floor attracted some of the chicks and elicited pecking responses. The present experiment did yield one important point, that injection of drugs into chick embryos can be accomplished successfully without impairing the health of the chicks. Other drugs, stimulants as well as depressants and those that enhance learn-

---

[1] Editors' note: The research design was a 3×9 split-plot factorial design (Chapter 5) with nine trials as one variable (repeated measures) and three drug injection conditions as the other. It is unfortunate that only three subjects were available for testing in the saline-injected group. The within-group variability in response times required more subjects be available to detect between-groups differences.

ing, could be injected into chick embryos, thereby opening up possibilities for further research in the area.

REFERENCES

Hess, E. H. Imprinting. *Science,* 1959, *130,* 133–141.

Remington's dictionary of pharmaceutical sciences. New York: Remington, 1965.

Sluckin, W. *Imprinting and early learning.* Chicago: Aldine, 1965.

Werner, G. Clinical pharmacology of central stimulant and anti-depressant drugs. *Clinical Pharmacology and Therapeutics,* 1962, *3,* 59–96.

PROJECT 10

Hoarding Behavior: The Effects of Deprivation on Hoarding Patterns in the Rat

MIKE GUERRA
University of the Pacific, 1969

(Abstract of paper presented at Western Psychological Association Convention, Los Angeles, 1970.)

Mowrer (1961) defined hoarding as the act of transporting food or objects from one area to another by rats who are satiated or have the opportunity for satiation. Mowrer suggested that hoarding is caused by the animal trying to eliminate its fear of hunger. In previous research deprivation has been cited as a major cause for the onset of hoarding (Stellar and Morgan, 1943; Licklider and Licklider, 1950; Baker, 1955; Marx, 1952). In each case it is implied that deprivation either created or increased the fear of hunger. However Bindra (1948) and Holland (1954) observed hoarding in rats that had never been deprived experimentally. Ross, Smith, and Woessner (1955) have summarized the research on hoarding by stating three main theoretical implications. They are: instinct as the basis of hoarding, learning as the basis of hoarding, and environmental factors and deprivation as the basis for hoarding.

The influence of a variety of environmental factors (e.g., consistency of food, appearance of food, temperature, etc.) have been investigated. (See Bindra, 1959.)

466

For example, foil-wrapped pellets were preferred to regular pellets (Licklider and Licklider, 1950). Other variables that have been found to affect hoarding are age, experience, frustration, emotionality, and strain of rat used.

The conceptual hypothesis in the present study is that there are two major bases for hoarding and whichever is stronger will determine the type of hoarding that will be manifested by the rats: (1) perceptual (texture, color, brightness, and novelty of the hoarding material) and (2) fear of hunger drive, which is greatly increased with food deprivation.

Hoarding was operationally defined as the act of transporting food or objects from one area to another by rats who are satiated or have the opportunity for satiation (Mowrer, 1961). The independent variables were the length of time the rat was kept on food deprivation. Three levels of deprivation were used starting with 0 hours of deprivation (Group I), 40 hours of food deprivation (Group II), and 76 hours of food deprivation (Group III). Two levels of type of food were used: foil-wrapped rat chow (FWP) or plain chow (PP). The dependent variables were: the total number of pellets transported from the hoarding cage to the home cage in a 25-min. test (PP + FWP), and the individual counts for plain pellets (PP) and foil-wrapped pellets (FWP) during the same 25-min. hoarding test.

The experimental hypotheses were: (H$_1$) Rats deprived of food for 40 hours will hoard more pellets than a control group, and rats given 76 hours of food deprivation will hoard more than either of the other groups; (H$_2$) hoarding that takes place before deprivation should be mainly of the foil-wrapped pellets; (H$_3$) the control group (Group I) should hoard significantly more FWP than PP; however, after deprivation Groups II and III should hoard significantly more (PP) than (FWP); (H$_4$) after several days of eating following deprivation, hoarding of PP by Groups II and III should decrease and hoarding of FWP pellets increase.

METHOD[1]

The Ss were nine naïve male albino Sprague-Dawley rats. Each animal was 30 days old on Day 1 of the experiment. The Ss were randomly assigned to the three groups. The rats weighed 100–150g. on Day 1. The Ss were maintained on *ad lib* water and rat chow at the onset of the experiment. The hoarding apparatus consisted of a circular wire mesh alleyway, 30″ long by 4″ in diameter, through which Ss were allowed access to the hoarding cage (8″ × 6″ × 6″). During testing the alley was connected to the Ss home cages allowing free access to the hoarding cage from the home cage. Home cages were darkened during testing and the hoarding cage and alley were illuminated by a 25 wt. lamp suspended over the hoarding cage.

Subjects were allowed five days to familiarize themselves with their new home cages. On Days 6, 7, and 8 of the experiment all Ss were allowed 10 min. to explore the hoarding apparatus. No food or objects were in the hoarding cage during

[1] Editors' note: The design was a 2 × 3 split-plot factorial (with two levels of type of food and three levels of deprivation) with repeated measures (seven trials). Insofar as the deprivation variable is concerned, the design is also a before-after design since the first three trials involved no deprivation for any group. The study suffers from the unusually small number of subjects.

the exploratory periods. On Day 9 hoarding tests were begun. Each rat was allowed to spend 25 min. in the hoarding apparatus. Fifty-five plain pellets (PP) and 55 foil-wrapped pellets (FWP) were mixed together and piled in the hoarding cage. Hoarding tests were repeated on Day 10 and 11. On Day 12 Group III was started on a 76-hr. "accumulative" deprivation schedule. Each rat was weighed just prior to the onset of deprivation. The 76-hr. accumulative schedule consisted of a 28-hr. period of deprivation at the end of which the rats were given one 6g. pellet of food. The Ss were allowed 30 min. to eat and then started on a 24-hr. period of deprivation. At the end of this period one 6g. pellet was given to the rats. A second 24-hr. period of deprivation was then begun. Thirty-six hours after Group III began deprivation, Group II began a 40-hr. accumulative deprivation schedule. The first period of deprivation lasted 16 hrs. the end of which coincided with the end of Group III's first 24-hr. period. One 6g. pellet of food was given to each rat and then a 24-hr. period of deprivation was started for Group II. On Day 15 of the experiment deprivation ended for all groups with the first 25-min. hoarding test. The rats were allowed to eat the food pellets in the hoarding cage. At the end of the hoarding test on Day 15 the rats were given abundant food. Hoarded pellets were removed at the end of each hoarding test to minimize terminal reinforcement (Holland, 1954). On Days 16, 17, and 18 of the experiment hoarding tests were repeated. The number of plain pellets (PP) and foil-wrapped pellets (FWP) hoarded was recorded for each rat on each test.

RESULTS AND DISCUSSION

During hoarding tests prior to deprivation very little hoarding was observed. The hoarding means for Groups I, II, and III before deprivation were: $\overline{X}_1 = 3.22$, $\overline{X}_2 = 0.11$, $\overline{X}_3 = 0.00$. Group I (control) hoarded the most, the hoarding confined to FWP. After deprivation Groups II (40 hrs.) and III (76 hrs.) hoarded great numbers of pellets (PP + FWP). The means for the groups were: Group I $\overline{X}_1 = 7.41$, Group II $\overline{X}_2 = 16.91$, Group III $\overline{X}_3 = 35.83$. Group I on all seven of the tests hoarded mainly FWP (113 FWP, 5 PP). Groups II (49 FWP, 154 PP) and III (139 FWP, 291 PP) preferred plain pellets to foil-wrapped pellets.

An analysis of variance and trend analysis showed the linear component of the Groups by Days interaction (PP + FWP) was significant ($F = 11.66$, $df = 2/36$, $p < .01$). These results support experimental hypothesis (H_1) which stated rats deprived of food for 40 hrs. would hoard more (PP + FWP) than the control groups and rats given 76-hr. deprivation would hoard more (PP + FWP) than either of the other groups. Hoarding taking place before deprivation was restricted entirely to FWP. This suggests support for (H_2) which predicted predeprivation hoarding would be mainly with FWP.

The control group (Group I) preferred FWP. This lends support to experimental hypothesis (H_3) that the nondeprived group (Group I) would hoard more foil-wrapped pellets (FWP) than plain pellets (PP).

After deprivation, PP were hoarded significantly more than FWP which supports experimental hypothesis (H_3) which stated Groups II and III would hoard more PP than FWP after deprivation. After deprivation, the number of FWP increased while PP reached a peak and then decreased. This supports experimental hypothesis (H_4) which stated that after several days of eating hoarding of FWP would increase and PP would decrease.

It was observed that many of the rats exhibited stereotyping of the hoarding pattern. The rats would wait at the opening of the alley in their home cages. They would sniff for a moment, then dash to the hoarding cage and pick up a pellet and run even faster back to their home cage. They would repeat this over and over, paying little attention to anything else. Two of the rats retrieved their tails a great deal after deprivation. One of the rats hoarded his tail *34 times* in addition to hoarding 51 pellets (PP + FWP) during his 25-minute test.

Most of the rats who did hoard great numbers, piled the hoarded pellets (both PP and FWP) neatly in a corner or along a wall of their home cage. They tended to pile the hoarded pellets away from their regular food pellets. On the first test after deprivation the rats spent 10–15 minutes eating. In each case, after eating they would drink for long periods then without hesitation run to the hoarding cage and begin hoarding plain pellets. The rats seemed to go through hoarding phases whereby they would become very active (jumping, running, sniffing, etc.) just before they would commence hoarding. Sometimes they would hoard so quickly the experimenter had trouble keeping up with the running count.

It is reasonable to say that not all hoarding is related to deprivation but hoarding that does take place because of deprivation differs motivationally from hoarding without deprivation. Deprivation-induced hoarding seems to be stronger than perceptual hoarding. Once deprivation hoarding subsides, perceptual hoarding again becomes dominant.

REFERENCES

Baker, R. A. The effects of repeated deprivation on the feeding behavior in rats. *Journal of Comparative and Physiological Psychology*, 1955, 48, 37–42.

Bindra, D. The nature of motivation for hoarding food. *Journal of Comparative and Physiological Psychology*, 1948, 41, 211–218.

Bindra, D. *Motivation: A systematic reinterpretation.* New York: Ronald, 1959, 72–79.

Holland, J. G. The influence of previous experience and residual effects of deprivation on hoarding in rats. *Journal of Comparative and Physiological Psychology*, 1954, 47, 244–247.

Licklider, L. C., and Licklider, J. C. Observation of the hoarding behavior in rats. *Journal of Comparative and Physiological Psychology*, 1950, 43, 129–134.

Marx, M. H. Infantile deprivation and adult behavior in the rat. *Journal of Comparative and Physiological Psychology*, 1952, 45, 43–49.

Mowrer, O. H. *Learning theory and behavior.* New York: Wiley, 1961, pp. 145–153.

Ross, S., Smith, W. I., and Woessner. Hoarding: An analysis of experiments and trends. *Journal of Genetic Psychology*, 1955, 52, 307–326.

Stellar, E., and Morgan, C. T. The role of experience and deprivation on the onset of hoarding behavior in rats. *Journal of Comparative and Physiological Psychology*, 1943, 47, 244–247.

APPENDICES

APPENDIX A
Review of Mathematical Notation and Operation Rules

ORDER OF OPERATIONS

Rule (1): Sets of terms within parentheses or brackets are treated as a single number.

To prevent ambiguity when several operations are involved in one equation or formula, symbols and terms are grouped within parentheses or brackets. For example,

$$(3 + 5) + 2(7 - 3) = (8) + 2(4),$$
$$= 8 + 8 = 16;$$
or
$$(4 + 6) \div (6 - 2) = 10 \div 4 = 2.5;$$
or
$$3\left[(7 - 1) \div (8 - 5)\right] = 3(6 \div 3),$$
$$= 3(2) = 6.$$

If several overlapping sets of parentheses or brackets are involved in an equation, the innermost grouping of operations is completed first. The grouped operations are completed in sequence from the innermost to the outermost grouping.

IMPLIED MULTIPLICATION

Rule (1): If numbers or symbols are enclosed in parentheses or brackets without any intervening signs or symbols, then multiply the numbers or symbols.

For example,

$$(3 + 2)(4 - 1) = (5)(3) = 15;$$
$$\text{or}$$
$$[2(6) \div 3][4 - 2] = (4)(2) = 8.$$

SUMMATION

The capital Greek letter sigma (Σ) is used to indicate summation.
For example,

$$\sum_{i=1}^{n} X = \sum_{1}^{n} X = \sum^{n} X = X_1 + X_2 + \cdots + X_n$$

if there are 4 values of X (n = 4) with $X_1 = 2$, $X_2 = 4$, $X_3 = 6$ and $X_4 = 8$, then

$$\sum^{4} X = 2 + 4 + 6 + 8 = 20$$

Rule (1): $\Sigma(X + Y) = \Sigma X + \Sigma Y$ where X and Y are both variables such that each value of X has a value of Y paired with it.

For example, if $X_1 = 2$, $X_2 = 4$, $X_3 = 6$, $X_4 = 8$ and $Y_1 = 1$, $Y_2 = 3$, $Y_3 = 5$, and $Y_4 = 7$, then

$$\Sigma(X + Y) = (2 + 1) + (4 + 3) + (6 + 5) + (8 + 7),$$

$$= (2 + 4 + 6 + 8) + (1 + 3 + 5 + 7),$$

$$\Sigma(X + Y) = 20 + 16 = 36.$$

Rule (2): $\Sigma(X - Y) = \Sigma X - \Sigma Y$ where X and Y are paired variables as above.

For example, if the same values of X and Y occur as in the previous example, then

$$\Sigma(X - Y) = (2 - 1) + (4 - 3) + (6 - 5) + (8 - 7),$$

$$= (2 + 4 + 6 + 8) - (1 + 3 + 5 + 7),$$

$$\Sigma(X - Y) = 20 - 16 = 4.$$

Rule (3): $\Sigma (X + C) = \Sigma X + nC$, where C is any constant.

For example, if $X_1 = 2$, $X_2 = 4$, $X_3 = 6$, and $X_4 = 8$, and $C = 2$, then

$$\Sigma (X + C) = (2 + 2) + (4 + 2) + (6 + 2) + (8 + 2),$$

$$= (2 + 4 + 6 + 8) + (2 + 2 + 2 + 2)$$

$$\Sigma (X + C) = 20 + 4(2) = 28.$$

Rule (4): $\Sigma (X - C) = \Sigma X - nC$, where C is any constant.
Rule (5): $\Sigma CX = C \Sigma X$, where C is any constant.

For example, if $C = 2$ and $X_1 = 2$, $X_2 = 4$, $X_3 = 6$, and $X_4 = 8$, then,

$$\Sigma CX = 2(2) + 2(4) + 2(6) + 2(8),$$

$$= 2(2 + 4 + 6 + 8),$$

$$\Sigma CX = 2(20) = 40.$$

Rule (6): $\Sigma (X \div C) = (1/C) \Sigma X$, where C is any constant.

CALCULATION OF MEANS

Since the mean is the $\Sigma X \div n$, the preceding rules for summation have the following implications about arithmetic means.

Rule (1): $\overline{C} = C$, where C stands for a constant. That is, $\overline{C} = \Sigma C/n = nC/n = C$.
Rule (2): $\overline{CX} = C\overline{X}$, where X is a variable and C is any constant.

For example, if $X_1 = 2$, $X_2 = 4$, $X_3 = 6$, $X_4 = 8$ and $C = 2$, then

$$\overline{CX} = \left[2(2) + 2(4) + 2(6) + 2(8) \right] \div 4,$$

$$= \left[2(2 + 4 + 6 + 8) \right] \div 4,$$

$$\overline{CX} = (2)(20) \div 4 = 10.$$

$$\overline{X} = 20 \div 4 = 5, \text{ and}$$

$$C\overline{X} = 2(5) = 10.$$

Rule (3): $\overline{X + C} = \overline{X} + C$, where X is a variable and C is any constant.
Rule (4): $\overline{X + Y} = \overline{X} + \overline{Y}$, where X and Y are variables.

For example, if $X_1 = 2$, $X_2 = 4$, $X_3 = 6$, $X_4 = 8$ and $Y_1 = 1$, $Y_2 = 3$, $Y_3 = 5$, and $Y_4 = 7$, then

$$\overline{X + Y} = \frac{(2 + 1) + (4 + 3) + (6 + 5) + (8 + 7)}{n = 4},$$

$$\overline{X + Y} = \frac{(2 + 4 + 6 + 8) + (1 + 3 + 5 + 7)}{4},$$

$$\overline{X + Y} = (20 \div 4) + (16 \div 4),$$

$$\overline{X + Y} = 5 + 4 = \overline{X} + \overline{Y} = 9.$$

ROUNDING NUMBERS

Rule (1): If the rightmost digit of a number to be "rounded" is less than 5, then we discard the excess. If, however, it is greater than 5 then the number is rounded up to the next largest number.

For example, when rounding to whole numbers, if the decimal fraction is less than 0.5, then the decimal is discarded and the whole number is unchanged. If the decimal fraction is greater than 0.5, the whole number is increased by one unit and the decimal fraction is discarded (4.4 = 4, 4.7 = 5).

Rule (2): By arbitrary convention (common practice) in the case that the rightmost digit is 5, if the number preceding the 5 to be dropped is an *even* number, then it is *not changed* when the 5 is discarded. However, if the number preceding the 5 is an *odd* number, then it is increased by one unit.

For example, 6.5 = 6, 7.5 = 8, 369.5 = 370, and 42.5 = 42.

SIGNIFICANT NUMBERS

There is much confusion about how many decimal places (significant figures) *should* be carried in a set of computations. Given that any set of data will contain error (including measurement error), it must be recognized that all data are approximations to the impossible ideal of errorless, perfectly measured scores. Furthermore, in any study the precision of measurement depends upon many factors including the equipment used. If a set of data points is relatively imprecise, it makes no sense to carry many more decimal places (significant figures) in computations with the data than the number of significant figures in the original data. For example, if the data is time measured to the nearest whole second, then calculating the mean to be 1.237986 seconds is an absurd waste of time.

Rule (1): According to Edwards (1967), the best single principle is to carry along one or two more figures in various computations than there are in the original data. Then the final answer is rounded back to either the number of significant figures in the original data, or a reasonable number. A "reasonable number" is that number determined from conventional practice or the logic of the statistics. For example, conventional practice is to report correlation coefficients in two decimal places (nearest hundredth). If the original data is measured to one significant digit in whole numbers, then if one rounded back the calculated value of r to the nearest whole number, only three possible values of r could exist, -1, 0, or $+1$. The informational value of r is nearly eliminated by such a procedure. The only way to determine conventional practice (in those cases where rational analysis does not lead to an immediate answer) is to examine the research literature in the psychological journals.

APPENDIX B

Table of Four-Place Logarithms

N	0	1	2	3	4	5	6	7	8	9	1 2 3	4 5 6	7 8 9
1.0	.0000	.0043	.0086	.0128	.0170	.0212	.0253	.0294	.0334	.0374	4 8 12	17 21 25	29 33 37
1.1	.0414	.0453	.0492	.0531	.0569	.0607	.0645	.0682	.0719	.0755	4 8 11	15 19 23	26 30 34
1.2	.0792	.0828	.0864	.0899	.0934	.0969	.1004	.1038	.1072	.1106	3 7 10	14 17 21	24 28 31
1.3	.1139	.1173	.1206	.1239	.1271	.1303	.1335	.1367	.1399	.1430	3 6 10	13 16 19	23 26 29
1.4	.1461	.1492	.1523	.1553	.1584	.1614	.1644	.1673	.1703	.1732	3 6 9	12 15 18	21 24 27
1.5	.1761	.1790	.1818	.1847	.1875	.1903	.1931	.1959	.1987	.2014	3 6 8	11 14 17	20 22 25
1.6	.2041	.2068	.2095	.2122	.2148	.2175	.2201	.2227	.2253	.2279	3 5 8	11 13 16	18 21 24
1.7	.2304	.2330	.2355	.2380	.2405	.2430	.2455	.2480	.2504	.2529	2 5 7	10 12 15	17 20 22
1.8	.2553	.2577	.2601	.2625	.2648	.2672	.2695	.2718	.2742	.2765	2 5 7	9 12 14	16 19 21
1.9	.2788	.2810	.2833	.2856	.2878	.2900	.2923	.2945	.2967	.2989	2 4 7	9 11 13	16 18 20
2.0	.3010	.3032	.3054	.3075	.3096	.3118	.3139	.3160	.3181	.3201	2 4 6	8 11 13	15 17 19
2.1	.3222	.3243	.3263	.3284	.3304	.3324	.3345	.3365	.3385	.3404	2 4 6	8 10 12	14 16 18
2.2	.3424	.3444	.3464	.3483	.3502	.3522	.3541	.3560	.3579	.3598	2 4 6	8 10 12	14 15 17
2.3	.3617	.3636	.3655	.3674	.3692	.3711	.3729	.3747	.3766	.3784	2 4 6	7 9 11	13 15 17
2.4	.3802	.3820	.3838	.3856	.3874	.3892	.3909	.3927	.3945	.3962	2 4 5	7 9 11	12 14 16
2.5	.3979	.3997	.4014	.4031	.4048	.4065	.4082	.4099	.4116	.4133	2 3 5	7 9 10	12 14 15
2.6	.4150	.4166	.4183	.4200	.4216	.4232	.4249	.4265	.4281	.4298	2 3 5	7 8 10	11 13 15
2.7	.4314	.4330	.4346	.4362	.4378	.4393	.4409	.4425	.4440	.4456	2 3 5	6 8 9	11 13 14
2.8	.4472	.4487	.4502	.4518	.4533	.4548	.4564	.4579	.4594	.4609	2 3 5	6 8 9	11 12 14
2.9	.4624	.4639	.4654	.4669	.4683	.4698	.4713	.4728	.4742	.4757	1 3 4	6 7 9	10 12 13
3.0	.4771	.4786	.4800	.4814	.4829	.4843	.4857	.4871	.4886	.4900	1 3 4	6 7 9	10 11 13
3.1	.4914	.4928	.4942	.4955	.4969	.4983	.4997	.5011	.5024	.5038	1 3 4	6 7 8	10 11 12
3.2	.5051	.5065	.5079	.5092	.5105	.5119	.5132	.5145	.5159	.5172	1 3 4	5 7 8	9 11 12
3.3	.5185	.5198	.5211	.5224	.5237	.5250	.5263	.5276	.5289	.5302	1 3 4	5 6 8	9 10 12
3.4	.5315	.5328	.5340	.5353	.5366	.5378	.5391	.5403	.5416	.5428	1 3 4	5 6 8	9 10 11
3.5	.5441	.5453	.5465	.5478	.5490	.5502	.5514	.5527	.5539	.5551	1 2 4	5 6 7	9 10 11
3.6	.5563	.5575	.5587	.5599	.5611	.5623	.5635	.5647	.5658	.5670	1 2 4	5 6 7	8 10 11
3.7	.5682	.5694	.5705	.5717	.5729	.5740	.5752	.5763	.5775	.5786	1 2 3	5 6 7	8 9 10
3.8	.5798	.5809	.5821	.5832	.5843	.5855	.5866	.5877	.5888	.5899	1 2 3	5 6 7	8 9 10
3.9	.5911	.5922	.5933	.5944	.5955	.5966	.5977	.5988	.5999	.6010	1 2 3	4 5 7	8 9 10
4.0	.6021	.6031	.6042	.6053	.6064	.6075	.6085	.6096	.6107	.6117	1 2 3	4 5 6	8 9 10
4.1	.6128	.6138	.6149	.6160	.6170	.6180	.6191	.6201	.6212	.6222	1 2 3	4 5 6	7 8 9
4.2	.6232	.6243	.6253	.6263	.6274	.6284	.6294	.6304	.6314	.6325	1 2 3	4 5 6	7 8 9
4.3	.6335	.6345	.6355	.6365	.6375	.6385	.6395	.6405	.6415	.6425	1 2 3	4 5 6	7 8 9
4.4	.6435	.6444	.6454	.6464	.6474	.6484	.6493	.6503	.6513	.6522	1 2 3	4 5 6	7 8 9
4.5	.6532	.6542	.6551	.6561	.6571	.6580	.6590	.6599	.6609	.6618	1 2 3	4 5 6	7 8 9
4.6	.6628	.6637	.6646	.6656	.6665	.6675	.6684	.6693	.6702	.6712	1 2 3	4 5 6	7 7 8
4.7	.6721	.6730	.6739	.6749	.6758	.6767	.6776	.6785	.6794	.6803	1 2 3	4 5 5	6 7 8
4.8	.6812	.6821	.6830	.6839	.6848	.6857	.6866	.6875	.6884	.6893	1 2 3	4 4 5	6 7 8
4.9	.6902	.6911	.6920	.6928	.6937	.6946	.6955	.6964	.6972	.6981	1 2 3	4 4 5	6 7 8
5.0	.6990	.6998	.7007	.7016	.7024	.7033	.7042	.7050	.7059	.7067	1 2 3	3 4 5	6 7 8
5.1	.7076	.7084	.7093	.7101	.7110	.7118	.7126	.7135	.7143	.7152	1 2 3	3 4 5	6 7 8
5.2	.7160	.7168	.7177	.7185	.7193	.7202	.7210	.7218	.7226	.7235	1 2 2	3 4 5	6 7 7
5.3	.7243	.7251	.7259	.7267	.7275	.7284	.7292	.7300	.7308	.7316	1 2 2	3 4 5	6 6 7
5.4	.7324	.7332	.7340	.7348	.7356	.7364	.7372	.7380	.7388	.7396	1 2 2	3 4 5	6 6 7

To obtain the mantissa for a four-digit number, find in the body of the table the mantissa for the first three digits and then, neglecting the decimal point temporarily, add the number in the proportional-parts table at the right which is on the same line as the mantissa already obtained and in the column corresponding to the fourth digit.

N	0	1	2	3	4	5	6	7	8	9	1	2	3	4	5	6	7	8	9
5.5	.7404	.7412	.7419	.7427	.7435	.7443	.7451	.7459	.7466	.7474	1	2	2	3	4	5	5	6	7
5.6	.7482	.7490	.7497	.7505	.7513	.7520	.7528	.7536	.7543	.7551	1	2	2	3	4	5	5·6		7
5.7	.7559	.7566	.7574	.7582	.7589	.7597	.7604	.7612	.7619	.7627	1	2	2	3	4	5	5	6	7
5.8	.7634	.7642	.7649	.7657	.7664	.7672	.7679	.7686	.7694	.7701	1	1	2	3	4	4	5	6	7
5.9	.7709	.7716	.7723	.7731	.7738	.7745	.7752	.7760	.7767	.7774	1	1	2	3	4	4	5	6	7
6.0	.7782	.7789	.7796	.7803	.7810	.7818	.7825	.7832	.7839	.7846	1	1	2	3	4	4	5	6	6
6.1	.7853	.7860	.7868	.7875	.7882	.7889	.7896	.7903	.7910	.7917	1	1	2	3	4	4	5	6	6
6.2	.7924	.7931	.7938	.7945	.7952	.7959	.7966	.7973	.7980	.7987	1	1	2	3	3	4	5	6	6
6.3	.7993	.8000	.8007	.8014	.8021	.8028	.8035	.8041	.8048	.8055	1	1	2	3	3	4	5	5	6
6.4	.8062	.8069	.8075	.8082	.8089	.8096	.8102	.8109	.8116	.8122	1	1	2	3	3	4	5	5	6
6.5	.8129	.8136	.8142	.8149	.8156	.8162	.8169	.8176	.8182	.8189	1	1	2	3	3	4	5	5	6
6.6	.8195	.8202	.8209	.8215	.8222	.8228	.8235	.8241	.8248	.8254	1	1	2	3	3	4	5	5	6
6.7	.8261	.8267	.8274	.8280	.8287	.8293	.8299	.8306	.8312	.8319	1	1	2	3	3	4	5	5	6
6.8	.8325	.8331	.8338	.8344	.8351	.8357	.8363	.8370	.8376	.8382	1	1	2	3	3	4	4	5	6
6.9	.8388	.8395	.8401	.8407	.8414	.8420	.8426	.8432	.8439	.8445	1	1	2	2	3	4	4	5	6
7.0	.8451	.8457	.8463	.8470	.8476	.8482	.8488	.8494	.8500	.8506	1	1	2	2	3	4	4	5	6
7.1	.8513	.8519	.8525	.8531	.8537	.8543	.8549	.8555	.8561	.8567	1	1	2	2	3	4	4	5	5
7.2	.8573	.8579	.8585	.8591	.8597	.8603	.8609	.8615	.8621	.8627	1	1	2	2	3	4	4	5	5
7.3	.8633	.8639	.8645	.8651	.8657	.8663	.8669	.8675	.8681	.8686	1	1	2	2	3	4	4	5	5
7.4	.8692	.8698	.8704	.8710	.8716	.8722	.8727	.8733	.8739	.8745	1	1	2	2	3	4	4	5	5
7.5	.8751	.8756	.8762	.8768	.8774	.8779	.8785	.8791	.8797	.8802	1	1	2	2	3	3	4	5	5
7.6	.8808	.8814	.8820	.8825	.8831	.8837	.8842	.8848	.8854	.8859	1	1	2	2	3	3	4	5	5
7.7	.8865	.8871	.8876	.8882	.8887	.8893	.8899	.8904	.8910	.8915	1	1	2	2	3	3	4	4	5
7.8	.8921	.8927	.8932	.8938	.8943	.8949	.8954	.8960	.8965	.8971	1	1	2	2	3	3	4	4	5
7.9	.8976	.8982	.8987	.8993	.8998	.9004	.9009	.9015	.9020	.9025	1	1	2	2	3	3	4	4	5
8.0	.9031	.9036	.9042	.9047	.9053	.9058	.9063	.9069	.9074	.9079	1	1	2	2	3	3	4	4	5
8.1	.9085	.9090	.9096	.9101	.9106	.9112	.9117	.9122	.9128	.9133	1	1	2	2	3	3	4	4	5
8.2	.9138	.9143	.9149	.9154	.9159	.9165	.9170	.9175	.9180	.9186	1	1	2	2	3	3	4	4	5
8.3	.9191	.9196	.9201	.9206	.9212	.9217	.9222	.9227	.9232	.9238	1	1	2	2	3	3	4	4	5
8.4	.9243	.9248	.9253	.9258	.9263	.9269	.9274	.9279	.9284	.9289	1	1	2	2	3	3	4	4	5
8.5	.9294	.9299	.9304	.9309	.9315	.9320	.9325	.9330	.9335	.9340	1	1	2	2	3	3	4	4	5
8.6	.9345	.9350	.9355	.9360	.9365	.9370	.9375	.9380	.9385	.9390	1	1	2	2	3	3	4	4	5
8.7	.9395	.9400	.9405	.9410	.9415	.9420	.9425	.9430	.9435	.9440	0	1	1	2	2	3	3	4	4
8.8	.9445	.9450	.9455	.9460	.9465	.9469	.9474	.9479	.9484	.9489	0	1	1	2	2	3	3	4	4
8.9	.9494	.9499	.9504	.9509	.9513	.9518	.9523	.9528	.9533	.9538	0	1	1	2	2	3	3	4	4
9.0	.9542	.9547	.9552	.9557	.9562	.9566	.9571	.9576	.9581	.9586	0	1	1	2	2	3	3	4	4
9.1	.9590	.9595	.9600	.9605	.9609	.9614	.9619	.9624	.9628	.9633	0	1	1	2	2	3	3	4	4
9.2	.9638	.9643	.9647	.9652	.9657	.9661	.9666	.9671	.9675	.9680	0	1	1	2	2	3	3	4	4
9.3	.9685	.9689	.9694	.9699	.9703	.9708	.9713	.9717	.9722	.9727	0	1	1	2	2	3	3	4	4
9.4	.9731	.9736	.9741	.9745	.9750	.9754	.9759	.9763	.9768	.9773	0	1	1	2	2	3	3	4	4
9.5	.9777	.9782	.9786	.9791	.9795	.9800	.9805	.9809	.9814	.9818	0	1	1	2	2	3	3	4	4
9.6	.9823	.9827	.9832	.9836	.9841	.9845	.9850	.9854	.9859	.9863	0	1	1	2	2	3	3	4	4
9.7	.9868	.9872	.9877	.9881	.9886	.9890	.9894	.9899	.9903	.9908	0	1	1	2	2	3	3	4	4
9.8	.9912	.9917	.9921	.9926	.9930	.9934	.9939	.9943	.9948	.9952	0	1	1	2	2	3	3	4	4
9.9	.9956	.9961	.9965	.9969	.9974	.9978	.9983	.9987	.9991	.9996	0	1	1	2	2	3	3	3	4

From Edwards, A. L. *Statistical Methods* (2d ed.), New York: Holt, Rinehart and Winston, 1967, pp. 432–433.

APPENDIX C

Table of Squares and Square Roots
of Numbers from 1 to 1000

Table of Squares and Square Roots of Numbers
From 1 to 1000

Number	Square	Square Root	Number	Square	Square Root
1	1	1.000	31	9 61	5.568
2	4	1.414	32	10 24	5.657
3	9	1.732	33	10 89	5.745
4	16	2.000	34	11 56	5.831
5	25	2.236	35	12 25	5.916
6	36	2.449	36	12 96	6.000
7	49	2.646	37	13 69	6.083
8	64	2.828	38	14 44	6.164
9	81	3.000	39	15 21	6.245
10	1 00	3.162	40	16 00	6.325
11	1 21	3.317	41	16 81	6.403
12	1 44	3.464	42	17 64	6.481
13	1 69	3.606	43	18 49	6.557
14	1 96	3.742	44	19 36	6.633
15	2 25	3.873	45	20 25	6.708
16	2 56	4.000	46	21 16	6.782
17	2 89	4.123	47	22 09	6.856
18	3 24	4.243	48	23 04	6.928
19	3 61	4.359	49	24 01	7.000
20	4 00	4.472	50	25 00	7.071
21	4 41	4.583	51	26 01	7.141
22	4 84	4.690	52	27 04	7.211
23	5 29	4.796	53	28 09	7.280
24	5 76	4.899	54	29 16	7.348
25	6 25	5.000	55	30 25	7.416
26	6 76	5.099	56	31 36	7.483
27	7 29	5.196	57	32 49	7.550
28	7 84	5.292	58	33 64	7.616
29	8 41	5.385	59	34 81	7.681
30	9 00	5.477	60	36 00	7.746

Table of Squares and Square Roots (Continued)

Number	Square	Square Root	Number	Square	Square Root
61	37 21	7.810	91	82 81	9.539
62	38 44	7.874	92	84 64	9.592
63	39 69	7.937	93	86 49	9.644
64	40 96	8.000	94	88 36	9.695
65	42 25	8.062	95	90 25	9.747
66	43 56	8.124	96	92 16	9.798
67	44 89	8.185	97	94 09	9.849
68	46 24	8.246	98	96 04	9.899
69	47 61	8.307	99	98 01	9.950
70	49 00	8.367	100	1 00 00	10.000
71	50 41	8.426	101	1 02 01	10.050
72	51 84	8.485	102	1 04 04	10.100
73	53 29	8.544	103	1 06 09	10.149
74	54 76	8.602	104	1 08 16	10.198
75	56 25	8.660	105	1 10 25	10.247
76	57 76	8.718	106	1 12 36	10.296
77	59 29	8.775	107	1 14 49	10.344
78	60 84	8.832	108	1 16 64	10.392
79	62 41	8.888	109	1 18 81	10.440
80	64 00	8.944	110	1 21 00	10.488
81	65 61	9.000	111	1 23 21	10.536
82	67 24	9.055	112	1 25 44	10.583
83	68 89	9.110	113	1 27 69	10.630
84	70 56	9.165	114	1 29 96	10.677
85	72 25	9.220	115	1 32 25	10.724
86	73 96	9.274	116	1 34 56	10.770
87	75 69	9.327	117	1 36 89	10.817
88	77 44	9.381	118	1 39 24	10.863
89	79 21	9.434	119	1 41 61	10.909
90	81 00	9.487	120	1 44 00	10.954

From A Simplified Guide to Statistics, 4th ed., by G. M. Smith. New York: Holt, Rinehart and Winston, 1962.

Table of Squares and Square Roots (Continued)

Number	Square	Square Root	Number	Square	Square Root
181	3 27 61	13.454	211	4 45 21	14.526
182	3 31 24	13.491	212	4 49 44	14.560
183	3 34 89	13.528	213	4 53 69	14.595
184	3 38 56	13.565	214	4 57 96	14.629
185	3 42 25	13.601	215	4 62 25	14.663
186	3 45 96	13.638	216	4 66 56	14.697
187	3 49 69	13.675	217	4 70 89	14.731
188	3 53 44	13.711	218	4 75 24	14.765
189	3 57 21	13.748	219	4 79 61	14.799
190	3 61 00	13.784	220	4 84 00	14.832
191	3 64 81	13.820	221	4 88 41	14.866
192	3 68 64	13.856	222	4 92 84	14.900
193	3 72 49	13.892	223	4 97 29	14.933
194	3 76 36	13.928	224	5 01 76	14.967
195	3 80 25	13.964	225	5 06 25	15.000
196	3 84 16	14.000	226	5 10 76	15.033
197	3 88 09	14.036	227	5 15 29	15.067
198	3 92 04	14.071	228	5 19 84	15.100
199	3 96 01	14.107	229	5 24 41	15.133
200	4 00 00	14.142	230	5 29 00	15.166
201	4 04 01	14.177	231	5 33 61	15.199
202	4 08 04	14.213	232	5 38 24	15.232
203	4 12 09	14.248	233	5 42 89	15.264
204	4 16 16	14.283	234	5 47 56	15.297
205	4 20 25	14.318	235	5 52 25	15.330
206	4 24 36	14.353	236	5 56 96	15.362
207	4 28 49	14.387	237	5 61 69	15.395
208	4 32 64	14.422	238	5 66 44	15.427
209	4 36 81	14.457	239	5 71 21	15.460
210	4 41 00	14.491	240	5 76 00	15.492

Table of Squares and Square Roots (Continued)

Number	Square	Square Root	Number	Square	Square Root
121	1 46 41	11.000	151	2 28 01	12.288
122	1 48 84	11.045	152	2 31 04	12.329
123	1 51 29	11.091	153	2 34 09	12.369
124	1 53 76	11.136	154	2 37 16	12.410
125	1 56 25	11.180	155	2 40 25	12.450
126	1 58 76	11.225	156	2 43 36	12.490
127	1 61 29	11.269	157	2 46 49	12.530
128	1 63 84	11.314	158	2 49 64	12.570
129	1 66 41	11.358	159	2 52 81	12.610
130	1 69 00	11.402	160	2 56 00	12.649
131	1 71 61	11.446	161	2 59 21	12.689
132	1 74 24	11.489	162	2 62 44	12.728
133	1 76 89	11.533	163	2 65 69	12.767
134	1 79 56	11.576	164	2 68 96	12.806
135	1 82 25	11.619	165	2 72 25	12.845
136	1 84 96	11.662	166	2 75 56	12.884
137	1 87 69	11.705	167	2 78 89	12.923
138	1 90 44	11.747	168	2 82 24	12.961
139	1 93 21	11.790	169	2 85 61	13.000
140	1 96 00	11.832	170	2 89 00	13.038
141	1 98 81	11.874	171	2 92 41	13.077
142	2 01 64	11.916	172	2 95 84	13.115
143	2 04 49	11.958	173	2 99 29	13.153
144	2 07 36	12.000	174	3 02 76	13.191
145	2 10 25	12.042	175	3 06 25	13.229
146	2 13 16	12.083	176	3 09 76	13.266
147	2 16 09	12.124	177	3 13 29	13.304
148	2 19 04	12.166	178	3 16 84	13.342
149	2 22 01	12.207	179	3 20 41	13.379
150	2 25 00	12.247	180	3 24 00	13.416

Table of Squares and Square Roots (Continued)

Number	Square	Square Root	Number	Square	Square Root
241	5 80 81	15.524	271	7 34 41	16.462
242	5 85 64	15.556	272	7 39 84	16.492
243	5 90 49	15.588	273	7 45 29	16.523
244	5 95 36	15.620	274	7 50 76	16.553
245	6 00 25	15.652	275	7 56 25	16.583
246	6 05 16	15.684	276	7 61 76	16.613
247	6 10 09	15.716	277	7 67 29	16.643
248	6 15 04	15.748	278	7 72 84	16.673
249	6 20 01	15.780	279	7 78 41	16.703
250	6 25 00	15.811	280	7 84 00	16.733
251	6 30 01	15.843	281	7 89 61	16.763
252	6 35 04	15.875	282	7 95 24	16.793
253	6 40 09	15.906	283	8 00 89	16.823
254	6 45 16	15.937	284	8 06 56	16.852
255	6 50 25	15.969	285	8 12 25	16.882
256	6 55 36	16.000	286	8 17 96	16.912
257	6 60 49	16.031	287	8 23 69	16.941
258	6 65 64	16.062	288	8 29 44	16.971
259	6 70 81	16.093	289	8 35 21	17.000
260	6 76 00	16.125	290	8 41 00	17.029
261	6 81 21	16.155	291	8 46 81	17.059
262	6 86 44	16.186	292	8 52 64	17.088
263	6 91 69	16.217	293	8 58 49	17.117
264	6 96 96	16.248	294	8 64 36	17.146
265	7 02 25	16.279	295	8 70 25	17.176
266	7 07 56	16.310	296	8 76 16	17.205
267	7 12 89	16.340	297	8 82 09	17.234
268	7 18 24	16.371	298	8 88 04	17.263
269	7 23 61	16.401	299	8 94 01	17.292
270	7 29 00	16.432	300	9 00 00	17.321

Table of Squares and Square Roots (Continued)

Number	Square	Square Root	Number	Square	Square Root
301	9 06 01	17.349	331	10 95 61	18.193
302	9 12 04	17.378	332	11 02 24	18.221
303	9 18 09	17.407	333	11 08 89	18.248
304	9 24 16	17.436	334	11 15 56	18.276
305	9 30 25	17.464	335	11 22 25	18.303
306	9 36 36	17.493	336	11 28 96	18.330
307	9 42 49	17.521	337	11 35 69	18.358
308	9 48 64	17.550	338	11 42 44	18.385
309	9 54 81	17.578	339	11 49 21	18.412
310	9 61 00	17.607	340	11 56 00	18.439
311	9 67 21	17.635	341	11 62 81	18.466
312	9 73 44	17.664	342	11 69 64	18.493
313	9 79 69	17.692	343	11 76 49	18.520
314	9 85 96	17.720	344	11 83 36	18.547
315	9 92 25	17.748	345	11 90 25	18.574
316	9 98 56	17.776	346	11 97 16	18.601
317	10 04 89	17.804	347	12 04 09	18.628
318	10 11 24	17.833	348	12 11 04	18.655
319	10 17 61	17.861	349	12 18 01	18.682
320	10 24 00	17.889	350	12 25 00	18.708
321	10 30 41	17.916	351	12 32 01	18.735
322	10 36 84	17.944	352	12 39 04	18.762
323	10 43 29	17.972	353	12 46 09	18.788
324	10 49 76	18.000	354	12 53 16	18.815
325	10 56 25	18.028	355	12 60 25	18.841
326	10 62 76	18.055	356	12 67 36	18.868
327	10 69 29	18.083	357	12 74 49	18.894
328	10 75 84	18.111	358	12 81 64	18.921
329	10 82 41	18.138	359	12 88 81	18.947
330	10 89 00	18.166	360	12 96 00	18.974

Table of Squares and Square Roots (Continued)

Number	Square	Square Root	Number	Square	Square Root
421	17 72 41	20.518	451	20 34 01	21.237
422	17 80 84	20.543	452	20 43 04	21.260
423	17 89 29	20.567	453	20 52 09	21.284
424	17 97 76	20.591	454	20 61 16	21.307
425	18 06 25	20.616	455	20 70 25	21.331
426	18 14 76	20.640	456	20 79 36	21.354
427	18 23 29	20.664	457	20 88 49	21.378
428	18 31 84	20.688	458	20 97 64	21.401
429	18 40 41	20.712	459	21 06 81	21.424
430	18 49 00	20.736	460	21 16 00	21.448
431	18 57 61	20.761	461	21 25 21	21.471
432	18 66 24	20.785	462	21 34 44	21.494
433	18 74 89	20.809	463	21 43 69	21.517
434	18 83 56	20.833	464	21 52 96	21.541
435	18 92 25	20.857	465	21 62 25	21.564
436	19 00 96	20.881	466	21 71 56	21.587
437	19 09 69	20.905	467	21 80 89	21.610
438	19 18 44	20.928	468	21 90 24	21.633
439	19 27 21	20.952	469	21 99 61	21.656
440	19 36 00	20.976	470	22 09 00	21.679
441	19 44 81	21.000	471	22 18 41	21.703
442	19 53 64	21.024	472	22 27 84	21.726
443	19 62 49	21.048	473	22 37 29	21.749
444	19 71 36	21.071	474	22 46 76	21.772
445	19 80 25	21.095	475	22 56 25	21.794
446	19 89 16	21.119	476	22 65 76	21.817
447	19 98 09	21.142	477	22 75 29	21.840
448	20 07 04	21.166	478	22 84 84	21.863
449	20 16 01	21.190	479	22 94 41	21.886
450	20 25 00	21.213	480	23 04 00	21.909

Table of Squares and Square Roots (Continued)

Number	Square	Square Root	Number	Square	Square Root
361	13 03 21	19.000	391	15 28 81	19.774
362	13 10 44	19.026	392	15 36 64	19.799
363	13 17 69	19.053	393	15 44 49	19.824
364	13 24 96	19.079	394	15 52 36	19.849
365	13 32 25	19.105	395	15 60 25	19.875
366	13 39 56	19.131	396	15 68 16	19.900
367	13 46 89	19.157	397	15 76 09	19.925
368	13 54 24	19.183	398	15 84 04	19.950
369	13 61 61	19.209	399	15 92 01	19.975
370	13 69 00	19.235	400	16 00 00	20.000
371	13 76 41	19.261	401	16 08 01	20.025
372	13 83 84	19.287	402	16 16 04	20.050
373	13 91 29	19.313	403	16 24 09	20.075
374	13 98 76	19.339	404	16 32 16	20.100
375	14 06 25	19.363	405	16 40 25	20.125
376	14 13 76	19.391	406	16 48 36	20.149
377	14 21 29	19.416	407	16 56 49	20.174
378	14 28 84	19.442	408	16 64 64	20.199
379	14 36 41	19.468	409	16 72 81	20.224
380	14 44 00	19.494	410	16 81 00	20.248
381	14 51 61	19.519	411	16 89 21	20.273
382	14 59 24	19.545	412	16 97 44	20.298
383	14 66 89	19.570	413	17 05 69	20.322
384	14 74 56	19.596	414	17 13 96	20.347
385	14 82 25	19.621	415	17 22 25	20.372
386	14 89 96	19.647	416	17 30 56	20.396
387	14 97 69	19.672	417	17 38 89	20.421
388	15 05 44	19.698	418	17 47 24	20.445
389	15 13 21	19.723	419	17 55 61	20.469
390	15 21 00	19.748	420	17 64 00	20.494

Table of Squares and Square Roots (Continued)

Number	Square	Square Root	Number	Square	Square Root
481	23 13 61	21.932	511	26 11 21	22.605
482	23 23 24	21.954	512	26 21 44	22.627
483	23 32 89	21.977	513	26 31 69	22.650
484	23 42 56	22.000	514	26 41 96	22.672
485	23 52 25	22.023	515	26 52 25	22.694
486	23 61 96	22.045	516	26 62 56	22.716
487	23 71 69	22.068	517	26 72 89	22.738
488	23 81 44	22.091	518	26 83 24	22.760
489	23 91 21	22.113	519	26 93 61	22.782
490	24 01 00	22.136	520	27 04 00	22.804
491	24 10 81	22.159	521	27 14 41	22.825
492	24 20 64	22.181	522	27 24 84	22.847
493	24 30 49	22.204	523	27 35 29	22.869
494	24 40 36	22.226	524	27 45 76	22.891
495	24 50 25	22.249	525	27 56 25	22.913
496	24 60 16	22.271	526	27 66 76	22.935
497	24 70 09	22.293	527	27 77 29	22.956
498	24 80 04	22.316	528	27 87 84	22.978
499	24 90 03	22.338	529	27 98 41	23.000
500	25 00 00	22.361	530	28 09 00	23.022
501	25 10 01	22.383	531	28 19 61	23.043
502	25 20 04	22.405	532	28 30 24	23.065
503	25 30 09	22.428	533	28 40 89	23.087
504	25 40 16	22.450	534	28 51 56	23.108
505	25 50 25	22.472	535	28 62 25	23.130
506	25 60 36	22.494	536	28 72 96	23.152
507	25 70 49	22.517	537	28 83 69	23.173
508	25 80 64	22.539	538	28 94 44	23.195
509	25 90 81	22.561	539	29 05 21	23.216
510	26 01 00	22.583	540	29 16 00	23.238

Table of Squares and Square Roots (Continued)

Number	Square	Square Root	Number	Square	Square Root
541	29 26 81	23.259	571	32 60 41	23.896
542	29 37 64	23.281	572	32 71 84	23.917
543	29 48 49	23.302	573	32 83 29	23.937
544	29 59 36	23.324	574	32 94 76	23.958
545	29 70 25	23.345	575	33 06 25	23.979
546	29 81 16	23.367	576	33 17 76	24.000
547	29 92 09	23.388	577	33 29 29	24.021
548	30 03 04	23.409	578	33 40 84	24.042
549	30 14 01	23.431	579	33 52 41	24.062
550	30 25 00	23.452	580	33 64 00	24.083
551	30 36 01	23.473	581	33 75 61	24.104
552	30 47 04	23.495	582	33 87 24	24.125
553	30 58 09	23.516	583	33 98 89	24.145
554	30 69 16	23.537	584	34 10 56	24.166
555	30 80 25	23.558	585	34 22 25	24.187
556	30 91 36	23.580	586	34 33 96	24.207
557	31 02 49	23.601	587	34 45 69	24.228
558	31 13 64	23.622	588	34 57 44	24.249
559	31 24 81	23.643	589	34 69 21	24.269
560	31 36 00	23.664	590	34 81 00	24.290
561	31 47 21	23.685	591	34 92 81	24.310
562	31 58 44	23.707	592	35 04 64	24.331
563	31 69 69	23.728	593	35 16 49	24.352
564	31 80 96	23.749	594	35 28 36	24.372
565	31 92 25	23.770	595	35 40 25	24.393
566	32 03 56	23.791	596	35 52 16	24.413
567	32 14 89	23.812	597	35 64 09	24.434
568	32 26 24	23.833	598	35 76 04	24.454
569	32 37 61	23.854	599	35 88 01	24.474
570	32 49 00	23.875	600	36 00 00	24.495

Table of Squares and Square Roots (Continued)

Number	Square	Square Root	Number	Square	Square Root
601	36 12 01	24.515	631	39 81 61	25.120
602	36 24 04	24.536	632	39 94 24	25.140
603	36 36 09	24.556	633	40 06 89	25.159
604	36 48 16	24.576	634	40 19 56	25.179
605	36 60 25	24.597	635	40 32 25	25.199
606	36 72 36	24.617	636	40 44 96	25.219
607	36 84 49	24.637	637	40 57 69	25.239
608	36 96 64	24.658	638	40 70 44	25.259
609	37 08 81	24.678	639	40 83 21	25.278
610	37 21 00	24.698	640	40 96 00	25.298
611	37 33 21	24.718	641	41 08 81	25.318
612	37 45 44	24.739	642	41 21 64	25.338
613	37 57 69	24.759	643	41 34 49	25.357
614	37 69 96	24.779	644	41 47 36	25.377
615	37 82 25	24.799	645	41 60 25	25.397
616	37 94 56	24.819	646	41 73 16	25.417
617	38 06 89	24.839	647	41 86 09	25.436
618	38 19 24	24.860	648	41 99 04	25.456
619	38 31 61	24.880	649	42 12 01	25.475
620	38 44 00	24.900	650	42 25 00	25.495
621	38 56 41	24.920	651	42 38 01	25.515
622	38 68 84	24.940	652	42 51 04	25.534
623	38 81 29	24.960	653	42 64 09	25.554
624	38 93 76	24.980	654	42 77 16	25.573
625	39 06 25	25.000	655	42 90 25	25.593
626	39 18 76	25.020	656	43 03 36	25.612
627	39 31 29	25.040	657	43 16 49	25.632
628	39 43 84	25.060	658	43 29 64	25.652
629	39 56 41	25.080	659	43 42 81	25.671
630	39 69 00	25.100	660	43 56 00	25.690

Table of Squares and Square Roots (Continued)

Number	Square	Square Root	Number	Square	Square Root
661	43 69 21	25.710	691	47 74 81	26.287
662	43 82 44	25.729	692	47 88 64	26.306
663	43 95 69	25.749	693	48 02 49	26.325
664	44 08 96	25.768	694	48 16 36	26.344
665	44 22 25	25.788	695	48 30 25	26.363
666	44 35 56	25.807	696	48 44 16	26.382
667	44 48 89	25.826	697	48 58 09	26.401
668	44 62 24	25.846	698	48 72 04	26.420
669	44 75 61	25.865	699	48 86 01	26.439
670	44 89 00	25.884	700	49 00 00	26.458
671	45 02 41	25.904	701	49 14 01	26.476
672	45 15 84	25.923	702	49 28 04	26.495
673	45 29 29	25.942	703	49 42 09	26.514
674	45 42 76	25.962	704	49 56 16	26.533
675	45 56 25	25.981	705	49 70 25	26.552
676	45 69 76	26.000	706	49 84 36	26.571
677	45 83 29	26.019	707	49 98 49	26.589
678	45 96 84	26.038	708	50 12 64	26.608
679	46 10 41	26.058	709	50 26 81	26.627
680	46 24 00	26.077	710	50 41 00	26.646
681	46 37 61	26.096	711	50 55 21	26.665
682	46 51 24	26.115	712	50 69 44	26.683
683	46 64 89	26.134	713	50 83 69	26.702
684	46 78 56	26.153	714	50 97 96	26.721
685	46 92 25	26.173	715	51 12 25	26.739
686	47 05 96	26.192	716	51 26 56	26.758
687	47 19 69	26.211	717	51 40 89	26.777
688	47 33 44	26.230	718	51 55 24	26.796
689	47 47 21	26.249	719	51 69 61	26.814
690	47 61 00	26.268	720	51 84 00	26.833

Table of Squares and Square Roots (Continued)

Number	Square	Square Root	Number	Square	Square Root
781	60 99 61	27.946	811	65 77 21	28.478
782	61 15 24	27.964	812	65 93 44	28.496
783	61 30 89	27.982	813	66 09 69	28.513
784	61 46 56	28.000	814	66 25 96	28.531
785	61 62 25	28.018	815	66 42 25	28.548
786	61 77 96	28.036	816	66 58 56	28.566
787	61 93 69	28.054	817	66 74 89	28.583
788	62 09 44	28.071	818	66 91 24	28.601
789	62 25 21	28.089	819	67 07 61	28.618
790	62 41 00	28.107	820	67 24 00	28.636
791	62 56 81	28.125	821	67 40 41	28.653
792	62 72 64	28.142	822	67 56 84	28.671
793	62 88 49	28.160	823	67 73 29	28.688
794	63 04 36	28.178	824	67 89 76	28.705
795	63 20 25	28.196	825	68 06 25	28.723
796	63 36 16	28.213	826	68 22 76	28.740
797	63 52 09	28.231	827	68 39 29	28.758
798	63 68 04	28.249	828	68 55 84	28.775
799	63 84 01	28.267	829	68 72 41	28.792
800	64 00 00	28.284	830	68 89 00	28.810
801	64 16 01	28.302	831	69 05 61	28.827
802	64 32 04	28.320	832	69 22 24	28.844
803	64 48 09	28.337	833	69 38 89	28.862
804	64 64 16	28.355	834	69 55 56	28.879
805	64 80 25	28.373	835	69 72 25	28.896
806	64 96 36	28.390	836	69 88 96	28.914
807	65 12 49	28.408	837	70 05 69	28.931
808	65 28 64	28.425	838	70 22 44	28.948
809	65 44 81	28.443	839	70 39 21	28.965
810	65 61 00	28.460	840	70 56 00	28.983

Table of Squares and Square Roots (Continued)

Number	Square	Square Root	Number	Square	Square Root
721	51 98 41	26.851	751	56 40 01	27.404
722	52 12 84	26.870	752	56 55 04	27.423
723	52 27 29	26.889	753	56 70 09	27.441
724	52 41 76	26.907	754	56 85 16	27.459
725	52 56 25	26.926	755	57 00 25	27.477
726	52 70 76	26.944	756	57 15 36	27.495
727	52 85 29	26.963	757	57 30 49	27.514
728	52 99 84	26.981	758	57 45 64	27.532
729	53 14 41	27.000	759	57 60 81	27.550
730	53 29 00	27.019	760	57 76 00	27.568
731	53 43 61	27.037	761	57 91 21	27.586
732	53 48 24	27.055	762	58 06 44	27.604
533	53 72 89	27.074	763	58 21 69	27.622
734	53 87 56	27.092	764	58 36 96	27.641
735	54 02 25	27.111	765	58 52 25	27.659
736	54 16 96	27.129	766	58 67 56	27.677
737	54 31 69	27.148	767	58 82 89	27.695
738	54 46 44	27.166	768	58 98 24	27.713
739	54 61 21	27.185	769	59 13 61	27.731
740	54 76 00	27.203	770	59 29 00	27.749
741	54 90 81	27.221	771	59 44 41	27.767
742	55 05 64	27.240	772	59 59 84	27.785
743	55 20 49	27.258	773	59 75 29	27.803
744	55 35 36	27.276	774	59 90 76	27.821
745	55 50 25	27.295	775	60 06 25	27.839
746	55 65 16	27.313	776	60 21 76	27.857
747	55 80 09	27.331	777	60 37 29	27.875
748	55 95 04	27.350	778	60 52 84	27.893
749	56 10 01	27.368	779	60 68 41	27.911
750	56 25 00	27.386	780	60 84 00	27.928

Table of Squares and Square Roots (Continued)

Number	Square	Square Root	Number	Square	Square Root
901	81 18 01	30.017	931	86 67 61	30.512
902	81 36 04	30.033	932	86 86 24	30.529
903	81 54 09	30.050	933	87 04 89	30.545
904	81 72 16	30.067	934	87 23 56	30.561
905	81 90 25	30.083	935	87 42 25	30.578
906	82 08 36	30.100	936	87 60 96	30.594
907	82 26 49	30.116	937	87 79 69	30.610
908	82 44 64	30.133	938	87 98 44	30.627
909	82 62 81	30.150	939	88 17 21	30.643
910	82 81 00	30.166	940	88 36 00	30.659
911	82 99 21	30.183	941	88 54 81	30.676
912	83 17 44	30.199	942	88 73 64	30.692
913	83 35 69	30.216	943	88 92 49	30.708
914	83 53 96	30.232	944	89 11 36	30.725
915	83 72 25	30.249	945	89 30 25	30.741
916	83 90 56	30.265	946	89 49 16	30.757
917	84 08 89	30.282	947	89 68 09	30.773
918	84 27 24	30.299	948	89 87 04	30.790
919	84 45 61	30.315	949	90 06 01	30.806
920	84 64 00	30.332	950	90 25 00	30.822
921	84 82 41	30.348	951	90 44 01	30.838
922	85 00 84	30.364	952	90 63 04	30.854
923	85 19 29	30.381	953	90 82 09	30.871
924	85 37 76	30.397	954	91 01 16	30.887
925	85 56 25	30.414	955	91 20 25	30.903
926	85 74 76	30.430	956	91 39 36	30.919
927	85 93 29	30.447	957	91 58 49	30.935
928	86 11 84	30.463	958	91 77 64	30.952
929	86 30 41	30.480	959	91 96 81	30.968
930	86 49 00	30.496	960	92 16 00	30.984

Table of Squares and Square Roots (Continued)

Number	Square	Square Root	Number	Square	Square Root
841	70 72 81	29.000	871	75 86 41	29.513
842	70 89 64	29.017	872	76 03 84	29.530
843	71 06 49	29.034	873	76 21 29	29.547
844	71 23 36	29.052	874	76 38 76	29.563
845	71 40 25	29.069	875	76 56 25	29.580
846	71 57 16	29.086	876	76 73 76	29.597
847	71 74 09	29.103	877	76 91 29	29.614
848	71 91 04	29.120	878	77 08 84	29.631
849	72 08 01	29.138	879	77 26 41	29.648
850	72 25 00	29.155	880	77 44 00	29.665
851	72 42 01	29.172	881	77 61 61	29.682
852	72 59 04	29.189	882	77 79 24	29.698
853	72 76 09	29.206	883	77 96 89	29.715
854	72 93 16	29.223	884	78 14 56	29.732
855	73 10 25	29.240	885	78 32 25	29.749
856	73 27 36	29.257	886	78 49 96	29.766
857	73 44 49	29.275	887	78 67 69	29.783
858	73 61 64	29.292	888	78 85 44	29.799
859	73 78 81	29.309	889	79 03 21	29.816
860	73 96 00	29.326	890	79 21 00	29.833
861	74 13 21	29.343	891	79 38 81	29.850
862	74 30 44	29.360	892	79 56 64	29.866
863	74 47 69	29.377	893	79 74 49	29.883
864	74 64 96	29.394	894	79 92 36	29.900
865	74 82 25	29.411	895	80 10 25	29.916
866	74 99 56	29.428	896	80 28 16	29.933
867	75 16 89	29.445	897	80 46 09	29.950
868	75 34 24	29.462	898	80 64 04	29.967
869	75 51 61	29.479	899	80 82 01	29.983
870	75 69 00	29.496	900	81 00 00	30.000

Table of Squares and Square Roots (Concluded)

Number	Square	Square Root	Number	Square	Square Root
961	92 35 21	31.000	981	96 23 61	31.321
962	92 54 44	31.016	982	96 43 24	31.337
963	92 73 69	31.032	983	96 62 89	31.353
964	92 92 96	31.048	984	96 82 56	31.369
965	93 12 25	31.064	985	97 02 25	31.385
966	93 31 56	31.081	986	97 21 96	31.401
967	93 50 89	31.097	987	97 41 69	31.417
968	93 70 24	31.113	988	97 61 44	31.432
969	93 89 61	31.129	989	97 81 21	31.448
970	94 09 00	31.145	990	98 01 00	31.464
971	94 28 41	31.161	991	98 20 81	31.480
972	94 47 84	31.177	992	98 40 64	31.496
973	94 67 29	31.193	993	98 60 49	31.512
974	94 86 76	31.209	994	98 80 36	31.528
975	95 06 25	31.225	995	99 00 25	31.544
976	95 25 76	31.241	996	99 20 16	31.559
977	95 45 29	31.257	997	99 40 09	31.575
978	95 64 84	31.273	998	99 60 04	31.591
979	95 84 41	31.289	999	99 80 01	31.607
980	96 04 00	31.305	1000	100 00 00	31.623

APPENDIX D

Table of Random Numbers

(Appendix D is reproduced from M. G. Kendall and B. B. Smith, Randomness and random sampling numbers. *Journal of the Royal Statistical Society*, 1938, *101*, 147–166, by permission of the Royal Statistical Society.)

COLUMN NUMBER

Row	00000 01234	00000 56789	11111 01234	11111 56789	22222 01234	22222 56789	33333 01234	33333 56789
				1st Thousand				
00	23157	54859	01837	25993	76249	70886	95230	36744
01	05545	55043	10537	43508	90611	83744	10962	21343
02	14871	60350	32404	36223	50051	00322	11543	80834
03	38976	74951	94051	75853	78805	90194	32428	71695
04	97312	61718	99755	30870	94251	25841	54882	10513
05	11742	69381	44339	30872	32797	33118	22647	06850
06	43361	28859	11016	45623	93009	00499	43640	74036
07	93806	20478	38268	04491	55751	18932	58475	52571
08	49540	13181	08429	84187	69538	29661	77738	09527
09	36768	72633	37948	21569	41959	68670	45274	83880
10	07092	52392	24627	12067	06558	45344	67338	45320
11	43310	01081	44863	80307	52555	16148	89742	94647
12	61570	06360	06173	63775	63148	95123	35017	46993
13	31352	83799	10779	18941	31579	76448	62584	86919
14	57048	86526	27795	93692	90529	56546	35065	32254
15	09243	44200	68721	07137	30729	75756	09298	27650
16	97957	35018	40894	88329	52230	82521	22532	61587
17	93732	59570	43781	98885	56671	66826	95996	44569
18	72621	11225	00922	68264	35666	59434	71687	58167
19	61020	74418	45371	20794	95917	37866	99536	19378
20	97839	85474	33055	91718	45473	54144	22034	23000
21	89160	97192	22232	90637	35055	45489	88438	16361
22	25966	88220	62871	79265	02823	52862	84919	54883
23	81443	31719	05049	54806	74690	07567	65017	16543
24	11322	54931	42362	34386	08624	97687	46245	23245

Table of Random Numbers (Continued)

COLUMN NUMBER

2nd Thousand

Row	00000 01234	00000 56789	11111 01234	11111 56789	22222 01234	22222 56789	33333 01234	33333 56789
00	64755	83885	84122	25920	17696	15655	95045	95947
01	10302	52289	77436	34430	38112	49067	07348	23328
02	71017	98495	51308	50374	66591	02887	53765	69149
03	60012	55605	88410	34879	79655	90169	78800	03666
04	37330	94656	49161	42802	48274	54755	44553	65090
05	47869	87001	31591	12273	60626	12822	34691	61212
06	38040	42737	64167	89578	39323	49324	88434	38706
07	73508	30908	83054	80078	86669	30295	56460	45336
08	32623	46474	84061	04324	20628	37319	32356	43969
09	97591	99549	36630	35106	62069	92975	95320	57734
10	74012	31955	59790	96982	66224	24015	96749	07589
11	56754	26457	13351	05014	90966	33674	69096	33488
12	49800	49908	54831	21998	08528	26372	92923	65026
13	43584	89647	24878	56670	00221	50193	99591	62377
14	16653	79664	60325	71301	35742	83636	73058	87229
15	48502	69055	65322	58748	31446	80237	31252	96367
16	96765	54692	36316	86230	48296	38352	23816	64094
17	38923	61550	80357	81784	23444	12463	33992	28128
18	77958	81694	25225	05587	51073	01070	60218	61961
19	17928	28065	25586	08771	02641	85064	65796	48170
20	94036	85978	02318	04499	41054	10531	87431	21596
21	47460	60479	56230	48417	14372	85167	27558	00368
22	47856	56088	51992	82439	40644	17170	13463	18288
23	57616	34653	92298	62018	10375	76515	62986	90756
24	08300	92704	66752	66610	57188	79107	54222	22013

Table of Random Numbers (Continued)

Row	00000 01234	00000 56789	11111 01234	11111 56789	22222 01234	22222 56789	33333 01234	33333 56789
				3rd Thousand				
00	89221	02362	65787	74733	51272	30213	92441	39651
01	04005	99818	63918	29032	94012	42363	01261	10650
02	98546	38066	50856	75045	40645	22841	53254	44125
03	41719	84401	59226	01314	54581	40398	49988	65579
04	28733	72489	00785	25843	24613	49797	85567	84471
05	65213	83927	77762	03086	80742	24395	68476	83792
06	65553	12678	90906	90466	43670	26217	69900	31205
07	05668	69080	73029	85746	58332	78231	45986	92998
08	39302	99718	49757	79519	27387	76373	47262	91612
09	64592	32254	45879	29431	38320	05981	18067	87137
10	07513	48792	47314	83660	68907	05336	82579	91582
11	86593	68501	56638	99800	82839	35148	56541	07232
12	83735	22599	97977	81248	36838	99560	32410	67614
13	08595	21826	54655	08204	87990	17033	56258	05384
14	41273	27149	44293	69458	16828	63962	15864	35431
15	00473	75908	56238	12242	72631	76314	47252	06347
16	86131	53789	81383	07868	89132	96182	07009	86432
17	33849	78359	08402	03586	03176	88663	08018	22546
18	61870	41657	07468	08612	98083	97349	20775	45091
19	43898	65923	25078	86129	78491	97653	91500	80786
20	29939	39123	04548	45985	60952	06641	28726	46473
21	38505	85555	14388	55077	18657	94887	67831	70819
22	31824	38431	67125	25511	72044	11562	52379	82268
23	91430	03767	13561	15597	06750	92552	02391	38753
24	38635	68976	25498	97526	96458	03805	04116	63514

Table of Random Numbers (Continued)

COLUMN NUMBER

4th Thousand

Row	00000 01234	00000 56789	11111 01234	11111 56789	22222 01234	22222 56789	33333 01234	33333 56789
00	02490	54122	27944	39364	94239	72074	11679	54082
01	11967	36469	60627	83701	09253	30208	01385	37482
02	48256	83465	49699	24079	05403	35154	39613	03136
03	27246	73080	21481	23536	04881	89977	49484	93071
04	32532	77265	72430	70722	86529	18457	92657	10011
05	66757	98955	92375	93431	43204	55825	45443	69625
06	11266	34545	76505	97746	34668	26999	26742	97516
07	17872	39142	45561	80146	93137	48924	64257	59284
08	62561	30365	03408	14754	51798	08133	61010	97730
09	62796	30779	35497	70501	30105	08133	00997	91970
10	75510	21771	04339	33660	42757	62223	87565	48468
11	87439	01691	63517	26590	44437	07217	98706	39032
12	97742	02621	10748	78803	38337	65226	92149	59051
13	98811	06001	21571	02875	21828	83912	85188	61624
14	51264	01852	64607	92553	29004	26695	78583	62998
15	40239	93376	10419	68610	49120	02941	80035	99317
16	26936	59186	51667	27645	46329	44681	94190	66647
17	88502	11716	98299	40974	42394	62200	69094	81646
18	63499	38093	25593	61995	79867	80569	01023	38374
19	36379	81206	03317	78710	73828	31083	60509	44091
20	93801	22322	47479	57017	59334	30647	43061	26660
21	29856	87120	56311	50053	25365	81265	22414	02431
22	97720	87931	88265	13050	71017	15177	06957	92919
23	85237	09105	74601	46377	59938	15647	34177	92753
24	75746	75268	31727	95773	72364	87324	36879	06802

Table of Random Numbers (Continued)

COLUMN NUMBER

5th Thousand

Row	00000 01234	00000 56789	11111 01234	11111 56789	22222 01234	22222 56789	33333 01234	33333 56789
00	29935	06971	63175	52579	10478	89379	61428	21363
01	15114	07126	51890	77787	75510	13103	42942	48111
02	03870	43225	10589	87629	22039	94124	38127	65022
03	79390	39188	40756	45269	65959	20640	14284	22960
04	30035	06915	79196	54428	64819	52314	48721	81594
05	29039	99861	28759	79802	68531	39198	38137	24373
06	78196	08108	24107	49777	09599	43569	84820	94956
07	15847	85493	91442	91351	80130	73752	21539	10986
08	36614	62248	49194	97209	92587	92053	41021	80064
09	40549	54884	91465	43862	35541	44466	88894	74180
10	40878	08997	14286	09982	90308	78007	51587	16658
11	10229	49282	41173	31468	59455	18756	08908	06660
12	15918	76787	30624	25928	44124	25088	31137	71614
13	13403	18796	49909	94404	64979	41462	18155	98335
14	66523	94596	74908	90271	10009	98648	17640	68909
15	91665	36469	68343	17870	25975	04662	21272	50620
16	67415	87515	08207	73729	73201	57593	96917	69699
17	76527	96996	23724	33448	63392	32394	60887	90617
18	19815	47789	74348	17147	10954	34355	81194	54407
19	25592	53587	76384	72575	84347	68918	05739	57222
20	55902	45539	63646	31609	95999	82887	40666	66692
21	02470	58376	79794	22482	42423	96162	49491	17264
22	18630	53263	13319	97619	35859	12350	14632	87659
23	89673	38230	16063	92007	59503	38402	76450	33333
24	62986	67364	06595	17427	84623	14565	82860	57300

References

Alder, H. L., and Roessler, E. B. *Introduction to probability and statistics.* (3d ed.) San Francisco: Freeman, 1964.

Allen, E. M. Why are research grant applications disapproved? *Science,* 1960, *132,* 1532–1534.

American Psychological Association, Ad-hoc Committee on Ethical Standards in Psychological Research. *Ethical principles in the conduct of research with human participants.* Washington, D.C.: A.P.A., 1973.

American Psychological Association, Committee on Precautions in Animal Experimentation. *Rules regarding animals.* Washington, D.C.: A.P.A., 1949.

American Psychological Association, Council of Editors. *Ethical standards of psychologists.* Washington, D.C.: A.P.A., 1953.

American Psychological Association, Council of Editors. Testing and public policy. Special issue of *American Psychologist,* 1965, *20,* 857–993.

American Psychological Association, Council of Editors. Congress and social science. Special issue of *American Psychologist,* 1967, *22,* 877–1041. (a)

American Psychological Association, Council of Editors. *Publication manual of the American Psychological Association.* Washington, D.C.: A.P.A., 1967. (b)

Amos, J. R., Brown, F. L., and Mink, O. G. *Statistical concepts. A basic program.* New York: Harper & Row, 1965.

Anastasi, A. *Psychological testing.* (3d ed.) New York: Macmillan, 1968.

Anderson, B. *The psychology experiment: An introduction to the scientific method.* (2d ed.) Belmont, Calif.: Wadsworth, 1971.

Animal Welfare Institute. *Basic care of experimental animals.* (Rev. ed.) New York: Animal Welfare Inst., 1965.

Ardrey, R. *The territorial imperative.* New York: Dell, 1966.

Ardrey, R. *The social contract.* New York: Dell, 1970.

Argranoff, B. W. Memory and protein synthesis. *Scientific American,* 1967, *216* (6), 115–122.

Asch, S. E. Effects of group pressure upon the modification and distortion of judgments. In E. E. Macoby, T. M. Newcomb, and E. L. Hartley (Eds.), *Readings in social psychology.* New York: Holt, Rinehart and Winston, 1951.

Atkinson, J. W. (Ed.) *Motives in fantasy, action, and society.* New York: Van Nostrand, 1958.

Ausubel, D., and Sullivan, E. *Theories and problems of child development.* (2d ed.) New York: Grune & Stratton, 1970.

Bachrach, A. J. *Psychological research: An introduction.* (2d ed.) New York: Random House, 1965.

Bach-y-Rita, P., Collins, C., Saunders, F., White, B., and Scadden, L. Vision substitution by tactile image projection. *Nature,* 1969, *221,* 963–964.

Baker, R. A. The effects of repeated deprivation on the feeding behavior in rats. *Journal of Comparative and Physiological Psychology,* 1955, *48,* 37–42.

Bandura, A. *Principles of behavior modification.* New York: Holt, Rinehart and Winston, 1969.

Bandura, A., Grusec, J. E., and Menlove, F. L. Some social determinants of self-monitoring reinforcement systems. *Journal of Personality and Social Psychology,* 1967, *5,* 449–455.

Bandura, A., and McDonald, F. J. Influence of social reinforcement and the behavior of models in shaping children's moral judgments. *Journal of Abnormal and Social Psychology,* 1963, *67,* 274–281.

Bandura, A., and Menlove, F. L. Factors determining vicarious extinction of avoidance behavior through symbolic modeling. *Journal of Personality and Social Psychology,* 1968, *8,* 99–108.

Bandura, A., and Walters, R. H. *Social learning and personality development.* New York: Holt, Rinehart and Winston, 1963.

Barber, T. X. The effects of "hypnosis" on pain: A critical review of experimental and clinical findings. *Psychosomatic Medicine,* 1963, *25,* 303–333.

Barber, T. X. *Suggested ("hypnotic") behavior: The trance paradigm vs. an alternative paradigm.* Harding, Mass.: Medfield Foundation, 1970.

Barber T. X., Calverley, D. S., Forginone, A., McPeake, J. D., Chaves, J. F., and Bowen, B. Five attempts to replicate the experimenter bias effect. *Journal of Consulting and Clinical Psychology,* 1969, *33,* 1–6.

Barber, T. X., and Silver, M. J. Fact, fiction, and the experimenter effect. *Psychological Bulletin Monographs,* 1968, *70,* 1–29. (a)

Barber, T. X., and Silver, M. J. Pitfalls in data analysis and interpretations. A reply to Rosenthal. *Psychological Bulletin Monographs,* 1968, *70,* 48–62. (b)

Barlow, H. B. Slippage of contact lenses and other artifacts in relation to fading and regeneration of supposedly stable retinal images. *Quarterly Journal of Experimental Psychology,* 1963, *15,* 36–51.

Barnett, S. A. *The rat. A study in behaviour.* Chicago: Aldine, 1963.

Barron, F. *Creative person and creative process.* New York: Holt, Rinehart and Winston, 1969.

Battig, W. F., and Spera, A. J. Rated association values of numbers from 0–100. *Journal of Verbal Learning and Verbal Behavior,* 1962, *1,* 200–202.

Baumrind, D. Some thoughts on ethics of research: After reading Milgram's "Behavioral study of obedience." *American Psychologist,* 1964, *19,* 421–423.

Beach, F. A. The snark was a boojum. *American Psychologist,* 1950, *5,* 115–124.

Beach, F. A. *Sex and behavior.* New York: Wiley, 1965.

Beach, F. A. Coital behavior in dogs. III. Effects of early isolation on mating in males. *Behavior,* 1968, *30,* 218–238.

Beauchamp, K. L. *Drive and maintenance schedule.* Unpublished doctoral dissertation, Claremont Graduate School, 1968.

Beauchamp, K. L., Chapman, A., and Grebing, C. Response by the calf to stimulus change. *Psychonomic Science,* 1967, *9,* 125–126.

Beauchamp, K. L., Matheson, D. W., and Scadden, L. A. Effect of stimulus change method on tactile-image recognition. *Perceptual and Motor Skills,* 1971, *33,* 1067–1070.

Beery, R. G., and Black, R. W. Reversal of magnitude of reward in differential conditioning. *Psychological Record,* 1968, *18,* 179–183.

Bell, C. R. Personality characteristics of volunteers for psychological studies. *British Journal of Social and Clinical Psychology,* 1962, *1,* 81–95.

Bell, J. E. *A guide to library research in psychology.* Dubuque, Iowa: William C. Brown, 1971.

Bem, D. J., Wallach, M. A., and Kogan, N. Group decision making under risk of aversive consequences. *Journal of Personality and Social Psychology,* 1965, *1,* 453–460.

Berger, S. M. Observer practice and learning during exposure to a model. *Journal of Personality and Social Psychology,* 1966, *3,* 696–701.

Bergmann, G., and Spence, K. W. Operationism and theory in psychology. *Psychological Review,* 1941, *48,* 1–14.

Bijou, S. W., and Baer, D. M. The laboratory-experimental study of child behavior. In P. H. Mussen (Ed.), *Handbook of research methods in child development.* New York: Wiley, 1960.

Bijou, S. W., and Sturges, P. T. Positive reinforcers for experimental study with children—consumables and manipulatables. *Child Development,* 1959, *30,* 151–170.

Bindra, D., The nature of motivation for hoarding food. *Journal of Comparative and Physiological Psychology,* 1948, *41,* 211–218.

Bindra, D., *Motivation: A systematic reinterpretation,* New York: Ronald, 1959, 72–79.

Black, R. W. Shifts in magnitude of reward and contrast effects in instrumental and selective learning: A reinterpretation. *Psychological Review,* 1968, *75,* 114–126.

Blackwell, H. R. *Psychophysical thresholds: Experimental studies of methods of measurement.* Ann Arbor: University of Michigan Press (Eng. Res. Bull. No. 36), 1953.

Blank, M. Effect of stimulus characteristics on dimensional shifting in kindergarten children. *Journal of Comparative and Physiological Psychology,* 1967, *64,* 522–525.

Blomgren, G. W., and Scheuneman, T. W. Psychological resistance to seat belts. Research Project RR-115, Northwestern University, Traffic Institute, 1961.

Blommers, P., and Lindquist, E. F. *Elementary statistical methods in psychology and education.* Boston: Houghton Mifflin, 1960.

Boice, R. Operant components of conditioned licking in desert rodents. *Psychological Reports*, 1968, *22*, 1161–1167.

Bolles, R. *Theory of motivation.* New York: Harper & Row, 1967.

Boneau, C. A. The effects of violations of assumptions underlying the *t* test. *Psychological Bulletin*, 1960, *57*, 49–64.

Borah, L. A., Jr. The effects of threat in bargaining: Critical and experimental analyses. *Journal of Abnormal and Social Psychology*, 1963, *66*, 37–44.

Boring, E. G. *Sensation and perception in the history of experimental psychology.* New York: Appleton, 1942.

Bower, G. H. A contrast effect in differential conditioning. *Journal of Experimental Psychology*, 1961, *62*, 196–199. (a)

Bower, G. H. Application of a model to paired associate learning. *Psychometrica*, 1961, *26*, 255–280. (b)

Bower, T. G. R. The visual world of infants. *Scientific American*, 1966, *215* (6), 80–92.

Boynton, R. M. The psychophysics of vision. In R. N. Haber (Ed.), *Contemporary theory and research in visual perception.* New York: Holt, Rinehart and Winston, 1968.

Bradburn, N. M. *N* achievement and father dominance in Turkey. *Journal of Abnormal and Social Psychology*, 1963, *67*, 464–468.

Bradley, J. I., and McClelland, J. N. *Basic statistical concepts. A self-instructional text.* Chicago: Scott, Foresman, 1963.

Brady, J. V. Ulcers in "executive" monkeys. *Scientific American*, 1958, *199* (4), 95–100.

Breland, K., and Breland, M. *Animal behavior.* New York: Macmillan, 1966.

Bridgman, P. W. *The logic of modern physics.* New York: Macmillan, 1927.

Bridgman, P. W. Remarks on the present state of operationalism. *Scientific Monthly*, 1954, *79*, 224–226.

Brown, R. *Social psychology.* New York: Free Press, 1965.

Bruner, J. S., Olver, R. R., Greenfield, P. M., Hornsby, J. R., Kenney, H. F., Maccoby, M., Modiano, N., Mosher, F. A., Olson, D. R., Potter, M. C., Reich, L. C., and Sonstroem, A. M. *Studies in cognitive growth.* New York: Wiley, 1966.

Buros, O. K. *The sixth mental measurements yearbook.* Highland Park, N.J.: Gryphon Press, 1965.

Butler, R. A. Discrimination learning by rhesus monkeys to visual-exploration motivation. *Journal of Comparative and Physiological Psychology*, 1953, *46*, 95–98.

Butler, R. A. Incentive conditions which influence visual exploration. *Journal of Experimental Psychology*, 1954, *48*, 19–23.

Byrne, W. L., Samuel, D., Bennett, E. L., Rozenzweig, M. R., Wasserman, E., Wagner, A. R., Gardner, F., Galambos, R., Berger, B. D., Margules, D. L., Fenichel, R. L., Stein, L., Corson, J. A., Enesco, H. E., Chorover, S. L., Holt, C. E., III, Schiller, P. H., Chiappetta, L., Jarvik, M. E., Leaf, R. C., Dutcher, J. D., Horovitz, Z. P., and Carlton, P. L. Memory transfer. *Science*, 1966, *153*, 658–659.

Caldwell, W. E., and Russo, F. An exploratory study of the effects of an A.C. magnetic field upon the behavior of the Italian honeybee (Apis Millifica). *The Journal of Genetic Psychology*, 1968, *113*, 233–252.

Calhoun, J. B. Population density and social pathology. *Scientific American*, 1962, *206*(2), 139–148.

Campbell, D. T., and Stanley, J. C. *Experimental and quasi-experimental designs for research.* Chicago: Rand McNally, 1963.

Candland, D. K. *Psychology: The experimental approach.* New York: McGraw-Hill, 1968.

Cantor, G. N. Responses of infants and children to complex and novel stimulation. In L. P. Lipsitt and C. C. Spiker (Eds.), *Advances in child development and behavior.* Vol. 1. New York: Academic Press, 1963.

Cantor, G. N., and Cantor, J. H. Observing behavior in children as a function of stimulus novelty. *Child Development,* 1964, *35,* 119–128.

Cantor, J. H., and Cantor, G. N. Functions relating children's observing behavior to amount and recency of stimulus familiarization. *Journal of Experimental Psychology,* 1966, *72,* 859–863.

Cantril, H. *Gauging public opinion.* Princeton: Princeton University Press, 1944.

Capaldi, E. J., and Lynch, D. Repeated shifts in reward magnitude: Evidence in favor of an associational and absolute (noncontextual) interpretation. *Journal of Experimental Psychology,* 1967, *75,* 226–235.

Carlborg, F. W. *Introduction to statistics.* Glenview, Ill.: Scott, Foresman, 1968.

Carmon, A. Stimulus contrast in tactile resolution. *Perception and Psychophysics,* 1968, *3,* 241–245.

Casteneda, A., and Fahel, L. S. The relationship between the psychological investigator and the public schools. *American Psychologist,* 1961, *16,* 201–203.

Chase, T. C., and Rescorla, R. A. The effect of magnesium pemoline on learning an active avoidance-passive avoidance discrimination. *Psychonomic Science,* 1968, *10,* 87–88.

Christophersen, E. R., Arnold, C. M., Hill, D. W., and Quilitch, H. R. The home point system: Token reinforcement procedures for application by parents of children with behavior problems. *Journal of Applied Behavior Analysis,* 1972, *5,* 485–497.

Clifton, M. The dread tomato addiction. *Outstanding Science Fiction,* Feb. 1958, 97–98.

Cochran, W. G. The χ^2 test of goodness of it. *Annals of Mathematical Statistics,* 1952, *23,* 315–345.

Cochran, W. G. Some methods for strengthening the common χ^2 tests. *Biometrics,* 1954, *10,* 417–451.

Cofer, C. N., and Appley, M. H. *Motivation: Theory and research.* New York: Wiley, 1964.

Coleman, C. The effects of embryonic drug stimulation with Methylphenidate on imprinting of chicks. Unpublished research. University of the Pacific, 1969.

Collier, G., and Marx, M. H. Changes in performance as a function of shifts in the magnitude of reinforcement. *Journal of Experimental Psychology,* 1959, *57,* 305–309.

Committee on Revision of Guide for Laboratory Animals. *Guide for laboratory animal facilities and care.* (3d rev. ed.) Institute of laboratory animal resources. National Research Council. United States Department of Health, Education, and Welfare. Bethesda, Md.: National Institutes of Health, Public Health Service, Publication Number 1024, 1968.

Conant, J. B. *On understanding science: An historical approach.* New Haven: Yale University Press, 1947.

Conger, J. J. The effects of alcohol on conflict behavior in the albino rat. *Quarterly Journal of Studies on Alcohol,* 1951, *12,* 1–29.

Coombs, C. H. *A theory of data.* New York: Wiley, 1964.

Coombs, C. H., Raiffa, H., and Thrall, R. M. Some views on mathematical models and measurement theory. *Psychological Review,* 1954, *61,* 132–144.

Cormack, R. H. Haptic illusion: Apparent elongation of a disc rotated between the fingers. *Science,* 1973, *179,* 590–592.

Cornsweet, T. N. Determination of the stimuli for involuntary drifts and saccadic eye movements. *Journal of the Optical Society of America,* 1956, *46,* 987–993.

Cornsweet, T. N. The staircase-method in psychophysics. *American Journal of Psychology,* 1962, *75,* 485–491.

Cornsweet, T. N. *Visual perception.* New York: Academic Press, 1970.

Corso, J. F. *The experimental psychology of sensory behavior.* New York: Holt, Rinehart and Winston, 1967.

Courts, F. A. *Psychological statistics.* Homewood, Ill.: Dorsey, 1966.

Crespi, L. P. Quantitative variation of incentive and performance in the white rat. *American Journal of Psychology,* 1942, *55,* 467–517.

Daniels, V. Communication, incentive, and structural variables in interpersonal exchange and negotiation. *Journal of Experimental Social Psychology,* 1967, *3,* 47–74.

Darbyshire, J. O., and Reeves, V. R. The use of adaptations of some of Piaget's tests with groups of children with normal and impaired hearing. *British Journal of Disorders of Communication,* Oct. 1969, *4* (2).

Day, R. *Human perception.* New York: Wiley, 1969.

Day, R. What not to look for when buying a used car. *Popular Science,* 1968, pp. 84–87.

Deese, J., and Hulse, S. H. *The psychology of learning.* (3d. ed.) New York: McGraw-Hill, 1967.

Dember, W. N. *The psychology of perception.* New York: Holt, Rinehart and Winston, 1960.

Dember, W. N. The new look in motivation. *American Scientist,* 1965, *4,* 409–427.

Dember, W. N., and Earl, R. W. Analysis of exploratory, manipulatory, and curiosity behaviors. *Psychological Review,* 1057, *64,* 91–96.

Denny, M. R., and Ratner, S. C. *Comparative psychology: Research in animal behavior.* (Rev. ed.) Homewood, Ill.: Dorsey, 1970.

Dethier, V., and Stellar, E. *Animal behavior.* (3d ed.) Englewood Cliffs, N.J.: Prentice-Hall, 1969.

Deutsch, M., and Krauss, R. M. The effect of threat upon interpersonal bargaining. *Journal of Abnormal and Social Psychology,* 1960, *61,* 181–189.

Dilger, W. C. The behavior of lovebirds. *Scientific American,* 1962, *206,* 88–98.

Ditchburn, R. W., and Pritchard, R. M. Stabilized interference fringes on the retina. *Nature,* 1956, *177,* 434.

Dollard, J., Doob, L. W., Miller, N. E., Mowrer, O. H., Sears, R. R., Ford, C. S., Hovland, C. I., and Sollenberger, R. T. *Frustration and aggression.* New Haven: Yale University Press, 1939.

Duncker, K. On problem-solving. *Psychological Monographs,* 1945, *58*(5), 1–112.

Dunham, P. J. Incentive contrast and deprivation factors in a discrete-trial bar-press situation. *Journal of Comparative and Physiological Psychology,* 1967, *67,* 485–487.

Dunham, P. J. Contrasted conditions of reinforcement: A selective critique. *Psychological Bulletin,* 1968, *69,* 295–315.

Dunham, P. J., and Kilps, B. Shifts in magnitude of reinforcement: Confounded factors or contrast effects. *Journal of Experimental Psychology,* 1969, *79,* 373–374.

Eacker, J. N. Behaviorally produced illumination change: Visual exploration and reinforcement facilitation. *Journal of Comparative and Physiological Psychology,* 1967, *64,* 140–145.

Ebbinghaus, H. *Uber das gedachtnis: untersuchungen zur experimentellen psychologie.* Leipzig: Dunker and Humblot. 1885, (Translated as *Memory: A contribution to experimental psychology,* by H. A. Ruger and C. E. Bussenius. New York: Teachers College, Columbia University, 1913.)

Edwards, A. L. *Statistical methods.* (2d ed.) New York: Holt, Rinehart and Winston, 1967.

Edwards, A. L. *The measurement of personality traits by scales and inventories.* New York: Holt, Rinehart and Winston, 1970.

Edwards, A. L. *Experimental design in psychological research.* (4th ed.) New York: Holt, Rinehart and Winston, 1972.

Edwards, A. L. *Statistical methods.* (3d ed.) New York: Holt, Rinehart and Winston, 1973.

Egan, J. P., and Clarke, F. R. Psychophysics and signal detection. In J. B. Sidowski (Ed.), *Experimental methods and instrumentation in psychology.* New York: McGraw-Hill, 1966, 211–246.

Ehrenfreund, D. The motivational effect of a continuous weight loss schedule. *Psychological Reports,* 1960, *6,* 339–345.

Eibl-Eibesfeldt, I. *Ethology: The biology of behavior.* New York: Holt, Rinehart and Winston, 1970.

Eisenberg, J. F., and Dillon, W. S. *Man and beast: Comparative social behavior.* Washington, D.C.: Smithsonian Institution Press, 1971.

Ellsworth, P., and Carlsmith, J. M. Effects of eye contact and verbal content on affective response to dyadic interaction. *Journal of Personality and Social Psychology,* 1968, *10,* 15–20.

Endler, N. S., Boulter, L. R., and Osser, H. (Eds.) *Contemporary issues in developmental psychology.* New York: Holt, Rinehart and Winston, 1968.

Estes, W. K. Learning theory and the new "mental chemistry." *Psychological Review,* 1960, *67,* 207–223.

Estes, W. K., Hopkins, B. L., and Crothers, E. J. All-or-none and conservation effects in the learning and retention of paired-associates. *Journal of Experimental Psychology,* 1960, *60,* 329–339.

Evans, C. R. *Prolonged after-images employed as a technique for retinal stabilization: Some further studies of pattern perception and some theoretical considerations.* National Physical Laboratory: Autonomics Division, Teddington, Middlesex, England, 1966.

Evans, C. R., and Drage, D. J. *Some notes on apparatus used to produce a prolonged after-image for studies of perfect retinal stabilization.* National Physical Laboratory: Autonomics Division, Teddington, Middlesex, England, 1967.

Evans, C. R., and Kitson, A. *An experimental investigation of the relation between the "familiarity" of a word and the number of changes in its perception which occur with repeated presentation as a "stabilized auditory image."* National Physical Laboratory: Autonomics Division, Teddington, Middlesex, England, 1967.

Evans, C. R., Longden, M., Newman, E. A., and Pay, B. E. *Auditory "stabilized images"; Fragmentation and distortion of words with repeated presentation.* National Physical Laboratory: Autonomics Division, Teddington, Middlesex, England, 1967.

Excline, R. V. Explorations in the process of person perception: Visual interaction in relation to competition, sex, and need for affiliation. *Journal of Personality,* 1963, *31,* 1–20.

Excline, R. V., Gray, D., and Schuette, D. Visual behavior in a dyad as affected by interview content and sex of respondent. *Journal of Personality and Social Psychology,* 1965, *1,* 201–209.

Excline, R. V., and Winters, L. C. Affective relations and mutual glances in dyads. In S. S. Tomkins and C. E. Izard (Eds.), *Affect, cognition, and personality,* New York: Springer, 1965, 319–350.

Fawl, C. L. Disturbances experienced by children in their natural habitats. In R. G. Barker (Ed.), *The stream of behavior.* New York: Appleton, 1963.

Fellows, B. J. Chance stimulus sequences for discrimination tasks. *Psychological Bulletin,* 1967, *67,* 87–92.

Ferster, C. B. The autistic child. *Psychology Today,* 1968, 2 (6), 34–37, 61.

Ferster, C. B., and Perrott, M. C. *Behavior principles.* New York: Appleton, 1968.

Filby, Y., and Frank, L. Magnesium pemoline: Effects on drl performance. *Psychonomic Science,* 1968, *10,* 265–266.

Fiske, D. W., and Maddi, S. R. *The functions of varied experience.* Homewood, Ill.: Dorsey, 1961.

Flanders, J. P. A review of research on imitative behavior. *Psychological Bulletin,* 1968, *69,* 316–337.

Flavell, J. H. *The developmental psychology of Jean Piaget.* Princeton: Van Nostrand, 1963.

Fleischman, P. R., Israel, J. V., Burr, W. A., Hoaken, P. C. S., Thaler, O. F., Zucker, H. D., Hanley, J., Ostow, M., Lieberman, L. R., Hunter, F. M., Rinsker, H., Blair, S. M., Reich, W., Wiedeman, G. H., Pattison, E. M., and Rosenhan, D. L. Assorted letters in *Science,* 1973, *180,* 356–369.

Forgus, R. H. *Perception: The basic process in cognitive development.* New York: McGraw-Hill, 1966.

Foss, V. *Experiments in visual perception.* Penguin Books, Baltimore, Maryland, 1966, 7–28.

Fowler, R. L., Jr. *Magnitude and delay of reinforcement in spatial discrimination learning.* Unpublished doctoral dissertation, University of Tennessee, 1963. Reported in Black, R. W. Shifts in Magnitude of reward and contrast effects in instrumental and selective learning: A reinterpretation. *Psychological Review,* 1968, *75,* 114–126.

Fox, R. P., Kramer, M., Baldrige, B. J., Whitman, R. M., and Ornstein, P. H. The experimenter variable in dream research. *Diseases of the Nervous System,* 1968, *29,* 698–701.

Frank, F. Untitled and unpublished research. Reported in J. S. Bruner, et al. *Studies in cognitive growth.* New York: Wiley, 1966, 193–202.

Franken, R. E. Stimulus change, exploration, and laten learning. *Journal of Comparative and Physiological Psychology,* 1967, *64,* 301–307.

Franken, R. E., Jones, C. E. B., and Hanley, D. A. Adaptation, intertrial interval, and response to preferred and non-preferred change. *Canadian Journal of Psychology,* 1968, *22,* 45–51.

Gaito, J. Statistical dangers involved in counterbalancing. *Psychological Reports,* 1958, *4,* 463-468.

Galanter, E. Contemporary psychophysics. In *New directions in psychology.* Vol. 1. New York: Holt, Rinehart and Winston, 1962.

Gallo, P. S., Jr. Effects of increased incentives upon the use of threat in bargaining. *Journal of Personality and Social Psychology,* 1966, *4,* 14–20.

Gay, W. I. (Ed.) *Methods of animal experimentation.* (3 Vols.) New York: Academic Press, 1968.

Geldard, F. A. *The human senses.* (2d ed.) New York: Wiley, 1972.

Gellermann, L. W. Chance orders of alternating stimuli in visual discrimination experiments. *Journal of Genetic Psychology,* 1933, *42,* 206–208.

Gergen, K., and Marlowe, D. *Personality and social behavior.* Reading, Mass.: Addison-Wesley, 1970.

Gessner, P. K. Evaluation of instruction. *Science,* 1973, *180,* 566–570.

Gibson, E. J. *Principles of perceptual learning and development.* New York: Appleton, 1969.

Gibson, E. J., and Walk, R. D. The "visual cliff." *Scientific American,* 1960, *202,* 64–71.

Gibson, J. J. *The senses considered as perceptual systems.* Boston: Houghton Mifflin, 1966.

Gibson, J. J., and Pick, A. D. Perception of another person's looking behavior. *American Journal of Psychology,* 1963, *76,* 386–394.

Gilbert, J. E., and Barber, T. X. Effects of hypnotic induction, motivational suggestion, and level of suggestibility on cognitive performance. *The International Journal of Clinical and Experimental Hypnosis,* 1972, *20*(3), 156–168.

Ginsberg, H., and Opper, S. *Piaget's theory of intellectual development: An introduction.* Englewood Cliffs, N.J.: Prentice-Hall, 1969.

Glanzer, M. Curiosity, exploratory drive, and stimulus satiation. *Psychological Bulletin,* 1958, *55,* 302–315.

Glasky, A. J., and Simon, L. N. Magnesium pemoline: Enhancement of brain RNA polymerases. *Science,* 1966, *151,* 702–703.

Glass, D. C., Cohen, S., and Singer, J. E. Urban din fogs the brain. *Psychology Today,* 1973, *6*(12), 94–99.

Glaze, J. A. The association value of nonsense syllables. *Journal of Genetic Psychology,* 1928, *35,* 255–267.

Glickman, S. E., and Hartz, K. E. Exploratory behavior in several species of rodents. *Journal of Comparative and Physiological Psychology,* 1964, *58,* 101–104.

Goffman, E. On facework. *Psychiatry,* 1955, *18,* 213–231.

Goodall, J. My life among wild chimpanzees. *National Geographic,* 1963, *124,* 272–308.

Goodwin, D. W., Powell, B., Bremer, D., Hoine, H., and Stern, J. Alcohol and recall: State-dependent effects in man. *Science,* 1969, *163,* 1358–1360.

Gottlieb, G. Prenatal behavior of birds. *Quarterly Review of Biology,* 1968, *43,* 148–174.

Granit, R. *Receptors and sensory perception.* New Haven: Yale University Press, 1955.

Granit, R. The development of retinal neuro-physiology. *Science,* 1968, *160,* 1192–1196.

Greenspoon, J. The reinforcing effect of two spoken sounds on the frequency of two responses. *American Journal of Psychology,* 1955, *68,* 409–416.

Gregory, R. *Eye and brain: The psychology of seeing.* New York: McGraw-Hill, 1966.

Gregory, R. *The intelligent eye.* New York: McGraw-Hill, 1970.

Guilford, J. P. *Fundamental statistics in psychology and education.* (4th ed.) New York: McGraw-Hill, 1965.

Haber, R. N. Discrepancy from adaptation level as a source of affect. *Journal of Experimental Psychology,* 1958, *56,* 370–375.

Haber, R. N. (Ed.) *Current research in motivation.* New York: Holt, Rinehart and Winston, 1966.

Haber, R. N. (Ed.) *Contemporary theory and research in perception.* New York: Holt, Rinehart and Winston, 1968.

Haber, R. N., and Hershenson, M. *The psychology of visual perception.* New York: Holt, Rinehart and Winston, 1973.

Hall, J. F. *Psychology of motivation.* Chicago: Lippincott, 1961.

Hall, J. F. *The psychology of learning.* Philadelphia: Lippincott, 1966.

Harlow, H. F. Learning set and error factor theory. In S. Koch (Ed.) *Psychology: A study of a science.* Vol. 2. New York: McGraw-Hill, 1959, 492–537.

Harlow, H. F. Love in infant monkeys, *Scientific American,* 1959, *200* (6), 68–74.

Harlow, H. F. The heterosexual affectional system in monkeys. *American Psychologist,* 1962, *17,* 1–9.

Harlow, H. F. Age-mate or peer affectional systems. In D. S. Lehrman, R. D. Hinde, and E. Shaw (Eds.), *Advances in the study of behavior,* Vol. 2. New York: Academic Press, 1969.

Harlow, H. F., Harlow, M. K., and Meyer, D. R. Learning motivated by a manipulation drive. *Journal of Experimental Psychology,* 1950, *40,* 228–234.

Hartry, A. L., Keith-Lee, P., and Morton, W. D. "Planaria: Memory transfer through cannibalism" reexamined. *Science,* 1964, *146,* 274–275.

Haslam, D. R. The effect of threatened shock upon pain threshold. *Psychonomic Science,* 1966, *6,* 309–310.

Haude, R. H., and Ray, O. S. Visual exploration in monkeys as a function of visual incentive duration and sensory deprivation. *Journal of Comparative and Physiological Psychology,* 1967, *64,* 332–336.

Hays, W. L. *Statistics for social scientists.* (2d ed.) New York: Holt, Rinehart and Winston, 1973.

Haywood, H. C., and Wachs, T. D. Effects of arousing stimulation upon novelty preference in rats. *British Journal of Psychology,* 1967, *58,* 77–84.

Hebb, D. O. *A textbook of psychology.* Philadelphia: Saunders, 1966.

Hebb, D. O. The mind's eye. *Psychology Today,* 1969, *2* (12), 54–57, 67–68.

Heckenmueller, E. G. Stabilization of the retinal image: A review of method, effects, and theory. *Psychological Bulletin,* 1965, *63,* 157–169.

Heinemann, E. G., Chase, S., and Mandell, C. Discriminative control of "attention." *Science,* 1968, *160,* 553–554.

Held, R., and Hein, A. Movement-produced stimulation in the development of visually guided behavior. *Journal of Comparative and Physiological Psychology,* 1963, *56,* 872–876.

Herring, F. H., Mason, D. J., Doolittle, J. H., and Starrett, D. E. The Virginia opossum in psychological research. *Psychological Reports,* 1966, *19,* 755–757.

Hess, E. H. Imprinting. *Science,* 1959, *130,* 133–141.

Hess, E. H. Attitude and pupil size. *Scientific American,* 1965, *212,* 46–54.

Hess, E. H., and Polt, J. M. Pupil size as related to interest value of visual stimuli. *Science,* 1960, *132,* 349–350.

Hilgard, E. R. *Hypnotic susceptibility.* New York: Harcourt Brace Jovanovich, 1965.

Hilgard, E. R., and Bower, G. H. *Theories of learning.* (3d ed.) New York: Appleton, 1966.

Hirayoshi, I., and Warren, J. M. Overtraining and reversal learning by experimentally naïve kittens. *Journal of Comparative and Physiological Psychology,* 1967, *64,* 507–510.

Holland, J. G., The influence of previous experience and residual effects of deprivation on hoarding in rats. *Journal of Comparative and Physiological Psychology,* 1954, *47,* 244–247.

Hollander, E. P. *Principles and methods of social psychology.* New York: Oxford University Press, 1967.

Hollender, M. H., Luborsky, L., and Scaramella, T. J. Body contact and sexual enticement. *Archives of General Psychiatry,* 1969, *20,* 188–191.

Holway, A. J., and Boring, E. G. The moon illusion and the angle of regard. *American Journal of Psychology,* 1940, *53,* 109–116.

Huff, D. *How to lie with statistics.* New York: Norton, 1954.

Hughes, R. N. Behaviour of male and female rats with free choice of two environments differing in novelty. *Animal Behaviour,* 1968, *16,* 92–96.

Hull, C. L. Simple trial-and-error learning: A study in psychological theory. *Psychological Review,* 1930, *37,* 241–256.

Hull, C. L. *Principles of behavior.* New York: Appleton, 1943.

Hurlock, E. *Developmental psychology.* (3d ed.) New York: McGraw-Hill, 1968.

Hurwitz, J., and Furth, J. J. Messenger RNA. *Scientific American,* 1962, *206* (2), 41–49.

Hyden, H., and Egybazi, E. Glial RNA changes during a learning experiment in rats. *Proceedings National Academy of Science,* 1963, *49,* 618–624.

Isaacs, W., Thomas, J., and Goldiamond, I. Application of operant conditioning to reinstate verbal behavior in psychotics. *Journal of Speech and Hearing Disorders,* 1960, *25,* 8–12.

Isaacson, R. L., Hutt, M. L., and Blum, M. L. *Psychology. The science of behavior.* New York: Harper & Row, 1965.

Jackson, C. R. *How to buy a used car.* New York: Chilton, 1965.

Jacobson, A. L., Babich, F. R., Bubash, S., and Jacobson, A. Differential-approach tendencies produced by injection of ribonucleic acid from trained rats. *Science,* 1965, *150,* 636–637.

Jensen, A. R., Kagan, J. S., Hunt, J. McV., Crowe, J. F., Bereiter, C., Elkind, D., Crowbach, L. J., and Brazziel, W. F. *Environment, heredity, and intelligence.* Cambridge, Mass.: Harvard Educational Review Reprint Series, No. 2, 1969.

Jensen, G. D., Bobbitt, R. A., and Gordon, B. N. Effects of environment on the relationship between mother and infant pigtailed monkeys *(Macaca nemestrina). Journal of Comparative and Physiological Psychology,* 1968, *66,* 259–263.

Johnson, H. H., and Solso, R. L. *An introduction to experimental design in psychology: A case approach.* New York: Harper & Row, 1971.

Jones, J. E. All-or-none vs. incremental learning. *Psychological Review,* 1962, *69,* 156–160.

Jones, M. B. Correlation as a dependent variable. *Psychological Bulletin,* 1968, *70,* 69–72.

Jones, T. B., and Kamil, A. C. Tool-making and tool-using in the Northern Blue Jay. *Science,* 1973, *180,* 1076–1078.

Jung, J. *Verbal learning.* New York: Holt, Rinehart and Winston, 1968.

Jung, J. *The experimenter's dilemma.* New York: Harper & Row, 1971.

Kamin, L. J., and Schaub, R. E. Effects of conditioned stimulus intensity on the conditioned emotional response. *Journal of Comparative and Physiological Psychology,* 1963, *56,* 502–507.

Kanzler, A. W. *Alcohol as a discriminative stimulus in the conditioned emotional response.* Unpublished doctoral dissertation, Claremont Graduate School, 1969.

Katz, M. M. Ethical issues in the use of human subjects in psycho-pharmacologic research. *American Psychologist,* 1967, *22,* 360–363.

Kelley, H. H. Experimental studies of threats in interpersonal negotiations. *Journal of Conflict Resolution,* 1965, *9,* 79–105.

Kelley, H. H. Interpersonal accommodation. *American Psychologist,* 1968, *23,* 399–410.

Kelley, H. H., Candry, J. C., Jr., Dahlke, A. E., and Hill, A. H. Collective behavior in a simulated panic situation. *Journal of Experimental Social Psychology,* 1965, *1,* 20–54.

Kelman, H. C. Human use of human subjects: The problem of deception in social psychological experiments. *Psychological Bulletin,* 1967, *67,* 1–11.

Kendall, M. G. *Rank correlation methods.* London: Griffin, 1948.

Kendler, H. H., and Kendler, T. S. Vertical and horizontal processes in problem solving. *Psychological Review,* 1962, *69,* 1–16.

Kerlinger, F. N. *Foundations of behavioral research.* (2d ed.) New York: Holt, Rinehart and Winston, 1973.

Kimble, G. A. *Hilgard and Marquis' conditioning and learning.* New York: Appleton, 1961.

Kimble, G. A. (Ed.) *Foundations of conditioning and learning.* New York: Appleton, 1967.

Kingsley, R. C., and Hall, V. C. Training conservation through the use of learning sets. *Child Development,* 1967, *38,* 1111–1126.

Kirk, R. E. *Experimental design: Procedures for the behavioral sciences.* Belmont, Calif.: Brooks/Cole, 1968.

Kleinke, C. L., Staneski, R. A., and Pipp, S. L. Effects of gaze, distance, and attractiveness on males first impression of females. Paper presented at Western Psychological Association Convention, Portland, 1972.

Kling, J., and Riggs, L. (Eds.) *Woodworth/Schlosberg's experimental psychology.* (3d ed.) New York: Holt, Rinehart and Winston, 1971.

Klopfer, P. H. Behavioral aspects of habitat selection: The role of early experience. *Wilson Bulletin,* 1963, *75,* 15–22.

Koch, S. (Ed.) *Psychology: A study of a science.* (6 vols.) New York: McGraw-Hill, 1959–1963.

Koch, S. (Ed.) *Sensory, perceptual, and physiological formulations.* Vol. 1. *Psychology: A study of a science.* New York: McGraw-Hill, 1959.

Krech, D., Rosenzweig, M., and Bennett, E. Relations between brain chemistry and problem-solving among rats in enriched and impoverished environments. *Journal of Comparative and Physiological Psychology,* 1962, *55,* 801–807.

Kruskal, W. H., and Wallis, W. A. Use of ranks in one-criterion variance analysis. *Journal of the American Statistical Association,* 1952, *47,* 583–621.

Kuhn, T. S. *The structure of scientific revolutions.* (2d ed.) Chicago: University of Chicago Press, 1970.

Kurtz, K. H. *Foundations of psychological research.* Boston: Allyn and Bacon, 1965.

Lamm, H. Will an observer advise higher risk-taking after hearing a discussion of the decision problem? *Journal of Personality and Social Psychology,* 1967, *6,* 467–471.

Langer, E. Human experimentation: New York verdict affirms patient's rights. *Science,* 1966, *151,* 663–666.

Langer, J. *Theories of development.* New York: Holt, Rinehart and Winston, 1969.

Lastrucci, C. L. *The scientific approach: Basic principles of the scientific method.* Cambridge, Mass.: Schenkman, 1963.

Lawick-Goodall, J. van. Mother-offspring relationship in free ranging chimpanzees. In D. Morris (Ed.) *Primate Ethology.* London: Weidenfeld and Nicolson, 1967.

Lawick-Goodall, J. van. Tool-using bird: The Egyptian vulture. *National Geographic,* 1968, *133,* 631–641.

Lefrancois, G. R. *Of children: An introduction to child development.* Belmont, Calif.: Wadsworth, 1973.

Leibowitz, G. Comparison of self-report and behavioral techniques of assessing aggression. *Journal of Consulting and Clinical Psychology,* 1968, *32,* 21–25.

Lenneberg, E. H. Understanding language without ability to speak: A case report. *Journal of Abnormal and Social Psychology,* 1962, *65,* 419–425.

Leuba, C. Toward some integration of learning theories: The concept of optimal stimulation. *Psychological Reports,* 1955, *1,* 27–33.

Levy, L. H. Reflections on replications and the experimenter bias effect. *Journal of Consulting and Clinical Psychology,* 1969, *33,* 15–17.

Levy, S. G. *Inferential statistics in the behavioral sciences.* New York: Holt, Rinehart and Winston, 1968.

Lewis, D. *Quantitative methods in psychology.* New York: McGraw-Hill, 1960.

Lewis, D., and Burke, C. J. The use and misuse of the chi-square test. *Psychological Bulletin,* 1949, *46,* 433–489.

Libby, W. F. Review of D. Irving. The German atomic bomb. *Science,* 1968, *160,* 175.

Licklider, L. C., and Licklider, J. C., Observation of the hoarding behavior in rats. *Journal of Comparative and Physiological Psychology,* 1950, *43,* 129–134.

Liddell, H. S. Conditioning and emotions. *Scientific American,* 1954, *190* (1), 48–57.

Lindesmith, A., and Strauss, A. *Social psychology.* (3d ed.) New York: Holt, Rinehart and Winston, 1968.

Lindquist, E. F. *Design and analysis of experiments in psychology and education.* Boston: Houghton Mifflin, 1953.

Lindzey, G., and Arsonson, E. (Eds.) *Handbook of social psychology.* (Rev. ed.) (5 vols.) Cambridge, Mass.: Addison-Wesley, 1967–1969.

Lockhead, G. R. A re-evaluation of evidence of one-trial associative learning. *American Journal of Psychology,* 1961, *74,* 590–595.

Logan, F., and Wagner, A. *Reward and punishment.* Boston: Allyn and Bacon, 1965.

Lore, R., Kam, B., and Newby, V. Visual and nonvisual depth avoidance in young and adult rats. *Journal of Comparative and Physiological Psychology,* 1967, *64,* 525–528.

Lorenz, K. *King Solomon's ring.* New York: Crowell, 1952.

Lorenz, K. The evolution of behavior. *Scientific American,* 1958, *199,* 67–78.

Lowe, G., and Williams, D. I. Light reinforcement in the rat: The effects of visual pattern and apparatus familiarization. *Animal Behaviour,* 1968, *16,* 338–341.

Luckiesh, M. *Visual illusions: Their causes, characteristics and applications.* New York: Dover, 1965.

Luttges, M., Johnson, T., Buck, C., Holland, J., and McGaugh, J. An examination of "transfer of learning" by nucleic acid. *Science,* 1966, *151,* 834–837.

Madaras, G. R., and Bem, D. J. Risk and conservatism in group-decision-making. *Journal of Experimental Social Psychology,* 1968, *4,* 350–365.

Maier, N. R. F., Julius, M, and Thurber, J. A. Studies in creativity: Individual differences in the storage and utilization of information. *American Journal of Psychology,* 1967, *80,* 492–519.

Maier, N. R. F., and Schneirla, T. C. *Principles of animal psychology.* New York: Dover, 1964.

Maier, R., and Maier, B. *Comparative animal behavior.* Belmont, Calif.: Brooks/Cole, 1970.

Malmstadt, H. V., Enke, C. G., and Toren, E. C. *Electronics for scientists.* New York: W. B. Benjamin, 1963.

Mandler, J. M. Overtraining and the use of positive and negative stimuli in reversal and transfer. *Journal of Comparative and Physiological Psychology,* 1968, *66,* 110–115.

Marlowe, D., Beecher, R. S., Cook, J. B., and Doob, A. N. The approval motive, vicarious reinforcement, and verbal conditioning. *Perceptual and Motor Skills,* 1964, *19,* 523–530.

Marquette, B. W., and Goulet, L. R. Mediated transfer in reversal and nonreversal shift paired-associate learning. *Journal of Experimental Psychology,* 1968, *76,* 89–93.

Marston, A. R. Determinants of the effects of vicarious reinforcement. *Journal of Experimental Psychology,* 1966, *71,* 550–558.

Martin, E. Short-term memory, individual differences, and shift performance in concept formation. *Journal of Experimental Psychology,* 1968, *76,* 514–520.

Marx, M. H. Infantile deprivation and adult behavior in the rat. *Journal of Comparative and Physiological Psychology,* 1952, *45,* 43–49.

Marx, M. H. (Ed.) *Theories in contemporary psychology.* New York: Macmillan, 1963.

Masserman, J. H., and Yum, K. S. An analysis of the influence of alcohol on experimental neurosis in cats. *Psychosomatic Medicine,* 1946, *8,* 36–52.

Matheson, D. W. *Facilitation of visual afterimages with auditory stimulation.* Unpublished doctoral dissertation, Claremont Graduate School, 1967.

May, R. B. Stimulus selection in preschool children under conditions of free choice. *Perceptual and Motor Skills,* 1963, *16,* 203–206.

May, R. B. Pretest exposure, changes in pattern complexity, and choice. *Journal of Comparative and Physiological Psychology* 1968, *66,* 139–143.

May, R. B., and Beauchamp, K. L. Stimulus change, previous experience, and extinction. *Journal of Comparative and Physiological Psychology,* 1969, *68,* 607–610.

McClelland, D. C., Atkinson, J. W., Clark, R. A., and Lowell, E. L. *The achievement motive.* New York: Appleton, 1953.

McConnell, J. V. Memory transfer through cannibalism in planarians. *Journal of Neuropsychiatry,* 1962, *3,* s42–s48.

McConnell, J. V. Comparative physiology: Learning in invertebrates. *Annual Review of Physiology,* 1966, *28,* 107–136.

McGill, T. E. (Ed.) *Readings in animal behavior.* New York: Holt, Rinehart and Winston, 1965.

McGinnies, E. *Social behavior: A functional analysis.* Boston: Houghton Mifflin, 1970.

McGuigan, F. *Experimental psychology: A methodological approach.* (2d ed.) Englewood Cliffs, N. J.: Prentice-Hall, 1968.

McNemar, Q. *Psychological statistics.* (4th ed.) New York: Wiley, 1969.

Mees, C. E. K. Scientific thought and social reconstruction. *Sigma Xi Quarterly,* 1934, *22,* 13–24.

Mehrabian, A. Immediacy: An indicator of attitude in linguistic communication. *Journal of Personality,* 1966, *34,* 26–34.

Mehrabian, A. Orientation behaviors and nonverbal attitude communication. *The Journal of Communication,* 1967, *17,* 324–332.

Mehrabian, A. Communication without words. *Psychology Today,* 1968, 2 (4), 53–55. (a)

Mehrabian, A. Inference of attitudes from the posture, orientation, and distance of a communicator. *Journal of Consulting and Clinical Psychology,* 1968, *32,* 296–308. (b)

Mehrabian, A. Relationship of attitude to seated posture, orientation, and distance. *Journal of Personality and Social Psychology,* 1968, *10,* 26–30. (c)

Meichenbaum, D. H., Gilmore, T. B., and Fedoravicius, A. Group insight versus group desensitization in treating speech anxiety. *Journal of Counseling and Clinical Psychology,* 1971, *36,* 410–421.

Milgram, S. Behavioral study of obedience. *Journal of Abnormal and Social Psychology,* 1963, *67,* 371–378.

Milgram, S. Issues in the study of obedience: A reply to Baumrind. *American Psychologist,* 1964, *19,* 848–852.

Miller, N. E. Comments on theoretical models. Illustrated by the development of a theory of conflict behavior. *Journal of Personality,* 1951, *20,* 82–100.

Miller, N. E., and Dollard, J. *Social learning and imitation.* New Haven: Yale University Press, 1941.

Miller, S. E., and Rokeach, M. Psychology experiments without subjects' consent. Letters in *Science,* 1966, *152,* 15.

Mills, J. (Ed.) *Experimental social psychology.* New York: Macmillan, 1969.

Modigliani, A. Embarrassment and social influence. *Dissertation Abstracts International,* 1967, *28*A, 295A.

Modigliani, A. Embarrassment, facework, and eye contact: Testing a theory of embarrassment. *Journal of Personality and Social Psychology,* 1971, *17,* 15–24.

Mood, A. M., and Graybill, F. A. *Introduction to the theory of statistics.* (3d ed.) New York: McGraw-Hill, 1963.

Morris, D. *The naked ape.* New York: McGraw-Hill, 1967.

Mosteller, F., Rourke, R. E. K., and Thomas, G. B., Jr. *Probability with statistical applications.* Reading, Mass.: Addison-Wesley, 1961.

Mowrer, O. H. *Learning theory and behavior,* New York: Wiley, 1961.

Mueller, C. G. *Sensory psychology.* Englewood Cliffs N.J.: Prentice-Hall, 1965.

Mullen, F. A. The school as a psychological laboratory. *American Psychologist*, 1959, *14*, 53–56.

Munn, N. L. *Handbook of psychological research in the rat.* Boston: Houghton Mifflin, 1950.

Murch, G. *Visual and auditory perception.* Indianapolis, Ind.: Bobbs-Merrill, 1973.

Mussen, P. H. (Eds.) *Handbook of research methods in child development.* New York: Wiley, 1960.

Mussen, P. H., Langer, J., and Covington, M. (ed.) *Trends and issues in developmental psychology.* New York: Holt, Rinehart and Winston, 1969.

Myers, J. L. *Fundamentals of experimental design.* Boston: Allyn and Bacon, 1966.

Nair, P. Untitled and unpublished research. Reported in Bruner, et al., *Studies in cognitive growth.* New York: Wiley, 1966, 187–192.

Natsoulas, T. Interpreting perceptual reports. *Psychological Bulletin*, 1968, *70*, 575–591.

Newsweek. The polls and the pols and the public. *Newsweek*, 1968, 72 (2), July 8, 23–27.

Noble, C. E. Measurement of association value (a), rated associations (a'), and scaled meaningfulness (m') for the 2100 CVC combinations of the English language. *Psychological Reports*, 1961, *8*, 487–521.

Nunnally, J. C., Jr. *Introduction to psychological measurement.* New York: McGraw-Hill, 1970.

Oppenheim, A. N. *Questionnaire design and attitude measurement.* New York: Basic Books, 1966.

Orzack, M. H., Taylor, C. L., and Kornetsky, C. A research report on the anti-fatigue effects of magnesium pemoline. *Psychopharmacologia*, 1968, *13*, 413–417.

Osgood, C. E. *Method and theory in experimental psychology.* New York: Oxford University Press, 1953.

Overton, D. A. State-dependent learning produced by depressant and atropine-like drugs. *Psychopharmacologia*, 1966, *10*, 6–31.

Palmer, R. R. *A history of the modern world* (2d ed.) New York: Knopf, 1958.

Payne, L. V. *The lively art of writing.* New York: Follett, 1965.

Petrie, A. *Individuality in pain and suffering.* Chicago: University of Chicago Press, 1967.

Plotnikoff, N. Magnesium pemoline: Enhancement of learning and memory of a conditioned avoidance response. *Science*, 1966, *151*, 703–704.

Plutchik, R. *Foundations of experimental research.* New York: Harper & Row, 1968.

Pritchard, R. M. Stabilized images on the retina. *Scientific American*, 1961, *204* (6), 72–78.

Proshansky, H. M., Ittelson, W. H., and Rivlen, L. G. *Environmental psychology.* New York: Holt, Rinehart and Winston, 1970.

Pulaski, M. A. S. *Understanding Piaget: An introduction to children's cognitive development.* New York: Harper & Row, 1971.

Rabinowitz, F. M., and Robe, C. V. Children's choice behavior as a function of stimulus change, complexity, relative novelty, surprise, and uncertainty. *Journal of Experimental Psychology*, 1968, *78*, 625–633.

Ratliff, F., and Hartline, H. K. The responses of Limulus optic nerve fibers to patterns of illumination on the receptor mosaic. *Journal of General Physiology*, 1959, *42*, 1241–1255.

Ratliff, F., Hartline, H. K., and Miller, W. H. Spatial and temporal aspects of retinal inhibitory interaction. *Journal of the Optical Society of America*, 1963, *53*, 110–120.

Razran, G. Russian physiologists' psychology and American experimental psychology. *Psychological Bulletin*, 1965, *63*, 42–64.

Reese, H., and Lipsitt, L. (Eds.) *Experimental child psychology.* New York: Academic Press, 1970.

Remington's dictionary of pharmaceutical sciences. New York: Remington, 1965.

Rheingold, H. L. (Ed.) *Maternal behavior in mammals.* New York: Wiley, 1963.

Rock, I. The role of repetition in associative learning. *American Journal of Psychology,* 1957, *70,* 186–193.

Rock, I., and Heimer, W. Further evidence of one-trial associative learning. *American Journal of Psychology,* 1959, *72,* 1–16.

Rock, I., and Kaufmann, L. The moon illusion. II. *Science,* 1962, *136,* 1023–1031.

Rodin, M., and Rodin, B. Student evaluations of teachers. *Science,* 1972, *177,* 1164–1166.

Rogers, C. R., and Skinner, B. F. Some issues concerning the control of human behavior: A symposium. *Science,* 1956, *124,* 1057–1066.

Rosenhan, D. L. On being sane in insane places. *Science,* 1973, *179,* 250–258.

Rosenthal, R. *Experimenter effects in behavioral research.* New York: Appleton, 1966.

Rosenthal, R. Unintended communication of interpersonal expectation. *American Behavioral Scientist,* 1967, *10,* 24–26.

Rosenthal, R., and Lawson, R. A longitudinal study of the effects of experimenter bias on the operant learning of laboratory rats. *Journal of Psychiatric Research,* 1964, *2,* 61–72.

Ross, H. L., and Campbell, D. T. Time series data in the quasi-experimental analysis of the Connecticut speeding crack-down. Unpublished manuscript, 1965. Cited in E. J. Webb, et al., *Unobtrusive measures: Nonreactive research in the social sciences.* Chicago: Rand McNally, 1966.

Ross, S., Smith W. I., and Woessner. Hoarding: An analysis of experiments and trends. *Journal of Genetic Psychology,* 1955, *52,* 307–326.

Rothblat, L. A., and Wilson, W. A., Jr. Intradimensional and extra-dimensional shifts in the monkey within and across sensory modalities. *Journal of Comparative and Physiological Psychology,* 1968, *66,* 549–553.

Rubin, E. *Visuell wahregenommene figuren: Studien in psychologischer analyse.* Teil I. Berlin: Gyldendalske Boghandel, 1921.

Ruch, F. L. Personality: Public or private. *Psychology Today,* 1967, *1* (6), 46, 58–61.

Runkel, P., and McGrath, J. *Research on human behavior: A systematic guide to method.* New York: Holt, Rinehart and Winston, 1972.

Runyon, R. P., and Haber, A. *Fundamentals of behavioral statistics.* Reading, Mass.: Addison-Wesley, 1967.

Russell, E. M. The effect of experience of surroundings on the response of Lebistes Reticulatus to a strange object. *Animal Behavior,* 1967, *15,* 586–594.

Sackett, G. P. The maturation and development of learning, motivated by change in light stimulation. Unpublished doctoral dissertation. Claremont Graduate School, 1963.

Sackett, G. P. Reward frequency and choice behavior in naïve and sophisticated monkeys and mentally retarded children. *Journal of Comparative and Physiological Psychology,* 1967, *64,* 151–153.

Sainsbury, P., and Barraclough, B. Differences between suicidal rates. *Nature,* 1968, *220,* 1252.

Sales, S. M. Stimulus complexity as a determinant of approach behaviour and inspection time in the hooded rat. *Canadian Journal of Psychology,* 1968, *22,* 11–17.

Sanford, F. H., and Capaldi, E. J. (Ed.) Advancing psychological science. Vol. I. *Philosophies, methods, and approaches.* Belmont, Calif.: Wadsworth, 1964.

Saravo, A. Effect of number of variable dimensions on reversal and nonreversal shifts. *Journal of Comparative and Physiological Psychology,* 1967, *64,* 93–97.

Sarbin, T. R. The scientific status of the mental illness metaphor. In S. C. Plog, and R. B.

Edgerton (Eds.), *Changing perspectives in mental illness.* New York: Holt, Rinehart and Winston, 1969, 9–31.

Sattler, J. A theoretical development and clinical investigation of embarrassment. *Genetic Psychology Monographs,* 1965, *71,* 19–59.

Scheffe, H. Statistical inference in the non-parametric case. *Annals of Mathematical Statistics,* 1943, *14,* 305–332.

Schiffman, H. R. Physical support with and without optical support: Reaction to apparent depth by chicks and rats. *Science,* 1968, *159,* 892–894. (a)

Schiffman, H. R. Texture preference in the domestic chick. *Journal of Comparative and Physiological Psychology,* 1968, *66,* 540–541. (b)

Schmidt-Koenig, K. Current problems in bird orientation. In D. S. Lehrman, R. A. Hinde, and E. Shaw, *Advances in the study of behavior.* Vol. 1. New York: Academic Press, 1965.

Schrier, A. M. Effects of an upward shift in amount of reinforcer on runway performance of rats. *Journal of Comparative and Physiological Psychology,* 1967, *64,* 490–492.

Scott, I. A. (trans. and ed.) *The Luscher color test.* New York: Random House, 1969.

Scott, W. A., and Wertheimer, M. *Introduction to psychological research.* New York: Wiley, 1962.

Searle, L. V. The organization of hereditary maze-brightness and maze-dullness. *Genetic Psychology Monographs,* 1949, *39,* 279–325.

Sechrest, L. Handwriting on the wall: A view of two cultures. Unpublished manuscript, Northwestern University, 1965. Cited in E. J. Webb, et al., *Unobtrusive measures: Nonreactive research in the social sciences,* Chicago: Rand McNally, 1966.

Selltiz, C., Jahoda, M., Deutsch, M., and Cook, S. W. Research methods in social relations. (Rev. ed.) New York: Holt, Rinehart and Winston, 1959.

Sharpe, P. B. *The effect of delayed introduction of a novel stimulus on rate of responding in children.* Unpublished master's thesis, University of Maine, 1951.

Sheridan, C. L. *Fundamentals of experimental psychology,* New York: Holt, Rinehart and Winston, 1971.

Shomer, R. W., Davis, A. H., and Kelley, H. H. Threats and the development of coordination: Further studies of the Deutsch & Krauss trucking game. *Journal of Personality and Social Psychology,* 1966, *4,* 119–126.

Sidowski, J. B. (Ed.) *Experimental methods and instrumentation in psychology.* New York: McGraw-Hill, 1966.

Sidowski, J. B., and Ross, S. (Eds.) Instrumentation is psychology. Special issue of *American Psychologist,* 1969, *24,* 185–384.

Siegel, S. *Nonparametric statistics.* New York: McGraw-Hill, 1956.

Siever, R. Science: Observational, experimental, historical. *American Scientist,* 1968, *56,* 70–77.

Silverman, I., and Schneider, D. S. A study of the development of conversation by a nonverbal method. *The Journal of Genetic Psychology,* 1968, *112,* 287–291.

Skinner, B. F. A case history in scientific method. *American Psychologist,* 1956, *11,* 221–233.

Skinner, B. F. Pigeons in a pelican. *The American Psychologist,* 1960, *15,* 28–37.

Sluckin, W. *Imprinting and early learning.* Chicago: Aldine, 1965.

Smith, M. B. Conflicting values affecting behavioral research with children. *American Psychologist,* 1967, *22,* 377–382.

Snedecor, G. W., and Cochrane, W. B. *Statistical methods.* (6th ed.) Ames, Iowa: Iowa State University Press, 1967.

Solomon, R. L. An extension of control group design. *Psychological Bulletin*, 1949, *46*, 137–150.

Solomon, R. L., and Lessac, M. S. A control group design for experimental studies of developmental processes. *Psychological Bulletin*, 1968, *70*, 145–150.

Sommer, R. Hawthorne dogma. *Psychological Bulletin*, 1968, *70*, 592–595.

Sommer, R. G. Guide to scientific instruments. Special edition of *Science*, 1972, *178*A.

Spearman, C. The proof and measurement of association between two things. *American Journal of Psychology*, 1904, *15*, 72–101.

Speer, N. E., and Hill, W. F. Adjustment to new reward: Simultaneous- and successive-contrast effects. *Journal of Experimental Psychology*, 1965, *70*, 510–519.

Spence, J. T., Underwood, B. J., Duncan, C. P., and Cotton, J. W. *Elementary statistics.* (2d ed.) New York: Appleton, 1968.

Staats, A. W. *Learning, language, and cognition.* New York: Holt, Rinehart and Winston, 1968.

Stass, J. W., and Willis, F. N., Jr. Eye contact, pupil dilation, and personal preference. *Psychonomic Science*, 1967, *7*, 375–376.

Steger, J. A. (Ed.) *Readings in statistics for the behavioral scientist.* New York: Holt, Rinehart and Winston, 1971.

Stellar, E., and Morgan, C. T., The role of experience and deprivation on the onset of hoarding behavior in rats. *Journal of Comparative and Phsyiological Psychology*, 1943, *47*, 244–247.

Stevens, S. S. *Handbook of experimental psychology.* New York: Wiley, 1951.

Stevens, S. S. Problems and methods of psychophysics. *Psychological Bulletin*, 1958, *55*, 177–196.

Stevens, S. S. Measurement, statistics, and the schemapiric view. *Science*, 1968, *161*, 849–856.

Stevenson, H. W., and Wright, J. C. Child psychology. In J. B. Sidowski (Ed.), *Experimental methods and instrumentation in psychology.* New York: McGraw-Hill, 1966.

Stilson, D. W. *Probability and statistics in psychological research and theory.* San Francisco: Holden-Day, 1966.

Stokes, A. W. (Ed.) *Animal behavior in laboratory and field.* San Francisco: Freeman, 1968.

Stricker, L. J. The true deceiver. *Psychological Bulletin*, 1967, *68*, 13–20.

Sutcliffe, J. P. A general method of analysis of frequency data for multiple classification designs. *Psychological Bulletin*, 1957, *54*, 134–137.

Swan, C. Individual differences in facial expressive behavior of preschool children. *Genetic Psychology Monographs*, 1938, *20*, 557–641.

Swets, J. A. Is there a sensory threshold? *Science*, 1961, *134*, 168–177.

Tate, M. and Clelland, R. C. *Nonparametric and shortcut statistics.* Danville, Ill.: Interstate Printers and Publishers, 1957.

Teger, A. I., and Pruitt, D. G. Components of group risk taking. *Journal of Experimental Social Psychology*, 1967, *3*, 189–205.

Terman, L. M. and Merrill, M. A. *Stanford-Binet intelligence scale: Manual for the third revision, form L-M.* Cambridge, Mass: Riverside Press, 1960.

Terrace, H. S. Discrimination learning with and without "errors." *Journal of the Experimental Analysis of Behavior*, 1963, *6*, 1–27. (a)

Terrace, H. S. Errorless transfer of a discrimination across two continua. *Journal of the Experimental Analysis of Behavior*, 1963, *6*, 223–232. (b).

Terrace, H. S. Discrimination learning and inhibition. *Science*, 1966, *154*, 1677–1680.

Thompson, R. W., and Knudson, G. R. Magnesium pemoline: Facilitation of one way and two way avoidance learning. *Psychonomic Science*, 1968, *11*, 155.

Thor, D. H., and Wood, R. J. The moon illusion. Paper presented at the meeting of the Midwest Psychological Association, Chicago, May 1968.

Thorndike, E. L., and Lorge, I. *The teacher's wordbook of 30,000 words*. New York: Teachers College, 1944.

Thorpe, W. H. *Learning and instinct in animals*. (2d ed.) London: Methuen, 1963.

Tighe, T. J., and Tighe, L. S. Discrimination shift performance of children as a function of age and shift procedure. *Journal of Experimental Psychology*, 1967, *74*, 466–470.

Timney, B. M., and Barber, T. X. Hypnotic induction and oral temperature; *The International Journal of Clinical and Experimental Hypnosis*, 1969, *17* (2), 121–132.

Tinbergen, N. *The study of instinct*. New York: Oxford, 1951.

Tinbergen, N. *Social behavior in animals*. London: Methuen, 1953.

Townsend, J. C. *Introduction to experimental method*. New York: McGraw-Hill, 1953.

Tryon, R. C. Genetic differences in maze learning in rats. *Yearbook of the National Society for the Study of Education*, 1940, *39*, 111–119.

Turabian, K. L. *A manual for the writers of term papers, theses, and dissertations*. Chicago: University of Chicago Press, 1955.

Turner, M. B. *Philosophy and the science of behavior*. New York: Appleton, 1967.

Ullmann, L. P., and Krasner, L. *Case studies in behavior modification*. New York: Holt, Rinehart and Winston, 1965.

Underwood, B. J. *Experimental psychology*. (2d ed.) New York: Appleton, 1966.

Underwood, B. J., and Keppel, G. One trial learning? *Journal of Verbal Learning and Verbal Behavior*, 1962, *1*, 1–13.

Underwood, B. J., and Schulz, R. W. *Meaningfulness and verbal learning*. Chicago: Lippincott, 1960.

von Békésy, G. *Sensory inhibition*. Princeton: Princeton University Press, 1967.

von Frisch, K. *Bees—their vision, chemical senses, and language*. New York: Cornell University Press, 1950.

Walk, R. D. The study of visual depth and distance perception in animals. In D. S. Lehrman, R. A. Hinde, and E. Shaw (Eds.). *Advances in the study of behavior*, New York: Academic Press, 1965.

Walk, R. D. Monocular compared to binocular depth perception in human infants. *Science*, 1968, *162*, 473–475.

Walk, R. D., and Bond, E. K. Deficit in depth perception of 90-day-old dark-reared rats. *Psychonomic Science*, 1968, *10*, 383–384.

Walk, R. D., and Gibson, E. J. A comparative and analytical study of visual depth perception. *Psychological Monographs*, 1961, *75*, 1–44.

Walk, R. D., Gibson, E. J., and Tighe, T. J. Behavior of light- and dark-reared rats on a visual cliff. *Science*, 1957, *126*, 80–81.

Walker, E. L. Psychological complexity as a basis for a theory of motivation and choice. In David Levine (Ed.), *Nebraska Symposium on Motivation*. Lincoln: University of Nebraska Press, 1964, 47–95.

Walker, H. M., and Lev, J. *Statistical inference*. New York: Holt, Rinehart and Winston, 1953.

Wallach, M. A., and Kogan, N. The roles of information, discussion, and consensus in group risk taking. *Journal of Experimental Social Psychology*, 1965, *1*, 1–19.

Wallach, M. A., Kogan, N., and Bem, D. J. Group influence on individual risk-taking. *Journal of Abnormal and Social Psychology*, 1962, *65*, 75–86.

Wallach, M. A., Kogan, N, and Burt, R. B. Are risk takers more persuasive than conservatives in group discussion? *Journal of Experimental Social Psychology*, 1968, *4*, 76–88.

Wallach, M. A., and Wing, C. W., Jr. Is risk a value? *Journal of Personality and Social Psychology*, 1968, *9*, 101–106.

Warkany, J., and Takacs, E. Lysergic acid diethylamide (LSD): No teratogenicity in rats. *Science*, 1968, *159*, 731–732.

Warren, J. M. An assessment of the reversal index. *Animal behaviour*, 1967, *15*, 493–498.

Warren, R. M. Verbal transformation effect and auditory perceptual mechanisms. *Psychological Bulletin*, 1968, *70*, 261–270.

Washburn, S. H., and DeVore, I. The social life of baboons. *Scientific American*, 1961, *204*(6), 62–71.

Waters, R. H., Rethlingshafer, D. A., and Caldwell, W. E. (Eds.) *Principles of comparative psychology*. New York: McGraw-Hill, 1960.

Weaver, W. *Lady luck: The theory of probability*. Garden City, N.Y.: Doubleday, 1963.

Webb, E. J., Campbell, D. T., Schwartz, R. D., and Sechrest, F. *Unobtrusive measures. Nonreactive research in the social sciences*. Chicago: Rand McNally, 1966.

Weil, A. T., Zinberg, N. E., and Nelsen, J. M. Clinical and psychological effects of marihuana in man. *Science*, 1968, *162*, 1234–1242.

Werner, G. Clinical pharmacology of central stimulant and anti-depressant drugs. *Journal of Clinical Pharmacology and Therapy*, 1962, *3*, 59–96.

Wertheimer, M. *Productive thinking*. New York: Harper & Row, 1945.

Wheeler, L. Toward a theory of behavioral contagion. *Psychological Review*, 1966, *73*, 179–192.

Wheeler, L., and Caggiula, A. R. The contagion of aggression. *Journal of Experimental Social Psychology*, 1966, *2*, 1–10.

Willems, E. P., and Rausch, H. L. (Eds.) *Naturalistic viewpoints in psychological research* New York: Holt, Rinehart and Winston, 1969.

Williams, S. R. *The ingredients of a successful research grant application*. Bethesda, Maryland: Office of Research and Development, Division of Chronic Diseases, National Institutes of Health, 1966.

Winer, B. J. *Statistical principles in experimental design*. (2d ed.) New York: McGraw-Hill, 1971.

Wolff, J. L. Concept-shift and discrimination-reversal learning in humans. *Psychological Bulletin*, 1967, *68*, 369–408.

Wolman, B. B., and Nagel, E. (Eds.) *Scientific psychology: Principles and approaches*. New York: Basic Books, 1965.

Wood, R. J., Zinkus, P. W., and Mountjoy, P. T. The vestibular hypothesis of the moon illusion. *Psychonomic Science*, 1968, *11*, 356.

Woodworth, R. S., and Schlosberg, H. *Experimental psychology*. (Rev. ed.) New York: Holt, Rinehart and Winston, 1954.

Wright, H. *Recording and analyzing child behavior*. New York: Harper & Row, 1967.

Yuwiler, A., Greenough, W., and Geller, E. Biochemical and behavioral effects of magnesium pemoline. *Psycholopharmacologia*, 1968, *13*, 174–180.

Zajonc, R. B., Wolosin, R. J., Wolosin, M. A., and Sherman, S. J. Individual and group risk-taking in a two-choice situation. *Journal of Experimental Social Psychology*, 1968, *4*, 89–106.

Zeaman, D., and House, B. J. The role of attention in retardate discrimination learning. In N. R. Ellis (Ed.), *Handbook of mental deficiency*. New York: McGraw-Hill, 1963, 159–223.

Zimbardo, P. G. The Stanford prison experiments. Paper and film presented at the Western Psychological Association annual convention, Anaheim, 1973.

Zinkus, P. W., and Mountjoy, P. T. The effect of head position on size discrimination. *Psychonomic Science,* 1969, *14,* 80.

Zucker, M. H. *Electronic circuits for the behavioral and biomedical sciences: A reference book of useful solid state circuits.* San Francisco: Freeman, 1969.

Index

Variable *(cont'd)*
  independent variable, 21, 40
  organismic variable, 22, 35, 45, 49
Variable programmer, 295
Variance, 28, 40, 128–129
  between-groups variance, 29, 50, 65, 67, 162, 333
  control of secondary variance, 31–35
  error variance, 29, 40
  extraneous variance, 29
  maximize primary variance, 30
  primary variance, 28–29, 40
  random variance, 29
  secondary variance, 29, 40
  systematic variance, 29
  within-group variance, 29, 50–51, 65, 67, 162, 333
Venn diagrams, 139
Vestibular hypothesis, 380–381
Vicarious reinforcement, 407
Visual cliff, 274, 382–385
  physical cliff, 383
  tactual (haptic) dominance, 384
  visual dominance, 384

Visual stabilization, 386
Voice-operated relay, 282
Von Frey hairs, 276

W

Warm-spot device, 279
White-noise, 270
Wilcoxon-Mann-Whitney Sum of Ranks Test, 316–322

X

X axis, 23

Y

Y axis, 23
Yes-no method, 257